Law Enforcement Bible® No. 2

Law Enforcement Bible No. 2

Edited by Detective Robert A. Scanlon

Foreword by Dr. William A. Mooney, Former Assistant Director, FBI

PUBLISHER:
Arthur H. Alintuck

MANAGING EDITOR:
Charlene S. Cruson

ASSOCIATE EDITOR:
Tucker Spirito

EDITORIAL CONSULTANT:
Robert F. Scott

RESEARCHERS:
Hadassa J. Goldsmith
Lottie L. Nielsen
Robert D. Scott

BOOK DESIGNER:
Caryn Seifer

COVER PHOTOGRAPHER:
Ray Wells

ARTIST:
Cheryl J.G. Handelman

FIREARMS CONSULTANT
Frank Gologorsky

Stoeger Publishing Company

"Admissibility of Confessions by Juveniles" reprinted with permission from the Center For Criminal Justice, Case Western Reserve University, Cleveland, Ohio.

"Hostage Negotiations: When Every Word Counts," reprinted from *Terrorism: Threat, Reality, Response* by Robert H. Kupperman and Darrell Trent, with the permission of the publishers, Hoover Institution Press. Copyright © 1979 by the Board of Trustees of the Leland Stanford Junior University.

Published by Stoeger Publishing Company
55 Ruta Court
South Hackensack, New Jersey 07606

Library of Congress Catalog Card Number: 81-84835
International Standard Book Number (ISBN): 0-88317-106-6
Manufactured in the United States of America

Distributed in the U.S. by Stoeger Industries, 55 Ruta Court, South Hackensack, New Jersey 07606, (201) 440-2700; in Canada, by Stoeger Canada Ltd., 165 Idema Road, Markham, Ontario, L3R 1A9, (416) 495-6682.

Foreword

"Hey, Sarge, where can I get more information on this?"

This question and others similar to it are heard over and over every day in criminal justice organizations throughout the world. The inquiry might refer to any of the numerous matters a law enforcement officer encounters in carrying out his or her daily responsibilities, and reflects a desire to gain knowledge and improve skills and techniques to perform more effectively.

While the answer to such a question is readily available in the 1980s, this was not always the case. Until 1915, the need for formal law enforcement training was generally not recognized by the law enforcement community.

Bruce Smith tells us that formal training facilities and programs were so rare prior to 1920 that their impact was negligible. Ten years later, a metropolitan police chief described the training of a recruit to the Wickersham Commission in the following manner:

> I say to him that now he is a policeman, and I hope he will be a credit to the force. I tell him he doesn't need anybody to tell him how to enforce the law—that all he needs to do is to go out on the street and keep his eyes open. I say, "You know the Ten Commandments and you go out on your beat, and you see somebody violating one of those Ten Commandments, you can be pretty sure he is violating some law."

In the next 50 years, our profession grew and improved. Municipal and state police academies were established. The Federal Bureau of Investigation, through its local police training schools and its National Academy at Quantico, Virginia, made substantial contributions to the developing profession. Colleges and universities became involved in criminal justice education. By 1962, there were 49 two-year and 40 four-year institutions offering degree programs in law enforcement fields in the United States. The Omnibus Crime Control and Safe Streets Act of 1968 lent a further impetus to the upgrading of law enforcement.

Today more than 1,000 institutions of higher learning are educating students in criminal justice fields. Various disciplines—psychology, sociology, law, medicine, management, organizational behavior and self-defense, to name a few—support the development of the profession. More and more books and scholarly publications are being published. Within the system itself, standards of education and training have improved at the state and municipal levels, experts have emerged with new problem-solving techniques and numerous associations and organizations have cropped up dedicated to communicating information and methods. So the sergeant today would not find it difficult to respond to an inquiry for more information on a particular topic.

Since you, the law enforcement officer, are engaged in the extremely complex role of directing and controlling human behavior, you must be educated and trained to perform the myriad tasks required of you in such an efficient and expert fashion that the public will recognize you as a true professional.

If we could rely on the concept—once trained, always trained—there would be no problem. Recruit and occasional in-service training programs might be sufficient. We live, however, in a time of change and the law enforcement officer can no longer function efficiently with the knowledge he had 5 or 10 years ago. Job changes, new laws, current interpretations of old laws, updated procedures and new police problems caused by economic, cultural, environmental or technological changes make continual training a personal, departmental and community responsibility.

Changes in the economic, socio-cultural, political-legal or technological aspects of society demand corresponding changes in people. To meet this demand, every law enforcement agency needs a comprehensive training program. This means not only recruit training, in-service training and specialized training, but also the professional development of each member of the department. Training, remember, ends only when you leave police service.

The LAW ENFORCEMENT BIBLE NO. 2 is written to assist law enforcement officers who are on the firing line each day in the seemingly endless battle with crime. It is a book for the rookie and the veteran police officer as well as for executives, administrators, supervisors and training officers—in short, for all police personnel. It would also be appropriate as a text for college-level classes or seminars.

Place the LAW ENFORCEMENT BIBLE NO. 2 in your department's library, the public library and your personal library. It makes available in a single volume articles and information that will add to your know-how and effectiveness. It brings to your fingertips the knowledge and experience the experts have gained over the years. The writers are people most of us will never have the opportunity to meet or hear. They are authorities in their respective fields and their articles represent some of the more significant writings in those fields. And they are easy to read, understand and apply to your own policing situations.

While a profession must possess or provide certain elements—a body of knowledge, a screening and preparation period, a code of conduct and self-policing procedures—you, the professional, also have an obligation to maintain your proficiency. This is accomplished by in-service training and continual self-development, part of which is reading what the experts say. Despite the well-developed, quality training programs found in law enforcement today, avid reading on an almost daily basis is a necessity.

So, when you are looking for more information related to your police profession, one source you know you can turn to is the LAW ENFORCEMENT BIBLE NO. 2. Read and study it. I have enjoyed it. I know you will.

—Dr. William A. Mooney

William A. Mooney, Ph.D., is a former assistant director of the FBI, where he was responsible for the human resources development of 20,000 employees. During his 25-year employment with the bureau, he held the positions of Deputy Assistant Director, Special Agent in Charge, Inspector, Section Chief and Assistant Director in charge of the FBI Academy's Training Division. He retired in 1976.

Dr. Mooney has written numerous law enforcement educational training documents, which have been developed for national and international law enforcement personnel. From 1966 through 1976, he traveled throughout the country lecturing and conducting seminars for executive and command-level criminal justice personnel. For two years after that, he was a consultant to the U.S. House of Representatives Committee on Appropriations.

Dr. Mooney, who received his Ph.D. from the Catholic University of America in 1975, is currently Associate Professor of Business Management and Administration at Mount Saint Mary College.

Acknowledgments

I would like to extend special thanks to the following agencies, police departments and individuals for their invaluable assistance with this LAW ENFORCEMENT BIBLE NO. 2:

• Bureau of Alcohol, Tobacco and Firearms; Federal Bureau of Investigation; National Automobile Theft Bureau; U.S. Customs Service.

• The police departments of New York City and the Port Authority of New York and New Jersey; the New Jersey police departments of Fair Lawn, Fort Lee, Hackensack, Leonia, Little Ferry and Oradell; and the Bergen County Prosecutor's Office and the Bergen County Police Department and Sheriff's Office

• Chief technical adviser Commissioner Charles Connolly of the Yonkers (N.Y.) Police Department; and other technical advisers—special agents John Walker, Russell Cestare and Robert Cozzolina, Dep. Inspector William Cox, Sgt. Pat Sardone, Sgt. John Miccolis; and members of the Quincy (Florida) Department of Public Safety—Director E.M. Spooner, Officer Howard Kinch and Officer Elaine K. Horton

• Photographers—Special Agent Allan Therrien, Det. Lt. John Hollowood, Lt. Stephen Fox, Sgt. Thomas Pierson, Sgt. John Riccardi, Det. Joseph Cleary, Sr. Inv. Richard Lau, Inv. Kenneth Nass, Inv. John Volpe, and Sheriff's Officer Howard Hass

—R.A.S.

Contents

Contents (Cont.)

Introduction

The first edition of the LAW ENFORCEMENT BIBLE, published in 1978, was a book for police officers by police officers. It contained a unique combination of elements found in no other law enforcement-oriented volume—articles by the experts, difficult-to-find reference material and a guide to weapons and equipment used by police personnel. The LAW ENFORCEMENT BIBLE NO. 2, a completely new and redesigned volume, contains the same sound and well-received components. And still there is no other book like it.

Endorsed as a supplementary text for students of ciminal justice, police science and related courses, volume No. 2 contains analyses of contemporary policing problems by a host of distinguished experts who write from practical experience as well as from many years of training:

• *John S. Farnam*, weapons training consultant from Wisconsin, writes on the necessity of developing quality weapons training and how to implement it • *Dr. Katherine Ellison*, a psychologist who worked with the N.Y.C.P.D., analyzes police stress and how you can cope with it • *Chief James Sewell* and former Training Sergeant *William Beckerman*, both from Florida, instruct us in the safest procedures for stopping motor vehicles • *Associate Judge Charles E. Moylan Jr.* of the Maryland Court of Special Appeals clears up some of the confusion surrounding search and seizure laws • *Lieutenant Joseph Keeney* of the

N.Y.C. Housing Authority P.D. gives a detailed picture of the policing program employed successfully in New York City's public housing • *Thomas Kissane*, associate professor of criminal justice at Iona College in New Rochelle, N.Y., addresses the problem of America's multimillion-dollar cargo theft • *Captain James Smith*, defense instructor for police academies in Colorado, teaches you how to use your handcuffs as weapons • *Carolyn F. Bailey*, President of the Minnesota Association of Women Police, outlines the telltale signs of child abuse and how the investigator can ensure the successful building of a case • Founder of the Sex Crimes Analysis Unit of the N.Y.C.P.D., *Harry O'Reilly* details effective techniques for investigating rape • *Deputy Chief Fire Marshal Joseph O'Dowd* describes the steps every arson investigator should take when probing into one of the nation's fastest growing crimes • No one is better qualified to discuss the worldwide crisis of hostage-taking than *Captain Francis A. Bolz Jr.*, coordinator of New York City's Hostage Negotiating Team • What tactics can corporations use against terrorists? *Richard Gallagher*, former FBI Assistant Director in charge of criminal investigation, proposes come concrete answers • The international trafficking of narcotics has not diminished since the French Connection expose, and *Patrick O'Carroll*, former Chief of Training of the United Nations Division of Narcotic Drugs, discusses the ramifications of the new Southwest Asian connection ● *George E. Goodreau Jr.,* who served as supervisor of the FBI's Latent Fingerprint Section, imparts his expertise on foolproof fingerprinting ● Hypnotherapist *Gary L. Griffiths* delivers the pros and cons of the new and controversial use of hypnosis as an investigative aid ● What better measure is there in evaluating the professionalism of law enforcement personnel than a well-written report? *Assistant Professor Leslie Bramble* tells how to write one correctly ● and I instruct on how to master the police officer's ultimate weapon—the shotgun; and how to handle evidence properly and testify in court.

To test your knowledge of the basic laws most-often applied on the job, we have included in the LAW ENFORCEMENT BIBLE NO. 2 a special question-and-answer section, "How Well Do You Know the Law?"

Because in law enforcement your life often depends on your gun, the wholly revised Weapons and Equipment Section includes detailed specifications on pistols, revolvers, rifles and shotguns used exclusively by police personnel. You will like the new format—it's easy to read and use for comparison. Also, in three separate articles we address the question, "What should I look for in an off-duty weapon, a holster or body armor?"

If you are a rookie just on the force, you may have wondered where you can obtain certain motor vehicle I.D. charts or, if you are a seasoned officer, you may be curious about joining a special-interest organization. In the Reference Section, we have jam-packed all sorts of information we hope will meet your on-duty and off-duty requirements. Every person in law enforcement should find especially pertinent the statistics on major crimes committed, excerpted from the FBI Uniform Crime Reports.

We hope you find the LAW ENFORCEMENT BIBLE NO. 2 a complement to volume No. 1, both of which you will want in your law enforcement library. We welcome reader comments and suggestions, so we can keep the volumes in the series interesting, useful and responsive to your law enforcement needs.

—Robert A. Scanlon

Detective Robert A. Scanlon began his career in law enforcement in 1960 as a patrolman with the Fair Lawn (N.J.) Police Department. He was later appointed to the Bergen County (N.J.) Police Department and since 1972 he has served as a detective with the Bergen County Prosecutor's Office.

His interest in firearms ranges from being an active competitive shooter (for which he has been awarded the title of Distinguished Expert) to conducting in-service training and firearms instruction for New Jersey prosecutors. He also instructs such agencies as the New Jersey S.P.C.A. on firearms safety and has lectured at various northeastern police academies, colleges, schools and civic groups. He is frequently called upon by the Superior Court and the County Grand Jury to testify as a firearms expert and serves as a firearms consultant to Stoeger Industries when he is not writing for Police Marksman Magazine *or working on his next book.*

Detective Scanlon has received four police commendations and, since editing the first LAW ENFORCEMENT BIBLE in 1978, he has received awards from the American Police Hall of Fame, the Veterans of Foreign Wars and the New Jersey Institute of Technology. He is a member of the N.J. State Honor Legion, the Police Emerald Society, the State Police Benevolent Association and the New York/New Jersey Detectives Crime Clinic.

Articles

Quality Weapons Training: When Your Life Depends on Your Gun

John S. Farnam

At no time in the history of the United States has the need for practical, job-related weapons training been more acute. Police officers are finding themselves in self-defense situations with greater frequency today than at any time during this century. As recently as 20 years ago, the majority of police officers never fired their weapons in self-defense during their entire careers. Today, the situation is reversed. Young officers coming into the system are aware that the probability of their being involved in at least one shooting incident during their first 10 years is greater than 50 percent. Before their careers end, they may be involved in several incidents—what's more, their careers may end with the first one if they are not fully prepared.

Despite this, however, many departmental weapons training programs are languishing. Outdated techniques are still being taught; weapons training in general still occupies the traditional back burner in many sectors. Unfortunately, the position of range officer has never exactly been the zenith of accomplishment in the law enforcement profession. It is often occupied by unenthusiastic individuals who are content to use yesterday's methods. The situation is changing, albeit slowly, because too many officers too often are finding themselves at the wrong end of the gun barrel.

Quality training, then, should be the mandate of the future. Those in leadership positions must become personally involved in a command effort to ensure that quality weapons training does happen. Sharp, energetic officers supported by their superiors must occupy the positions of range officers.

In working with departments of every description, I've seen many training programs ranging from excellent to abominable. After years of study, I've identified 10 criteria that seem to typify the best programs and can be used as a yardstick in evaluating other police weapons training programs.

1. The Training Must Be Regularly Scheduled. Once an officer graduates from the academy and starts his regular duties, weapons training is often haphazard at best. It is important that shooting exercises be scheduled at regular intervals at least four times a year and that the schedule be adhered to. It is not uncommon for a department to contract with me or other training consultants to conduct a training program several times a year simply because that is the only way they can get one positively scheduled on the calendar. A flexible schedule is no schedule; every-

In weapons training courses, officers should be taught the difference between the haphazard use of available cover and the best use of it. Here an officer who came under fire while out in the open is properly using the vehicle to protect himself and return fire. Another effective position would be crouched down in front of the car with his head below the hood and his right knee fully bent and almost touching the ground.

thing, it seems, becomes more important than weapons training. Your range officer must successfully battle the activities that steal training time, and he must have backing. Once the word gets out that weapons training *will* go as planned, the grumbling will subside, and your training program can proceed as scheduled.

2. *The Training Must Be Compulsory*. This is a real bugaboo. Compulsory training in most departments must be mandatory for everyone below the rank of lieutenant. The only one who can make a compulsory rule stick is the chief himself. It is very difficult for me during one of my programs to get a chief to do anything more than observe briefly. Almost always he has something else to do. The chief must realize, however, that if he consistently makes an exception of himself, his staff officers will start imitating him. When that happens, the whole program will collapse, because anyone who really doesn't want to

shoot (and these are usually the ones who most need the training) knows that with a little imagination he can usually get out of it. Leaders should lead. You won't have to look very far to find an excuse for not going to the range when you've been scheduled—any old excuse will do. And if you're the chief, nobody is going to argue with you. But, you'll never know if your weapons training program is worthwhile, if your equipment is worthwhile, if your range facility is worthwhile or if your people are worthwhile unless you yourself get out from behind your desk, strap on your gun, go down to the range and actually shoot that day's training exercise right alongside your people— and accept the score you actually earned. There is no substitute for having the chief on the range, because if he's there, you can bet all the majors, captains and lieutenants will be there, too. Compulsory weapons training means just that—and it starts at the top.

3. *The Training Must Be Job-Related.* Is our weap-

ons training really relevant? In all areas of law enforcement, the officer must be trained to perform the tasks he will be expected to do on the job. However, in the education business we have a bad habit of training people in a sterile environment, and nowhere will you find more sterile training than on the range. We know, for instance, that the majority of shooting incidents involving police officers take place during hours of darkness or in reduced light. Wouldn't it make sense, then, to conduct most of our weapons training in reduced light? Why don't we? If we claim to be preparing the officer for what he will actually encounter on the job, the answer is, because we're lazy and afraid to counter tradition. We all know how important the skillful use of cover is to the survival of an officer in a shooting incident. Do we routinely require the officer to use cover during live-fire exercises? We are limited only by our sense of commitment and our imagination.

4. The Training Must Be Performance-Oriented. "Train the way you fight, because you will fight the way you've been trained"—so goes an old military adage, and it's true. *Everything* that is done routinely on the range will be done on the street. Every habit learned on the range will be applied automatically in the street—for better or worse. Therefore, we no longer train officers to get killed; we train them to survive. Becoming more common now is the "hot

A vehicle can provide adequate cover for an officer during a gun battle. Note how between the vehicle and the officer's arms (which are positioned correctly), his entire vital area is protected.

Occasions will arise when an officer stopping a vehicle will be attacked before he has a chance to exit his vehicle. At these times, he will have to fire at his attackers with his left hand (most often the weak hand). It is very important that firearms training include training for use of the weak hand so proficiency still results.

range." This means officers don't go around with an empty gun—even on the range. Officers are taught to keep their weapons loaded at all times. They no longer drop their brass in buckets at stations along the course. They are required to use their duty gear: if they carry speedloaders, they use them; if they carry beltloops, they use them, etc. They don't reload out of a pocket unless that's where they actually keep their ammunition. They should perform on the range exactly as they would in an actual gunfight. To the greatest extent possible they should practice with service ammunition also.

That goes for tactics, too. It's not enough to lecture about individual tactics, like the use of cover. Officers learn tactics like they learn anything else—by doing. The bottom line is: Anything we expect them to do in the street, we had better train them to do on the range. The training *is* the test.

5. The Training Must Be Realistic. A shooting incident is about as stressful a situation as can be imagined, so whatever the officer is trained to do, he must be able to apply easily under stress. In recent years, some interesting discoveries have come to light about stress. While under stress, for example, fine coordination and decision-making abilities are severely reduced. This is why all those slick martial arts tricks that look so easy on the mat become very difficult and don't usually work when applied in actual situations on the street. Since stress has this affect on coordination and mental processes, we must

During an armed encounter, an officer should stay behind his vehicle's door until a backup unit arrives on the scene. Shown are two different angles of the proper positions and stances. Note how the officer's arm is rested against the vehicle's frame, providing balance and a point of rest.

ensure that the techniques taught to law enforcement officers will hold up in the most desperate of stressful environments.

In view of the foregoing, three things should be eliminated from the weapons training program to the greatest extent possible: complicated, intricate movements; visual cues; and conditional branching. Everything the officer does with the weapon should involve only general movements with the hands and arms. The more complicated the technique, the higher the probability that it will break down under stress and, therefore, the more thoroughly it must be ingrained. Officers should be able to do everything by feel and by sound. Everything officers do with a weapon, they should be able to do in the dark. Remember, they should be trained for all environments, and if they require visual cues before executing a move—they won't be able to function in reduced light.

Conditional branching is a data-processing term that refers to a split in a computer flow chart. In other words, the computer must make a decision and go one way or another. If a student is asked to make a lot of critical decisions under stress, he will fall apart. So, no

longer are five different shooting techniques taught based on the distance to the target. Rather, only one technique is taught so the officer will master it with the objective that he will shoot that way regardless of the range. The technique should be step-by-step and unconditional so the shooter has no decisions to make other than the one to shoot.

For the range officer teaching a course, make sure that what you are teaching these people will hold up and serve them well in a high-stress environment. Create a stressful environment (to the greatest extent possible) during training and *test* what you've been teaching. Old techniques and procedures that do not prove their worth under this kind of testing must be discarded—no matter how enshrined or traditional they are. The new generation of electronic targeting equipment such as the Duelatron by ATS is very helpful. Your department should have one.

6. The Training Must Stress the Basics. All education is repetitive. Nearly everything you do routinely, from walking to driving, you learned by repeating it over and over. There is no such thing as instinct shooting. You were no more born with an innate ability to operate a firearm than you were with an innate ability to operate a motor vehicle. Everything you know about weapons and shooting you *learned*. You learned it from television, from movies and maybe even a little from range training. Unfortunately, most of what is on TV relating to firearms is useless, having not the slightest connection with reality. So, when students report to the range having watched thousands of hours of TV cop shows as they were growing up, the training expert's work is cut out for him.

What the trainees learned from watching TV, they will have to unlearn as they learn the proper techniques. It will take a long time. All their high-stress moves must be properly learned and then repeated and repeated until they are so thoroughly ingrained, the student will react properly and automatically when the situation calls for the use of firearms. The basics should be repracticed and restressed during some part of every training exercise.

The most important basics are shooting, reloading and use of cover. In shooting, the firing stroke (draw and firing position) and trigger control should be emphasized. The stroke is important because that is what will position the weapon at the point where it will hit. Trigger control is critical, especially with the double-action weapons, because a sloppy trigger press will cause a miss even when a shooter has a good stroke.

In our training courses, we no longer tell our people to count their rounds. It's too unreliable because when students try to tally their rounds in a high-stress environment, they're nearly always wrong. As a rule, they will actually have fired from two to three times as many rounds as they think they have or that they recall firing. Instead, we tell them to reload as soon after the initial exchange as they can, regardless of how many rounds they have expended. Our officers carry a minimum of 18 rounds on their person because instances in which officers have expended more than 18 rounds are almost unheard of. In domestic gunfighting, encounters are usually violent and over quickly. So, we no longer try to conserve ammunition. We stress to the officer that he must keep his weapon loaded so it will be ready when he needs it. "Load when you want to, not when you *have* to," we tell them.

Maximum reloading time (with the weapon loaded

When using a tree or telephone pole as cover during a gun battle, the proper—and safest—position (left) is directly behind it with as little of the body exposed as possible. In the improper position (right), the officer's entire vital area is vulnerable.

with empty cases or an empty magazine to a loaded weapon held in a position to fire) for the double-action revolver is six seconds using speedloaders; twelve seconds using a dump pouch or loops. Maximum time for magazine changing in autos is three seconds. Reloading should also be practiced in the dark.

Shooters should be taught to use cover right from the beginning. The skillful use of cover involves recognizing what constitutes cover, moving to a position of cover, taking maximum advantage of the cover and shooting from behind it. The "jack-in-the-box" technique, which calls for a shooter to extend his head and shoulders out into the open, extend his arms, fire, then withdraw is no longer advocated. In the preferred method, the "Roll-out," the shooter gets into a position to fire while still behind cover, then rolls out with his gun, arms and chest, moving as a whole unit, until he sees the target, fires, then rolls back. The shooter should roll out in a different place each time to confuse the adversary about his exact position.

With the shotgun, the basics must be learned in the same way. Most working police officers don't have the slightest notion of what to do with a shotgun. It is the forgotten weapon. Carrying, firing and reloading under fire must be repeated and trained for in the same way handgun techniques are. The shotgun is by far the most versatile and effective weapon of law enforcement and should be emphasized and used more than it is now. Students should understand that the handgun is a close, defensive weapon. It is not what you use when you get caught flat-footed and have to shoot your way out with what you have with you. If you have time, the shotgun is the weapon of choice. If you get into a situation in which the people involved may be armed, and you approach with anything less than a shotgun—you must have suicidal tendencies.

7. The Training Must Be Varied and Enjoyable. Boring training is as unnecessary as it is inexcusable. With all the things there are to learn and all the challenges there are to meet—there is no reason for any shooter to be bored. Officers at the practice range should look forward to a new challenge every time they have a shooting exercise. They should learn new things, trying new courses all the time. They should know the basics, but be constantly required to apply new things to new situations.

Getting stuck in a groove is how PPC evolved. When the PPC (Practical Police Course) was shot to the exclusion of any other course, special "PPC guns" and "PPC holsters," neither of which have the slightest utility outside the PPC range, became popular. Shooters started using "mellow-wads" that barely had enough velocity to cut through the target paper.

Using a basic handgun position taught in weapons training courses, the officer is kneeling behind his vehicle for protection while firing his weapon. Most of his body is protected by the vehicle.

Barricades that were supposed to be used as cover were, and in some places still are, being used as a support for the gun. The whole thing has degenerated into irrelevance. Don't let this happen to your program. Keep it fresh by introducing new challenges.

One standard exercise guaranteed to spice up a range exercise is shooting up a car. The best way to show students how to use a vehicle for cover is to drag an expendable vehicle onto the range and actually use it as a prop. (The vehicle can be one of the department's tow-aways or a junk from a local salvage yard.) The students can practice firing from the vehicle or from behind it, and if someone inadvertently hits it, no harm is done. This exercise is useful for demonstrating the incredible resistance of most cars to penetration by handgun bullets. Each student is given the opportunity to test the penetration of his weapon and ammunition.

Movies are another addition that can be used to add zest to the training session. Motorola Teleprograms has an excellent series of films on aspects of police shootings, as does Calibre Press and Harper and Row.

I've run many courses in abandoned houses, expendable house trailers, even junk yards. I've also set up jungle lanes in wooded sites. Such props can be used to teach tactics. Role-playing exercises and guest lecturers are also useful.

As range officer, if you are really doing your job, your people should be looking forward to every training exercise and should not be saying things like, "Do we have to shoot *again*?"

8. *The Training Must Be Complete.* Just as there is more to successful gunfighting than just launching bullets, there is more to weapons training than merely teaching the physical operation of the weapon. The complete weapons training program should include shooting (handgun and shotgun), reloading, tactics and legal and psychological implications. Students need to know not only how to shoot, but when and when not to shoot.

No police officer is ready for the street unless he can hit any reasonable target with his handgun or shotgun on demand and under stress. A good stroke and a good trigger will produce a hit. In training, don't only do a lot of shooting, do a lot of hitting. Reloading should be learned along with shooting.

Tactics include recognition of danger signs, use of cover, movement, target identification (decision-making) and situation engineering. Again, it's not enough merely to talk about tactics. Training scenarios must be set up that compel the shooters to use the individual tactics being taught. Human figure targets are very useful for teaching target recognition—the widest selection is available from Advance Training Systems.

Most departments have a policy of "self-defense only" with regard to the use of deadly force—even if state statutes permit the use of deadly force under some less drastic circumstances. Every officer must understand what the policy is and be trained accordingly. Topics such as the shooter's psychological reac-

Because the majority of police patrol units are now equipped with shotguns, weapons training courses should include instruction and practice on handling them during armed encounters. Defensive positions are basically the same as for handguns, but simulated practice situations provide invaluable training. Here the officer is using the vehicle's door to protect his body while returning fire.

tion to violent death (called "after-burn") must also be addressed.

9. *The Training Must Be Documented.* No one can deny the usefulness of carefully maintained records in a civil or criminal case. Whenever an officer shoots someone in the line of duty, the department may be sued. Not only will the city be sued, but each of the officers involved—the chief, the training officer, the manufacturer of the ammunition—anyone the injured party thinks he can get money from. You can't avoid being sued, but you can avoid being sued successfully.

Neat, carefully maintained training records look impressive in court and convey the impression of conscientiousness and professionalism. Every weapons training session, no matter how small or informal must be carefully recorded, with every attending officer properly credited. If the training officer on the stand responds to a question about the department's weapons training program with, "Well, sir, we qualify once a year," it's all downhill from there.

10. *The Training Must Be Cost-Effective.* Training is as difficult to sell as life insurance, because that's what it really is. When the city fathers spend money, they want to see something for it. If equipment is purchased, they can see physically where the money has been spent. But, when dollars go toward training, results are the only tangible evidence.

Since it's so difficult to get money committed to training, as much quality training as possible should be squeezed out of each dollar. Some savings can be gleaned through dry-fire practice, since it does not consume ammunition. Skip-shooting is also an excellent exercise. An exciting part of any training exercise is a bowling-pin shoot—a reactive target is always good therapy for the shooter. The bowling pins are usually donated or can be had at nominal cost. Steel falling plates make another excellent reactive target that can be used over and over and can be made at low cost.

Quality training doesn't just happen, you have to make it happen. Even the expenditure of a lot of money on new training equipment will not automatically guarantee good training. What will guarantee good training is a firm commitment to it that begins with the top people. Until now, most of the training innovations have come about because the men demanded up-to-date training, not because it was pushed on them by superiors. This is not as it should be. The department leadership should be pushing for better training all the time. They should be open to new ideas, new techniques, new equipment.

Law enforcement personnel will live or die as a result of the training they have received. Don't wait until your people are involved in a shooting incident to provide quality training—the time for that training is now.

Officer John S. Farnam of the Juneau County Sheriff's Department in Wisconsin is a weapons training consultant who supervises weapons training programs for police and civilians in the U.S. and abroad. A graduate of Cornell College, Farnam is a contributing author to Combat Handguns *and* American Handgunner *magazines, a staff consultant for the Advanced Training Systems of Motorola Teleprograms and a lecturer for officer survival courses conducted by the Traffic Institute at Northwestern U.*

The Stress Syndrome of the Modern Police Officer

Katherine W. Ellison, Ph.D.

Physically, policing may not be the most dangerous occupation in our society, but emotionally it ranks number one. Scientists, police administrators and individual officers are becoming aware that the stress involved in policing has the potential not only to affect health and well-being, but also a policeman's ability to do his job. And as stress reduces the efficiency of an individual officer, it will diminish the effectiveness of the entire organization.

Stress is a complex concept, with psychological and physiological aspects. In *The Stress of Life,* Dr. Hans Selye defines stress in physiological terms as the body's nonspecific response to any demand placed on it, whether the demand is pleasant or not. That is to say, any change, or any event experienced by the individual as change (and the individual's definition of the situation is very important), is stressful to some degree. However, not all change, or even all negative change, necessarily leads to negative consequences. Some change is essential for people to function well; also, individuals differ in the extent to which they seek or avoid change. For example, some police officers join the force because they are looking for excitement and adventure; they need and thrive in an environment in which things are constantly happening. Others join because they want security; they may work best on assignments involving well-ordered routine.

Because some stress is helpful, what are the conditions under which stress can lead to physical and psychological damage? The answer seems to lie in the intensity of the stressful situation, or stressor, its duration and its meaning to the individual. But when the individual is confronted with too many stressful events, or those which are too severe, in too short a period of time, with too few personal, organizational or societal supports, that stress leads to trouble.

Responses to Stress

Physical. The body responds to stress in ways that are similar, regardless of the nature of the stressful event. In the first stage of what Selye has called the "general adaptation syndrome," an *alarm* reaction develops. Resistance falls below normal, the heart rate increases, while the blood pressure, body temperature and muscle tone decrease. In response to these changes, the brain releases a hormone which increases the secretion of the stress hormones—adrenalin and cortisone—from the adrenal gland. The body then enters a stage of *resistance,* in which the blood pressure rises, and possibly temperature and blood volume. The body is mobilized for coping. Often the coping mechanisms are successful, and the body returns to normal. If, however, the stress is severe or long-lasting, the person enters a stage of *exhaustion,* in which many of the symptoms of the alarm phase reappear and other physical symptoms may set in.

Psychological Crisis Reactions. Prolonged stress may cause psychological reactions, one of which is "crisis." A crisis reaction is subjective, based on the way a person feels. It is also a time when people are particularly susceptible to change, a turning point from which the individual may emerge with psychological damage, or strengthened and better able to cope with future stressful situations.

Crisis may result from several different kinds of stressors. First, there are the normal developmental events: the things that happen to most people in our society as they grow older—marriage, the birth of children, beginning a new job, retirement, and the like. Because these events happen to most people, it is possible to plan for them, at least to some extent, and planning tends to lessen the impact of stressful events.

Other stressful life situations are accidental. These occur suddenly and are viewed by the victim as unpredictable and arbitrary, so that he asks, "Why did this happen to me?" These events include accidental deaths, natural disasters, sudden illnesses and crime victimization. Events of this sort can cause crisis reactions not only in the victims, but also in what sociologists call their "significant others," i. e., family and friends. They can also cause crisis reactions in professionals called to work with these victims.

A third kind of stressor comes from chronic conditions, such as a family, neighborhood or job situations

The routine stopping of a motor vehicle is sometimes cause for an officer to fear for his life; he may find he has stopped a wanted criminal, a violent drunk or drug abuser or even encounter gunfire as he approaches. This type of stop has become so hazardous in recent years, a full discussion of proper stopping techniques is included, beginning on page 32.

The desk officer in a busy police department is under constant stress. He must make instant decisions on subjects of major proportions. Only if things get unusually hectic, may he rely on the assistance of another officer.

that are maladaptive, chaotic and disruptive. These situations are especially likely to be stressful if the person feels he has no control over his fate. In these situations, stress usually builds slowly (in contrast to the accidental stressors), with chronic feelings of low-level anxiety and malaise. This state is punctuated from time to time by periods of acute distress, often triggered by the "straw that broke the camel's back." It is at these times that symptoms of psychological distress flare up, sometimes expressed in depression, sudden outbursts of temper, alcoholic binges, domestic disputes, physical symptoms, such as ulcers, and even suicide attempts or psychotic episodes.

Chronic stressors may also lead to a kind of behavior called "learned helplessness." A person who at one point in his life has learned that nothing he does makes any difference, that he is powerless to gain

rewards or avoid punishment, may respond by ceasing to try. He becomes depressed and apathetic. This condition persists even if the situation changes so the person *could* control rewards and punishment.

People's overt reactions in crisis vary tremendously, as you can see in the accompanying chart.

But just as there are stages in physiological reactions, so crisis reactions also tend to occur in stages. The first phase, the *acute* crisis phase, begins with the precipitating incident and lasts a few hours or perhaps a day. Typically, it is characterized by denial ("This can't be happening to me."), by disruption, so that the normal coping mechanisms don't work and the person feels anxious, threatened and out of control, and often guilty.

The guilt may be straightforward: "I must have done something wrong," or it may be projected onto another person. The crime victim who angrily tells the responding officer, "If you had been out there doing your job instead of giving out tickets, this wouldn't have happened to me," is an example of this phenomenon.

The person in crisis may also regress, and act and think in childlike ways. As a result, he cannot be expected to think and act rationally. His perceptions are distorted; people under stress make particularly unreliable eyewitnesses. Finally, the person in crisis is open, vulnerable and suggestible. His "defenses are down."

BEHAVIOR AND RESPONSE IN CRISIS

In crisis situations, behavior and responses differ markedly from individual to individual, but listed below are some typical reactions. People in crisis may display several of these reactions at the same time or at different times:

Anger	Fear
Anxiety attacks	Feelings of going crazy
Apathy	Frustration
Changes in sexual response	Guilt
Clinging dependency	Headaches
Compulsive actions	Hives, blemishes and
Confusion	other skin reactions
Crying jags	Hypersensitivity
Denial	Laughing / joking
Depression	Nightmares
Desire for action	Obsessive thoughts
Desire for revenge	Panic
Disbelief	Phobias
Disrupted eating habits	Repression
Disrupted sleeping patterns	Self-hatred
Distrust	Shock
Extreme calm	*Sympathy for the aggressor

*This reaction is particularly prevalent in the individuals who have been kidnapped or taken hostage for long periods of time. The victims, owing their lives and safety to the caprice of the offender, are relieved and grateful to be alive. Most victims react with extreme passivity, some even come to feel sorry for the offender or to express positive emotions about him.

To oversimplify somewhat, the needs of people in this acute crisis phase are relatively straightforward. They need to regain some control, or at least the feeling that they have some control, over their lives. They need to be able to feel that they can *do* something to make the situation better. They need to

understand what is happening and why, to be able to predict—to know what to expect—and, in many cases, to ventilate. For adults, ventilation means "getting it out of your system," usually by talking about what has happened, and then to begin to plan for constructive action. Finally, the person in crisis needs the support of his social network—his friends, family, superiors and co-workers and, especially, the support of the authorities to whom he turns for help.

The second phase in crisis reaction involves *coping and recovery*—the feeling that everything is all right, that the individual is coping and has recovered. At this time, he wants to get on with the business of living, to try to forget what has happened, not to talk about it. He begins to integrate the experience into his life and his perceptions of himself. This feeling, however, is commonly interrupted by flashbacks in which the person remembers the crisis-producing event and relives the emotional experiences. When this occurs, he may again need someone to talk to.

These last two responses, integration and flashback, may alternate for some time. Under favorable circumstances, if the individual's needs are met, the flashbacks become less frequent and less severe, until he feels totally recovered. With mild stresses, this process can take a few hours or days; with severe stresses, such as the loss of a family member, up to a year or more. Here, again, the person in crisis needs the help and support of those with whom he interacts and trusts. With such help, he can go on to be stronger. Without it, and without personal strengths, the normal defense mechanisms that arose to help him cope become permanent habits which can hinder his long-range ability to deal with future stresses: the nightmares a person expects after witnessing an especially grisly wreck do not lessen in intensity, but become a permanent part of his sleep.

A special reaction to chronic job stress has been found in those people whose jobs involve a great deal of contact with the public in roles that involve interpersonal management tasks, particularly "human service-delivery" roles. This reaction has been called "burnout." It is the tendency to cope with stress by a form of distancing, which not only hurts the professional person, but is damaging to his ability to serve the public. Distancing, of course, is a matter of degree, and some distancing—objectivity—is necessary to allow an individual to work in difficult situations. How, then, is burnout different from the normal defenses which facilitate competence?

A number of symptoms point to a person who is burning out, many of which may be seen in police officers. The officer becomes cynical and develops negative feelings about everyone outside the police world. He may begin to talk of civilians as other than human, and to withdraw from contact with them. Withdrawal is further characterized by sharp distinctions between his job and personal life. As described by Christine Maslach in *Human Behavior,* a major symptom of burnout is "the transformation of a person with original thought and creativity on the job into an autonomic bureaucrat." The individual withdraws from personal involvement by "going by the book," rather than by the unique circumstances of each situation.

Coping mechanisms of this sort may work in the short run, but they do take their toll. A person who is burned out often develops physical symptoms, such as ulcers, anxiety attacks and insomnia. He may seek relief in alcohol, drugs or tranquilizers. Family life deteriorates, and divorce and suicide rates climb.

It is important to emphasize that certain crisis reactions, and even burnout, are not necessarily indicators of a "weak" or "sick" personality, but may be a normal, understandable defense against overwhelming stress.

Special Stress Factors in Policing

A number of different factors contribute to stress in policing. Classified into four general categories they are: (1) stressors external to the police organization; (2) stressors inherent in the police role; (3) stressors in the organizational structure and in supervisory style; and (4) stressors resulting from individual personality factors.

Stressors external to the police organization include conditions such as the political atmosphere of the jurisdiction in which an officer works, public policy, laws and the problems of the courts and other parts of the criminal justice system. While it is important to acknowledge their potential impact, these factors lie largely out of the control of anyone within the police organization. They are a constant with which and around which police administrators and officers must work.

So, too, stressors inherent in police work are factors largely out of the control of anyone in the police organization. These include taking the responsibility for the lives of others; working with people in crisis, with people who hate police, with criminals; handling responsibility and authority; boredom, and the like. Accidental stressors come in the form of assignments that can cause crisis reaction for even the most hardened officers: cases involving children who have been killed or injured, disaster work, involvement in shooting incidents and the wounding or death of a fellow

An everyday routine assignment such as traffic control bears its own stress. Many officers are injured annually by vehicles operated by drivers under the influence of alcohol or drugs.

officer. Certain particularly stressful assignments include youth work, sex crimes investigation and undercover assignments, especially undercover narcotics work. Although the department cannot control these events, administrators and supervisors should be aware that they may lead to crisis reactions and see that officers receive training and support in dealing with these situations.

An important, often neglected, source of stress in policing is found in the structure of the organization and in supervisory styles. Job stress is exacerbated and indeed may be caused by certain traditional police practices. One of the more devastating of these is the indiscriminate use of the "military model."

The military model sees police skills as technological. It assumes that every assignment requires skills that do not vary greatly from individual to individual or with the setting. It views discretion as unimportant and inappropriate for all but top brass. While there are skills and assignments in policing for which such a model is appropriate, for others it is not.

Many, if not most, police tasks involve managing people. Different individuals accomplish these tasks differently, depending on factors such as personality style, size and appearance, sex, and the like. Thus, while both can do the job, a small person may handle a bar brawl differently than a large one, and a male officer may use different techniques in interviewing a child than would a female. Thus, the person who is an excellent homicide investigator may be less adept as a polygraph examiner.

Unlike the combat soldier, the police officer usually works alone or with a single partner. He is continually called upon to exercise discretion. Untrained in its exercise, told it is not part of his job and inappropriate for one of his rank, seldom rewarded for the many instances when he does exhibit judgment, but often punished if actions attract adverse public attention, he learns to take the conservative path, not to make waves, to go by the book even when such action may be damaging to his larger mandate to serve and protect.

Role conflict and ambiguity is another stress factor in some police organizations: not knowing what is expected of you, or how to get rewards and avoid punishment. Many departments have regulations that are ambiguous or conflicting. Often, too, there is a clash between the demands of the three basic functions of the police: law enforcement, peace keeping and provision of service. This may be seen, for example, in the directives for handling domestic disputes. A law enforcement orientation calls for arrest, while a service-delivery model emphasizes mediation. The "right" approach often depends on the situation, and this comes back to the exercise of discretion.

Another form of role conflict is overload—the situation about which officers say, "We don't object to the things we are asked to do, and we don't find them inappropriate, but we can't meet all the demands at once." In such situations, it is important that priorities be set.

The essence of the strain that comes from organizational or supervisory styles is the individual's perception that he lacks control over his working conditions. This happens when his requests for assignment to, or removal from, certain jobs are repeatedly ignored, and when he feels that rewards come only from those he knows. It is made worse by lack of consistent feedback about performance, or workable suggestions for improvement. Often, lower ranking officers develop a perception of "we" versus "they" within the department, the belief that "bosses" and "workers" are on different sides.

Contributing to the stress caused by lack of control over working conditions is the paradoxical fact that in the exercise of his duties, the officer has enormous control over the lives of others. He can detain and question them, and even deprive them of their liberty, at least for a short time, or of their lives.

No discussion of the stressors in organizational structure can ignore the issue of shift work. Research has consistently shown that rotating shifts have an adverse effect on physical condition and an officer's ability to work at maximum efficiency.

Indicators of stress due to organizational style include such gauges of low morale as absenteeism, "sabotage" of group goals, high turnover and a department constantly in turmoil because of rumors.

The stress factors heavily emphasized by most researchers and police administrators have been those resulting from individual personality factors. They include such elements as the individual's personality type, his past history of coping, his definition of the situation as a stressor or a challenge and other events that have been taking place in his life. Such an emphasis leads to solutions involving better selection procedures and in-service screening to weed out the "inadequate" personality.

While this must be a part of any meaningful stress prevention program, by itself it is insufficient for a number of reasons. It implies that a careful job analysis has been made and, by reason of it, a good definition of the requirements for the job has been articulated. This is seldom true. Furthermore, civil service restrictions may limit flexibility in personnel decisions.

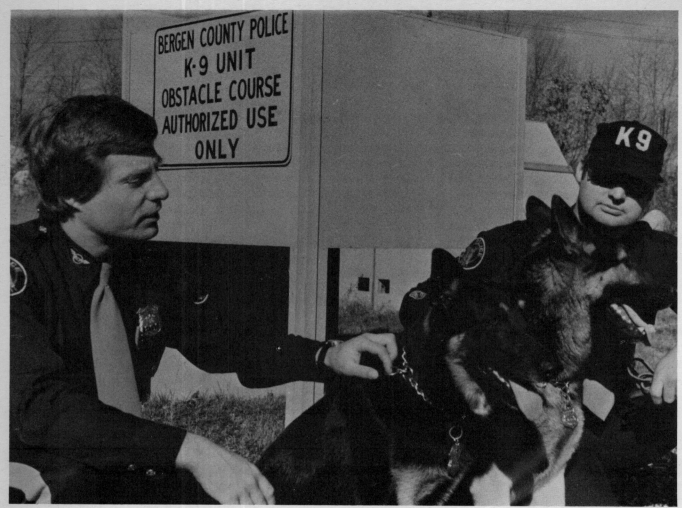

Officers who work special assignments such as SWAT or K-9 are a special breed. They are selected because they usually can make quick, discreet decisions and remain calm and composed under the stress of their specialized tasks. Many departments even require them to undergo psychiatric examination before they are assigned.

Even if the personality type best suited to perform competently can be identified, and people who fit this type are successfully recruited, a problem remains. *The best, healthiest, most dedicated officer will succumb to stress if the organizational pressures are great enough.* Indeed, some of the insulating qualities that help to counteract burnout—and that could be used as a basis for selection—are undesirable for other reasons. For example, people with rigid personalities suffer less role conflict, but rigidity of behavior is not an asset in many stressful jobs where discretion plays an important part. So, too, the psychopath is less likely to feel the stressors, but he is the one who will end up charged with corruption. Put another way, some people never burn out because they were never on fire to begin with.

Danger Signals of Stress

Certain behaviors or changes in behavior *may* signal that stress is beginning to overwhelm an individual. "May" is emphasized, because supervisors and friends must avoid the temptation to play amateur analyst and jump to conclusions too quickly. This does not mean that such signs should be ignored; they can, however, be checked out cautiously before conclusions are made that require action. The key words in determining whether a behavior is a natural, transient reaction or evidence of continuing problems are "excessive," (as compared with others doing the same job) and "prolonged" (an occasional bad day should not be cause for alarm).

Some of the symptoms that may alert supervisors or peers to overwhelming stress in a colleague are listed below. Changes you can look for in yourself are also outlined.

Danger Signals of Stress

Personality Changes:
1. A mild-mannered, reasonably sociable and even-tempered officer becomes aggressive, unreasonable and short-fused, exploding at supervisors or fellow officers with little justification.
2. An officer who normally handles difficult situations calmly and effectively lately seems to let these situations get out of control, characterized by:
   - Great increase in physical involvement; numerous arrests for the most trivial offenses that seemingly could have been avoided
   - Suddenly finding it necessary to lodge resisting arrest charges against arrestees in these cases
   - Numerous civilian complaints of abuse
3. A stable officer starts to show unusual highs, rapidly followed by periods of depression:
   - Talks of feeling hopeless, expresses despair
   - Withdraws from social contacts and even from family members
4. Officer changes his drinking patterns and displays indications of drug use, including abuse of aspirin, antacids, tranquilizers and prescription drugs:
   - Even in the most tension-filled circumstances, is "always on cloud nine"

Changes in Appearance:
1. Officer changes grooming habits:
   - A well-groomed officer becomes sloppy and loses interest in his appearance; hair untidy, beard unshaven, uniform soiled and wrinkled
   - A more casual officer suddenly develops Marine-Corps, foot-locker style of dress
   - Gains or loses weight
   - Suddenly concerned with physical condition; has passion for weightlifting, running, etc.
   - Always tired, appears lethargic, even though claiming to sleep well
   - Appears to have trembling hands, facial tics

Changes in Work Habits:
1. Officer's efficiency dramatically increases or decreases relative to the efficiency of other officers doing the same job.
2. Officer may ride fine line between bravery and recklessness in serious confrontations and develops an "I-don't-give-a-damn" attitude.
3. Officer sleeps at command post rather than at home.
4. Officer's spouse calls department to discuss problems, especially those linked to physical assaults.
5. Normally punctual officer frequently arrives late.
6. Officer often requests short-notice excusals.

Prevention of Stress-Related Disorders

Although stress is inevitable in policing, it need not lead to long-term damage; burnout is not inevitable. Strategies should include evaluation and change at multiple levels: organizational and supervisory, as well as individual.

Changed strategies at the organizational level, while perhaps the most important, are also the most difficult. In a department with severe morale problems, the strategies of the technique called "organizational development" may be helpful. (For a description of this process, see R.W. Boss', "It Doesn't Matter If You Win or Lose, Unless You're Losing: Organizational Change in a Law Enforcement Agency," *Journal of Applied Behavioral Science,* 1979.) For those who feel the need for a less drastic solution, the first step is to recognize that a problem exists. This should be followed by a review of departmental priorities and a restructuring of department regulations to reflect

An officer in his riot gear. Whether assigned to the scene of a civil disturbance or to an industrial strike, this officer knows his chances of confrontation are high—and so is his stress pattern.

priorities, if necessary. To minimize role conflict and role ambiguity, superiors should attempt to provide clear directions concerning tasks to be performed and the means for their accomplishment. Any confusion in authority and responsibility relationships should be resolved, and overlaps in authority areas eliminated, so no man has to serve two masters. Efforts should be made to guarantee that adequate channels of communication exist, allowing employees to obtain information, thereby reducing uncertainties.

STRESS SYMPTOMS

The stress symptoms listed below can be warning signs to the individual. Self-diagnosis and especially self-medication should be strictly avoided; however, presence of these symptoms in the individual should not be written off as hypochondria or malingering:

Change in sleep patterns
Chronic illness for which a doctor can find no specific cause
Chronic tiredness
Dependence on alcohol to relax
Dependence on drugs, including daily use of tranquilizers
Edginess and constant irritability
Headaches
Heart symptoms, i.e., acute anxiety attacks
Obsessive thinking without action, especially dwelling on how bad things are and how little one can do
Tics, muscle tension

Also important is a frank, soul-searching review of reward structure, consistent with the priorities that have been established. Even though supervisors, including chiefs, have little control over financial rewards, they do control working conditions, shifts, assignments and recognition.

Despite resistance to doing away with traditional authoritarian structures, programs have been developed to give officers some degree of control and participation in planning. One such structure is team policing. Other innovative programs that have the potential for reducing stress include organized recreation, retirement planning, programs aimed at preventive health care (both physical and mental health), programs for families and programs aimed at improving community relations.

At the supervisory level, it is important to realize that the basic principles of good supervision not only lead to a more efficient organization, but also reduce stress. The first-line supervisor is the street officer's basic contact with the organization, a force for socialization, as well as the first person able to detect and deal with early signs of problems. Programs aimed at supervisors must begin with adequate training, both in basic principles of supervision, and in recognition and reduction of stress-related disorders. Of special importance is training in checking out what might be symptoms of stress in nonthreatening, nonjudgmental ways. At this, as at all, levels, emphasis must be on prevention. By the time an officer's behavior becomes so bizarre or inappropriate that consideration is given to the drastic step of removing his weapon, helping him becomes much more difficult.

Because people in crisis often need to let off steam, supervisors should encourage regular informal get-togethers—ones in which members of a unit gather to discuss the events of the day. This form of ventilation can be very useful, if properly controlled. If not, it can lead to the kind of disaster described in Joseph Wambaugh's novel, *The Choirboys*.

Individual solutions to stress have received the most attention. One of the more important ones is a comprehensive program of physical fitness, including proper diet and weight control, enough sleep or rest and a regular program of exercise. (One program that is particularly useful for those who dislike exercise is the Royal Canadian Air Force Exercises book.) These condition the individual to withstand increased tension and also work off some of the tension.

The individual can be taught to recognize the buildup of tension and how to deal with it, including physical methods of relaxation. Some people find that music helps them relax, others use various forms of meditation or deep muscle relaxation. Another strategy, borrowed from behavior modification methods of psychotherapy, is cognitive behavior modification. In this technique, you can learn to rehearse normally stress-producing situations in ways that decrease the tension.

An important and difficult strategy for the individual involves a serious appraisal of one's life and priorities. As Selye puts it, "A better way (than drugs or meditation) to handle stress involves taking a different attitude toward the various events in our lives." He believes that the worst of all modern social stresses is purposelessness. A person needs to ask himself questions such as, "Why am I doing this? What is it giving me?" "If I am truly miserable, what can I do to change it?" It is important to keep realistic standards for what can and can't be changed, to realize one's own possibilities and limitations. No individual officer alone can significantly reduce crime, put all the "bad guys" away or change the court system. He can, however, do the best possible job in the most professional manner and remind himself constantly of the importance of the work he is doing.

Having asked these questions, an officer must work to minimize grousing, worry, feeling sorry for himself or expressing illogical, damaging statements about himself ("I'm no good" "Nobody understands me," and the like). Worry is both self-perpetuating and self-escalating. After saying, "What, if anything, did I do wrong?" the next question should be, "How can I do better next time?" It is often helpful to find someone trustworthy to talk to for constructive suggestions, or to observe the tactics of someone you respect.

Sometimes the person an officer trusts is a family member. The issue of taking the job home is hotly debated, with arguments for and against it. There is a difference, of course, between talking out some of the joys and frustrations of the job and keeping them bottled up until they erupt in other ways, such as ranting and raving at your children. Studies published in the *FBI Law Enforcement Bulletin* (see "Police Stress: A Possible Approach" by J.P. Leyden, December 1977) have shown that most wives want to know what is worrying their police husbands and want to share their worries. It is better that the wives—and the children—know that the officer is frustrated because of the job than to think that they have somehow done something wrong.

Finally, you can forget your own troubles by doing something for others, like helping your neighbor with some repair work, for example.

Professional Help

Some departments have sought to help their members deal with the symptoms of job-related stress—depression, alcoholism, suicide attempts or manic episodes—by employing psychologists or other counselors. Such professionals have the potential to be of help, particularly to an officer suffering the effects of acute stress. Unfortunately, their effectiveness is often compromised because their first loyalty is to the department. As such, it is their duty to identify officers who are "unfit" to carry out their regular duties and recommend corrective measures. Often these measures involve removing the man from his regular assignment and scheduling him on a "rubber gun" squad (inside assignment). While this may be necessary for the good of the department, it is often devastating to the officer. To be deprived of his former authority and status is a disgrace. Few will feel free to admit serious problems, or even trifling ones, to some-

one who has the power to use these revelations against them.

A private counselor may be of more help. Since many a mental health professional may perhaps hold some negative attitudes about police, such a person should be chosen with care. He should have experience working with officers and an understanding of their unique problems.

Another kind of support is often provided by social-science professionals who are involved with the department in some way, but have no formal input into officers' records or other forms of individual evaluation. Some may be researchers hired by the department on a consulting basis who work closely with officers on projects of interest to both. For example, one department hired a social worker to assist the station and take responsibility for some of the service-delivery problems confronting the officers, for which they had neither training, resources nor interest. At first the officers were suspicious, but after finding that the social worker could be trusted, they would often drop in to discuss a case, share solutions and insights or bring up problems. Many researchers who spend time "on the bricks" with officers find them eager to talk about the rewards and problems of the job. Those who realize this as potentially more than idle chit-chat or griping can sometimes perform a valuable service.

The prevention of stress-related disorders in police officers requires reorientation: an increased concern by the organization for the needs of the officer and an increased understanding by the individual of his own potential and limitations. The fact that so many officers perform capably under stress is testimony that it is possible to do well the difficult job of policing. Stress management is a skill important to such a task, and programs for stress reduction represent an important step in recognizing the complexity of the profession and in taking positive, effective steps to meet the challenge.

Katherine W. Ellison, Ph.D., is an assistant professor in the Department of Psychology at Montclair State College in New Jersey and Associate Director of the Center for Responsive Psychology in Brooklyn, New York. She received her doctorate in social psychology from the City University of New York. Because of her expertise in victimology, sex crimes, eyewitness identification, organizational change, supervision and stress, she has served as a consultant and lecturer to law enforcement agencies throughout the country since 1972. She has published various articles in journals such as Police Chief *and the* FBI Law Enforcement Bulletin. *She is co-author with Robert Buckhout of* Psychology and Criminal Justice, *(Harper & Row, 1981).*

Stop that Vehicle and Stay Alive

**Chief James D. Sewell and
William D. Beckerman**

The figures are too well-known to many of us in the law enforcement community. From 1976 through 1979, 403 officers were killed and more than 214,000 assaulted in the line of duty in the United States. In Florida, where both authors are active in law enforcement administration and education, 26 officers were murdered and nearly 27,000 were assaulted during the same time period.

These murders and assaults occurred in a variety of circumstances: responding to burglaries, robberies, other crimes in progress, handling prisoners, during other arrests and dealing with mentally deranged persons. Two specific types of violence-producing situations stand out, however; 69 officers were killed and 67,030 assaulted while handling disturbance calls, and 52 were murdered and 23,057 assaulted while engaged in traffic pursuits and stops; statistics for 1980 indicate that an additional 17 officers were killed performing traffic control duties. This latter category is responsible for more than 10 percent of our nationwide officer assault statistics.

If these figures are an accurate representation of an officer's vulnerability, particularly during traffic stops, why do they continue to rise? Why do trained officers too many times forget the basics of training

and experience, fail to request backups in an obvious felonious situation or neglect to pay strong attention to intuition, and find themselves in a shooting situation in a "routine" vehicular stop?

Probably because we in law enforcement have a tendency to classify too many stops as "routine." When we first graduate from the academy, the traffic stop is one of our most stressful events; it is here that we must deal with the public in a potential confrontation and confront *ourselves* when we face imminent danger. These stops become easier as we perform them more often. Finally, we start to see them as less stressful and, ultimately, less dangerous. While familiarity reduces the stress of many of our law enforcement activities, it can also breed contempt for those measures of safety that we learned at the academy, that were emphasized by the vets who trained us and that subconsciously we know we must follow. We develop a false sense of security and take too seriously the media image of "super cops." Requesting a backup threatens our self-image of personal strength and implies that we cannot handle our job. We become convinced that the hazards and the dangers will occur only to other officers and, in doing so, we forget to practice rules constantly which will maximize our

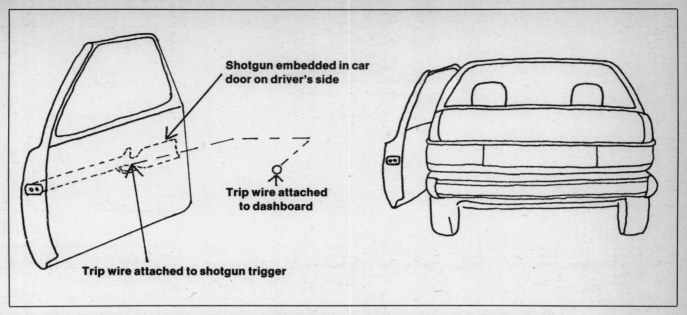

Shotgun embedded in car door on driver's side

Trip wire attached to dashboard

Trip wire attached to shotgun trigger

Concealed shotgun built into the door panel of a motor vehicle. Reproduced from a special report on *Disguised Weapons,* published by the U.S. Dept. of the Treasury, 1979.

personal safety. That's when we get hurt.

Vehicular stops, then, can and should be viewed as a major source of danger for the law enforcement officer. They can be divided into two categories: routine, or "moderate-risk," in which there is no indication of a particular problem; and "high-risk," in which there is a high potential for violence and confrontation. While many of the guidelines for a moderate-risk vehicular stop hold true for high-risk circumstances, such as the availability of backup units, oftentimes a modification in your normal strategy is required. A number of basic concerns apply to both kinds of stops and should be part of your automatic routine when making a vehicular stop:

1. Plan your stop before you even turn on your blue lights; think through a variety of alternatives and "what-if's" prior to the stop.

2. Immediately assume control of the situation and firmly direct the actions of the driver and passengers of the stopped vehicle.

3. Take steps that emphasize your protection and the public's; your major concern with every stop is your survival.

4. Assume that every stop has the potential to be high-risk and don't consider any stop to be routine.

5. Always be observant and keep your guard up.

6. Don't forget the basic "how-to" rules you learned at the police academy and practice them always.

7. Any effective vehicular stop takes time; don't allow circumstances to force you to rush through it in

such a manner that you compromise your own safety.

But where are the critical danger spots in which you face the greatest risk? In a particularly good overview of police officer survival during traffic stops published in the February 1981 *FBI Law Enforcement Bulletin,* William Thomas and Frank Boyer, of the Division of Law Enforcement Training in the Kentucky Department of Justice, enumerated a number of "points of vulnerability" in a routine traffic stop. These points, listed below, suggest those times during a stop when an officer must be most vigilant and prepared for trouble:

• When the officer first makes the stop, but before exiting the police unit

• While he is searching for items (citation pad, notebook, etc.) he needs

• While the violator's or passenger's hands are removed from the officer's sight in order to find an operator's license, vehicle registration or other identification

• When the officer returns to his cruiser with his back to the stopped vehicle

• While sitting in the cruiser writing the citation

• During the officer's second approach to deliver the citation

• While the officer is engaged in a second encounter with the violater

• When the officer turns his back to return to the cruiser and reenter service

The key to a safe vehicular stop, then, is to analyze the

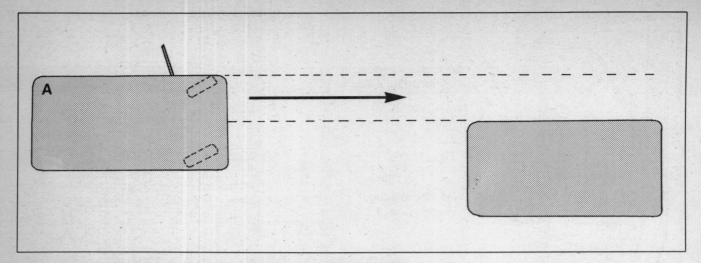

Proper positioning of a police vehicle (A) in a moderate-risk motor vehicle stop.

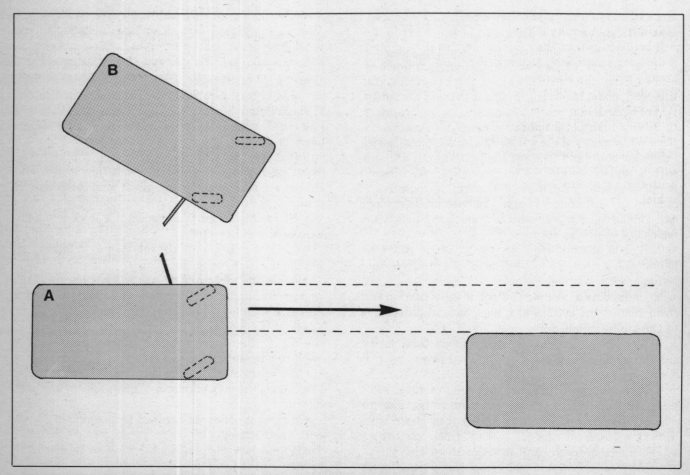

Proper positioning of police vehicle (A) and backup unit (B) in a high-risk motor vehicle stop.

When approaching the suspect vehicle, check the trunk to make sure it is not ajar and concealing an additional passenger.

As you pass the rear portion of the suspect vehicle, check the back seat for hidden persons, weapons or possible contraband.

steps in a stop and emphasize those points which will maximize your safety. The components of a stop that will be discussed in the remainder of this article are: radio communication; site selection; stopping the vehicle; establishing control and a zone of safety; approaching the vehicle; control of the violator; and terminating the stop.

Radio Communication. Your best friend in any vehicular stop—and in most other situations—is your radio. Once you have decided that a stop is necessary, run a wants/warrants check on the vehicle tag and wait for its return before you attempt to stop the vehicle. Always use the radio to notify your dispatcher and other officers when you are making a stop, your exact location and the license plate number and description of the stopped vehicle. Once you have relayed this information to headquarters, be sure your microphone is still accessible throughout the stop; leave it on your steering wheel where it can easily be reached or hang it out your open driver's window.

Site Selection. While you're waiting for the records check to return, follow the target vehicle at a distance of about one car length for every 10 mph. That will allow you adequate room to maneuver if the driver attempts any evasive tactics and will reduce some of the time with which the driver-occupants of that car can decide they're your target and begin to prepare for you.

Select the location for your stop carefully. A variety of factors connected to the road itself must be considered prior to pulling a vehicle over. The road/shoulder width should be enough to allow both vehicles to leave the road and allow traffic to pass safely. Stops on hills or curves, which restrict the vision of approaching drivers, should be avoided to increase your safety and the safety of others. Finally, be sure that the site of your stop is not so congested with people that it affords the "bad-guy" extra protection while you are restrained from returning gunfire because of fear of hitting an innocent bystander. Most often he will not share that concern. When stopping a driver at night, try to position him in the light for clearer observation and use the shadows to increase your own protection. Remember, the site of a stop is critical to increasing your safety.

Stopping the Vehicle. Once you have decided to make the stop, have received your information on the radio and have selected the site, it's time to notify the driver that he should pull over. Turn on your blue lights, and initially tap your horn; flash your headlights or spotlight to gain attention if the car still has not stopped. Use your siren only as a last resort. And, regardless of the actions of the violator, never pull alongside and motion him over to the side of the road; you're only increasing your vulnerability and setting yourself up for the violator to brake and become *your* pursuer.

Establishing Control and a Zone of Safety. Once the violator starts to pull to the side of the road, remember that the best position for you in a moderate-risk stop is 15 feet behind and three feet to the left of the stopped vehicle. In a high-risk stop, allow yourself more room, about 30 feet, for both safety and maneuverability. As you park, turn your vehicle steering wheel to the left so your tires can afford you protection from ricochets and low gunfire. Make sure your driver's window is rolled down so you can hear any unusual noises that might arouse your suspicion. Use your public address system to ask the driver to turn off the engine of his car, but leave your own car engine running.

Particularly at night, use your lights to assist you in control. Train your bright headlights on the car and direct your spotlight at the car's inside rearview mirror. This will improve your illumination and your ability to observe the subject car, and will also increase your psychological control over its occupants. *Never* place yourself in a situation where you silhouette yourself in your own lights and make yourself a target.

Prior to exiting your patrol car, observe the stopped vehicle and its occupants. If you see anything suspicious, do not hesitate to request backup units. Remember, requesting assistance is not a sign of weakness or inability to handle your job; it's a sign of intelligence and common sense. If backups are needed, order the driver of the stopped vehicle to throw his keys out the window and maintain control of the situation at a safe distance until your backups arrive.

If nothing initially arouses your suspicions, exit your vehicle and prepare to approach the stopped car carefully. Unsnap your service holster and keep your gun hand free. Pause to analyze the situation again prior to leaving the safety of your car.

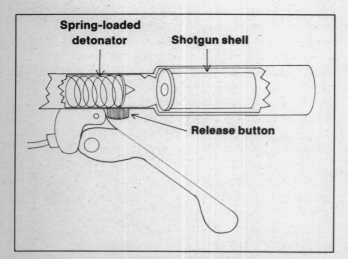

Shotgun built into the handlebars of a motorcycle. Reproduced from the Florida Criminal Activity Bulletin, published by the Florida Department of Law Enforcement.

Approaching the Vehicle. The canons of an approach are the simple precautions you have heard since you entered the academy. Take your time and be observant. Closely watch the movements of the driver and any passengers. Check the trunk and make sure it is not ajar and possibly concealing an additional passenger. If the vehicle is a van, make sure the rear doors are locked, and there is no threat from inside. Look in the back seat for any hidden passengers or weapons. Look for little things—an out-of-place or changed license plate, damage to any doors or windows or furtive movements by the driver or his passengers—which should raise your suspicions and therefore signal danger.

Always maintain firm control of the violator and direct him to the safest location for your protection. Note the officer has her gun hand free and is keeping the door between herself and the violator.

Remember, too, that the driver of the other car has in his control a weapon weighing thousands of pounds: his automobile. Always use your zone of safety in your approach and don't place yourself between the two cars. You could easily be crushed if the stopped driver suddenly shifted his car into reverse and floored the accelerator. His ability to control his car is another reason to demand that he turn off the motor once his car is pulled safely to the side of the road.

Beware of other tricks of the trade used by criminals. A shotgun could be mounted inside the door of an automobile and fired by pulling a guidewire attached to the dash board. Motorcyclists have also been known to turn their cycle handlebars into a single-shot shotgun and fire upon unsuspecting officers. So stay abreast of the state of the art on how officers are being killed and assaulted and learn from these tragedies how to protect your life.

At night, remember that you can use shadows to your benefit. Keep the stopped vehicle in the light—as much light between the street lights and your headlights and spotlight as possible—and *you* stay in the shadows unless, or until, you must approach the vehicle. At times, it may even be advantageous to approach the car from the passenger's side to increase your time and ability to observe what's happening inside and to maximize your use of shadows.

Never silhouette yourself in your own headlights during an approach and, if you're the backup unit on a high-risk stop, turn off your headlights *and* emergency lights just before you arrive on the scene; the officer you're assisting could otherwise lose his cover of darkness, his night vision and his life.

Control of the Suspect. Again, your training and experience are the best guides for successful—and safe—control of the suspect. Always keep the passengers and the driver in the car until you are ready for him to exit. When you approach the vehicle, never stand where the suspect or his passengers may have an easy shot at you; stand off center and slightly to the rear of the driver's door so he has to turn to respond to your inquiry. Two things act in your favor: 1) the speed with which he can turn with a weapon is reduced while your ability to observe and respond to that danger is somewhat increased; and 2) because he has to move to meet your commands, your psychological control of the situation is increased. When you first approach the vehicle, ask for a driver's license and/or other form of identification and have the driver produce it with his left hand; the odds are on your side that the person's left hand will be his non-gun hand.

Remember, too, that this kind of a traffic stop is an emotion-laden situation; you should take steps to reduce the tension and decrease your own risk. Always speak to the violator in a courteous, well-modulated tone. Refer to him with respect, and never do anything which is overtly offensive or designed to affront the individual. Remember that you are a professional; never provoke a confrontation—verbal or physical—with someone you have stopped.

Particularly if there are passengers in the car,

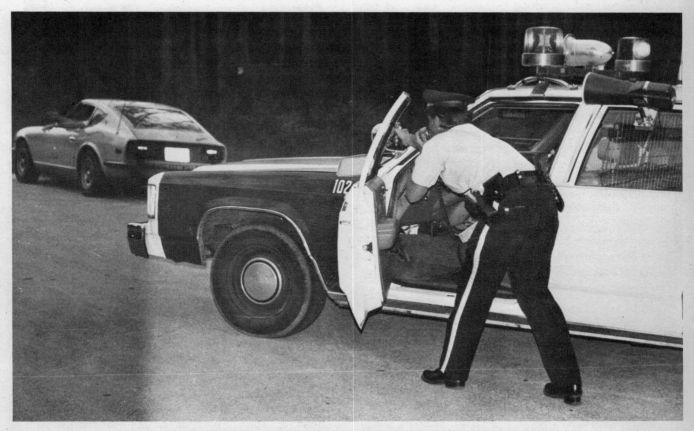

In a high-risk situation, use your public-address system to control the stopped vehicle and its occupants, while using your vehicle as a defensive shield. The officer here has his weapon drawn, and the suspect has both arms out the window of his vehicle where the officer can see them.

Always place the violator where you can keep him within your peripheral vision, especially as you write the citation.

remove the driver and bring him back to your vehicle to write the citation. This will allow you continued observation of the individual and the vehicle, reduce the passengers' influence on the driver's behavior and reduce points of danger as you reapproach the car. Never let the driver get too close; have him stand at the front of your patrol car, while you stand behind the open patrol car door to write a citation. In this position, you can use your peripheral vision to observe the driver continually while you are writing. Your vehicle again serves as a shield for your protection and you have easy access to both your shotgun and your radio. Remember, always think survival.

A number of officers and experts in the field of police survival have additional suggestions to improve your safety in high-risk stops. To reduce the potential for danger in "those cases where the police officer has an explainable justification for feeling that his safety is in jeopardy," Thomas and Boyer, for instance, advocate a number of other steps which make great use of the vehicle to protect the officer. More important, they require the suspect to come to the officer's cruiser as soon as the stop is effected and the officer is prepared.

Central to their approach is the need for effective planning of the stop and execution based on the potential danger faced in any stop. They suggest a number of modifications to normal stopping procedures, such as changing the location of writing the ticket to the rear of the police cruiser. Thus, with the violator easily within the peripheral vision of the officer, the officer is not required to turn his back on the violator at any time; he is no longer vulnerable while sitting in his cruiser writing the citation; and he can more easily observe and respond to potential

danger signs. This technique is especially useful when the subtle, though oftentimes indescribable, feelings of danger are aroused and an officer feels that, based on experience and intuition, something about the stop is just "not right."

Control of the violator and any passengers in a high-risk stop is critical. It cannot be emphasized too strongly that any officer performing one of these stops should wait until the arrival of backup units before exiting his vehicle. The occupants should be controlled and brought from their vehicle by the use of the cruiser's public address system once there is adequate firepower from the officer and his backup units. Each individual in the stopped vehicle should be commanded to exit the vehicle one at a time through the driver's side doors, instructed to walk backward to the patrol cars and secured before the next individual exits the vehicle. In such cases, assume that each individual is armed. Verbal command over the individuals should be exercised by a single officer, usually the driver of the initial stopping vehicle. Time should be utilized to gain and maintain psychological control but the situation should never be rushed. Clear and distinct verbal commands should reinforce the obvious control of the police over the situation.

Terminating the Stop. No stop is complete until the stopped vehicle is again on the road or its occupants are in custody and the vehicle has been secured. Even in the moderate-risk stop, in which you have given the violator a citation or a warning, don't let your guard down until you have watched the driver reenter the traffic lane from the safety of your patrol car. It becomes a safer task if the driver has had to join you at the cruiser to receive his citation or warning and has to return *by himself* to his car. With that point of vulnerability thus reduced, your safety is increased.

If your vehicular stop was high-risk and you safely took the violators into custody, be sure to check the vehicle and trunk to make sure there is no one hidden within. Following your departmental procedures, inventory the vehicle and secure it, or call a wrecker and take it to your impound site. Use the same care to inventory and seize the vehicle that you did to take its occupants into custody; don't lose potential court cases through careless handling of property.

Checklist for Safe Vehicular Stops

Perhaps one of the best tools for safely performing a vehicular stop is to be prepared with a mental checklist of specific steps to use. Once you have observed a violation or made a decision to stop a vehicle that is suspicious or contains known criminals, have these steps in your mind and make sure you have rehearsed them enough so your responses are automatic.

1. Decide that the stop is necessary because: you have observed a traffic violation, the vehicle appears suspicious or its description matches that of a known violator.

2. Run a wants/warrants check on the license plate and wait for its return *before* you stop the vehicle.

3. Follow the car at a distance of about one car length for every 10 miles per hour of speed; such a distance will allow you quickly, yet safely, to respond to any actions of the violator.

4. Choose a location for the stop which maximizes your safety, the safety of the violator and the safety of the public.

5. If the vehicle contains a known or probable felon, request backup units and wait for their arrival *before* attempting the vehicular stop.

6. In simple traffic stops, make sure your citation book and any other items you need are accessible on your front seat so you will not have to search for them when the stop is made.

7. Once your wants/warrants check has returned and you have chosen the site for the stop, pull the violator over. The best position for you in a routine vehicular stop is 15 feet behind and three feet to the left of the stopped vehicle. In a high-risk stop, expand that distance of safety. Make sure that, when you park, you turn your steering wheel to the left so your tires can afford you some protection from richochets and low gunfire.

8. Radio in a full description of the vehicle, occupants and location of the stop *before* exiting your vehicle. Leave your microphone where it is easily accessible, either out the driver's window or on the steering wheel.

9. Before exiting your patrol car, observe the vehicle and its occupants: Is there anything suspicious at this point? If so, request and wait for your backups. Use your public-address system to establish control over the vehicle and its occupants.

10. Prior to approaching the vehicle, use your public-address system to ask the driver to turn off the engine of his car. Leave your own car engine running.

11. Carefully approach the stopped vehicle. Look for little things that may indicate danger, and utilize your training, experience, common sense and intuition to maintain your safety.

12. Always keep your holster unsnapped and your gun hand free during the stop.

13. Control the driver. Make him follow your instructions. If the driver is not alone, remove him from the vehicle and lead him to a location which allows you to control the individual as well as to observe passengers. Never allow the driver to get so close that he can pose a more immediate threat to you.

14. Never illuminate yourself with your own headlights.

15. Remember, no traffic stop is routine and each one poses a threat to your safety.

16. Finally, remember that no vehicular stop is complete until the driver of the stopped vehicle has reentered the traffic lane or until you have the driver or any passengers in custody and the vehicle is properly secured.

James D. Sewell is Chief of the Criminal Intelligence Bureau (CIB) the Florida Department of Law Enforcement. He was formerly the International Inspector of the CIB's Office of Inspector General and a lieutenant with the Florida State University Department of Public Safety, where he supervised the support service section. A graduate of the FBI National Academy, Chief Sewell holds B.S., M.S. and Ph.D. degrees in criminology from Florida State University.

William D. Beckerman is an instructor at the Lewis M. Lively Law Enforcement Training Center in Tallahassee, Florida. A 10-year veteran of Florida police service, he has served as a special agent in the state's Department of Law Enforcement, as Personnel and Training Sergeant in the Leon County Sheriff's Department and as Field Deputy and Investigative/Patrol Sergeant of the Alachua County Sheriff's Department. Beckerman holds an M.S. in criminal justice from Eastern Kentucky University.

Mastering the Ultimate Police Weapon— the Shotgun

Detective Robert A. Scanlon

The shotgun is a smooth-bore weapon that derives its name from the types of projectiles, or shot, which are fired from it. The projectiles vary in size, from the rifled slug—a single, large projectile of 72 caliber (12 gauge)— to the shotshell which contains over 2,400 separate, minute lead pellets.

The three loads most commonly issued by law enforcement agencies are the rifled slug, no. 00 buckshot and no. 4 buckshot. When the rifled slug is employed, the shotgun changes from a close-quarter weapon to one with a medium range. The one-ounce lead slug performs like a rifle bullet and can be extremely accurate at distances of 100 yards or so. Yet, unlike a rifle projectile, the average slug has a hollow base and loses most of its energy upon impact, so the chances of it ricocheting are almost nil. With training, most police officers using a shotgun can easily strike and kill a man at 80 to 100 yards. The rifled slug can easily penetrate a car door and still have enough energy left to fatally wound a person seated inside.

In contrast to the no. 4 buckshot, the 00 buckshot is a shell casing containing nine pellets of 33 caliber. When this type of shell is fired at a person from a distance of 60 yards, the pattern is such that at least one of the pellets will strike the target. When used at close range, this same shell could easily take a person's head off. In fact, there have been stories of 00 buckshot striking a man in the stomach at close range and nearly cutting him in half. This load was the most widely used by law enforcement until about 1976, when the no. 4 buckshot load became popular with many major agencies.

A no. 4 buckshot shell contains 27 pellets of 24 caliber. Tests con- ducted by the armed forces and the Los Angeles Police Department reveal that at seven yards the patterns of no. 4 buckshot were slightly over three inches greater in diameter than the 00 buckshot. At 25 yards, the diameter was increased by almost a foot. The most potent no. 4 buckshot was ultimately adopted as the standard service load by the New York and Los Angeles police departments, and by numerous other city departments.

The principal pump guns used by American law enforcement agencies are: the Savage M-69 RH, High Standard M-811, Winchester M-1200, Remington M-870 and Ithaca M-37. Some departments, however, have begun using semiautomatics. While it's true that semiautomatics can fire faster than pump guns, they also can malfunction, causing precious time to be wasted in clearing the action. An-

The Auto-Burglar, a 20-gauge shotgun, is only 26½ inches overall. Because of its size, this weapon is classified as a pistol in many states.

other problem is that some of the special accessories, such as the "Ferret" barricade gas shell manufactured by AAI, may not function properly in a semiauto. Nevertheless, for departments that prefer semiautos, the most widely used and least troublesome ones are the High Standard M-8245, the Remington 1100 and the "Massive Monster," Ithaca's 10-guage Magnum Roadblocker.

Narcotics arrest squads and robbery stakeout teams have found that nothing delivers two shots faster than the old faithful double barrel. When used by stakeout teams, the double tubes are usually loaded with one slug and one no. 4 buckshot—a truly deadly combination. The most popular double-barreled guns are the Stevens M-311, and the FIE Brute, which is only 30 inches long overall and is

available in either 12 or 20 gauge. Other high-performance shotguns include the Zabala double barrel, which is even shorter than the Brute (only 28 inches overall), and the old standby Auto-Burglar, a 20-gauge sawed-off weapon with a 12-inch barrel, full pistol grip and an overall length of 26½ inches. Except for the Auto-Burglar, all these weapons have barrels of at least 18 inches and overall lengths of at least 26 inches to meet minimum federal regulations.

Throughout the recent history of the United States, the shotgun has been held in high esteem by law enforcement officers—from sheriffs and the stagecoach guards of the 1800s to the big city cops and federal agents of today. Because of the weapon's capabilities and versatility, a majority of officers and experts consider the shotgun to be

the best defensive and backup weapon in the police arsenal.

The shotgun is carried primarily on dangerous assignments, such as stakeouts and raids, where the police are led to believe that the persons they are seeking are armed and dangerous. When officers go on a raid where there is the possibility of encountering armed adversaries, the shotgun greatly increases their feeling of confidence. The size of the muzzle opening on a 12-gauge shotgun is .729 of an inch. This penny-sized opening pointed in the direction of an adversary tends to intimidate the toughest criminals and, in most cases, stops trouble before it starts.

This reaction by criminals is proof enough of the weapon's value to the law enforcement community; however, the weapon can be invaluable in everyday, routine police duties. The shotgun, for example, is carried when transporting payrolls and deposits to and from banks, or when a heavy-duty weapon is needed to kill a dangerous or fatally injured animal. (In the latter situation a handgun would be impractical and even dangerous to bystanders because of possible ricocheting.)

Ironically, although the shotgun is a law enforcement officer's most effective and versatile weapon, it is often a police department's most neglected piece of equipment. Compounding this problem, many

The FIE Brute has 19-inch barrels and is 30 inches overall. It can be obtained in 12, 20 or .410 gauges.

U.S. police forces are inadequately trained to use the weapon and, consequently, the weapon is generally abused and improperly maintained. In many police vehicles, for example, a shotgun is placed in a rack standing against the vehicle's dashboard and is sometimes used by officers as an ashtray or hat rack. Telltale rust spots along the barrel and on the receiver are common signs of the neglected department shotgun. Yet, when the need arises for the use of shotguns, these same mistreated weapons will be expected to function flawlessly.

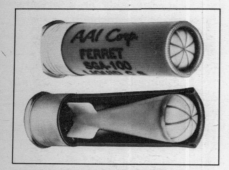

Exterior and interior views of the Ferret 12-gauge barricade shell which dispenses tear gas after penetrating an obstacle. Note the fins on the bottom of the projectile, which account for its accuracy.

If mistreatment of the shotgun were not reason enough to educate and train officers in the proper use and functioning of the weapon, there is another reason: two-officer patrol cars in the big cities are being phased out, and the one-officer cars are being fitted with shotguns in place of partners. Cities such as New York and Detroit have expanded their training programs for officers who are assigned to shotgun-equipped, one-man patrol cars, and other major departments throughout the country are doing the same. Aside from the training programs of these major departments, however, shotgun

training is generally inadequate across the country. Officers are often not given enough practice time with the weapon and are unable to handle it with self-confidence and proficiency.

Despite these facts, there seems to be a prevailing belief among police administrators that even without sufficient training an officer can take the shotgun from his dashboard rack whenever necessary and protect himself and others by virtue of the weapon's capabilities alone. This belief is erroneous; when an officer encounters a life-threatening situation, only his self-confidence along with his mastery of the weapon will determine whether he will emerge from the confrontation alive.

Shotgun Training

Mastery of the shotgun, particularly in instances of armed confrontation, should include an officer's ability to reload his weapon quickly and efficiently. During armed encounters it is often necessary for the officer to reload without looking away from his adversary even for an instant. Such reloading expertise can only be developed through weeks of intense, supervised training.

Standard Loading Techniques. The officer should first grip the weapon in his left hand and put the safety on while keeping his fingers away from the trigger *(Photo 1)*. The left elbow should be kept against the body, with the weapon held parallel to the body and the muzzle well above the head of the tallest person present. The shells to be loaded should be kept in an accessible right-side pocket containing only the shells. Loading should be accomplished with the right hand. Because the uniformed officer carries additional equipment, such as a holster, cuffs and nightstick, the trainee can use the

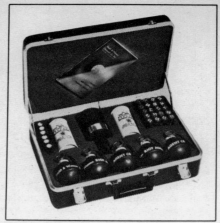

The S & W Tear Gas Kit contains five baseball-type tear-gas grenades, 20 shotshells containing CS gas and an attachment for a 12-gauge shotgun from which canisters of tear gas can be launched. The six blank shotshells on the left of the kit are used for propelling the canisters.

right-rear pocket of his uniform pants to hold extra shells.

If the officer feels he will use the shotgun immediately, he should drop a shell into the ejection port and close the action with his right hand *(Photo 2)*. Other shells can then be loaded into the magazine. If the weapon is to be placed in a vehicle rack or carried to a scene of action, the chamber should always be kept free of shells *(Photos 3 and 4)*.

Combat Loading. These techniques were designed by the FBI for the pump shotgun, but a firearms instructor can easily alter them for other types of weapons. In combat loading, a right-handed shooter should hold the weapon by the pistol grip with the right hand, keeping it parallel to the ground *(Photo 5)*. By keeping the stock against the right hipbone, the officer can immediately fire from the hip if the need arises. Of course, if time allows the weapon can be fired from the shoulder. In combat loading, a right-handed shooter should carry extra shells in a left or rear pocket. When grasping a shell,

The initial steps for loading a shotgun: (1) grip the weapon using the weak hand (usually the left) and put on the safety, keeping your left elbow against your body. Keep the muzzle well above the head of the tallest person present. (2) For immediate use, open the action, put a round in the ejection port and close the action; load the remaining rounds in the magazine. (3) No shell should be placed in the chamber if the weapon is to be transported.

The correct stance (4) when firing a shotgun from the hip position; bend your front leg to help absorb recoil. (5) In a combat situation, a right-handed shooter should hold the weapon against his left hip, parallel to the ground so he can fire immediately. (6) To load, place the shell in the ejection port from under the receiver; seat the round, then move your left hand forward to grip the forearm, moving it forward to close the action and chamber the round.

Another method of loading during combat is (7) to pass the left hand over the top of the slightly canted receiver and drop the round into the ejection port from above. (8) Feel for the trigger guard and move your hand forward until you feel the loading port. Practice this procedure without looking at the gun; it will prepare you for any fire fight in the dark. Once loaded, bring the gun to a modified port arms position (9) before changing your position.

the shooter should keep it at the base of his fingers *(Photo 6)*. Use of the method in emergency situations allows the officer to grasp the forend of the weapon to steady and fire the shotgun accurately without dropping the shell. All loading should be done without looking at the weapon so the officer can be alert for a potential adversary. (The FBI suggests that instructors teaching this type of course allow students to practice the procedure several times while *looking* at the gun in order to master the loading techniques.)

There are two acceptable methods for loading the first round when the shotgun is empty and the action open. In the first method, the left hand passes under the action and raises the hand-held shell until it slips into the ejection port *(Photo 5)*. The left hand is then moved forward while grasping the foregrip, thus closing the action and chambering the round.

The second and less desirable method is to cant the weapon slightly to the left *(Photo 7)*. At this point, the officer's left hand passes over the weapon and the shell is dropped into the ejection port. The foregrip is then moved forward, closing the action and chambering the round. To reload spare shells in the magazine tube,

the left hand is brought under the weapon; once the head of the shell is in the magazine tube, seat it fully by pressing with the thumb *(Photo 8)*. To aid in locating the loading port, the shooter can first press the shell against the trigger guard, then move it slowly forward until it is seated properly. This type of training for combat situations is also useful if the officer is confronted with a firefight at night or is inside an unlighted building, a warehouse, for example. Once the weapon is reloaded and the officer wishes to change positions, the shotgun should be held at a modified port arms position *(Photo 9.)*

Combat Skeet Course. This combat skeet course is fired on a standard skeet field and consists of five phases, with five shells being fired in at each phase for a total of 25 shells. (See no. 10 for diagram of course).

Phase A. The officer starts at station 1 with five no. 9 shotshells and an unloaded weapon. On command, he will load one round into the chamber and one round into the magazine (using combat loading techniques) and come to the ready gun position, announcing when he is ready *(Photo 9)*. During this sequence he will be presented with five moving clay birds to shoot. The first bird will be re-

leased within four seconds from either the low or high house (one located at each end of the skeet field) at the instructor's discretion. From the first report of firing, the instructor will count off four seconds, then release another bird to the shooter. In the case of doubles (two birds at one time), the four seconds is counted from the second shot. In all, the officer will receive three single birds either from the low or high house and one set of doubles. Any of the five potential shots not fired are counted as misses.

Phase B. This phase is fired from position 2 and the clay bird targets are presented in similar fashion as in Phase A, but the sequence should vary.

Phase C. This phase is fired from position 6 following the same instructions as with Phase B.

Phase D. This phase is to be fired from position 7 and follows the shooting pattern as in Phase A.

Phase E. The officer starts at station 4, loads the weapon with two rounds and brings his shotgun to the ready gun position. At this point, the officer begins to walk toward position 8. As the shooter walks, he is presented with five bird targets in a varied sequence.

This course can be altered to suit the particular needs of a de-

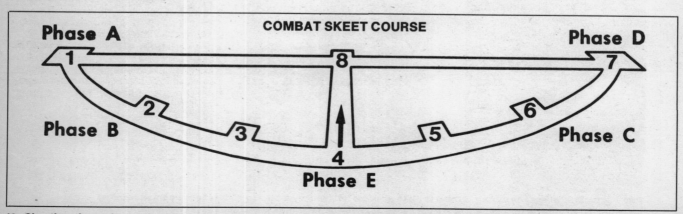

10. Shooting phases for combat skeet course. Each shooter fires five shells at each of the five phases, for a total of 25 shells.

SHOTGUN COURSE NO. 6

For this practice course, use one silhouette (11), ten rounds of no. 00 buckshot and two rifled slugs on a Practical Police Course (P.P.C.). At 50 yards, with no time between shots, load two slugs; fire one standing (12) and one kneeling (13).

At 25 yards, in 30 seconds, load four rounds and come to ready gun position. On the whistle, load a fifth round into the magazine (14) and fire one round. Load a sixth round into the magazine and continue to fire until you have fired all six shots. At 15 yards, in 10 seconds, load four rounds and come to ready gun position. On the whistle, chamber the first round and fire all four rounds (15).

INSTRUCTOR'S SHOTGUN COURSE

This shotgun practice course calls for four silhouette targets (16) and two barricades, one placed at 60 yards from the targets, and the other, at 25 yards; 10 rounds of no. 00 buckshot and 10 rifled slugs.

At 60 yards, load four rounds of rifled slugs; come to ready gun position. On the whistle, while standing, fire two rounds with the strong hand (17) and two with the weak hand (18); one round each target.

At 60 yards, reload with four rounds of rifled slugs; come to ready gun position. Using the barricade, on the whistle, fire two rounds around the clock standing (19) and kneeling (20) using your strong hand.

Still using the barricade at 60 yards, fire two rounds standing (21) and kneeling (22) with your weak hand. Reload two no. 00 buckshot, then two slugs.

Jog to the 50-yard line and fire two rounds strong hand while kneeling; use two targets. Then jog to the 25-yard line and fire two rounds the same way (23). At 25 yards, move behind the barricade (24), and reload with four rounds of buckshot. Fire all four rounds around the clock, one shot at each target. Reload four more rounds of buckshot. Advance to the 15-yard line; from a hip-shooting position, fire one round at each target.

partment or agency. In tests run by the FBI, it was found that the average shooter hits about three fewer targets than on an ordinary sport skeet course. However, use of the Combat Skeet Course along with combat loading techniques reflects a higher degree of realism in police shotgun training. Such training could give an officer the edge when it really counts.

Shotgun Course No. 6. As they have done with other weapons, the FBI staff instructors have developed combat training courses for the shotgun. Of the eight devised, this is the most practical one for the average department. Score five points for each slug hit, one point for each buckshot hit. Total possible score is 100 points; the qualifying score, depending on departmental requirements, can be between 60 and 70 points.

Instructor's Shotgun Course. Use four targets per shooter and a barricade at 60 and 25 yards, 10 rounds of no. 00 buckshot and 10 rifled slugs on a P.P.C. field. Using a scoring method of one point for each of the rifled slugs and one point for each of the buckshot (with nine pellets to each round), you get a total of 100 points. Because this course is often used to qualify instructors, the qualifying score starts at 70.

The importance of shotgun training cannot be overemphasized. Since the shotgun is the police officer's most important backup weapon, he should be properly trained in its use so he acquires the self-confidence to use it with skill and accuracy.

Editor's Note: For detailed specifications of shotguns designed for law enforcement, and for new shotgun products, see page 213.

How Well Do You Know the Law?

As a uniformed officer or detective working on the street, you might find yourself in any of the following situations, which were created to test your knowledge of the law.

Many details in these stories are taken from actual incidents involving search and seizure, probable cause and wiretapping. After reading them, answer the questions that follow each scenario and find out just how sharp your knowledge of proper police investigative procedures really is. Major court decisions based on actual cases are discussed as well.

Remember, at the scene of a crime, it is not unusual for an officer to make an error in judgment. But, if you're going to make a mistake, let it be on the next few pages instead of on the street, where it could mean the loss of a conviction, a case—or even a life.

Saturday Night Accident

On Saturday night, October 4, Detective Dave Rutland, a 20-year veteran of police work, was driving through a tunnel joining two Eastern cities when he observed a blue 1979 Chevrolet being driven in an erratic manner. The vehicle, occupied by only a driver, was traveling at an excessive rate of speed and was weaving from lane to lane.

As the Chevrolet disappeared out of sight around a curve, Det. Rutland heard a crash. The traffic slowed, then stopped. Rutland got out of his car and walked toward the accident. He saw that the Chevrolet had struck the rear of a van traveling in the same direction. The van's occupants, two adults and two young children, sustained extensive injuries from the collision. Rutland observed that both vehicles were severely damaged and could not be driven.

He then walked over to the blue automobile and observed that the driver, a white male of about 25 years of age, appeared to be in a stupor—as if under the influence of alcohol or drugs. About that time, two patrol units from the tunnel authority police arrived. One unit contained two uniformed officers and the other, a uniformed lieutenant. One of the officers and the lieutenant approached the driver of the Chevrolet, who, by this time, had gotten out of his vehicle and was staggering on the roadway. The officers spoke with him for a minute, then placed him under arrest and put him in the back of a patrol car which had a wire mesh cage separating the front and back seats.

Rutland walked to the driver's side of the Chevrolet and saw that the driver had left the front door open. He looked inside and observed about ten 38-caliber cartridges on the floor of the vehicle on the driver's side. He immediately went to the uniformed lieutenant, identified himself and told him what he had observed earlier in the tunnel and about the cartridges in the car. The lieutenant and Rutland walked to the Chevrolet, and the lieutenant, observing the cartridges, began a search of the vehicle.

Rutland said, "Lieutenant, you'd better not search this car without a warrant; it could blow the case." The lieutenant turned sharply to Rutland, straightened up and replied, "Let's get something straight. I appreciate your help, but I'm in charge of this scene. I'll take whatever action I deem fitting and necessary." Holding out his hand with the loose cartridges he added, "Besides, I've got probable cause." The lieutenant returned to search the vehicle as Rutland stood shaking his head. "Not really, lieutenant," he told him, "because this vehicle is incapable of being moved under its own power. You should get a search warrant."

Under the driver's seat, the lieutenant found a half-filled box of 38-caliber cartridges, which had broken open when the accident occurred. He also found a 38-caliber Smith & Wesson round butt revolver. After securing the evidence, he thanked Rutland for his assistance and asked him to stop at the department's station house outside the tunnel and give a statement, which the detective did.

Questions:

1. Since Det. Rutland was off duty, should he have minded his own business and not become involved with the incident?
2. Did the officer and the lieutenant handle the driver of the car correctly?
3. Was Det. Rutland's advice to the lieutenant regarding a search warrant correct?
4. Was the lieutenant's response to Rutland's advice appropriate?
5. Upon learning about the cartridges, what should the lieutenant have done immediately?

(Answers appear on page 55.)

Kansas City Stakeout

At approximately 8:30 p.m. on June 20, two D.E.A. agents were on a stakeout in downtown Kansas City, Kansas. Agents Brewer and Mitchell were standing near the corner of Fifth Street and Minnesota Avenue waiting for a meet to go down. The meet was to be between a known international narcotics courier and a local member of a large narcotics syndicate.

They stationed themselves in the doorway of a small shoe repair shop that was closed. About 8:45 p.m., the agents observed two men, who appeared to be in their mid-40s, standing across the street halfway down the block. Three different times the men walked to a jewelry store, which was directly across from the agents, peered through the window, then returned to their former positions. Shortly after the third trip to the store window, the men began to argue. The argument lasted about 10 minutes and became heated to the point where a fist fight appeared imminent.

Suddenly, the taller of the two men turned and started across the street heading in the direction of the two agents. He crossed the street and stepped onto the curb when the agents saw the man stop short and grab his left trouser leg near the knee. A small-frame revolver dropped out onto the street. The man quickly picked up the gun and stuck it back into his waistband. He looked around cautiously to see if anyone had seen him and, when he spotted the two agents, he took off down the street in the opposite direction.

The agents instantly made their move. They strode down the street and overtook him by the middle of the block. Drawing their weapons, they placed him under arrest, ordered him to interlock his fingers and place them on his head. Agent Brewer searched the man and found an old model Harrington and Richardson 32 caliber, fully loaded, in his waistband. In the man's coat pocket, Brewer also found a stocking mask.

Once the man was handcuffed behind his back, agent Mitchell turned his attention to the man's partner, who was still across the street watching the arrest being made. Seeing that he was now the focus of Mitchell's attention, the man turned and began running down the street toward Minnesota Avenue. Mitchell turned back to his partner, "I'm gonna get the other guy." Brewer replied, "What for, we got nothing on him." Mitchell answered as he started running up the street, "He's gotta have a gun, too." Mitchell chased the suspect to Minnesota Avenue, then south on Minnesota about another half-block when he saw the suspect throw something to the ground near some garbage cans. Mitchell stopped by the garbage cans and found that the suspect had discarded a Beretta 380-caliber automatic pistol. He picked up the weapon and continued the chase.

Within the next block, just before reaching Chestnut Avenue, the suspect ran out of steam and fell exhausted to the pavement. Mitchell, who was by now not in much better shape, overtook the suspect and handcuffed him behind his back while he was still on the ground. After helping the suspect to his feet and advising him of his rights, Mitchell searched him and found a stocking mask in his back pants pocket.

Two Kansas City police officers on routine patrol observed what was taking place and stopped to investigate. Agent Mitchell identified himself and advised the uniformed officers of what had occurred. A second marked patrol unit was called to the scene and the two agents and their prisoners were transported to police headquarters. Both suspects, who by now had been identified as Stephen Meanio and Juan Alverez, were charged with illegal possession of firearms.

Questions:

1. Did the agents' observations provide enough probable cause to effect an arrest?
2. Was it correct for the agents to frisk or search the subjects?
3. Was Agent Mitchell correct in pursuing the other man?
4. Should the agents have abandoned the narcotics stakeout to arrest the two men?

(Answers appear on page 55.)

A Family Affair

On Friday, July 12, Sergeant Bob Edwards, a 17-year police veteran, was working the four-to-midnight shift. He was assigned to radio patrol with rookie patrolman Joe Decker, who only one month before had graduated from the academy.

The first two hours passed uneventfully. At 6:10 p.m. they responded to a call about a family dispute at 361 North Fourth Avenue. When they arrived at the location, both officers took their nightsticks and started up the stairs to the house. As they reached the door, it was opened by a woman who identified herself as Mrs. Helen Walsh. She was crying and holding a bloody towel over her face as she begged the officers to come in and help her.

When they entered the house, the officers observed a man standing in the living room. Mrs. Walsh identified him as her husband, Steve, whom she claimed had "beat her up." As Mrs. Walsh spoke, she removed the towel from her face, exposing a bloody nose and a badly split upper lip. The woman pleaded, "Please get that animal out of the house." Patrolman Decker appeared upset and agitated by the damage to the woman's face and looked at Steve Walsh angrily. Edwards kept calm and explained to Mrs. Walsh, "We can't just force your husband to leave his home unless you sign a complaint. Then we can arrest him." Mrs. Walsh replied excitedly, "No, no, I don't want him arrested. I just want him out of here until he sobers up." Decker lost control and voiced his anger, "You don't want him arrested? Look what he did to your face!"

Steve Walsh, who had obviously been drinking, laughed and remarked, "Why don't you boys run along and write some old lady a ticket." Decker spun around, pointed his finger at Walsh and said, "Watch your mouth, buddy." The smile drained from Walsh's face. Edwards stepped between the two men and spoke to Decker in a whisper, "Keep cool and don't get involved. He's been drinking and is trying to aggravate you. Besides, we didn't witness the assault and, if she won't sign a complaint, there's nothing we can do." Decker appeared to calm down and regain his composure.

Mrs. Walsh was by now becoming insistent that the officers force her husband to leave the house. As Edwards again tried to explain the law to Mrs. Walsh, Walsh suddenly stepped between the officer and his wife. He put his face close to his wife's and shouted, "Look, tramp, the boys in blue told you, they can't throw me out of my own house." Reacting impulsively, Decker grabbed Walsh by the shirt and started pulling him toward the front door. Walsh retaliated by swinging at Decker, who blocked the punch, and without hurting him forced Walsh against a wall and handcuffed him. At police headquarters, Decker charged Walsh with disturbing the peace and assault on a police officer.

Questions:

1. Was Sergeant Edwards' interpretation of the law correct?
2. Do the police have the right to force a man from his home at the request of his wife?
3. Were Patrolman Decker's actions toward Walsh justified?
4. Was the arrest of Steve Walsh valid?
5. Should Decker face departmental charges based on improper conduct?

(Answers appear on page 56.)

Stopping a Suspect Vehicle

State Trooper Eric Fredericks, 10 years with the California Highway Patrol, was on routine duty on Highway 1 along the Pacific Palisades. It was Sunday, February 2.

At 7:30 p.m. he was traveling south when he observed a dark blue 1979 Ford sedan bearing Colorado plates. Occupied by four black males, it was pulling out of a gas station. Traffic was light and, when the vehicle entered the roadway and headed south, Fredericks noticed that the front seat passenger turned several times to look at his troop car. After a short distance, Fredericks noticed that the driver was also busy looking in his rearview mirror, instead of watching the speedometer—the Ford was traveling 10 miles an hour over the speed limit. Fredericks decided to stop the sedan but, keeping in line with department procedures, he radioed his position to headquarters along with the plate number of the Ford and requested a backup.

As he switched on his flashing lights and the Ford started to pull over, Fredericks observed the front seat passenger look back at him, bend forward as if putting something under the front seat, then straighten up and glance back again. Once the vehicle had stopped, the trooper, without waiting for his backup, got out of his car and approached the Ford.

Fredericks asked the driver, later identified as Leroy Thompson, for his license and registration. Thompson produced a valid license, but stated that the vehicle was owned by the man seated next to him. The trooper walked around to the right front window and asked the man for the registration. Calvin Cooper produced a valid registration for his automobile, but Fredericks, still bothered by Cooper's actions prior to the stopping, asked him to step out from the sedan, whereupon the trooper patted him down for weapons. No weapons were found, but Fredericks discovered that Cooper was wearing an empty shoulder holster designed to hold a small-frame revolver. Cooper was ordered by the officer to stand by the right front fender.

Fredericks then searched under the seat where Cooper had been seated and found a cloth bag containing several hypodermic needles and eighteen 38-caliber cartridges. Fredericks asked Cooper and the three other occupants of the sedan about the ownership of the bag. No one spoke; they just shook their heads. Fredericks ordered the two men seated in the rear of the vehicle to keep their hands in plain sight and get out of the car. They, too, were patted down and, again, no weapons were found. However, William Cooper, Calvin's brother, was also wearing an empty shoulder holster designed for a small-frame revolver.

At this point a backup unit driven by Trooper Nick Vargas arrived at the scene. Taking Fredericks to the side, Vargas asked, "What have you got, Eric?" He answered, "Two guys wearing empty shoulder holsters, a bag of cartridges under the front seat—but no guns yet." Vargas thought for a moment, then asked, "Do you think you have enough to search the car?" Fredericks shot back, "I've arrested enough of these guys to know when they have guns—and I'm certain these guys have guns in that car."

With his backup now at the scene to watch the four men, Fredericks began to search the interior of the vehicle. On the floor near the back seat he found a paper bag containing three handguns: two small-frame 38-caliber revolvers and one 32-caliber automatic. The four men were placed under arrest and transported to state police headquarters.

Questions:
1. Was Trooper Fredericks correct in stopping the sedan?
2. Was the trooper following procedure in not waiting for his backup and asking Calvin Cooper to get out of the car?
3. Was Fredericks correct in patting down Calvin Cooper?
4. Did the trooper have probable cause to search the automobile?
5. Do you think the arrest would stand up in court?
(Answers appear on page 56.)

Drug Bust

Todd Williams, aged 19, of Columbus, Ohio, was stopped by a Columbus police officer Thursday afternoon, March 12, for what the officer first thought was drunken driving. As the officer approached Williams' car, he got out unsteadily and had to keep a hand on the car for support. The officer noticed classic signs of narcotics use: Williams' dilated pupils, despite the bright and sunny weather, his incessant talking and his overly alert and hyperactive behavior—he could barely stand still. The officer asked him if he had been drinking, to which Williams replied, "I don't drink." The officer then asked, "What kind of dope you been using?" Almost without thinking, Williams said nervously, "I only did one line of coke, man, that's all."

Williams was placed under arrest, patted down for weapons and transported to police headquarters. There he was searched and on his person was found six foil-covered packets containing white powder, which later tested out to be cocaine. It was also ascertained that Williams had a prior conviction for possession of narcotics. He was charged with being under the influence of narcotics and possession of a controlled dangerous substance. After a preliminary hearing, Williams' case was referred to the county prosecutor's office for presentation to a grand jury.

Several weeks later Williams' lawyer, James Waxman, visited the prosecutor to plea bargain. The prosecutor told the attorney that if his client pleaded guilty to charges against him and cooperated with the members of the narcotics squad by giving them useful information about his supplier, he would recommend that Williams be enrolled in a narcotics program instead of being sentenced to jail. The lawyer left the meeting after assuring the prosecutor that he would discuss the offer with his client.

The following week, Mr. Waxman informed the prosecutor that Williams decided to accept the plea offer. The prosecutor had an accusation drawn up and Williams pleaded guilty before Judge Robert Durkin of the Superior Court. Sentencing was delayed so the defendant could fulfill his part of the bargain.

That same afternoon, Williams met with Lt. Furness of the Narcotics Squad. He told the lieutenant that his supplier was a certain Curtis Mann and that Mann always kept a large quantity of drugs at his pad. Lt. Furness knew Mann was a big-time drug dealer; he asked Williams if he could get an undercover cop into Mann's pad to make a buy and Williams replied, "Sure I can."

On Sunday evening, April 19, Williams and Detective Jack Hunter, an undercover officer, drove to Mann's apartment on North Third Street. After parking the car, they entered the fashionable apartment building and took the elevator to the seventh floor. At apartment 7D Williams knocked and, shortly after, both men heard the peephole in the door open and close. The door opened and Mann ushered them in. Williams introduced Hunter to Mann and, after some conversation, he sold Hunter a half-ounce of cocaine for $1,200. After leaving the apartment, Hunter and Williams returned to the squad office, field-tested the suspected cocaine, then logged it into the evidence locker and met with Lt. Furness.

A week later, on April 26, Detective Hunter made a return visit with Williams to Mann's apartment and purchased another half-ounce of cocaine. At that same meeting, arrangements were made for Hunter to purchase two ounces of cocaine for $4,000 on Tuesday, May 12. After leaving Mann's apartment, Hunter followed the same routine of returning to his office, field-testing the suspected coke and logging it into the evidence locker. A second meeting with Lt. Furness took place. After hearing the results of the investigation conducted by Hunter, the lieutenant decided that at the time of the two-ounce buy, Mann would be arrested.

That same day, Detective Hunter signed four complaints against Curtis Mann: two for possession of a controlled dangerous substance and two for sale of a controlled dangerous substance. During the next few days, Hunter prepared his affidavit and application for a search warrant. On the morning of May 8, the papers were presented to Superior Court Judge Goldman, who, after reading the affidavit, signed the search warrant.

On the morning of May 12, five members of the squad—Lt. Furness, Det. Hunter, Sgt. Flynn, Det. Morgan and Det. Norris—met to discuss the upcoming raid. Hunter sketched the details of Mann's four-room apartment; Furness assigned Morgan to cover the rear of the building while the rest went in. The lieutenant, Flynn and Norris would stay down the hall from Mann's apartment and, after Hunter was inside for five minutes, they would break down the door. Before leaving the squad room, Hunter told them that the apartment had a fire-resistant, metal-covered door which would take several shots from the squad's 40-pound steel battering ram to open it.

The officers used two cars for transportation, and parked them around the corner on Madison Avenue. Hunter walked openly around the corner and into the apartment house. He walked down the first floor hallway, opened a fire-exit door leading to an alley and let the other officers in. They all got into the elevator and started up. Furness, Flynn and Norris got off at the sixth floor and walked upstairs; Hunter rode to seven. At apartment 7D, Hunter knocked and heard the peephole click open and shut. After unlocking the door and looking up and down the hallway, Mann motioned Hunter inside. In the living room, the two men talked about the buy and how the exchange would be made.

Suddenly a tremendous blast shook the door, then another. Mann jumped to his feet yelling, "Shit. Cops!" and bolted toward the bedroom. Hunter drew his gun, showed his badge and announced to Mann that he was a cop. Mann froze and raised his hands as a third smash against the door sent it flying open and the three detectives rushed inside. Mann was handcuffed and read his rights by Hunter, as the other officers began a thorough search of the apartment. In addition to the two ounces Hunter was to buy, the officers uncovered another one-ounce bag of coke, more than 1,000 amphetamines and a half-load (15 decks) of heroin. Before leaving the apartment, Flynn said to Furness, "You know, Lieutenant, this guy has three color televisions. I'm gonna seize them; I bet they're hot." "Good idea," Furness replied.

At police headquarters, Curtis Mann was booked on the four charges Hunter had made against him, plus a third charge of possession made by Hunter. Flynn entered the television serial numbers into the computer and was overjoyed to find that two of them had been reported stolen in Cleveland six months earlier. Flynn charged Mann with an additional complaint for possession of stolen property.

Questions:

1. When Williams was first arrested, should the officer have tried to find the cocaine on the initial

patdown?

2. Should the officer have called for a backup before stopping Williams?

3. Was Williams' case correctly handled?

4. Were two buys from Mann enough to justify a search warrant?

5. Did Detective Hunter conduct a proper undercover investigation?

6. Was it appropriate to seize the televisions?

7. Can Mann be charged with possession of stolen property?

(Answers appear on page 56.)

Wiretaps—Do's and Don'ts

It was Tuesday evening, January 10. Bill Keane of the Rockland County (New York) Organized Crime Task Force received a call from one of his informers. Joseph Penny, a paid informer, had been working for Detective Keane for a little over a year. During that time, Penny had provided information that had led to more than 10 arrests. On this occasion, Penny told Keane a gambling operation was going on at Crecca's Luncheonette on Elm Drive in Pearl River, New York. Penny went on to say that the owner was known as "Tony C" and was about 45 years old.

Keane asked him how the action was getting in. Penny replied, "Some comes in across the counter, but most of it comes in by phone. The number is 647-3661 and the caller has to use the code 'Sammy's well' to get the action in."

That afternoon Keane went to the County Criminal Identification Bureau and ran a check on the name Anthony Crecca. Keane found Crecca had a record of three convictions—two for assault and one for violation of the state's gambling laws. The following morning Keane went to the district attorney's office in New City and got a subpoena for the telephone company to turn over the last two month's toll sheets for number 647-3661. After picking up the tolls at the phone company's business office, Keane returned to the task force office and scrutinized them with his partner, Detective Vic Ulinsky. They found that most of the outgoing calls were made to one number in New Jersey between the hours of 10 a.m. and 3 p.m. Ulinsky turned to Keane with a smile. "Man, it looks like your snitch came up with another good one."

"Yeah, he's one of the best around. From the times of the phone calls, which are probably lay-offs, it looks like a lottery operation."

Ulinsky smiled, "A big lottery operation and . . . this guy could be connected with the mob."

The following morning around 11, the two detectives, dressed in undercover work clothes, drove in an unmarked van down Elm Drive past the luncheonette. They saw that the store was situated in the heart of a middle-class suburban neighborhood, a location they knew would make a surveillance difficult, if not impossible. They observed four cars parked at the curb in front of the store and one late-model silver Mercedes double-parked with the motor running. As they passed, Keane got the plate numbers of three of the vehicles. Ulinsky drove two blocks past the location, turned around and headed back toward the store. Keane then got the plates of the remaining two cars, one, a 1979 Buick with New York plate number AFD 300 and the other, the silver Mercedes 709 KND, of New Jersey. At 11:30 a.m. the next day, Ulinsky, again dressed in work clothes drove a van-type delivery truck to Elm Drive, parked across the street from the luncheonette and went in to have lunch. Inside the rear of the van, Keane watched the store through a ¼-inch hole in the door and during the next 40 minutes, he took down the license plate numbers of 15 vehicles whose drivers or passengers had gone into the store.

Upon returning to their office, the two officers checked that day's list against the first and found only one vehicle that showed up on both, the 1979 Buick. Ulinsky ran a check with the Department of Motor Vehicles and found that the car was owned by Donald Amier of the Bronx, New York. A check was run on Amier which revealed that at age 29 he had been arrested three times for violation of the state gambling laws. A further check with the State Police Organized Crime Unit revealed that Amier was a known numbers runner for the gambling operations controlled by a major crime family based in Westchester County, New York.

The following day, two different members of the task force drove to the area of the luncheonette and obtained seven more plate numbers. On this test, the silver Mercedes showed up again. A check revealed the owner to be Gus Mestaro, a known convicted gambler and underworld figure who lived in Paramus, New Jersey. Keane was now in possession of enough evidence to conclude that there was a gambling operation of substantial size going on that was most likely under the protection of a major crime family.

At about 2 p.m. that afternoon, Keane met with Penny at an outdoor public phone booth three blocks from Crecca's luncheonette. With Keane standing next to him, Penny called in a numbers bet to Crecca, using the code, "Sammy's well." After returning to their office, Keane and Ulinsky sat down with their superior, Lt. Joe Conlon, and laid out everything they had—the information, the tolls, the lists of the vehicles observed at the store and their owners, some of whom were members of organized crime families or known convicted gamblers. The detectives told Conlon more information could probably be obtained, but due to the location of the luncheonette, physical surveillance was dangerous and could blow the investigation. Lt. Conlon agreed and suggested that Keane apply to the district attorney for authorization for a wiretap and also make application for an "Interception of Wire Communication." The two detectives returned to their desks and immediately started work on the tedious and exacting job.

In his application for the wiretap, Keane included the following:

1. His authority (department)
2. Name of the person who was to install the wiretap, and his experience
3. What type of crime they were investigating and what type of evidence they were expecting to obtain
4. The type of building to be bugged and the phone number
5. The number of days he wanted the tap to run (maximum 30 days) and hours of the day (10 a.m. through 4 p.m.)
6. His personal background and experience as a police officer
7. How he first got his information about the operation (through an informer and how he had formerly been reliable)
8. Name and description of suspect and other unknown individuals
9. What had been done by Keane so far to corroborate the facts related by the informer and the results of these efforts
10. Why it would be dangerous to the investigation to continue using other means of surveillance
11. An assurance that every effort would be made to minimize or eliminate interception of those calls not pertaining to violations of the gambling laws
12. Finally, a request that the judge order the New York Bell Telephone Company to furnish all the necessary information and assistance to ensure a successful wiretap

On January 18, District Attorney Mellone signed the application for authorization and the following afternoon Judge Tracy of the County Superior Court reviewed and signed the wiretap order, which was to run for 14 days.

Once set up, the tap went well and the detectives were able to ascertain that numerous bets were coming in by phone and the outgoing toll calls to Gus Mestaro in New Jersey were lay-offs. On the fifth day of the tap, Keane was off and detectives Kell and White were running the wire. About 4:05 that afternoon, Keane stopped in the wire room to see how things were going. He was angry to find the equipment still running plus Kell and White in a fit of laughter while listening to a conversation.

Keane asked, "What the hell is going on? You're supposed to shut down at 4."

Kell was still laughing as he answered, "You should hear this—two broads telling each other about their affairs." Keane blew his top, "Are you guys trying to blow this case?"

Keane shut off the equipment and stormed out of the room. He went directly to Lt. Conlon and told him what had taken place in the wire room. Conlon immediately took Kell and White off the case and reassigned them. The wiretap ran for the remainder of the two weeks without a hitch and more than enough evidence was obtained to justify arrest and search warrants for Tony Crecca and his building, plus Donald Amier and his vehicle. Evidence was also gathered against Gus Mestaro; Keane signed a complaint against him, and the New Jersey authorities got a search warrant for his house based on probable cause from Rockland County. Further information was obtained that gave the Westchester County District Attorney's Office probable cause to secure search warrants for several locations known to be run by members of organized crime. When the warrants were served, gambling records were recovered and seized at Crecca's store and Mestaro's home. Numbers bets and records were also found on the person of Donald Amier.

Questions:

1. Did Detective Keane follow proper investigative procedures?
2. Did Keane have all the necessary information in his application?
3. Was the wiretap handled properly?
4. Can a law enforcement agency handling an investigation give evidence to an outside agency to act as probable cause?

(Answers appear on page 57.)

ANSWERS

Saturday Night Accident

1. No. As a police detective, Rutland acted correctly.
2. No. One of them should have searched the driver before placing him in the police vehicle. Had the driver been armed, one of the officers could have lost his life.
3. Yes. According to the Carroll Doctrine, his recommendations were correct.
4. No. Instead of getting angry at Rutland, the lieutenant should have listened to him. He should have realized that Rutland, a detective, might have been better versed on the laws of search and seizure.
5. The lieutenant should have checked with the uniformed officer to verify that the driver had been searched.

The Carroll Doctrine. *Carroll v. United States* (267 U.S. 132, 1925). This Supreme Court decision provides that the police may search an automobile without a warrant whenever two preconditions exist: 1) the police have probable cause to believe that the automobile contains evidence of a crime; and 2) the situation demands that an immediate and warrantless search be undertaken because the vehicle is drivable.

On December 16, a probable cause hearing was held before Judge Alfred Lecus of the Superior Court. After hearing the case, Judge Lecus suppressed the evidence and ruled that condition one in the Carroll Doctrine had been met in that the cartridges were in plain view, giving the lieutenant probable cause to believe a gun was also in the car. However, in the judge's opinion, the second condition of the doctrine was not met. Because of the totally disabled condition of the Chevrolet and the fact that it could not be driven away, a search warrant should have been obtained. The case was thrown out of court.

Kansas City Stakeout

1. Yes. Under the rules of the Plain View Doctrine, it was a valid arrest.
2. Yes. A frisk differs from a search in that: A frisk, or a patting down of the subject's clothing to ensure the officer's safety by making sure the suspect is not armed, may be taken on mere suspicion; a complete and thorough search of an individual may be undertaken once he is under arrest.
3. Yes. He had probable cause.
4. Yes. The stakeout was not abandoned because, up until the time of the arrests, neither of the subjects the agents were waiting for had arrived on the scene. In addition, the detectives—witnesses to an unexpected illegal occurrence—had an obligation to see that the law was enforced, regardless of the mission to which they were initially assigned.

Plain View Doctrine. *Coolidge v. New Hampshire* (*supra* n.6); *Warden v. Hayden* (387 v.s. 294, 1967); *Marron v. United States* (275 v.s. 192, 1927). This case involves the Plain View Doctrine which is exclusively a rationale for warrantless searches. It is nevertheless a legitimate exception to the warrant requirement because the Fourth Amendment proscribes unreasonable seizures as well as unreasonable searches. The Plain View Doctrine states that three conditions must come together before a warrantless seizure may take place under its authority:

1) A prior valid intrusion; 2) the inadvertent sighting of evidence in plain view; and 3) probable cause to believe that what is sighted is evidence.

The doctrine holds that if a police officer is already in the course of an undercover assignment, he satisfies condition number one; conditions two and three are self-explanatory.

On July 20, a probable cause hearing was held before Judge Arthur Byrne of the County Superior Court. After hearing the testimony of the defendants and agents Brewer and Mitchell, Judge Byrne ruled that in the case of defendant Meanio, who had been crossing the street, the agents met all three aforementioned conditions. Because they were in the area on an undercover assignment, condition one was satisfied. When the agents saw the gun fall from Meanio's clothing and then observed him pick it up, condition two was met. The judge went on to state that as experienced police officers, the agents recognized the object that fell from Meanio's trousers as a handgun, which is usually an illegal object for a citizen to possess on the street, so condition three was met.

In the case of defendant Alverez, the man Agent Mitchell chased and arrested, Judge Byrne ruled that the arrest was valid. The judge stated that condition one of the Plain View Doctrine was met for the same reason as in the Meanio case. He went on to say that conditions two and three were met because it was reasonable for the agents to assume that, after watching two men who were together for a period of time and acting suspiciously, if one of them was arrested for possession of a weapon and the other fled, there was probable cause to believe the second man was also armed. This probable cause gave the officer grounds to stop and frisk. The motion for the suppression of the evidence was denied and the defendants were ordered to stand trial.

In August, both defendants pleaded guilty to the charges in Superior Court and were sentenced.

A Family Affair

1. Yes. He did not witness the assault. No police action could appropriately have been taken if Mrs. Walsh would not sign a complaint.
2. No. A man or woman cannot be forced from his or her home, even at the request of the spouse. Only in the event that a lawful arrest can be made on other charges can a party be forced to leave.
3. No. He did not act in a professional manner. A law enforcement officer should remain neutral and not take sides.
4. Yes. Although Decker initiated the action, Walsh was not injured or in danger of being injured; thus he had no right under the law to resist arrest. In a case where a person is arrested and is beaten or in danger of being injured by an arresting officer, he may resist. Even in these circumstances, the force used must only be enough to overcome the imminent danger.
5. Yes. Initially, he became too emotionally involved in the husband/wife dispute, which prevented him from acting objectively. Later on, however, Decker, knowing Mrs. Walsh had already been assaulted, became justifiably concerned for her safety when the husband approached her and began to shout.

On September 3, a hearing was held in Room 241 of the Marix County Courthouse before Judge William Rapp. After hearing the testimony, Judge Rapp found Steven Walsh guilty of a reduced charge, or "simple assault." The judge stated that his decision to reduce the charge stemmed from the fact that the defendant had been drinking and that Officer Decker had not sustained any injuries.

Stopping a Suspect Vehicle

1. Yes. The driver was in violation of a motor vehicle law.
2. No. Knowing that the furtive movements of Calvin Cooper could have meant personal danger to him, the trooper should have waited for his backup. Only at the time of a hearing or trial, however, could a judge rule on this point.
3. Certainly. Once an officer makes a decision, such as the one Fredericks made, he should follow through and completely protect himself by patting the subject down.
4. Yes. The subject's suspicious movements plus the discovery that he was wearing an empty shoulder holster were reasons to assume a gun was in the auto. Fredericks' finding of cartridges under the seat added to the probable cause.
5. This would be for the judge at the probable cause hearing to decide after taking all the evidence into account. He would have to consider several things: the experience of the officer; the reason for initially stopping the vehicle; the movements of Calvin Cooper, which the trooper found furtive; and the way in which probable cause was found.

On March 12, a probable cause hearing was held in Los Angeles County Court House, Room 961, before Superior Court Judge Amos Van Dyke. The judge held that because the initial stopping of the sedan was legal and the actions of defendant Cooper would have appeared furtive to any experienced officer, and because Trooper Fredericks confined his initial search to the area where Cooper was sitting, the arrest was legal. The defendants were remanded for trial.

Drug Bust

1. No. The initial patdown was to find out if the subject had a weapon.
2. Yes. At the time he stopped Williams, the officer thought he would be dealing with a drunk and—as all streetwise cops know—drunks are unpredictable.
3. Yes. Much plea bargaining revolves around a defendant either turning state's evidence and testifying for the state, or assisting undercover officers.
4. Yes. In every respect.
5. Yes. After making the buy, he immediately returned to his office, field-tested the evidence and logged it in, which would be important for showing continuity and building a solid case.
6. No. The search warrant was limited to drugs. That a person owns three television sets does not provide probable cause to believe they are stolen property.
7. No. For the reasons stated in answer 6, the television sets were illegally seized.

On June 19, a probable cause hearing was held before Judge Robert Durkin of the County Superior Court. After hearing all the testimony, Judge Durkin ruled that the officers had enough probable cause for a search warrant and so the narcotics evidence seized was legally obtained. The judge did add, however, that the evidence concerning the stolen televisions was to be suppressed because the search warrant was limited to illegal drugs. He went on to say that no mention of stolen property had been made in the affidavit and that a person living in a fashionable apartment and owning three television sets does not necessarily create an air of suspicion. Judge Durkin stated that if Sergeant Flynn had merely noted the serial numbers of the television sets, run them through the N.C.I.C. computer and ascertained they had been stolen, he could have then obtained a search warrant, seized the evidence properly and pressed charges against Mann according to the law.

Wiretaps—Do's and Don'ts

1. Yes. Keane did everything he could, such as checking telephone numbers, the backgrounds of suspects and ascertaining that known gamblers frequented the store.
2. Yes. He followed the guidelines set forth in Federal Statutes Title III which sets the standards for state statutes, such as:
   a) Who may apply for surveillance orders
   b) Subject matter (types of crimes)
   c) What and when approval can be granted
   d) Who may authorize the order
   e) Length of time a wiretap can be run (30 days maximum; extensions may be applied for)
   (The only restriction that does not apply to state statutes is toward the persons empowered to authorize the wiretap. On the state level, the Attorney General or any one of the county prosecutors can authorize it.)
3. No. Allowing the wire to run over the specified time is illegal, and failure to report it could mean suppression of the evidence collected.
4. Yes. As long as evidence is collected legally, it can be used by a different law enforcement agency for prosecution of criminals or probable cause for warrants.

Katz v. United States (389 v. 347, N. 14, 1967). This case placed electronic surveillance within the limits of the Fourth Amendment, i.e., a warrant is required for a wiretap.

Berger v. United States (388 U.S. 41,60, 1967). This case outlined the standards of particularity which such a warrant must meet under the Fourth Amendment.

United States v. Pacheco (489 F 2d. 554, 5th Cir., 1974.) This case defined lottery bets as part of gambling operation.

On March 16, a suppression hearing was held in the Rockland County Superior Court before Judge Alfred Marcos. The hearing lasted an entire day with Judge Marcos hearing all the testimony, including the facts that Kell and White listened to a private conversation after the time specified in the warrant.

The judge in his decision remarked that the information and evidence gathered prior to the wiretap were obtained properly. The applications were prepared correctly and signed by persons in authority to do so. He hesitated before saying, "Anything irrelevant to an investigation that does not provide evidence of the commission of crime should not be intercepted. Because the monitors never know exactly what they are about to hear until they hear it, their efforts at minimization are usually not completely successful. . . ." He continued, "Although interception of a single irrelevant portion of a conversation is not grounds for suppression, the monitor must make a reasonable effort to minimize the greatest possible number of irrelevant conversations." The judge declared, "In this case, there has been at least one flagrant violation of the guidelines set down in Title III 18 U.S.C.S. 2510 (4) 1970, *United States v. McLeod.* Therefore, I hold the evidence collected through the electronic surveillance suppressed and not usable by the State in the prosecution of the defendants."

Search and Seizure: Understanding the Fourth Amendment

Associate Judge Charles E. Moylan Jr.

The law of search and seizure is not a single subject — such as the law of confessions, double jeopardy or identification—but an umbrella term embracing a whole curriculum of subjects including standing to object, search incident to lawful arrest, the Carroll Doctrine, the Plain View Doctrine, consent searches and stop and frisk. Because the curriculum is so vast, it cannot be reduced to something subject to immediate and total recall. A checklist of questions should be relied on as investigative circumstances demand. The first and most fundamental questions on the list are:

1. Is the Fourth Amendment applicable?

2. Has the Fourth Amendment been satisfied:

More important than the two questions themselves is the direction lurking between them: Do not go on to question two unless and until the answer to question one is, "Yes." Indeed, if the answer is, "No, the Fourth Amendment is not applicable," then the second question is immaterial.

There are various ways in which the Fourth Amendment may be deemed inapplicable so as not to require satisfaction. It may not cover the particular place searched. Obviously, the writ of the Fourth Amendment does not extend to places where American law generally does not extend—the Sierra Madre Mountains, downtown London or the suburbs of Paris, for instance. Even on American soil there are places not protected by this amendment. The classic example is the Open Fields Doctrine, first articulated by the Supreme Court in 1924 *(Hester v. United States),* which protects the sacred precincts of the home. This extends even beyond the four walls of the main house to the family living area or zone of habitation called the curtilage. The protection also covers the store, the barn, the garage, the automobile *(Carroll v. United States,* 1925) and even the suitcase *(United States v. Chadwick,* 1977; *Arkansas v. Sanders,* 1979). It does not, however, cover all of one's real property. *(Air Pollution Variance Board v. Western Alfalfa Corp.,* 1974). So it becomes important to be able to identify the constitutionally protected perimeter. Within that perimeter, the basic commandment to government is to be reasonable and measured by such subcriteria as warrants, probable cause and exigency controls. Outside the protected perimeter there are no such requirements, at least according to the Fourth Amendment, and the subcriteria of warrants, probable cause and exigency are immaterial considerations.

A second way in which the Fourth Amendment may be inapplicable is in those cases when the searching and seizing is done by an individual citizen

According to the Open Fields Doctrine, the probe for evidence outside the perimeter of a residence does not require a search warrant.

private citizens. The Supreme Court has not had occasion to map boundary lines with any precision. Although the precise border between private action and state action may not be clear, it is beyond dispute that such a line does exist and that it determines whether the Fourth Amendment and its Exclusionary Rule is applicable or not.

A third, and quantitatively very significant, way in which the Fourth Amendment may be inapplicable is where the search takes place in a constitutionally protected area and where the searcher is a governmental agent, but the defendant on trial is not the individual whose Fourth Amendment protection was violated. This is the very complex and rapidly developing subject of standing to object. The standing requirement is a limitation on the operation of the Exclusionary Rule. The basic principle involved is that one person may not vindicate the Fourth Amendment rights of someone else, but must be a member of the aggrieved class before he will be permitted to litigate the Fourth Amendment merits. Classically, this required a defendant, when challenged, to establish a property interest in the item seized and/or the place searched (*Combs v. United States,* 1972).

instead of a governmental agent. The principle involved is that the entire Bill of Rights, including the Fourth Amendment, is by definition a set of limitations upon government as government and is not directed to the private citizen in any way. The inapplicability of the Exclusionary Rule where a private citizen searches in a manner that would be forbidden a governmental agent was pointed out clearly by the Supreme Court in 1921 in *Burdeau v. McDowell.* When a private citizen acts at the request of a policeman or in conjunction with a policeman, that private person becomes, for Fourth Amendment purposes, the agent of the policeman and the Exclusionary Rule does apply (*Coolidge v. New Hampshire,* 1971). When the private citizen acts exclusively alone with no police involvement, encouragement or acquiescence, the Exclusionary Rule is inapplicable regardless of the circumstances surrounding the search. (*Walters v. United States,* 1980).

The line between state action and the actions of the private citizen is a blurred one. The rulings vary from state to state as to whether intermediate functionaries, such as private investigators, high school principals, teachers and department store security personnel, are defined as governmental agents or

A frisk is the initial patting down or superficial searching of a suspect's clothing to remove any weapon(s) he may have been carrying or at least to ascertain that he is not armed. This is necessary to safeguard the lives of the officers and any passersby and does not require a search warrant.

In 1960, the Supreme Court significantly liberalized the standing requirement in the case of *Cecil Jones v. United States* in two separate respects. In those cases where a defendant was charged with unlawful possession of contraband, he was extended automatic standing with no requirement on his part to establish anything. The thrust of the reform was to remove the defendant from the horns of a dilemma, whereby his very testimony required to establish standing might later come back to haunt him on the merits of guilt or innocence. In 1968, the Supreme Court promulgated its decision in *Simmons v. United States,* wherein it ruled that a defendant was free to testify on such preliminary issues as the suppression of evidence secure in the knowledge that that testimony could not be used by the state to prove its case in chief. As a consequence of *Simmons v. United States,* the reason for establishing the automatic standing rule no longer existed, and in 1980 the Supreme Court, in *United States v. Salvucci* and *Rawlings v. Kentucky,* expressly abolished the rule of automatic standing. Thus, there is no defendant who is relieved of the responsibility, when appropriately challenged, of establishing affirmatively that he enjoyed in the first instance the constitutional protection that was ostensibly violated.

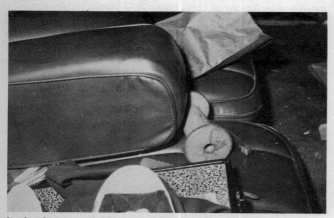

In simple terms, the Plain View Doctrine encompasses all evidence that is in the open and can easily be observed. A trained police officer would recognize the "slap hammer" under the armrest as the tool of a car thief.

The second great liberalization of *Cecil Jones v. United States* was to extend standing derivatively through the host to all those persons legitimately on the premises who were searched because they were guests, licensees or invitees of the host. Although this variety of standing still appears to be valid when the place of search is a fixed premises, the Supreme Court held in 1978 in *Rakas v. Illinois* that such standing is

not available to one who, though legitimately present, is merely a passenger in an automobile.

As a general proposition, the Supreme Court now determines the coverage of the Fourth Amendment, that is, standing to object, by looking to the 1967 decision of *Katz v. United States* and asking whether there was or was not a reasonable expectation of privacy. The court measures this reasonable expectation of privacy both subjectively and objectively. If the defendant believes subjectively that he has the expectation of privacy, it is necessary to ask whether this expectation is one which society objectively is prepared to recognize as reasonable. If, under the totality of the circumstances, there is both a subjective and objective reasonable expectation of privacy, then there is Fourth Amendment coverage and the person enjoying that coverage has standing to litigate the Fourth Amendment merits (*Smith v. Maryland,* 1979).

When the Fourth Amendment does apply, then and only then must American courts approach the second question of amendment satisfaction. At this point, it becomes important to recognize the problems of: 1) initial intrusion; and 2) scope.

Both *Coolidge v. New Hampshire* (*Supra* n.6) and *Terry v. Ohio* (1968) provide excellent discussions of these two distinct considerations. When considering the reason for the initial intrusion into a house, a car, a citizen's liberty by way of arresting him, the interest being guarded is the zone of privacy. That interest is protected primarily by requiring that a warrant be obtained before that zone of privacy may be breached. This is the core value of the Fourth Amendment. While the zone of privacy does not enjoy absolute protection and must yield to the investigative imperative, we seek to safeguard the basic value, however, by requiring that, whenever feasible, the decision to breach the zone of privacy must be made by the neutral and detached magistrate, representing the independent judicial branch of government, rather than be made unilaterally within the executive branch of government. This limitation upon the executive branch applies not only to policemen but also to prosecutors, attorneys general, governors and even presidents (*United States v. United States District Court for Eastern Michigan,* 1972). The basic principle involved is that the executive branch of government is charged with enforcing the laws and with apprehending and prosecuting wrongdoers. Committed as it should be to this vital mission, that branch of government cannot be expected to be the watchman of its own possible overzealousness. The essential purpose of the warrant requirement is to

The Fourth Amendment calls for the police to minimize their activities when conducting an authorized search. In this case, searching the two-piece crucifix for gambling slips was not improper. Had the warrant specified weapons only, however, this evidence would have been suppressed.

interpose the neutral and detached judicial figure between the executive branch of government and the citizenry. The spirit of this requirement is simply the courtroom manifestation of the basic American value that you cannot be the umpire calling the balls and strikes at the same time you are a member of one of the competing teams.

Obtain a warrant whenever possible. If the circumstances are such that it is possible to obtain a search and seizure warrant, the policeman must do so. If the circumstances provide for obtaining an arrest warrant, the policeman must obtain one. But of course, there are exceptions. To justify traveling the exceptional, warrantless route, there must be exceptional circumstances to legitimize such a departure, and the burden is always upon the state to show the special necessity to permit the exceptional invstigative approach. This centrality of the warrant requirement was well articulated by the Supreme Court in *Coolidge v. New Hampshire* (403 U.S. at 454-455):

> [T]he most basic constitutional rule in this area is that "searches conducted outside the judicial process, without prior approval by judge or magistrate, are *per se* unreasonable under the Fourth Amendment—subject only to a few specificially established and well-delineated exceptions." The exceptions are "jealously and carefully drawn," and there must be "a showing by those who seek exemption . . . that the exigencies of the situation made that course imperative . . . [T]he burden is on those seeking the exemption to show the need for it."

Even assuming a constitutional initial intrusion into the zone of privacy, either by virtue of a validly issued warrant or under one of the permitted exceptions to the warrant requirement, law enforcement officers do not have free rein to search endlessly for anything. The Founding Fathers sought to protect our citizens from the general warrant or unrestricted rummaging about that had in part provoked the American Revolution. The Fourth Amendment seeks to ensure that a search which begins legitimately does not suddenly degenerate into an opportune exploration. The particularity clause provides that the warrant describe in detail "the place to be searched and the persons or things to be seized." In short, it sets the limitations of the search. Similarly, whenever a warrantless search is permitted, there are built-in limitations. The permitted scope of any search is whatever is necessary to serve the legitimate purpose for which that search began—but not one bit more. Once the police find what they are looking for, they should not linger looking for some extra bonus, but should terminate the search. In the process of looking, they should look only in places where the items sought would most likely be found. Regarding scope limitations, the basic commandment of the Fourth Amendment is, "Min-

imize, minimize, minimize." Or as the FBI National Academy teaches, "Don't look for an elephant in a matchbox."

Although the Fourth Amendment contemplates that a warrant will be obtained whenever it can be, exceptions are permitted when necessity demands. Seven well-recognized exceptions to the warrant requirements are:

1. Search incident to lawful arrest
2. The Carroll Doctrine, or so-called automobile exception
3. The suitcase exception
4. Hot pursuit or general emergency
5. Stop and frisk
6. The Plain View Doctrine
7. Consent

With each exception, it is important to look at the purpose for which it was invented and what the limitations are under that exception. Indeed, with respect to limitations, a knowledge of the purpose is indispen-

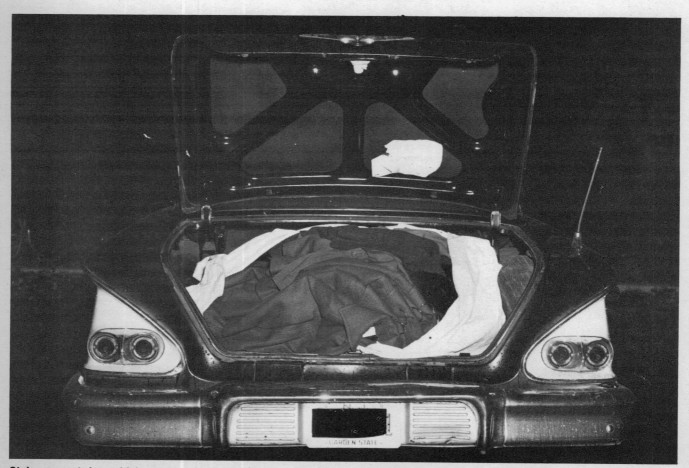

Stolen property in a vehicle can be seized without a warrant under certain circumstances. One condition the Supreme Court has stated is, "If the police may seize a car warrantlessly, they may search it warrantlessly."

sable because permitted scope is always whatever is necessary to serve that purpose—nothing more.

Search Incident to Lawful Arrest. This is the oldest and quantitatively the most significant of the exceptions. The purpose for the initial intrusion is simple enough—to obtain a lawful arrest. The difficulty with this exception is in determining its geographic scope. Given a lawful arrest, what shall be the permitted search perimeter? The Supreme Court vacillated over this issue for an appreciable time until it got down to fundamentals in *Chimel v. California* in 1969. The purposes of a search incident are: 1) to disarm the arrestee in order to protect the life of the arresting officer, and to prevent an escape; and 2) to prevent the destruction of potential evidence by the arrestee. In *Chimel,* the Supreme Court finally determined that the necessary search perimeter to serve these two purposes was anything within "the reach, lunge or grasp" of the arrestee. This is occasionally described as the wingspan or the wingspread of the arrestee. In basic terms, a danger zone exists within which an arrestee can possibly do either of the two wrongful things that the exception was designed to prevent him from doing. When a trial judge determines what that danger zone is, he has outlined the zone within which the police are permitted to take the necessary preventive measures. The purpose of the exception is not to enable the police to obtain evidence as such, but is rather to enable them to prevent the arrestee from destroying or secreting evidence.

The Carroll Doctrine, or so-called Automobile Exception. The 1925 decision of *Carroll v. United States* provided that the police may search an automobile or automobile equivalent, in contrast to a fixed premises,

When searching the area near a crime scene for a specific type of evidence, such as a gun, any other evidence recovered can be legally seized. Note the white package containing cocaine near the gun.

warrantlessly whenever two preconditions coalesce: 1) probable cause to believe that the automobile or automobile equivalent contains evidence of crime; and 2) an exigency requiring that an immediate warrantless search be undertaken, arising from the character of the automobile as something then moving or at least readily movable. In 1970, the Supreme Court decision of *Chambers v. Maroney* made it clear that the arrest of the driver of the automobile does not remove the exigency. The police are, therefore, not required to drive or tow an automobile to their own impounding lot or to place a guard over it, then obtain a warrant before proceeding further. With respect to an automobile at least, the Supreme Court has held in effect that if the police may seize it warrantlessly, they may search it warrantlessly.

The Suitcase Exception. With respect to suitcases, boxes and other containers, the Supreme Court has held that such containers may be seized warrantlessly to extinguish the exigency arising out of their possible disappearance. However, unlike the case of the automobile, the police are required to hold such suitcases, etc., in their custody unsearched and not proceed further until a properly issued search warrant is obtained. If such warrant is not forthcoming, the suitcase must be returned unsearched (*United States v. Chadwick, supra* n. 3; *Arkansas v. Sanders, supra* n. 3).

Hot Pursuit. The exigent circumstances exception is difficult to delineate. Basically, even the threshold of the home or other fixed premises, which will not yield to a warrantless search for evidence, will yield to a warrantless crossing when there is some emergency or threat that involves a danger to life and not just a danger to evidence. The classic instance of such an emergency is "hot pursuit," the circumstance that led to the recognition of this exception by the Supreme Court in the 1967 decision of *Warden v. Hayden.* "Hot pursuit," however, is not the only exigency that will justify the warrantless crossing of the threshold. In 1978, the Supreme Court indicated in *Mincey v. Arizona* that a warrantless investigation may be made of a murder scene and in *Michigan v. Tyler* that a warrantless investigation may be made of a fire scene, although both of those cases pointed out that the prerogative to enter and process the scene warrantlessly does terminate once the emergency situation has ended.

Stop and Frisk. The key to understanding the stop-and-frisk exception is to appreciate that the stop and the frisk really is two distinct investigative techniques (*Terry v. Ohio, supra* n. 17; *Sibron v. New York,* 1968). Since both a stop and a frisk represent in-

The officer who stopped this vehicle for a motor vehicle violation and observed the ignition lock punched out (ignition key hole on steering column is missing) would have probable cause to believe the car was stolen.

trusions to a citizen's freedom, they are reviewable under the reasonableness standard of the Fourth Amendment. Because the stop is less intrusive than a full-blown seizure of the person (custodial arrest) and because the frisk is less intrusive than a full-blown search of the person, these two lesser intrusions are permitted by reasons less substantial than probable cause. These are referred to as "reasonable suspicion," "good cause to believe," or "articulable suspicion." It is not enough, however, to know how much suspicion is needed; it is also necessary to know what must be suspected.

To determine that, we must look separately at the purpose of the stop and frisk.

The stop is crime related. To justify it, a police officer must have articulable suspicion to believe that a crime has occurred, is then occurring, or is about to occur. The purpose of the frisk, however, is not to solve or to prevent crime, but to protect the life and limb of the stopping officer. To justify a frisk, there must be suspicion to believe that the person stopped may be armed. Both the stop and the frisk each have their own scope limitations. The stop must be right on the street and may not involve transporting the person stopped any great distance away, such as to the station house. The stop, moreover, may last for only a brief period of time. The scope limitation upon the frisk is that it must be limited to a pat-down of the exterior of the clothing surface. This is all that is required to detect the presence of weapons and, under the ever-present commandment to minimize, it is all that will be permitted.

The Plain View Doctrine. This exception differs from all the others in that it does not serve as justification for even the most minimal of searches. It is exclusively a rationale for warrantless seizures. Nonetheless, it is a legitimate exception to the warrant requirement for the reason that the Fourth Amendment proscribes unreasonable seizures just as surely as it proscribes unreasonable searches. Three conditions must come together before there may be a warrantless seizure under the authority of the Plain View Doctrine. They are: 1) a prior valid intrusion; 2) the inadvertent spotting of evidence in plain view; and 3) probable cause to believe that the item spotted is evidence.

If a policeman is already legitimately inside a constitutionally protected area to make a valid arrest, is in hot pursuit of a fleeing felon, is in the course of an undercover assignment or is executing a search warrant, these are the prior valid intrusions contemplated by the Plain View Doctrine. No threshold has to be crossed to make a Plain View Doctrine seizure, because that boundary has already validly been crossed before the spotting of the evidence occurs. The evidence that is ultimately seized must be seen in plain view; one does not undertake a search to discover it. The inadvertence requirement guards against the contrived plain view, whereunder the entry is a mere subterfuge to get a look around. The final requirement is that, even when something is inadvertently seen in plain view, there must be probable cause to believe that it is, indeed, evidence before its seizure may be justified (*Stanley v. Georgia,* 1969).

Consent. The basic principle underlying the consent exception is that any constitutional protection, including a Fourth Amendment protection, may be waived. Only two fundamental requirements are involved. If we are dealing with third-party consent, it is necessary to determine whether the person who agrees to the search is one who has the legal authority to give valid consent (*United States v. Matlock,* 1974). If, on the other hand, we are dealing with first-party consent, where it is the ultimate defendant himself who consents to the search, the critical issue is whether the consent is voluntary. No single factor will make consent valid or invalid; the totality of the circumstances must be reviewed. All things considered, if the consent that is forthcoming is deemed to be the product of a free will, voluntary though not necessarily volunteered, such consent is valid and constitutional. If, on the other hand, the consent is the product of a will overborne by force or intimidating psychological pressures, such consent is invalid and unconstitutional (*Schneckloth v. Bustamonte,* 1973).

When you look at all of the exceptions to the warrant requirement in aggregate, remember that these are just what their names imply—*exceptions.* The warrantless approach is the exceptional approach, justified only by an exceptional exigency and requiring that the exceptional circumstances be shown. The normal—the expected—investigative approach is to gather probable cause and submit it to the neutral judicial figure so he may make the ultimate determination of whether the search and seizure should proceed.

Charles E. Moylan Jr. has been Associate Judge of the Court of Special Appeals of Maryland since 1970. His previous posts in the law profession included State Attorney of Baltimore City, Deputy State's Attorney and Assistant State's Attorney. Judge Moylan has also taught at the University of Maryland, the University of Baltimore and other academies, and has lectured to prosecutorial and judicial groups in 46 states on search and seizure, trial tactics, confrontation, compelled self-incrimination and many other law-related topics. Judge Moylan, who received his Doctor of Jurisprudence degree from the University of Maryland Law School, has had 11 essays and articles published in law reviews and journals.

Meeting the Challenge of Policing Public Housing

Lieutenant Joseph D. Keeney

Policing public housing projects remains a relatively new aspect of police administration and very little has been written that can form the basis for a public housing security program. Experience in New York City with the Housing Authority Police Department indicates that if the municipality and the local housing authority devote attention and provide resources to the projects, the goal of providing decent and safe housing can be met successfully.

All of us remember the terrible riots that occurred during the 1960s in many of the nation's largest cities. Few large cities escaped the kind of violence and destruction that took place in Newark, Detroit, New Haven and Watts. Many of these riots occurred in the vicinity of a public housing complex where, historically, all of the pressures of daily living impact directly on the poor. There were no such riots or disorders in New York City, although it is reasonable to assume that the poor in New York are no better off than the poor in any of the nation's other large urban centers.

The fact that New York City was relatively free of disturbance is attributable to the progressive policies of the city administration and the professionalism of the New York City Police Department. Also bearing on the success is the fact that Housing Authority police officers with a deep sense of community concern and commitment were generally able to police the public housing projects in a manner which prevented development of large scale disorders. That the New York City Housing Authority makes such a deep commitment to the preservation of the quality of life in its public housing projects may have been directly responsible for the prevention of occurrences which were so devastating to other large urban areas. In my opinion, the old-fashioned "beat cop" is effective where all other systems seem to fail and is the main reason why the Housing Authority Police Department relies so heavily on its Project Community Officer Program.

How the N.Y.C. Housing Authority Works

The New York City Housing Authority is responsible for the operation and management of 256 public housing developments throughout the city of New York. These developments provide housing for 169,073 families numbering 523,000 persons. In addition, the New York City Housing Authority operates a very extensive leased housing program in the private housing market which adds an additional 26,000 housing units. The properties of the Authority are valued at approximately three billion dollars and the annual operating budget is slightly over five hundred million dollars. The Authority currently employs approximately 14,500 persons, many of whom are also tenants of the Authority.

The police service for such a large-scale operation is in itself significant. In 1952, the Authority established the Housing Authority Police Department with the appointment of 47 officers from an open competitive civil service list. This small force impacted so favorably on the quality of life in the city's housing projects that in 1956, by an act of the New York State Legislature, its members were accorded police officer status under the provisions of the New York State Criminal Procedure Law.

The Housing Authority Police Department is charged with the responsibility of protecting life and safeguarding persons on or about Housing Authority property, maintaining the public peace, preventing crime, detecting and arresting offenders and guarding and protecting Housing Authority property from acts of destruction, vandalism, theft and nuisance within the buildings and on the property of the Authority.

The New York City Police Department is similarly charged by the New York State Legislature with the responsibility of providing the tenants of public housing with the same service it provides to the citizenry of the city of New York. The N.Y.C. Police Department and the N.Y.C. Housing Authority Police Department have concurrent jurisdiction with regard to providing police service to the tenants of public housing projects. Housing Authority developments are patrolled by both departments, and the tenants may request police service from either the municipal police department or the N.Y.C. Housing Authority Police Department.

The Authority's police department represents a significant portion of its total operating budget, or slightly more than 60 million dollars annually with approximately 96 percent attributable to personnel costs.

Organization of Personnel. Since the mid-1970s the police department has been confronted with a severe and continuing fiscal crisis and has, as a result, engaged in a strenuous program of cutback management which has sought to maximize the productiv-

Because many of the duties and training requirements of the New York City Housing Authority police are identical to those of the N.Y.C.P.D., cooperative programs have been established between the two groups. Here officers from both departments take firearms training at the N.Y.C.P.D. range at Rodman's Neck, City Island, N.Y.

ity of the officers on patrol by appointing civilians to those positions not requiring the assignment of a sworn officer. The current status of the 1,712-member force breaks down as follows:

ORGANIZATION OF PERSONNEL
1,712

Officers

Title	Quota	In Service
Chief	1	1
Deputy Chief	1	1
Inspector	1	1
Deputy Inspectors	4	2
Captains	17	14
Lieutenants	65	57
Sergeants	146	113
Detectives	—	60
Police Officers	1,701	1,178
Total	1,936	1,427

Civilians

Police Administrative Aides	80
Clerks, Typists, etc.	48
Community Assistants	157
Total	285

The Housing Authority Police Department is organized in a traditional "line and staff" type structure. The Chief of Housing Police, Charles Henry, is the chief executive officer of the department and he is but one of the department directors within the Housing Authority. The chief of housing police, under the direction of the police commissioner of the police department of the city of New York, reports to the general manager and the chairman and the members of the Housing Authority. The chief of housing police is assisted in the administration of the department by a deputy who assumes the duties of the chief in his absence. Four major bureaus report directly to the chief: the Patrol Bureau, Detective Bureau, Support Services Bureau and the Internal Affairs Bureau.

Staff support is furnished by such units and functions as the 1) Office of Disciplinary Trials; 2) Community Relations Unit; 3) Community Service Officer Program; and 4) Planning Unit.

During the early 1960s, through negotiations with the collective bargaining representatives for housing police and superior officers, an agreement was made among the police benevolent associations, the Housing Authority and the city of New York, providing for a system of "parity" which governs and controls the salaries of all Housing Authority police personnel.

Each rank within the Housing Police Department, with respect to salary and working conditions, is pegged to the corresponding rank in the New York City Police Department. Entry level salaries for police officers of both departments are identical, and this concept continues through the ranks up to and including the rank of inspector.

In August 1979, Mayor Edward I. Koch presented a program of coordination of police service delivery which involved the New York City Police Department, the New York City Transit Authority Police Department and the Housing Authority Police Department. The three departments, all formerly autonomous, were placed under the overall direction of the police commissioner of the New York City Police Department. There are regularly scheduled meetings between the housing police chief and the police commissioner, as well as a free exchange of information and mutually cooperative programs.

All police officer positions within the Housing Authority Police Department are filled from competitive civil service testing, which is administered by the N.Y.C. Department of Personnel. Medical and physical standards are identical to those used for the municipal police department. In addition, recent appointees to the Housing Authority P.D. have participated in the 21-week recruit training program conducted at the N.Y.C.P.D. Police Academy. Regular members of the Housing Authority P.D. fully participate in the firearms training program of the city police department.

Patrol Bureau. The Patrol Bureau is responsible for furnishing direct first-line police service to the Authority's housing developments. It is, of course, the largest unit within the department and has assigned one inspector, two deputy inspectors, 11 captains, 38 lieutenants, 76 sergeants and 1,090 police officers.

The patrol force is structured into nine police service areas that operate in a manner very similar to a large city police precinct. The various police service areas have anywhere between 85 to 170 police officers assigned and each of the service areas is commanded by a captain. Each area provides the protective services for public housing developments located within the specified territorial jurisdiction of that area.

The commanding officer of the police service area holds direct control and responsibility for the operation of his command and he meets frequently with the various commanding officers of the local N.Y.C.P.D. precincts, the elected representatives of the tenant associations within his command area as well as the civilian managers of the various housing projects.

Police officers and superior officers, i.e., sergeants

and lieutenants, work in rotating shifts which provide for a controlled distribution of the patrol force (8 a.m. to 4 p.m.; 4 p.m. to 12 p.m.; 12 to 8 a.m.). Each tour of duty is actually eight hours and 35 minutes long; 243 tours are scheduled per year, with 27 vacation days allowed.

The motorized equipment assigned to the nine police service areas consists of 78 marked radio motor patrol cars, 12 unmarked radio motor patrol cars, 60 two-wheel scooters, 18 three-wheel scooters and three 15-passenger marked vans.

The cornerstone of the housing police patrol has always been the uniformed officer on foot patrol. The typical "hi-rise" residential building within Authority developments ranges from six to 30 stories, and most have a front entrance and either a basement or rear entrance.

The officer on patrol is required to check and inspect the lobby and watch for suspicious persons, vandals and disruptive and disorderly conditions. Mailboxes which are usually located in the lobby are given particular attention, as they are extremely inviting targets for criminals. Where conditions warrant, plainclothes officers working with postal authorities frequently stake out such crime-prone locations.

Continuing his patrol, the officer will generally cause the elevators to return to the lobby floor where they can be inspected for safe operation and the existence of any criminal activity. If satisfied with their operation and condition, the officer will then proceed to the uppermost floor where he will inspect the roof landing and the roof for any sign or presence of criminal activity. At this point, the officer must be extremely alert, as such areas provide perpetrators with seclusion as well as a warm and well-lighted area.

After leaving the roof, the officer descends via the stairs, stopping on each floor of the building to inspect apartment doors for any signs of tampering and even keys left carelessly in locks.

After checking each floor, the officer must proceed to the various basement rooms which in some buildings may house a community room, laundry area, tenant storage spaces and Housing Authority facilities such as paint shops, maintenance areas and offices.

The officer is required to note the address and the time of inspection in his memorandum book. Should any hazardous condition exist, he is required to remain at the scene, if such poses a threat to life or a potential for serious injury. Minor problems are reported to the manager of the development for repair by the project maintenance staff.

Each officer on patrol is equipped with a radio transceiver, which keeps him in constant contact with the department's communications unit, located at department headquarters in Manhattan.

Officers are also assigned to radio motor patrol and supplement the patrol coverage at developments which are not routinely covered by foot patrol officers. In addition, the radio motor patrol officers respond and assist the foot patrol officers where assignments pose or present danger to the responding officers on foot.

In addition to radio motor patrol and foot patrol, the N.Y.C. Housing Authority uses enclosed three-wheel scooters. They are especially effective in inclement weather and they provide high police visibility.

Requests for police service received at Housing Police Headquarters are dispatched by radio to field units and are responded to by available foot patrol officers or radio motor patrol cars.

The department's patrol force operates on a combination of random patrol and directed patrol. Random patrol within the assigned sector and post is engaged in with the following basic exceptions:

1. Special Post Conditions. These are established by the police service area commander based on crime analysis and complaints received from the public. Prior to their tour of duty, officers are advised of post conditions and are required to respond at designated times, and to correct conditions or arrest offenders as necessary. Officers having handled a post condition are required to record information relative to the

Housing Authority developments range in size from six-story buildings on small tracts of land to very large complexes involving many hi-rise buildings. Police patrols must be flexible and skilled enough to patrol both types of developments effectively.

A uniformed officer enters a marked housing police patrol car. Housing Authority police vehicles are conspicuously marked and are painted orange and blue, the official colors of the city and the Housing Authority.

A Housing Authority officer observing from a building rooftop, one of the areas he must frequently check for the presence of any disorder or criminals.

condition on a special post condition board maintained at the police service area. When a condition is cleared, the special condition is removed from the board.

2. Park and Walk. There is no adequate way to patrol a hi-rise building in a patrol car and only foot patrol can provide the special presence required to maintain good police-tenant relations. Officers are periodically directed to park the patrol car at a particular development and for a specified period of time conduct foot patrol at the location. While doing so, the officers are equipped with radios and may be summoned to respond to an emergency situation. The park-and-walk program allows the department to maximize the presence of its reduced patrol force.

In an effort to establish closer liaison with the tenant community, the department has developed a program in which designated officers, referred to as Project Community Officers, report for duty at particular housing projects and perform duty exclusively at those locations. These uniformed officers are assigned to work tours of duty that are dictated by criminal activity, post conditions, particular events and community needs. The project community officers work closely with tenant groups, youth gangs and management in an effort to establish a better understanding of and working relationship with the police. The project community officer is an attempt on the part of the housing police department to restore the old "beat cop" to the police scene and reestablish the relationship lost by the excessive use of the impersonal patrol car tour of duty.

The project community officer soon gets to know most of the tenants, their concerns, their problems and with this knowledge he can work personally to alleviate some of the conditions that negatively affect the quality of life.

Police work, however, also demands effective crime fighting techniques. When a serious crime wave erupts in a public housing project, the tenants are suddenly confronted with concerns which, when added to their normal daily concerns, become almost intolerable. When such conditions occur, it is necessary to recognize the condition quickly so the total crime fighting force can be brought to bear on the problem.

The New York City Police Department and the Housing Authority Police Department have had great success with the special task forces created to respond to serious crime problems at particular housing projects. The excellent technical services the New York City Police Department is able to furnish, when combined with the community support and information sources developed by the community-oriented housing police, frequently lead to the arrest of the responsible person(s). Recently, such combined efforts resulted in the arrest of two young men involved in a series of homicides in housing projects on the lower East Side of New York, and in the arrest of an individual who had perpetrated an extensive series of rapes in Harlem. Apprehensions such as these tend to

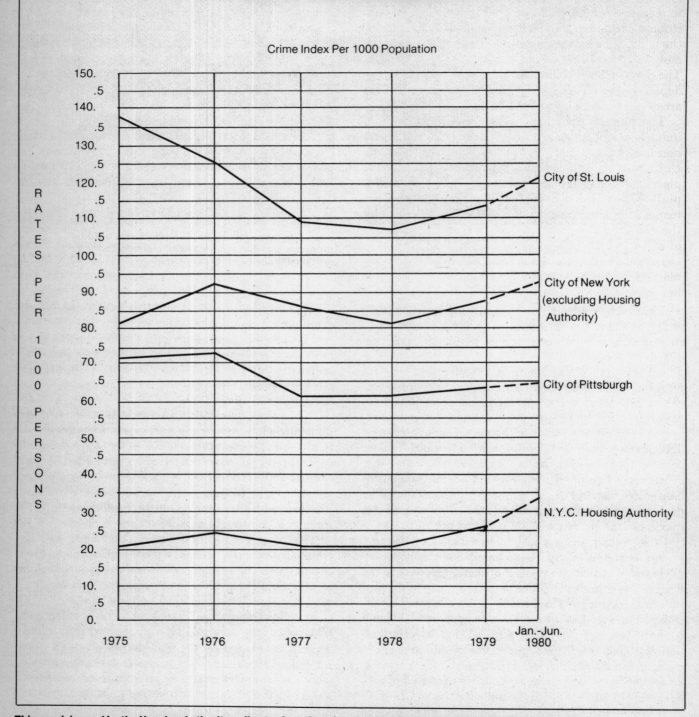

NEW YORK CITY HOUSING AUTHORITY
POLICE DEPARTMENT
STATISTICS AND RECORDS UNIT

Crime Index Per 1000 Population

RATES PER 1000 PERSONS

150.
.5
140.
.5
130.
.5
120.
.5
110.
.5
100.
.5
90.
.5
80.
.5
70.
.5
60.
.5
50.
.5
40.
.5
30.
.5
20.
.5
10.
.5
0.

City of St. Louis

City of New York
(excluding Housing
Authority)

City of Pittsburgh

N.Y.C. Housing Authority

1975   1976   1977   1978   1979   Jan.-Jun.
1980

This graph is used by the Housing Authority police to show the crime rate per thousand residents in their combined projects. St. Louis and Pittsburgh are used for comparison because, like the Housing Authority projects, they have more than 500,000 residents. The New York City crime rate is included to show how it compares with the others when the Housing Authority crime statistics are excluded.

show the value of good police work accompanied by spirited community involvement.

The Housing Authority Police Department has recently developed a Robbery Task Force in an effort to reduce the number of robberies in housing projects. Robberies and burglaries impact especially heavily on the poor and must be responded to if a police department is to gain or retain the respect of the community. The Robbery Task Force, although only recently deployed, has yielded excellent results and significant arrests have been made.

The unit, composed of anti-crime, stake-out and uniformed contingents, is deployed at a particular housing project based on extensive crime analysis. Uniformed officers are deployed in an effort to displace street robberies in an area that is saturated with plainclothes (anti-crime) officers and stake-out teams. The basic concept appears to be effective and the department is currently considering the addition of a fourth element—a decoy aspect.

Detective Bureau. The Detective Bureau is commanded by a deputy inspector and has five detective lieutenants, five detective sergeants, 60 detectives and 16 police officers assigned to it. The Detective Bureau is subdivided into the following squads:

1. Headquarters Squad. This unit conducts special investigations as directed by the chief of housing police and the detective commander and sensitive investigations of criminal activity involving Housing Authority operations such as stolen paychecks, forgery and the like.

2. Homicide/Major Case Squad. This unit investigates all homicides and certain designated major cases occurring on Housing Authority property on a city-wide basis. This squad works closely with its corresponding squad in the N.Y.C.P.D. and furnishes technical assistance to each of the detective squads responsible for the investigation of crimes in each borough of the city.

3. Crimes Against the Elderly Squad. This group operates on a city-wide basis and through extensive crime analysis concentrates its efforts exclusively with respect to the prevention and detection of perpetrators of crimes against the elderly. The Crimes Against the Elderly Squad maintains very close contact with the community relations personnel and corresponding squads in the N.Y.C.P.D.

Support Services Bureau. The Support Services Bureau is responsible for the operations of the communications, personnel services, statistics and records, police academy, repair, medical and firearms training units.

Internal Affairs Bureau. The Internal Affairs Bureau has the mandate and mission of any internal inspections function, namely, the investigation of complaints of misconduct, corruption or other undesirable conduct by members of the department.

In addition, the Civilian Complaint Investigation Unit within the Internal Affairs Bureau is responsible for the conduct of investigations of all civilian complaints and performs the basic function of civilian complaint review.

The Internal Affairs Bureau works very closely with the Office of the Special State Prosecutor, the N.Y.C. Department of Investigation, the various district attorneys and other law enforcement agencies and inspectors general.

Community Service Officer Program. The New York City Housing Authority Community Service Officer Program (HACSO) is operated through Federal Community Development funds by the N.Y.C. Housing Authority under the terms of a contract with the city of New York. The purpose of the program is to provide supplemental security services in housing projects and other public spaces within the community development areas. These services include unarmed uniformed patrols, foot and vehicular escorts, emergency assistance, crowd control and the reporting of hazardous conditions.

The program is administered by the Housing Authority Police Department and is under the command of a police lieutenant. The operation of the program is divided into three geographical areas, each under the direction of a police sergeant. In addition to furnishing service to the tenants of the Authority, the community service officers engage in educational programs which help in securing high school equivalency diplomas and in preparation for civil service testing. Many community service officers have gone on to jobs in the police and the corrections fields.

Lieutenant Joseph D. Keeney is aide to the chief of the New York City Housing Authority Police Department. During the last 10 of his 20 years with the department, he has been involved with almost every major crime or incident in the Housing Authority's 260 developments and he is frequently consulted by municipal housing authorities across the country regarding their policing programs. A recipient of five commendations from his department, Lt. Keeney holds a B.S. degree in business administration.

Stolen in Transit: Combating Cargo Theft

Thomas P. Kissane

If Hercules were to visit Earth today—in particular, the United States—he would be hard-pressed to understand why we permit the piracy of cargo throughout our country. He would probably instruct us that, were it not for his efforts in clearing the brigands from ancient Attica, Athens would not have flourished, Alexander could never have cleared the Mediterranean Sea of pirates, trade routes would not have been established and Western civilization would not have prospered under Greek and later Roman leadership. After Caesar's conquests, the most important mission of the Legions was to police the roadways to keep them open for trade with Rome. Without free and unencumbered trade, progress is retarded, the political entity atrophies and a barbaric period of disorder results, until a new authority, which can maintain free trade, is asserted. The dramatic growth of the U.S., which has provided so much for so many, can, in large measure, be attributed to its extensive transportation network.

The early corduroy roads permitted the surplus wheat crop of the eastern states to be transported by wagon cart to the mountain men of Kentucky for processing. Eventually this grain returned to the East as whiskey. The loaded barges of the Erie Canal carried people and property to the new settlements in the Ohio Valley and returned to the East loaded with furs and timber.

The process of the nation's development was accelerated by the vast amounts of goods imported from England as a result of the Industrial Revolution. The United States met the challenge of distributing this surplus of English goods by implementing a railroad system linking the Atlantic and Pacific oceans. The inhabitants of these once-inaccessible areas were eager customers for imports.

Conversely, the fatted cattle of the western states, no longer made lean by a trek to the packing houses of the Midwest, were eagerly sought by the people of the East for their succulent tenderness and reasonable price.

What made the U.S. grow was not so much bountiful crops, well-educated people or a productive temperate climate, but rather the ability to harvest and transport goods throughout the country in a safe, swift and economic manner.

We must beware of losing this great capability today. Such a loss would pose a greater threat to national security than the militaristic taunt of any foreign nation. Unfortunately, the effects of such a

Aerial view of Port Newark, New Jersey. Here, as in so many other large, busy seaports around the country, the security problems for the law enforcement agencies that police them are enormous. Warehouses have many doors and several loading bays—each one a potential entrance for a thief.

Often, when a small truck or van containing valuable cargo is stolen by professional thieves, they set the empty vehicle on fire to eliminate any traces of evidence.

danger cannot be overdramatized. Cargo theft is a multifaceted challenge, and the greatest of these challenges is the "elusive" criminal receiver. Because identification of property and proof of criminal intent are difficult evidentiary problems in courtroom presentation, the marketing of stolen property is relatively risk-free for the "fence," while it maximizes his profits. If the purchasers of stolen goods were more questioning about their suppliers' sources, perhaps there would be less larceny in our society, lower insurance premiums, cheaper bargains for the consumer and a more efficient and functional system of trade for all.

Some states have instituted a triple penalty statute to try to limit the resale of stolen merchandise. If a complainant can prove he was to be the owner of goods stolen in transit, he may sue the "receiver" for three times the value of the goods stolen.

With regard to cargo security, the transportation industry is in a state of upheaval. Those involved in all modes of transportation—trucking, shipping, railroad and air—are redefining their roles and accepting greater responsibility for preventing theft of cargo.

Throughout the tenures of former Presidents Ford and Carter, the federal government played a voluntary supervisory role in prevention of cargo theft primarily by awarding grants to industry and sponsoring educational programs designed to combat the crime. During these two administrations, an annual "Report to the President" from the secretary of transportation was instituted. This report gave the secretary responsibility for evaluating the federal government's interaction with industry to reduce the incidence of theft-related loss of goods in transit and for making recommendations for program improvements.

Under the policies of the Reagan administration, however, government's overall involvement in cargo theft prevention has been severely curtailed. The first report to President Reagan on March 31, 1981, from Secretary of Transportation Drew Lewis, resulted in significant monetary cutbacks previously awarded to industry by the Department of Transportation and, in general, turned all cargo theft prevention activities over to the private sector and local governments. Today, the federal government serves the transportation industry only in an advisory capacity.

President Reagan's call for volunteers in the industry to assume a major role in reducing cargo theft is gradually being answered by industry leaders all across the country. In the Northeast, for example, the New York/New Jersey area has formed its own group known as the Cargo Security Council of New York and New Jersey.

Many kinds of devices are employed to combat cargo theft. At one receiving area, eight-feet-high chain-link fences are placed six-feet apart and topped with barbed wire to prevent thieves from slipping stolen items over or under the barricade to waiting accomplices.

Of all cargo-packed motor carriers, this type is most often the target of thieves — stolen from parking lots at truck stops while the drivers are having their meals. Note that the trucking company name plates have been removed from the rear doors to prevent identification.

Seminars, now organized and funded by private industrial sectors, are being conducted to train law enforcement and corporate personnel to combat cargo theft. One such seminar was conducted in October 1981, under the auspices of the aforementioned Cargo Security Council. Another was hosted by Iona College in New Rochelle, New York (the only American college that includes as part of its undergraduate curriculum a course on the prevention of cargo theft).

Well-received by the attendees, both seminars covered such topics as: the business of transportation, problems of cargo losses, charting the organized crime investigation, managerial practices, physical security measures, security seals, local law enforcement and the transportation company, cargo crime investigation and prosecution, questioned document analysis, investigation of drug shipment thefts and transportation crime evidence and prosecution. Although many

of the law enforcement attendees were skilled and experienced investigators, their expertise was in the area of street crimes. They agreed that cargo theft investigations differed from general police investigations in that the primary emphasis was studying the paper flow. To conduct a successful investigation and prosecution in transportation crime requires a knowledge of this documentation and a close audit of the paper trail to apprehend the culprits.

By investing a few hours of employee time in seminars such as these, industry would obtain trained public officers who, while performing their general duties, would be better able to assist the transportation industry in achieving its mission—a profitable cost-effective service for its customers.

Designing a Security Program

Anyone interested in developing an in-house securi-

Month	Hijacks 1978		Hijacks 1979		Grand Larceny 1978		Grand Larceny 1979		Combined Totals 1978		Combined Totals 1979	
	No.	Value	No.	Value	No.	Value	No.	Value	No.	Value	No.	Value
January	5	$ 197,934	12	$ 458,632	7	$ 143,000	8	$ 370,425	12	$ 340,934	20	$ 829,057
February	4	89,320	9	294,014	8	839,700	6	150,000	12	929,020	15	444,014
March	8	238,868	15	483,125 *	5	370,622	9	580,000	13	609,490	24	1,018,125
April	7	295,600	5	133,467	4	126,000	7	233,546	11	421,600	12	367,013
May	4	310,000	11	447,794	7	169,800	6	912,000	11	479,800	17	1,359,794
June	4	18,000	6	68,700	10	265,000	7	178,000	14	283,000	13	246,700
July	13	692,555 *	7	69,575	8	171,500	1	25,000	21	864,055	8	94,575
August	9	306,970	14	438,300	4	80,000	8	182,266	13	386,970	22	620,566
September	12	424,046	8	144,200	2	30,000	5	304,024	14	454,046	13	448,224
October	7	528,500	13	569,356	5	130,000	12	1,009,900	12	658,500	25	1,579,256
November	7	808,770	14	484,985 *	7	267,600	5	76,934	14	1,076,370	19	561,919
December	10	412,800	18	184,630 *	7	385,800	9	202,000	17	797,800	27	386,630
Totals	90	$4,323,363	132	$3,731,778	74	$2,978,222	83	$4,224,095	164	$7,301,585	215	$7,955,873

* Attempt thwarted, not included

ty program has many resources available to him. Specifically, a transportation security director should acquire three publications that together will become his working manual:

DOT P 4200.2 "Guidelines for the Physical Security of Cargo," May 1972, U.S. Government Printing Office, Washington, D.C. 20590 (pub. #0-288-637)

DOT P 4200.5 "Cargo Security Handbook for Shippers and Receivers," September 1972, U.S. Government Printing Office, Washington, D.C. 20590 (pub. #0-288-636)

U.S. Army FM 19-30 "Cargo Theft and Organized Crime," March 1979, U.S. Government Printing Office, Washington, D.C. 20590 (pub. #52006)

The transportation security director, having gathered his resource material should draw up an organizational chart within the department so all members of security can be made aware of their roles and responsibilities according to the director's policy. In addition, during this time the director should develop a list of training needs and outline a draft of his potential training program. After he has established the broad outline of the program, the security director should delegate the finalization of the curriculum document to a training coordinator. Upon its completion, the director should review the appropriateness and quality of its contents and, finally, direct the training coordinator to implement the program.

When designing his initial plan, the director should allow time in his schedule for "external relations." A few hours a month spent in amicable face-to-face conversation with local law enforcement officers and prosecutors will return great dividends because it eliminates many man-hours ordinarily wasted in pre-court and court proceedings. Although cargo theft is, of necessity, low on the local law enforcement officer's

VALUE OF GOODS STOLEN/RECOVERED IN MOTOR FREIGHT TRANSIT
First Quarter Fiscal Year 1980

City	Number of Thefts	Value of Goods Stolen	Value of Goods Recovered
New York	210	$ 622,036	$ 3,360
Miami	113	149,649	454
Baltimore	56	31,615	9,200
Los Angeles	45	180,409	1,965
Houston	41	34,240	5,713
Chicago	22	61,112	24,000
San Francisco	13	3,264	0
New Orleans	7	18,073	5,290
Boston	3	17,937	0
Total	510	$ 1,118,335	$ 49,982

order of priorities, with crimes against persons receiving paramount attention, members of the criminal justice system tend to help those who appear to be helping themselves.

After formulating his training program and perhaps attending a security seminar, the security director should proceed to administer his security program. (In 1979, legislation was introduced in New York State that provides for a mandatory 40-hour training program for all security guards. In time, such legislation will be a requirement throughout the United States.) By having his curriculum well designed and his training effort documented, the security director will ultimately be in a position to effect a savings to his company when such guard training becomes mandatory.

Above all, the director should resist the temptation to obtain a police recruiting training document for use as his training outline. Although some of the subjects contained in such a document are of value, they do not contain training hour modules specifically addressed to the needs of security officers, nor do they provide for necessary site-specific training. Attention to the development of an effective job-related program will be repaid to the corporation by the efficient performance of the members trained.

In brief, the basis for an effective cargo security program requires that the security director:

Develop an Overview of the Problems.
- Familiarize himself with specific problems associated with the site
- Solicit assistance from operations personnel by designing an instrument or by personal interviews
- Develop rapport with local law enforcement personnel and prosecutors
- Seek rapport with other security directors in re-

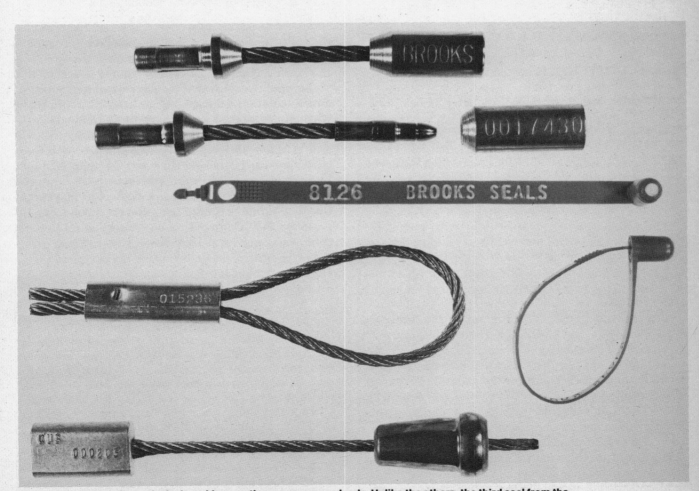

Assorted high-security seals designed for one-time use on cargo loads. Unlike the others, the third seal from the top is made of plastic rather than steel and is used when a simple record is the only type of security needed. Without exception, all security bands must be severed to obtain the cargo; a severed band usually signals that the cargo has been tampered with.

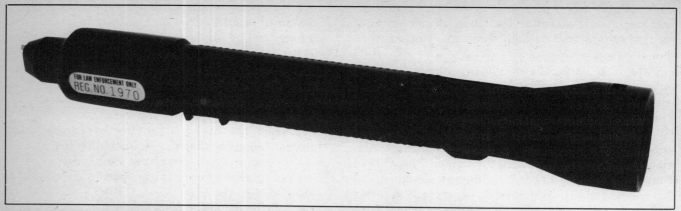

"The Source" is a nonlethal, high-frequency electronic defense weapon and flashlight designed exclusively for law enforcement and security personnel by Captain James A. Smith of Florida. When the prongs at the bottom of the device are pressed against the human body, a static charge, capable of penetrating one-quarter inch of clothing, is generated. Unlike other such electronic devices, however, The Source is completely safe, producing only one 500 millionths of one ampere. Nonetheless, the jolting vibration it emits allows an officer to prod an attacker or suspect safely, disperse a group of strikers, break up a fight between employees or aid in many other routine security or police-related tasks.

lated fields
• Isolate and identify training needs with regard to barriers, CCTV, locking systems and seals

React to the Problems.
• Develop liaison with local industry associations
• Join appropriate self-help programs, e.g., Operation Alert
• Draw up an organizational chart for the department so all employees will be aware of their authority and responsibilities
• Write a manual of procedure to be distributed to personnel on a need-to-know basis
• Assign a training coordinator from among his subordinates to be responsible for developing a training program according to the director's plan
• Involve himself with the training program by lecturing at training sessions and providing for expert guest lecturers

Inspect and Update His Program. In the transportation industry, problems and their solutions shift constantly. The security director must frequently inspect and review his losses and update methods to curtail them. An excellent way to keep in touch with the current state of the art is to join the American Society of Industrial Security. As a member of this prestigious organization, the security director will receive *Security Management Magazine,* which contains current security information written by experts in the field of security management.

Many persons, especially law enforcement officers, claim that the best crime prevention methods are those that result in a swift, effective investigation and conviction of the responsible parties. Although it is difficult to argue against the wisdom of such a statement when professional criminals are involved, the truth is that with extremely limited governmental resources, overcrowded court calendars, overburdened law enforcement agencies, whose top priority is with crimes against persons, those individuals battling cargo theft cannot be afforded the luxury of swift and effective investigations. Nonetheless, if the experts are correct when they tell us that 80 to 85 percent of these losses are employee-related, a good crime-prevention program directed at this may be the best and surely the more cost-effective means of halting cargo theft. Moreover, security specialists contend that over a period of time there is generally a three-dollar return in profit for every dollar spent for an effective "target-hardening" program. American industry could not make a sounder investment.

Thomas P. Kissane is Associate Professor of Criminal Justice at Iona College in New Rochelle, New York, where he instructs classes and establishes the curriculum for the college's police science program. From 1965 to 1974, he served as a captain of the N.Y.P.D., where he was also Commanding Officer and city-wide coordinator of the Burglary Larceny Division, exercising line authority over 1,000 investigators and supervisors throughout the city.

Kissane's most highly praised achievement was his project direction of the Cargo Theft Investigation Prevention Program, in which he developed a two-week training course for police chiefs in 16 major U.S. cities concerned with transportation theft. During his 40-year career, he has received a total of 20 awards for outstanding law enforcement achievements.

Using Your Handcuffs As Weapons

Captain James A. Smith

When people envision the conditions under which policemen work, they usually assume every officer has a patrol partner. In reality, over 75 percent of the officers on duty in the 4,000 plus counties across the United States work by themselves. In many cases, even with a partner, an officer will be dealing with several subjects at one time and will need all the help he can get while waiting for additional cover, *if* he has a chance to call for it.

For decades, the law enforcement officer has used handcuffs solely for the purposes of restraint—cuffing someone's hands so he can be transported to a given area or to prevent injury to the suspect, the officer or a third party. Now, after years of field work, study and practice, specialized tactics are becoming more common so handcuffs can be used as defensive weapons as well.

Since their inception, handcuffs have been made of metal, but now they are being manufactured in plastic and nylon, and come in long thin strips. Probably the best known are "Therocuff"; once put into place, these strip cuffs must be cut off with a special tool. These restraints are usually carried in a uniformed officer's hatband or on the sun visor of the police cruiser (passenger side). These keyless-type cuffs are especially useful when a large number of subjects are to be restrained or arrested in situations such as barroom fights, antiwar demonstrations, riots or raids.

Although opinions differ, your handcuffs should be worn on your strong-hand side (right side if you are right-handed), not the side that looks good. If the cuffs are on the wrong side, you will not be able to reach across for them with your strong hand while holding onto a suspect with your other hand. It is a must to have the cuffs near the hand you automatically respond with, so you can get to them effortlessly.

Some officers find it difficult to put handcuffs on a suspect—even one who willingly lets these restraints be placed on him. The subject's skin gets pinched by techniques that are performed clumsily. Some officers are taught to keep the eyelets or openings of the cuffs facing out so removal is easier at the booking desk or receiving area. The jailer who makes this type of request obviously has not been out in the field or has never had to contend with a drunk, a rioter or a junkie under adverse conditions. It may be dark, raining or snowing; you may be rolling on the floor or the ground with a suspect, or fighting someone in the back seat of a car. At these times, you will be happy just to get the cuffs on. (These are also reasons why your cuffs should be worn on your strong-hand side.) You may be

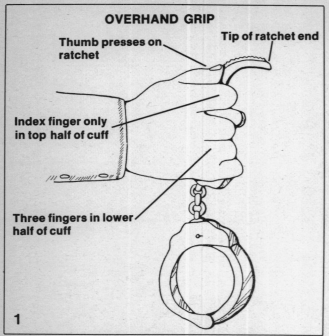

OVERHAND GRIP

Thumb presses on ratchet

Tip of ratchet end

Index finger only in top half of cuff

Three fingers in lower half of cuff

1 In the overhand grip, three fingers are placed inside the lower half of the cuff. The index finger is placed on the inside of the upper half and pressure is applied by placing the thumb on the ratchet. This is a basic grip when using handcuffs as a defensive weapon.

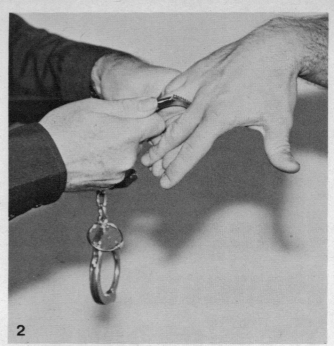

2 Using the proper overhand grip, force the point of the ratchet into either the center of the top of the hand or between any two fingers on the subject's hand. This method causes great pain and is especially useful for controlling drug users, alcoholics and mental patients.

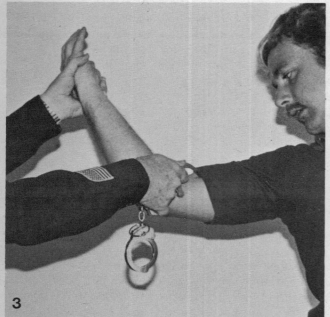

3 The overhand method can also be used to apply pressure to a subject's bicep muscle or armpit. This again will cause great pain and tend to throw the subject off balance, thus allowing you to control the situation. Remember, do not strike with the ratchet, rather drive it in using even pressure.

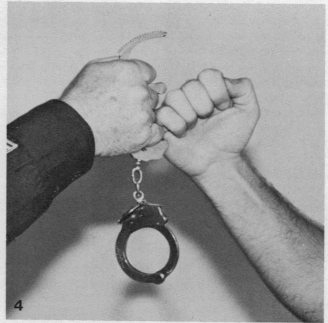

4 Still using the proper overhand method, handcuffs can be effective when someone throws a punch at you. Holding the cuffs sideways would cause the subject's fist to strike any one of the three points of the cuffs, causing pain. You should follow up immediately with a takedown.

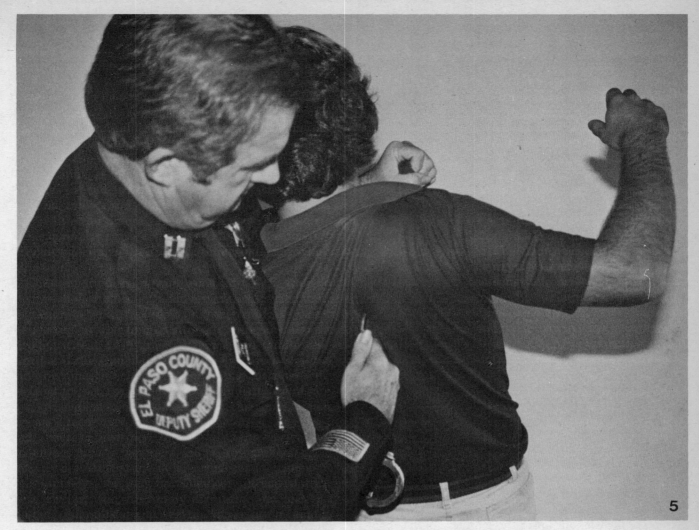

5

When attempting to control a subject from the back, the overhand method can be used effectively. Place your free hand around the neck as shown, and with moderate pressure place the ratchet against the subject's shoulder blade, which will cause him extreme pain. As with all uses of the cuffs, only enough pressure should be used to force the subject to obey your commands.

bringing someone through a crowded bar or through an apartment complex where all the neighbors are shouting and grabbing at you. How well will you be able to handle the situation and defend yourself? Adept use of your handcuffs can help you control the situation and help you protect your life and the lives of others.

Whatever your position in law enforcement—city patrolman, county constable, state trooper or park ranger—you will find using handcuffs practical, particularly when you are on duty alone. The two basic grip positions—the overhand and the underhand—can be used in numerous ways. Practice these frequently with a partner or another patrolman to improve your skill in adapting handcuffs to your indivi-

dual on-duty assignments and needs. Be prepared for the unexpected predicaments you may encounter.

Overhand Position. As *Figure 1* shows, the thumb is placed behind the ratchet and the index finger placed directly on the upper part of the cuffs, as though you were aiming a gun; the other three fingers of the hand are in the lower half of the cuffs. The following are five ways you can use the overhand position to control a suspect who resists arrest or begins to assault you when you tell him he is under arrest. By using the proper techniques with your cuffs, you can keep control of the situation without severe injury to yourself or the suspect.

1. Taking the tip of the ratchet, press down in the center of the top of the hand as shown in *Figure 2.* Do not strike the hand, rather hold onto the subject's hand with your free hand and pull toward you. This usually causes a great deal of pain and is a common method of moving a suspect to a wall or car. Another effective way to move a subject, for example, an alcoholic or a drug user, is to press the ratchet end lightly between any two fingers, using your other hand to hold the suspect's hand.

2. In the chest area, there is a small hollow point at the base of the sternum in the middle of the rib cage; if you press in—gently but firmly—with the tip of the ratchet, while pulling one of the subject's arms toward you, even a very strong man will freeze in position.

3. The clavicle, or collarbone, area between the shoulder and the neck is very sensitive. Take the cuffs in your strong hand and press down with the tip of the cuffs behind the subject's right or left clavicle while stepping toward him and holding onto his arm with your free hand; he should immediately go down. (When pressing on the right clavicle, hold onto the right arm; left clavicle, left arm.)

4. You can control a suspect by using the overhand position on the biceps of the upper arm or by applying pressure with the cuffs to the armpit area or a little below. Here again, hold onto the subject's arm with your free hand. (*Figure 3*).

5. The overhand grip can also be used effectively when someone throws a punch at you. Holding the cuffs sideways would cause the subject's fist to strike the points of the cuffs, resulting in extreme pain. (*Figure 4*).

Underhand Position. This position calls for the same grip you would use shooting a pistol. It is a strong grip with your lower three fingers in the shank of the cuff, your index finger only in the upper portion under your thumb, which is then wrapped around the lower three fingers (*Figure 6*). Practice the underhand position in the following ways:

1. Press the tip of the ratchet upward into the palm of the subject's hand, which is facing downward; with your other hand, press down on top of his hand. This is painful and will usually and effectively restrain a person. A variation of this is to use your thumb, rather than your free hand, over the person's hand. This is particularly useful in moving a suspect through an unruly crowd.

The next two positions are especially helpful against a suspect who is resisting arrest:

2. Using the underhand grip, press the tip of the ratchet into the lower rib cage or kidney area to release the side headlock the suspect has on you (*Figure 7*).

3. If the suspect tries a bear hug, pressing the tip of

the ratchet into his spine should release him at once; then you can employ other means to take him down and keep him under control (*Figure 8*).

Other Effective Uses For Handcuffs. Because most routine police duties involving the restraint of criminals and lawbreakers do not require the use of your firearm, an assist from a nonlethal device such as handcuffs, goes a long way. For example:

● To remove a subject who refuses to release his grip from his auto's steering wheel, hold onto the subject's closest hand with your free hand and press the ratchet of the cuffs with your strong hand against his wrist (use the overhand grip), or press into the side of his arm above the elbow or against his rib cage (underhand grip). This should help pry him loose. Also, be sure to balance yourself by the open car door by bending one knee and placing that foot on the floorboard to prevent the subject from striking you with his arm.

● To subdue a "kicker" who is tearing up the back of a cruiser or patrol car, try to grasp one of his legs and remove his shoe or boot. Using the underhand grip, press the ratchet into the arch of his foot with your strong hand while holding the foot with your free hand. He'll calm down.

● When you find you must walk a subject through an unruly crowd, you can side walk him from behind much more easily by placing the tip of the cuffs (use overhand grip) under the shoulder blade with one hand while putting your other arm around his neck (*Figure 5*). You can also use the tip of the cuffs effectively in his lower spine, making sure the butt end of the cuff is on his belt or firmly against his back. Once the subject starts to move, however, it is important that you do not press any harder than you have to or he will become desensitized to the pain. But do keep the tip of the cuffs against him at all times. Try not to walk directly behind him, either, since he may try to snap-kick you with his feet. Side walk him; it's safer. This technique is particularly effective in winter when a subject has heavy clothing on.

● If, for instance, you are moving a suspect to a wall for proper cuffing, you can use the cuffs as come-alongs before you get there by applying either the overhand or underhand cuff grip to the top or underside of the suspect's hand. To complete the procedure at the wall, make the suspect bend over to waist level with the top of his head against the wall, his feet away from the wall and his other arm behind his back. All his weight will be toward his head and he will not be able to move from the wall. Open the prong of the unused cuff and snap it around his wrist very deliberately. If the suspect gives you any difficulty, you

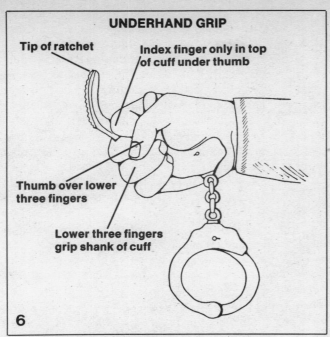

UNDERHAND GRIP

Tip of ratchet

Index finger only in top of cuff under thumb

Thumb over lower three fingers

Lower three fingers grip shank of cuff

6

To secure the underhand grip, place the lower three fingers around the shank of the cuff. Put the index finger on top of the upper portion and secure your hand by locking the thumb over the lower three fingers.

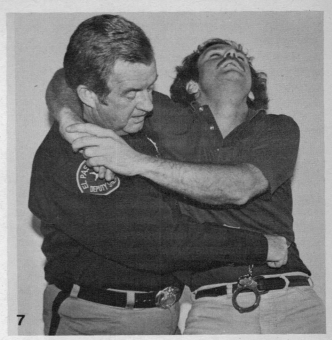

7

During a fight, especially when you are in close quarters, a suspect could easily grab you in a headlock. The underhand grip can be used with the point of the ratchet pressed into the man's lower rib cage or kidney area. Because of severe pain, the suspect will immediately release his grip.

8

During a confrontation in which an offender grabs you in a bear hug, using the underhand grip, press the point of the ratchet into the person's spine area. This should force him to release his grip immediately.

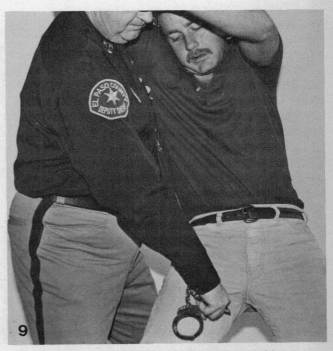

9

When an officer is held forcibly against a wall or partition by a subject, use the underhand method and press the ratchet into the upper thigh or groin area. Even the strongest subject will release his hold.

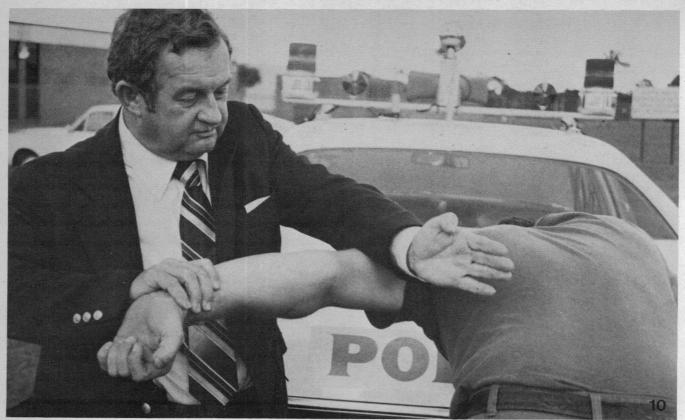

To control a spinning subject, grab his arm and pull him toward you, while you pivot behind his back. Bend his arm, throwing all your weight against it.

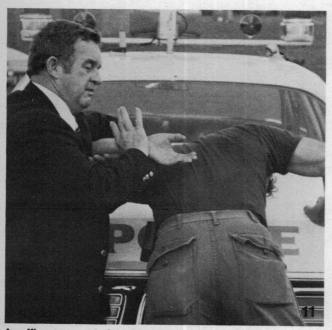

An officer can control a subject much larger than himself with only one hand once this move is completed. The other hand is then free to reach for the handcuffs and secure the subject.

still have the other open cuff to push between his should blades or his spine to control him. Knowing you can use your cuffs this way will help you maintain control of the suspect and the situation at all times.

• Using the underhand grip, you can release the hold even an extremely strong person may have on you. With a little pressure, press the ratchet into the inner thigh area or the groin, as shown in *Figure 9.*

• You have taken a suspect by the arm and have brought him down using the clavicle takedown. You roll him onto his abdomen, but you decide not to cuff him because other people in the vicinity are giving you difficulty, and your backup has not arrived. Here is a tip you can use to maintain control of the situation.

Keep the suspect's face and head down with his nose and mouth facing the ground. By using the overhand position with the handcuffs in the center of his back between his shoulder blades, you will prevent him from moving his torso. Put one foot on one side of his face and bend your other leg so that knee is on the other side of his face; he will not be able to turn his head in either direction. The smallest amount of pressure will be painful and he will be prevented from encouraging help from friends or any onlookers. He will have to do what you say, because the position you must assume for this restraining technique places you right next to his ears. If he is kicking, just press down on his back with your cuffs and he will stop. Have him put his hands behind his back, but still do not cuff him. With the cuffs in position, if someone in the crowd tries to attack you, you can control him as well. Of course, always keep your gun hand free just in case.

● As we all know, a suspect will sometimes come apart at the seams after he is told he is under arrest. He may react aggressively and try to flee. With your left foot forward, catch his wrist with your right hand as he spins toward you. Bringing your left arm down in a blade-like fashion, throw your entire weight forward, keeping your left hand in the blade form so the hand is facing up (*Figure 10*). Bend his arm back with your right hand and lock it behind his back (*Figure 11*). You can then reach down and take your cuffs, because the suspect will be held fast in a very painful position. This will also enable you to drive your knee into his groin area, if necessary. In most cases, you can lock anyone of any size and hold him no matter what your physical stature.

● Before placing a subject in a patrol car, side face him after cuffing to prevent yourself from being snap-kicked in the groin area. If possible, wrap his shirt tail around the chain between the cuffs; this will facilitate moving the subject by pulling down on the fabric. If the prisoner refuses to get into the car, merely pull down on his collar or his hair and, at the same time, lift up on his shirt tail; this will cause him to fall forward into the auto. If he needs any further prodding, you can always push him with your knee. Also, with your back to the cruiser, no one can get behind you.

An important point to remember in regard to hand-cuffs is that once a suspect is cuffed, most officers do not search thoroughly. They will usually search the hair, collar and pat down the suspect in routine fashion only to find he has uncuffed himself sometime during the trip. This can cause injury—even death—not only to the arresting officer, but to those officers assisting in the apprehension of the suspect if he has escaped. In addition to the usual areas, check his watchband, belt and packs of matches.

Watchband: a handcuff key can easily be concealed between the back of the watch and the skin. Because the suspect's hands will be behind him, he may be able to get to the key and unlock the cuffs.

Belt: many belts have zipper linings that may contain money, jumper wires, handcuff keys, narcotics, etc.; therefore, always remove the belt.

Packs of matches: it is easy to hide a key in a pack or box of matches in a back pants pocket.

If a person with a criminal nature has been handled before and does not want to be apprehended, he can escape with a little ingenuity. So be sure to check *everything*. It may save your life and the lives of others as well.

Captain James A. Smith, associated with law enforcement for over 25 years, is a certified defense instructor for police academies in Colorado and is certified in jail operations by the National Institute of Corrections, the Department of Justice and the Bureau of Prisons. He has taught defense tactics in police departments and academies around the U.S., as well as to the FBI, CID, Military Police, Air Police, U.S. Air Force Academy, U.S. Marshals and State Patrol.

An active member of the International Association of Chiefs of Police, Captain Smith has invented a nonlethal police and security weapon called "The Source" and gives seminars worldwide in its use.

Child Abuse: The Unspeakable Crime

Sergeant-Investigator Carolyn F. Bailey

Child abuse may be broadly defined as inflicted physical injury or sexual maltreatment of a child by a parent, guardian or someone responsible for the child's care. Most people, including police officers, find it difficult to believe that parents sexually assault, injure and kill their own children. But mounting reports of child abuse emphasize the reality of the problem. Children are often seen with extensive bruising, severe burns, permanent mutilations and other evidence of deliberate attack. The following are actual examples.

Case No. 1: Battering. A four-year-old boy was brought to the police station by a woman who had been asked by his mother to babysit for him so her welfare worker would not see him when the mother answered the door. The child had multiple bruises, lacerations and swellings over his entire body. The outer skin on his buttocks, lower back and thighs was gone; his waist was dotted with pinch and puncture marks; and some hair on his head appeared to have been pulled out close to the scalp. Subsequent X-rays showed two previous leg fractures. No area of his body was left untraumatized. The child pleaded continually, "Please don't take me home." The mother later admitted, "I swatted and swatted him because he kept on screaming." Then she set him in a large laundry pail full of boiling water.

Case No. 2: Sexual Abuse. School authorities questioned an eight-year-old girl after observing what appeared to be rope burns on both of her wrists. The child related that her father and mother had been hanging her nude by the wrists over the bedroom door and putting objects up her vagina. Her father had been having intercourse with her, and her mother had been instructing the child to suck on her breasts and vagina. During the sexual assaults, her parents took photographs which were later confiscated.

Although child abuse has been present throughout history, it has been the focus of increasing recognition and concern since 1962, when Drs. C. Kempe and Ray Helfer defined the "Battered Child Syndrome." Today all states have laws that require the reporting of suspected cases of child abuse and have penalties for failure to report. Many states do not define a specific crime of child abuse, and existing criminal statutes, most often directed toward adult victims, are not always applicable or adequate. Available statistics are often incomplete because such offenses may be classified as murder, assault, rape, sodomy, etc., and are not specifically identified as child abuse. The statistical figures remind us that these are real children, who cry, ache and listen in the night for footsteps of an angry parent who may burst into the bedroom and cause further pain.

Many agencies, including police, schools, social services, medical personnel and field nursing, attorneys, courts and mental health professionals become involved in child abuse, and the teamwork of all of them is required to deal most effectively with the problem and assure the children's protection. There are many multi-disciplined child abuse teams now functioning successfully that have coordinated information and available services.

Police officers in the past have frequently shied away from these stressful and demanding cases, arguing that it is a problem for social service agencies. Many professionals involved in the treatment of these offenders are becoming aware that the effectiveness and outcome of treatment is greatly increased if facilitated through the criminal court process, and they are increasingly seeking police involvement. Assaults, both sexual and physical, are, in fact, crimes, and the children in our community are entitled to the same protection under the law as are adults. The traditional function of the police is the protection of persons and property. In addition, police are uniquely capable of providing emergency and 24-hour service. Reports of suspected child abuse require highly skilled investigations that develop uncontaminated admissible evidence. No longer can the police turn away or argue that this is someone else's problem.

The investigation of physical abuse of children is generally conducted differently than those cases of sexual abuse, even though physical abuse is frequently involved in complaints of sexual abuse. To avoid confusion, physical and sexual abuse investigations are treated separately in the following text.

Identifying Physical Abuse

Identification of Physical Abuse. Unlike most crimes reported to police, the investigator in a suspected case of child abuse may first be confronted with determining if a crime has actually been committed or if injuries, for example, are accidental. A persistent problem is differentiating between willful and accidental causation. Since it is generally accepted that many cases of child abuse go undetected, identification becomes imperative.

Cases often go undetected because:

1. Many abused children are not old enough to talk. The majority of battered children are younger than four years of age, although abuse occurs at all ages. A child may not yet be able to talk or may be afraid to

State governments have created agencies to investigate all the complaints within their jurisdictions relating to child abuse. They are responsible for determining if complaints are valid and, if so, to what extent. If it is found that a crime has been committed, the county prosecutor is notified and investigation proceeds. If, however, no crime has occurred, but the family is in need of counseling, the agencies will see that it is provided.

tell what happened because of fear of reprisal.

2. Parents who beat their children can be very deceptive. They may be disarmingly cooperative, overprotective, neat and orderly. They often have opportunities to prepare their explanations and can be glib liars.

3. Children do accidentally injure themselves in various ways and are often found with bruises, skinned knees, cut fingers, etc. Parents can often think of reasonable explanations for injuries, and no suspicion might be aroused.

4. Abuse usually takes place in the absence of witnesses who might report or testify. A preschool child may have limited contacts outside the home, so an injury might be concealed unless medical personnel or police are called.

These reasons not only contribute to the lack of detection of child abuse, but to the difficulty in prosecuting these cases.

The alert police officer is in an excellent position to recognize such assaults, through community contacts as well as during investigations. Child abuse should be suspected when any of the following conditions are present.

1. A marked discrepancy exists between the nature of the injury and the alleged cause as described by the parents. A few parents offer no explanation for the injury, but most offer some excuse, such as the child fell, usually off the sofa or down the stairs, or the child was hit by another child, often younger, etc. If the given cause of the injury seems unusual or does not satisfactorily explain it, check further for inconsistencies and visit the scene. Medical studies have shown that very few children sustain serious life-threatening injuries from their falls. Investigators should be suspicious of child abuse if a child has a serious head injury, with or without a skull fracture, when the cause of the injury is reported to be a fall from a bed, sofa or crib.

2. *An unusually long interval exists between the occurrence of the injury and the time the parents seek medical care.* Wouldn't most responsible parents immediately rush a child to the hospital rather than wait several hours? A lengthy time lapse may be suspicious and should be investigated. Immediate action, however, may also be significant. Many parents, after they have severely beaten their children, are terrified, horror-stricken, panicky, and their first thought is to get medical help for their children.

3. *Fractures are present in children under four years of age,* especially children who cannot yet crawl. The ease with which a child can be seized by the arms and legs as "handles" causes common injuries to the long bones.

4. *Visible injuries to the skin are present.* These include:

• *Bruises.* Bruises are characterized by a bluish discoloration of the skin, the result of pressure that breaks the tiny blood vessels under the skin.

Bruises on the jaw and neck may be of a "fingertip" nature, suggesting gripping. Fingertip-type marks on the chest or upper arms may be indicative of shaking. These injuries are potentially very serious and are believed to be a significant cause of mental retardation because the brain is damaged when it strikes the skull. Blood vessels in the brain may be ruptured as a result of shaking, and the child may become semi-comatose. These injuries do not occur spontaneously. If the injury is the result of childbirth, obvious abnormalities exist from the time the child is born; they won't just "happen" later.

Bruising of the cheeks and sides of the head may suggest blows or slaps with an open hand or fist while more localized bruises or a severe injury to the skull or brain may indicate blows against hard objects, such as furniture. The presence of a laceration of the inner upper lip with some tearing, including torn crenulins, is a striking feature which may result from a blow or efforts to silence a child.

It is difficult to estimate the age of bruises accurately because shock varies. Bruises normally fade and disappear in about two weeks, while scars may linger after many weeks or months. For this reason, it is important to describe in a report the full extent of the injuries, including the coloring, exact location, etc.

Photographs are essential before the injuries heal.

• *Burns.* Approximately 16 percent of burns on children are the result of abuse and result from cigarettes, stoves, radiators, heated instruments, boiling liquids, etc. Dunking burns are common as punishment for children who are poorly toilet trained, and typically show a straight line of exposure. The most difficult burns to identify appear to be those resulting from splashing of hot grease, for example. Burns to the buttocks, soles of the feet and hands are common; scars on the top of the hands, rather than the palms, are particularly suspicious.

• *Marks on the skin* inflicted by certain objects, such as ropes and buckles. Scrape marks from ropes or objects used to restrain children are most often found on the wrists, neck and ankles. Marks from bites and belt buckles may show clear imprints on the skin. Examine the injuries carefully, always considering the possible instruments used. Many causes become obvious.

• *Ear injuries.* These are often overlooked and are suspicious. Examine the external ears for evidence of trauma by pinching, twisting and pulling.

5. *The injury is recurrent.* This is probably one of the most significant indications of child abuse. A history of accidents or injuries which is not consistent with the age of the child may be strong evidence in court. Include all information obtained which shows the child had previous similar "accidents." Even if this may not have been a deliberate injury, the fact that the incident repeated itself causing another injury may indicate parental neglect.

6. *The child fails to thrive.* This is a medical diagnosis denoting severe developmental lags that may have multiple causes. Often identified with the first two years of life, the most extreme example is the infant who literally is starved to death due to insufficient caloric intake. In such cases, the parents often say the child receives sufficient food, but fails to gain weight. Failure to thrive is associated with parental indifference or rejection of the child. To make this judgment, medical personnel must use very accurate measurements (two percentiles or more).

7. *The parents exhibit telltale clues.* These are the parents who:

• are *evasive or contradictory* regarding circumstances under which the injury occurred. Careful coordination with all medical personnel, etc., may disclose inconsistencies in statements given by parents. Some may not volunteer information at all.

• are obviously *demanding, anxious and discipline-oriented.* Battering parents commonly place unreasonable demands in performance on their children,

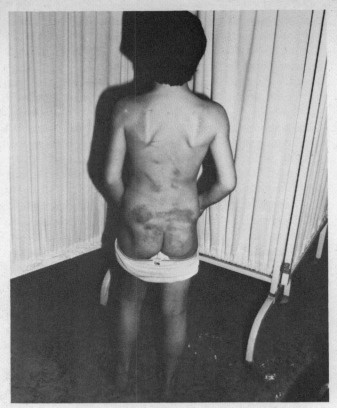

This 12-year-old boy was beaten by his divorced mother's boyfriend, a relatively common phenomenon that occurs when the friend or second husband feels jealous because the child is competing with him for the mother's attention. When investigating such cases, look at the relationships in the household for possible causes of child abuse.

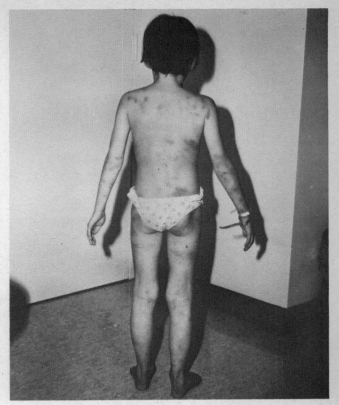

This 10-year-old boy is another victim of child abuse. Statistics show that most child abusers were themselves abused as children and often beat their children for little or no logical reason. Some circumstances that have provoked abuse are as seemingly minor as children playing the television too loud, crying, feeling sick or taking too long to finish dinner.

and as a result they tend to discipline too early. An example of this might be the parent who says his four-month-old "got out of hand" or the parent who expects his six-month-old to be toilet trained.

• *complain agitatedly* of difficulties with their children, especially about excessive crying and the inability to cope with it. They may also express fearfulness of being alone with their child and appear anxious when anyone watches them care for him, especially during feeding.

• *do not empathize* with the child. They may not seem to know or care what their child needs or wants, and they seem to resent it when the concern of others focuses on the child rather than on themselves. They may respond favorably to the investigator who sympathizes with their problems rather than the child's injuries. They have become preoccupied with themselves and have little perception of how the child feels. They may be using the child to serve their own needs, and the child—learning to avoid abuse—begins to

take care of the parents. Close observation may reveal the parent-child role reversal even with the very young child.

• *reject, criticize or blame* their child. Although the parents may now regard the child as a necessary part of their lives, the child may have been the result of an unwanted pregnancy which aggravates later resentment of the child. After the child's birth, the parents may begin to attribute negative characteristics to the child and become hostile toward him.

• *seldom touch or look* at the child.

• *fear the outside world,* distrust those in authority and do not seek help. They may be socially isolated and lonely.

• *were beaten themselves* as children. An argument given by parents that is cause for suspicion is that they would not do such a thing because they themselves were subjected to this and they know what it feels like. Through repeated disappointments and failures, any person can develop a low self-image and feelings of

With the recent upsurge of sex crimes and child abuse cases reported to the police, many of the larger police agencies have created units of specialists trained to handle them.

worthlessness, then turn around and perpetuate similar situations. Parents are no exceptions.

● *show little or no concern* about the injury, treatment or prognosis, do not inquire about the child's discharge date and tend not to visit the child in the hospital.

● *exhibit violent feelings* and behavior.

8. *Crisis situations exist.* Events that produce frustration and stress that the parent cannot handle may result in uncontrolled actions against the child. A situation that may seem minor to one parent may appear monumental to the parent who feels overwhelmed and unable to handle the stress involved. Day-to-day problems, such as worrying about paying the household bills, listening to the incessant barking of a neighbor's dog, and the like, may provoke a crisis situation. Special problems, such as caring for a child who is retarded, hyperactive or autistic, are inherently volatile and require extreme patience and steady nerves. Some parents just can't cope. For the mother who is cooped up day after day with her children and has no way of getting away from the home environment, a minor incident could be transformed into a tragedy. As the investigating officer, when looking into the circumstances surrounding a potential child abuse case, pay special attention to the parents' perceptions about the incident; they may be clues that a crisis existed that led to the child's injuries.

Investigating Physical Abuse

1. *Protection and Removal of the Child.* The police officer's first responsibility in investigating child abuse is the protection of the child. If the child's safety is endangered and immediate protection is needed, the child should be removed from the home by court order. Since removal is very frightening to a child, the officer should try to keep the effects of removal from being detrimental to the child. In making the decision about removal, the age of the child should be considered as well as the extent of the injuries and any previous known injuries, any bizarre or unusual punishment indicating extreme personal problems or disturbances and the child's own fear and attitude. When the situation is sufficiently dangerous to necessitate the removal of one child, brothers and sisters may also be assumed to be in comparable danger, unless there is clear evidence otherwise.

2. *Medical Care.* If immediate medical attention is required, the officer should transport the child to an emergency hospital or arrange for medical care to be administered. Medical examination is also helpful in verifying and identifying injuries even when treatment may not be required. The officer should observe the physical condition of the child and describe the injuries in detail in reports.

3. *Photographing the Injuries.* Visible injuries should be photographed as soon as possible. Some injuries fade or disappear quickly, and this evidence should not be lost because of delay. Photographs are helpful in illustrating the extent of injuries to the court as well as possibly demonstrating how the injury may have occurred, particularly when the history given by the parent is inconsistent with the injury. Photographs have posed few problems legally as long as the photographer and child have a legal basis for being in the place where the photos are taken (for example, a child who is in protective custody versus a child at home where parents refuse admission). The admissibility of the photographs in court is a matter to be handled by the attorneys, and the arguments by the defense are primarily that the photos will bias a jury. Generally, if the photos are instructive to the jury to understand the nature and extent of injuries, they will be admitted into evidence. It is helpful to document injuries through both photography and medical testimony.

4. *Gathering Pertinent Facts and Building a Case.* In initiating the investigation, determine all the facts from the reporting source. If the reporter is a medical professional, estimate as closely as possible when the injury occurred. The significance of the time frame is obvious in that it can more closely assist in establishing who may have been present with the child when the injury took place. The doctor may also be able to suggest how the injury may have occurred, particularly if fractures are involved, or determine whether injuries or repeated injuries are old or are in different stages of healing. Obtain background medical history to ascertain if there have been repeated injuries, lack of appropriate medical care or incidents of neglect.

This may require additional inquiries to area hospitals or doctors.

If the reporting source is a relative, neighbor or friend, he may be an essential witness, so explore all details about which he may be aware. Most often there are no eyewitnesses, and evidence is primarily circumstantial. If approached properly, relatives, neighbors and friends are often excellent sources of information.

Do not overlook the possibility of obtaining information from even a very young child. Children who are two or three years old may not qualify as witnesses in court, but may provide direction in the investigation, and a person who has obtained information directly from the child immediately after the offense may be an excellent corroborating witness.

Visit the scene of the injury at the earliest possible time, preferably before it has been disturbed. If it involves a claim of a fall from the crib, highchair, sofa, stairs, etc., measurements, photographs, descriptions and diagrams are appropriate. Collect and preserve physical evidence, such as instruments used to inflict injuries, broken furniture, clothing, etc. Evidence of a laboratory nature should be obtained when available. If the officer uses the approach that the investigation is merely routine, many permission difficulties in obtaining crime-scene evidence will be overcome.

Talk to the nonoffending parent, preferably without the suspect present. If this is done before the parents have an opportunity to compare their accounts, this can be particularly enlightening. If the nonoffending parent is a witness, obtain a written statement immediately because he/she may later change his/her story in an attempt to protect the suspect. It is important to have all available facts about the injury at this time to overcome denial, indecision or apathy. It may be encouraging to emphasize the possible future danger to the child or other children.

In questioning a possible suspect, allow the suspect to describe the circumstances of the injury without pressure. Interrogation can follow as further background information is collected. If the suspect is initially very defensive, it may be effective to point out that the officer's position is simply to make a routine determination of the cause of injuries. Again, written and recorded statements may be indicated, and delay may prevent obtaining these in the future. The sooner you talk to the suspect, the more likely the suspect will make incriminating and contradictory statements.

If the child is present during this time, observe the attitude of the parents toward the child, the child's response and their interrelationship. The battered child, for example, may be eager to please the abusive parents, and you may observe the child picking up things for the parent and otherwise performing to gain acceptance. Several courts, including the Minnesota Supreme Court (*State v. Daniel Loss*) and the South Dakota Supreme Court (*State v. Barbara and Daniel Best*) have admitted the "Battered Child Syndrome" into evidence as it applies to the defendant. The court's recognition of the battered child syndrome may allow more social history into evidence than in other cases. Police should be careful to obtain all evidence, whether it appears admissible or not, because of the variance of admissibility in these cases and because the information may later be useful to social services agencies or in a juvenile court to assure the protection of the child.

In addition to witnesses, the officer should interview anyone who may have received a different explanation from the parent concerning the injuries. Inconsistencies have been noted from paramedics, emergency room personnel, physicians, social workers, neighbors and relatives. An advantage in these cases is that social workers are often available to provide corroborating or rebuttal testimony, and they are not bound by the extensive rules of admissibility as are police officers. Social workers also can be of assistance in supporting and reassuring witnesses, especially during the time before trial.

Canvass the neighborhoods, not only the presently occupied area, but other places in which the family resided. There may be witnesses in the area such as mailmen, milkmen, garbage men, etc. Even if they have no knowledge about the present offense, they may be able to establish a previous similar pattern of conduct by the suspect.

Contact school authorities if the victim or other children in the family are of school age. School authorities are in a good position to monitor the child's care, particularly if the child often stays at home or is sent home with ailments. The school provides an opportunity to interview children without parental interference. Since the child is not viewed as a suspect, parental permission is not required.

Contact law enforcement agencies, welfare departments and any other agencies in the area(s) where the family has resided. Frequently, this is beneficial and may reveal a progression of abuse. Many of these families move frequently and seek varied sources of assistance so a continuous history is not accumulated. If procedures set by various agencies with whom you must deal, such as hospitals or schools, are found to be a hurdle, encourage meetings to develop changes in policy.

Keep informed of current scientific reporting and research, especially regarding causation of injuries, which is useful in identifying and prosecuting these cases.

Remain open-minded during the investigations, do not jump to conclusions and always remember that your job is to seek the truth. Control your emotions, do not overreact and do not respond until you are well prepared.

Recognizing Sexual Abuse

Researchers unanimously agree that the reported incidence of sexual abuse represents only a small amount of the actual cases, and estimate that sexual abuse affects 10 to 14 percent of all families. It is generally recognized that communities skilled in the identification of and intervention in sexual abuse receive increasing reports and show a sharp rise in offenses. Some departments are recording more cases of sexual abuse than reports of all other sexual assaults combined. Unlike rape, which has shown a greater concentration in the cities, incest permeates both the rural and the urban communities. The stigma, shame and guilt, which tend to reduce reporting of all sex crimes, is especially prevalent in sexual abuse cases involving children.

Criminal statutes generally describe incest as sexual intercourse between relatives nearer than first cousins with the knowledge of the relationship. For investigative purposes, the broader range of sexual abuse cases are included because investigative techniques are similar. Actual intercourse may not take place in the sexual abuse case, but sodomy or other molesting may. And while in some instances the offender is not a blood relation, the child views the relationship as incestuous because the offender—a stepfather or a mother's boyfriend—is serving as a parent and lives in the home.

Since father/daughter sexual abuse cases are the most often reported to police, in the following text the offender will be referred to as "he" and the victim/child as "she." It should be emphasized, however, that many male children are victims of sexual abuse, with female adults as the perpetrators. The possibility that male children may be involved should be paramount in the investigator's consideration of these cases. Also, during the investigation of father/daughter incest cases, it frequently has developed that brother/sister incest (or incest between other relatives) is also involved.

It is helpful during the investigation to have a working knowledge of sexual abuse because it can assist you not only in identifying these cases, but in dealing with the family and anticipating what will happen. Expert testimony on the nature and characteristics of sexual abuse may be allowed in some court presentations. The following are generally accepted assumptions.

1. The child who reports being sexually abused is telling the truth. It is so rare that a child will lie about sexual abuse that, unless there is specific information otherwise, it is important that you believe the child. Often no one else has. The incestuous father can usually think of motives for why the child would lie and tries to evade the truth. The mother, who prefers to avoid confronting it and to "sweep it under the rug," will often ignore the child's report. The police officer and other professionals, confused and having difficulty dealing with it, waste time wondering what happened.

Children often tell no one, especially at the time of the first molesting, and find it very difficult when they do decide to tell. After reporting, the child may later be coerced by the family into retracting her report through threat of disgrace, violence and family disruption. If the sexual abuse is not reported before the child becomes a teenager, the child may become self-destructive, i.e., truant, hostile, delinquent, promiscuous, drug dependant, suicidal, etc.; in short, other serious effects may result.

2. Incest is invariably damaging to the victim and the other family members. Some researchers have recently argued that incest is normal sexual behavior. It is unlikely that they have had any direct contact with victims, who are totally disrupted and feel exploited. Therapists who see the devastation among victims agree that incest severely scars them, with damage that cannot be underestimated. Since the experience remains indelibly etched in the mind, the long-term effects are overwhelming.

Most of these children do not fully comprehend what has happened and should not be expected to give informed consent. The child becomes the object to fulfill adult needs. The young victim has been taught to respect and obey adults and is seduced into a game without knowing the consequences. Often the child knows very little about sex, even though she is experiencing it, and later sex education is helpful. Bribes of affection, gifts or money are frequent. Fear and violence or the threat of violence are often present. Increasingly, younger and younger children are involved who require urgent care.

3. Other children in the family are often or are likely to be sexually abused unless there is effective intervention. All children in the family should be questioned and frequently will corroborate each other. The first victim is often the oldest daughter, even if the report to authorities is from a younger child. Without treatment, the risk of repeated abuse is constant over a period of years, and emergency protective placement of the children out of the home is often appropriate, even when an offense has not occurred recently.

4. Physical abuse of the wife and children is often present concurrently. The father often has a history of conflict with his own mother and a tendency toward violence and punishment of women.

5. Chemical dependency, most often alcoholism, in the father is frequently present.

6. The incestuous father is often uncooperative and unchangeable without outside control. The father should be immediately separated from the family, and criminal as well as juvenile court action is often indicated. The authority of the criminal justice system adds assurance for continued treatment, where treatment is appropriate.

7. The mother should be considered unreliable and a direct participant in the sexual abuse. Even if the mother accepts the child's story, she will likely fail to act or protect the child; she may even blame a very young child for seduction. She, too, may be chemically dependent and a previous incest victim.

8. The child who reported the abuse must be protected. This is the primary concern, and if unprotected, the child is often subjected to further abuse and rejection. The immediate family tends to condemn the victim who reports the abuse. The child feels isolated, disgraced and betrayed. She believes she is bad and worthless, accepting the blame and responsibility for what her father has done. Avoid further condemnation of her.

Investigating Sexual Abuse

Although other agencies frequently offer services in sexual abuse cases, a police investigation should be conducted regardless of what, if any, court action is contemplated. Sexual abuse cases involve the most severe accusations of parental maladjustment and require documented evidence for successful court presentations. Investigative skills are required that are often not available in nonpolice professions which traditionally have offered their services.

Probably more than any other type of offense, *the incest investigation must be initiated and completed as quickly as possible* after the report is brought to the attention of outside authorities. It is urgent that every family member be carefully questioned immediately after they are aware of the investigation

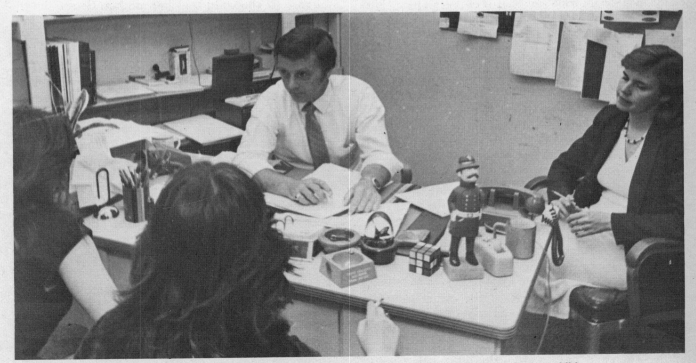

When a male investigator or officer interviews young females who are possible victims of either sex crimes or child abuse, a female officer should also be present. Having another woman there often reduces the victims' feelings of inhibition and embarrassment, so relating the details of the crime(s) is easier.

and that this is documented, because attitudes often change quickly and evidence is lost. When the police are conducting an investigation, it is important that other associated professionals coordinate with police and that their direct contact with witnesses is curtailed until the immediate investigation is completed.

Occasionally, the police may be called to the scene of the offense after a specific incident has been discovered. Such calls are volatile and can be more dangerous than most domestic situations. The officer may be confronted with a drunken, angry and violent offender in a location that often is other than the family home.

1. Gathering Pertinent Facts. If the reporting source is someone other than the victim, as much detailed information as possible should be obtained before the initial contact with the victim. How did the reporter obtain the information? Was it direct observation, suspicion or verbal complaints from a family member? Carefully prepared background information greatly facilitates the questioning of the victim.

Generally, when a report is received, the child has provided information or there are corroborating witnesses. In some cases when a report is vague or indirect, it is essential to obtain information from the child who is reported to be the victim. Indirect reports may include information that a child is openly displaying sexual behavior beyond that normally expected, or the child demonstrates unusual sexual awareness, very specific facts, and the child is less than six years of age.

The child who is the victim should be interviewed first before proceeding to contact other family members. If the parents are aware that the child is to be questioned, they may interfere and attempt to prevent the interview. This is an extremely difficult interview, upon which the entire outcome of the investigation is based. The victim must be supported, reassured that she is not to blame, and the victim must trust that the results of providing the report will be an improved lifestyle or she will not provide complete information.

If the victim herself has initiated the report, the investigator has an advantage, because the child has already decided she can no longer tolerate the sexual abuse and desires a change. If the initial report is made by a social worker who may already have a comfortable relationship with the child, the social worker should bring the child in for a statement. When the child has sought help, often her primary concern is finding a place to live. She frequently doesn't care where she lives as long as it is not with her father or the incestuous relative. However, if the victim is asked what she would like more than anything else in the world, she usually will respond, "To be home with my mother, brothers and sisters without my father there."

When possible, the offender, rather than the child, should be removed from the home. But in cases in which the mother is not supportive and the offender is likely to be released from custody and become violent, for example, it may be too risky to allow the child to remain in her own home. The child may be reluctant to tell her mother about the incest because she is ashamed and feels her mother is "too weak" to deal with the reality of incest (and she often is). In these cases, because of the need to protect the child, she must be separated from the home environment. Unfortunately, she may later interpret this as punishment and experience increased feelings of guilt and responsibility for what has happened.

In questioning the victim, determine from the child the most recent offense, including a detailed sequence of events and the specific act itself; the duration of offenses, including the initial contact, the nature and frequency of sexual abuse, and any specific dates available; any possible witnesses (friends, babysitters and other relatives are sometimes witnesses and even additional victims); who the child has told about the offense (if the child told her mother, determine the mother's response).

2. Medical Examination. A medical examination of the child may be indicated if intercourse or penetration is reported. Although incest is seldom reported immediately after the offense when sperm may be present, the medical examination may demonstrate the extent of penetration and provide treatment for possible injuries and venereal disease (uncommon among these victims). This examination is especially traumatic for the incest victim and should be carefully handled and tactfully explained to the child.

3. Questioning the Parents. The parents of the victim should never be questioned together. The presence of the husband or wife can greatly limit or distort the information obtained. It is usually easier to maintain control of the case and less likely to create an immediate crisis if the mother can be located alone and questioned before the incestuous father is aware the complaint has been made. Although the mother frequently expresses surprise about the incest—even though the child may report having told her—the mother may later relate earlier suspicions, which should be noted in reports. The mother is usually receptive to the child's temporary removal from the home, although her willingness seems to decrease as the age of the child decreases. Unless she has actually witnessed the sexual abuse and summoned police to the scene, the mother is frequently reluctant to separate from her husband.

The mother in these cases should be considered extremely unreliable during the entire investigation. Even if she initially accepts the offense as valid, she may later deny it or blame the child. She is frequently very protective of her husband and feels dependent on him. If the mother can provide corroborating evidence, such as in witnessing the offense, a written statement should be obtained immediately because she may later refuse to provide any information. If the officer explains to the mother that he is aware this is a very difficult situation for her, that there will be professionals to help her and the family and that the police responsibility is to assure the child's safety, the mother may be more likely to cooperate. She may retaliate if the officer is quick to condemn her husband rather than seek facts and explanations. It is important to convey to the mother the validity of the offense rather than argue about it, because the investigation proceeds more smoothly and the situation is far easier for the child.

Physical evidence, such as pornographic magazines, contraceptives, etc., should be obtained as quickly as possible and may be available from the mother at the time of the initial notification.

Questioning of the father can be most effective in the police station. Frequently, the father will come in voluntarily if asked and if immediate arrest is not indicated. An emotional approach in questioning the father may be effective, because the father often will express guilt about the incest and relief that the "secret" is out. Encouraging him to explain the difficulties he experienced in his childhood and in his marriage, especially with regard to sex, allows him an opportunity to "save face." If you become aware that he is an incestuous father who appears to feel that sexual abuse is appropriate, justified (as with certain religious arguments) and acceptable, a matter-of-fact approach may be more effective.

Avoid expressing your own personal feelings or responding negatively as the father describes his behavior or it may inhibit his willingness to relate information. An accepting nod without verbal approval can be encouraging. If the father admits the sexual abuse, an attempt should be made to obtain specific details, especially where dates may be available. Information, which corroborates the child's account, such as the exchange of money, lends further credibility to the complaint.

The investigation should be referred to the local child protection agency, which can provide services to the family and considerable assistance during the investigation. Many prosecution cases are successful as a result of the ongoing support provided to the witnesses by the social services agencies.

There has been a tendency to overreact to incest as a nameless sexual evil with disastrous effects. If we are irrational about sex, it is because we choose to look at sex irrationally. We cannot afford to think irrationally at a time when a child comes to us in serious need of common sense and good judgment. It is important to respond to the child with warmth, objectivity and acceptance, so the child does not become beset by sexual fears. The investigative process, if handled with discretion and professionalism, should not become a demoralizing and ineffective experience for the victim. Despite the potentially detrimental consequences of incest, we in law enforcement can and should help the child recognize sex as a necessary and meaningful part of life, one of the intimate ways in which people can relate to one another other.

Sergeant-Investigator Carolyn F. Bailey has served with the St. Paul Police Department in Minnesota for more than 20 years. Before joining the force, she was a social worker in the Ramsey County (Minnesota) Welfare Department. Sgt.-Inv. Bailey, who received her B.A. in social work at the University of Minnesota, serves on the boards of 11 councils, task forces and associations, most of which are concerned with child abuse and neglect as well as sexual assaults and offenses. She is also co-founder of the Ramsey County Child Abuse Team, Vice President of the International Association of Women Police and President of the Minnesota Association of Women Police. She has written several articles and training manuals dealing with protection against sexual assault and incest.

Essentials of Effective Rape Investigation

Harry O'Reilly

In the past decade, society's increasing sensitivity to the needs of victims of sexual assault has precipitated improved services to victims. Hospital procedures have been formalized, rape crisis centers have evolved and a new breed of criminal investigator—the sex crime specialist—has emerged. The successful sex crime investigator in contemporary police service is a caring professional who calls upon both stress management and investigative skills to help the victim survive the psychological crisis of rape, while fulfilling the police functions of successful investigation, apprehension and prosecution.

While every working police officer should know the essentials of investigating sexual assault, efforts should be made by police administrators to train specific individuals in the attitudes and skills necessary to investigate sexual assault cases successfully.

In larger departments and county prosecutors' offices, specialized units have evolved whose personnel are exclusively assigned to the investigation of sex crimes. For example, the New York City Police Department, prior to fiscal cutbacks, had over 150 personnel assigned full time to various sex crime investigation and analysis units. Smaller police agencies, however, may not be able to afford the luxury of assigning personnel to a specialized unit. In such departments, the task of investigating sexual assault cases falls on detectives or patrol officers who must conduct these investigations, in addition to performing their other routine tasks.

Defining Rape

There are many legalistic definitions of rape, but essentially rape is the forcible vaginal penetration of a female by a male without her consent and against her will. In some jurisdictions, the term "rape" has been replaced by the term "sexual assault" and includes anal penetration of a male or female victim. In any case, rape may generally be described as a forcible theft of sex.

To prosecute a rape case successfully, it is necessary to prove several elements:

1. Lack of Consent—that the sexual act occurred against the will and over the objection and resistance (verbal or physical) of the victim. In most jurisdictions, intercourse with persons who are unconscious or physically or mentally incapable of resistance is also considered rape.

2. Penetration—that the assailant's penis penetrated the inner space of the victim's anus or vagina,

All photos by Paul Bondi

Be sure to photograph the scene. Signs of turmoil, such as upset furniture and broken objects, will help corroborate forcible compulsion and refute a defense attorney's contention that consenting sex occurred.

no matter how slightly. Ejaculation, rupturing of the hymen and total penetration need not be accomplished. However, in most cases, penetration is proven by the presence of semen in the vagina or anus and by medical examination, which discloses injury to or reddening of the vaginal or anal areas of the victim.

3. Forcible Compulsion—that the sexual act was committed by the use of verbal or physical force and against the will of the victim. This can most often be proven by the presence of bruises and marks on the victim's body; by torn clothing; by disorder, disheveled bedclothes and overturned furniture and objects which indicate that a struggle occurred; and by testimony of persons who heard screams, abusive language or a struggle that would corroborate the victim's allegation that force was used.

4. Identification—that the accused person is, without a doubt, the person who committed the crime. This is proved by eyewitness identification, finger-prints and other physical evidence linking the accused to the victim.

One of the major problems confronting the police officer investigating a rape case is his lack of understanding of what rape is. Rape is a violent assault manifested in a sexual act. Because of misconceptions about both the crime of rape and about human sexuality, many officers view the rape crime as "just another sexual experience" and do not feel or show sympathy and compassion to the victim.

The crime of rape is far removed from, and is a corrupt, distorted abuse of, the beautiful act of love. The rapist uses sexuality as a means of degrading, defiling and punishing his victim. The sexual act is stripped of all tenderness and decency and is reduced to its most primitive form. The rape victim does not experience sexual gratification or pleasure; on the contrary, since her body was not ready to receive sex, she experiences a painful, burning penetration. The life-threatening assault on her person places her body in a state of rigidity and muscular tension—the exact opposite of the psychological and physiological relaxation necessary to the enjoyment of sexual intercourse. Mentally, she is deprived of her autonomy—the freedom of choice, the right to decide for herself—and this loss of control over her life is an important component of rape. Performing actions against your will is a painful experience for any human being to endure. If law enforcement officers and other criminal justice professionals can learn to view the crime of rape in this perspective, their attitudes toward and their treatment of victims of sexual assault will improve. A greater degree of complainant cooperation and, ultimately, more successful prosecutions of sex offenders will result.

Dealing With Rape Victims and Their Families

Some police professionals believe erroneously that displays of tenderness, sympathy and gentleness are unmanly and unprofessional. On the contrary, the mature, intelligent police officer realizes that expressing compassion and gentleness are as much a part of his makeup and job requirements as is the ability to be tough and "ass kicking" when the need arises. Of course, working with a steady diet of pain, suffering and misery can take its toll on anyone. In varying degrees, all of us become hardened and cynical; few of us retain the wide-eyed innocence and blind faith in human nature we may have held when we got into harness and went out on a police beat for the first time. Yet, the hardest and most negative of us is capable of displaying tenderness and love for his fellow man in certain circumstances. Helping an injured child, making a death notification, comforting an elderly person who has been mugged—all are situations which require the police officer to display compassion and sympathy. The same gentleness and care must be displayed toward rape victims as well. If the police officer would stop and reflect on what his feelings would be if he or one of his loved ones were similarly victimized, and what kind of treatment he would accept from a brother or sister officer, he would more readily respond to the rape victim's need for sensitive treatment. When the police officer realizes that rape is perhaps the ultimate form of criminal violation, and when he acknowledges that the rape victim needs and deserves his compassion and concern as much as the child with the broken arm, he will have achieved a milestone in his personal and professional development.

Doctors Katherine Ellison and Morton Bard, psychologists who have worked closely with specialized police units dealing with rape victims, have described behavior by which police officers may help to ease the pain of the rape victim, while gathering information and evidence that will help develop their case. Briefly outlined and paraphrased, they suggest:

1. Avoid verbal or physical displays of force. The rapist was tough and hard and the victim probably has had about all she can handle of "tough guys." This is a time for you to be gentle and supportive, not aggressive.

2. Don't be judgmental. Don't second-guess the actions that caused her to be victimized, even if she did something careless or stupid. Avoid statements such as, "That wasn't too smart" or "Maybe you should have . . . ." Your role is to fix blame on the rapist, where it belongs, and to *relieve* the victim of shame and guilt, rather than deepen her crisis with recrimination and criticism. If she did something thoughtless, she surely knows about it by now and has paid the price. She does not need you to remind her of her error.

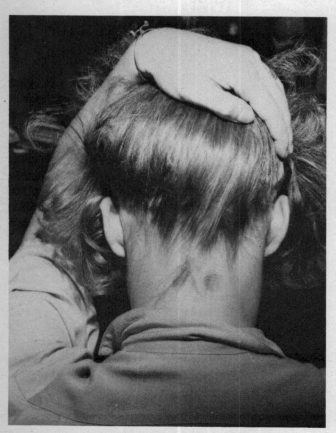

Bruise marks which will help to prove forcible compulsion may be hidden by long hair. Locate and photograph those marks.

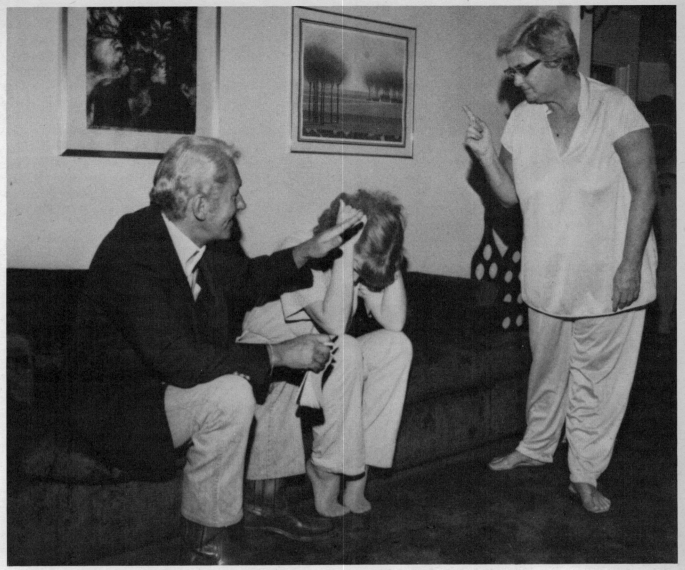

Deal with the victim's family as the need arises. Fend off the anger of the critical mother or outraged father or husband and protect the victim from any further abuse—verbal or physical.

3. While you are eliciting the details of the rape, the victim will be relating intimate sexual incidents that may be awkward or embarrassing to hear. Do not display shame, reluctance to listen—or even anger or disgust toward the rapist. She may misconstrue your statements or even your facial expressions as being critical of *her*. Remain as objective and reassuring as possible. Let her know that she is not shocking or embarrassing you. Let her talk; she needs to ventilate her feelings, and you need to be a good listener.

4. Be tactful and supportive in dealing with the victim's family. Establish a feeling of rapport, and assure them that the victim was not at fault. Without

frightening them, make them aware of the seriousness of the victimization to her and encourage them to give her the love and support necessary to survive the crisis. If the victim submitted without a struggle, assure them that she acted correctly to survive a life-threatening experience and that she should not be blamed or criticized.

5. Put the family to work on the investigation. Tell them to listen carefully when she talks about the attack and to pass on to the investigator any new information that comes out in conversation. They may pick up some facts that have been overlooked. Ask them to inquire discreetly in the neighborhood. Many

witnesses who will not confide in the police will give information to the family of the victim.

6. Deal with the anger of family members. Many parents react violently toward the victim, especially if she has violated some family rule or curfew, which set the stage for the rape. Do not allow her to be physically struck or verbally browbeaten. Do not allow family members to talk about retaliation and revenge toward the rapist in the presence of the victim. Explain that this will only make things worse for her. If she knows her family is willing to beat up or kill someone because of the rape, it implies a stigma toward her and her family, and it will increase her feelings of shame and guilt. If they *do* take revenge, she will feel guilty and responsible if it results in the arrest of a loved one. Talk to the family about her need for affection, tenderness and support at this time. Tell them that they belong with her, dealing with her feelings, not out in the street looking to satisfy their own feelings of anger and rage.

7. Demystify police and court procedures for the victim and her family. Remember that police and court systems which you understand and routinely work with can seem confusing, complex and often unfair to persons who have not dealt with the criminal justice system. Explain and clarify things for them, and give them strength and support throughout the entire procedure, from the initial interview through the trial.

Duties of the Dispatcher

The police dispatcher plays a vital role in the rape investigation. Any sign of frivolity, negativity, indifference or other forms of unprofessional behavior from him might cause the victim to hang up and change her mind about reporting. Consequently, the dispatcher should appear concerned and sympathetic and make every effort to comfort the victim and put her at ease. Assure her that the ordeal is over and help will be on the way soon. Be sure to do the following:

1. Get the victim's name and *exact* address, including apartment number and telephone number.

2. Ask if there are any injuries requiring medical attention. If so, dispatch ambulance or first aid. When appropriate, notify the hospital emergency room that the victim is en route so the medical assistance network will be alerted and activated.

3. Find out exactly when the crime occurred. If within a reasonably short time, get a preliminary physical description of the suspect, method and direction of escape, vehicle and license plate number, if possible. If the crime occurred relatively earlier, so advise the units on patrol when issuing the radio

alarm. *Always* advise the patrol units if the suspect is armed and with what weapon.

4. Dispatch the appropriate police unit to the scene. Avoid sending unnecessary units that might bring undue attention or embarrassment to the victim.

5. If available and if in accordance with department policy, contact a rape crisis center or other counseling group to respond either to the hospital or to the residence, as appropriate. Do this *only* if the complainant has indicated she is agreeable.

6. Keep the victim on the line (or, if you are too busy, connect her with another member of the department who can speak to her) and continue to put her at ease until the appropriate unit arrives at her home.

7. Tell the victim not to wash or douche. Explain that, although her natural instincts are to want to wash immediately, it is in her best interests, for both medical and investigative purposes, not to wash until after the medical examination. Assure her that as soon as her treatment at the hospital is finished, she will be permitted to clean up.

8. Instruct her to keep herself and others away from the scene of the crime and not to touch anything so the crime scene will be preserved and the evidence protected.

9. Advise her, if she is able, to ask any neighbors or others who may have witnessed the crime or the escape of the assailant to remain on the scene.

If the complainant reports in person or stops a patrol unit and makes a complaint, if the report is made by a third party, or if other circumstances exist whereby the dispatcher is not involved in the initial reports, the above considerations should be taken care of by the first officer responding to the scene.

Duties of the Responding Officer

At the Scene. Provide first aid and medical assistance as appropriate. Reassure the victim that she is safe now. Display a positive and supportive attitude, and in calm, soft tones, conduct your preliminary interview as you would other investigations, obtaining the necessary information: who, what, where, when, how and why.

Do *not* ask personal or embarrassing questions about the sexual details of the crime beyond those questions necessary to establish that a rape, in fact, has been committed and to prepare your preliminary report. Detailed questions are more appropriately asked by the detective who will perform the investigation. However, if you are a member of an agency in which you, as a uniformed officer, are responsible for the entire investigation, you will be required to perform the tasks contained in this section in addition to those delineated under "Duties of the Investigating Officer."

After putting the victim at ease and eliciting the preliminary information, make the necessary notifications to the patrol commander, the detective bureau, the hospital, emergency service or lighting units to illuminate the crime scene in order to search—whatever assistance is necessary at the scene. Remember that in smaller jurisdictions where rapes are uncommon, a sexual assault case is serious enough to be brought to the attention of your police chief, and failure to notify him could be a source of embarrassment to him—and to you.

If an alarm has not yet been transmitted, do so at this time. If appropriate, initiate roadblocks and an area search. However, at all costs, avoid creating a circus atmosphere that will bring undue attention to the victim. It is not necessary for large numbers of units that are not directly involved in the case to pull

Do not leave the victim alone upon completion of the interview at the crime scene. She will need the support of a friend, family member or rape counselor.

up at the victim's home. All units whose presence is not essential should be directed to resume patrol or participate in an area search rather than to congregate at the crime scene.

It is *vital* that to every degree possible the anonymity of the victim be protected. Our society does not yet perceive the rape victim in the proper perspective. While robbery and burglary victims are the object of sympathy and support from neighbors, all too often the rape victim is viewed as a freak, and becomes the target of condemnation, criticism and neighborhood gossip. In many cases, rape victims even change their residence as a result of shame and embarrassment once their victimization becomes known in the neighborhood. Therefore, during neighborhood canvasses, or when questioned by curious local residents, officers should downplay the sexual aspects of the crime. During a door-to-door canvass, for example, the officer might say, "Your neighbor was robbed" (or mugged or assaulted or burglarized) and we are looking for witnesses." People will usually cooperate, even if you tell them only part of the truth.

Search the crime scene for obvious pieces of evidence—weapons, torn clothing, objects that may contain the suspect's fingerprints—and safeguard them for processing and transporting by detectives. Take notes describing the evidence you have found, as well as the location, and make a sketch of the area where each item was recovered. Include in your notes a description of the physical appearance of the victim and her emotional condition. Was she distraught? Hysterical? Crying? Angry? Hair and lipstick mussed? Clothing torn? Bedroom upset? Drawers pulled out and dumped on the floor?

Safeguard the crime scene. Determine through conversations with the victim exactly where the suspect was, where he walked, what he touched, how he entered and exited, whether or not he used the bathroom. After determining the scope of his movements within the area, confine the crime scene and prevent intrusions by civilians or other police officers. This may be done by utilizing barriers, rope or by simply locking doors. Hold the scene until properly relieved by detectives or crime scene technicians.

Write a verbal portrait of any signs of disorder regarding other conditions that relate to both the victim and the premises that might help at some future time to prove that force was used. Remember that a few weeks or months from now when the case comes to trial, the victim will be healed and composed and your memory may be clouded by having dealt with many other cases in the interim.

Make discreet efforts to locate witnesses in the area

Process for fingerprints bottles, cans or glasses from which the assailant may have taken a drink.

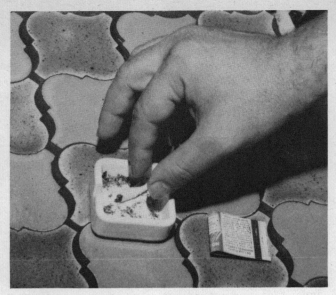

Handle cigarette butts carefully—they may contain fingerprints or saliva that can be blood typed.

and make notes of the names and addresses of all parties involved in the case. If you do locate witnesses, separate them so you will get unprejudiced reports of the perceptions of each witness. If you allow them to confer, often the stronger personalities dominate and you will get a concensus, rather than accurate individual statements.

About the press: In most jurisdictions there is a standing arrangement whereby the identity of a sex crime victim will not appear in print. On occasion, however, eager, ambitious reporters after the "big story" violate this traditional journalistic credo. Your response at the scene to members of the press should be a polite, "No comment." Refer them to your superior officer for further information.

In cases in which the crime is reported immediately after occurrence, if the victim is agreeable, she may accompany the police in a search of the area of the suspect. But if significant time has elapsed between the time of the rape and the time of reporting, the victim should be transported to the hospital without delay.

At the Hospital. If you are the officer designated to transport the victim to the hospital, ensure that she is treated with dignity and that she is not subjected to any further shame or embarrassment. Help her with the administrative and enrollment procedures. Do what you can to cut through routine and red tape. If possible, isolate her from the waiting room crowd until she is ready to be treated by a gynecologist.

Make sure that she is given appropriate medication

Together with the victim, check the refrigerator to see what food or liquid has been consumed by the assailant. Process the appropriate areas for fingerprints.

to prevent venereal disease, and that she is apprised of her options regarding the possibility that she is pregnant. In larger hospitals, formal protocol exists to deal with rape victims, but in rural areas or in locales where rapes are infrequent, emergency room staffs may be unaware of these considerations; if they are ignored, an unwanted pregnancy or a venereal disease could result.

Be sure that medical evidence requirements are fulfilled. They include:

1. Documentation on medical reports that the victim was *forcibly* penetrated, such as signs of trauma in the vaginal area, ruptured hymen, rectal bleeding, etc.

2. Documentation of scratches, marks and bruises, particularly in concealed areas—neck, inner thighs, breasts, etc. In addition to documenting these traumas in writing, photographs should be taken of *all* signs of violence that appear on the victim's body and face. Marks on the breasts, buttocks or genitals should

be photographed by a female—preferably a police officer—but if one is unavailable, by a victim advocate, nurse or doctor. The person who takes the pictures should sign an affidavit to that effect or, if a Polaroid camera is used, indicate on the reverse side of the photo the victim's name, date and location where the photo was taken, and the name and signature of the person who took the photograph. *Under no circumstances* should a male officer take photographs of the private bodily areas of a female victim. If necessary, enlist the assistance of a female hospital employee or even another patient or visitor. The practice of male officers taking the photographs is usually a matter of convenience; but it is unnecessary, degrading and shameful to the victim and should be avoided even if it means additional delay or expense to the police agency.

Wet-mount slides must be prepared from smears taken from the vagina, anus and mouth of the victim. Hospital personnel will prepare these slides and de-

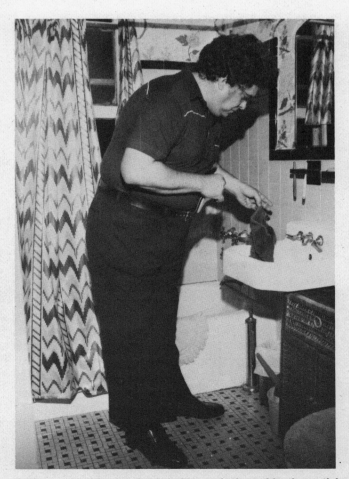
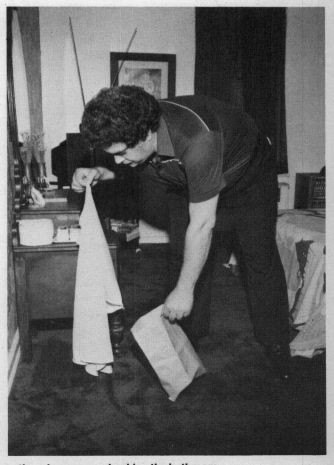

Gather semen, blood-stained clothing and other evidentiary articles from the crime scene, checking the bathroom, especially, for soiled towels, etc. Use paper sacks—not plastic bags—to prevent putrefaction of organic material.

liver them to the officer to be transported to the crime lab. The officer should obtain a copy of the medical report from the hospital. This report should contain a notation signed by the victim releasing the hospital from responsibility of allowing the police to have a copy of this report. This will preclude the necessity of having to subpoena the report, which is a complicated, time-consuming process.

Torn or blood-stained clothing should be taken from the victim and passed on to the officer. In anticipation of this, the officer should advise the victim, family or friends to bring a change of underwear or other clothing to the hospital. Remember that articles containing blood or semen stains should not be placed in plastic bags or containers, since the absence of oxygen will cause putrefaction and destroy their evidentiary value. Rather, brown sacks or grocery bags which are porous should be used, sealed and properly labeled.

Pubic hair combings should be made by medical staff, in the event that there was a transference of pubic hair between the assailant and the victim. Personnel taking combings should comb the victim's pubic area, place hairs in a clean envelope that has been properly labeled with the date, time, victim's name and the name of the person taking the combings. Where the victim indicates she scratched the assailant, scrapings of skin fragments should be taken from under the victim's fingernails for future comparison with the skin of a suspect. Several envelopes should be properly labeled and scrapings from each fingernail should be placed in a separate clean envelope.

Upon conclusion of the medical examination and evidence-gathering procedures, the victim should be transported promptly to her residence.

Duties of the Detective/Investigator

At the Scene of Investigation. If the victim has not yet been to the hospital, see that she receives the necessary attention. Either accompany her yourself or have her transported by a uniformed officer, depending upon the circumstances or the procedures of your department. If the crime occurred sometime in the past, you may decide to take the statement *prior* to taking her to the hospital. There are no hard and fast rules.

When taking the victim's statement, your initial manner and approach should convey your genuine concern for her. You should assure her that she is not just another case. Once she responds to your sincerity and your support, begin the interview. Follow a logical sequence of questioning. Start at the beginning and work your way through the testing and threat stages of the rape. Note the exact words that the suspect used when he first approached the victim, the exact words of the threat, and an exact description of the weapon. "Knife" or "pistol" are not sufficient. Specifics, such as a "serrated-edged kitchen knife" or a "chrome-plated automatic" can be the clues to the successful solution of a case.

When questioning the victim relative to the actual assault, be sure to ask about any conversations, requests, boasts, apologies or pet names that the rapist may have verbalized. These can be important clues to his personality type and even to his identity. Ask her about any genital deformities or scars he may have had. Did he have trouble achieving an erection? Was he impotent? Was he incapable of ejaculation? How many times did he ejaculate? All the details of the sexual act, while difficult for you to ask and for her to answer, may be vital to the identification, apprehension and prosecution of the rapist, and they must be elicited.

Many victims have difficulty in talking about anal or oral sex that may have been a part of the sexual assault. They feel dirty and degraded and will withhold details of this part of the crime unless the information is drawn out of them discreetly and sensitively. Experience has shown that such terms as "sodomy" and "unnatural acts" are threatening to victims and cause them to recoil. An excellent way of obtaining this information is to phrase it in the following manner: "Quite often in our experience the criminal forces his victim to endure other acts. Did anything like this happen?" In these two sentences you have told her that you have heard of such things before and that you will not be shocked. You have acknowledged that she was forced and did not play a willing part. You have avoided labeling the acts or passing value judgments and you have enabled her to answer with a nod of the head. It is important that you elicit this information, because it may dictate additional medical treatment that might not be forthcoming unless the question is asked; furthermore, sodomy is a separate crime and warrants an additional charge in the arrest and prosecution processes.

The next set of questions should focus on the termination stage, how the rapist made his departure: Was he apologetic? Boasting? Did he set a time limit? Threaten to come back? Try to make a date? His parting statements are extremely important: How did he leave? In an auto? On foot? Running? Walking? In which direction? These facts will give investigative direction and assist you in deciding where your canvass will be conducted.

Allow the victim to converse freely. Lead her through the sequence of events in a logical, orderly fashion and, when you have the entire story, get a detailed description of the assailant. You will have already gotten a preliminary description for the purpose of sending an alarm. Now, you will seek an in-depth description. Beginning from his head, work your way down. *Ask for specifics.* Never ask, "Tell me what he looked like." She is not an expert observer, as you presumably are. The following is a sequence of inquiries you might make:

Hair color?
Hair style?
Hair density? Thick? Bald? Receding hairline?
Eyes—Color? Size? Crossed or defects?
Wearing glasses? What kind?
Eyebrows—Bushy? Thin? Arched?
Nose—Flat? Broken? Pointed?
Moustache? Thin? Thick? Droopy?
Mouth—Full lips? Thin?
Teeth—Gold? Missing? Braces? Crooked?
Voice—Harsh? Refined? Accent? Speech defect?
Breath—Odor? Foul? Sweet? Alcohol? Garlic?
Beard? Van Dyke? Full? Scant?
Body—Stout? Slender? Skinny? Fat? Muscular?
Height—No guessing; compare her estimate to your own height
Weight—Determine same as height
Jewelry? Earrings? Necklace? Rings? Watch? Bracelet?
Clothing—Be specific: Brand name? Color? Insignia? School name? Embroidery?
Scars? What part of body? How big?
Marks? Moles? Birthmarks? Where?
Tattoos? Where? What kind?
Odors? Foul? Oily? Paint? Cologne? What brand?
Shoes—Shined? Scuffed? Boots? Dress shoes? Work shoes?

Statements and descriptions, using the above described interview techniques, should be taken from all witnesses. Eliciting a step-by-step description may provide you with a clue that might otherwise have been overlooked and which could ultimately be the key to solving the case. Remember to look for the unusual and the unique.

Process the crime scene for evidence. Look for objects that the rapist may have touched—glasses, cups, bottles, pocketbooks, cigarette packs, etc. Gather any stained or torn items of clothing. Look for blood and semen stains, particularly on bed clothes and garments the victim was wearing. Look for foreign objects, such as pubic hairs, buttons or cigarette butts that the assailant may have left behind. Be sure to check the bathroom on the chance that he may have wiped blood or semen on a towel or face cloth. Process points of entry and exit for fingerprints. Photograph the entire scene, with particular attention to points of entry and exit and any signs of struggle or disorder. Do not permit unauthorized persons into the crime scene until you are satisfied that you have gathered every scrap of information and evidence.

The Follow-up Investigation

If there is no immediate apprehension of the suspect, the following steps should be taken as soon as practicable:

1. Have the victim view photographs of subjects previously arrested for sex crimes, then photographs of any other likely suspects in your photo file. Remember that most criminals are opportunists rather than specialists, and a violent criminal who assaults or robs someone is equally capable of rape. If the victim is agreeable, perhaps you might wish to take her to a neighboring jurisdiction or to a large nearby city to view the photos on file at that police department.

2. Conduct an M.O. search of previously reported sex offenses and of previous arrest reports to compare the M.O. used in this case with past cases. If appropriate, develop an M.O. and physical description file on sex offenders in your jurisdiction, to which you may refer upon receiving a reported sexual assault case.

3. Prepare composite drawings, using Identi-kit, Photo-fit or an artist. If your department does not employ or have access to an artist, you might establish contact with a local high school or college art department and use an art student or teacher on a paid or voluntary basis to do drawings for you.

4. Conduct both photo and in-person lineups when appropriate. In-person lineups should be viewed by the victim through a one-way mirrored window. Be fair in conducting lineups and use photos or individuals who resemble the suspect in general physical appearance. Many otherwise successful cases have been lost due to faulty lineup procedures. When in doubt as to proper lineup techniques, consult with your prosecutor's office and ask for direction.

5. Recanvass the area of occurrence. Many good citizens who are approached in the immediate aftermath of a crime are intimidated and frightened and refuse to cooperate. But after a short while, conscience pangs will cause them to give up valuable information if they are given the opportunity. Go back and knock on doors again. Many cases have been solved by the simple, basic practice of going back again.

Procedures in the Event of an Arrest

Persons accused of rape will most often deny their guilt and will use one of two defenses:

1. Incorrect Identification. "You have the wrong guy." "It wasn't me." In such cases, corroborative witnesses and physical evidence placing the accused at the scene are essential.

2. Victim Consent. "She *let* me, and now she's trying to make trouble for me." "She's mad 'cause I wouldn't pay her." In these cases, it is necessary to take photographs of marks, bruises and disordered furniture and to collect torn clothing and other objects that will prove forcible compulsion.

Regardless of denial, be sure to protect the rights of the suspect. The law mandates this and you are sworn to uphold the law. Further constitutional requirements are strictly enforced and failure to comply with constitutional guidelines may result in the dismissal of a case. Advise the accused of his rights in the proper manner and in accordance with your department's policy. Suppress the temptation to use unnecessary force. As reprehensible as his actions may have been, the offender is protected under the law, and any self-indulgent violence on your part could weaken your case against him.

Gather evidence from the suspect as appropriate. Since such steps as taking blood or pubic hair samples or undergarments of the suspect can be touchy civil rights issues, confer with your prosecutor and obtain court orders, if necessary. Utilize search warrants to obtain evidence or clothing from the suspect's home or auto. Should he agree to make a statement, have him reduce it to writing or have it taken by a stenographer or an assistant prosecutor, whichever is appropriate to your jurisdiction. From the point of arrest on, begin to think prosecution. Put all reports and documents together in a neat package for delivery to the prosecutor. Ensure the proper handling and processing of evidence. Prepare yourself, your complainant and your witnesses to testify competently. Assist the prosecutor in all phases of trial preparation and prosecution. And, equally important, support and guide your complainant through the harrowing and frightening process of the trial, which often reopens old wounds and rekindles old fears and insecurities.

Essentially, the two keys to successful rape investigation are the development of policing skills and interpersonal skills. A combination of sound investigative techniques and a positive, supportive attitude will result in greater victim cooperation, which increases the likelihood of making arrests and obtaining convictions. Increased convictions, in turn, enhance the image of the officer as a police professional and a sympathetic, caring human being. No victim of rape can ever be the same person after the assault as she was before, but using the proper investigative techniques will help the victim cope with the crisis and better ensure her psychological readjustment.

For almost 20 years, Henry T. (Harry) O'Reilly was a member of the New York City Police Department, spending 14 years in the detective bureau until he retired in 1977 with the rank of Detective Sergeant. He served for three years as a Supervisor of the Sex Crimes Analysis Unit, the agency he helped found and develop. Today, it is a highly acclaimed prototype for comparable units throughout the country, and O'Reilly has contributed to establishing programs and policies for these units.

He is currently the director of the Institute for the Study of Investigative Services at the Criminal Justice Center of John Jay College of Criminal Justice in New York City, where he teaches a course on sex crime investigation. O'Reilly has recently become affiliated with Harper and Row Media, presenting nationwide seminars on a variety of investigation-related topics.

Arson or Accident?

Deputy Chief Fire Marshal
Joseph F. O'Dowd

During the last decade, arson has become America's fastest growing and most complex crime. Statisticians estimate that arson is being committed at an escalating rate of 23 percent a year. In 1979, for example, fire marshals in New York City investigated more than 10,000 suspicious fires and made approximately 700 related arrests. Many experts in the field have blamed this alarming growth on the fact that there is and has been an absence of a nationally coordinated program to fight the crime.

Arson does not occur only in large cities, although the media would indicate that this is the case. Arson is just as prevalent in suburbs and rural areas, but a farmer burning down an old barn in Kansas for the insurance money doesn't have the news appeal of a fancy Chicago or Los Angeles restaurant leveled by a suspicious fire.

Unlike fires that have not been set maliciously, arson is difficult to investigate. First, incendiary fires burn hotter and more completely than accidental fires; thus, evidence of arson is frequently destroyed. Second, because there are rarely any witnesses to the crime and often no complainant other than a suspicious insurance investigator, identification and conviction of the arsonist are especially difficult.

Two questions must be answered in every arson investigation: What was the motive for the fire, and who was the arsonist? Several studies have recently been conducted to determine the major motives for arson. Although vandalism was the reason in many cases, the most common motives were the collection of insurance money and the concealment of other crimes. Insurance investigators and police detectives have compiled a list of typical arson offenders and their most common motives:

1. Criminals attempting to conceal other crimes such as murder or burglary

2. Business people caught in a financial crisis seeking to collect insurance money

3. Individuals driven by greed to collect insurance money

4. Juvenile vandals acting on impulse or attempting to gain social dominance or recognition

5. Pyromaniacs and other emotionally disturbed persons impelled by their mental illness

6. Those who set fires as an act of terrorism, during violent protests, riots, etc.

7. Persons acting out of revenge or jealousy

Detecting and Investigating the Fire

Because of the difficulties connected with arson investigation, it is essential that the first uniformed police or fire officials at the scene have a basic knowledge of the elements of arson investigation. They can provide the trained arson investigator who arrives later with vital information to conduct a comprehensive physical examination of the fire scene and make a determination as to the fire's cause and origin. Thus, successful arson investigation is the result of teamwork between officers, who detect evidence at fires, and fire investigators, who conduct the in-depth investigation that follows. Indications of an incendiary fire can be detected through alertness and keen observation; conversely, carelessness and failure to discover and preserve evidence may ultimately cause the perpetrator to escape justice.

Unlike an incendiary fire, or one that the fire investigator has determined through physical examination of the fire scene and interviews with witnesses to be set intentionally and not traceable to any accidental causes, a suspicious fire is a determination made by the chief officer in command of a fire operation and is one reason why the fire investigator is called in.

A fire is suspicious if: there are indications that it may have been deliberately or maliciously set and all accidental causes have not been eliminated; a threat to a person, organization or establishment preceded the fire; a series of similar fires preceded the fire; the premises, usually locked, are found unlocked; and goods or belongings were removed prior to the fire.

At the fire scene the chief officer should be on the lookout for these telltale signs of arson:

1. *Ignition Devices*—combustible mechanical, chemical or electrical substances placed at the point of origin and used to ignite the fire;

2. *Trailers*—cotton waste, rags, paper, fluids, excelsior and other materials arranged to spread the fire from its point of origin to other areas of an occupancy;

3. *Accelerants*—gasoline, kerosene, turpentine, alcohol, paint thinner or even cut or disconnected gas lines used to make the fire spread rapidly;

4. *Protected Areas*—clean or unburned areas left by stock, furniture, etc., covering shelves, floors or other combustible areas.

In addition to these, a fire may also be suspicious if there is evidence of two or more separate and distinct fires burning simultaneously, if there is an eyewitness to the setting of the fire, or an actual confession to the crime. Other factors, of course, may also serve as evidence of arson, but before proof of arson can be established, every piece of evidence may require corroboration.

Outside the Premises. Police officers and fire officials have an excellent opportunity to make observations that a fire investigator cannot be expected to make. In fact, arson might well be overlooked unless the officials first at the fire scene remain alert.

Initially, pay special attention to persons leaving the premises or vehicles leaving the vicinity of the fire in what could be interpreted as a suspicious manner. Make mental notes of the appearance, age, sex and dress of these people and write down the license numbers and descriptions of the vehicles. Observe also whether the vehicles' doors and windows were open or closed and if windows were obstructed to block the outside view. In addition, upon arrival fire officials and police officers must be observant of everyone still at the scene. Was anyone arguing or fighting? Did anyone attempt to obstruct the firefighting operations? Check for persons frequently seen at fires and showing too much eagerness to provide assistance and information. Keep an eye out for persons with injuries, too. Injuries or burns, sometimes the result of the flash of flammable vapors from accelerants spread by the arsonist, should be noted on the forehead, cheeks, under the chin and nose and on the hands and arms of any individuals.

If the building's occupants claim they were in bed during the outbreak of the fire, notice their dress with an eye toward such improbabilities as tied shoelaces, men wearing ties and other apparel that might indicate they were not in bed. Record any comments made by occupants of the building or neighbors. What was said by the person who first discovered the fire is particularly important. Let the person talk freely and get names and addresses. In general, look, listen and get all possible vital information for your report as well as for the fire investigator. Record information, but do not interrogate. Damage to the case may occur, or a witness might refuse to cooperate as a result of amateurish or overzealous questioning.

Observe the outside of the premises, and note any visible flames. Jot down on what floors, on what side of the building, through how many windows the flames were seen and if they were going through the roof. Observe also the characteristics of the flames: Were they gently rolling and quiet or violently driving and blowtorch-like? Were the flames accompanied by a roaring sound or sounds of explosion? Note how rapidly the flames spread and their color. The color of the smoke and flames during the fire's early stages plus subsequent changes in color are partial indicators of the presence of gasoline, kerosene, turpentine and

An incredible amount of heat is given off by fire, and incendiary fires burn particularly hot because of the use of accelerants. Here the victim's body was completely consumed.

windows that were nailed shut, opened skylights and doors. Check also for the presence of pry tools, pry marks or broken locks.

Look for, but don't disturb, any evidence of trailers, plants or incendiary devices, and for any unexplained rapid extension of fire or a separate fire. If suspicion of a second fire is aroused, take special care in recording the evidence: the investigator must be able to prove that it was not a normal spread of the first fire. This requirement emphasizes the importance of noting the fire's position when first arriving at the scene.

Check for any irritating, noxious or toxic gases and the odor of petroleum products. Fire investigating officers should become familiar with all the various odors associated with arson so they can accurately detect them during investigation and describe them if they are called as witnesses in a trial. Specifically, look for the presence of any flammable accelerants. Check if flammable liquids are in areas where they would not normally be found. Distinguish between flammable liquids located throughout an area or when they are found just above the fire floor. Note also possible indicators of the use of flammable liquids, such as charring of the floor, low burn marks on walls and under or on the lower part of the door. This charring can be identified by broken patterns or puddle-like concentric circle burns on the floor. With final regard to accelerants, check for any excessive fire damage when compared to the burning time: Accelerants increase damage and cause the fire to spread unusually fast.

Make an examination of structural damage made

Arsonists frequently pile up flammable materials for use as accelerants to get a good start for their fires. In this instance, the fire was discovered before it was able to spread.

Fire officials and investigators must always be on the lookout for telltale signs of arson. Note the trail of burned gasoline on the pavement leading to and up the wall into the window of this burned-out building.

Not all suspicious fires are the result of arson. Many ghetto fires are started by persons who cook or dry clothes on gas heaters, something the fire investigator must probe into to determine the nature of a fire.

other accelerants. Try to determine if the flames were part of a separate and distinct fire or part of the spreading main fire. Check for out-of-service hydrants, or ones that are knocked over, blocked or clogged with rubbish and if all caps were removed.

Inside the Premises. The physical evidence a police officer usually discovers inside the premises before and during operations can be defined as something material, visible and tangible.

To gather physical evidence begin by asking: Were there any signs of forcible entry? Was the door locked or unlocked? After gaining entry into the building, note if an attempt was made to block the door with furniture or other items to prevent firefighters and law enforcement officials from entering. Look for signs of burglary, for example, opened windows or

This basement wall was blown out by an explosion, caused when a flammable liquid leaked from the upper floor, vaporized and then exploded. Note the liquid-stained wall by the staircase. Both the explosion and the stained wall were reported by the investigator as evidence of arson.

before the fire, e.g., holes in the walls where papers could have been stuffed or accelerants placed. Note whether the sprinkler system or standpipe valves were turned off or if they might have been previously damaged or out of order. Always leave doors, baseboards, mouldings, window frames, etc., intact where possible. Unnecessary removal or damage could hinder or delay the fire investigator's physical examination of the scene.

During your investigation, note the removal of expensive or personal items prior to the fire and substitution of contents, i.e., expensive furniture replaced with poor-quality furniture. Try to detect unusual locations of fire: in closets, under steps or porches, in desk drawers and note furniture with burn marks underneath or on the lower parts. Finally, note the dates of newspapers found at the fire scene, especially those that may have been used to ignite the fire.

Overall, to the greatest extent possible, try to determine the path of heat travel back to the point of origin; establish an approximate burning time; evaluate the combustion characteristics of the material involved; fit known facts to various possibilities.

As soon as possible after your on-site investigation, begin a follow-up investigation. Here are some consid-

erations that would warrant looking into and some tips to keep in mind:

1. Determine if more than one fire occurred in the same structure during the recent past.

2. If a fire occurs during building renovation, determine if there was lack of capital to complete the work or if the renovations were not to the satisfaction of the owner.

3. A fire occurring on a holiday or weekend is not necessarily reason to absolve an out-of-town owner or landlord from involvement in a suspected arson; indeed, this situation alone could be reason to question the owner.

Handling Evidence

Collecting, packaging and preserving evidence is vitally important to a complete and proper investigation. Many of the legal problems associated with evidence could be avoided if all the evidence were collected by the fire investigator; however, since he may arrive on the scene at a much later time, fire personnel may be required to identify, safeguard, collect and preserve evidence.

Safeguarding procedures must be taken by the officer in charge where a fire was not extensive and the fire units have been returned to service. No one should be allowed into the premises until the fire investigator arrives. Although contamination is seldom a problem associated with the collection of evidence, it can become a problem if evidence is not properly packaged and preserved. One way of guarding against contamination is to use a completely airtight container

Locating the point of origin is essential to every arson investigation. Here that point is shown by the charring of the lower portion of the 2 x 4, an indication of the use of an accelerant.

made from nonodorous material, for example, a previously *unused* one-gallon metal can. Evidence should be cut or folded to fit into the can and the top must be clamped securely into place as soon as possible.

A sample of flammable liquids, most of which float on water, may be skimmed from the surface of the water used to put out the fire. Enclose the sample in a clean new can or a clean glass jar with a tight-fitting lid. Do not use a jar with a rubber seal around the lid —it may react with the sample and contaminate the evidence. Also try to avoid the use of plastic containers for storing flammable liquids. Vapors may escape through plastic and evidence may be tinged by the deterioration of the container. Plastic bags can be used in an emergency, but they should be new and of heavy gauge. For proper packaging, place the evidence in one bag, tie it closed, then place in another bag, tie it closed, and put the evidence into a can or jar as soon as you can obtain one.

Because continuity of evidence is as important as proper packaging and preservation, do not remove evidence from its container once you have sealed it unless absolutely necessary. As soon as possible, submit the evidence to the fire investigator, who will testify to its continuity. Should the fire investigator be unable to pick up the packaged evidence soon after you call him, request that the photo unit take pictures of the evidence. Ordinarily, evidence is labeled and marked as to where it was found at the fire scene soon after packaging; however, never label, mark or alter evidence in any way before photos are taken.

Finally, evidence cannot be left in an office unless it is under lock and key or someone signs and stays with it. Continuity of evidence is essential to any case: Guard it carefully. A break in continuity breaks the chain of evidence and may seriously detract from the professionalism and value of your entire investigation.

Joseph F. O'Dowd, Deputy Chief Fire Marshal of the New York City Fire Department, has served 20 years in the department. O'Dowd, who holds a B.S. degree in criminal justice from the FBI Academy, is also adjunct professor at Rockland Community College of Criminal Justice in New York State and the John Jay College of Criminal Justice in New York City.

Hostage Negotiations: When Every Word Counts

Captain Francis A. Bolz Jr.

Many hostage situations have occurred in recent years, but none have been so indelibly inscribed as the "Olympic Tragedy" that took place in Munich, Germany. During the course of the 18½ hours this event encompassed, 11 Israeli athletes, five Black September Arabs and one Munich policeman lost their lives. Three other Arab commandos were captured; as the result of another airplane hijack, they were later released. This episode, as it unfolded, was destined to become the classic hostage confrontation, one that would be the basis for the formulation of plans and guidelines by the New York City Police Department for dealing with this new form of criminality.

At 4:00 a.m. that September day, eight Arab terrorists, armed with automatic weapons as well as 10 hand grenades packed in athletic bags, gained entry to the Olympic Village by scaling a small fence. The civilian security guards were accustomed to "not seeing" athletes who might be out past the training curfew, climbing over these fences. The commandos split up into two groups and proceeded to enter the building that housed the Israeli Olympic team. Four entered through the basement and four via the front door. A confrontation took place at the apartment door where a coach was shot as he attempted to slam the door, and an athlete was shot as he tried to escape. Nine athletes were taken hostage and kept prisoner in several rooms. The rest of the team managed to escape and sound the alarm that "four" terrorists were holding the athletes hostage.

Selection of this location was apparently not by chance. During the Olympic games, more than 3,000 news writers from all over the world were in Munich to ensure global coverage. By 8:00 a.m. that day the entire world was aware of the events unfolding and the resultant deaths.

Between 8:00 and 10:00 a.m. various attempts at negotiation were made by the local police and the German government, as well as by many foreign diplomatic personnel at the highest levels, to effect the release of the hostages. Each of the efforts was fruitless—as were the offers of money, alternate hostages and safe conduct out of Germany. The Arabs demanded the release of some 200 Arab prisoners who were being held in Israeli prisons. Israel, considering itself in a state of war, would not consider the release. The Arabs also warned the Federal Republic that if the Israeli athletes were taken from Germany, their lives would probably be lost. For this reason, the officials were requested not to permit Israelis to be taken from Germany. At this time one of the Israelis who had escaped noted that the Arab who was negotiating was, in fact, an additional man and not one of the "four" he remembered. Attributing the miscount to the excitement at the time, the police updated their intelligence information to prepare for five perpetrators.

The only solution remaining was liberation by force. Deadlines were set and passed, but the possibility of more deaths constantly loomed. Because the compound was constructed like a fortress, direct assault would surely cost police lives. In addition, it was unlikely that they would be able to rescue the hostages before their captors executed them, so plans for direct assault were scrapped. (There was no chemical agent that would work so fast that the captors would be deterred from killing their hostages.)

A plan had to be devised that would bring the Arabs and their hostages out of the building to a location that would afford the police a better tactical advantage. It was decided that an airplane would be brought to the old NATO airport at Furstenfeldbruck and passage would be given the captors and the athletes to the airport. At that location, marksmen would then be used to neutralize the Arabs and bring about the safe release of the hostages. A second airport nearby had to be covered in the event the Arabs diverted to that location.

German law at that time was not specific as to whether an order to shoot to kill could be given. At the end of World War II the Federal Republic of Germany abolished capital punishment. The necessity to direct the sharpshooters to kill the terrorists created a strong psychological problem among the police personnel. Each airport was covered by five sharpshooters, as the new intelligence had indicated there were five captors.

At approximately 9:00 p.m., the hostages and their captors were moved from the Israeli compound by bus to the makeshift helipad near the Olympic Village, then by two helicopters to the Furstenfeldbruck airport. At this time the deficiency of the police intelligence first came to light. It was ascertained that there were actually eight perpetrators.

Because of the quick succession of events, the police were unable to increase the number of sharpshooters at the airports to coincide with the number of terrorists. A plan was quickly developed whereby it was assumed that the leaders themselves would probably want to check out the airplane while the hostages stayed in the helicopters. As soon as possible, they were to be neutralized and then the rest would probably capitulate. Two captors did check out the aircraft. As they returned to their helicopters, the order was given and they were shot by police sharpshooters. One was killed almost instantly, the second only wounded.

But the other terrorists did not capitulate. Instead, a hand grenade was thrown into one helicopter and the other helicopter was machine-gunned. When the shooting stopped, all nine hostages, five Arabs and one Munich policeman were dead. Three Arabs were captured.

And so the tragic events ended, but not the memory or the lessons learned that day.

The New York Plan

Because of these events and the possibility of similar confrontations taking place in New York City, site of the United Nations headquarters, a plan was needed to cope with such an eventuality.

Chief Simon Eisdorfer, Commanding Officer of the Special Operations Division of the N.Y.C.P.D., called together representatives of the Police Academy, the Patrol Division, the Emergency Service Division, the Detective Bureau (which I represented) and the Psychological Services Section. A set of guidelines for dealing with barricaded felons and hostage situations was developed that sought to eliminate any impulsive or uncoordinated actions which might unnecessarily cost human life. Various specific responsibilities and functions based on past experience and ability fell to the Patrol Division, the Emergency Service Division and the Detective Bureau.

Patrol Division. Patrol Officers are usually first on the scene. Their duties are the initial confrontation and containment of the perpetrator, the evacuation of innocent bystanders and neighbors and the gathering of the initial intelligence of the operation. In addition, in New York City, to ensure unity of command, clear-cut authority and responsibility, the Patrol Borough Commander is in charge of the entire situation, with Specialty Units acting as staff personnel. The reason for this command framework is that the senior officer who is most familiar with the locality involved will be able to make more knowledgeable decisions. He will also be left to deal with the community when the Specialty Units pack up their "hardware" and move on. Thus, the borough commander makes the decisions as to whether or not deadly physical force will be used in a controlled and contained situation. Of course, this does not preclude the use of force in a personal emergency involving self-defense. (Good cover and a "display of force" will usually discourage any attack by the perpetrator.)

Emergency Service. The Emergency Service Division is the firearms battalion of the New York City Police Department. More than 200 men and

Vehicles used for SWAT teams and other anti-terrorist units contain assorted types of equipment, including such firearms as M-1 carbines, submachine guns, sniper rifles and shotguns. Gas guns, gas masks, bulletproof vests, spare ammo, floodlights and many other items are also transported so officers are prepared for any situation that may arise.

women are specially trained in rescue techniques and are charged with bringing the trucks and rescue equipment as well as the heavy weaponry of the department to the scene of hostage confrontations.

Well-trained and disciplined, they come equipped with bullet-resistant garments and body armor, shotguns, scoped rifles, machine guns, tear gas and sufficient walkie-talkie radios on a dedicated frequency to ensure clear and unimpeded communication within the inner perimeter of the operation. The Emergency Service personnel relieve the Patrol Forces who initially contained the perpetrator, so that they may assume control of the outer perimeter and take over crowd control.

Detective Bureau. Detectives traditionally have been charged with investigation, interrogation and interviews. This experience gives them certain practical psychological insights that, coupled with extensive clinical training, make them extremely well qualified to act as negotiators in hostage confrontations. They are also charged with the establishment of liaison with other departments and agencies and with the control and operation of the mobile portion of the plan, if movement from one location to another is required to gain tactical advantage.

Phases of the Plan. The plan, based upon what was learned in Munich, was structured in three parts, or phases. Patrol, emergency and detective units re-

A hooded terrorist stands on the balcony of the hotel that accommodated the Israeli athletes at the 1972 Olympic Games in Munich, West Germany. Terrorists held the athletes hostage until a rescue attempt was made by the German police.

spond and carry out specially delineated duties and responsibilities.

Phase I is the location of the site at which the hostages are held. This is where the captor(s) and his hostages are contained and police personnel and resources are consolidated. This is also where the all-important gathering of intelligence must start and continue throughout the operation. The effect of this operation upon the community is greatly influenced by the initial response and the control and discipline of firepower on the part of the Patrol and Emergency Service units. Communication via dedicated special radio frequency enables all police personnel directly involved to be informed as to what is taking place. By eliminating any ignorance of the situation, we eliminate fear. By eliminating fear, we cut down on the

A sniper is an important backup to the negotiator. An elevated position permits the sniper a better view of the scene and target, but when he must be on the ground to shoot, as this sniper is, a bulletproof vest must be worn if he is to be adequately protected.

possibility of uncontrolled gunfire on the part of the police. This phase is parallel to the Israeli compound in Munich.

Phase II is the mobile portion of the operation. If a demand is made for a vehicle or transportation to another location that would afford a tactical advantage, removing the operation from a fortress-like location, as in Munich, to another location, would accomplish this in a controlled operation on wheels. The same discipline and coordination are carried out from the Phase I location to the destination. The Detective Bureau is responsible for and in command of the caravan as it moves and takes up a new location. The detectives escorting the procession would take up containment positions and lock the perpetrator into this new location, pending the moving up of the Emergency Service Unit, which is considered Phase III.

Phase III is for all intents and purposes a duplication of Phase I in that containment, consolidation and intelligence are commenced again, with the Emergency Service moving up to relieve the detectives on containment positions. It is not inconceivable that a situation could leapfrog to three or four locations before it was concluded. During each of these moves, though it is tricky for the police, who would prefer not to move, it is also difficult for the perpetrator(s), so all units are constantly on the alert to seize the advantage if he makes a mistake.

Courses of Action. In hostage situations there are generally four courses of action that can be followed:

1. Direct assault. At any time, with personnel equipped with body armor and cut-down shotguns, the location where the perpetrator is holding hostages can be assaulted. However, before this is attempted, many things must be known: the layout of the building or apartment, the number of perpetrators and their armament, whether or not they may have changed clothing, and so on. A premature charge could cost the lives of police officers as well as the hostages.

2. Selected sharpshooters. These expert gunmen have the capability of staying long distances from the captor and, with rifles equipped with 9-power scopes, of shooting the captor without exposing themselves. Again, intelligence is extremely important. On one occasion in another jurisdiction, a hostage was used as a shield for the perpetrator to look out of a window and a rifle appeared to be protruding from under the arm of the hostage. A sharpshooter saw the weapon and fired, killing the hostage in the window. Other possible barriers exist. If one perpetrator is shot, a second or third might feel all is lost and kill the

Courtesy Harper & Row

When a hostage situation occurs, a safe assembly area should be set up outside the danger zone where SWAT officers can prepare themselves and their equipment before receiving assignments.

hostage and himself.

3. Chemical agent. Despite having the capability and equipment to flood an area with tear gas to hamper the captor, no gas is so fast working that it will immobilize him and prevent him from killing hostages before they can be rescued. In addition, it must be known whether a hostage suffers from any respiratory ailment that might be adversely affected by tear gas. Also, what is the atmosphere in the location where the gas will be used? The most effective chemical agent projectiles are the "hot" burning type that produce a gas, yet these have been known to start fires. All of this must be considered from an intelligence point of view.

4. Contain and negotiate. This is the format of the plan used in New York. Note that the first three courses of action are violence-oriented, and once committed to an action, deescalation is unlikely. But if containment and negotiations fail, the scale of tactics must be improved, fortified with more intelligence than at the outset.

Why negotiate? The locking in of a perpetrator will generally stop the action in a given situation. This cessation in and of itself will somewhat help the situation. Negotiators are used to buy time from the perpetrators, thereby permitting transference to take place between the captor and his hostages.

The term "transference" and the phenomenon might best be explained by an example. Did you ever notice when traveling by air how extremely friendly the other passengers are? They will start up a con-

Communication is extremely important in any hostage situation. Small groups of officers assigned to block avenues of escape, such as the back of a house or building, must be kept apprised of the ever-changing hostage events taking place elsewhere. Note the officer holding a walkie-talkie, which is necessary for communication, and the sniper wearing extra-long armor.

versation with a total stranger, tell him where they are going, who they are going to see, and so on, and even show photos of their kids or grandchildren. Why? Because they are afraid of flying. They are in a crisis and they seek other human beings with whom to share this crisis. On the other hand, if a fellow starts talking to a young lady on the local subway or bus, she is apt to hit him on the head with her pocketbook or call a policeman to have him stop bothering her.

This transference, or crisis adjustment, is the phenomenon that keeps hostages, perpetrators and negotiators alive in these life-and-death situations. The more time spent together, the less likelihood that the captor will take the life of a hostage.

Negotiation actually treats these people in crisis situations and engages them in a form of therapy to alleviate the anxiety and tensions that the captor is experiencing. This training and experience are based upon the theories and program established by Dr.

Harvey Schlossberg, who was a full-time detective in the New York City Police Department, as well as the director of the department's Psychological Services Bureau. Working with other members of the N.Y.C.P.D., Dr. Schlossberg developed profiles of the hostage-taker type. They fall into three (over-simplified) categories:

• The professional criminal—He is the man who robs banks or stores for a living. While committing a holdup, his escape is blocked and he takes a hostage as a "ticket to freedom." He is perhaps the easiest to deal with. He is rational and, after a given period of time, will generally see the futility of getting further involved or killed over a simple robbery attempt. Weighing the odds, he will come to terms with the police.

• The psychotic—Because of his psychological problems, this person presents a difficult and more complex problem. He tends to be irrational and is,

For SWAT and other technical units and routine police work, the 12-gauge shotgun is the most versatile weapon available. Here the officer is armed with a pump-action shotgun and is properly positioned behind the vehicle door for maximum protection.

Courtesy Harper & Row

therefore, less predictable in his actions. Often suffering from feelings of inadequacy, he now finds himself in a position of great power and is generally unable to handle this new-found authority. He is usually highly charged and emotionally tense. By treating this anxiety, we expend a great deal of his physical and psychological energies, bringing him down to a position where he can rationalize and accept help.

• The terrorist group—These persons are the most difficult to deal with. Many rationalize their behavior as necessary to put forward their "cause." Many are charged up, as were the kamikaze pilots of World War II, ready to die for their cause. Time influences their decisions, and the resolve to die deteriorates as time passes. It also permits them to make mistakes which a negotiator must always be ready to capitalize on.

In the New York plan, almost anything can be negotiated, with two exceptions: 1) weapons—if the subject has a bogus weapon or ammunition, giving

him a weapon would create a real danger; and 2) additional hostages. Hostages are not exchanged; whoever the captor has in the beginning will be kept throughout. Police personnel especially would not be exchanged. This would change an objective operation to a subjective one if a member of the "police family" were being held. This is much like a doctor operating on his own children; it is not done because of the emotional problems involved.

Credibility must be maintained. You cannot be caught in a lie to the perpetrator, otherwise you will be useless as a negotiator. The negotiator is the semi-authority figure between the captor and the ultimate authority.

Why detectives as negotiators? It takes a singular type of individual to deal unarmed, face-to-face with an armed felon holding a hostage. He must be cool, resourceful, mature and, above all, effective in verbal communication. Successful detectives have developed

During hostage negotiations, the most dangerous moment is when the negotiator first exposes himself to the terrorist. At this time, the officer does not know how heavily armed the person is, or how he will react. The windbreaker worn by the officer is lined with Kevlar®, a bullet-resistant material.

these attributes through their experience in dealing with the public, interviewing witnesses and interrogating suspects.

Selection of Negotiators. The following criteria are used to select the members of the Hostage Negotiating Team: They are volunteers only; in good physical condition and psychologically sound; have a mature appearance; a good speaking voice; are outgoing; are skilled interrogators and are representatives of various ethnic and racial groups with, if possible, the ability to speak a foreign language; have a college education and other special qualifications.

More than 70 members of the New York City Detective Bureau have been selected and trained as hostage negotiators, two of whom are women, 12 black, 12 Hispanic and the balance Caucasian. The languages spoken by the group include Italian, Spanish, German, Hebrew, Yiddish, Greek, Polish, Portuguese, Russian, Ukrainian and Croatian. In addition, other members of the department who are not members of the group speak Arabic, Chinese and Japanese and are available as translators.

Training of Negotiators. The group underwent an intensive four-week training course conducted at various locations throughout the city. The course consisted of the following subjects: psychology, physical training, use of firearms and electronic equipment as well as operation of the emergency rescue ambulance and escape and chase vehicles, cooperation with other agencies and retraining updates regarding current

A member of a SWAT team hangs from a rappelling rope while attempting to pry open the rear window of a building occupied by armed terrorists. Note the M-16 on his back and the 12-gauge Remington Model 870 shotgun held by his backup.

hostage situations.

• Psychology—The greatest emphasis was placed on intensive psychological training to prepare team members to analyze various situations and develop strategies using psychological techniques rather than force to obtain the safe release of hostages. The point of this training was to provide a basis for understanding and anticipating the hostage-taker's moves as well as his possible reactions to police tactics. Role-playing and the use of crisis intervention therapy were learned.

• Physical training—This encompassed general upgrading of the physical condition as well as weapon-disarming methods and techniques of unarmed self-defense.

• Firearms—Firearms training included the qualification with 38 caliber revolver, 9mm submachine gun, 223 caliber sniper, scope rifle, shotgun (double barrel and pump), 37mm tear gas launcher, 25 caliber automatic and 22 caliber Derringer. Candidates wore bullet-proof vests during the firing of all weapons.

• Electronic equipment—All members had to qualify in the use of miniphone wireless transmitters and recorders and in the use of electronic tracking devices that utilize range and relative-bearing features, which can be quite valuable during Phase II.

• Emergency rescue ambulance—Each team member learned to operate the emergency rescue ambulance, a full-track armored personnel carrier. This training also included the use of its auxiliary equipment, that is, the public address system, intercom, radio equipment, fire-fighting system and first-aid gear. The ERA has been used to establish contact with heavily armed, barricaded hostage-takers.

• Vehicle operation—Instruction was given in the operation of escape and chase vehicles. Special attention was paid to those streets and routes from various locations in the city to airports or other destinations that would offer the team the best tactical advantages.

• Liaison—Hostage-team candidates received two days of training on jurisdictional matters and cooperation with other agencies, including the FBI and the Federal Aviation Administration. One day of training was held at John F. Kennedy International Airport and LaGuardia Airport with the Port of New York and New Jersey Authority Police, where the team integrated its plan with their emergency programs.

• Retraining—In addition to the initial program, debriefings are scheduled to critique every significant hostage situation that occurs anywhere in the world. During such critiques, "Monday morning quarterbacking" and speculations are encouraged. From the situations under study, officers gain new insights and learn new techniques.

Working Detectives. Members of the Detective Bureau Hostage Negotiating Team are working detectives who are assigned to various squads throughout the city. Once their training as hostage negotiators is completed, they return to their permanent commands, resume their normal investigative duties and are called to respond to situations as they happen.

The "New York Plan," as it has been labeled by law enforcement agencies that have been trained by Dr. Schlossberg and myself, has been used effectively in many jurisdictions in the United States and Canada. Our department has shared its experience with other departments and other countries and the program has been applied successfully throughout the world. The one overriding principle that permeates the entire program is that life is sacred—the life of the hostage, of the police officer and even that of the captor. Since the program's inception in 1973, we have never lost a hostage, a police officer or even a perpetrator.

But no two hostage situations are alike, and there can be no standardized format—only guidelines. While each situation is treated as it unfolds, the discipline of firepower and the establishing of communication by informed, well-trained units seem to permit this program to work successfully.

Francis A. Bolz Jr. is a captain in the New York City Police Department and has been the coordinator of the department's Hostage Negotiating Team since its inception in 1973. He has successfully negotiated many hostage cases, responded to over 75 percent of the city's hostage call-outs, which occur at an average rate of 22 times per year, and has gained the safe release of more than 200 hostages. With Dr. Harvey Schlossberg, Captain Bolz has devised a training method for negotiators and has now trained—in addition to over 70 members of the N.Y.C.P.D.'s Hostage Negotiating Team—more than 1,500 domestic and foreign law enforcement agency representatives.

Corporate Tactics Against Terrorists

Richard J. Gallagher

American industry is threatened by hostile action from three types of perpetrators: terrorists, criminals and psychopaths.

Terrorists. The term "terrorism" has no precise definition and means different things to different people. It is used to describe almost any act of violence by political extremists and thereby encompasses spectacular crimes that are not really terroristic. Terrorism is sometimes described as mindless, senseless or irrational violence. But, more accurately, it is violent criminal activity designed to intimidate and induce fear for political purposes.

Terrorism is nothing new. Throughout the centuries, numerous acts of terrorism have been committed around the globe. During the last several years, however, terrorist activities have increased. Almost on a daily basis, the media report incidents of terrorism. The world was shocked by the events that took place in Munich, Germany, on September 5, 1972. Blood stained the Olympic flag as television transmitted the events as they happened. The terrorist was the actor; the entire world, his audience. In the wake of Munich, hostage incidents perpetrated by criminals and psychopaths received increasing media attention, especially as these groups adopted terrorist tactics.

Many terrorist groups have been active in the United States over the past several years. They represent the left—for example, the New World Liberation Front; and the right—the Ku Klux Klan. They include radical Marxist groups, ethnic nationalist groups, Puerto Rican nationalist groups and anti-Castro Cuban groups. William Webster, Director of the Federal Bureau of Investigation, identified the most prominent groups in the U.S. in 1976-77:

1. The Armed Forces of Puerto Rican National Liberation (FALN), whose bomb factory was uncovered in Chicago in November 1976;

2. The New World Liberation Front (NWLF), which has claimed responsibility for a series of violent acts in western states; and

3. The Coordination of United Revolutionary Organizations (CORU), a Cuban-exile group formed in 1976, which has admitted participation in bombings of airline offices and other facilities in San Juan, Puerto Rico; Fort Lauderdale, Florida; Washington, D.C.; and locations abroad.

The FALN, which has claimed responsibility for more than 100 bombings in the past six years in major U.S. cities, including Philadelphia, San Francisco, Washington, Chicago and New York, escalated its activities in 1980. Gun-wielding members took over the campaign headquarters of former President

The explosives most commonly used by terrorists in the U.S. are: (left) wire with blasting caps attached; (center, from top) a pipe bomb, a one-pound package of TNT, a stick of gelatin dynamite, a half-pound package of TNT; (right, top) a fragmentation hand grenade; and (right, bottom) a 60mm blasting timer fuse.

Carter and Vice President Mondale in Chicago on March 15, 1980. They spray-painted the walls with such slogans as, "Free Puerto Rico—Statehood Means Death—FALN." About the same time, they took control of the New York City headquarters of George Bush, a Republican candidate for the presidency, and tied up campaign workers. Ironically, these incidents occurred just before the first presidential primary ever held in Puerto Rico.

In April 1980, Carlos Torres, a leading suspect in FALN bombings in Chicago, Washington and New York, was arrested in the windy city. Torres had been on the FBI's Most Wanted List since 1977. During the same month, FBI agents raided a suspected FALN hideout in Jersey City, New Jersey, and seized a quantity of explosive devices, including military fire bombs, timers and ammunition, as well as a number of disguises and a book on makeup. Also found was a diagram of the electrical and security systems for

Madison Square Garden in New York City, the site of the 1980 Democratic National Convention. In addition, profiles and background information concerning about 100 leading corporate executives and industrialists in the U.S. were discovered.

The New World Liberation Front, a band of radical Marxists, made headlines primarily for its bombing operations directed against public utilities, business firms, foreign diplomatic establishments and federal, state and local government installations. The NWLF is dedicated to the destruction of the American capitalist system, support of the oppressed people of the world and a "class war toward a classless society that is firmly controlled by the people." The NWLF has concentrated its bombing efforts in the San Francisco Bay area. In the more than 70 of its bombings between 1974 and 1979, property damage has exceeded several million dollars.

CORU is the umbrella under which several terrorist

groups have functioned. Omega 7, the most active of these anti-Castro terrorist groups, has operated in the New York/New Jersey area, as well as in Puerto Rico.

Among the other terrorist organizations active in the U.S. in recent years are:

• The Revolutionary Communist Party (RCP). Its members call for a violent class war against "U.S. imperialists" and demand that workers "rise in arms, forcibly smash and dismantle the armed forces and political apparatus of the bourgeoisie and create in their place the organs of power of the armed working class."

In January 1979, RCP demonstrators with press credentials infiltrated the White House welcoming ceremony for Vice Premier Teng Hsiao-ping of China, crying out, "Murderer! Traitor!" In August, Bob Avakian, chairman of the RCP, son of a superior court judge and once a student at the University of California, told an audience at the Convention Center in Los Angeles that "the masses must arm themselves and kill the slave masters."

• The Croatian group. These terrorists have carried out 12 actions since 1972, including the 1976 hijacking of a TWA plane which was eventually flown to Paris. The Croatians took over the German Consulate in Chicago in 1978, holding the staff hostage for 10 hours. In March 1980, they claimed credit for bombing a Yugoslav bank office in New York City.

• Iranian student groups. Condemned by the Attorney General in 1979 for committing acts of violence against the family of the Shah in Los Angeles, many of the students were deported or were to be deported from the U.S. under the direction of the Department of Justice. However, between November 1979—when the U.S. Embassy in Iran was seized and Americans taken hostage by Iranian students—and March 1980, more than 11,000 Iranians, as reported by the *Houston Chronicle,* had been admitted to the U.S. under a lax immigration inspection policy. The FBI warned that some of these newcomers may have been terrorists.

In April 1980, FBI Director Webster stated that the FALN, the Croatian Freedom Fighters and the Omega 7 had created the most problems. Of the 52 domestic terrorist incidents in 1979, the FALN was deemed responsible for 30, while the count for Omega 7 stood at 10. In appraising the overall trend, Webster said the events suggested that the U.S. was developing a "serious capacity" for political assassinations, similar to the type committed by the Puerto Rican independence groups.

In 1979, terrorist activity resulted in 22 deaths, 165 injuries and in excess of $6.6 million in property damage in the U.S. and Puerto Rico. Eighty-five percent were successful bombings, while 15 percent were attempts. Eight of those killed were terrorists themselves, seven were intended victims, six were innocent bystanders and one was a law enforcement officer.

While the U.S. has been spared the political kidnappings experienced in other parts of the globe—the kidnapping of German industrialist Dr. Hanns-Martin Schleyer, for example, in Cologne, Germany, in September 1977, or that of Italian political leader Aldo Moro in Rome in March 1978—increased activity by terrorists in 1980 accounted for 1,800 actual and attempted bombings, 34 deaths, 154 injuries and property damage in excess of $12,300,000, almost twice that reported in 1979.

Criminals. Criminals sometimes adopt terrorist tactics and choose businesses or members of the business community as their targets. In recent years, criminal-type kidnappings and hostage takings have been experienced along those lines. In July 1979, for example, Mrs. William Dedrick, wife of a bank vice president, was kidnapped from her home in West Milford, New Jersey, and a $230,000 ransom was paid for her release. In February 1980, a banker in Landover, Maryland, was abducted but escaped before a ransom was delivered. The same month, a man sought for another bank robbery held seven people hostage for a day in a Berea, Ohio, bank. In another bank in Redondo Beach, California, during the same time period, a gunman held six hostages captive and shot a woman teller to death.

All segments of our society, however, not just business people or bankers, have been recent victims of the criminal kidnapper: sons of famous entertainers and chairmen of the board as well as daughters of publishers and leading fashion designers.

Psychopaths. In many ways, psychopaths may represent the greatest potential threat to corporations or corporate executives because their behavior is difficult to predict.

The terrorist actions of a psychopath may be triggered by a real or imagined affront, by a direct or indirect relationship to a corporation or by publicity. The publicity may involve an executive or some action by a corporation, or the psychopath may copy the publicized actions of the terrorist or the criminal.

In 1976, for example, Anthony Kiritsis, a former Army firearms instructor, borrowed $130,000 from the Meridian Mortgage Company in Indianapolis, Indiana, to purchase a 17-acre tract of land on which he planned to build a shopping center. An executive of the company refused to extend the deadline for repay-

Courtesy MTI Teleprograms

Some terrorists are revolutionaries who commit crimes, such as bank robberies, to fund their political activities. Others are criminals or psychopaths who adopt terrorist tactics and choose businesses, such as banks, as their targets. In attempting to intimidate their victims, most terrorists come well-armed with fully automatic weapons.

ment of the loan which was about to fall due. Kiritsis contended that the bank official had been responsible for dissuading several potential lessees from locating on his property and that he, Kiritsis, faced foreclosure and bankruptcy.

Kiritsis strapped a sawed-off shotgun around the executive's neck and marched him in shirtsleeves onto the streets of Indianapolis. The temperature was a chilling five degrees. Kiritsis wanted complete immunity from prosecution or psychiatric treatment, cancellation of his $130,000 mortgage debt and a public apology for the wrongs done him by the mortgage company.

When Kiritsis surrendered after 63 hours, he cried, "Get the cameras on, get those cameras on. I'm a goddamned national hero and don't forget it." Kiritsis was tried and found not guilty by reason of insanity.

The corporation faces similar incidents involving disgruntled employees with real or imagined grievances, outsiders triggered by adverse publicity involving the company or persons seeking publicity for a cause.

Targets. Those people or organizations that are often the targets of terrorists are:

1. Individuals of wealth or influence;

2. Political candidates because of their views on issues;

3. Corporate leaders because of their symbolic value, their influence in a community or their wealth; and

4. Corporations because of the products they manufacture, their effect on the environment, their acquisition or reorganization of other corporations or their profits.

Information concerning individuals, political candidates, corporations and corporate leaders is readily available in the U.S. because of media publicity. And, unfortunately, although more and more individuals of wealth and prominence are becoming targets, the ability of law enforcement at all levels to meet the challenge is being increasingly restricted.

Restrictions on Law Enforcement

The three levels of law enforcement—federal, state and local—operate within jurisdictional limits. Many crimes, such as those of occupation (i.e., embezzlement by a banker), assault and trespassing are local violations within the investigative jurisdiction of the local law enforcement authorities only.

As many corporations move from the big cities like New York and Chicago to rural areas for more space, lower taxes or whatever, they lose the protection of the large city department with its trained and specialized personnel and with no federal jurisdiction. They

are dependent on small departments that are not accustomed to handling the many problems that arise. In many instances of terrorist threats, the FBI cannot assist in the investigation because of the jurisdictional restraints.

Restrictions on the FBI. In April 1976, the Attorney General adopted guidelines limiting FBI investigations of U.S. citizens or domestic organizations to those instances where a violation of a federal criminal law is involved or where there is an immediate threat of violence; such investigations must be reviewed on an annual basis.

On July 31, 1979, a bill was introduced in the U.S. House of Representatives "to create a charter for the FBI and for other purposes." The purpose of this legislation was to (1) define the duties and responsibilities of the FBI, except as to foreign intelligence collection and foreign counterintelligence investigation, (2) confer upon the FBI and codify the statutory authority necessary to discharge those duties and responsibilities and (3) establish procedures for the discharge of those duties and responsibilities.

The charter (Charter For the Use of Informers), introduced by Senator Ted Kennedy in 1980, set forth guidelines for use by the FBI of informants and

The first floor outer wall of a terrorist bomb factory after a homemade bomb accidentally exploded, killing two terrorists. The brick outer wall and the wooden inner frame were completely blown out. Had such a blast taken place in a crowded restaurant or bank, for instance, the death and injury toll would have been extensive.

undercover agents, physical, mail or electronic surveillances, access to third party records, access to tax information and the use of other sensitive investigative techniques. Congress, however, shelved the charter and never acted upon it.

Impact of the Freedom of Information and Privacy Statutes. In 1974, the U.S. Congress passed legislation for publishing central and field operations requiring that each Federal Agency publish in the Federal Register a description of its central and field organizations and established places and the employees from whom and the method whereby the public may obtain information from the agency. The Privacy Act was enacted into law in the same year. Among other things, this act permits an individual to determine what records pertaining to him are collected, maintained, used or disseminated by such agencies. Both acts provide for exemption where there are important public policy considerations.

When records are requested, the law requires that each agency make them available within 10 days. In narrowly defined or unusual circumstances or in cases of a sensitive nature, the time limit may be extended for no more than 10 additional days. While this law pertains to federal agencies, several of the states have passed similar legislation.

The FBI alone has received more than 85,000 requests for information since the enactment of these laws. Each working day it receives approximately 60 new requests for records. More than 300 people are assigned to handle these requests, including 34 lawyers. About 16 percent of the requests are made by or on behalf of prisoners in jails or penitentiaries throughout the country.

Several state law enforcement officers have shown a reluctance to furnish information to federal authorities for fear of disclosure under these laws. Consequently, the ability of law enforcement to obtain information from the general public, hospitals, hotels, insurance companies, newspapers, public utilities and private companies has been limited.

The Response

From Law Enforcement. Following the "Munich Massacre" at the 1972 Olympiad, the FBI and the New York City Police Department recognized that concluding hostage situations safely required both trained and skilled hostage negotiators. Now, almost all police departments have trained hostage negotiators.

Before Munich, law enforcement in the U.S. followed three basic precepts in dealing with a hostage situation:

1. Try to overcome the offender with superior manpower or firepower;

2. Attempt to drive the offender from his concealed position by the use of chemical agents; and

3. Attempt to lure the offender into the open into the sights of a marksman.

After Munich, law enforcement adopted a fourth option—negotiation to bargain with the offender to release the hostages and surrender without violence.

From the Government. In the wake of the Munich tragedy, the U.S. Congress amended the Federal Kidnapping Statute to cover an internationally protected person if this person were in the U.S., regardless of the place where the offense was committed or the nationality of the victim or the alleged offender. In addition, two other laws were enacted. One makes it a crime to injure, damage or destroy willfully any property—real or personal—in the U.S. belonging to a foreign guest. The other makes it a crime to assault, imprison, intimidate, threaten, harass or use violence against a foreign official or official guest.

From Industry. Industry, realizing it was vulnerable and that it needed to take steps to minimize its risks and develop a response capability in the event of an incident, began examining its executive protection programs and the security of its sites. As a result, corporate security departments were formed or expanded.

To assist corporations, MTI Teleprograms, formerly Motorola, of Schiller Park, Illinois, a leading producer of police training films and programs, published the *Executive Protection Manual* for corporation officials.

Working with 10 U.S. multinational corporations, MTI Teleprograms also developed a system by which a company could use traditional management skills in times of crises, rather than rely on intuitive or emotional responses. MTI Teleprograms' "Crisis Management System" has three phases:

1. Pre-event preparation. Identify as many issues as possible, research the issues and develop policies, programs, tactics and tools in advance;

2. During the event. Establish control over events and outcomes by using these policies, programs, tactics and tools; and

3. Post-event phase. Debrief, evaluate and adjust the system to improve future performance.

To handle these phases, management should adopt three lines of corporate defense—information collection and analysis, preventive programs and a response system to manage an incident if one does occur.

Information collection and analysis. The corporation should gather information from legitimate sources on threats of terrorism and analyze the strengths and weaknesses of the terrorist to determine what real threats the company faces. It should analyze propaganda and the media used by the terrorist, including the legitimate as well as the so-called radical alternative or underground media, the use of informants and political information services.

An effective information collection program requires the development of threat profiles of all a company's operations, based on past threats to the company and to other similar companies. It also requires the development of management briefing programs, and the establishment and maintenance of effective liaison with all appropriate law enforcement agencies.

Risk management principles should be used to ensure that the company's risk assessment provides the most comprehensive and objective data.

Preventive programs. Total protection is impossible—it is not cost effective and not adaptable to the lifestyle of American executives. Some risk must be assumed, although the company should do all it can to minimize that risk. To do that, a preventive program should include:

1. Security officer. Every corporation, no matter how small, should employ a security officer or someone responsible for security. In the medium to large corporation, it may be necessary to have a separate security department. Because every corporation is unique, a security officer is in the best position to evaluate the security needs of the corporation on a cost-effective basis. It should be his responsibility to prepare the company security system and to oversee it. He should be responsible for site security and

Periodic meetings between leaders of industry and law enforcement personnel to discuss and exchange ideas can lead to the creation and adoption of programs to improve overall corporate security.

WANTED FOR ESCAPE
JOANNE CHESIMARD
ESCAPED NOVEMBER 2, 1979, WHILE SERVING LIFE TERM FOR MURDER OF A NEW JERSEY STATE TROOPER

Remarks: Subject escaped from Clinton Reformatory for Women with the aid of three black males and one white female. Serving life term, plus 26 to 33 years consecutive, for the murder of a New Jersey State Trooper on May 2, 1973. Self proclaimed revolutionary, member Black Liberation Army.

DESCRIPTION
Joanne Deborah Byron Chesimard
AKA: Assata Shakur
Alias: Justine Henderson; Joanne Byron; Barbara Odoms; Joanne Chesterman; Joan Davis

Sex & Race . . . . Female, Negro
Age / DOB . . . . 33 yrs. — 7/16/47
POB . . . . New York City, NY
Height / Weight . . . . 5'6" — 138 lbs
Hair . . . . Black, various styles
Complexion . . . . Medium
Scars . . . . Round scar, left knee, bullet wounds
left shoulder and underside of right arm
Mother' address . . . . 100-33 Elgar Place, Bronx, NY

S.S. No. 051-38-5131
S.B.I. No. 335640A
F.B.I. No. 11102J7
F.P.C. AAAAAA0711AAAAAA0410

ATTENTION: **Subject may be dressed in Muslim clothing or in mens' clothing**

ANY INFORMATION NOTIFY
New Jersey State Police
Fugitive Unit
West Trenton, New Jersey 08625
Telephone: (609) 882 - 2000 Ext. 440

Joanne Chesimard, leader of the Black Liberation Army, a black terrorist group, was sentenced to life imprisonment for the 1973 murder of a New Jersey state trooper. She escaped from a state prison in 1979 with the aid of an unknown white female and three unknown black males and still heads the list of most-wanted female criminals in America.

executive protection and, in many cases, should coordinate the response plan.

2. Site security. While it would be impossible to set forth a program that would cover all the steps a company could adopt to ensure the security of its facilities, some basics should be undertaken:

• Survey of the physical facilities and the offices of the executive with regard to access control, fencing, lighting, alarm system, emergency plans (fire, bomb) and evacuation plans

• Communication with local law enforcement as to jurisdiction of law enforcement and its capabilities and response time

• Establishment of programs for handling mail

• Establishment of plans for dealing with bomb threats—notification of key personnel, responsibility for the search, coordination with police, fire and other agencies, and evacuation procedures

• Establishment of security training programs for employees.

• Set up of employee information programs.

3. Executive protection. The most important aspect of any executive protection program is developing the awareness in the executive that he or she could be a target. If the executive takes some simple preventive steps, the possibility of a kidnapping or other terrorist act may be reduced. Protecting the executive includes the following:

• Home survey, which involves such things as alarms, lighting and locks on doors and windows. A survey could determine the most cost-effective way of protecting the home in line with the lifestyle of the executive and his family. (This survey could be done along with the office survey.)

- Communication system (a) in the home, by which those inside the house can communicate with those outside without opening the door and (b) in the executive's auto, since most kidnappings and assassinations occur while the victim is traveling to and from work.
- Program for handling mail.
- Program for dealing with threats, including bomb threats.
- Ready access to important telephone numbers—police, fire, FBI, hospital, rescue squad—as well as the exact location and most direct routes to the police station, fire department and hospital.
- Program for family members and household help covering all the above suggestions. It is important that the entire household participate in an awareness program. Threats are diminished just by not opening the door for a stranger, not furnishing personal information over the phone about the family and by being cautious about accepting packages.
- Travel control program, with regard to both company and commercial aircraft; also driver training for the executive as well as for company drivers.
- Hostage survival program.

Corporate response system. The only viable response to a coercive terrorist threat is an organized response requiring policies, resources, communications, analysis and decision-making that go beyond the usual boundaries of the corporate security department. This response is provided by a multi-disciplinary team of high-level executives whose aim is not to investigate and gather intelligence information, rather to minimize losses of all corporate assets in crisis situations by: gathering information in pre-event activity for use when an incident occurs; analyzing threats; considering alternatives and recommending the most desirable action to top management; and establishing communications with the adversary, top management, government, law enforcement, the family of the victim, employees, the press, the public and all company resources, both internal and external.

Of course, no single strategy can provide an adequate defense—the sum total of all three lines of defense working together is essential. Also, the risks and problems are different in each company. The program necessary for each corporation varies with the individual corporate structure, its executives, its location and its business. Each company must prepare its defenses in accordance with its needs, and its defenses must be planned, budgeted and implemented into the total system. Remember, what is successful in one company may not necessarily work in another.

Basic configuration of the crisis management team. MTI Teleprograms devised a Crisis Management Team (CMT) designed to accommodate the widest possible range of organizational options, crisis situations and geographical locations. The team could vary from one to 20 in size, but five to seven people is probably the most desirable.

MTI's suggested team consists of:

1. Leader. A member of top management responsible for the selection, motivation and supervision of the CMT. His responsibilities include developing, training and evaluating the team, as well as integrating all outside resources.

2. Legal officer. Many problems of a legal nature occur that require the expert knowledge of a member of the legal department. He is responsible for ransom laws and liabilities of the corporation and provides guidance and counsel to the team.

3. Finance officer. He ensures the availability of funds to meet demands, secures funds to operate the team and should be aware of the currency laws in various countries.

4. Personnel officer. This person assists the victim's family in time of crisis, is responsible for company records and, along with the medical department, should be aware of any medical problem of the victim.

5. Security officer. This member is the liaison with law enforcement and provides protective services to management, employees, facilities and families of the victim. This team member also provides the continuity among the other members of the CMT.

6. Liaison person. In a rare negotiation situation, this individual would communicate with the kidnapper, possibly supported by an outside consultant. In the U.S., hostage negotiation is usually handled by federal or state law enforcement.

In some instances, the actual team composition will be small and include only legal, personnel and security officers. In other cases, the CMT must have internal support from other disciplines within the company—communications, medical, director of facilities, insurance, etc. Many companies, for example, are obtaining kidnap insurance. While there has been increasing publicity about availability of such insurance, the less said about whether a company has such a policy, the better. Still, the CMT must have access to company insurance information and kidnap insurance should not be considered the whole program—just one part.

The CMT should have outside resources available.

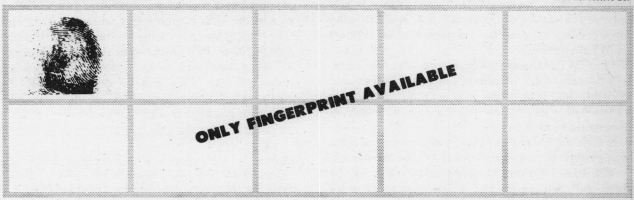

WANTED BY FBI

Entered
NCIC
I. O. 4633
9-24-74

PATRICIA CAMPBELL HEARST

ALIASES: Patricia Hearst, Tania

FBI No. 325,805 L10

ONLY FINGERPRINT AVAILABLE

Date photographs taken unknown

DESCRIPTION
AGE: 20, born February 20, 1954, San Francisco, California
HEIGHT: 5'3"   EYES: brown
WEIGHT: 110 pounds   COMPLEXION: fair
BUILD: small   RACE: white
HAIR: light brown   NATIONALITY: American
SCARS AND MARKS: mole on lower right corner of mouth, scar near right ankle
REMARKS: hair naturally light brown, straight and worn about three inches below shoulders in length, however, may wear wigs, including Afro style, dark brown of medium length; was last seen wearing black sweater, plaid slacks, brown hiking boots and carrying a knife in her belt

CAUTION
PATRICIA HEARST, A SELF-PROCLAIMED MEMBER OF THE SYMBIONESE LIBERATION ARMY, REPORTEDLY HAS BEEN IN POSSESSION OF NUMEROUS FIREARMS, INCLUDING AUTOMATIC WEAPONS. SHE MAY BE ACCOMPANIED BY WILLIAM HARRIS IDENTIFICATION ORDER 4610 AND EMILY HARRIS IDENTIFICATION ORDER 4632, WHO ARE ALSO SUBJECTS OF FEDERAL WARRANTS. PATRICIA HEARST AND WILLIAM HARRIS ALLEGEDLY HAVE USED GUNS TO AVOID ARREST. ALL THREE SHOULD BE CONSIDERED ARMED AND VERY DANGEROUS.

A Federal warrant was issued on May 20, 1974, at Los Angeles, California, charging Patricia Hearst with violation of the National Firearms Act (Title 26, U. S. Code, Section 5861(d)). On June 6, 1974, after an indictment was returned by a Federal Grand Jury, San Francisco, California, a Federal warrant was issued charging her with bank robbery and use of a weapon during commission of a felony (Title 18, U. S. Code, Sections 2113(a), (d) and 924).

IF YOU HAVE INFORMATION CONCERNING THIS PERSON, PLEASE CONTACT YOUR LOCAL FBI OFFICE. TELEPHONE NUMBERS AND ADDRESSES OF ALL FBI OFFICES LISTED ON BACK.

C. M. Kelley
Director
Federal Bureau of Investigation
Washington, D. C. 20535

Identification Order 4633
September 24, 1974

Patty Hearst, daughter of millionaire publisher William Randolph Hearst, was kidnapped on February 4, 1974, from her apartment on the campus of the University of California by Symbionese Liberation terrorists. Two weeks later she assisted the S.L.A. in a California bank robbery, after which she became the FBI's most-wanted female criminal. Hearst was captured by FBI agents on September 15, 1975, in San Francisco and was tried the following year for bank robbery. She was convicted and sentenced to seven years in prison.

The most important, of course, is the law enforcement community. A crisis consultant should be available to the team leader, as well as the newest scientific techniques for threat analysis.

The hostage taker in many cases determines whether an intermediary is to be used and who that intermediary will be. However, the CMT should have an intermediary available if one is needed.

Eight steps are usually involved in the development of an organization's competence to handle crisis situations:

1. The Crisis Readiness Survey is a study of an

organization's threat history in every area of operation. This survey provides an assessment of current capability to handle these threats, a study of management structure and style, a recommendation of appropriate crisis management configuration and a plan to achieve readiness.

2. The Charter is a mandate from top management to create a CMT. The charter includes the selection of members, delineation of the team's limits of authority and the commitment of top management to support the CMT operations.

3. The CMT Introduction is the process of familiarizing selected CMT members with their roles and responsibilities. It involves a general orientation to CMT and the assignment of functional responsibilities to team members.

4. Individual Preparation is the orientation of individual members and assumption of the functional responsibilities. Pre-event responsibilities must be fulfilled and integrated and event/post-event roles must be carefully developed.

5. The Simulation of a realistic crisis is set up to test "actual" operation of the CMT as a unit. This step provides the opportunity for the team to crystallize as an interdisciplinary unit and for individual members to evaluate their own performances.

6. Evaluation of the objective analysis of CMT operations and capabilities and the process of revision is necessary to hone the team into its most effective configuration.

7. Follow-up Training consists of the reorientation and updating of the team to relevant issues. This may also involve the broadening of interdisciplinary skills.

8. On-Going Threat Assessment is crucial to the maintenance of the CMT in a state of readiness. Such assessment requires a comprehensive program of evaluation of threats that could emerge as crises.

In today's world, where the number of terrorist attacks has increased, where crime in all major categories in the U.S. is increasing, where we have encountered many hostage incidents involving criminals and psychopaths, it is imperative that corporations take all steps necessary to neutralize crises with a minimum of loss. This can be accomplished through awareness, training, advanced preparation and the ability to respond in an organized manner.

Richard J. Gallagher is a former assistant director in charge of the criminal investigative division of the FBI. Since his retirement from the bureau in 1977 which ended a 35-year career, he has been a consultant to multinational corporations on crisis management, hostage survival and white collar crime. He assists U.S. police departments in devising hostage negotiation strategies and also lectures and coordinates seminars dealing with terrorism and white collar crime.

He has written numerous articles on cargo security, crime resistance and white-collar crime and has co-authored a police training manual.

The recipient of a Master of Laws degree from the George Washington University Law Center, Gallagher also holds a Juris Doctor degree from Harvard Law School.

Drug Watch: Breaking the Southwest Asian Connection

Patrick O'Carroll

Early in April 1980, Peter Bensinger, administrator of the U.S. Drug Enforcement Administration (DEA) and his aids met with executive officers of the International Association of Chiefs of Police, police chiefs of the major cities in the U.S. and several state police units. The topic of their discussions was the escalating illicit narcotic traffic from Southwest Asia, specifically, Afghanistan, Iran, Pakistan and Turkey, the countries that make up the Golden Crescent.

Bensinger told the assembled officers that the heroin flooding Europe from Southwest Asia had also reached the shores of the United States and was being widely distributed throughout the country. Fred Rody, his deputy and a veteran narcotic investigator, commented on the return of the French Connection and described how former French violators were processing and manufacturing heroin from Southwest Asian opium.

Abe Azzam, DEA's intelligence chief monitoring Southwest Asia explained that Afghanistan, Iran and Pakistan were expected to produce about 1,600 tons of opium, much of which would be shipped to Turkey, a major transit point. From there, Turkish couriers would carry it into Europe to meet the heroin demand in Germany and Italy, and a large part of it would be transported to the U.S. Azzam explained that 1,600 tons of opium was more than nine times the combined production of Mexico and the Golden Triangle countries of Thailand, Laos and Burma. (It is significant also because only about 80 tons of opium was responsible for the heroin traffic to the U.S. in the '60s and early '70s.) He concluded that even if 1,000 metric tons of opium were bought by the inhabitants of Southwest Asia, an estimated 40 to 60 tons of heroin could still be available for export. (This estimate is based on a conversion ratio of 10 kilograms of opium to produce one kilo of heroin, or 2.2 pounds.)

As formidable as this production potential is to those countries battling the influx of illegal narcotics, another equally great challenge is supressing the special breed of people who produce the opium. Control of the opium production in Southwest Asia means controlling the 15 million Pashtuns who have stood for centuries in the land corridors between Khurasan and the Indian subcontinent. (In Pakistan, they are called Pashtuns or Pakhtuns; in Afghanistan they are known as Pathans, pronounced P'tans.) Of those members of the tribe engaged in opium production and drug trafficking, about 7.5 million live in the Northwest Frontier Province of Pakistan and the

The U.S. Customs Service ship-searching squad is charged with uncovering narcotics hidden in cargo vessels traveling from international ports. Here the contraband—six pounds of cocaine—was found in the shaft alley area of the vessel a few hours after it tied up at a Brooklyn, N.Y., pier.

other half in Afghanistan.

This tribe, fiercely independent, has never been conquered in any meaningful sense, although their territory has been invaded time and time again because the land they inhabit is the gateway to India through the Khyber Pass. The Pathans are considered by many to be the best resistance fighters in the world. Their passion for independence, their experience in mountain warfare and their code of "badal," or blood vengeance, make these bearded knife-wielding sharpshooters tough adversaries.

Challenging the Problem

Ironically, the emergence of Southwest Asia as a leading source of illicit opium is largely the result of successful law enforcement measures to combat drug trafficking. During the last 20 years, the world has witnessed the French Connection change to the Mexican Connection to the Golden Triangle Connection and now to the Golden Crescent Connection.

The changes in production locations and shifts and disruptions in trafficking patterns is due to effective law enforcement, government controls plus opium eradication, crop substitution and other controls. These disruptions often buy time for the international community to concentrate on long-term solutions. Ideally, a continuous and constant pressure on the narcotics problem through close cooperation among the various concerned governments and agencies will eventually cause the narcotics problem to be solved.

Narcotics are smuggled in many ingenious ways. More than 248 pounds of pure heroin were found in this 1967 Citroen seized by U.S. Customs at San Juan, P.R., on May 29, 1971. Of the total, 18 half-kilo bags were discovered in the factory-built panel between the gas tank and the rear seat; 56 half-kilo bags in the false rear floor and 65 half-kilo bags in the false trunk floor compartment.

Although law enforcement strategies play an important part in any intervention program, worldwide social, economic and political influences also have an impact on the drug trafficking world.

Probably the most important factor in countering the narcotics problem is the demand of the people of a particular country that their government do something about the problem. For instance, the admirable work of Detective Eddie Egan of the N.Y.P.D. in busting the French drug trade was not followed up by the French police until the people demanded some official action. When a 17-year-old schoolgirl overdosed and died on some heroin that was a spillover from a processing lab in Marseilles, it caused a sensation. Within one year, French police located and seized 11 heroin laboratories.

If heroin overdose is one of the factors that shapes the will of the people, the statistics concerning heroin overdose in the Federal Republic of Germany are chilling. Related deaths have increased from nine in 1969 to 378 in 1978 and to 601 in 1979. The figure for 1979 represents 9.69 deaths per million population, almost six times the present reported U.S. rate estimated to be 1.64 per million. Not surprisingly, the government and the people of the Federal Republic of Germany are working daily to counter the heroin problem in their country.

Another great internal pressure working against the narcotics trade is the Islamic religion. It is the second largest after Christianity, with more than 750 million adherents; in the Golden Crescent more than 92 percent of the population is Muslim. According to the Quaran and the Hadith, the Muslims' holy books, intoxicating substances such as alcohol and opiates cloud the brain and prevent true union with God.

Since the 1950s, governments of the region recognized that heroin spillages were occurring in the big cities, and that opium usage was on the rise. A saying in the region, "Opium is like Allah's finger—it smites and it heals," emphasizes the paradox of the drug. Used properly, opium is one of the greatest analgesics ever discovered by man; when abused, it is the deadliest of drugs. In Teheran, the government sees opium and its derivatives as smiting the population, while Islamic officials teach lessons to narcotics addicts and other violators. In July 1980, for example, a roving Islamic judge, Ayatollah Sadegh Khalkhali, hanged seven men and one woman on a Teheran street for narcotics offenses and other crimes. Since then many other drug offenders have met the same fate.

Another pressure on opium production is the United Nations' constant encouragement to governments of this region to make the economic and political decisions necessary for controlling opium production. In 1974, Turkey, with the help of the United Nations, established limited poppy cultivation in seven of its 67 provinces. Cultivation is now controlled under a strict licensing system. Farmers are banned from lancing the poppies to produce opium gum and must sell the dried capsules to the government at a guaranteed price to be processed for pharmaceuticals. According to reports by the International Narcotic Control Board of the United Nations, this system has been very successful, with no evidence that poppy cul-

Forty-three bricks of marijuana were found concealed throughout the automobile, including those discovered in the door panel by U.S. Customs Inspector Lloyd Hanson while on duty at San Ysidro, Calif.

Dogs can be especially helpful for use in narcotics detection. U.S. Customs Service narcotic detector dog, "Lucky," checks inbound mail and baggage at John F. Kennedy International Airport. He is being put through his paces by Customs Dog Handler Donny Brown.

tivation has been resumed in Turkey.

In Pakistan, the United Nations Fund for Drug Abuse Control (UNFDAC) has established a pilot income substitution project in the Buner subdivision of the North West Frontier Province. Basically, the project is a rural development program offering land leveling and irrigation schemes, credit for farm machinery and crop substitution. The farmers who participate must agree to total elimination of poppies from the selected fields. This small-scale project is not expected to have any dramatic impact on overall opium production in Pakistan; nevertheless, it is a positive step toward countering the growth and spread of Pakistan's opium, and in the long term perhaps a major contribution.

Since its inception in 1946, the Commission on Narcotic Drugs, an agency within the United Nations, has been a very important factor in advising the Economic and Social Council of the U.N. (ECOSOC) in international narcotics matters and has helped to provide a brake on the escalating opium production of Southwest Asia. The agency's Subcommission on Illicit Drug Traffic and related Matters in the Near and Middle East, whose members are from Southwest Asia, provides valuable information that aids in developing barriers against the opium traffic in Southwest Asia.

Aside from all these factors working against opium production and dispersal, Southwest Asia's political problems also inhibit narcotics trafficking. One of the most noteworthy conflicts is that the Pathans are busy fighting off Russian invaders and do not have time to be involved in the production and sale of opium. This situation may be temporary but, nevertheless, it certainly has had some impact on the flow of opium to the West.

In Iran there is a battle between fundamentalism and modernity, or the old versus the new and, among other problems, the uncertain new regime is now attempting to quell an internal revolt of about four million Iranian Kurds who want regional autonomy and preservation of their language and culture.

In Turkey, the government has put the population under military control and curfew and is battling daily with leftist groups who are trying to seize control of the government. There is also some difficulty internationally over control of the main route between the narcotics producers in Southwest Asia and consumers in Turkey. Turkey has a huge outflow of migrant workers, particularly to West Germany, and some of them are supplementing their income by being couriers of narcotics.

In Afghanistan, the Russians seem bogged down fighting the Pathans who easily slip back and forth across Pakistan's 1,300 mile border.

Worldwide Law Enforcement Efforts

Like the U.S., France and the Fed. Rep. of Germany, the countries that make up the Golden Crescent are not immune to the social and economic ill-effects of opium. The people in Southwest Asia seem to be recognizing that drug availability can cause addiction and a variety of related problems; further, there is a growing determination to check the spread of the drug. In fact, an Iranian representative at a United Nations meeting touched on this point, stating that opiates remain a constant menace on the Iranian scene and that heroin is an ever-increasing threat to Iran's population, 50 percent of whom are under the age of 20.

In Iran, law and order is maintained in the cities by a police force and in the rural areas by a gendarmerie. There are about 300 police stations in the towns and cities of Iran, and about 70,000 officers and men in the towns and villages. Many of these officers, particularly senior officials, have been trained in the U.S. or through the United Nations. According to reliable information, as much as 80 percent of them have survived the revolution and have remained in their posts. The narcotics policing force under the Shah had kept a lid on the narcotics problem; today, however, they are hampered in their effort to control it because they are simultaneously battling escalating crime.

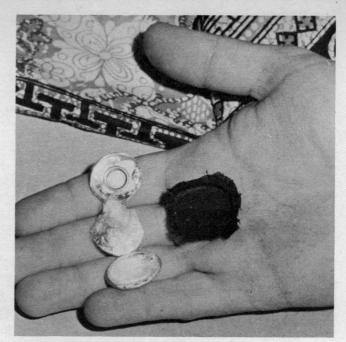

One heroin smuggling operation between Thailand and certain U.S. cities was broken up when U.S. Customs Service narcotic detector dogs discovered the powder in the buttons of women's dresses imported from Bangkok. The buttons, each containing one gram of heroin, were professionally put together and probably would have gone undetected with just a casual examination.

At the beginning of the revolution, 300,000 weapons of all descriptions fell into the hands of the public and are still unrecovered by the government. Also, when the Shah's regime fell, the revolutionaries released as many as 30,000 common criminals from jail and only about 2,000 of those prisoners are back in jail today.

The Turkish Narcotic Force is controlled by the Ministry of Interior. Today, as in the past, the force has been effective both nationally and internationally. One of the immense tasks they face today is the screening of their 1.5 million guest-arbeiten (migrant workers) who travel like commuters between Turkey and West Germany. Better controls are being devised to suppress the smuggling operations of a number of these workers.

The Pakistan Narcotic Control Board, the narcotics force in Pakistan, tries to keep firm controls on narcotics traffic. Because the government writ does not extend to the tribal areas of the North West Frontier Province, its work has been hampered. In other areas of Pakistan where the force can operate freely and enforce the laws, and in the international forum of the United Nations, it has continued to make a contribution in the fight against narcotics traffic.

In Afghanistan, before the Russian invasion, there had been a trained force of narcotics experts. Although part of the regular police forces, the narcotics unit reported directly to the general in charge of the police forces. Although some of these officers had received police training in the U.S. and West Germany, the majority received their narcotics training from the U.N. Division of Narcotic Drugs. Seizure of drugs in Afghanistan through the years indicates that a tremendous amount of opium is produced in Afghanistan and that the narcotics unit was highly motivated and professional. Opium seizures in Afghanistan have increased from 14 tons in 1977 to 23 tons in 1978 to 48 tons in 1979. No confirmed reports concerning the activities of the Afghan narcotics force have been available since December 27, 1979, the date Soviet forces deposed Amin and installed the Babrak Karmai regime in Kabul. In fact, since U.S. narcotics agents were expelled from Afghanistan when the Soviet Union invaded the country and from Iran when the Shah's regime was overthrown, post-1979 information relating to southwest Asian drug trafficking filters clandestinely from narcotics secret agents to the CIA, and statistics are difficult, if not impossible, to acquire.

Finally, Interpol's narcotic drug unit is also involved in an attempt to halt the surging flood of opium from Southwest Asia. The organization, which has a number of officers in Southwest Asia who are detached from police forces, has recently established a regional liaison officer for this area.

Despite the factors at work to combat the Golden Crescent narcotics trafficking—the will of the people of various nations, the Islamic religion, political unrest, the role of the United Nations, worldwide law enforcement efforts, etc., their impact is extremely difficult, if not impossible, to gauge. One valuable measuring tool, however, is the effectiveness of enforcement in identifying the problem, evaluating its pervasiveness and combating it by arresting suspects and seizing drugs.

In August 1980, Billie Ashcraft, U.S. Narcotic boss stationed in Britain, and I met with Phil Connelly, Britain's senior intelligence chief. I asked him if the dire predictions about the Southwest Asia connection were true and if they really had such an enormous opium production capability. Connelly explained, "Yes, the Southwest Asia Connection is the new threat and is our top enforcement priority. To give you an idea of the extent of the traffic, our statistics show that we have seized 23 kilos of heroin that originated in Southwest Asia versus 8 kilos from Southeast Asia."

That same month I spoke with Abe Azzan of the U.S. DEA's Office of Intelligence. During our discussion he referred to a chart showing results of DEA's monitoring of the street traffic in the U.S. and stated, "Our men and the police forces in the U.S. are making good seizures. We're working closely with the police forces in Region 17, which includes Europe and Southwest Asia. In the Near and Middle East, we're building up a stone wall through cooperation with our counterparts overseas."

A new phase in the battle against drugs continues. It is difficult to surmise when the battle, let alone the war, will be won. Still, along with the cooperation of Interpol and international law enforcement agencies, numerous social, economic and political pressures are adversely affecting the drug traffic in Southwest Asia. What is needed now is time, patience and the continued close interaction and support among governments and law enforcement agencies throughout the world.

From 1972 through 1979, Patrick O'Carroll was Chief of Training of the United Nations Division of Narcotic Drugs. For three years prior to that, he was Assistant to the Director in the Washington, D.C., Bureau of Narcotics and Dangerous Drugs. In his 36 years of law enforcement, O'Carroll has taught more than 40 criminal justice courses to local, state and federal law enforcement officers throughout the country. As director of nearly 300 police science and criminal justice seminars and a frequent guest lecturer, he has contributed to the training of approximately 2,000 law enforcement officials from 92 countries.

Fingerprinting Tools and Techniques

George E. Goodreau Jr.

During the past 100 years the science of fingerprinting —the reproduction of patterns or whorls that appears on the end joints of the fingers—has come to be recognized as one method that can positively determine the identity of anyone who has been fingerprinted and whose prints have been maintained in an available file. Among the many individuals who contributed to the advancement of the science during this time were three pioneers: Dr. Henry Faulds, Sir Edward Richard Henry and Sir Francis Galton.

Dr. Faulds was a Scottish doctor who worked in a hospital in Tokyo. In an 1880 article published in the English scientific journal *Nature,* he discussed his studies of fingerprints and made several suggestions about the future of printer's ink for taking permanent record prints, or known prints, for comparison purposes. Dr. Faulds also wrote about the potential identification of criminals through fingerprints left at scenes of crimes. He himself demonstrated the practical application of his theory by establishing the identity of an individual who had been drinking some of his rectified laboratory spirits. The culprit's identity was revealed by the greasy finger marks left on the bottle. This is certainly one of the earliest latent fingerprint identifications of modern times.

Sir Edward Richard Henry developed a system in 1896 for finding the prints of a single individual in a file of numerous prints. The basic Henry system with modifications and extensions is currently used by the FBI, which houses the largest known collection of prints. All the systems in use in English-speaking countries are based on the system devised by Henry.

Sir Francis Galton was a noted British anthropologist who studied fingerprints during the 1880s and in 1892 published a book entitled *Finger Prints.* His studies scientifically established the individuality and permanence of fingerprints. Galton also devised the first scientific method for classifying fingerprint patterns by dividing them into loop, whorl and arch types. He is further responsible for naming the ridge characteristics by which all fingerprints are identified today. These Galton details are: ending ridges; forking ridges; islands (now called extremely short ridges or dots); and enclosures (now called islands to describe a ridge that forks or divides into two and then rejoins to become one ridge).

Classifying Fingerprints

Generally, fingerprints are classified into three types of Galton-named patterns: loops, representing 60-65 percent of all patterns; whorls, representing 30-35 percent; and arches, representing five percent.

TYPES OF PRINTS

Loop

Loop

Central pocket loop

Double loop

Tented arch

Plain arch

Plain whorl

Accidental

Loops, the most common pattern, are of two types: those that open toward the thumb (known as radial) and those that open toward the little finger (known as ulnar). Loops are classified not only by their size, but by their direction. A loop looks like a hairpin and has at least one ridge that comes in from either side, doubles back on itself and exits or tends to exit on the same side of the pattern on which it came in. Loops are counted, that is, all ridges intervening between the only delta and core of the loop are counted. The ridge count of any particular loop may be from one to any number, although ridge counts over 30 are very uncommon. (Delta is the fourth letter of the Greek alphabet and is represented by an isosceles triangle. In a loop print, the delta is where the ridge, running in three different directions, comes together to form an isosceles triangle without the angles. The core is in the approximate center of the loop and is within, or on, the innermost looping ridge.)

Arches, the least common of all patterns, are characterized by ridges that enter on either side of the print and exit on the other side or tend to exit on the other side, making a rise or a curve in the center. Arches are subdivided into two categories—plain arch or tented arch. Unlike the plain arch, the tented-arch pattern has one or more ridges that diverge from the general flow of the ridges and form an angle or up-thrust.

Whorls are of four types: plain; central pocket-loop-type; double-loop-type; and accidental. All whorls have two or more deltas. Any pattern that has three or more deltas is an accidental. All whorls do not look alike, but are characterized by ridges that travel in a circular pattern. The differences between plain whorls and central pocket-loop-type whorls are of use only to technicians who work with large amounts of inked prints. Double-loop-type whorls have two deltas with two-loop formations in the pattern. Accidentals are very rare and usually comprise a combination of two different types of patterns (not the plain arch) or those that have more than two deltas.

Whorls are traced from the extreme left delta toward the right delta. The tracing may be either inner-meeting or outer (I-M-O). Loops are either given I or O or SM or L, depending on the number of ridge counts and the finger on the hand bearing that print. The classification formula (usually indicated on the fingerprint card in the upper right-hand corner) is a shorthand compilation of the types, sizes and positions of the patterns contained in the 10 fingers printed on the card. This is Henry's part of the science of fingerprints that enables the technician to go quickly to the part of the fingerprint file containing all prints with the same classification formula and search through the prints for a match with the current print.

Each print of the current card is compared with every print in the same classification formula by the Galton details to make sure the ridges on the fingers coincide in all respects on the two cards in question. All prints with the same classification formula will have the same types of patterns on each finger. This by no means implies that prints with the same classification formula belong to just one individual. There may be several thousand individuals with the same classification. To lessen the number of prints to be individually compared, the FBI uses other items to segregate prints. Prints of females are filed separately from those of males and are further divided by age: 1-30; 31-54; 55-74; and 75 and older. Scars, amputations and intentional mutilations are also used to subdivide a classification.

Fingerprints: Proof-positive I.D.

Fingerprints are used as positive means of identification for two reason: (1) each fingerprint is unique, i.e., the ridge characteristics or Galton details on one person's finger will never exactly match the ridge characteristics on any other person's finger; and (2) the ridge characteristics are permanent. The ridges formed before birth enlarge as a child becomes an adult. Of course, ridges may be destroyed through permanent scarring, but scars merely destroy the

Bergen County (N.J.) Sheriff's I.D. Officer Howard Haas is shown dusting a weapon used in a homicide for latent prints. The regular and illuminated magnifying glasses on the table and the bottle of white dusting powder are for use against the dark finish of the weapon.

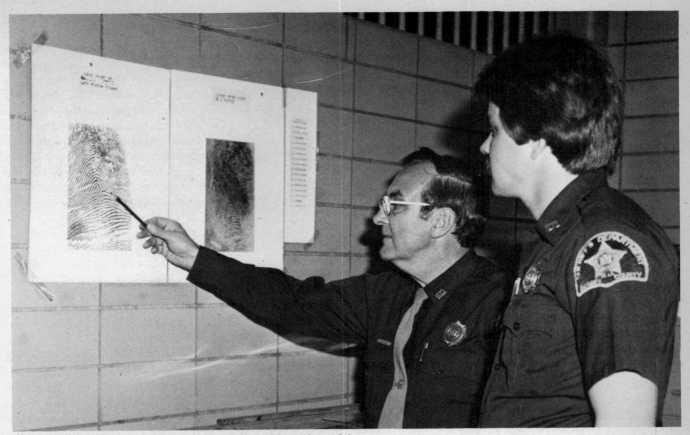

A fingerprint comparison chart being prepared as evidence for a trial.

ridges that are already present. These ridges are not replaced by different ridge characteristics but by scar tissue, which has no ridges.

Fingerprints may be inked prints or latent prints. Inked fingerprints are usually made under optimum conditions and are made with highly contrasting materials, usually black printer's ink on a white card or sheet of paper. These prints are clear and easy to classify and disclose the ridge details that appear in each of the 10 fingers printed on the card. Latent, or hidden, prints refer to those prints collected at a crime scene and differ from inked prints in that they are chance impressions left on objects a person has handled. Latent fingerprints are usually transferred to an object by a thin film of perspiration covering the ridges. Latent prints also may be deposited on handled objects by any foreign substance covering the fingers.

Developing Latent Prints. Both inked and latent fingerprints positively prove one of two things: that the person whose print is on an item was in the presence of that item or that he had possession of that item. The presence or absence of latent prints can be determined only by examining the item. No investigator can positively say that an object was or was not handled without first examining it for the presence of prints. Latent fingerprints cannot be aged, that is, the time they were deposited on an object cannot be accurately determined unless an investigation is conducted. Only by discovering when the object in question was last cleaned, washed or polished or when and if the object was exposed to the weather can it be known when prints were deposited.

Latent prints must be developed so they can be readily discerned by the eye. They may be developed with powder and a brush or with chemicals. The best method to use depends entirely on the surface on which the latent prints are found.

1. Powder Method. If the surface bearing the suspected latents is one that water will not penetrate, it should be examined with powder and a brush. Powders can be purchased from chemical supply houses and are available in many different colors. Black powder should be used on light objects and gray powder on dark or black objects. The examiner should always strive for contrast between the ridge characteristics of the latent print being developed and the color of the object on which the print is being developed.

If you are developing latent prints, always wear gloves and handle the object as little as possible. Hold the object only by the corners or by those areas where no latent prints could be developed. Never powder a wet object; let it dry first. Handle the brush lightly and dip only the tips of the bristles in the powder. Gently tap the brush with a finger to shake some of the powder onto the surface and cover the surface with short strokes, leaving the bristles on the brush straight or with very little bend. Friction between the ends of the bristles and the surface is always present, but if the bristle ends are pressed too hard against the surface, the prints will be rubbed off. Heavy-handed examiners have probably destroyed more latent prints than they have developed.

After the presence of latents is determined, they may be accentuated by following the flow of the ridges with the bristle tips. Travel parallel with the ridges, not across them. Preservation of powdered latent prints sometimes calls for a little ingenuity on the part of the examiner. These types of prints are extremely fragile and can be completely destroyed inadvertently. I have known some examiners who have lifted the latent prints on the object and then wiped the object clean. These examiners first covered the object with transparent semi-stiff plastic or covered only the area

It is important when fingerprinting a subject to print completely the entire joint to below the first crease in the finger and to roll the finger fully from nail to nail, as demonstrated here.

where the latent print was developed with plastic and then taped it down. Plastic is used because the latent print can be seen through it and because plastic, a nonporous substance, will not absorb the moisture that adheres the powder to the latent print.

Some courts are now demanding that the object bearing the print be shown and explained to the jury. When the examiner explains to the jury how the print was developed, the latent print on the object—completely visible through the plastic—makes a highly effective exhibit. The plastic also prevents the accidental or deliberate erasure of the latent print when handled by others in the courtroom during the trial. (This has happened in the past.)

Finally, although powders are always used in developing latent prints on nonporous surfaces, those prints left in blood, grease or dirt, as well as prints impressed in paint, wax, gum, soap, putty or dust will be destroyed by the addition of powders of any type, no matter how carefully applied. The only way these types of prints may be preserved is on the article itself or by photography.

2. Chemical Method. If the surface to be examined absorbs moisture, for example, paper, cardboard or untreated and unpainted wood, chemicals should be used. Chemicals develop better-quality prints on these items than powder. Police departments sometimes use powder on these substances, but with mixed results. With chemicals there is no need to cope with the friction between the ends of the bristles of the brush and the surface of the latent-print-bearing item. In addition, more so than powders, chemicals will develop latent prints on moisture-absorbing objects long after the prints are deposited. I have developed latent prints on checks that were more than seven years old with the chemical Ninhydrin (triketohydrindene hydrate), probably the best chemical available for developing latent prints.

Chemicals are placed on latent prints that were made by the perspiration that is exuded from the sweat pores on the palms of the hands and soles of the feet. These pores in the hands and feet are located on the tops of the ridges, not in the spaces between the ridges. Hypothetically, if every sweat pore on each ridge of a hand or foot was exuding perspiration and if all the body's chemicals were present, a perfect reproduction of the ridges would be captured. Since perfect reproduction does not happen in reality, you have to work with what can be developed.

Ninhydrin develops latents containing small amounts of proteins, called amino acids, in the perspiration. (Ninhydrin powder can be purchased at chemical supply houses, but it is more economical for police departments to mix their own solutions. Two-thirds of an ounce or 20 grams of powder should be dissolved in one gallon of acetone. This solution is highly volatile and should be kept in a tightly corked glass bottle or metal can. Use it only in a well-ventilated room and do not smoke—the fumes are highly explosive.) A Ninhydrin powder solution may be applied with a brush to the surface, it may be sprayed on the surface with a spray gun or the object may be dipped in the solution. After the specimen has come in contact with the solution, the latent prints will gradually appear upon exposure to room-temperature air. Although over a period of 72 hours optimum development of the latents is attained, development may be hastened by applying a steam iron to the surface of the specimen.

Latents obtained by using Ninhydrin are purpled-red in color and are fairly permanent. On some items, however, such as paper or cardboard, the stains gradually disappear, possibly because of chemicals in the specimens. The surface that has been sprayed or painted, or the object that has been dipped in the solution is not viable for further development of latents if the surface or item is handled indiscriminately or without gloves. Contamination may be claimed and allowed by the court and the item disallowed as evidence at the trial.

Should it be desired that the item that has been examined and that bears stains of Ninhydrin be returned to its original state as closely as possible, a solution of one part ammonium hydroxide to two parts distilled water can be used. Place this solution in a glass or steel tray and immerse the specimen in it until the Ninhydrin stain disappears. Remove the object from the ammonia solution and wash it in a bath of running water, then press it dry with a warm iron. Be careful, though—specimens made of certain types of paper will disintegrate in this solution.

In addition to Ninhydrin, other chemicals, such as iodine (as fumes) and poisonous silver nitrate (in crystal form), can be used to develop latent prints on porous substances. Iodine fuming has never been a very popular method for developing identifiable latent prints, but it can develop latents containing large amounts of fat or oil. While perspiration exuded from the pores on the palms contains only traces of fat and oil, the fingers, coming in contact with the face, hair or scalp, may transfer sebaceous matter to an object. Iodine crystals may be bought by the pound at chemical supply houses and an iodine fuming gun can be constructed very easily (see illustration).

Silver nitrate, also readily available from chemical supply houses, may be used to develop latent prints containing a small amount of salt. This chemical,

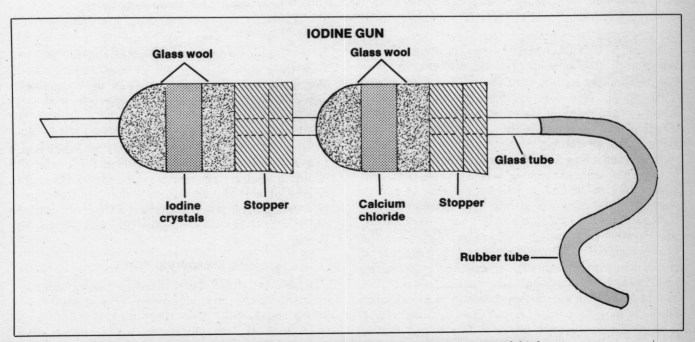

IODINE GUN

Glass wool Glass wool

Iodine crystals   Stopper   Calcium chloride   Stopper   Glass tube

Rubber tube

The iodine fuming method of removing prints, while not popular, is useful in developing latents containing large amounts of fat or oil. To assemble the "gun," you'll need: two gooch tubes, two cork or rubber stoppers to fit the tubes, glass wool, iodine crystals, calcium chloride, a glass tube 4 inches long and a rubber tube 8 inches long. This diagram shows how these materials fit together. The gun can only be used once, since the chemicals oxidize easily.

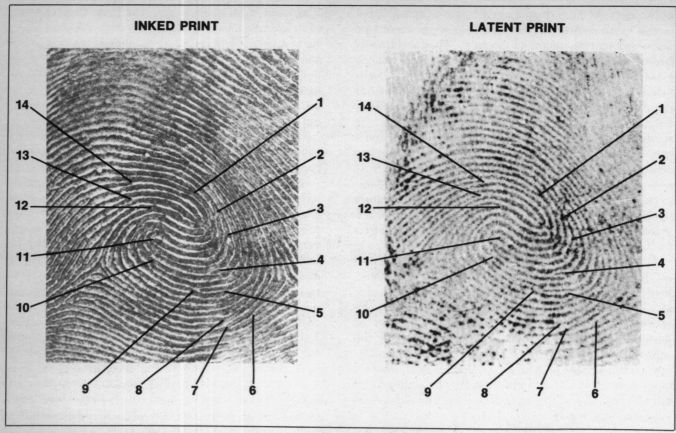

INKED PRINT

LATENT PRINT

A comparison chart prepared by a fingerprint expert for presentation at trial. To be accepted as evidence in a court of law, between eight and 12 points of identification must be identical; this print has 14.

however, is expensive and the results obtained may not justify the expenditure. To use, dissolve two ounces of silver nitrate crystals in one gallon of distilled water. This solution may be painted on the paper or cardboard, or the item may be dipped in the solution. The specimen is then dried and exposed to strong light, preferably sunlight.

When the silver nitrate comes in contact with salt in the latent print, a chemical reaction takes place and silver chloride is formed. Silver chloride is a very unstable substance and strong light breaks it down further. The latent print appears as a dark brown print against a lighter tan background. As long as the item is exposed to light, the print and the background will continue to darken until all contrast between the print and the background disappears. This solution should be kept in a dark brown bottle in a dark, cool place. It may be used over and over as long as the solution is clear—once it becomes dark brown it must be discarded. Don't pour it down a sink, though, because silver chloride will cause corrosion. Avoid getting this solution on skin and clothes. Skin touched

by it will become dark brown but will fade; clothes will turn the same color but are permanently damaged. For some unknown reason, prints developed with silver nitrate are of better quality in winter than in summer.

Above all, care and good judgment should be used in all phases of fingerprint investigation. Whenever a fingerprint examination is conducted for a case, the ultimate goal is the verdict. All potentially crime-related objects should receive latent-print examination because it is possible that even the most unlikely object may be the one that links the guilty party to the crime.

Comparing Prints

I have frequently been asked by law enforcement officials, "How do you compare fingerprints?" The joking response is, "Very carefully." The serious answer, however, lies with the technician who is doing the comparing. He should make sure that ending ridges, forking ridges, islands and enclosures on the two prints being compared are in relatively the same position. Once an entire series of these details appears in the same position in two prints, an examiner can make an identification. Inked prints, the basis for the science of fingerprints, are usually recorded at the arrest or immediately thereafter and should be taken carefully so that easy and accurate determination of the ridges can be made. Ironically, some inked prints I have encountered were of such poor quality that I could identify suspects with better-quality latent prints.

The area needed to identify any unknown latent print with a known inked print is very small, and positive identification can be made from a very small part of the finger. I once made an identification on a latent print that was 7/32 of an inch long by 3/32 of an inch wide at its widest part (it was shaped like an arc). It is not the amount of the latent print that is developed or that can be compared with the inked print available, but the amount or number of ridge characteristics that appear in the same relative position in the two prints being compared that determines whether or not the latent and the inked prints are from the same finger. On the two prints referred to above, there were more than 10 points of identity in common.

Only officers or investigators experienced in fingerprints should be allowed to work on latent prints, unless they are under the supervision of a qualified expert who will consistently monitor their work. They should be experienced in classifying fingerprints and inked comparisons, and in filing and searching for inked prints. Officers and investigators with little or no experience in fingerprints can be trained to protect evidence at crime scenes, develop latent prints (especially powdered) and photograph or lift latent prints. Only experience can aid a law enforcement official in evaluating the worth of a crime-scene latent and making the comparison between a borderline latent and a known inked print from a suspect. Even inexperienced people can compare a good, clear latent print with an inked print and identify a suspect.

What is a good latent print? This question is frequently asked of me on the witness stand. My answer is the same at all times, "One that has been identified." The best-quality latent print is worthless if it is never identified, or if it is identified as that of a fellow officer who was not mindful or careful where he put his hands or did not wear gloves at a crime scene. This last point can be very embarrassing, incidentally, if the question is asked of the examiner on the witness stand.

Only those with considerable experience in all phases of fingerprinting should attempt to qualify and testify as fingerprint experts. They should work under the tutelage of an experienced and qualified expert for some time before appearing in court to present testimony. Of course, they are not precluded from appearing as experts in crime-scene examinations or as takers of inked prints for comparison with latent prints developed at the crime scene itself. Crime-scene investigation for latent prints is based on an officer's experience and apprenticeship with a more experienced person. Evaluation of latent prints collected at the crime scene and determination of identification, however, should be left to the experts in the field.

The value of a fingerprint file of inked prints depends on the expertise of the agencies or officers who contribute to it. Generally, very little training is needed to enable an officer to take good prints; the procedure can be accomplished simply and satisfactorily in a very short time. Poor prints are usually caused by one or more of the following: 1) use of inks other than printer's ink; 2) printer's ink where the oil has separated from the color; 3) failure to clean the equipment or the fingers of foreign substances or to dry the fingers of perspiration just before printing; 4) too much ink on the slab, rendering the inked print useless for comparison and too dark and smudged to be classified correctly; 5) too little ink on the slab, resulting in prints that are too light for comparison and classification; 6) failure to roll the finger completely from nail to nail or to print completely the entire joint to below the first crease in the finger; and 7) allowing the fingers to slip or twist while being rolled.

Because no two people—even identical twins—have the same fingerprints, the science of fingerprinting remains the only infallible means of positive identification known to man. Thus, any law officer who properly applies his knowledge of fingerprinting in his investigative work can only increase his success rate in the prosecution of crime.

George E. Goodreau Jr. was a supervisor in the FBI's Latent Fingerprint Section in which he served for 20 of his 38 years with the bureau. Before he retired, Goodreau conducted thousands of fingerprint examinations and was frequently called upon by federal and state courts throughout the nation to give expert testimony regarding fingerprint findings. In addition, he served the FBI by identifying the victims of civil disasters. Today he is sought by U.S. police departments as a lecturer on the proper techniques of developing and preserving latent prints.

Pros and Cons of Investigative Hypnosis

Gary L. Griffiths

Occasionally, a crime occurs which by its very savagery makes even a multiple homicide case seem rather a commonplace occurrence. The Stanislaus County California Sheriff's Office was confronted with just such a case on the 29th of September, 1978, when their detectives were called to investigate the brutal rape and maiming of a 15-year-old girl. After having kidnapped, raped and forcibly sodomized her, her attacker chopped off both of her forearms with an axe, and stuffed her body into a drainage tunnel, leaving her for dead. Miraculously, the girl survived and was able to flag down a passing motorist, who took her to a hospital. Upon being questioned by detectives, however, the girl could remember only sketchy details of the incident and could not provide more than a partial description of the perpetrator.

Had this incident happened as little as five years earlier, the investigation would probably have ground to a halt. It is the most frustrating feeling in the world to have to write an unsolved case on a serious crime committed by a dangerous perpetrator because the victim or witness is unable to recall enough details of the incident to provide solid leads. Investigators can only watch and wait, with half of their minds hoping for a similar crime with fresh clues to give them a second crack at the perpetrator, while the other half

hopes no other young girl will be mutilated or killed in the same grisly manner.

Fortunately, investigators in this case were afforded a third option, one which is rapidly gaining acceptance nationwide in law enforcement circles: hypnosis. One of the detectives had been trained in its use as an investigative tool and, after preliminary investigation failed to develop any substantive leads, he placed the victim under hypnosis. The detective succeeded in obtaining the name of the perpetrator and other useful information, which led to his location. Also, the girl gave an excellent physical description of the subject, and completed a police artist's sketch which was remarkably accurate. This information was corroborated by other witnesses, which resulted in the perpetrator's conviction and a long prison sentence.

What exactly is this 20-year-old investigative tool called hypnosis? There are many definitions of the term, but virtually all practitioners would agree that hypnosis is an altered state of consciousness, a superconcentration of the subconscious mind, whereby the subject can recall a repressed or forgotten event with greater accuracy and detail than he or she would otherwise. While hypnosis produces an altered, or heightened, state of consciousness, the subject is nev-

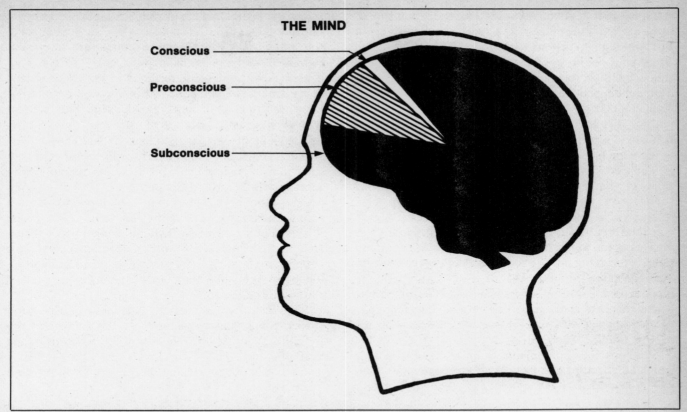

THE MIND

Conscious

Preconscious

Subconscious

Only the smallest fraction of the mind is used to focus the conscious attention. The preconscious mind is the memory center which stores stimuli for later recall at the conscious level. The subconscious is by far the largest part of the mind. It receives repressed stimuli from the censor and also independently records and stores information directly from each of the five senses at all times.

er unconscious or asleep; in fact, the opposite is true. The hypnotized individual is fully aware of himself and his surroundings, but his attention is concentrated exclusively on the matter at hand.

The two most successful methods of inducing hypnosis from within 10- to 15-minutes are permissive and progressive relaxation inductions. During permissive induction the hypnotist asks the subject to close his eyes and relax and take a few deep breaths. The hypnotist then encourages the subject to relax, phrasing his suggestions with the words "if you will" to remind the subject that he, not the hypnotist, is in full control. Progressive relaxation induction is accomplished by instructing the subject to concentrate on making one part of his body—frequently the feet —totally relaxed. The subject is then told to relax another part of his body, then another, until he is completely relaxed. Usually, the hynotist deepens the hypnosis by having the subject visualize a peaceful, pleasant scene, or by counting forward or backward.

Several hundred law enforcement officers from all over the United States have received specialized train-

ing in the induction and use of hypnosis for investigative purposes. These hypno-investigators fully understand the methods of obtaining information through hypnosis, and what types of information may be elicited. While all investigators learn to obtain detailed and accurate information from victims and witnesses, they should also have a basic understanding of hypnotic techniques to be able to determine intelligently whether hypnosis will be of value in any given investigative situation.

Psychodynamics of the Mind

Before investigative hypnosis can be understood, it is essential to understand the basic functioning of the human mind. It is divided into three basic areas, each with a specialized function: the conscious, the preconscious and the subconscious (sometimes called the unconscious). The mind faithfully records every bit of information from every one of the five senses every split second of a person's existence. Its capacity is virtually limitless.

According to the latest psychological theories, the

mind is capable of storing some 10 quadrillion bits of information. This number is so vast it is meaningless, but perhaps a clearer understanding could be achieved if you stopped to think there have been more than 62 billion seconds since the time of Christ. If a human being could live that long—roughly 1981 years —he could store 160,000 bits of information *per second* for that entire time and still have room for more! It is obvious that only the tiniest fraction of the mind is used for focusing the conscious attention.

The Conscious Mind. The conscious mind consists solely of what your attention is focused on at any given time, recording input from whatever sense or combination of senses with which you are perceiving your surroundings. Right now, for example, you, the reader, are seeing the words in this article, and your conscious mind is receiving input from your visual nerve centers. The conscious mind is also analogous to a pair of binoculars focused on a given object. The object on which they are focused will be recorded as memory, but the myriad of other objects outside this rather narrow field of focus will not.

The conscious mind also contains a censor through which all stimuli must pass to enter the preconscious

(memory center). This censor changes or removes entirely those stimuli it perceives as being harmful to the individual's ego. These memories are said to be repressed and are transferred directly to the subconscious without being retained in the preconscious as a memory to be recalled. This is undoubtedly what happened to the mutilated rape victim. The incident was so traumatic that all of the vital details were washed out of her preconscious by the censor. The situation need not even be outwardly traumatic. Persons who witness a bank robbery, for example, may repress details such as the perpetrator's features or a license number because they subconsciously fear a second confrontation with the dangerous robber, even if he is in police custody. It should be emphasized here that these persons are *not* being uncooperative or suppressing evidence for fear of becoming involved. They genuinely don't remember having seen or heard the vital details.

The Preconscious Mind. This area of the mind stores things that were formerly the subject of the individual's conscious attention, and keeps them available for recall with the proper stimulus. It is much larger in area than the conscious mind, and

THE CENSOR

From the Conscious Mind

CENSOR

Safe
Safe
Safe

Repressed

To the Preconscious For Recall

To the Subconscious Mind

The censor in the conscious mind edits out stimuli which are perceived as being harmful to the individual. These stimuli are said to be repressed and go directly to the subconscious, without being retained as memories.

receives only "safe" memories. The preconscious also automatically cross-refers and categorizes information, grouping similar data together. This becomes, however, the primary cause of inaccurate information from eyewitnesses. Thus, when a witness describes a bank robbery, the information recalled and given to the investigator may be contaminated with memories the person may have seen of a movie or TV show about a similar incident.

The Subconscious Mind. The subconscious consists of about seven-eighths of the brain. It independently records and directly stores every stimulus from every one of the five senses *at all times*, not just what the conscious attention is focused on, and no matter what the conscious condition of the individual. Even though intoxicated by liquor or drugs or unconscious due to physical trauma, the subconscious mind continues to function.

In one case, the Los Angeles Police Department was able to solve a homicide by hypnotizing a witness who was too high on drugs and alcohol to remember what took place. Under hypnosis, the witness gave an excellent description of the suspect, and details of an argument which had taken place prior to the shooting. In another unusual case, police arrested two robbers based on details of a conversation that took place between them after they supposedly knocked the victim unconscious. The victim's auditory nerve center continued to function, and he repeated the conversation under hypnosis, even though he never consciously heard it.

The subconscious also receives and stores "unsafe" memories directly from the censor and receives old, unused memories from the preconscious—things one has "forgotten."

How Investigative Hypnosis Aids Recall

At present, there is some controversy about whether hypnosis does, in fact, increase memory and, if so, to what extent. Clinical and experimental studies have shown that hypnotically enhanced memory is, at best, only marginally superior to conscious-level recall. These studies, however, were conducted in carefully defined research settings, where the participants knew that experiments with memory were being undertaken. In fact, in the latest of these studies using videotapes of a traffic accident, the subjects had pre-knowledge that they were expected to remember as many details as possible.

The actual experience of law enforcement agencies that employ hypno-investigators have been far more dramatic, with hypnosis yielding substantially more information in the majority of cases. While hypnosis may only slightly improve the quality of memory in a deliberately remembered occurrence, the real usefulness of investigative hypnosis is in removing the confusion and trauma associated with a criminal incident, or in recovering "routine" memories which were of no significance at the time of the incident.

The Witness' Mental Perceptions. Typically, a witness to a crime of violence or exciting event perceives only a small portion of the entire scene at the conscious level. Thus, the witness records only the main theme of the occurrence. Even if the person has the presence of mind to look for a license number or distinguishing feature, this information may be consciously or unconsciously viewed as threatening, and may become confused or forgotten. Once the witness has been hypnotized, he can be asked to go back to the time of the incident and scan it several times, with the hypno-investigator suggesting each time that the witness remember the details more clearly, vividly and accurately than before.

When sufficient details are brought forward by repetitive scanning, the witness can be requested to review the incident, describing the events just as though he were watching them happen all over again. The witness can then be requested to "stop action" at any given moment and view the scene just as though it were a color picture or slide. This way he can "zoom in" on the details that need to be clarified.

This method works best with general information, such as the description of a perpetrator or a narration of the action; however, when the incident is brought to the conscious level of awareness in this manner, distorting factors from the preconscious may be reintroduced. To eliminate or minimize this distortion in obtaining details where the structure of the answer is known (such as letters and numbers on a license plate or letters on a street sign) the hypno-investigator may utilize a technique called "ideomotor response." This is simply linking a muscular reaction, such as a finger signal, to the subconscious mind. Thus, the index finger may typically be made to twitch for a "yes" answer and the little finger for a "no." The thumb is usually keyed to "I don't want to tell you," a psychological safety valve. These signals come directly from the subconscious mind and bypass all conscious control. This is considered a more accurate method of gaining some types of information than scanning, but may only be used, obviously, when the questions can be answered with a simple yes or no.

Thus if a license plate number is desired, the witness should first be asked, "Did you see a license plate?" If the answer is yes, the witness should then be asked, "Was the first character on the plate a

A witness to an exciting event tends to concentrate only on the "main theme" of the event and may miss vital details.

Under hypnosis a witness can be taken back mentally to the time of the incident, so the scene may be viewed without excitement. The scene can then be "frozen" at any given time, allowing the witness to concentrate on important details.

letter? A number?" If a yes response is received to the letter, then ask, "Was the first letter A? B? C?" etc., until the entire alphabet has been checked; then go for the second character. This is tedious and time consuming, and sometimes more than one response will be received for any given character. If so, both characters should be checked, or the hypno-investigator may be able to determine which is correct by further questioning. Confusion in letters and numbers is not uncommon but may mean, for example, that the witness also observed a parking sticker number and is confusing it with the license plate number.

Although use of this technique for sharpening blurred memories is effective and widely used among hypno-technicians, some experts, notably Harry Arons, forensic hypnotist and Director of the Ethical Hypnosis Training Center in South Orange, New Jersey, are critical of the technique. According to Mr. Arons and his associates, gathering information in this manner could be challenged in a court of law as "forcing a response" or as "unduly suggestive." Nonetheless, in light of accurate information sometimes obtained by this method, a potential court battle is a small reason for not using it as an investigative technique, especially when a particularly heinous crime is involved.

The witness can be hypnotically instructed to "zoom in" and see details that he may have missed before.

The Victim's Mental Perceptions. The victim of a crime of violence is usually much more traumatized than the witness. Frequently, he will not remember anything about the perpetrator, except the muzzle of the gun, which he will faithfully describe as being anywhere from the size of an eight-inch howitzer to the size of a railroad tunnel. For the traumatized victim who can only remember that cavernous muzzle, the hypno-investigator can remove most of the fear

and trauma that blocks perception by having the victim visualize a TV or movie screen where he can watch a filmed documentary about the incident from the safety of his own chair and describe what is happening.

Once the trauma has been removed by this depersonalization, the victim can watch the documentary several times, each time being instructed to remember the details more calmly, clearly and accurately than before. Again, the victim may be requested to "stop action" or "zoom in" on details.

Under hypnosis, the witness can be asked to review and recall details such as license plate numbers.

The interviewee should be asked if he has ever seen the perpetrator before and, if so, under what circumstances. Hypnosis can induce hypermnesia, or greatly increased recall, and the interviewee may have seen the perpetrator at some address, in some vehicle or in association with some other person known to the interviewee.

Problems With Hypnotically Obtained Information. Unfortunately, as every law enforcement officer knows when dealing with an eyewitness, you must take into consideration the fact that people will see and remember things differently. Hypnotically obtained information is often more accurate than conscious-level recall, but the information may still be jumbled. The investigator should always remember that hypnotically obtained information is subject to the same discrepancies as an eyewitness testimony. For this reason, it is vital to attempt to verify all leads developed through hypnosis with supporting physical or testimonial evidence. If, for example, a six-digit license number is obtained, the digits may all be correct, but in the wrong order. This happened to me on one occasion, when the victim under hypnosis described her assailant's vehicle as having a yellow license plate with the numbers 1-4-5-0-7-9 in black. When the case was solved, the perpetrator owned a vehicle bearing old Alabama plates with the numbers 5-4-1-1-0-7-9 in black on a yellow background. For some unknown reason, the victim had transposed the first three numbers, and there was an extra "1" in the actual number. If the number originally obtained is not the right one, the state DMV computer should be utilized to check out all possible combinations of the characters received during the session.

The way a person tries to remember something may also affect recall. In an investigation I was involved with, the victim, under hypnosis, came up with the name "Walton" as having been on the perpetrator's military fatigue uniform. Her mother, who was watching the procedure on closed-circuit TV exclaimed, "That's right! When she got home she said the name was just like that family on TV — The Waltons!" Actually, the name was different, but was very similar to "Walton." The girl, in attempting to remember the name, had apparently associated it with a name with which she was more familiar, and it was this associated name that was evoked under hypnosis.

Another factor to be considered is the close correla-

The victim of a crime of violence is usually so traumatized that he will not remember anything except the cavernous muzzle of the loaded gun.

tion between the meaning of an event and the ability of a witness to recall it. The more emotion involved, the better the recall. For example, a bank teller who witnessed a robbery would be able to remember much more at both the conscious and subconscious levels than she would if she had merely cashed a check that later proved to be stolen. I used hypnosis in one such check-cashing case, and found that the teller was unable to go back to the check in question, but kept focusing her attention on a check she had later cashed. This second check also turned out to be stolen, and she had been disciplined for cashing it, even though she had cleared it with the bank manager. She was so emotional and indignant over this second check that it blocked her perception of the check in question. However, she spontaneously came out of hypnosis and informed me of the problem rather than furnish incorrect or misleading information.

Perhaps the most important consideration for the hypno-investigator is to ensure that no memory artifacts are created as a result of the hypnosis session. A hypnotized person is extremely suggestible, and may actually create a detail of an incident in response to a carelessly worded question. Great care must be taken in the phrasing of suggestions given to the hypnotized interviewee. Obviously, no hypno-investigator should say, "Joe Doakes is the man who raped you, isn't he?" Yet, it would be relatively easy to ask without considering the consequences, "Did you get a good look at the passenger in the car?" Here the suggestion is more subtle, but nevertheless the phrase "the passenger" implies that there was one. Accordingly, it is possible, although unlikely, that in response to this question, the interviewee would fantasize having seen a passenger and provide a detailed description of someone who never existed. Further, in hypnotherapy there is little concern for whether memories elicited under hypnosis are historically accurate, inasmuch as what the subconscious mind believes to be true *is true* — for that person. Accordingly, there is little value in distinguishing fact from fantasy for therapeutic purposes. For this reason, it is essential that investigative hypnosis be performed by a hypno-investigator who will ensure that no leading or suggestive questions are asked. The interviewee should be encouraged to relate his experience in a narrative fashion, with questions being used only to focus the narrative, not to suggest specific details or answers.

Another aspect of eyewitness testimony that is of heightened concern during hypnosis is confabulation —the tendency of a person to fill in the details of an event which he does not clearly recall with fantasy or speculation. This occurs in both hypnotic and normal

Under hypnosis, the trauma can be removed and the victim will be able to see the details as they really were.

interviews, but is of special concern in hypnosis because the person may view these fantasies as realities and be unable to distinguish them from actual memories. Some agencies that routinely utilize mental health professionals for investigative hypnosis have experienced difficulties regarding confabulation and how to deal with it. Unfortunately, most mental health professionals, even though experienced in clinical hypnosis, have very little expertise with this problem.

As a precautionary measure, every word spoken from the time the interviewee enters the hypno-investigator's office until he is released after the post-hypnotic interview should be recorded. It is possible for an unscrupulous hypnotist to convince the witness that the main suspect—who may be a suspect only through the most tenuous of circumstantial evidence—is, in fact, the perpetrator. If this suggesting is deliberately and skillfully done, the witness may emerge from the interview convinced that the suspect is the perpetrator and no amount of cross-examination will shake his testimony, because *he will remember seeing the suspect committing the crime.*

Hypnosis may help the victim remember having seen the perpetrator before and enable him to describe where and under what circumstances.

The only way to safeguard against charges of manipulation is to record every word of each session, including all conversations before and after the actual hypnosis session. Also, this recording will be available for perusal by expert psychiatrists and psychologists for both prosecution and defense, who will be able to testify whether or not anything said during the interview might have inadvertently been suggestive or biased.

If possible, a videotape should be utilized with at least one audiotape for backup, as videotapes are more difficult to tamper with and will be more credible to a jury in this post-Watergate era. All persons present during the session should be fully identified on tape and should appear on camera if video is used. If the equipment distracts the interviewee, a room with a two-way mirror should be utilized; however, all parties to the interview must be made aware that the session is being recorded and must consent to this procedure.

Hypnosis as a Lie Detection Technique

Another constant problem for hypno-investigators is the widespread belief among the public as well as law enforcement officers that hypnosis somehow ensures truthfulness or can be used to detect lies with 100 percent accuracy. Such is definitely *not* the case. A person normally will not practice deliberate deception under hypnosis, but neither will he usually practice it in the waking state. The subconscious mind does not lie, and ideomotor responses are considered to be true subconscious responses; however, the subconscious mind can always be overridden by the conscious mind. Although an experienced hypnotist can usually differentiate between a conscious ideomotor response and a true subconscious response, the differences are highly subjective and usually will differ from subject to subject. Considering the efficiency and reliability of present-day polygraph techniques, hypnosis should never be used as a truth-ensuring or lie-detecting technique by law enforcement hypnotists. Only under the most unusual circumstances should a suspect be hypnotized by a law enforcement hypnotist, and in any such procedure, the results should be regarded with a good deal of skepticism. Actually, hypnosis of suspects is counterproductive in that the suspect can lie without displaying the nervous signs that experienced interrogators look for as indicators of deception. Also, this procedure will firmly fix the details of the fictitious story in the suspect's mind, and it will later be impossible to trip him up with inconsistencies, as there will be none.

Occasionally, of course, the most innocent-appearing witness will make a statement under hypnosis that in some way may be self-incriminating. If this happens, the procedure should be immediately terminated, the person dehypnotized and advised of the nature of the statement made under hypnosis. The interview should be "cleansed" by informing the new suspect that the statement made under hypnosis cannot be used in court against him, and he should be advised of his rights and interviewed utilizing normal interrogation techniques.

The Status of Hypnosis in the Courts and Law Enforcement

Concomitant with the dramatic upsurge in the usage of hypnosis by law enforcement agencies has been the ever-increasing number of court decisions concerning the admissibility of hypnotically influenced testimony. Although American courts have almost unanimously ruled that exculpatory statements made by accused persons under the influence of hypnosis are inadmissible, they have consistently allowed witnesses to testify to facts remembered after participating in investigative hypnosis sessions for the purpose of memory enhancement. Most courts follow the principle of past recollection refreshed, as articulated by the 9th U.S. Circuit Court of Appeals in *Kline v. Ford Motor Company:*

> She was testifying about her present recollection of events that she had witnessed. That her present memory depends on refreshment claimed to have been induced under hypnosis goes to the credibility of her testimony, not to her competence as a witness. Although the device by which recollection was refreshed is unusual, in legal effect her situation is not different from that of a witness who claims that his recollection of an event that he could not remember was revived when he thereafter read a particular document.

The same appellate court later applied this same doctrine to criminal cases (robbery and homicide), stating ". . .we see no reason for a different result in the context of a criminal case."

Attempts to exclude hypnotically influenced testimony have been based on the following five arguments:

1. That all hypnotically influenced testimony is inherently untrustworthy;

2. That the use of hypnosis denies the right of the accused to confrontation and cross-examination under the Sixth Amendment, because once the witness undergoes hypnosis, he is not the same person who witnessed the incident, and therefore cannot be properly cross-examined;

3. That investigative hypnosis techniques have not

gained general acceptance in the scientific community and therefore have not met court-mandated standards for acceptance as scientific evidence;

4. That the use of investigative hypnosis denies due process because it is "unnecessarily suggestive" when used on a witness; and

5. That the use of investigative hypnosis destroys evidence (memories) which might have proven beneficial to the accused.

The first argument was soundly rejected by the 9th U.S. Circuit Court of Appeals on two occasions, and the second and third arguments were presented to the U.S. Supreme Court in the case of *Quaglino v. California*. The court, denied certiorari, upholding Quaglino's conviction, which was based largely on hypnotically obtained testimony. In refusing to rule on this case, the court did not set a precedent, although it indicated that it found the arguments over the constitutional issues to have little merit. Generally, the only time hypnotically influenced testimony has been excluded from court has been in cases where the questioning under hypnosis was clearly suggestive. Investigative hypnosis sessions conducted along the guidelines given in this article should yield results that will be admissible in most jurisdictions. Some courts, however, such as the New Jersey Supreme Court, have mandated additional requirements specifying that the sessions be conducted only by a mental health professional not associated with law enforcement. At present, only the supreme courts of Arizona and Minnesota have ruled that hypnotically obtained information is inadmissible in their jurisdictions.

Today there are probably more than a thousand hypno-investigators employed by law enforcement agencies throughout the United States. Accurate statistics are difficult to come by, since there are several sources for such training; however, the Society for Investigative and Forensic Hypnosis, an international society dedicated to upholding the highest standards of professional, moral and ethical conduct on the part of its members, numbers more than 500 and is growing rapidly. Generally, state and local law enforcement agencies train sworn officers to perform as hypno-investigators, although some use the services of outside mental health professionals. Most federal agencies, however, have adopted a conservative posture about investigative hypnosis, seeing it only as a last resort when all conventional leads have been exhausted, or when the information is vital to the case and clearly can be obtained in no other manner. To date, federal agencies have used mental health professionals to perform the actual inductions, with questions being asked by specially trained investigators who ensure quality and legal sufficiency. Preparations are underway in some of these agencies, however, to switch the entire procedure to hypno-investigators, with mental health professionals acting only as consultants in the event problems should arise. This latter procedure is probably the best one to adopt to ensure that adequate precautions are taken from both legal and mental-health standpoints.

Ever since hypnotism was first used for law-enforcement purposes, various police department and governmental studies have been undertaken to determine the value and accuracy of hypnotically obtained information. One of the most scientific, up-to-date studies was conducted by the FBI from August 1975 through March 1980. In analyzing its findings, the bureau reported that, in spite of the FBI practice of using hypnosis as a last resort on "dead-end" cases, 35 percent of these cases were solved through information given by hypnotized individuals. Moreover, the bureau estimated that only 10 to 12 percent of these cases would have eventually been solved without the use of hypnosis. The FBI also reported that in cases where information obtained under hypnosis could be corroborated or refuted, 87 percent of the hypnotically obtained information proved to be accurate.

If the present trend continues, within the next decade this newest of forensic sciences may well prove to be as vital to law enforcement efforts as the discovery of positive identification by means of fingerprint comparison. It will almost certainly prove to be of as much benefit to law enforcement as the polygraph, which is now considered one of law enforcement's most valuable tools. No law enforcement agency will have to settle for "I don't remember" or "It all happened too fast" as answers to questions in important cases. Hypnotism is already solving "unsolvable" cases and will undoubtedly save more lives by helping to remove dangerous felons from society.

Gary L. Griffiths, a graduate of the Washington School of Professional Hypnosis, is a certified hypnotist and clinical hypno-therapist. He assisted the CID in developing a policy on the use of investigative hypnosis and now instructs classes in it to Army Criminal Investigation students. In addition to the seminars on investigative and forensic hypnosis he gives to civilian law enforcement, criminal justice and mental health professionals, he has written for several professional journals and recently collaborated on a study for the U.S. Air Force Command and Staff College on the uses of hypnosis in the military.

Doing It Right: How to Handle Evidence and Testify in Court

Detective Robert A. Scanlon

Evidence is defined as anything that can be used in a court of law. There are three main categories:

Direct evidence—statements or testimony by persons who were eyewitnesses to a crime;

Real evidence—demonstrative evidence, i.e., a tangible object, such as a weapon, that can be perceived by the jury; and

Indirect evidence—that which tends to prove the fact at issue, for example, the firearm purchase forms showing the ownership of the weapon used by the accused in a crime.

The responding officer first at the scene must realize that making arrests for crimes—without obtaining proper evidence and securing it—is a waste of valuable time. Therefore, once he arrives, his first action should be to safeguard the scene by keeping unauthorized persons away. In this manner, the uniformed officer ensures that any valuable evidence that may be present will not be accidentally destroyed.

When covering crime scenes where a body is present, the officer should ascertain if the person is dead or only badly injured. If the person is still alive, the officer should administer first aid and radio for an ambulance, without disturbing the scene. If the detectives do not arrive before the injured victim is moved to a hospital, the uniformed officer should mark or, if possible, sketch out the position of the body.

He must also be prepared to take a declaration from a badly injured or dying victim and put it in writing. Should the victim die, this declaration could become an important exhibit at trial. If there is a dead body at a crime scene, the distance of the body should be noted in relation to fixed objects at the scene and, most important, notes of all actions and observations should be recorded in essay form, especially if a homicide is involved.

As another aid to the detectives, the officer should get the names and addresses of everyone present at the scene. If there is someone present whom the officer feels may have taken part in the crime, that suspect should be detained until the detectives arrive.

Once the detectives are on the scene and take over the investigation, the uniformed men should fill them in on what has transpired and what actions they have taken. These same uniformed men should then return to their headquarters and file formal reports while the details are still fresh in their minds.

Most criminal cases are not tried for about a year from the time of the crime. Each case has to travel the same route. Once the crime has been committed, an

This German Walther P-38 in 9mm caliber was found in an attache case on the front seat of a suspect's vehicle. In certain circumstances, in order to secure evidence an officer must show probable cause to search the vehicle before any weapon can be seized and the suspect arrested.

Dime bags of heroin—85 of them—and more than a pound of marijuana seized during a narcotics raid. Each item of evidence must be initialed by the arresting officers, so they can be positively identified by them at time of trial.

investigation follows and, if all goes well, the criminal is identified and apprehended. Then he is booked, arraigned and bail is set. Within a week, a preliminary hearing is held by a local magistrate and the case is forwarded to the county prosecutor's office to be prepared for presentation to a grand jury. Within six to eight weeks, the case is presented to the grand jury and if they feel the evidence is conclusive, they will vote a true bill and an indictment is handed down. The case is then added to the bottom of a probably already overcrowded trial calendar. A well-organized and detailed report will be extremely important at trial time, especially considering that between the commission of this crime and the trial date, an officer may be called to assist at a dozen other different crime scenes.

For the detective whose role in handling and completing a criminal investigation is more complicated than that of the uniformed officer, taking notes, writing reports and eventually testifying should be utmost in his mind at all times. All evidence and deductions are to be noted and every lead should be investigated. Nothing should be taken for granted. Everything a detective observes should be recorded—even if it doesn't seem important at the time—then filed.

Before moving a body or seizing and securing any evidence, the detective should take photographs of the undisturbed crime scene. In some cases, specialists from Bureau of Criminal Identification (BCI) units or evidence collection units are called in to do this. Good, clear photographs are especially important because:

1. They may reveal significant evidence that was overlooked by detectives at the scene;

2. They will give an accurate picture of the crime scene as it was before anything was moved; and

3. Most important, they will help refresh the investigators' memories before and during the trial, thus aiding in recalling a true clear mental image of the crime scene.

Photos can be of major importance in acquainting the judge and jury with the original scene and details. They will also give them a better understanding of how the testimony, evidence and exhibits presented relate to or with the accused, either through his use, association or possession.

Basically, two types of real evidence should be looked for and secured at crime scenes:

Immovable—such as footprints, fingerprints, tire marks and markings on objects too large to move. This type of evidence is preserved by photographing, sketching, or lifting and casting.

Movable—such as firearms, stains, debris, liquid, documents, etc., which can be seized and preserved by the case detective for comparison and analysis at the crime lab and eventually used in court.

All evidence should be taken in adequate amounts to allow the necessary tests to be conducted. Each piece of evidence should be marked properly and tagged for identification, wrapped to ensure safety from damage and preserved, if necessary, e.g., blood, and transported properly and carefully. Any material or evidence sent to a crime lab for comparison testing with evidence obtained at a crime scene should be marked clearly and separately.

At the time of the trial, the manner in which the detective gathered and marked evidence will demonstrate his investigative proficiency or carelessness. All evidence that is seized should be immediately secured, even though some evidence may later prove to be of no value and can be eliminated. The continuity of the possession of the evidence from the crime scene to headquarters, to the lab and to the prosecutor's office should be unbroken. Each person who handles the evidence should sign a receipt. One word of caution: make sure as few persons as possible handle the evidence.

If the detective conducts a proper investigation, handles the evidence in accordance with established procedures and makes the arrest without violating the defendant's rights, he has a potentially solid case. The final step, however, is presenting the case in court. If your report and notes are in order and the presentation goes smoothly, it is likely a conviction will result. If the defendant does get off, which may happen, you will at least have the satisfaction of knowing it wasn't because you conducted a poor investigation.

Giving Expert Testimony

When called upon to testify in a court of law, every police officer is duty-bound, as is every citizen, to state the pertinent facts truthfully and properly as he knows them. While court testimony is the potential duty of every American, for police officers intimately involved in the upholding of justice, the task is vitally important. When a detective or patrolman takes the stand before a judge and jury, his testimony becomes the final and most severe test of his competence. Furthermore, the outcome of the trial is the measure by which an officer's pretrial investigation will be judged by his superiors and the public.

At a crime scene, all the investigating officer's decisions and methods of procedure should be influenced by his ultimate goal—the presentation of evidence before a jury. Collection and preservation of evidence—including finding and questioning witnesses, search and ultimate arrest of a suspect, painstaking interrogation of that suspect, preparation of exhibits and detailed reports of his procedures during the investigation and, finally, the establishment of evidence continuity—culminate at the trial.

The value of these pretrial man-hours and accumulated bits of evidence hinge on the witness-stand testimony of the officer and on the impression his demeanor leaves with the jury. Fair or not, jurors are not only interested in what the testifying officer says, but how he says it—his attitude and his manner of presentation. If, for example, the jury gets the impression that the officer is biased against the defen-

The importance of photographs in the collection of evidence cannot be overstressed. The interior of a robbery suspect's vehicle is shown as it was when police officers stopped it. When the photo is displayed in court, the judge and jury will clearly see that the evidence was in plain view. Note the gloves on the seat and the knife handle protruding from the paper bag on the floor.

dant, his testimony could be weakened and, even worse, could sway the jury's verdict and unjustly affect the fate of the defendant. In addition, professional, responsible testimony precludes giving guess-answers, or concealing or distorting the facts.

When an officer is sworn in to testify, he is before the critical eye of the court and must meet the challenge of the defense lawyer's cross-examination. Regardless of how proficiently and professionally his investigation was carried out, a poor presentation by the investigating officer could render his prepared statements and evidence useless. Therefore, his appearance, his conduct and his self-control on the stand plus the way in which he relates his testimony are significant.

Personal Appearance. First impressions *are* registered by jurors. An officer's clothes should be neat and clean, whether he is wearing a uniform or civilian

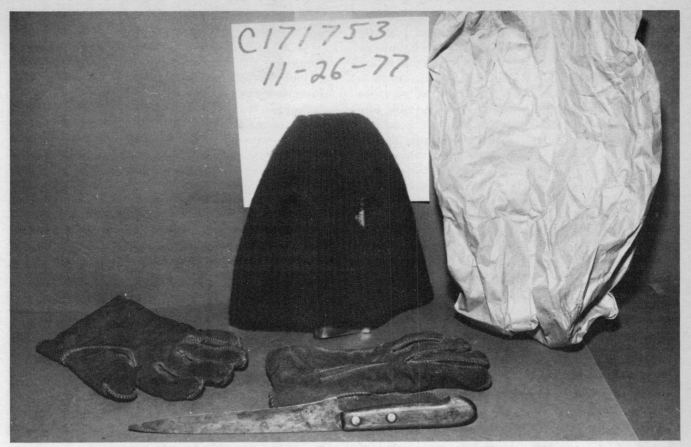

The same articles are laid out for possible identification by the victim of the robbery. All items seized as evidence in violent crimes should be photographed as shown to prevent the loss of evidence.

attire. He should stand erect while being sworn in and, when the clerk asks for his name, rank and precinct or department, the response should come in a loud, clear, confident voice. The officer, too, should sit straight in the chair and hold his head up.

Preparedness. A controlled, self-assured manner can be gained with some pretrial preparation. The officer about to testify should carefully refresh his recollection of the facts before entering the courtroom by reviewing all notes and reports relevant to the case. Once sure of the facts, the officer should put all related papers away. Any notes used while testifying must be shown to the defense attorney upon his request and may trigger an unexpected line of questioning.

Procedures During Testimony. During testimony, the officer should speak loudly and clearly, so the prosecuting and defending attorneys, the judge and the jury can hear. A bad impression is created when an officer mumbles or his voice is inaudible, prompting the judge to ask him to speak up. When answering questions, the testifying officer should not be over-

Two electric typewriters where they were hidden by a perpetrator after a burglary. Often a burglar will attempt to hide stolen property near the scene of the crime so he can return later with a vehicle to retrieve it. Again, always photograph the evidence where found.

anxious to respond; answers should be thought out, then spoken. The witness should wait until the attorney has asked his complete question before attempting to answer. Information should not be volunteered and, if at all possible, answers should be a straightforward "yes, sir" or "no, sir." If he has cause to speak to the judge, the officer should address him as "Your Honor." If the officer doesn't know the answer to a particular question, he should simply state, "I don't know." Answers must always be truthful and impartial and, of course, the facts should never be slanted, distorted or twisted in an attempt to obtain a certain decision.

If a question is misleading, vague or confusing or if the officer believes that a question was asked deliberately to anger or badger him, he should politely ask to have the question repeated or rephrased; he should not lose his temper. Handling a difficult question in this manner not only makes the officer appear unflappable, it gives him extra time to collect his thoughts. Often the prosecuting attorney will raise a formal objection in response to suggestive questioning by the defense attorney. In such instances, the testifying officer should have enough self-control not to answer until after the judge has ruled on the objection.

Similar difficulties arise when an officer encounters a defense attorney who insists on yes or no answers to complicated questions. In cases like this, the officer should state politely to the judge that he cannot adequately answer the question put to him with a simple "yes" or "no." If the judge rules that the witness answer as directed by the attorney, then he is required to do so, but in most cases the judge will allow a proper and complete answer.

Police officers sometimes make the serious error of trying to cover up or ignore an honest mistake in their testimony. An honest mistake is not perjury and, if corrected promptly, you are likely to influence the jury favorably; however, if you wait and the defense attorney brings it out, your credibility could suffer.

If an officer is asked his opinion, he should be especially deliberate and cautious with his reply. Sometimes solicitation of a witness' opinion is inadmissible if the prosecutor properly objects. Again, the officer has to use restraint and refrain from answering until the prosecutor has had time to object. Keep in mind, however, that a witness cannot object to questions. If such a question is not countered with an objection or if the officer is directed by the judge to answer, he must do so.

A police officer testifying should be on guard for two pitfalls that could discredit him and nullify his testimony. The first is arguing with the defense attorney—no officer should permit himself to be drawn into a verbal brawl no matter how much he is provoked into one. The defense attorney has the right to question the witness and the witness is obliged to answer. The second pitfall is prejudice. Above all, the officer as witness must remain impartial. If he is asked a question regarding the defendant, his answer should be given honestly, without hesitation. When the jury realizes that the police officer who made the arrest and conducted the subsequent investigation is not anxious to conceal anything, his testimony will be strengthened.

Giving impartial, professional testimony and projecting the attitude of a conscientious public servant require discipline and self-control and are duties not easily accomplished. Fortunately, for the officer determined to be an exemplary courtroom witness, the rewards are many. He will gain the immediate confidence of the judge and jury, the approval of his superiors, the respect of the American people and the knowledge that there's no truer testimony than the sworn statements made by a responsible law enforcement officer.

Good Report Writing: Mark of the Police Professional

Asst. Professor Leslie Bramble

In all criminal justice agencies, written reports are indispensable; indeed, almost every official action taken by a police officer must be reported in writing. These communications help those in positions of command keep track of routine police operations, learn about new developments within their area of command and evaluate whether new law enforcement programs are effective. In the most general sense, written reports enable superior officers to base their important everyday decisions on the advice of their specialists— the street cops.

The common element in all police reports which sets them apart as a distinct species of writing is their element of responsibility. On a daily basis, all public safety officers communicate with each other, with criminal justice agencies and with the public. To a significant extent, the contents of their written reports can determine whether suspects are arrested and, if arrested, whether they are convicted and sentenced.

Deficient report writing can do more than damage a police officer's career; it can seriously detract from the department's professional image. Any report that contains misspellings or grammatical errors is hardly impressive; a good report, however, may positively influence a police officer's career to the extent that promotion may result.

Good reports also contribute to good public relations. A detailed, informative and responsible report shown either to a trial jury as evidence or a representative of the media in reference to a major investigation, can reflect the honesty and competence of the officer and his department.

Further, police field reports, when published in newspapers, police publications or news releases, often improve police relations within the community. Reports help isolate specific crime threats and through them public safety officers can suggest specific crime countermeasures to community organizations so they can assist the police. For example, through his report a public safety officer can alert members of a P.T.A. group about attempted sexual attacks in the community or warn senior citizens that the elderly are becoming the targets of muggers. Finally, he can outline the preventive measures being taken by police to counter these attacks and suggest how citizens can avoid becoming victims. Thus, a well-written and comprehensive report can do much to gain the public's respect, cooperation and support.

Of course, written reports specifically serve the law enforcement community. Detectives must have

The handling of a fatal accident should never be routine. Detailed notes should be taken and a clear, informative and complete report made. This apparent accident may actually be a homicide; only careful gathering and securing of evidence as well as proper documentation will assure a solid case.

a complete account of the initial investigation conducted by patrol officers first on the scene, if they are to carry out their investigations successfully. Without a report containing all pertinent facts and leads relevant to the crime, a detective's work would be seriously handicapped.

Prosecutors, too, know that even minor offenses demand a thorough investigation. The prosecutor's initial awareness of a particular case may stem from the line officer's report. From it the prosecutor will develop and evaluate his overall strategy for the trial and determine the proper witnesses to

subpoena. Judging by how well-executed the report is, the prosecutor may also use the responding officer's report to measure the officer's potential effectiveness on the witness stand. This impression may then influence the state's position in any subsequent plea bargaining. The report must provide all necessary information in easily understandable language; otherwise, the prosecutor can neither prosecute the case successfully nor properly protect the officer testifying on the witness stand.

Events occurring months, sometimes even years earlier, must be

related in detailed testimony under oath. During testimony, the officer relies on memory, notes and his formal report for his information. Memory, of course, is frequently dulled, notes are too often fragmentary, disorganized and difficult to interpret under the stress of courtroom testimony. Consequently, a well-organized, formal report that permits the officer to relate the facts quickly and easily is his most reliable source of accurate information.

The Qualities of a Good Report

All the principles of good writing—accuracy, clarity, completeness and conciseness plus a discussion of the basic who, what, where, when, why and how—apply to good report writing. Some of the questions an officer should ask himself before starting his report are: Who will read the report? How much will the readers need to know? And, of course, do I have all the necessary information to write a proper report and answer all relevant questions?

In addition, a good report should be self-sufficient, i.e., anyone who reads it should be able to comprehend what has taken place without having to guess or consult the officer's files for any missing pieces. To ensure that your report is self-sufficient, read it over several times to make sure no facts have been omitted and no information is vague, misleading or subject to more than one interpretation.

An officer who investigates a community problem or crime and follows it up with a report often starts his work with preconceived expectations of the outcome. Although this practice should be avoided, when it is based on experience and knowledge, anticipating results is understandable. When it is based on mere prejudice or, even worse, on self-interest, the problem is much more serious. As difficult as it may sometimes be, you should conduct every investigation impartially so you will not fail to uncover evidence that may contradict conclusions you expected or hoped to reach.

Writing the Report

Most reports you will write have at least three, sometimes four, main parts: introduction, body, conclusions and recommendations.

The introduction should state the subject and purpose of the report. For a brief informal report, a

Often when a patrol-car officer on duty alone receives an emergency call, he is unable at the time to write down such details as the time and destination of the call. To facilitate incorporating these essentials into his report, the officer can usually rely on the dispatcher, who fills out a card on each call relayed to patrol units.

REPORT OF INVESTIGATION

POLICE DEPARTMENT Glen Dale

ALL SPACES TO BE FILLED IN:

Number of Defendants

ADULTS — JUVENILES

Defendant #1	Last Name	First	Initial	Alias	Address	Home Phone
	Doe	John	E	Jack	17-81 Summit Ave Paterson, N.J.	None

DOB	Sex	Height	Weight	Social Security #	REIN ☒	Occupation	Prints ☒
4-16-38	M	5'10"	160	134-66-4185	NCIC ☐	Unemployed	Photo ☐

Place of Employment | Business Phone | Municipal Judge

Crime	Statue	Bail	Bondsman	Phone
B+E	2C:18-2	500.	EMPIRE BONDING CO.	742-0611
Poss Gun	2C:39-5		Address of Bondsman 14 Eagle St. Paterson NJ	
			Attorney Walter Moore	Phone 742-0091
			Address of Attorney 196 Main St Paterson NJ	

Defendant #2	Last Name	First	Initial	Alias	Address	Home Phone
	Smith	William	—	None	416 River Rd. Newark	None

DOB	Sex	Height	Weight	Social Security #	REIN ☒	Occupation	Prints ☒
7-13-38	M	6'2"	195	164-22-4180	NCIC ☐	Unemployed	Photo ☐

Place of Employment | Business Phone | Municipal Judge

Crime	Statue	Bail	Bondsman	Phone
B+E	2C:18-2	5000.	EMPIRE Bonding Co	742-0611
Poss Gun	2C:39-5		Address of Bondsman 14 Eagle St. Paterson NJ.	
			Attorney	Phone
			Address of Attorney	

Victim	Last Name	First	Initial	Address	Home Phone
	James	Lopo		86 Rock Rd, Glen Rock N-J	673-8184

DOB	Occupation	Place of Employment	Business Phone
4-18-76	Counter Man	Garden St. Ice Cream Co	671-0800

Individual Reporting Crime James Lopo | Home Phone

Date | Time | Reported to Whom | Location of Crime

Details of Crime	Date	Time	Latent Prints	Collected by
B+E	87-81	9:30P	Yes	Det. Edwards

Investigating Officer	Photographs	By Whom	Collected by
Ptl. Woods	Yes		Det. Edwards

Statement: Defendant # 1	Taken by	Arresting Officer(s) Defendant #1
Written ☒ Oral ☐ None ☐	Det King	Ptl. Woods

Statement: Defendant #2	Taken by	Arresting Officer(s) Defendant #2
Written ☐ Oral ☒ None ☐	Ptl. Woods	Ptl. Woods

Brief synopsis — including circumstances of arrest

Counter man heard noise in rear of store, he checked + saw two men run out back door which had been locked. He called the police + Ptl. Wood arrested two defts. one block away running toward hiway

USE BLANK PAPER FOR ADDITIONAL INFORMATION AS REQUIRED.

A police officer often has to appear in court to testify about an incident two or three years after it has occurred. This hand-written report can barely be read, even though it was only completed a short time ago. Imagine the condition of this same report three years from now after it has been handled numerous times.

REPORT OF INVESTIGATION

POLICE DEPARTMENT GLEN DALE

Number of Defendants
ADULTS — JUVENILES

ALL SPACES TO BE FILLED IN:

Defendant #1	Last Name	First	Initial	Alias	Address	Home Phone
	DOE	JOHN	E	JACK	17-81 SUMMIT AVENUE PATERSON, N.J.	NONE

DOB	Sex	Height	Weight	Social Security #	REIN ☒	Occupation	Prints ☒
4/16/28	M	5'10"	160	143-66-4789	NCIC ☐	UNEMPLOYED	Photo ☐

Place of Employment

Business Phone | Municipal Judge W. HENRY ESQ.

Crime	Statue	Bail	Bondsman	Phone
BURGLARY	2C:18-2	$5,000.	EMPIRE BONDING COMPANY	742-0611
Crime POSS.WEAPON	Statute 2C:39-5	Bail	Address of Bondsman 14 EAGLE STREET, PATERSON, N.J.	
Crime	Statute	Bail	Attorney WALTER MOORE Esq.	Phone 742-0081
Crime	Statute	Bail	Address of Attorney 196 Main Street, PATERSON, N.J.	

Defendant #2	Last Name	First	Initial	Alias	Address	Home Phone
	SMITH	WILLIAM		NONE	486 RIVER ROAD, NEWARK, NJ	NONE

DOB	Sex	Height	Weight	Social Security #	REIN ☒	Occupation	Prints ☒
2-13-38	M	6'2"	195	164-22-4860	NCIC ☐		Photo ☐

Place of Employment

Business Phone | Municipal Judge W. HENRY ESQ.

Crime	Statue	Bail	Bondsman	Phone
BURGLARY	2C:18-2	$5,000.	EMPIRE BONDING COMPANY	742-0611
Crime POSS.WEAPON	Statute 2C:39-5	Bail	Address of Bondsman 14 EAGLE STREET, PATERSON, N.J.	
Crime	Statute	Bail	Attorney ROBERT WEGNER Esq.	Phone 742-0081
Crime	Statute	Bail	Address of Attorney 196 MAIN STREET, PATERSON, N.J.	

Victim	Last Name	First	Initial	Address	Home Phone
	LOPO	JAMES		16-32 ROCK ROAD, GLEN ROCK, N.J.	623-8184

DOB	Occupation	Place of Employment	Business Phone
4-18-26	COUNTER MAN	GARDEN STATE ICE CREAM CO.	621-0800

Individual Reporting Crime: JAMES LOPO

Address: FOREST AVENUE, GLEN DALE, N.J. Home Phone

Date	Time	Reported to Whom	Location of Crime
8-7-81	9:30PM	GLEN DALE POLICE HQ.	SEE ABOVE

Details of Crime:	Date	Time	Latent Prints	Collected by DET. J. EDWARDS
BURGLARY	8-7-81	9:30PM	Yes	

Investigating Officer PTL. D. WOODS	Photographs YES	By Whom DET. J. EDWARDS

Statement: Defendant # 1 Written ☒ Oral ☐ None ☐	Taken by DET. J. KING	Arresting Officer(s) Defendant #1 PTL. WOODS
Statement: Defendant # 2 Written ☐ Oral ☒ None ☐	Taken by PTL. D. WOODS	Arresting Officer(s) Defendant #2 PTL. WOODS

Brief synopsis – including circumstances of arrest

COUNTER MAN HEARD NOISE IN REAR OF STORE, HE CHECKED AND FOUND TWO MALES

RUN OUT THE BACK DOOR, WHICH HAD BEEN LOCKED EARLIER. HE CALLED THE POLICE

AND PTL. WOODS APPREHENDED THE TWO DEFTS. A BLOCK AWAY.

USE BLANK PAPER FOR ADDITIONAL INFORMATION AS REQUIRED.

The officer who appears in court to testify with this report will certainly give the jurors a favorable impression of his professional competence.

subject line may sometimes be an adequate introduction. Sometimes it is helpful to the reader to include in the introduction important background information or to mention briefly any conclusions you have drawn.

The body of the report should present a clearly organized account of the report's subject, for example, the results of a test or the status of an investigation. The amount of detail to include in the body depends on the complexity of the subject and the reader's familiarity with it.

In the conclusion of the report, you should summarize your findings and comment on their significance. Finally, make recommendations for a course of action that will remedy the problems discussed in the body of the report.

The following steps are suggestions on how to approach writing your report and may be modified as the circumstances dictate:

1. Analyze and plan your assignment as a whole, so you have in mind a picture of the kind of report you must produce and what you must do to produce it.

2. Form a general, tentative plan for presenting your material, including a preliminary outline of the report and what elements to include.

3. Gather the facts of the case and interpret their significance.

4. Revise your tentative plan so your outline reflects your final ideas about organization.

5. Write a first draft of the report, with your conclusions and recommendations.

6. Revise and rewrite as necessary, typing everything neatly

7. Reread the report carefully to be sure it contains no errors.

Word Processing in Report Writing. The paperwork explosion

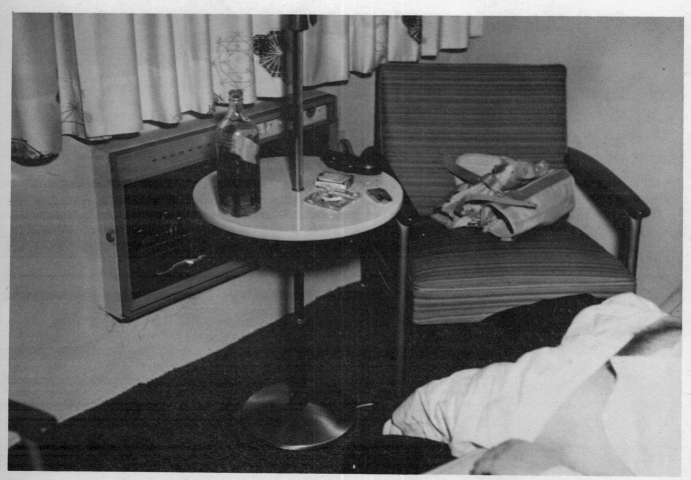

The uniformed officer first at a crime scene must include in his report every detail he observes. These would include in this case: the position of the body on the bed; the Colt Detective Special and the bottle of Johnnie Walker scotch on the lamp table; a surgical brace on the corner chair; and the victim's trousers and underwear pulled halfway down. Because the killer may not be brought to trial for over a year, the need for a complete and well-written report is evident.

has affected organizations of every size and type, including police agencies. Departments are often inundated with paperwork and, unfortunately, report writing is a major contributor to the problem. But keeping on top of the necessary, though time-consuming, task of writing formal communications is important for reasons other than preventing a paperwork backlog. First, the primary objective of policing is actively to fight crime and uphold the law, not to sit typing reports. Second, most states now have speedy trial programs in effect to assure the swift administration of justice; consequently, officers must have their reports completed and ready for the prosecuting attorneys within about 48 hours after the arrest of a suspect.

Among the new technologies many government and law enforcement agencies are using to meet the flood of paperwork is word processing, a modern method for producing reports and other written communications rapidly, accurately and inexpensively. The automated business equipment used in word processing consists basically of automatic typewriters and dictating machines.

Overall, word processing equipment is useful in repetitive communications, such as form letters; for combined repetitive and variable typing with standard paragraphs stored in a memory bank for certain kinds of memos, etc.; for transcription typing, where the operator enters data from the transcriber into the automatic typewriter; and for test preparation, editing and review.

While the use of word processing has grown considerably in law enforcement agencies throughout the country, many departments now using word processing technology have not yet realized the system's full potential because of the special difficulties in adapting law enforcements' many and ever-changing needs to the equipments' characteristics. Still, the practical application of word processing has aided law enforcement enormously, not only because it speeds the preparation of reports, but because it has helped free officers from clerical responsibilities and given them more time for their policing duties.

Leslie Bramble is an assistant professor of criminal justice at County College of Morrison in Dover, New Jersey. He holds degrees in education, sociology, public safety and administration and is currently studying for his Ph.D. in criminal justice at Fordham University. He was previously a staff investigator of the Bergen County prosecutor's office.

Weapons and Equipment

Off-Duty and Special Assignment Weapons

The law enforcement officer has little trouble when it comes to choosing an on-duty handgun. His department usually issues a regulation weapon or, in a few instances, gives him a choice between two already-designated weapons. Unfortunately, these firearms are not always the best available to meet the needs of the street officer. When equipment is needed, a list of minimal requirements is drawn up by the department and sent to various manufacturers who, in turn, submit bids for the various items. All things considered, most often the manufacturer who turns in the lowest bid gets the contract. This type of purchasing system is sufficient when the product is a typewriter, for example, because if the typewriter malfunctions, no one gets hurt. But if an officer's weapon fails to function, is defective or operates improperly, the officer could be seriously injured or even killed.

In contrast, the choice of an off-duty or undercover weapon is left to the discretion of the individual officer. He should therefore take great care and consider many factors before reaching a decision: the purpose for carrying the weapon and the type of environment (urban, suburban, rural), which will determine the size of the weapon, its caliber and barrel length; and the climate, which determines the type of finish on the gun

(blue, nickel, stainless steel, etc.) and, more important, influences the kind of clothing the officer will wear. The weight, thickness and amount of clothing worn is directly related to his ability to conceal his weapon; therefore, clothing must be taken into account when determining the frame size suitable for the weapon. The size of the frame can be influenced by the height, weight and build of the officer. Naturally, a large-frame officer could conceal a larger weapon better than a small-frame officer, but all gun-carrying officers should guard against selecting a weapon that might interfere with their usual activity and reveal that they are armed. In addition, two other factors must be considered when purchasing an off-duty weapon: the calibers authorized by the department; and the calibers recommended as the best manstoppers.

Because choosing an off-duty weapon is so important, the final selection should not be made without devoting considerable time and thought. Police officers know that a shoot-out could happen suddenly and unexpectedly, and they must keep in mind that bringing their weapons into play must be accomplished in the least amount of time with the most accuracy. They should practice drawing their weapons over and over until the motion is executed with ease and speed. Also,

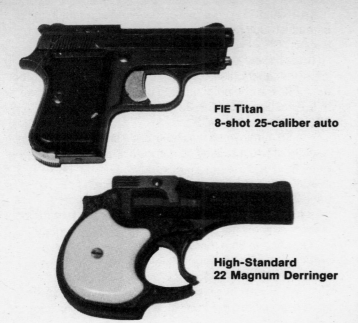

**FIE Titan
8-shot 25-caliber auto**

**High-Standard
22 Magnum Derringer**

One of the most underrated yet widely used calibers is the 38 Special. A large percentage of all the police in this country carry duty weapons of this caliber, but few officers realize the work and research that has gone into beefing up the cartridge. Until about 1974 the 158-grain 38 Special cartridge had a measured velocity of only about 870 feet per second (fps), and the slugs were solid lead or copper-jacketed solid steel. Now, manufacturers such as Smith & Wesson, Remington and Super-Vel offer the 38 Special caliber in a jacketed hollow-point cartridge that moves out of a four-inch barrel at almost 1300 fps. The Glaser Safety Slug Company manufactures a 38 Special cartridge that moves at almost 1600 fps. The velocity of the Safety Slug surpasses all but one of the current 357 Magnum slugs. That one is also produced by Glaser Safety Slug and moves out at just over 1615 fps. That's moving!

Colt Detective Special

if at all possible, officers should carry their off-duty or hideout weapons in the same positions on their persons so they become accustomed to the weight of the gun and learn to move naturally.

Unless an officer is working on special assignment or under dangerous circumstances in which concealment of a small-frame weapon, such as a 25-caliber semi-automatic or a two-shot 22-caliber Magnum derringer, is called for, he should carry the best manstopper available he can handle.

Semiautomatic pistols in 380, 9mm and 45 calibers, used in conjunction with the proper ammunition, provide adequate stopping power; however, revolvers in 38 Special, 357 and 41 and 44 Magnum calibers used with the right cartridges are also more than adequate as manstoppers.

Revolvers are manufactured in several different designs, such as the small, lightweight, magnesium-frame hammerless S&W Centennial and the S&W Airweight Bodyguard. Excellent for undercover officers, both these weapons weigh only 14½ ounces and are available in 38 Special caliber. When drawn from beneath clothing, the hammer spur cannot snag because it is covered by a shroud. The two most widely used of the conventional steel-frame, snub-nosed revolvers are the five-shot, 19-ounce S&W Chief's Special, and the six-shot, 12½-ounce Colt Detective Special.

Smith & Wesson makes the only 9mm revolver that doesn't have to be loaded with half-moon clips. A specially designed cylinder enables the Model 547 to be loaded with 9mm ammo in the same manner as any other revolver. This six-shot weapon is built on the combat-tested K frame and comes with a heavy barrel in lengths of three or four inches.

For officers who feel the need for an off-duty gun that

**Browning DBA
in 45 caliber**

**S & W Model 547
6-shot double action**

carries a slightly more potent punch than a 38 caliber, a good choice is the 357 Magnum. Leading in this category is the S&W Model 19 Combat Magnum. This weapon is available with a 2½- 4- or 6-inch barrel, and weighs between 31 and 35 ounces. Another popular selection is the Colt Python in 357 Magnum, available with a 2½-, 4-, 6- or 8-inch barrel, but it is slightly heavier in weight—between 33 and 43 ounces. The Python has a marginally larger frame and is about twice as expensive; however, it is truly a beautiful weapon. Also in this class of larger frame weapons is the Dan Wesson Model 14-2, which has four interchangeable barrels on a 357 Magnum frame. This versatile design is an economical purchase because the officer would have, in effect, four weapons in one.

Recently, the Sturm Ruger Company has gained a foothold in the law enforcement market by producing the Security Six and Police Six—both strong, well-made weapons at competitive prices. These handguns have lured such large accounts as the New Jersey State Police, Pennsylvania State Police, Boston P.D., New Orleans P.D., Los Angeles County Sheriff's Office and the U.S. Armed Forces, which have replaced their aging blue-finish Colt revolvers with stainless steel, Ruger Security Six Revolvers in 357 Magnum caliber.

Undercover Guns. When concealment is of primary importance for officers assigned to work undercover, for example, the choice of backup weapons narrows down to five calibers: 25 ACP, 22 Magnum, 22 Long Rifle, 38 Special and 380 ACP.

The 25 auto, which fires a 50-grain slug with a muzzle velocity of 810 fps, is by no means a manstopper, but when fired at close range with accuracy it can be deadly. When faced with a situation where he has to bring his weapon into play, an undercover officer doesn't necessarily have to kill his adversary if wounding him would allow the officer time to escape immediate danger. At one time there were plenty of 25 autos around but, with the import ban on small weapons, Browning, Beretta, Colt and Walther 25s are hard to come by. If you have a chance to pick up a used one in good shape, grab it—it will give you years of excellent performance.

Another of the reliable, sought-after backup weapons is High-Standard's two-shot derringer in 22 Magnum caliber. The cartridge comes in a jacketed hollow point and moves out at over 1200 fps. A lot of people don't realize the tissue damage it can cause; those who do are the ones who carry it.

Sterling Arms produces small-frame automatics in both 25 and 22 L.R. calibers. Both these weapons weigh a pound and make perfect pocket guns. Like the 22 Magnum, the 22 L.R. is underrated, but stop and think about a small, lightweight, hollow-nose slug moving about 1110 fps, and you can imagine the extensive injury it could cause.

The A.M.T. Company has marketed a new weapon called the Back-Up. This is a good choice for both undercover and uniformed officers who wish to carry a

**S & W Model 39
9-shot double-action 9mm**

**S & W Model 59
15-shot double-action 9mm**

American Arms TP-70
25-caliber auto

Walther Model 9
7-shot 25-caliber auto

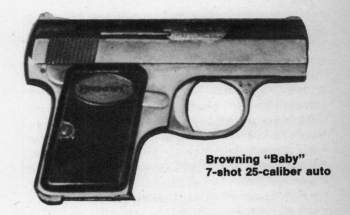

Browning "Baby"
7-shot 25-caliber auto

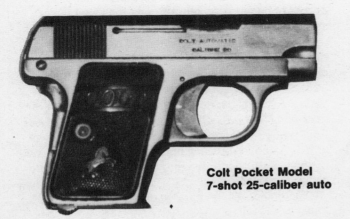

Colt Pocket Model
7-shot 25-caliber auto

Colt Junior Auto
22 shot, 25 caliber

backup gun on duty that delivers some punch and is also small enough to double as an off-duty gun. In these days of high inflation, the gun is a godsend. Produced in 380 caliber (9mm Kutz), this cartridge, when used with a hollow-point slug, moves out at a healthy 984 fps. While the Back-Up in 380 caliber is not a super-powerful manstopper, it does the job.

Of the new stainless-steel frame models on the market, two are dependable: the C.O.P. and the TP-70, both by American Arms (M & N Dist.). The C.O.P., a four-barreled 357 Magnum, is used primarily for personal protection. The gun is reliable and safe to operate and, although it weighs a light 28 ounces, it gives quite a jolt when fired. This weapon is not for constant use, but when an undercover officer's life is on the line, it will provide the manstopping power he'll need. The TP-70 is a double-action, 25-caliber automatic and a perfect hide-out gun. In addition to the usual advantages of small-frame hide-out guns, it is made from stainless steel. This feature is a plus for the undercover officer who is forced to carry his gun against his skin, because quality stainless steel will not corrode or rust from body salt.

Semiautomatics. Automatic pistols have been the standard issue for law enforcement agencies throughout Europe for decades, but the American law enforcement system has stuck to the wheelgun, except for a small percentage of the departments located in New Jersey, Texas, Illinois and California. The largest police department in the United States to change over and issue semiautomatics was the Illinois State Police in 1967. It chose the S&W double-action 9mm, Model 39, and the 1700 troopers are required to carry it both on and off duty.

Of all the departments converting to automatics, none has been in major cities with populations of over one million, where the crime rate is highest. Ironically, the officers in those large cities are the ones most likely

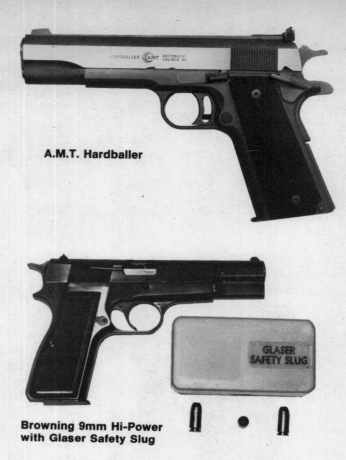

A.M.T. Hardballer

**Browning 9mm Hi-Power
with Glaser Safety Slug**

to become involved in a fire fight and need the extra firepower of the automatics, which usually hold nine to 15 rounds. Reasons for this failure to change are based on the tightening of city budgets and the shortages of funds allotted for law enforcement in general.

Despite the large departments' inability or reluctance to change weapons, officers who are given their own choice of backup and off-duty weapons are buying semiautos in ever-increasing numbers. Manufacturers sensitive to this trend have attempted to meet law enforcement demands by making their weapons smaller and more compact while retaining firepower. At the 1981 Shot Show, for example, O.D.I. introduced its Viking. A 45-caliber double-action semiauto, it is available with 4¼- or 5-inch barrels. It was so well received that the New Orleans P.D. ordered enough of them to arm its narcotics officers, and orders have been placed by the U.S. Border Patrol and the Marshals Service for use as duty weapons.

Calibers most in demand are the 9mm, 45 and 380. There has been a long-running controversy over which is the better manstopper—the 9mm or the 45 caliber. Both are powerful, of course, but the 9mm has been

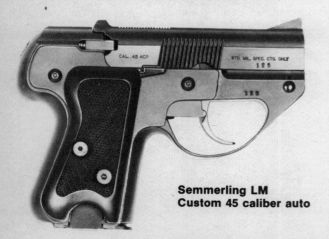

**Semmerling LM
Custom 45 caliber auto**

standard cartridge for handguns and submachine guns for numerous armies since the 1930s, and it probably won't be long before our own armed forces adopt it. If you have any doubts about its manstopping power, check the statistics on soldiers killed in World War II, and remember that more men have been killed with the 9mm than any other cartridge. The 9mm 100-grain slug moves out at muzzle velocities of between 1080 and 1839 fps, according to the slug weight. The highest velocity belongs to the 96-grain Glaser Safety Slug. Only the 200-grain 44-caliber Magnum has more shocking power than that.

There are numerous weapons on the market chambered for the 9mm, but the three most popular are the S&W nine-shot double-action Model 39, the S&W 15-shot double-action Model 59 and the 14-shot Browning Hi-Power. The Hi-Power is an old warhorse that's been around since 1935 and, although the weapon is single action, it is as popular today as when it was first manufactured. The Navy Arms Co. is issuing a redesigned Mamba, a 9mm semiautomatic made entirely of stainless steel. This weapon was conceived by joint West German and South African technology and will also be available in the near future in 45 caliber.

The newest additions to the field of 9mm semiautos are from Smith & Wesson. These weapons are a direct outgrowth of the models entered by them in the U.S. Government's program to select a new 9mm handgun to replace the 45-caliber Colt 1911 autoloader. The new models 439 and 459 have steel-alloy frames, and their major differences from the old models 39 and 59 are new sights protected by metal wings, new extractors and new firing pins. Steel-frame models (nos. 539 and 559) are also available.

The 45-caliber automatic has been in use since 1911 and was designed by John Browning, the same Browning who designed the B.A.R. and the Browning Hi-Power. Because of its often exaggerated manstopping power, the 45 auto is without a doubt the most sought-after off-duty weapon on the market—and its price reflects it.

The 45 caliber slug is generally slower moving than the 9mm. It travels at about 900 fps when used with a Federal 225-grain hollow point and at about 1000 fps with a 185-grain hollow point by Winchester-Western. However, it will produce nearly 400 pounds of muzzle energy—truly a manstopper.

So many law enforcement and security officers carry automatics today, particularly 45s, that the king of semiautomatics, Jeff Cooper, has opened a training school in Arizona called the American Pistol Institute, better known as Gunsite. Other weapons experts have opened combat training schools: Lance Weber in Colo-

Colt Combat Commander

S & W Model 459 15-shot double-action 9mm semiautomatic

M-S Safari Arms Enforcer 45-caliber semiauto

rado and John Farnam in Wisconsin. At these schools, persons interested in becoming proficient with a handgun can train for a fee.

Stainless steel is being more widely used in the production of 45s as well as the other caliber automatics. The A.M.T. "Hardballer" in 45 caliber is all stainless steel, as is the shortened 45-caliber Enforcer from M-S Safari Arms, which has a custom look about it. The action of this weapon is rough and leaves a lot to be desired, but with a little work it can handle most ammo well.

Stoeger Industries imports a line of semiautomatics from Llama of Spain, available in stainless steel and blue finishes. These guns come in double action, controlled by a newly patented ball-bearing design. The weapons are the same size as the Colt Commander, but sport a custom look. A redesigned, completely adjustable rear sight is milled into the slide. The 45 caliber holds eight rounds. The 9mm comes in two models: a nine-shot

version with an alloy frame; and a redesigned 13-shot clip version with a steel frame. These weapons have a smooth action and are beautifully made. Other popular models are available. Llama produces a small, sturdy single-action weapon that's easy to conceal, as does Astra with its 380 Constable. For double-action fans, there are three imported super models on the market: the Beretta M-84, a 13-shot weapon; Browning sells the same model with a slightly different slide, also manufactured by Beretta; and the Walther model PPK/S, perhaps the finest double-action weapon ever produced. First manufactured in 1929, today it is imported from West Germany by Interarms and is still considered a coveted purchase by law enforcement officers. In 1955, the gun cost about $75; today it would cost about $600. Interarms manufactures a PPK/S in this country also.

Custom Guns. Custom handguns for law enforcement and security personnel first became popular in 1964 when Paris Theodore, the owner and founder of

The Asp, customized S & W Model 39 by Armament Systems

Mini-combat Browning customized by Austin Behlert

Customized S & W Model 39 by the Devel Corporation

The Devel, customized S & W Model 59, by the Devel Corporation

Seecamp double-action conversion by Behlert

Behlert's 44 Magnum customized S & W Model 29

Seventrees Ltd. of New York City created the Asp. This was a unique, beautiful, compact, easy-to-conceal weapon made from an S&W Model 39 in 9mm. For the first time in the history of American law enforcement, a plainclothes officer could totally conceal a high-powered automatic, and Seventrees was given a large government contract to supply law enforcement agencies with the weapon. After delivering only 250 units, however, the company went under. In 1976, Armament Systems and Procedures, Inc., brought the Asp back onto the market in all its glory.

A second combat conversion developed from the S&W Model 39 is the 9mm Devel, produced by the Devel Corporation. This weapon is compact and has the same eight-round capacity as the Asp, but is slightly longer and heavier. Also, the finish on the Asp is black, whereas the Devel's is brushed nickel.

Throughout the United States, if you talk to officers in tune with custom handguns, a familiar name always crops up: Austin Behlert. Behlert and his son Frank are custom gunmakers located in Monmouth Junction, New Jersey. They do custom work on such weapons as the S&W models 39 and 59. Their custom Colt 45 automatic called the Bobcat is a classic, and their cut-down and reworked Browning Hi-Power has to be seen to be appreciated.

Also adept at customizing the action of combat weapons while not reducing their size is Cylinder and Slide, Inc.

There is no getting around or away from it, custom weapons are beautiful, expensive and practical. If you like small compact semiautos that pack a wallop, and you can handle the price, be assured you'll never need to purchase a second off-duty or backup weapon.

Pistols

The following firearms specifications sections have been compiled exclusively with the law enforcement officer in mind. They contain only the weapons and calibers normally stipulated for use by law enforcement.

A.M.T.

COMBAT GOVERNMENT ("HARDBALLER")

Calibers: 45 ACP and 9mm
Capacities: 8 rounds with 7-round magazine in 45; 10 rounds with 9-round magazine in 9mm; 15-, 20- and 25-round magazines available in 45
Action: Single
Barrel Length: 5 inches
Overall Length: 8½ inches
Weight: 38 ounces
Grips: Diamond-pattern checkered walnut
Sights: Fixed combat style
Finish: Satin stainless steel
Additional Features: Extended combat safety; loaded chamber indicator; custom-fitted barrel bushing; adjustable target-type trigger

TDE BACKUP

Caliber: 380 ACP
Capacity: 6 rounds with 5-round magazine
Action: Single
Barrel Length: 2½ inches
Overall Length: 5 inches
Weight: 17 ounces
Grips: Smooth wood
Sights: Fixed, open and recessed
Finish: Brushed stainless steel
Additional Features: Smallest 380 made in U.S.; stainless steel construction; concealed hammer; blowback operation

American Arms

TP-70

Calibers: 22 and 25 ACP
Capacity: 7 rounds with 6-round magazine
Action: Double
Barrel Length: 2.6 inches
Overall Length: 4.72 inches
Weight: 12.6 ounces
Grips: Checkered composition
Sights: Fixed
Finish: Stainless steel
Additional Features: Stainless steel construction; manual and magazine safeties

Astra

CONSTABLE

Caliber: 380 ACP
Capacity: 8 rounds with 7-round magazine; 15-round magazine available

Action: Double
Barrel Length: 3½ inches
Overall Length: 6⅝ inches
Weight: 26 ounces
Grips: Molded plastic
Sights: Fixed
Finishes: Blue and chrome
Additional Features: Nonsnagging hammer; nonglare rib on slide

Bauer

AUTOMATIC PISTOL

Caliber: 25
Capacity: 7 rounds with 6-round magazine
Action: Single
Barrel Length: 2¼ inches
Overall Length: 4 inches
Weight: 10 ounces
Grips: Plastic pearl or checkered walnut
Sights: Fixed
Finish: Satin stainless steel
Additional Features: Stainless steel construction; magazine and manual safeties

American Arms
TP-70

Astra
Constable

Pistols

**Bauer
Automatic Pistol**

Beretta Model 84

Beretta

MODEL 70S

Caliber: 380 ACP
Capacity: 8 rounds with 7-round magazine
Action: Single
Barrel Length: 3.5 inches
Overall Length: 6.5 inches
Weight: 23 ounces
Grips: Checkered black plastic
Sights: Fixed
Finish: Blue-black
Additional Features: Side lever indicates empty magazine;
  steel alloy frame

MODEL 84

Caliber: 380 ACP
Capacity: 14 rounds with 13-round magazine
Action: Double
Barrel Length: 3¾ inches
Overall Length: 6½ inches
Weight: 23 ounces
Grips: Smooth black plastic or wood
Sights: Fixed ramp front; white-outlined adjustable rear
Finish: Blue-black
Additional Features: Harrem block slide safety-loaded
  chamber indicator

MODEL 92S

Calibers: 9mm Parabellum and 9mm
Capacity: 16 rounds with 15-round magazine
Action: Double
Barrel Length: 4.9 inches
Overall Length: 8.5 inches
Weight: 33.8 ounces
Grips: Smooth walnut or plastic
Sights: Fixed
Finish: Blue-black
Additional Features: Hammer drop safety

Bernardelli

MODEL 80

Caliber: 380 ACP (9mm short)
Capacity: 8 rounds with 7-round magazine
Action: Single
Barrel Length: 3.5 inches
Overall Length: 6.5 inches
Weight: 26.8 ounces
Grips: Checkered plastic with thumbrest
Sights: Ramp-style front; adjustable rear
Finish: Blue
Additional Features: Slide stays open after last shot

Browning

**Browning
9mm Hi-Power**

9mm HI-POWER

Calibers: 9mm Parabellum and 9mm
Capacity: 14 rounds with 13-round magazine; 22-round
  magazine available
Action: Single
Barrel Length: 4 21/32 inches
Overall Length: 7¾ inches
Weight: 32 ounces
Grips: Hand-checkered walnut
Sights: Fixed or adjustable
Finishes: Blue-black and chrome
Additional Features: Cock and thumb safeties; cannot
  be fired with the magazine removed

Pistols

Browning

Browning Model BDA-45

MODEL BDA-45

Caliber: 45 ACP
Capacity: 8 rounds with 7-round magazine
Action: Double
Barrel Length: 4¼ inches
Overall Length: 7 25/32 inches
Weight: 29 ounces
Grips: Checkered black plastic
Sights: Fixed blade front with white dot; white-outlined square notched rear adjustable for windage
Finish: Blue-black
Additional Features: Square trigger guard; decocking lever allows hammer to be lowered onto locked firing pin; slide stays open after last shot

MODEL BDA-380

Caliber: 380 ACP (9mm short)
Capacity: 13 rounds with 12-round magazine
Action: Double
Barrel Length: 3 13/16 inches
Overall Length: 6¾ inches
Weight: 23 ounces
Grips: Smooth walnut with inset Browning medallion
Sights: Fixed front; white-outlined rear adjustable for windage
Finishes: Blue-black and nickel
Additional Features: Combination safety and decocking lever automatically lowers cocked hammer to half cock; may be operated by both left- and right-handed shooters

Bushmaster

BUSHMASTER

Caliber: 223
Capacities: 20 rounds with 19-round magazine; also 30-round magazine plus 1
Action: Semiautomatic
Barrel Length: 11½ inches

Overall Length: 20½ inches
Grips: Black molded nylon
Sights: Blade front and rear
Finish: Black matte
Additional Features: Only pistol that fires 223 ammunition

Colt

COMBAT COMMANDER

Calibers: 45 ACP, 9mm Luger and 38 Super
Capacities: 8 rounds with 7-round magazine in 45 ACP; 10 rounds with 9-round magazine in 9mm and 38 Super
Action: Single
Barrel Length: 4¼ inches
Overall Length: 7⅞ inches
Weight: 36 ounces
Grips: Sandblasted walnut panels
Sights: Fixed blade front; square notched rear
Finishes: Blue and nickel
Additional Features: Lanyard-style hammer; thumb and grip safeties

LIGHTWEIGHT COMMANDER

Caliber: 45 ACP
Capacity: 8 rounds with 7-round magazine; 15-, 20- and 25-round magazines available
Action: Single
Barrel Length: 4¼ inches
Overall Length: 7⅞ inches
Weight: 27 ounces
Grips: Sandblasted walnut grips
Sights: Fixed blade front; square notched rear
Finish: Blue
Additional Features: Top of slide sandblasted to reduce glare; grooved trigger and hammer spur; grip and thumb safeties; high-strength alloy frame

Bushmaster

Pistols

**Colt
Combat Commander**

GOLD CUP NATIONAL MATCH MK IV

Caliber: 45 ACP
Capacity: 8 rounds with 7-round magazine; 15-, 20- and 25-round magazines available
Action: Single
Barrel Length: 5 inches
Overall Length: 8¾ inches
Weight: 38½ ounces
Grips: Checkered walnut
Sights: Undercut front; Colt-Elliason adjustable rear
Finish: Blue
Additional Features: Serrated target hammer; special trigger; thumb and grip safeties

GOVERNMENT MODEL MK IV

Calibers: 45 ACP, 9mm Luger and 38 Super
Capacities: 8 rounds with 7-round magazine in 45; 10 rounds with 9-round magazine in 9mm and 38 Super
Action: Single
Barrel Length: 5 inches
Overall Length: 8⅜ inches
Weight: 38½ ounces
Grips: Sandblasted walnut panels
Sights: Ramp front; notched fixed rear
Finishes: Blue and nickel
Additional Features: Grip and thumb safeties; grooved trigger; accurized barrel and bushing

Detonics

45 PISTOL

Caliber: 45 ACP

Capacity: 7 rounds with 6-round magazine; 15-round magazine available
Action: Single
Barrel Length: 3¼ inches
Overall Length: 6¾ inches
Weight: 29 ounces
Grips: Checkered walnut
Sights: Fixed blade front; notched fixed rear; may be ordered with adjustable rear sight
Finishes: Blue, nickel, hardchrome and stainless steel
Additional Features: Self-adjusting barrel; full clip indicator in magazine

FIE

MODEL A27B, THE BEST

Caliber: 25 ACP
Capacity: 7 rounds with 6-round magazine
Action: Single
Barrel Length: 2½ inches
Overall Length: 4⅝ inches
Weight: 13 ounces
Grips: Checkered walnut
Sights: Fixed
Finish: Blue
Additional Features: Steel construction; thumb and magazine safeties; exposed hammer

TITAN

Caliber: 25 ACP
Capacity: 7 rounds with 6-round magazine
Action: Single
Barrel Length: 2 7/16 inches
Overall Length: 4⅝ inches
Weight: 12 ounces
Grips: Checkered nylon
Sights: Fixed
Finishes: Blue and chrome
Additional Features: Simple takedown for cleaning and repair

E380, TITAN II

Caliber: 380 ACP
Capacity: 7 rounds with 6-round magazine
Action: Single
Barrel Length: 3⅞ inches
Overall Length: 5⅝ inches
Weight: 20 ounces
Grips: Checkered nylon
Sights: Fixed
Finishes: Blue and chrome
Additional Features: Equipped with magazine disconnector so weapon cannot be fired when magazine is removed; standard slide safety plus firing pin block

Pistols

Heckler & Koch

MODEL HK4

Calibers: 25, 380, 32 ACP and 22 LR
Capacities: 8 rounds with 7-round magazine in 25;
9 rounds with 8-round magazine in 380
Action: Double
Barrel Length: 3 11/32 inches
Overall Length: 6 3/16 inches
Weight: 16½ ounces
Grips: Black checkered plastic
Sights: Fixed blade front; notched rear adjustable for windage
Finish: Black matte
Additional Features: Basic weapon available in 380 ACP; conversion kits for other calibers available

MODEL P9S

Calibers: 45 ACP and 9mm Parabellum
Capacities: 8 rounds with 7-round magazine in 45;
10 rounds with 9-round magazine in 9mm

Action: Double
Barrel Length: 4 inches
Overall Length: 7.6 inches
Weight: 30 ounces
Grips: Checkered plastic
Sights: Combat style; target sights also available
Finish: Black matte
Additional Features: Delayed roller-locked bolt system

MODEL VP70Z

Caliber: 9mm
Capacity: 19 rounds with 18-round magazine
Action: Double
Barrel Length: 4.57 inches
Overall Length: 8.03 inches
Weight: 29 ounces
Grips: Black stippled plastic
Sights: Based on light-and-shadow principle; ramp front; channeled rear
Finish: Black matte
Additional Features: Recoil-operated receiver is solid plastic; parallel-type revolver trigger and direct firing pin ignition ensure readiness to fire and allow loaded weapon to be carried safely

Heckler & Koch Model HK4

Heckler & Koch Model VP 70Z

Iver Johnson

PP30 SUPER ENFORCER

Caliber: 30 M1
Capacity: 5 rounds; 15- and 30-round magazines available
Action: Single
Barrel Length: 9½ inches
Overall Length: 17 inches
Weight: 68 ounces
Grips: American walnut with finger grooves on forend
Sights: Fixed blade front; rear adjustable for windage and elevation
Finish: Blue
Additional Features: Pistol is based on a carbine action

X300 PONY

Caliber: 380 ACP
Capacity: 7 rounds with 6-round magazine
Action: Single
Barrel Length: 3 inches
Overall Length: 6 inches
Weight: 20 ounces
Grips: Checkered walnut
Sights: Blade front; notched rear adjustable for windage and elevation
Finishes: Blue, nickel and military matte
Additional Features: Steel construction; loaded chamber indicator; inertia firing pin; thumb safety locks hammer

Pistols

Iver Johnson PP30 Super Enforcer

Iver Johnson X300 Pony

Llama Double-Action Automatic

L.E.S.

P-18

Calibers: 9mm Parabellum, 30 Luger and 45 ACP
Capacities: 19 rounds with 18-round magazine in 9mm
and 30 Luger; 11 rounds with 10-round magazine in
45 ACP
Actions: Double and single
Barrel Length: 5½ inches
Weight: 36 ounces
Grips: Checkered resin
Sights: Post-type front; V-notched rear adjustable
for windage
Finish: Black matte
Additional Features: All stainless steel; gas-assisted
action

Llama

DOUBLE-ACTION AUTOMATIC

Caliber: 45 ACP
Capacity: 8 rounds with 7-round magazine; 15-, 20- and
25-round magazines available
Action: Double

Barrel Length: 4¼ inches
Overall Length: 7¾ inches
Weight: 40 ounces
Grips: Smooth walnut
Sights: Ramp blade front; rear adjustable for windage
and elevation
Finishes: Polished blue and satin chrome
Additional Features: Steel construction; ball-bearing
action hammer shoe

LARGE-FRAME AUTOMATIC

Calibers: 38 Super, 9mm and 45 ACP
Capacities: 10 rounds with 9-round magazine in 9mm
and 38; 8 rounds with 7-round magazine in 45;
25-round magazine available in 45
Action: Single
Barrel Length: 5 inches
Overall Length: 8½ inches
Weight: 40 ounces
Grips: Smooth teakwood on satin models; smooth walnut
on blued models
Sights: Patridge-type front; square notched rear adjustable
for windage
Finishes: Blue and satin chrome
Additional Features: Checkered back strap machined
from steel; plain front strap

Pistols

Llama

SMALL-FRAME AUTOMATIC

Caliber: 380
Capacity: 8 rounds with 7-round magazine; 15-round magazine available
Action: Single
Barrel Length: 3 11/16 inches
Overall Length: 6½ inches
Weight: 23 ounces
Grips: Modified thumbrest; black plastic grips
Sights: Patridge-type front; square notched rear adjustable for windage
Finishes: Blue and satin chrome
Additional Features: External wide-spur serrated hammer; straight blowback action; thumb, half-cock and magazine safeties

**Llama
Small-Frame Automatic**

**Llama
Large-Frame Automatic**

9mm AUTOMATIC

Caliber: 9mm Parabellum
Capacity: 14 rounds with 13-shot magazine; 9-round magazine also available
Action: Double
Barrel Length: 4¼ inches
Overall Length: 8⅛ inches
Weight: 38½ ounces empty
Sights: Ramp front, notched
Additional Features: Lightweight version available

Mauser

Mauser Model HSc

MODEL HSc

Caliber: 380
Capacity: 8 rounds with 7-round magazine
Action: Double
Barrel Length: 3.75 inches
Overall Length: 6 inches
Weight: 23.3 ounces
Grips: Checkered walnut
Sights: Fixed battle type
Finish: Black matte
Additional Features: Steel construction; thumb and magazine safeties; exposed hammer; matte nonglare sight channel

MODEL HSc 80

Caliber: 380 ACP
Capacity: 13 rounds with 12-round magazine
Action: Double
Barrel Length: 3.75 inches
Overall Length: 6.25 inches
Weight: 26.4 ounces
Grips: Stippled walnut panels

Pistols

M & N Distributors
C.O.P.

Navy Arms Mamba

M-S Safari Arms
Enforcer

M-S Safari Arms

ENFORCER

Caliber: 45 ACP
Capacity: 8 rounds with 7-round magazine
Action: Single
Barrel Length: 3.8 inches
Overall Length: 7 inches
Weight: 35 ounces
Grips: Checkered wood
Sights: Ramped blade front; rear adjustable for windage
and elevation
Finishes: Satin hardchrome and ebony
Additional Features: Internal parts coated with Teflon®
to eliminate lubricating; finger grip and stippling on
front strap; match model available with 5-inch barrel

Sights: Open fixed sights
Finishes: Blue and matte
Additional Features: Exposed hammer; combat trigger
guard; matte sight channel

Navy Arms

MAMBA

Caliber: 9mm Parabellum
Capacity: 16 rounds with 15-round magazine
Action: Double
Barrel Length: 5 inches
Overall Length: 8.5 inches
Weight: 42 ounces
Grips: Hard checkered composition; also available in wood
Sights: Ramp front; rear drift adjustable for windage
Finish: Stainless steel
Additional Features: May be carried safely in cocked and
locked positions; adjustable trigger stop; self-cleaning
rifling system; optional magazines of 20, 25, 35 and
40 rounds.

M&N Distributors

C.O.P.

Caliber: 357 Magnum
Capacity: 4 rounds
Action: Double
Barrel Length: 3¼ inches
Overall Length: 5½ inches
Weight: 28 ounces
Grips: Checkered composition
Sights: Fixed and open
Finish: Satin stainless steel
Additional Features: Weapon is only one-inch wide and has
four barrels

Pistols

O.D.I.

VIKING

Calibers: 45 ACP and 9mm
Capacities: 8 rounds with 7-round magazine in 45; 10 rounds with 9-round magazine in 9mm
Action: Seecamp double action
Barrel Length: 4¼ inches
Overall Length: 7⅞ inches
Weight: 36 ounces
Grips: Teakwood
Sights: Serrated ramp front; ⅛-inch notched rear
Finish: Satin stainless steel
Additional Features: Made from 17-4 and 400 series stainless steel

Semmerling

MODEL LM-4

Caliber: 45 ACP
Capacity: 5 rounds with 4-round magazine
Action: Double

O.D.I. Viking

**Semmerling
Model LM-4**

Overall Length: 5 inches
Weight: 22 ounces
Grips: Checkered cocobolo or ebony
Sights: Fixed serrated ramp front; square notched rear
Finishes: Blue and hardchrome
Additional Features: Each round must be chambered by hand; kits available to make weapon even thinner than standard model

Sile-Bennelli

MODEL B-76 DA

Caliber: 9mm Parabellum
Capacity: 9 rounds with 8-round magazine
Action: Double
Barrel Length: 4¼ inches
Overall Length: 8 1/16 inches
Weight: 34 ounces
Grips: Checkered high-gloss walnut
Sights: Blade front with white face; rear adjustable for windage; both sides outlined with white bars for fast sighting
Finish: Blue-black
Additional Features: Steel construction; external parts blued; internal parts hardchrome plated; fixed breech; locked barrel; stainless steel inertia firing pin; loaded chamber indicator

Sile-Seecamp

SILE-SEECAMP II

Caliber: 25 ACP
Capacity: 9 rounds with 8-round magazine
Action: Double
Barrel Length: 2 inches
Overall Length: 4⅛ inches
Weight: 10 ounces
Grips: Checkered walnut
Sights: Smooth no-snag contoured slide
Finish: Brushed stainless steel
Additional Features: Stainless steel construction; inertia operated firing pin; hammer follows slide down to safety rest after each shot—no manual safety needed; magazine safety disconnector

Smith & Wesson

MODEL 39

Caliber: 9mm Parabellum
Capacity: 9 rounds with 8-round magazine; 14-round magazine available
Action: Double
Barrel Length: 4 inches

Pistols

**S & W
Model 439**

**S & W
Model 459**

Overall Length: 7 7/16 inches
Weight: 26½ ounces
Grips: Checkered walnut with S&W monogram
Sights: Fixed ⅛-inch serrated ramp front; Patridge-type rear adjustable for windage
Finishes: Blue and nickel
Additional Features: Falling block thumb safety

MODEL 59

Caliber: 9mm Parabellum
Capacity: 15 rounds with 14-round magazine; 25-round magazine available
Action: Double
Barrel Length: 4 inches
Overall Length: 7 7/16 inches
Weight: 27½ ounces
Grips: High-impact molded checkered nylon
Sights: ⅛-inch serrated front; notched rear with micrometer click adjustment for windage
Finishes: Blue and nickel
Additional Features: Two clips

MODEL 439

Caliber: 9mm Parabellum
Capacity: 9 rounds with 8-round magazine; 14-round magazine available
Action: Double
Barrel Length: 4 inches
Overall Length: 7 7/16 inches
Weight: 27 ounces
Grips: Checkered walnut
Sights: ⅛-inch serrated square ramp front; fully adjustable square notched rear
Finishes: Blue and nickel
Additional Features: Protective shields on both sides of

rear sight; magazine disconnector; new extractor design; new trigger-actuated firing pin lock plus regular rotating safety; steel-alloy frame

MODEL 459

Caliber: 9mm Parabellum
Capacity: 15 rounds with 14-round magazine; 25-round magazine available
Action: Double
Barrel Length: 4 inches
Overall Length: 7 7/16 inches
Weight: 28 ounces
Grips: Checkered high-impact nylon
Sights: ⅛-inch serrated square ramp front; fully adjustable square notched rear
Finishes: Blue and nickel
Additional Features: Protective shields on both sides of rear sight; magazine disconnector; new extractor design; new trigger-actuated firing pin lock plus regular rotating safety; steel-alloy frame

Star

MODELS BKM and BM

Caliber: 9mm Parabellum
Capacity: 9 rounds with 8-round magazine; 14-round magazine available
Action: Single
Barrel Length: 3.9 inches
Overall Length: 7.2 inches
Weight: 25 ounces
Grips: Checkered walnut
Sights: Fixed
Finishes: Blue; BM also available in chrome
Additional Features: External hammer; magazine and thumb safeties

Pistols

**Star
Model PD**

**Sterling
Model 300**

**Sterling
Model 450**

Star

MODEL PD

Caliber: 45 ACP
Capacity: 8 rounds with 7-round magazine; 15-round magazine available
Action: Single
Barrel Length: 3.9 inches
Overall Length: 7 inches
Weight: 25 ounces
Grips: Checkered walnut
Sights: Ramp front; rear sight milled into slide and adjustable for windage and elevation
Finish: Blue
Additional Features: Grooved front strap; thumb safety; nylon recoil buffer

Sterling

MODEL 300

Caliber: 25 ACP
Capacity: 7 rounds with 6-round magazine
Action: Single
Barrel Length: 2½ inches
Overall Length: 4½ inches
Weight: 13 ounces
Grips: Black Cycolac
Sights: Fixed
Finishes: Blue and stainless steel
Additional Features: Steel construction

MODEL 400 MK II

Caliber: 380 ACP
Capacity: 8 rounds with 7-round magazine; 15-round magazine available
Action: Double
Barrel Length: 3¾ inches
Overall Length: 6½ inches
Weight: 26 ounces
Grips: Hand-checkered walnut
Sights: Fixed
Finishes: Blue and stainless steel
Additional Features: Steel construction

MODEL 450

Caliber: 45 ACP
Capacity: 9 rounds with 8-round magazine
Action: Double
Barrel Length: 4¼ inches
Overall Length: 7½ inches
Weight: 35 ounces
Grips: Checkered walnut

Pistols

Sights: Blade front; rear adjustable for windage and elevation
Finish: Blue
Additional Features: Designed for law enforcement and military personnel

Steyr

Steyr Model GB

MODEL GB

Caliber: 9mm Parabellum
Capacity: 19 rounds with 18-round magazine
Action: Double
Barrel Length: 5.4 inches
Overall Length: 8.9 inches
Weight: 32 ounces
Grips: Checkered walnut
Sights: Post front; fixed, open and notched rear
Finish: Blue
Additional Features: Gas-operated blowback-delayed action

Targa

MODEL TA380XE

Caliber: 380 ACP
Capacity: 13 rounds with 12-round magazine
Action: Single
Barrel Length: 3.88 inches
Overall Length: 7.38 inches
Weight: 28 ounces
Grips: Smooth hardwood
Sights: Fixed front; rear adjustable for windage and elevation
Finishes: Blue and satin nickel

Additional Features: Steel construction; magazine, firing pin and thumb safeties

Universal

3000 ENFORCER

Caliber: 30 M1 carbine
Capacity: 5 rounds; 15- and 30-round magazines available
Action: Single
Barrel Length: 10¼ inches
Overall Length: 17¾ inches
Weight: 72 ounces
Grips: American walnut with hand guard
Sights: Gold bead ramp front; peep sight rear adjustable for windage and elevation
Finishes: Blue, gold, nickel and Teflon®

Vega

STAINLESS 45

Caliber: 45 ACP
Capacity: 8 rounds with 7-round magazine; 15-, 20- and 25-round magazines available
Action: Single
Barrel Length: 5 inches
Overall Length: 8⅜ inches
Weight: 40 ounces
Grips: Diamond-pattern checkered walnut
Sights: Choice of fixed or combat-style; rear sight adjustable for windage and elevation
Finish: Satin stainless steel
Additional Features: Stainless steel construction; grip and thumb safeties (exact copy of Colt 1911); top of slide, front and back straps sandblasted, remaining areas highly polished

Walther

MODEL P-38

Calibers: 9mm Luger and 30 Luger
Capacity: 9 rounds with 8-round magazine; 14-round magazine available
Action: Double
Barrel Length: 4 15/16 inches
Overall Length: 8½ inches
Weight: 28 ounces
Grips: Black checkered plastic
Sights: Fixed
Finishes: Matte; polished blue available on special order
Additional Features: Imported from Germany; safety blocks firing pin from falling onto chambered cartridge; chamber-loaded indicator

Pistols

Walther

MODEL P-38K

Caliber: 9mm Luger
Capacity: 9 rounds with 8-round magazine; 14-round magazine available
Action: Double
Barrel Length: 2¾ inches
Overall Length: 6⅜ inches
Weight: 26 ounces
Grips: Black checkered plastic
Sights: Fixed front; rear adjustable for windage
Finish: Black matte
Additional Features: Imported from Germany; streamlined version of P-38; hammer decocking lever

Walther
Model P-38K

MODEL PP

Caliber: 380 ACP
Capacity: 8 rounds with 7-round magazine; 15-round magazine available
Action: Double
Barrel Length: 3.9 inches
Overall Length: 6.7 inches
Weight: 23.8 ounces
Grips: Black checkered plastic
Sights: Fixed with white markings
Finish: Blue
Additional Features: Imported from Germany; extra magazine with finger rest; chamber-loaded indicator

Walther
Model PP

MODEL PPK/S

Caliber: 380 ACP
Capacity: 8 rounds with 7-round magazine; 15-round magazine available
Action: Double
Barrel Length: 3.3 inches
Overall Length: 6.1 inches
Weight: 23.8 ounces
Grips: Black checkered plastic
Sights: Fixed with white markings
Finish: Blue
Additional Features: Two models available, one is imported from Germany, the other is manufactured in U.S.; chamber loaded indicator; extra magazine with thumbrest

Walther
Model PPK/S

Revolvers

It should be noted that all revolvers chambered for the 357 Magnum cartridge can also safely chamber and fire the 38 Special caliber cartridge.

Astra

MODEL 357

Caliber: 357 Magnum
Capacity: 6 rounds
Action: Double
Barrel Lengths: 4, 6 and 8½ inches
Overall Length: 11¼ inches with 6-inch barrel
Weight: 39 ounces with 6-inch barrel
Grips: Checkered hardwood; magna style
Sights: Adjustable rear sight
Finishes: Blue and chrome
Additional Features: Wide spur hammer and trigger; floating firing pin

Charter Arms

BULLDOG

Caliber: 44 Special
Capacity: 5 rounds
Action: Double
Barrel Lengths: 3 and 6 inches
Overall Length: 7¾ inches with 6-inch barrel
Weight: 19 ounces with 6-inch barrel
Grips: Hand-checkered American walnut bulldog or square butt
Sights: 9/64-inch Patridge-type front; square notched fixed rear
Finishes: High-luster blue and stainless steel

POLICE BULLDOG

Caliber: 38 Special
Capacity: 6 rounds
Action: Double
Barrel Length: 4 inches
Overall Length: 9 inches
Weight: 20½ ounces
Grips: Checkered walnut; magna-style square butt
Sights: Full-length front; fully adjustable combat rear
Finish: Blue
Additional Features: Steel frame; unbreakable firing pin; wide hammer and trigger

TARGET BULLDOG

Calibers: 357 Magnum and 44 Special
Capacity: 5 rounds
Action: Double
Barrel Length: 4 inches
Overall Length: 9 inches
Weight: 20½ ounces
Grips: Checkered walnut; magna-style square butt
Sights: Full-length ramp front; fully adjustable milled-channel square notched rear
Finish: High-luster blue

UNDERCOVER

Caliber: 38 Special
Capacity: 5 rounds
Action: Double
Barrel Lengths: 2 and 3 inches
Overall Lengths: 6¼ and 8 inches
Weights: 16 and 17½ ounces
Grips: Smooth walnut
Sights: Patridge-type ramp front; square notched rear
Finishes: High-luster blue and nickel

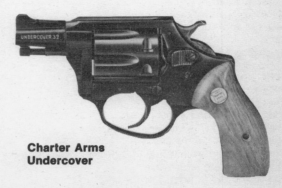

Charter Arms Police Bulldog

Charter Arms Undercover

Revolvers

**Colt
Detective Special**

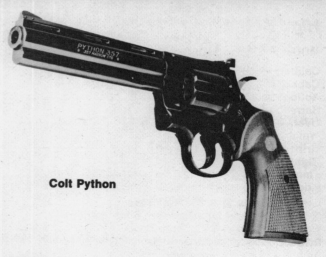

Colt Python

Colt

DETECTIVE SPECIAL

Caliber: 38 Special
Capacity: 6 rounds
Action: Double
Barrel Length: 2 inches
Overall Length: 6⅞ inches
Weight: 21½ ounces
Grips: Checkered walnut; round butt
Sights: Fixed ramp front; square notched rear
Finishes: Blue and polished nickel

DIAMONDBACK

Caliber: 38 Special
Capacity: 6 rounds
Action: Double
Barrel Lengths: 2½ and 4 inches
Overall Lengths: 7½ and 9 inches
Weights: 24 and 28½ ounces
Grips: Checkered walnut; target style
Sights: Ramp-style front; adjustable rear
Finishes: Blue and polished nickel
Additional Features: Ventilated rib; grooved trigger; wide hammer spur

LAWMAN MARK III

Caliber: 357 Magnum
Capacity: 6 rounds
Action: Double
Barrel: Heavy; 2 and 4 inches long
Overall Lengths: 7¼ and 9⅜ inches
Weights: 32 and 35 ounces
Grips: Checkered walnut; round butt with 2-inch barrel; square butt with 4-inch barrel
Sights: Fixed blade front; fixed square notched rear
Finishes: Blue and polished nickel

PYTHON

Caliber: 357 Magnum
Capacity: 6 rounds
Action: Double
Barrel Lengths: 2½, 4 and 6 inches
Overall Length: 11¼ inches with 6-inch barrel
Weight: 43½ ounces with 6-inch barrel
Grips: Oversized checkered walnut
Sights: Ramp-type front; adjustable rear
Finishes: Royal blue and nickel
Additional Features: Ventilated rib; fast-cocking wide hammer; grooved trigger; available with 8-inch barrel

TROOPER MARK III

Caliber: 357 Magnum
Capacity: 6 rounds
Action: Double
Barrel Lengths: 4 and 6 inches
Overall Length: 9½ inches with 4-inch barrel
Weight: 39 ounces with 4-inch barrel
Grips: Oversized checkered target-style grips; square butt
Sights: Fixed ramp front; adjustable rear blade
Finish: High-luster blue
Additional Features: Target hammer; grooved trigger

FIE

D-38 DERRINGER

Calibers: 38 Special and 38 S&W
Capacity: 2 rounds
Action: Single
Barrel: Tipped up; 3 inches
Overall Length: 4¾ inches
Weight: 14 ounces
Grips: Checkered white nylon
Sights: Fixed
Finish: Chrome
Additional Features: Spur trigger

Revolvers

High Standard

MODELS 9194 and 9306

Caliber: 22 Magnum
Capacity: 2 rounds
Action: Double; top break
Barrel Length: 3½ inches
Overall Length: 5 inches
Weight: 11 ounces
Grips: Smooth white or black plastic
Sights: Fixed and open
Finishes: Blue and nickel
Additional Features: Steel parts encased in a black anodized alloy housing; dual extraction; hammerless

CRUSADER—MEDIUM FRAME

Caliber: 357 Magnum
Capacity: 6 rounds
Action: Double
Barrel Lengths: 4¼ and 6½ inches
Overall Lengths: 9¾ and 11¾ inches
Weights: 40 and 44 ounces
Grips: Checkered walnut; magna style
Sights: Blade on ramp front; completely adjustable rear
Finish: Blue

CRUSADER—LARGE FRAME

Calibers: 44 Magnum and 45 Colt
Capacity: 6 rounds
Action: Double
Barrel Lengths: 4¼, 6½ and 8⅜ inches
Overall Lengths: 9⅞, 12⅛ and 14 inches
Weights: 43, 48 and 52 ounces
Grips: Smooth walnut; magna style
Sights: Blade on ramp front; completely adjustable rear
Finish: Blue

Llama

COMANCHE

Calibers: 38 Special and 357 Magnum
Capacity: 6 rounds
Action: Double
Barrel Lengths: 4 and 6 inches
Overall Lengths: 9¼ and 11 inches
Weights: 36 and 39 ounces
Grips: Checkered walnut; oversized target style
Sights: Serrated quick-draw front ramp; square notched rear adjustable for windage and elevation
Finishes: Blue and satin chrome
Additional Features: Case-hardened hammer and trigger; wide spur-type hammer; wide-grooved target-type trigger; serrated front and back strap

SUPER COMANCHE IV

Caliber: 44 Magnum
Capacity: 6 rounds
Action: Double
Barrel Length: 6 inches
Overall Length: 11¾ inches
Weight: 50 ounces
Grips: Checkered walnut; oversized target style
Sights: Serrated quick-draw front ramp; square notched rear
Finish: Blue
Additional Features: Case-hardened hammer and trigger; wide spur-type hammers; wide-grooved target-type trigger; serrated front and back straps

**High Standard
Crusader—Medium Frame**

Llama Comanche

**Llama
Super Comanche IV**

Revolvers

Mitchell Arms

DERRINGER

Caliber: 38 Special
Capacity: 2 rounds
Action: Single
Barrel Length: 2¾ inches
Overall Length: 5¼ inches
Weight: 11 ounces
Grips: Checkered walnut
Sights: Open and fixed; ramp front
Finish: Polished blue
Additional Features: Steel construction

Rossi

MODEL 31

Caliber: 38 Special
Capacity: 5 rounds
Action: Double
Barrel Length: 4 inches
Overall Length: 8¾ inches
Weight: 22 ounces
Grips: Checkered wood
Sights: Ramp front; low-profile rear adjustable for windage and elevation
Finishes: Blue and nickel
Additional Features: Target trigger; wide-spur target hammer

MODEL 68

Caliber: 38 Special
Capacity: 6 rounds
Action: Double
Barrel Length: 3 inches
Overall Length: 7½ inches
Weight: 22 ounces
Grips: Checkered wood
Sights: Ramp front; low-profile rear adjustable for windage
Finishes: Blue and nickel
Additional Features: Combat styled

Ruger

POLICE SERVICE-SIX Models 107 and 108

Calibers: 9mm Parabellum and 357 Magnum
Capacity: 6 rounds
Action: Double
Barrel Lengths: 2¾ and 4 inches; 4-inch heavy
Overall Length: 9¼ inches with 4-inch barrel
Weight: 33½ ounces with 4-inch barrel
Grips: Checkered American walnut; semi-target style
Sights: Patridge-type front; fixed square notched rear
Finishes: Blue and stainless steel
Additional Features: Strong steel frame; barrel, rib and ejector rod housing combined into one unit

SECURITY SIX Model 117

Caliber: 357 Magnum
Capacity: 6 rounds
Action: Double
Barrel Lengths: 2¾, 4 and 6 inches; 4-inch heavy
Overall Length: 9¼ inches with 4-inch barrel
Weight: 33½ ounces with 4-inch barrel
Grips: Hand-checkered American walnut; semi-target style
Sights: Patridge-type front; completely adjustable rear
Finishes: Blue and stainless steel
Additional Features: Hard steel construction; sighting rib along top of barrel; wire coil springs

SPEED-SIX

Calibers: 38 Special, 9mm and 357 Magnum
Capacity: 6 rounds
Action: Double
Barrel Lengths: 2¾ and 4 inches
Overall Length: 7½ inches with 2¾-inch barrel
Weight: 31 ounces with 2¾-inch barrel
Grips: Diamond-pattern American checkered walnut
Sights: Patridge-type front; square notched rear
Finishes: Blue and stainless steel
Additional Features: Round-butt lightened version of the Security Six designed for use by plainclothes and off-duty officers; hammer without spur available on special order

Rossi
Model 68

Ruger
Speed-six

Revolvers

Smith & Wesson

BODYGUARD Model 38

Caliber: 38 Special
Capacity: 5 rounds
Action: Double
Barrel Length: 2 inches
Overall Length: 6⅜ inches
Weight: Airweight—14½ ounces; standard—20½ ounces
Grips: Checkered walnut; service type
Sights: 1/10-inch serrated ramp front; square notched rear
Finishes: Blue and nickel

S & W Model 19

CHIEFS SPECIAL Model 36

Caliber: 38 Special
Capacity: 5 rounds
Action: Double
Barrel Lengths: 2 and 3 inches
Overall Length: 6½ inches with 2-inch barrel
Weight: 19 ounces with 2-inch barrel
Grips: Checkered walnut; service type
Sights: 1/10-inch serrated ramp front; square notched rear
Finishes: Blue and nickel with 2-inch barrel; blue only with 3-inch barrel

S & W Model 586

CHIEFS SPECIAL Model 60

Caliber: 38 Special
Capacity: 5 rounds
Action: Double
Barrel Length: 2 inches
Overall Length: 6½ inches
Weight: 19 ounces
Grips: Checkered walnut; service type
Sights: Fixed 1/10-inch serrated ramp front; square notched rear
Finish: Stainless steel

COMBAT MAGNUM Model 19

Caliber: 357 Magnum
Capacity: 6 rounds
Action: Double
Barrel Lengths: 2½, 4 and 6 inches
Overall Length: 9½ inches with 4-inch barrel
Weight: 35 ounces with 4-inch barrel
Grips: Checkered Goncalo Alves; target style
Sights: ⅛-inch Baughman Quick Draw front with 2½- and 4-inch barrels; ⅛-inch Patridge front with 6-inch barrel; S&W micrometer click rear adjustable for windage and elevation
Finishes: Blue and nickel
Additional Features: Price varies according to accessories, such as target hammer and trigger; available with white-outlined rear sight

COMBAT MAGNUM Model 66

Caliber: 357 Magnum
Capacity: 6 rounds
Action: Double
Barrels: Square butt—4 and 6 inches; round butt—2½ inches long
Overall Length: 9½ inches with 4-inch barrel
Weight: 35 ounces with 4-inch barrel
Grips: Checkered Goncalo Alves; target-style grips on square-butt models
Sights: ⅛-inch S&W red ramp front on ramp base; S&W micrometer click rear adjustable for windage and elevation
Finish: Stainless steel
Additional Features: Stainless steel construction

DISTINGUISHED COMBAT MAGNUM Model 586

Caliber: 357 Magnum
Capacity: 6 rounds
Action: Double
Barrel Lengths: 4 and 6 inches
Overall Length: 9¾ inches with 4-inch barrel
Weight: 42 ounces with 4-inch barrel
Grips: Checkered Goncalo Alves
Sights: S&W red ramp front; S&W micrometer click rear adjustable for windage and elevation; white-outlined notch
Finish: Blue and nickel
Additional Features: Model 686 is same weapon except in stainless steel

Revolvers

Smith & Wesson

COMBAT MASTERPIECE Model 15

Caliber: 38 Special
Capacity: 6 rounds
Action: Double
Barrel Lengths: 2 and 4 inches
Overall Length: 9⅛ inches with 4-inch barrel
Weight: 34 ounces with 4-inch barrel
Grips: Checkered walnut
Sights: ⅛-inch Baughman Quick Draw on plain ramp front; S&W micrometer click rear adjustable for windage and elevation
Finishes: Blue and nickel
Additional Features: May be ordered with target hammer and trigger

HIGHWAY PATROLMAN Model 28

Caliber: 357 Magnum
Capacity: 6 rounds
Action: Double
Barrel Lengths: 4 and 6 inches
Overall Length: 11¼ inches with 6-inch barrel
Weight: 44 ounces with 6-inch barrel
Grips: Checkered walnut; service type; walnut target grips at extra cost
Sights: ⅛-inch Baughman Quick Draw front on plain ramp; S&W micrometer click rear adjustable for windage and elevation
Finish: Blue

K-38 MASTERPIECE Model 14

Caliber: 38 Special
Capacity: 6 rounds
Action: Double
Barrel Lengths: 6 and 8⅜ inches
Overall Length: 11⅛ inches with 6-inch barrel
Weight: 38½ ounces with 6-inch barrel
Grips: Checkered walnut
Sights: ⅛-inch plain Patridge front; micrometer click sight rear adjustable for windage and elevation
Finish: Blue
Additional Features: May be ordered with target hammer, trigger and grips

K-38 COMBAT MASTERPIECE Model 15

Caliber: 38 Special
Capacity: 6 rounds
Action: Double
Barrel Lengths: 2 and 4 inches
Overall Length: 9⅛ inches with 4-inch barrel
Weight: 34 ounces with 4-inch barrel
Grips: Checkered walnut; service type
Sights: ⅛-inch S&W red ramp front on ramp base; S&W micrometer click rear adjustable for windage and elevation
Finish: Stainless steel

S & W Model 10

S & W Model 13

MILITARY & POLICE AIRWEIGHT Model 12

Caliber: 38 Special
Capacity: 6 rounds
Action: Double
Barrel Lengths: 2 and 4 inches
Overall Length: 6⅞ inches with 2-inch barrel
Weight: 18 ounces with 2-inch barrel
Grips: Checkered walnut; magna-style round or square butt
Sights: Fixed ⅛-inch ramp front; square notched rear
Finishes: Blue and nickel

MILITARY & POLICE Model 10

Caliber: 38 Special
Capacity: 6 rounds
Action: Double
Barrel Lengths: 2, 4, 5 and 6 inches; 4-inch heavy
Overall Length: 9¼ inches with 4-inch barrel
Weight: 30½ ounces with 4-inch barrel
Grips: Checkered walnut; magna-style round or square butt
Sights: Fixed ⅛-inch ramp front; square notched rear
Finishes: Blue and nickel

Revolvers

MILITARY & POLICE Model 13

Calibers: 38 Special and 357 Magnum
Capacity: 6 rounds
Action: Double
Barrel: Heavy; 4 inches long
Overall Length: 9¼ inches
Weight: 34 ounces
Grips: Checkered walnut; square butt
Sights: Fixed ⅛-inch ramp front; square notched rear
Finishes: Blue and nickel
Additional Features: K-Frame

MILITARY & POLICE Model 64

Caliber: 38 Special
Capacity: 6 rounds
Action: Double
Barrel Lengths: 2 and 4 inches
Overall Length: 9¼ inches with 4-inch barrel
Weight: 34 ounces with 4-inch barrel
Grips: Checkered walnut; service type
Sights: Fixed ⅛-inch serrated ramp front; square notched rear
Finish: Stainless steel

MILITARY & POLICE Model 65

Caliber: 357 Magnum; also fires 38 Special
Capacity: 6 rounds
Action: Double
Barrel: Heavy; 4 inches long
Overall Length: 9¼ inches
Weight: 34 ounces
Grips: Checkered walnut; service type
Sights: Fixed ⅛-inch serrated ramp front; square notched rear
Finish: Stainless steel

MILITARY & POLICE Model 547

Caliber: 9mm
Capacity: 6 rounds
Action: Double
Barrel Lengths: 3 and 4 inches
Overall Length: 8⅛ inches with 3-inch barrel
Weight: 32 ounces with 3-inch barrel
Grips: Checkered walnut round butt target with 3-inch barrel; checkered square-butt Magna Service with 4-inch barrel
Sights: ⅛-inch serrated ramp front; ⅛-inch square notched rear
Finish: Blue
Additional Features: Half-moon clips not required for loading

MODEL 27

Caliber: 357 Magnum
Capacity: 6 rounds
Action: Double
Barrel Lengths: 3½, 5, 6 and 8⅜ inches
Overall Length: 11¼ inches with 6-inch barrel
Weight: 45 ounces with 6-inch barrel
Grips: Checkered walnut; service type
Sights: Choice of any S&W target front; S&W micrometer click rear adjustable for windage and elevation
Finishes: Blue and nickel

MODEL 29

Caliber 44 Magnum
Capacity: 6 rounds
Action: Double
Barrel Lengths: 4, 6 and 8⅜ inches
Overall Length: 11⅞ inches with 6-inch barrel
Weight: 47 ounces with 6-inch barrel
Grips: Checkered Goncalo Alves; special oversized target type
Sights: ⅛-inch S&W red ramp front; S&W micrometer click rear adjustable for windage and elevation
Finishes: Blue and nickel

S & W Model 65

S & W Model 547

Revolvers

Smith & Wesson

S & W Model 57

MODEL 57

Caliber: 41 Magnum
Capacity: 6 rounds
Action: Double
Barrel Lengths: 4, 6 and 8⅜ inches
Overall Length: 11⅜ inches with 6-inch barrel
Weight: 48 ounces with 6-inch barrel
Grips: Checkered Goncalo Alves; oversized target type
Sights: ⅛-inch S&W red ramp front; S&W micrometer click rear adjustable for windage and elevation
Finishes: Blue and nickel

Taurus

MODEL 65

Caliber: 357 Magnum
Capacity: 6 rounds
Action: Double
Barrel Length: 4 inches
Weight: 34 ounces
Grips: Checkered walnut; target type
Sights: Fixed ramp front; square notched rear
Finishes: Blue and satin nickel

MODEL 66

Caliber: 357 Magnum
Capacity: 6 rounds
Action: Double
Barrel Lengths: 3, 4 and 6 inches
Weight: 35 ounces with 4-inch barrel
Grips: Checkered walnut; target grips with 4- and 6-inch barrels; target-style magna grips with 3-inch barrel
Sights: Serrated ramp front; micrometer click rear adjustable for windage and elevation
Finishes: Blue and satin nickel

MODEL 82

Caliber: 38 Special
Capacity: 6 rounds
Action: Double
Barrels: Heavy; 3 and 4 inches
Overall Length: 9¼ with 4-inch barrel
Weight: 34 ounces with 4-inch barrel
Grips: Checkered walnut; service type
Sights: Fixed ramp front; square notched rear
Finishes: Blue and satin nickel

MODEL 83

Caliber: 38 Special
Capacity: 6 rounds
Action: Double
Barrel Length: 4 inches
Weight: 34½ ounces
Grips: Checkered walnut; target type
Sights: ¼-inch ramp front; micrometer click rear adjustable for windage and elevation
Finishes: Blue and satin nickel

PROTECTOR Model 85

Caliber: 38 Special
Capacity: 5 rounds
Action: Double
Barrel Length: 3 inches
Weight: 21 ounces
Grips: Brazilian hardwood; smooth service type
Sights: Fixed, square and notched rear
Finishes: Blue and satin nickel

Taurus Model 66

Taurus Model 83

Revolvers

**Taurus
Model 86**

**Dan Wesson
Model 8**

TARGET MASTER Model 86

Caliber: 38 Special
Capacity: 6 rounds
Action: Double
Barrel Length: 6 inches
Weight: 35 ounces
Grips: Checkered walnut; target type
Sights: Patridge-type micrometer click rear adjustable
for windage and elevation
Finish: Blue

Dan Wesson

MODELS 8 and 14

Calibers: Model 8—38 Special; Model 14—357 Magnum
Capacity: 6 rounds
Action: Double
Barrels: Optional and interchangeable; 2½, 4, 6 and
8 inches long
Overall Length: 9¼ inches with 4-inch barrel
Weight: 34 ounces with 4-inch barrel

Grips: Checkered walnut; optional and interchangeable
Sights: ⅛-inch serrated blade on front ramp; integral rear
with frame
Finish: Blue

MODELS 9 and 15

Calibers: Model 9—38 Special; Model 15—357 Magnum
Capacity: 6 rounds
Action: Double
Barrel Lengths: 2½, 4, 6 and 8 inches; Model 15 also
available with 10-, 12- and 15-inch barrels
Overall Length: 9¼ inches with 4-inch barrel
Weight: 36 ounces with 4-inch barrel
Grips: Checkered walnut; magna style; optional and
interchangeable
Sights: ⅛-inch serrated interchangeable blade front; click
graduated rear adjustable for windage and elevation
Finish: Blue
Additional Features: Wide tang trigger with overtravel
stop; wide-spur hammer with short double-action travel; for
sporting use

Rifles

American Arms

180 AUTO CARBINE

Caliber: 22 LR
Capacity: 177
Action: Automatic
Barrel Length: 16½ inches
Overall Length: 36 inches
Weight: 5¾ pounds
Stock: High-impact plastic stock and forend
Sights: Blade front; peep-type rear adjustable for windage and elevation
Additional Features: Available in selective fire version for law enforcement agencies; Laser-lok laser beam sight available at extra cost

Armalite

MODEL AR-180

Caliber: 223 (5.56mm)
Capacity: 5 rounds; 20- and 40-round magazines available
Actions: Automatic and semiautomatic
Barrel Length: 18½ inches
Overall Length: 38½ inches
Weight: 6½ pounds
Stock: Nylon folding rear stock; fiberglass forend
Sights: Post front adjustable for elevation; flip up "L"-type rear adjustable for windage and elevation
Finish: Black matte
Additional Features: Safety lever accessible from both sides of weapon; flash suppressor

Browning

HIGH-POWERED AUTO

Calibers: 243, 270, 30-06, 308
Capacity: 5 rounds with 4-round magazine
Action: Automatic
Barrel: Round and tapered; 22 inches long
Overall Length: 43 inches
Weight: 7⅜ pounds
Stock: French walnut; checkered pistol grip and forend
Sights: Hooded ramp front with gold bead; folding leaf rear
Finish: Blue
Additional Features: The receiver, made from one solid bar of steel, is tapped for scope mounts and is completely free of exposed screws, pins or holes; gold trigger on Grade IV model

MODEL BBR

Calibers: 25-06, 270, 30-06, 7mm Rem. Mag., 300 Win. Mag.
Capacities: 4 rounds with 3-round magazine in Mag. calibers; 6 rounds with 5-round magazine in all other calibers
Action: Bolt action
Barrel Length: 24 inches
Overall Length: 44½ inches
Weight: 8 pounds
Stock: American walnut with checkered grip and forend; anti-warp inlays of structural aluminum in barrel channel
Sights: None; clean barrel is drilled and tapped for scope mounts
Finish: Blue
Additional Features: Rotary-type bolt with nine engaging locking lugs and a recessed bolt face

**Browning
High-Powered Auto**

**Colt
AR-15 Sporter**

Rifles

Colt

CAR-15, Collapsible Stock

Caliber: 223 Remington (5.56mm)
Capacity: 5 rounds; 20-, 30- and 40-round magazines available
Action: Semiautomatic
Barrel Length: 16 inches
Overall Length: Stock extended—39 inches; folded—32 inches
Weight: 5.8 pounds
Stock: Nylon-coated aluminum stock and forend
Sights: Post front; rear adjustable for windage and elevation
Finish: Black military matte
Additional Features: Collapsible stock

R-15 SPORTER

Caliber: 223 Remington (5.56mm)
Capacity: 5 rounds; 20-, 30- and 40-round magazines available
Action: Semiautomatic
Barrel Length: 20 inches
Overall Length: 39 inches
Weight: 7.6 pounds with 20-round magazine
Stock: High-impact plastic stock and forend
Sights: Post front; rear adjustable for windage and elevation
Finish: Black military matte

Demro Products

MODEL XF-7

Calibers: 45 ACP and 9mm Parabellum
Capacities: 5 rounds; 15- and 30-round magazines available in 45; 32-round magazine available in 9mm
Actions: Automatic and semiautomatic
Barrel Length: Auto—10 inches; Semiauto—16⅞ inches
Overall Length: Auto, stock extended—30½ inches; folded—20 inches
Weight: Auto—7½ pounds
Stock: High-impact synthetic forearm and pistol grip; metal folding stock
Sights: Removable front blade; rear adjustable for windage and elevation
Finish: Black military matte
Additional Features: Delayed blowback firing system operates on an open bolt

Fabrique Nationale

F.N.-F.A.L. ASSAULT RIFLE

Caliber: 308 Winchester (7.62mm NATO)
Capacity: 20-round magazine
Actions: Automatic and semiautomatic
Barrel Length: 24½ inches
Overall Length: 44½ inches
Weight: 9½ pounds
Stock: Synthetic stock with ventilated forend
Sights: Fixed blade front adjustable rear
Finish: Black military matte
Additional Features: Trigger has three positions—automatic, semiautomatic and three-shot bursts

F.N.-F.A.L. PARATROOPER

Caliber: 308 Winchester (7.62mm NATO)
Capacity: 20-round magazine
Action: Automatic and semiautomatic
Barrel Length: 24.5 inches
Overall Length: 42.6 inches
Weight: 8.2 pounds
Stock: Skeleton folding stock
Sights: Fixed blade front; adjustable rear protected by wings on both sides
Finish: Black military matte
Additional Features: Trigger has three positions—automatic, semi-automatic and three-shot bursts

FNC PARATROOPER

Caliber: 223 (5.56mm)
Capacity: 30-round magazine
Action: Automatic and semiautomatic
Barrel Length: 18 inches
Overall Length: 45 inches
Weight: 8 pounds
Stock: Skeleton-type tube steel
Sights: Battle fixed ramp front with protective wings; rear adjustable for windage and elevation; protective wings on both sides
Finish: Black military matte
Additional Features: Uses same magazine as M-16; trigger has three positions—automatic, semiautomatic and three-shot bursts

Heckler & Koch

MODELS HK91 A-2 and A-3

Caliber: 308 Winchester (7.62mm NATO)
Capacity: 20-round magazine; 30- and 40-round magazines available
Actions: Automatic and semiautomatic
Barrel Length: 17.7 inches
Overall Lengths: A-2—40.35 inches; A-3—33.07 inches
Weight: Approximately 10 pounds
Stocks: High-impact black plastic on A-2; retractable metal on A-3
Sights: Fixed covered post front; rear aperture adjustable for windage and elevation
Finish: Black military matte

Rifles

Heckler & Koch
Model HK93

Heckler & Koch

MODELS HK93 A-2 and A-3

Caliber: 223 Remington (5.56mm)
Capacity: 25-round magazine
Actions: Automatic and semiautomatic
Barrel Length: 16.1 inches
Overall Lengths: A-2—37 inches; A-3—30 inches
Weights: A-2—7.9 pounds; A-3—8.6 pounds
Stocks: High-impact black plastic on A-2; retractable metal on A-3
Sights: Fixed covered post front; rear aperture adjustable for windage and elevation
Finish: Black military matte

Iver Johnson

PM 30P M1 CARBINE

Caliber: 30 M1
Capacity: 5 rounds; 15- and 30-round magazines available
Action: Semiautomatic
Barrel Length: 18 inches
Overall Length: Stock extended—35½ inches
Weight: 5½ pounds
Stock: American walnut
Sights: Blade aperture front with protective wings; adjustable for windage and elevation
Finish: Blue
Additional Features: Paratrooper stock; telescoping wire stock available

Remington

MODEL 700 ADL

Calibers: 22-250 Rem., 222 Rem., 243 Win., 270 Win., 6mm Rem., 25-06 Rem., 30-06, 308 Win.

Capacities: 7 rounds with 6-round magazine in 222 Rem.; 6 rounds with 5-round magazine in all other calibers
Action: Bolt action
Barrels: Round and tapered; 22 and 24 inches long
Overall Lengths: 41½ and 43½ inches
Weight: 7 pounds
Stock: Checkered walnut with RKW finish
Sights: Ramp front with gold bead; removable step adjustable rear with screw adjustment for windage
Finish: Blue
Additional Features: Side safety; receiver tapped for scope mounts

MODEL 700 BDL

Calibers: 222 Rem., 223 Rem., 22-250 Rem., 25-06 Rem., 243 Win., 6mm Rem., 308 Win.
Capacities: 7 rounds with 6-round magazine in 222 and 223 Rem.; 6 rounds with 5-round magazine in all other calibers
Action: Bolt action
Barrel: Heavy; 24 inches long
Overall Length: 43½ inches
Weight: 9 pounds
Stock: American walnut; Monte Carlo style with cheekpiece; custom checkering on grip and three sides of forend
Sights: None; fitted with Remington 40XB scope bases
Finish: Blue
Additional Features: Designed for maximum and minimum range precision shooting; hinged floorplate; quick release swivels and strap

MODEL 700 CLASSIC

Calibers: 22-250 Rem., 222 Rem., 243 Win., 270 Win., 6mm Rem., 25-06 Rem., 30-06, 308 Win.
Capacities: 6 rounds with 5-round magazine in 222 Rem.; 7 rounds with 6-round magazine in all other calibers
Action: Bolt action
Barrel Length: 24 inches

Rifles

Remington Model 700 BDL

Remington Model 700 Classic

Remington Model 7400

Overall Length: 43½ inches
Weight: 9 pounds
Stock: American walnut; Monte Carlo style with cheekpiece; custom checkering on grip and three sides of forend
Sights: Hooded ramp front with gold bead; removable step adjustments for windage and elevation
Finish: Blue
Additional Features: Side safety; receiver tapped for scope mounts; left-handed action in 270 Win. and 30-06 available

MODEL 7400

Calibers: 30-06 and 308 Winchester
Capacity: 5 rounds with 4-round magazine
Actions: Automatic and semiautomatic
Barrel Length: 24 inches
Overall Length: 42 inches
Weight: 7½ pounds
Stock: Walnut with fleur-de-lis checkering
Sights: Flat-faced gold bead on front ramp; step adjustable rear with windage adjustment screw

Finish: Blue
Additional Features: Receiver drilled and tapped for scope mounts; removable clip magazine; basket-weave checkering available

MODEL 7600

Calibers: 243 Win., 280 Rem., 6mm Rem., 30-06, 308 Win.
Capacity: 5 rounds with 4-round magazine
Action: Pump action
Barrel Length: 22 inches
Overall Length: 42 inches
Weight: 7½ pounds
Stock: Walnut with fleur-de-lis checkering
Sights: Blade on ramp front; step adjustable rear with windage adjustment screw
Finish: Blue
Additional Features: Receiver drilled and tapped for scope mounts; removable clip magazine; basket-weave checkering

Rifles

Ruger

MINI-14

Caliber: 223 Remington (5.56mm)
Capacity: 5 rounds; 10-, 20- and 30-round magazines available
Actions: Automatic and semiautomatic
Barrel Length: 18½ inches
Overall Length: 37½ inches
Weight: 6⅓ pounds
Stock: American hardwood; steel reinforced
Sights: Ramp front; rear adjustable for windage and elevation
Finishes: Blued steel and stainless steel
Additional Features: Paratrooper model available

AC-556 SELECTIVE FIRE AUTOMATIC

Caliber: 223 (5.56mm)
Capacity: 5 rounds; 20-, and 30-round magazines available
Actions: Automatic and semiautomatic
Barrel Length: 18½ inches
Overall Length: 37¼ inches
Weight: 6½ pounds
Stock: American walnut stock; heat-resistant ventilated fiberglass hand guard
Sights: Stud-type protected front; military rear adjustable for windage and elevation
Finishes: Blued steel and stainless steel
Additional Features: Fire mechanism consists of a positive three-position selector lever for automatic, semiautomatic and three-shot bursts; flash hider; military bayonet stud; fiberglass hand guard

AC-556F SELECTIVE FIRE AUTOMATIC

Caliber: 223 (5.56mm)
Capacity: 5 rounds; 20- and 30-round magazines available
Actions: Automatic and semiautomatic
Barrel Length: 13 inches
Overall Length: Stock folded—23¾ inches
Weight: 8 pounds
Stock: American walnut stock; heat-resistant ventilated fiberglass hand guard with blued steel folding stock
Sights: Stud-type protected front; military rear adjustable for windage and elevation
Finishes: Blued steel and stainless steel
Additional Features: Firing mechanism has the same positive three-position selector lever as the AC-556

MODEL 77R

Calibers: 22-250 Rem., 220 Swift, 243 Win., 6mm Rem., 308 Win.
Capacity: 6 rounds with 5-round magazine
Action: Bolt action
Barrels: Round and tapered; 24-inch length in 220 Swift; 22 inches in all other calibers
Overall Length: 42 inches with 24-inch barrel
Weight: 6¾ pounds
Stock: Hand-checkered American walnut
Sights: Ramp front with gold bead; folding leaf rear with adjustments for windage and elevation; optional scope mounts and rings available
Finish: Blue
Additional Features: Hinged floorplate; fully adjustable trigger; diagonal bedding system; integral scope mount bases

Ruger Mini-14

Ruger AC-556 Selective Fire Automatic

Rifles

Savage

110S SILHOUETTE RIFLE

Caliber: 308 Winchester
Capacity: 6 rounds with 5-round magazine
Action: Bolt action
Barrel: Heavy, tapered and free floating; 22 inches
Overall Length: 43 inches
Weight: 8½ pounds
Stock: Special silhouette stock of select walnut; high-fluted stippled grip and forend
Sights: None; receiver drilled and tapped for scope mounts
Finish: Blue
Additional Features: Receiver has satin blue finish to reduce glare; top tang safety available in right-handed action only

Sig

AMT AUTO RIFLE

Caliber: 308 Winchester
Capacity: 20-round magazine
Actions: Automatic and semiautomatic
Barrel Length: 18¾ inches
Overall Length: 39 inches
Weight: 9½ pounds
Stocks: Walnut stock and forend
Sights: Adjustable post front; adjustable aperture rear
Finish: Blue-black military matte
Additional Features: Right side cocking lever; loaded chamber indicator; no-tool takedown

Springfield Armory

MODEL BM-59

Caliber: 308 Winchester (7.62mm Nato)
Capacity: 5-, 10- and 20-round magazines
Action: Semiautomatic
Barrel Length: 25 1/16 inches with suppressor
Overall Length: 43½ inches
Weight: 9½ pounds
Stock: American walnut or birch with simulated walnut heat-resistant fiberglass hand guard; walnut hand guard available
Sights: Military square blade front; full click adjustable rear aperture
Finish: Parkerized
Additional Features: Commercial equivalent of U.S. M-14 service rifle; provisions for automatic fire

Steyr Mannlicher

MODEL M PROFESSIONAL

Calibers: 270 Winchester and 30-06 Springfield
Capacity: 5 rounds with 4-round magazine
Action: Bolt action
Barrel Length: 23.6 inches
Overall Length: 43 inches
Weight: 7.5 pounds
Stock: Synthetic ABS Cycolac
Sights: With or without iron sights
Finish: Parkerized
Additional Features: Barrel drilled and tapped for scope; choice of single or double triggers

**Ruger
AC-556F Selective Fire Automatic**

**Savage
110S Silhouette Rifle**

Rifles

**Winchester
Model 70 XTR**

Steyr Mannlicher

MODEL SMG

Caliber: 9mm Parabellum
Capacity: 25- and 32-round magazines
Actions: Automatic and semiautomatic
Barrel Length: 10.2 inches
Overall Lengths: Stock extended—24 inches, folded—18.3 inches
Weight: 6.5 pounds
Stock: Wire type; retractable
Sights: Blade front; diopter rear
Finish: Black military matte
Additional Features: Cyclic rate of fire is 550 rounds per minute

SSG MARKSMAN

Caliber: 308 Winchester
Capacity: 5 rounds; 10-round magazine available
Action: Bolt action
Barrel Length: 25.6 inches
Overall Length: 44.5 inches
Weight: 8.6 pounds
Stock: Synthetic Cycolac or walnut
Sights: Hooded blade front; folding leaf rear
Finish: Parkerized
Additional Features: Removable spacers in butt section adjust weapon from 12 to 14 inches; available with Startron night scope or Kahles scope

Universal

1003 AUTOLOADING CARBINE

Caliber: 30 M1
Capacity: 5-, 15- and 30-round magazines
Action: Automatic
Barrel Length: 18 inches
Overall Length: 35½ inches
Weight: 5½ pounds
Stock: American walnut inletted for issue sling and oiler
Sights: Blade military-type front with protective wings; rear adjustable for windage and elevation
Finish: Blue
Additional Features: Receiver tapped for scope mounts

Winchester

MODEL 70 XTR

Calibers: 222 Rem., 243 Win., 7mm Rem. Mag., 30-06, 308 Win.
Capacities: 4 rounds with 3-round magazine in 7mm Rem. Mag., 6 rounds with 5-round magazine in all other calibers
Action: Bolt action
Barrel Lengths: 222 Rem., 30-06 and 308 Win.—22 inches; all other calibers—24 inches
Overall Lengths: 222 Rem.—42½ inches; all other calibers—44¼ inches
Weight: 7½ pounds
Stock: American walnut; kiln dried, sized and turned; real cut checkering; all-weather and wear-resistant finish
Sights: Hooded ramp front; leaf-style rear with adjustments for windage and elevation; optional scope mounts and rings
Finishes: Blue and black matte
Additional Features: Exclusive three-position safety; wide serrated trigger; detachable sling swivels; special matte finish on receiver to reduce glare

Shotguns

FIE

BRUTE

Calibers: 12, 20 and .410 gauge
Capacity: 2 rounds
Type: Double barrel
Barrel Length: 19 inches
Overall Length: 30 inches
Weight: 5⅛ pounds
Stock: Walnut stock and forend
Sights: None
Finish: Blue
Additional Features: Manufacturer recommends that the weapon be fired from the waist and hip, not near the face

Ithaca

MAG 10 ROADBLOCKER

Caliber: 10 gauge
Capacity: 4 rounds with 3-round magazine
Type: Automatic action
Barrel Length: 22 inches
Overall Length: 42 inches
Weight: 11¼ pounds
Stock: American walnut; checkered grip and forend
Sights: Optional; rifle sights or front bead
Finish: Blue matte
Additional Features: Piston, cylinder, bolt, charging lever, action release and carrier made of stainless steel; low recoil force; countercoil gas action

37 M&P

Caliber: 12 gauge
Capacity: 5 rounds with 4-round magazine; 8 rounds with 7-round magazine
Type: Pump action
Barrel Length: 20 inches
Overall Length: 39¾ inches
Weight: 7¼ pounds
Stock: Oil-finished walnut
Sights: Brass bead front
Finishes: Standard commercial and satin chrome
Additional Features: Interior metal parts are parkerized; external parts are parkerized and sandblasted

37 M&P with pistol grip

Caliber: 12 gauge
Capacities: 5 rounds with 4-round magazine; 8 rounds with 7-round magazine
Type: Pump action
Barrel Lengths: 18 and 20 inches
Weight: 6½ pounds
Stock: Oil-finished wood forearm; high-impact nylon pistol grip
Sights: Steel bead front
Finishes: Parkerized and matte chrome
Additional Features: Sling swivels and nylon web sling

Ithaca 37 M&P

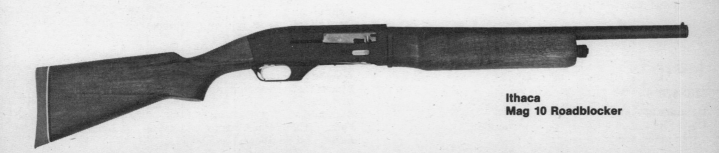

Ithaca Mag 10 Roadblocker

Shotguns

**Ithaca
37DS Police Special**

**Laser
LPC 87S**

**Laser
LPC 87P**

Ithaca

37DS POLICE SPECIAL

Caliber: 12 gauge
Capacities: 5 rounds with 4-round magazine; 8 rounds with 7-round magazine
Type: Pump action
Barrel Length: 20 inches
Overall Length: 40 inches
Weight: 7¼ pounds
Stock: Walnut
Sights: Rifle sights
Finishes: Standard commercial and satin chrome
Additional Features: Interior metal parts are parkerized, external parts are parkerized and sandblasted

Laser

LPC 87P

Caliber: 12 gauge
Capacity: 5 rounds with 4-round magazine
Type: Pump action

Barrel Length: 18 inches; 12½ inches on special law enforcement order
Overall Length: 30 inches; 24½ inches on special order
Weight: 7¼ pounds
Stock: Oil-finished wood forearm; high-impact nylon pistol grip
Sights: Steel bead front
Finish: Black military matte
Additional Features: Weapon is built on the Remington 870 and is specially equipped with a laser aiming device that pinpoints a target at night; batteries are in extended pistol grip

LPC 87S

Caliber: 12 gauge
Capacity: 5 rounds with 4-round magazine
Type: Pump action
Barrel Length: 20 inches
Overall Length: 41 inches
Weight: 9¼ pounds
Stock: Oil-finished wood forearm; high-impact plastic nylon rear stock
Sights: Blade front; folding leaf rear
Finish: Black military matte
Additional Features: Same as LPC 87P

Shotguns

Marlin

120 MAGNUM

Caliber: 12 gauge; 2¾- and 3-inch shells
Capacities: 2¾-inch shells—6 rounds with 5-round magazine; 3-inch shells—4 rounds with 3-round magazine
Type: Pump action
Barrel Length: 20 inches
Overall Length: 40½ inches
Weight: 7¾ pounds
Stock: Checkered American walnut stock and forend
Sights: Rifle sights; adjustable rear drilled and tapped for scope mounts
Finish: Blue
Additional Features: Steel receiver; matte finish on top of receiver to reduce glare

Mossberg

500 ATP-6 and 500 ATP-6S

Caliber: 12 gauge
Capacity: 6 rounds with 5-round magazine; 1 round less with 3-inch shells
Type: Pump action
Barrel Length: 18½ inches
Overall Length: 37¾ inches
Weight: 6¾ pounds
Stock: Stained walnut stock and forend
Sights: ATP-6—none; ATP-6S—rifle sights
Finishes: Blue
Additional Features: Factory-installed sling swivels

500 ATP-8 and 500 ATP-8S

Caliber: 12 gauge
Capacity: 8 rounds with 7-round magazine; 1 round less with 3-inch shells
Type: Pump action
Barrel Length: 20 inches
Overall Length: 39¾ inches
Weight: 7 pounds
Stock: Stained walnut stock and forend
Sights: ATP-8—none; ATP-8S—rifle sights
Finish: Blue
Additional Features: Factory-installed sling swivels

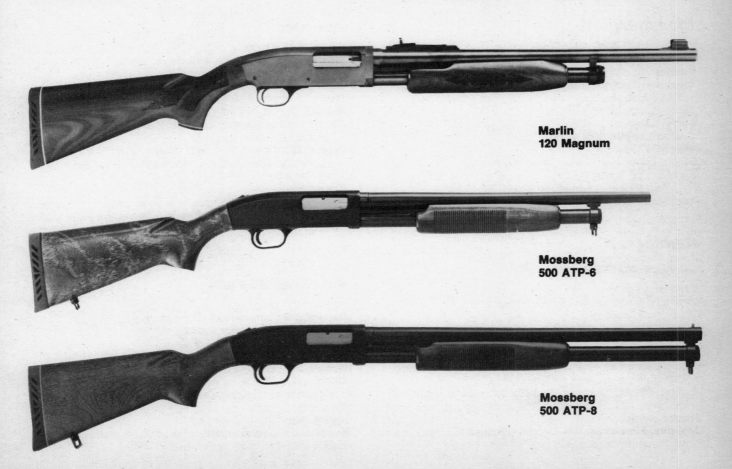

Marlin 120 Magnum

Mossberg 500 ATP-6

Mossberg 500 ATP-8

Shotguns

**Mossberg
500 ATP-8SP
Special Defense Enforcement**

**Remington
870 Brushmaster**

Mossberg

500 ATP-8SP SPECIAL DEFENSE ENFORCEMENT

Caliber: 12 gauge
Capacity: 8 rounds with 7-round magazine; 1 round less
  with 3-inch shells
Type: Pump action
Barrel Length: 20 inches
Overall Length: 39¾ inches
Weight: 7 pounds
Stock: Oil-finished walnut stock and forend
Sights: Rifle sights
Finishes: Blue and parkerized
Additional Features: Equipped with accessory lug

Remington

870 BRUSHMASTER

Caliber: 12 gauge
Capacity: 5 rounds with 4-round magazine
Type: Pump action
Barrel Length: 20 inches
Overall Length: 40½ inches
Weight: 7 pounds
Stock: Lacquered American walnut; checkered grip and
  forend; finger grooves on forend
Sights: Rifle sights; rear adjustable for windage and
  elevation
Finish: Blue
Additional Features: Top of receiver matted to reduce glare;
  solid steel construction

870 POLICE

Caliber: 12 gauge
Capacity: 5 rounds with 4-round magazine
Type: Pump action
Barrel Lengths: 18 and 20 inches
Overall Length: 40½ inches with 20-inch barrel
Weight: 7½ pounds with 20-inch barrel
Stock: Lacquered American walnut with lateral and
  vertical grooves
Sights: Metal bead front with 18-inch barrel; rifle
  sights with 20-inch barrel; rear adjustable for windage
  and elevation
Finish: Blue
Additional Features: Barrels interchangeable with special
  tools; 7- and 8-shot magazine extensions available; folding
  stock available at extra cost

MODEL 1100 DEER GUN

Caliber: 12 gauge
Capacity: 5 rounds with 4-round magazine
Type: Gas-operated autoloading
Barrel Length: 22 inches
Overall Length: 42½ inches
Weight: 7¼ pounds
Stock: Lacquered American walnut; checkered grip and
  forend; finger grooves on forend
Sights: Rifle sights, rear adjustable for windage and elevation
Finish: Blue
Additional Features: Choked for both rifled slugs and buck
  shot

Shotguns

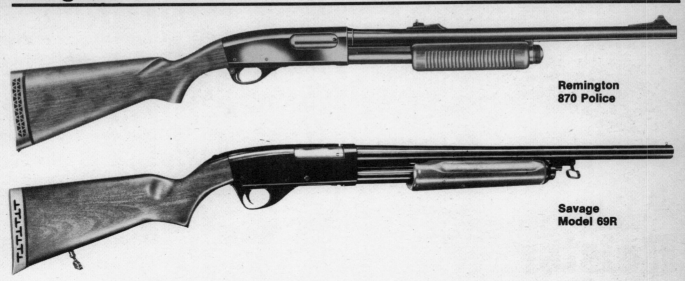

Remington 870 Police

Savage Model 69R

Savage

30 SLUG GUN

Caliber: 12 gauge; 2¾- and 3-inch shells
Capacity: 5 rounds with 4-round magazine
Type: Pump action
Barrel Length: 21 inches
Overall Length: 40½ inches
Weight: 7¼ pounds
Stock: Commercial-finished walnut; checkered grip; finger grooves on forend
Sights: Rifle sights
Finish: Blue

MODEL 69R

Caliber: 12 gauge
Capacity: 5 rounds with 4-round magazine
Type: Pump action
Barrel Length: 20 inches
Overall Length: 40 inches
Weight: 6¾ pounds
Stock: Walnut-finished hardwood stock and forend
Sights: White-finished metal bead front
Finish: Blue
Additional Features: Full pistol grip; finger grooves on forend; steel frame

MODEL 69-RXL

Caliber: 12 gauge
Capacity: 7 rounds with 6-round magazine
Type: Pump action
Barrel Length: 18¼ inches
Overall Length: 38¼ inches
Weight: 6¼ pounds

Stock: Walnut-finished hardwood stock and forend
Sights: White-finished metal bead front
Finish: Blue
Additional Features: Steel frame

Savage-Stevens

MODEL 311-R

Caliber: 12 gauge
Capacity: 2 rounds
Type: Double barrel
Barrel Length: 20 inches
Overall Length: 35¾ inches
Weight: 6¾ pounds
Stock: Walnut-finished hardwood stock and forend
Sights: White-finished metal bead front
Finish: Blue
Additional Features: Double triggers; hammerless lockup with coil springs; fast hammer fall and positive extraction

Winchester

1200 DEFENSE GUN

Caliber: 12 gauge
Capacity: 5 rounds with 4-round magazine
Type: Pump action
Barrel Length: 18 inches
Overall Length: 38⅝ inches
Weight: 6 pounds
Stock: American walnut; checkered forend
Sights: Metal bead front
Finish: Black matte
Additional Features: Receiver is rustproof aluminum; twin action slide bars provide action without binding

A Holster For Every Need

Not all law enforcement officials who carry handguns use holsters to secure them. Many incorrectly carry a semiautomatic pistol by tucking it in their jacket pocket, waistband or pants pocket when in plain clothes. This method of securing a weapon invites accidental loss of the weapon, which could be particularly dangerous when chasing a felon; and accidental discharge, a result of the repositioning of the improperly secured weapon.

Holsters, like handguns, are manufactured in various styles for various purposes, and certain guidelines should be followed when choosing them. Selection of a holster should be made by first considering the frame size and caliber of your weapon—whether it is your on-duty issue or your own off-duty gun. Second, the holster should fit your weapon and hold it in a position so it can be carried comfortably and not inter-fere with your normal activity. Third, your holster should be the best one available for your weapon, that is, it should be well constructed and made of durable materials.

Holsters for Uniformed Officers. The holster used by a uniformed officer is totally different from the type needed to conceal the weapon of an off-duty or plain-clothes officer. This is especially true if the uniformed officer is issued a six-inch barreled revolver. If the officer is assigned to patrol-car duty, the weapon should be carried in a swivel-type rig. This allows the holster to be rotated into position along the officer's leg so the butt of the weapon does not jam into the officer's rib cage while driving his patrol vehicle. When the officer leaves the vehicle, the holster automatically swivels back into an easily accessible position.

Mandatory use of a swivel holster does not mean an officer has a small selection from which to choose. On the contrary, this type of rig is produced by many holster manufacturers in numerous styles, such as front break, clam shell and thumb break. A patrol-car officer who carries a four-inch barreled weapon could use either a swivel-type rig or a high-ride, front-break holster. In contrast, a foot-patrol or motorcycle officer could use any type of uniform holster on the market—swivel, clam shell, front break, cross draw, canted border patrol or belt side.

Some departments, such as the Connecticut State Police, who are strictly motor-patrol officers, carry their weapons in a cross-draw fashion. Although there is great debate as to the value of carrying a weapon in this position, several manufacturers, for example, Bianchi, Jack-ass and Roy's Custom Leather (Baker), all produce excellent equip-

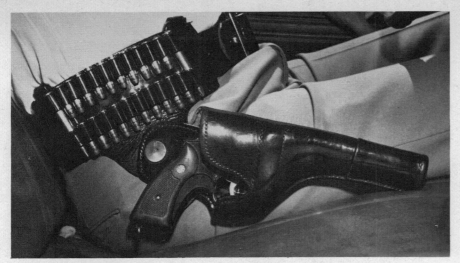

A uniformed officer on patrol, carrying a six-inch barreled weapon in a Jay-Pee swivel holster. Note that the weapon is secured by a clip that fits inside the trigger guard.

ment designed for officers who prefer this style. In fact, these manufacturers, and others, produce exceptionally fine pancake and high-ride holsters that can be worn on either side of the body in an easily concealable position.

The oldest and perhaps the most secure method of carrying a handgun is in a belt holster, whether it is worn on the officer's gun-hand side, cross draw or inside the pants. The FBI is the police agency perhaps most famous for carrying its four-inch barreled revolvers in a strong-side, high-ride belt holster, with the grip canted forward.

Holsters for Plainclothes Officers.

The plainclothes officer has different needs: he must choose a weapon and holster for concealability and easy access. The trend today is toward custom shoulder rigs produced by such firms as Bianchi, Alessi, Rogers and Safariland. In addition, many companies are producing different styles of leg and ankle holsters that are extremely popular, especially during the warm weather months when jackets are usually not worn.

Shoulder Holsters.

Off-the-shelf shoulder holsters are available from many manufacturers for all popular large-frame handguns. Bianchi and Safariland, the two leaders in these types of rigs, manufacture old standby models that are made for semiautos as well as revolvers. With models such as Bianchi's X-15 and X-2100 and Safariland's Model 101, the holster must be anchored to the wearer's belt to hold the weapon firmly. Another well-made, popular model that is secured in the same manner is the Brauer Brothers' Model K. Because today's fashionable trousers for men often do not have belt loops, this design is sometimes a problem; nonetheless, these holsters are frequently the first choice by law enforcement officers who carry large-frame handguns.

For small-frame revolvers and automatics, there is a wide variety of rigs on the market: the Bianchi Model 9-R, the Smith & Wesson Model 03 and the Bucheimer Model 600, to name a few. These three models hold the weapon in an upside-down position. Other types of shoulder rigs, such as the Hoyt Models 101 and 101A, feature front-break holsters that position the weapon low on the wearer's side and secure it to his belt. Unlike the Bianchi, Smith & Wesson and Bucheimer models, the Hoyt rigs are among the new breed of shoulder holsters that contain an extra cartridge and handcuff holder under the armpit opposite the weapon.

Big favorites among federal agents and plainclothes officers are custom-made by manufacturers such as Rogers and Alessi, whose holsters contain extra ammo and cuffs but don't have to be anchored. This concept serves a dual purpose: it gives the wearer extra ammo in an easily accessible place; and it adds weight to the weaponless side of the rig, providing better balance. As an added advantage of having all equipment attached to one rig, the odds are against a plainclothes officer taking

Shoulder rig Model X-15 by Bianchi for large-frame autos.

A common but incorrect and potentially dangerous method for plainclothes officers to carry their weapons.

his gun with him and forgetting extra ammo or cuffs. The shoulder straps on the Rogers rig are thin and designed with Velcro so they are easy to adjust for concealment and comfort. The shoulder straps of the Alessi rig are made of wide, soft elk hide which, together with the rig's balanced weight, allow the holster to be worn during an entire tour of duty without discomfort. With this rig, the

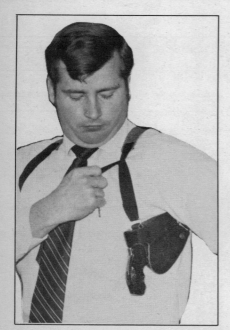

This shoulder holster by Rogers features Velcro and leather strip shoulder straps to hold the weapon secure.

officer also gets a custom-fitted holster for his particular weapon, which eliminates any possible movement of the weapon.

Today's female police officers like to carry their off-duty or plainclothes weapons in shoulder rigs like their brother officers, but conventional off-the-shelf shoulder rigs do not position the weapon correctly for the average female body. They are not contoured for the female breast outline and bulges can be seen. This problem is alleviated with custom rigs that can be adjusted so the portion of the holster and weapon on the front of the wearer's body fit snuggly, hug the body and stay concealed.

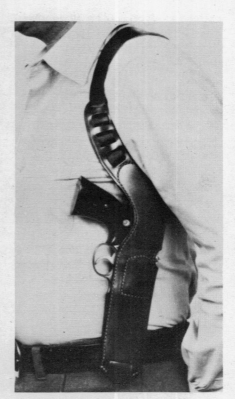

Bianchi shoulder rig Model X-2100 for large-frame revolvers, fastened to the wearer's belt.

It is important for the male or female officer who wears a shoulder rig to make sure that any shirt or blouse pockets are kept empty.

This Alessi shoulder rig is one of the few that can be adjusted to fit the contour of the female form.

Should the need arise to draw the weapon, a pocket not flush against the body could cause the weapon's sights or hammer to become snagged.

Ankle Holsters. Little was heard about the ankle holster until Popeye Doyle used one in the 1973 movie, *The French Connection*. That exposure, along with the popularity of men's flair pants, made the ankle holster a natural. Today, ankle holsters are rapidly growing in demand and the vast majority of detectives and federal agents own one type or another to conceal a backup gun or to use during the hot summer months. Uniformed officers are caught up in the same trend and use ankle holsters off duty for the same reasons.

If a gun is to be worn in an ankle holster, it should be kept out of sight by observing the following: 1) have the trousers legs lengthened slightly because they will ride up when you sit; 2) take care not to cross your legs when seated, because the trousers will ride up even more, exposing the holster; 3) strap the holster on the inside of the leg opposite your gun hand; and 4) do not wear ankle holsters with straight-leg trousers—the outline of the gun will be visible.

To conceal the weapon, ankle holsters must be properly designed to grip the wearer's ankle. Most of the models available keep the weapon secure by means of a safety strap that crosses under or behind the hammer. These safety straps are held by either a button snap or Velcro fastener. The Velcro method is probably the better of the two, because the ring inside the button snap has a tendency to expand slightly with use. This may cause the snap to open without the wearer realizing it and the weapon could be lost.

A De Santis ankle holster fitted for a custom Asp automatic.

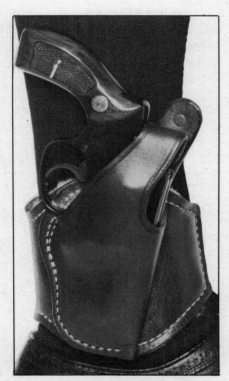

This Bianchi ankle holster uses a snap to keep the safety strap secured.

As with shoulder rigs, fitting female officers with ankle holsters designed for mén poses some problems. Models held in place by either leather straps with buckles or Velcro fit loosely on the female ankle, even when fastened in the tightest position. This is not to say the holster will fall off but, again, any slippage of the holster would betray the fact that the officer is carrying a gun. Major manufacturers have recently turned their attention to sizing ankle holsters for females, but until they are marketed, most female officers will remain unable to wear ankle holsters with complete comfort and confidence and will run the risk of having them noticed.

Leg Holsters. The leg holster is fast becoming the rival to the ankle holster in popularity. A relatively recent development, the leg holster is made from two strips of leather or two pieces of elastic material fastened together by snaps or Velcro, with the holster positioned somewhere in between.

The rules for wearing and hiding an ankle holster also apply to the leg holster; and it must fit the wearer correctly and hold the weapon securely in place. A law enforcement officer chasing a suspect may need to run several blocks, climb a few flights of stairs or even jump a fence. An improperly fitted holster could cause the weapon to fall out or become lost. Even worse, it could cost the officer his life. A weapon carried in either a leg or ankle holster should be worn often so the wearer

becomes accustomed to the added weight and learns to walk without favoring the leg holding the gun. It is essential that the wearer practice drawing his weapon from these unconventional holsters so the motion becomes second nature. While most leg holsters are made of leather, Safariland uses a skin-like material that is wrapped around the wearer's leg and is secured by a zipper which runs down the holster's entire length. The pouch-type holster is then secured in place by strips of Velcro. The other popular

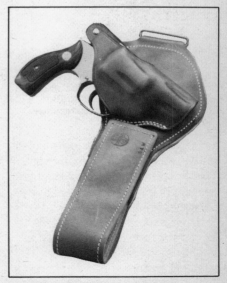

The holster on this Cobra Gunskin ankle rig is custom made for the S & W Model 36.

models of leg and ankle rigs are manufactured by Alessi, Bianchi, Jackass and Jay-Pee.

Offbeat Holsters. Some manufacturers have broken out of more traditional molds and devised unique holsters to meet the ever-changing needs of law enforcement. Bianchi, a company whose name is synonymous with high-grade holsters, offers the Scorpion, a shoulder rig that can be used as a one- or two-gun system. The weapon is held horizontally and is secured by metal thumb snaps. The harness has a two-inch-wide elastic strap that fits across the shoulders and another two-inch-wide strap that extends across the upper back so the weight of the rig is distributed evenly for comfort.

Boot holster by Seldeen Leathersmiths made specifically for the Smith & Wesson Model 36. Here the weapon is pictured with Rogers' molded grip.

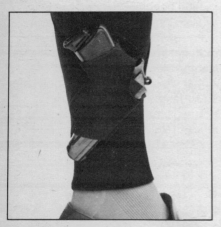

This unique leg holster by Safariland features a skinlike material that extends around the wearer's leg. The holster is held on by a Velcro fastener.

Cobra Gunskin, a custom holster maker, has designed the Comvest. This shoulder rig features a double harness of burnished calfskin that can be easily adjusted to any size. The holster is custom-molded with a sight track to fit each weapon; it is double reinforced with saddle stitching and has a silicone suede lining. The rig is very comfortable because of the double-thick elk hide straps that extend over the wearer's

shoulders. This holster is available for both automatics and revolvers.

Among the holsters produced by the De Santis Holster and Leather Company is its Shellhammer Model 3. This high-ride, strong-side holster features a unique six-cartridge holder attached with Velcro to a leather extension that runs along the wearer's belt from the holster.

De Santis also offers a different twist for officers who like to carry a large-frame gun in a shoulder rig—the Model 8 swivel shoulder rig. In this pivoting holster, the weapon is held securely and upright by a positive snap device. When the device is released, the butt of the gun tilts down and can be drawn. This rig has been adopted by numerous SWAT teams across the country. The manufacturer also has an attachment for its shoulder rigs that permits an officer to carry a portable radio in an upside-down position under the armpit opposite his weapon.

The Fury Leather Company believes it has improved upon some of the features associated with a good shoulder holster: conceal-

ment, comfort, quick release and a safely secured weapon. In its horizontal holster, the gun is held in place by means of a Velcro holster strap, and the wide shoulder strap has a strip of foam rubber between the wearer's shoulder and the leather. This provides a cushion for the weight of the weapon and also prevents slippage. The rig is secured by means of a heavy elastic strip that fits across the wearer's back and fastens to his belt or belt loop. The leather is double stitched and riveted at stress points.

Although boots are so prevalent in today's world of fashion, most holster manufacturers have overlooked the problems this footwear presents to law enforcement officers who like to carry off-duty guns on their legs. Seldeen Leathersmiths, however, has designed a boot holster specifically for the Smith & Wesson Model 36. Available through mail order, the holster comes with a kit consisting of several pieces of Velcro and a tube of glue for attaching the Velcro to the boot. With very little time and effort on your part, the holster will fit com-

Cobra also produces a nylon shotgun sling designed for use by SWAT teams and is equipped to hold 15 extra shotgun shells.

Holsters come in all types, shapes and sizes to meet various law enforcement needs: mini-holsters—(A) for large automatics and (B) for small-frame revolvers by 4-D Marketing and Development Company; (C) belt holsters, like this Shellhammer model by De Santis, with its uniquely attached cartridge holder; and hi-ride models, such as (D) Cobra Gunskin's Stingray which is made for large-frame autos and (E) Alessi's custom model made for Hi-Power 9mms.

fortably inside your boot. Seldeen also offers a unique belt holster for a large-frame, single-action automatic: the weapon is held in the holster with no round in the chamber, but while drawing the gun, the holster activates the slide and chambers a round.

Safariland has an unusual holster: a beautifully styled vest made of washable nylon and cotton polyester. The holster is made with a cuff pocket and ammo pouch and can be specifically ordered to fit Colt or S&W two-inch revolvers or any medium-frame automatic. In addition, the vest is constructed so that

holsters for different weapons are interchangeable. The vest, with accessories, is available in sizes small, medium, large and extra large. Safariland is also working on holsters made of plastic which will be marketed in the near future.

Smith & Wesson has designed an ankle holster—the Model 28, which differs from others in that it rides just above the ankle, almost to the point of being a leg holster. The holster is held in place by one wide strip of Velcro which wraps around the wearer's leg.

Top-Line and A&B Industries have produced nylon holsters and

carrying pouches for cuffs, ammo and portable radios which they claim are unsurpassed in comfort and wearability. They are made from nine-ounce nylon, have a double-moisture barrier and are coated with polyurethane, which virtually eliminates rusting. Available are shoulder and belt holsters for medium- and large-frame weapons, and ankle and leg holsters for small-frame guns. The holsters and accessory pouches are held secure by means of Velcro strips.

The 4-D Marketing and Development company has its Mini-Holster for wear inside the pants. The

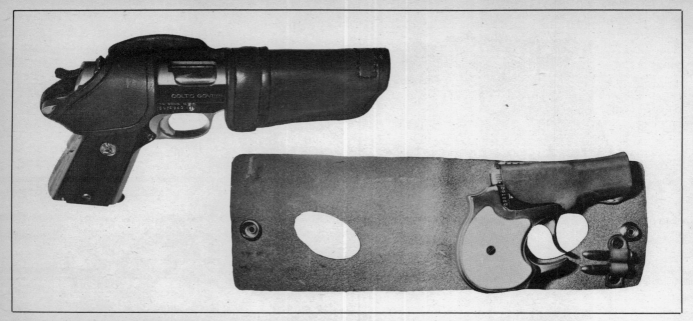

In Seldeen Leathersmith's rig for single-action automatics (left), the weapon can be loaded and cocked while still in the holster. Similarly, the Wallat holster (right) by Jackass Leather fits into the wearer's back pocket when folded in half; the opening in the holster permits the weapon, here a High Standard 22 Magnum derringer, to be fired without opening the wallet.

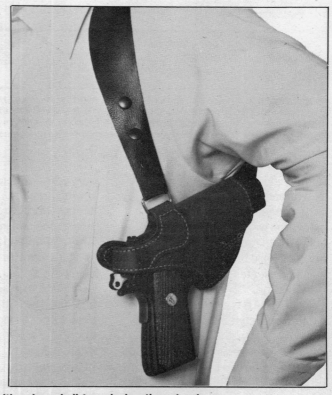

Two models by Bianchi: one rig (left) holds the weapon upside down with a clam-shell-type design; the cut-outs allow it to be slipped through a belt and worn at the waist. The Scorpion model (right) holds large-frame autos such as this Colt Commander, which is being carried cocked; note how the wearer's shirt pocket is empty and flush against the body.

holster is designed to carry a pistol or revolver inside the trouser waistband without the usual bulk of a conventional holster. The rig is held outside the trousers by a clip that fits over the waistband, so it can be used with beltless trousers. The Mini-Holster comes in two models, one for small-frame revolvers and one for large-frame semiautos; each is constructed from a material called Inmont Porvair, reported to outwear leather. An ammo drop pouch of the same material allows ammunition to be carried or stored over a long period of time without the traditional worry of leather-induced corrosion forming on the cartridge casings.

Guidelines for Purchasing.

Whether you are considering a production line, off-the-shelf job or a custom rig, first think about your

The Smith & Wesson Model 28 is the only ankle holster designed to be worn above the ankle. Compared to conventional ankle holsters, this allows for a longer holster that can hold a larger frame revolver.

The proper way to carry a weapon inside the waistband. This inside pants holster by Alessi does a nice job of hiding an S & W Model 59.

duty assignment and try to envision job situations that would necessitate your using a handgun. If, for example, you are considering a combat speed holster, remember that the holster should have as little leather covering the weapon as is practical. The grip of the weapon should be exposed so that, when necessary, the officer can make the proper contact. If he has to make a grip adjustment while drawing, his speed and hitting accuracy will be hindered.

Once the uses for a weapon are established and you have determined what type of holster you will carry, concentrate on holster construction. This begins with top-grade quality leather. The leather should be form-fitted to the weapon it will hold, yet should be pliable. If the leather appears to be thin and rigid—like cardboard—chances are it will not stand up to heavy-duty use and will probably crack. Check the holster stitching very carefully to be sure it is strong enough to withstand the weapon's constant pressure. Inspect the seams to see if they are all sewn tightly and inquire as to the type of thread used. Nylon thread is

the best because it is at least 20 times stronger than an equivalent thickness of linen thread. In some of the more expensive holsters, the thread is coated with a lubricant to prevent it from drying out and splitting.

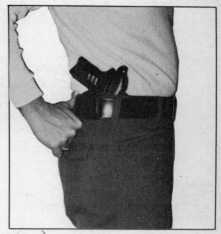

De Santis' inside-the-pants belt holster for small-frame autos completely hides the contour of the weapon.

As an added precaution, look over the safety straps on the thumb break holsters. Velcro straps are the best and safest, but if you prefer button snaps, check the side of the snap that makes contact with your weapon to make sure it is covered. This covering will protect the finish of the weapon and will also eliminate the possibility of the snap snagging on the weapon's sight or hammer when it is drawn.

Ultimately, keep in mind that holsters, like guns, are obtainable in cheap and expensive models. Be smart and buy the better model; there is no such thing as a good cheap holster. The wrong choice of a holster by someone in law enforcement could literally mean life or death. The extra years of wear and service you'll get from the better holster will more than compensate for the extra money you'll spend for the initial purchase.

Police Body Armor

In March 1974, the Law Enforcement Assistance Administration (LEAA), then part of the Department of Justice, requested the U.S. Army Biomedical Laboratory (ABL) in Maryland to develop body armor for use by law enforcement officers.

The LEAA specified that the armor had to be lightweight, inconspicuous and comfortable, and give law enforcement personnel good protection during surprise assaults and face-to-face confrontations with handgun-armed persons. In addition, the armor material was to be suitable for use as an undershirt, sport coat or as the inner lining of a raincoat, tunic or raid jacket and be durable and inexpensive to maintain.

The materials tested by laboratory researchers were Du Pont's Hi-Tenacity Nylon, Nylon Felt, Hi-Tenacity Rayon, Kevlar 29 and Kevlar 49; Union Carbide's Thornel Graphite Yarn; and Stackpol Monsanto's X-55 Fiber and X-500 Felt. After 12 months of testing, the results showed the only material that met all the requirements was DuPont's Kevlar 29.

Because efforts to prevent projectile penetration were important, an assessment of weapons injuries to law enforcement officers at the time of the ABL testing showed that in 80 percent of injuries, the 38 Special cartridge was used. The researchers tested the 38 Special projectile, which traveled at 800 fps, and the 22 Long Rifle projectile, which traveled at 1110 fps. To prevent penetration from both projectiles, only seven layers of 400/2 denier Kevlar 29 were necessary. Although the protection level of the vests could be raised to stop 9mm and 357 Magnum caliber projectiles, such stopping capabilities made the armor less lightweight and comfortable when worn for extended periods of time.

Additional data was obtained from the Maryland Institute for Emergency Medicine to ascertain the amounts of trauma received by the body of a person wearing body armor when struck by a projectile. Results indicated that the trauma levels for an officer wearing seven layers of 400/2 Kevlar 29 when struck with a 38 Special or 22 Long Rifle projectile were acceptable.

Finally, researchers, curious to know the stopping power of Kevlar 29 against the threat of a knife attack, ran a set of tests using a M-16 bayonet, a switchblade knife with a four-inch blade, a butcher-knife with a ten-inch blade and an ice pick. Only the ice pick pene-

LOCATION OF FATAL FIREARMS WOUNDS

Head: 38

Torso: 59

Below Waist: 3

Total: 100

According to FBI Uniform Crime Report figures, of the 100 fatal firearms wounds inflicted to police officers in 1979, almost 60 percent hit the torso area —ample justification for requiring body armor for on-duty use.

velocity projectiles, and soft-material armor (nylon) for stopping shrapnel. These protective armors were eventually modified for law enforcement so they were less conspicuous and cumbersome and more suitable for everyday use.

Since 1974, however, many new types of body armor constructed almost exclusively of Kevlar have come onto the marketplace. New scientific knowledge has been obtained from the protective armor development efforts of the Department of Justice, and intense competition has arisen among body armor manufacturers. New body armor configurations have been developed; some are made of 1,000 deniers of Kevlar 29, while others are of several layers of laminated or coated Kevlar 29. These variations are all created with one goal in mind: to produce a superior product that can save the lives of law enforcement officers.

While some form of defense is better than none, this large-frame detective is only partially protected. His armor is improperly fitted, leaving vulnerable the major arteries that run across his chest, as well as other vital areas.

trated the Kevlar 29.

The tests also suggested an almost endless list of law enforcement-related uses for Kevlar 29: for example, in emergency ropes, ladders and stretchers, embassy curtains, armored car door panels and protective panels to shield airline flight crews from hijackers.

Until the time of the ABL research and the widespread use of Kevlar, body armor had primarily been developed for and used by the military. Military armor was of two general types: various hard-faced armor (steel or ceramic) for stopping high-

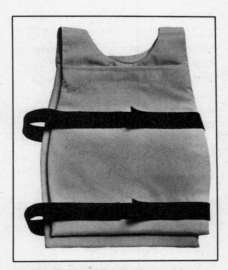

Burlington Industries produces this Model-7800, which only partially protects the wearer due to its reduced size. It weighs only about four pounds and will stop both the 9mm and 357 caliber projectiles.

Now, soft body armor has reached the technological level where it can be produced to stop almost all

handgun projectiles, at the same time allowing the wearer to continue to function with little hindrance.

With ever-increasing numbers of shootouts, ambushes and assaults against law enforcement personnel across the country, body armor has become standard equipment for the police officer. In fact, in many areas of the country, police officers are issued and are required to wear body armor while on duty. This new policy is, in part, a positive reaction to the annual statistics released by the FBI Uniform Crime Reports, which in recent years have indicated a rise in the murders of law enforcement officers. During the past five years, for instance, 500 law enforcement officers have been killed in the line of duty, while nearly 100,000 more have received injuries. In 1979 alone, of the 106 officers who died in the line of duty, 94 percent were killed by firearms. Of that percentage, 59 officers suffered fatal wounds in the torso area which would have been protected had the officers been wearing body armor.

No single vest protects against all calibers at all distances; such a vest would be too heavy and impractical for everyday use. Most soft body armor, however, is designed and tested to protect the wearer at about 9 to 10 feet or more from a specified caliber weapon. (According to the FBI, the average gun battle occurs at about seven feet.)

This armor by Safariland is equipped with long panels, so it can be tucked into the wearer's trousers and keep a flat contour.

To find the thickness of Kevlar that should be worn, law enforcement officers should first consult their departments' firearms instructor or county prosecutor's office and check the statistics on calibers of weapons confiscated from criminals in the area. They should also consider the caliber of weapon issued

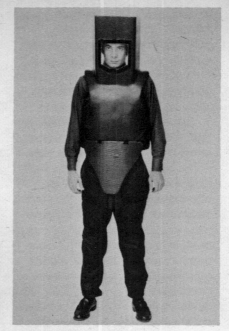

Protective Materials Company manufactures this lightweight suit for professional bomb handlers. It protects the wearer's vital organs and major arteries, while allowing complete mobility.

by their departments, because more frequently law enforcement officers are being killed with their own weapons, with the guns their assailants seize from them. By taking these factors into account, officers can determine the minimum threat they can expect to face while on duty.

For basic protection against the most-often-used 38 Special caliber, which, since 1974 has been upgraded to travel at up to 1300 fps, the law officer requires a vest made of at least seven plies of Kevlar R, 29/100 denier, with a 31 x 31 square weave. A vest made to these specifications would weigh only about 2½ pounds.

Another important consideration in choosing body armor is water

repellency, because rain and perspiration reduce the protective quality of the material. To be sure of getting maximum protection, a police officer should buy a vest made of waterproof Kevlar or encase his vest in a waterproof fabric. This latter alternative is better because the process used to make Kevlar waterproof reduces the fabric's capacity to "breathe," making the vest hot and uncomfortable.

Despite its light 7¾ pounds, this glass-reinforced plastic armor used for special assignments will protect the wearer from 9mm, 357 Magnum and 12-gauge shotgun projectiles.

When it comes to soft body armor, the bottom line for law enforcement is: Use it. You or your department may buy the best armor vest on the market, but if it is kept in a closet at home or in the trunk of your patrol car, it cannot protect you from injury or death.

Directory of Manufacturers and Suppliers

BODY ARMOR

American Body Armor and Equipment Company
100 Ricefield Lane
Hauppauge, New York 11787
(516) 271-0019

Armorshield
Federal Laboratories
Saltsburg, Pennsylvania 15681
(412) 639-3511

Armor of America
1760 Stewart Avenue
Santa Monica, California 90402
(213) 828-6023

Armour of America
P.O. Box 1405
Beverly Hills, California 90202
(213) 478-7725

Burlington Industries
1345 Avenue of the Americas
New York, New York 10038
(212) 333-5160

Blauer Manufacturing Company
160 North Washington Street
Boston, Massachusetts 02114
(617) 227-1300

Life Shield Vest Company
3425 Gratiot Avenue
Detroit, Michigan 48207
(313) 571-9428

Logistics International
P.O. Box 15243
Plantation, Florida 33318

Protective Apparel Corp. of America
333 Sylvan Avenue
Englewood Cliffs, New Jersey 07632
(201) 871-0108

Protective Materials Company
York Street
Andover, Massachusetts 01810
(617) 475-6397

Point Blank Body Armor, Inc.
14 West 17th Street
New York, New York 10011
(212) 929-3220

Safariland Ballistics, Inc.
1941 South Walker Avenue
Monrovia, California 91016
(213) 357-7902

Second Chance Body Armor
Box 587
Central Lake, Michigan 49622
(800) 253-7090

Smith & Wesson
P.O. Box 2208
Springfield, Massachusetts 01101
(413) 781-8300

FIREARMS

A.M.T.
(See Arcadia Machine and
Tool Company)

Action Arms Ltd.
4567 Bermuda Street
Philadelphia, Pennsylvania 19124
(215) 744-3400

American Arms International
(Available through M & N Distributors)

**Arcadia Machine and
Tool Company (A.M.T.)**
Santa Clara
Arcadia, California 91006
(213) 574-9749

Armalite
118 East 16th Street
Costa Mesa, California 92627
(714) 548-7701

**Armanent Systems
and Procedures, Inc.**
Box 356
Appleton, Wisconsin 54912
(414) 731-8893

Astra
(Available through Interarms)

Auto Ordnance Corp.
Box ZG
West Hurley, New York 12491
(914) 679-7225

Bauer Firearms Corporation
34750 Klein Avenue
Fraser, Michigan 48026
(313) 294-9130

Austin Behlert
(See Custom Guns, Inc.)

Beretta U.S.A. Corp.
17601 Indianhead Highway
Acco Keck, Maryland 20607
(301) 283-2191

Bernardelli
(Available through Interarms)

Browning
Route 1
Morgan, Utah 84050
(801) 876-2711

Bushmaster Firearms Company
803 Forest Avenue
Portland, Maine 04103
(207) 775-3324

Century Arms Company
3-5 Federal Street
St. Albans, Vermont 05478
(802) 524-9541

Charter Arms Corporation
430 Sniffens Lane
Stratford, Connecticut 06497
(203) 377-8080

Colt Industries, Firearms Division
150 Huyshope Avenue
Hartford, Connecticut 06102
(203) 278-8550

Commando Arms Company
Box 10214
Knoxville, Tennessee 37919
(615) 523-3393

Crown City Arms
P.O. Box 1126
Cortland, New York 13045
(607) 753-0194

Custom Guns, Inc.
Box 227
Monmouth Junction, New Jersey 08852
(201) 329-2284

Cylinder and Slide
P.O. Box 937, 523 North Main
Freemont, Nebraska 68025
(402) 721-4277

Detonics Corporation
2500 Seattle Towers
Seattle, Washington 98101
(206) 624-9090

Demro Products Inc.
345 Progress Drive
Manchester, Connecticut 06040
(203) 649-4444

Devel Corporation
3441 West Brainard Road
Cleveland, Ohio 44122
(216) 292-7723

Excam Import Company
4480 East 11th Avenue
P.O. Box 3483
Hialeah, Florida 33013
(305) 681-4661

Fabrique Nationale
(Available through Steyr Daimler Puch)

FIE
P.O. Box 4866, Hialeah Lakes
Hialeah, Florida 33014
(305) 685-5966

Heckler & Koch
933 North Kenmore Street, Suite 218
Arlington, Virginia 22201
(703) 243-3700

High Standard Inc.
31 Prestige Park Circle
East Hartford, Connecticut 06108
(203) 289-9531

Interarms
10 Prince Street
Alexandria, Virginia 22313
(703) 548-1400

International Distributors Inc.
7290 Southwest 42nd Street
Miami, Florida 33155
(305) 264-9321

Ithaca Gun Company, Inc.
123 Lake Street
Ithaca, New York 14850
(607) 273-0200

Iver Johnson's Arms, Inc.
Wilton Avenue Off South Street
Middlesex, New Jersey 08846
(201) 752-4994

L. E. S.
2301 Davis Street
North Chicago, Illinois 60064
(312) 473-9484

Laser Products Corporation
18285 Mount Baldy Circle
Fountain Valley, California 92708
(714) 962-7728

Llama
(Available through Stoeger Industries)

M & N Distributors
3040 West Lomita Boulevard
Torrance, California 90505
(213) 530-9000

Mandall Shooting Supplies, Inc.
7150 East 4th Street
Scottsdale, Arizona 85252
(602) 945-2553

Mannlicher
(See Steyr Mannlicher)

Marlin Firearms Company
100 Kenna Drive
North Haven, Connecticut 06473
(203) 239-5621

Mauser
(Available through Interarms)

The Merrill Company
704 East Commonwealth
Fullerton, California 92631
(714) 870-8530

Mitchell Arms Company
116 East 16th Street
Costa Mesa, California 92627
(714) 548-7701

O. F. Mossberg & Sons, Inc.
7 Grasso Avenue
North Haven, Connecticut 06473
(203) 288-6491

M-S Safari Arms Company
P.O. Box 23370
Phoenix, Arizona 85062
(602) 269-7283

Navy Arms Company
689 Bergen Boulevard
Ridgefield, New Jersey 07657
(201) 945-2500

North American Arms Company
310 West 700 South Street
Provo, Utah 84601
(801) 375-8074

O. D. I., Inc.
1244A Greenwood Avenue
Midland Park, New Jersey 07432
(201) 444-4557

**Pacific International
Merchandising Corporation**
2215 J Street
Sacramento, California 95816
(916) 446-2737

Plainfield Inc.
292 Vail Avenue
Piscataway, New Jersey 08854
(201) 981-0131

Remington Arms Company, Inc.
939 Barnum Avenue
Bridgeport, Connecticut 06602
(203) 333-1112

Rossi
(Available through Interarms)

Ruger
(See Sturm, Ruger & Company, Inc.)

Sako
(Available through Stoeger Industries)

Savage-Stevens
(See Savage Arms Company)

Savage Arms Company
Springdale Road
Westfield, Massachusetts 01085
(413) 562-2361

Semmerling Corporation
P.O. Box 400
Newton, Massachusetts 02160

Sig
(Available through Mandall Shooting Supplies)

Sile-Bennelli
(Available through Sile Distributors)

Sile-Seecamp
(Available through Mandall Shooting Supplies)

Sile Distributors
7 Centre Market Place
New York, New York 10013
(212) 925-4111

Smith & Wesson
2100 Roosevelt Avenue
Springfield, Massachusetts 01101
(413) 781-8300

Springfield Armory
420 West Main Street
Geneseo, Illinois 61254
(309) 944-5138

Star
(Available through Interarms)

Sterling Arms Corporation
211 Grand Street
Lockport, New York 14094
(716) 434-6631

Steyr
(See Steyr Daimler Puch)

Steyr Mannlicher
(See Steyr Daimler Puch)

Steyr Daimler Puch of America Corporation
Sporting Arms Division
85 Metro Way
Secaucus, New Jersey 07094
(201) 865-2284

Stoeger Industries
55 Ruta Court
South Hackensack, New Jersey 07606
(201) 440-2700

Sturm, Ruger & Company, Inc.
Lacey Place
Southport, Connecticut 06490
(203) 259-7843

Targa
(Available through Excam Import Company)

Taurus
(Available through International Distributors, Inc.)

U.S. Repeating Arms Company
(Available through Winchester Arms Co.)

Universal Firearms Company
3740 East 10th Court
Hialeah, Florida 33013
(305) 836-7786

Valmet Sporting Arms Inc.
7 Winchester Plaza
Elmsford, New York 10523
(914) 347-4440

Vega
(Available through Pacific International
Merchandising Corp.)

Dan Wesson Arms, Inc.
293 Main Street
Monson, Massachusetts 01057
(413) 267-4081

Walther
(Available through Interarms)

Winchester-Western
275 Winchester Avenue
New Haven, Connecticut 06504
(203) 789-5000

GRIPS

Bianchi
100 Calle Cortez
Temecula, California 92390
(714) 676-5621

Bullshooter's Supply
9625 East 3rd Street
Tucson, Arizona 85732
(602) 298-6924

Colt Industries
150 Huyshope Avenue
Hartford, Connecticut 06102
(203) 278-8550

Eagle Grips
Box 819
Berkeley, Illinois 60163

J. M. Evans
5078 Harwood Road
Sunny Dale, Calfornia 95124
(408) 737-2424

E. M. Fuzzy Farrant
1235 West Vine Avenue
West Covina, California 91790
(213) 338-8301

Fitz Grips
Box 49797
Los Angeles, California 90049

Franzite Sports Inc.
P.O. Box 683
Park Ridge, Illinois 60068

Herrett's Stocks
Box 741
Twin Falls, Idaho 83301
(208) 733-1498

Jean St. Henri
6525 Dume Drive
Malibu, California 90265
(213) 457-7211

Hogue Custom Combat Grips
P.O. Box 460
Morro Bay, California 93428
(805) 528-5788

Mustang Grips
2425 South Keller
Industry, California 92390
(213) 699-0581

Pachmayr Gun Works, Inc.
1220 South Grand Avenue
Los Angeles, California 90015
(213) 748-7271

Sanderson Custom Pistol Stocks
17965 Fenton
Detroit, Michigan 48219
(313) 568-2434

Jay Scott Grips
35 Market Street
Elmwood Park, New Jersey 07407
(201) 796-4554

Rogers Grips
10601 Theresa Drive
Jacksonville, Florida 32216

Sile Distributors
7 Centre Market Place
New York, New York 10013
(212) 925-4111

Western Gunstock Manufacturing Company
550 Valencia School Road
Aptos, California 95003
(408) 688-5884

John W. Womack
3006 Bibb Street
Shreveport, Louisiana 71108
(318) 635-7687

HOLSTERS

A & B Industries, Inc.
7852 Hamilton Avenue
Cincinnati, Ohio 45223
(513) 522-2994

Alessi Custom Holsters
2465 Niagara Falls
Tonawanda, New York 14150
(716) 691-5615

American Sales and Manufacturer
Box 677
Laredo, Texas 78040
(512) 723-6893

Armament Systems Products Unltd.
P.O. Box 18595
Atlanta, Georgia 30326

Baker Holsters
(See Roy's Custom Leather)

Belt Slide Inc.
P.O. Drawer 15303
Austin, Texas 78761
(512) 255-1805

Bianchi Gunleather
100 Calle Cortez
Temecula, California 92390
(714) 676-5621

Ted Blocker Custom Holsters
Box 821
Temple City, California 92390
(213) 442-5772

Edward Bohlin
931 North Highland Avenue
Hollywood, California 90038
(213) 463-4888

Bosselmann
P.O. Box 900
Tombstone, Arizona 85638

Boyt Holster Company
Box 1108
Iowa Falls, Iowa 51026
(515) 646-4626

Brauer Brothers Manufacturing Company
2012 Washington Street
St. Louis, Missouri 63103
(314) 231-2864

Browning Holsters
Rt. 4 Box 624-B
Arnold, Missouri 63010

J. M. Bucheimer Company
Box 280, Airport Road
Frederick, Maryland 21701
(301) 662-5101

Chase Leather Products
507 Alden Street
Fall River, Massachusetts 02722
(617) 678-7556

Cobra Gunskin
1865 New Highway
Farmingdale, New York 11735
(516) 752-8544

Courtland Boot Jack Co. Inc.
270 Lafayette Street
New York, New York 10021
(212) 966-5686

G. William Davis
Box 446
Arcadia, California 91006
(213) 445-3872

**De Santis Holster and
Leather Goods Company**
1601 Jericho Turnpike
New Hyde Park, New York 11040
(516) 354-5957

El Dorado Leather Company
8406 Magnolia, Suite-E
Santee, California 92971
(714) 449-4920

El Paso Saddlery Company
Box 27194
El Paso, Texas 79926
(915) 544-2233

4-D Marketing and Development Company
Box 19157
Detroit, Michigan 48219
(313) 535-6737

First Chance Holsters
c/o Robert A. Strong Company
105 Maplewood Avenue
Gloucester, Massachusetts 01930
(617) 281-3300

Fury Leather Company
2204 Niagara Street
Niagara Falls, New York 14303
(716) 282-7080

Garth Company
P.O. Box 14354
Tampa, Florida 33690

The Gun Protector
Rt. 1, Box 303
McKinney, Texas 75069

H. J. Herman Leather Company
Route 1
Skiatook, Oklahoma 74070
(918) 396-1226

Hoyt Holster Company
Box 69
Coupeville, Washington 98239
(206) 678-6640

The Hunter Corporation
3300 West 71st Street
Westminster, Colorado 80030
(303) 427-4626

Don Hume Leather Goods
Box 351
Miami, Oklahoma 74354

Jackass Leather Company
7383 North Rogers Avenue
Chicago, Illinois 60626
(312) 338-2800

Jay-Pee
(Available through
Courtland Boot Jack Company)

John's Custom Leather
525 South Liberty
Blairsville, Pennsylvania 15717
(412) 459-6802

Kirkpatrick Leather
Box 3150
Laredo, Texas 78041

Koplin Manufacturing, Inc.
P.O. Box 231
Berlin, Wisconsin 54923
(414) 361-0400

Lawman Leather Inc.
Box 4772
Scottsdale, Arizona 85258
(602) 991-5277

George Lawrence Company
306 Southwest 1st Street
Portland, Oregon 97204
(503) 228-8244

Leathercrafts
710 South Washington
Alexandria, Virginia 22314
(703) 549-2506

Milt Sparks
Box 7
Idaho City, Idaho 83631
(208) 392-6695

Milwaukee Holster Company
Box 559
Milwaukee, Wisconsin 53201
(414) 445-7330

S. D. Myres Saddle Company
Box 357
Mills, Massachusetts 02054

K.L. Null Holsters Ltd.
RD 5, Box 197
Hanover, Pennsylvania 17331

Old West Inc. Leather Products
Box 2030
Chula Vista, California 92012
(714) 429-8050

Ranger Leather Products
Box 3198
East Camden, Arkansas 71707

Renegade Holster and Leather Co.
Box 31456
Phoenix, Arizona 85046
(602) 971-5900

Rogers Holsters
St. Johns Bluff Road
Jacksonville, Florida 32216
(904) 641-9434

Roy's Custom Leather
Box 852
Magnolia, Arkansas 71753
(501) 234-1566

Safariland Leather Products
1941 Walker Avenue
Monrovia, California 91016
(213) 357-7902

Safety Speed Holster Co. Inc.
910 South Vail
Montebello, California 90640
(213) 423-4140

Seldeen Leathersmiths
222 Ramona Place
Camarillo, California 93010
(805) 482-5702

Seventrees Leathersmiths Ltd.
Rd 5, Box 197
Hanover, Pennsylvania 17331
(717) 632-6873

Smith & Wesson
2100 Roosevelt Avenue
Springfield, Massachusetts 01101
(413) 781-8300

Snick Products
P.O. Box 480009
Los Angeles, California 90048
(213) 466-6771

Robert A. Strong Company
105 Maplewood Avenue
Gloucester, Massachusetts 01930
(617) 281-3300

Top-Line
(See A & B Industries, Inc.)

Viking Leathercraft
Box 2030
Chula Vista, California 92012
(714) 423-8991

SCOPES

American Import Company
1167 Mission
San Francisco, California 94103
(415) 863-1506

Bianchi
100 Calle Cortez
Temecula, California 92390
(714) 676-5621

Burris Company, Inc.
Box 747
Greeley, Colorado 80632
(303) 356-1670

Bushnell Optical Company
(Div. of Bausch & Lomb)
2828 East Foothill Boulevard
Pasadena, California 91107
(213) 577-1500

Colt Industries
150 Huyshope Avenue
Hartford, Connecticut 06102
(203) 278-8550

Fontaine Ltd., Inc.
11552 Knott Street, Suite 2
Garden Grove, California 92602
(714) 892-4473

Jason Empire Inc.
P.O. Box 12370
Overland Park, Kansas 66212
(913) 888-0220

Kahles of America
Division of Del-Sports, Inc.
Main Street
Margaretsville, New York 12455
(914) 586-4103

Kassnar Imports
P.O. Box 6097
Harrisburg, Pennsylvania 17112
(717) 652-6101

Leupold & Stevens, Inc.
P.O. Box 688
Beaverton, Oregon 97075
(503) 646-9171

Lyman Gun Sight Products
Route 147
Middlefield, Connecticut 06455
(203) 349-3421

Redfield Company
5800 East Jewell Avenue
Denver, Colorado 80224
(303) 757-6411

Sears Roebuck & Company
825 South St. Louis
Chicago, Illinois 60607
(312) 875-2500

Southern Precision Import
3419 East Commercial
San Antonio, Texas 78215
(512) 224-5801

Swift Instruments, Inc.
952 Dorchester Avenue
Boston, Massachusetts 02125
(617) 436-2960

Tasco Sales Inc.
2600 Northwest 26th Street
Miami, Florida 33122
(305) 591-3670

John Unertl Optical Company
3551-5 East Street
Pittsburgh, Pennsylvania 15214
(412) 321-2215

United Binocular Company
9043 South Western
Chicago, Illinois 60620
(312) 445-6166

Universal Sporting Goods, Inc.
7920 Northwest 76th Street
Medley, Florida 33166

Weatherby, Inc.
2781 Firestone Boulevard
South Gate, California 90280
(213) 569-7186

W.R. Weaver Company
7125 Industrial Avenue
El Paso, Texas 79915
(915) 778-5281

Williams Gun Sight Company
7389 Lapeer Road
Davison, Michigan 48423
(313) 653-2131

Carl Zeiss Inc.
444 Fifth Avenue
New York, New York 10018
1-800-446-1807

Reference

Facts and Figures on Major U.S. Crimes

All law enforcement officers have a common goal: to arrest and bring to trial those who break the law. Uniformed officers are assigned to patrol their counties, cities and towns conspicuously in an attempt to eliminate possible opportunities for the commission of crimes and handle the initial investigation of those which do occur. Plainclothes officers, on the other hand, have the responsibility of performing major criminal investigations and handling them to completion.

It is important, therefore, for police officers to know about the nature of the major crimes committed throughout the country and their frequency of occurrence. The following section provides the most current information from the latest FBI Uniform Crime Reports published by the U.S. Department of Justice on murder, aggravated assault, forcible rape, robbery, arson, burglary, larceny-theft and motor vehicle theft. Included are the nature, trends, frequency, rates of increase, rates of clearance and types of persons arrested for these eight major categories of crime.

In addition, of poignant interest to all law enforcement officers are statistics on the why, when, where and how 1,141 officers were killed in the line of duty during the 10 years from 1970 through 1979.

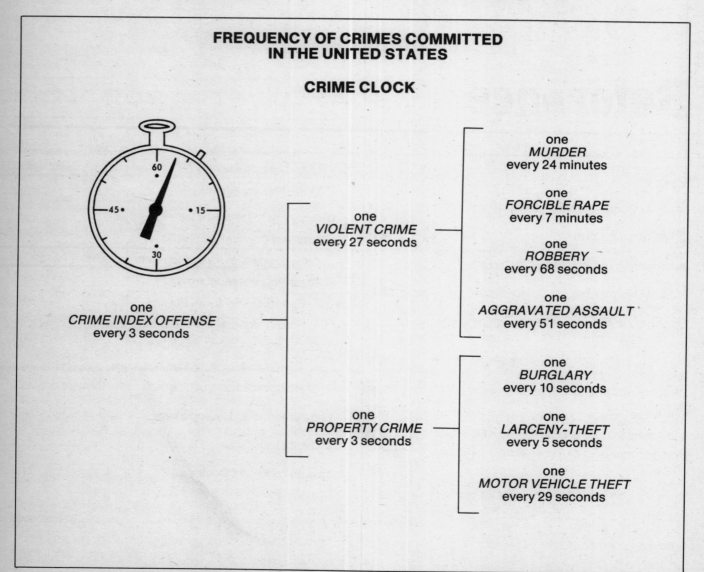

FREQUENCY OF CRIMES COMMITTED IN THE UNITED STATES

CRIME CLOCK

one
CRIME INDEX OFFENSE
every 3 seconds

one
VIOLENT CRIME
every 27 seconds

one
MURDER
every 24 minutes

one
FORCIBLE RAPE
every 7 minutes

one
ROBBERY
every 68 seconds

one
AGGRAVATED ASSAULT
every 51 seconds

one
PROPERTY CRIME
every 3 seconds

one
BURGLARY
every 10 seconds

one
LARCENY-THEFT
every 5 seconds

one
MOTOR VEHICLE THEFT
every 29 seconds

This crime clock illustrates the annual average ratio of government index offenses to fixed time intervals. It should not be interpreted merely as a representation of the regularity with which any of the crimes are committed.

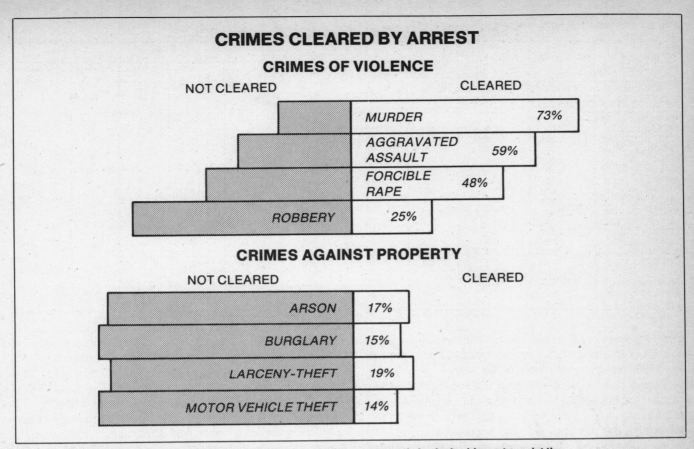

CRIMES CLEARED BY ARREST

CRIMES OF VIOLENCE

NOT CLEARED   CLEARED

MURDER	73%
AGGRAVATED ASSAULT	59%
FORCIBLE RAPE	48%
ROBBERY	25%

CRIMES AGAINST PROPERTY

NOT CLEARED   CLEARED

ARSON	17%
BURGLARY	15%
LARCENY-THEFT	19%
MOTOR VEHICLE THEFT	14%

Unlike crimes of violence, which usually provide crime scenes with some type of physical evidence to assist the investigating officer in clearing the crime, crimes against property usually have no actual crime scenes and thus have significantly lower clearance rates. For example, in crimes of arson, most, if not all, of the evidence is destroyed; similarly, for motor vehicle theft, the vehicle—if found—will most likely be abandoned and will reveal scant evidence.

Murder and Nonnegligent Manslaughter

Murder and nonnegligent manslaughter are defined in the Uniform Crime Reports as the willful killing of one human being by another.

These are crimes the police are virtually powerless to stop because of several uncontrollable factors. One is that the vast majority of murders are committed on the spur of the moment and in the heat of passion. Another, and perhaps more important, factor is that most of these crimes are committed by the victim's friend, lover, relative or acquaintance. This type of murder is classified as not premeditated.

In contrast, premeditated murders are those which are carefully planned and calculated by the murderer before being carried out. Such murders are committed for any of several reasons: to silence an informer; to cover up another crime; to take revenge; or, in the case of organized crime, to set an example by killing a member who has violated a rule or code. These crimes are usually carried out by either a professional hit man or the vengeful person himself, acting alone or with an accomplice.

Not included in this offense classification are deaths caused by negligence, suicide or accident; justifiable homicides, which are the killings of felons by law enforcement officers in the line of duty or by private citizens; and attempts to murder or assaults to murder, which are termed aggravated assaults. Finally, persons declared mentally incompetent or adjudged insane, who cannot be held accountable for their actions and are institutionalized for their crimes in lieu of standing trial, are not included in these statistics.

Volume. In the United States during 1979, there were an estimated 21,456 murders representing approximately two percent of the total violent crimes.

A geographic breakdown of murder by region revealed that 42 percent of the murders occurred in the Southern States, which account for the largest regional population. Twenty-one percent were reported by the North Central States; 20 percent by the Western States;

Age, Sex and Race of Murder Victims, 1979

Age	Number	Percent[1]	Sex		Race					
			Male	Female	White	Negro	Indian	Chinese	Japanese	All Others
TOTAL...............	20,591		15,777	4,814	11,154	8,934	140	43	23	297
PERCENT............		100.0	77.6	23.4	54.2	43.4	.7	.2	.1	1.4
Infant (under 1).....	163	.8	94	69	87	70	1	1		4
1 to 4....................	336	1.6	171	165	194	130	2	3	2	5
5 to 9....................	178	.9	103	75	109	61	2			6
10 to 14.................	203	1.0	121	82	124	77	1			1
15 to 19.................	1,866	9.1	1,387	479	1,098	728	17	1	3	19
20 to 24.................	3,465	16.8	2,665	800	1,842	1,545	22	7	4	45
25 to 29.................	3,337	16.2	2,645	692	1,645	1,620	21	4	3	44
30 to 34.................	2,525	12.3	2,063	462	1,253	1,217	16	8	1	30
35 to 39.................	1,824	8.9	1,453	371	925	857	9	3	3	27
40 to 44.................	1,404	6.8	1,115	289	740	631	16	2	1	14
45 to 49.................	1,232	6.0	956	276	699	505	12	4		12
50 to 54.................	1,044	5.1	844	200	578	442	7	2	2	13
55 to 59.................	805	3.9	654	151	453	333	5	2	3	9
60 to 64.................	603	2.9	453	150	364	229	3	2	1	4
65 to 69.................	470	2.3	331	139	308	154	1	2		5
70 to 74.................	316	1.5	194	122	221	85	1	2		7
75 and over...........	443	2.2	225	218	322	119				2
Unknown..............	337	1.8	303	74	192	131	4			50

[1]Because of rounding, percentages may not add to total.

and 17 percent by the Northeastern States.

December had a higher frequency of murder offenses in 1979 than any other month of the year.

Trend. Nationally, the number of murders increased 10 percent from 1978 to 1979, and all four geographic regions registered upswings. The Southern States reported a rise of 11 percent; the Northeastern and Western States, 10 percent each; and the North Central States, seven percent.

Suburban areas and large core cities of 250,000 or more people recorded seven and 14 percent upswings, respectively. In rural areas, the volume of murders was down 2 percent.

Nature. Murder victims were male in approximately three of every four instances in 1979. On the average, 54 of every 100 victims were white, 43 were black and the remainder were of other races.

During 1979, 16,955 offenders were identified in connection with the murders of 15,040 victims. Most of the victims (14,024) were slain in single-victim situations. Of these, 12,429 were killed by single offenders and the remainder by more than one offender. Concerning homicides involving multiple victims, 815 persons were killed by 357 offenders in incidents involving one assailant and multiple victims, and 201 victims were slain by 207 offenders in multiple victim/multiple offender situations.

In 1979, firearms predominated as the weapons most often used in the commission of murders throughout the nation. In both the North Central and Southern Regions, firearms were used in 65 percent of the murders; in the Western States, they were employed in 58 percent; and in the Northeastern States, they were used in 53

percent. Nationwide, 63 percent of the murders were committed through the use of firearms. Handguns were the weapons used in 50 percent of all murders.

A comparative study for the years 1975 through 1979 showed a decrease in the use of firearms to commit murder. In 1975, firearms were used in 66 percent of all murders, while 63 percent of all murders in 1979 were perpetrated with these weapons. An analysis of weapons used to commit murder for these five years is shown in tabular form.

Murder, Type of Weapon Used, 1975-1979 (in percent)

Year	Total		Fire-arms	Knife or other cutting instruments	Unknown or other dangerous weapons	Personal weapons
	Number	Percent[1]				
1975	18,327	100.0	65.8	17.7	7.5	9.0
1976	16,605	100.0	63.8	17.8	12.2	6.2
1977	18,033	100.0	62.5	19.1	12.9	5.6
1978	18,714	100.0	63.6	18.8	11.8	5.7
1979	20,591	100.0	63.3	19.2	11.9	5.6

[1]Because of rounding, percentages may not add to total.

Motives. That murder is largely a societal problem beyond the control of the law enforcement community is emphasized by the relationship of the murder victim to the offender. Fifty-two percent of the murder victims in 1979 were acquainted with their assailants, and one of every five victims was related to the offender.

The greatest percentage of murders in 1979 (43 percent) according to the following chart, resulted from arguments. Seventeen percent occurred as a result of felonious activity, and five percent were suspected to be the result of some felonious act.

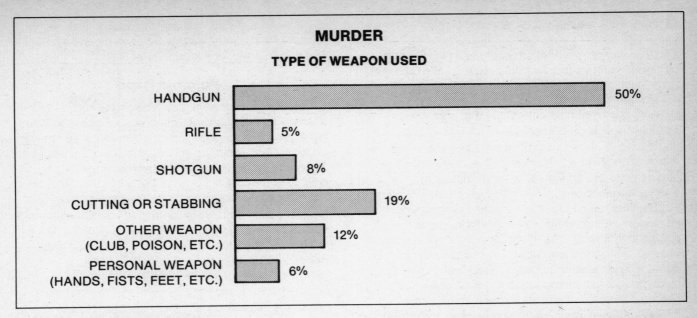

MURDER

TYPE OF WEAPON USED

HANDGUN	50%
RIFLE	5%
SHOTGUN	8%
CUTTING OR STABBING	19%
OTHER WEAPON (CLUB, POISON, ETC.)	12%
PERSONAL WEAPON (HANDS, FISTS, FEET, ETC.)	6%

Murder Circumstances/Motives, 1976-1979 (in percent)

	1979	1978	1977	1976
TOTAL	20,591	18,714	18,033	16,605
PERCENT[1]	100.0	100.0	100.0	100.0
FELONY TOTAL	16.9	16.7	16.7	17.7
Robbery	10.5	10.2	9.9	10.3
Narcotics	1.9	1.7	1.7	1.8
Sex offenses	1.6	1.4	1.7	1.8
Other felony	2.9	3.3	3.4	3.8
SUSPECTED FELONY	5.3	5.6	5.9	7.0
ARGUMENT TOTAL	42.9	45.5	46.6	48.3
Romantic triangle	2.4	2.7	2.8	2.8
Influence of alcohol or narcotics[2]	4.5	5.3	5.3	5.8
Property or money	3.0	3.5	3.3	3.9
Other arguments	33.0	33.9	35.2	35.7
OTHER MOTIVES OR CIRCUMSTANCES	17.2	18.3	16.6	18.6
UNKNOWN MOTIVES	17.7	13.8	14.2	8.5

[1]Because of rounding, percentages may not add to totals.
[2]Murders committed during arguments while under the influence of narcotics are not counted in felony murders.

Clearances. The clearance rate for murder in 1979 was higher than for any other Crime Index offense. City and suburban law enforcement agencies were successful in clearing 73 percent of the murders during the year, while those in rural areas cleared 83 percent. In 1979, persons under 18 years of age accounted for five percent of the willful killings cleared by law enforcement in cities and rural areas; seven percent of those cleared in suburban areas involved only persons in that age group.

Persons Arrested. Arrests of youthful offenders under 18 years of age for murder decreased 12 percent during the period 1975-1979, and adult arrests for that offense fell nine percent in the same period. In 1979, 44 percent of all persons arrested for murder were under age 25, and nine percent were under 18. The 18- to 22-year age group, accounting for 25 percent of the total 1979 murder arrests, showed the heaviest involvement in this offense. Whites made up 49 percent of the total arrestees for murder in 1979, blacks constituted 48 percent, and the remaining three percent were of other races.

Aggravated Assault

Aggravated assault is the unlawful attack by one person upon another for the purpose of inflicting severe or aggravated bodily injury. This type of assault is usually accompanied by the use of a gun, knife or other weapon, or by means likely to produce great bodily injury or death. There are several subclassifications of this crime, the penalties for which are based on the severity of the injuries suffered during the attack.

The statistics are inflated because attempts to commit more serious crimes, such as murder, are included.

This reflects the philosophy that it is not necessary for an injury to result when a weapon is present which could and probably would result in serious personal injury if the crime were successfully completed. In other words, barroom brawls, family scuffles and threats with a knife at a football game automatically fall into the aggravated assault category.

However, when a person attempts to murder another using a firearm, knife or bludgeon—but the victim survives—the crime is often downgraded to the most serious subclassification of aggravated assault.

Trend. In 1979, an estimated 614,213 aggravated

assaults were committed, an increase of 10 percent over 1978 and 27 percent over 1975. Cities with 250,000 or more population recorded a nine-percent upswing over the previous year, and rural and suburban areas each reported eight-percent increases for the same period.

Rises were reported in the volume of aggravated assaults for each geographic region. The increases were 13 percent in the Western States, 11 percent in the North Central States, 9 percent in the Southern States and 8 percent in the Northeastern States.

A comparison of aggravated assault from 1975 to 1979 revealed that the use of firearms as weapons increased eight percent; assaults with knives or other cutting instruments rose 11 percent; assaults with blunt objects or other dangerous weapons increased 28 percent; and those aggravated assaults committed through the use of personal weapons climbed 18 percent. The following table shows by region the aggravated assaults in 1979 by type of weapon used.

Aggravated Assault, Type of Weapon Used, 1979 (in percent)

Region	Total[1] all weapons	Fire- arms	Knives or other cutting instru- ments	Other weapons; (clubs, poison, etc.)	Personal weapons; (hands, fists, feet)
Northeastern States	100.0	14.9	24.5	30.1	30.5
North Central States	100.0	23.8	21.3	28.7	26.1
Southern States	100.0	27.3	24.1	25.4	23.2
Western States	100.0	23.1	19.1	27.8	30.0
Total	100.0	23.0	22.5	27.6	26.9

[1]Because of rounding, percentages may not add to totals.

Clearances. Collectively, city law enforcement agencies cleared an average of 59 per 100 cases of aggravated assault in 1979. This relatively high clearance rate was consistent with high rates for other crimes against persons. Persons under 18 years of age, exclusively, were identified in 11 percent of the city clearances.

Suburban and rural agencies reported 58 and 70 percent aggravated assault clearance rates, respectively. Persons under age 18 accounted for 13 percent of suburban clearances and six percent of those in rural areas.

Persons Arrested. Arrests for aggravated assault during the period 1978-1979 were up nine percent. Since 1975, arrests of persons 18 years of age and over for aggravated assault rose 11 percent, and arrests of persons under age 18 increased less than one percent.

Persons 21 years of age and over accounted for 69 percent of the 1979 aggravated assault arrests. Arrests of males for this offense outnumbered those of females by 7 to 1.

Whites made up 61 percent of the arrests for aggravated assaults; blacks, 37 percent; and all other races accounted for the remainder.

Forcible Rape

Forcible rape is defined as "the carnal knowledge of a female forcibly and against her will." Rape is a violent crime that often creates significant physical and mental problems and can bring social and economic disruption to the lives of the victims, their families and friends, and society as a whole.

The number of reported rapes per 100,000 women has more than doubled in the last 10 years, making rape appear to be the fastest rising crime of violence among the four most frequently reported crimes of violence— murder, aggravated assault, rape and robbery.

Unfortunately, it is not known whether the incidents of rape are actually increasing or whether the statistics reflect the increased willingness of victims to come forward and report crimes of rape that previously went unreported. The crime of forcible rape, however, constitutes less than one percent of the crimes reported in the UCR and six percent of the four categories of violent crime.

According to FBI reports, the majority of reported rapists are between 15 and 24 years of age. Separate studies show that more than half the rape victims are under 21. Statistics further indicate that among teenagers, in particular, the rapist and his victim often know each other through friends, family or casual acquaintances.

Trend. The number of forcible rape offenses in 1979 totaled an estimated 75,989, up 13 percent over 1978 and 35 percent over 1975. During 1979, 39 percent of the forcible rapes occurred in cities with 250,000 or more inhabitants. In the suburban areas, forcible rape offenses rose 12 percent, and the rural areas registered a four-percent increase over 1978. All regions indicated upsurges in the volume of forcible rape offenses with increases of 16 percent in the North Central States; 14 percent in the Southern States; 12 percent in the Northeastern States; and 11 percent in the Western States.

Nature. Of all reported offenses in this category during 1979, 76 percent were rapes by force. Attempts or assaults to commit forcible rape made up the remainder. Forcible rape, a violent crime against the person, has been recognized by law enforcement as one of the most underreported of all Index crimes, primarily because of the victims' fear of their assailants and their embarrassment over the incidents.

Clearances. Both the cities and the suburban areas reported 48 percent of known forcible rapes were

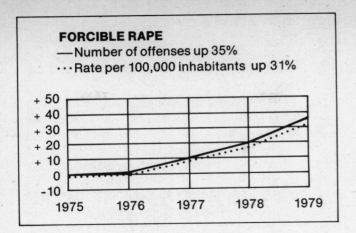

FORCIBLE RAPE
— Number of offenses up 35%
··· Rate per 100,000 inhabitants up 31%

cleared by arrest or exceptional means, i.e., hearings, in 1979. The rural areas recorded a 65-percent clearance rate. Of the total clearances for forcible rape, suburban areas had 11 percent involving only persons under the age of 18, while the cities and rural areas each reported nine percent involving that age group alone.

Persons Arrested. Total 1979 arrests for forcible rape increased nine percent from 1978 figures and 14 percent from those for 1975. Incarceration of persons under 18 years of age increased five percent from 1975 to 1979 while adult arrests climbed 16 percent for the same time period.

Fifty-seven percent of the forcible rape arrests in 1979 were of males under the age of 25, with 30 percent of the arrestees in the 18- to 22-year age group. Fifty percent of the persons arrested for forcible rape in 1979 were white, 48 percent, black. The remainder included all other races.

(For additional information on the criminal investigation of rape, please see "Essentials of Effective Rape Investigation," page 98.)

Robbery

Robbery is a crime defined as the taking of valuables from a victim or victims by the use of force, threat of force or violence, thus putting that victim in fear.

This crime has two classifications: strong-armed robbery, including incidents in which the victim is mugged; and armed robbery, which occurs when the robber uses a weapon. The type of weapon need not be a gun or knife; an ordinary broom handle would be considered a weapon under the law if it caused the victim to be in fear of bodily injury or death.

Robbery is considered one of the more violent crimes. When a person carries a weapon while committing a crime, he knows beforehand he might be forced to use it. Thus, there is always the chance of a robbery becoming a case of felonious murder.

Trend. The 1979 robbery volume totaled an estimated 466,881. This increased 12 percent from the previous year but rose less than one percent from 1975.

Cities over 250,000 in population as well as suburban areas reported 12-percent rises in robbery offenses in 1979 as compared to their 1978 volumes. A six-percent increase was also recorded by rural areas.

Geographically, all four regions experienced an upsurge in robbery from 1978 to 1979. In the Southern States the increase was 17 percent; in the Northeastern States, 14 percent; in the Western States, 10 percent; and in the North Central States, four percent.

Nature. During 1979, the average value loss per robbery was $532, for a total reported loss of $248 million. The impact of this violent crime on the victim cannot be measured in terms of monetary loss alone. While the target of a robbery is money or property, many victims of this crime suffer serious personal injury.

Nationally, nearly half of the reported robberies committed in 1979 were perpetrated on the streets or highways; the average loss for this type of robbery was $355. Bank robbery, which climbed 51 percent between 1975 and 1979, accounted for less than two percent of all 1979 robberies. The highest average loss per bank robbery incident was $3,613.

Increases were also reported for convenience store holdups, up 15 percent and street robberies, up five percent. In the same five-year period, gas or service station holdups fell 17 percent, robberies of commercial or business establishments other than those listed above declined eight percent and residential robberies dropped seven percent.

In 1979, 40 percent of all reported robberies were committed through the use of firearms, 38 percent by strong-arm tactics (hands, fists, feet, etc.), 13 percent by the use of knives or cutting instruments and nine percent through the use of other weapons.

Robbery, Types of Weapons Used, 1979 (in percent)

Region	Total all weapons[1]	Armed			Strong-armed
		Firearms	Knives or other cutting instruments	Other weapons	
Northeastern States......	100.0	30.5	17.0	11.6	40.9
North Central States......	100.0	42.6	10.2	11.5	35.8
Southern States............	100.0	47.7	10.3	6.9	35.0
Western States..............	100.0	41.9	13.0	7.7	37.4
Total........................	100.0	39.7	13.2	9.4	37.7

[1]Because of rounding, percentages may not add to totals.

Clearances. Rural law enforcement agencies were successful in clearing 43 percent of the robbery

ROBBERIES
1975-1979

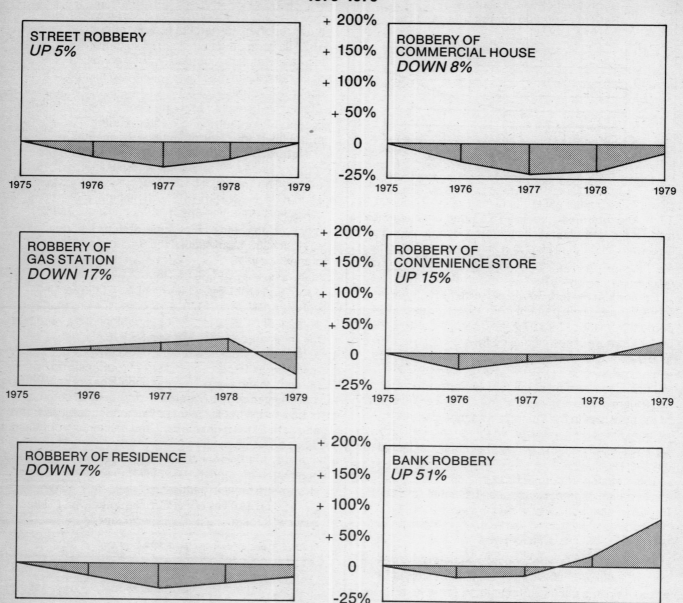

STREET ROBBERY
UP 5%

1975 1976 1977 1978 1979

ROBBERY OF COMMERCIAL HOUSE
DOWN 8%

+ 200%
+ 150%
+ 100%
+ 50%
0
-25%

1975 1976 1977 1978 1979

ROBBERY OF GAS STATION
DOWN 17%

1975 1976 1977 1978 1979

ROBBERY OF CONVENIENCE STORE
UP 15%

+ 200%
+ 150%
+ 100%
+ 50%
0
-25%

1975 1976 1977 1978 1979

ROBBERY OF RESIDENCE
DOWN 7%

1975 1976 1977 1978 1979

BANK ROBBERY
UP 51%

+ 200%
+ 150%
+ 100%
+ 50%
0
-25%

1975 1976 1977 1978 1979

offenses reported for 1979, while the suburban areas cleared 28 percent and the cities 25 percent. Of the robbery clearances reported, 20 percent in the suburban areas, 16 percent in the cities and 12 percent in the rural areas involved only persons under 18 years of age.

Persons Arrested. Nationally, arrests for robbery rose three percent in 1979 when compared to 1978. Increases in the volume of arrests for these offenses

were experienced in the suburban areas with a seven-percent upswing; in the rural areas with a four-percent rise; and in the cities with a two-percent rise.

Data on arrests disclosed that 74 percent of the persons arrested for robbery were under 25 years of age, 55 percent were under 21, and 31 percent were under 18 years of age.

An average of 7 out of every 100 persons arrested for robbery during 1979 were female. Arrests of women for this offense increased six percent when compared to 1978.

From the standpoint of race, 57 percent of those arrested were black, 41 percent were white and two percent were of other races.

Burglary

Burglary is the unlawful entry of a structure by a person with the intent to commit a felony or theft therein.

This crime is perhaps the one most often investigated by the suburban or rural police officer. In a majority of these cases, the burglar—who is often a narcotics addict looking for valuables to support his habit—chooses well-to-do communities as locales of his crimes.

In a burglary perpetrated against a dwelling, that home or apartment is usually unoccupied. The burglar, if he knows the law, prefers it this way. If a homeowner were asleep in his house and was awakened by a perpetrator who put him in fear, the classification of the crime would become robbery. In almost every state, the penalty for robbery is double that for burglary.

It should be noted that the use of force to gain entry is not required to classify a crime as burglary. In this report, burglary is broken down into three subclassifications: forcible entry; unlawful entry where no force is used; and attempted forcible entry.

Trend. The five-year trend, 1975-1979, indicated burglary offenses rose one percent. Nationally in 1979, with an estimated 3,299,484 offenses, the burglary volume increased six percent over 1978. For the year, cities 250,000 and over in population reported an increase of six percent; the suburban areas, a five-percent increase; and the rural areas, a three-percent rise. An upswing was registered in all regions, with the Southern States up 10 percent; the Northeastern and North Central States both having six-percent increases; and the Western States showing a two-percent upturn.

Burglary represents a substantial financial loss. In 1979 burglary victims suffered losses totaling $2.1 billion. The average dollar loss per burglary was $644.

BURGLARIES
1975-1979

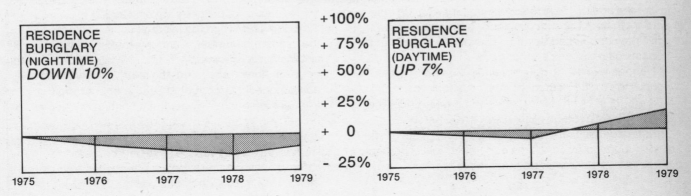

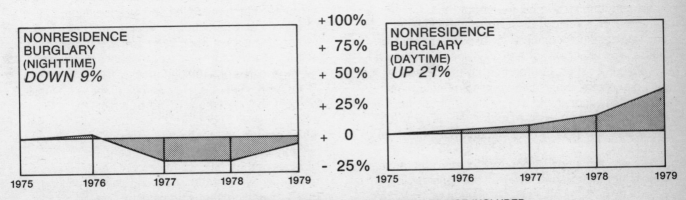

BURGLARIES OF UKNOWN TIME OF OCCURRENCE ARE NOT INCLUDED

Clearances. In 1979, adults were involved in 68 percent of all burglary offenses cleared, and only young people under 18 years of age were offenders in the remaining 32 percent. Thirty-six percent of the burglary clearances in the suburban areas and 29 percent of those in the rural areas involved solely persons under age 18.

Of the burglaries reported within their jurisdictions in 1979, law enforcement agencies in rural areas cleared 19 percent; those in the suburban areas recorded a clearance rate of 15 percent; and agencies in cities with 250,000 or more inhabitants obtained clearances in 13 percent of these crimes.

Persons Arrested. In the UCR, the arrests of several persons may account for the clearance of but one crime. Likewise, with the arrest of one individual, law enforcement agencies may clear numerous offenses, which is often true in cases of burglary. In analyzing the 1975-1979 period, an 11-percent decline in burglary arrests was seen. Arrests of individuals under the age of 18 dropped 16 percent, and arrests of adult burglary offenders fell five percent.

When the 1978-1979 burglary figures were compared, an increase of six percent was seen for total burglary arrests of persons 18 years of age and over, while a decrease of six percent was seen for persons under the age of 18. Arrests for burglary were up one percent in both the suburban and rural areas, while they decreased less than one percent in the nation's cities.

Nationally in 1979, persons under 25 years of age accounted for 83 percent of all arrests for burglary, and 49 percent of all arrested for this crime were under the age of 18. An average of six of each 100 persons arrested for this crime during 1979 were female. Of the total burglary arrests, whites accounted for 69 percent, blacks for 29 percent, and other races for the remainder.

Larceny-Theft

Larceny-theft, the most frequently recurring and pervasive crime in the U.S., is the unlawful taking, carrying, leading or riding away of property from the possession or constructive possession of another. It covers crimes such as larceny-from-the-person, which includes pocket-picking and purse-snatching. Also included are shoplifting, bicycle thefts, thefts from motor vehicles and thefts of motor vehicle parts and accessories in which no use of force, violence or fraud occurs.

Larceny and theft are common crimes and range from minor thefts, some of which are considered disorderly persons offenses, to cases in which large sums of money or valuables are taken. In such cases, the classification is upgraded to a felony.

Certain types of thefts, such as pocket-picking and purse-snatching, border dangerously close to being robbery. Should the person being victimized become aware of the crime being attempted—and resist—the circumstances that follow could lead to a charge of robbery.

Motor vehicle theft, a crime committed frequently and in large number, is treated in a separate section that follows this one. Embezzlement, con games, forgery and printing and passing of worthless checks are such specialized crimes that they have been omitted from the statistics entirely.

Trend. With 6,577,518 offenses estimated in 1979, the volume of larceny-thefts rose 10 percent from 1978. The rural areas showed an increase of 13 percent; in the suburban areas, a 10-percent upturn was registered; and cities with populations of 250,000 or more reported an upswing of seven percent.

The larceny-theft trend showed little variation among the regions. The Northeastern States reported an 11-percent increase; the Southern and Western States experienced upswings of 10 percent; and the North Central States showed a rise of nine percent.

Nature. For each reported larceny-theft in 1979, the average value of property stolen was $256, up from $219 in 1978. When the average value was applied to the estimated number of larceny-thefts, the loss to victims nationally was $1.7 billion. While a portion of the goods stolen is recovered, the relatively low clearance percentage for larceny-thefts (19 percent) and the frequent absence of owner identification on recovered property indicate the overall loss due to this criminal activity is not substantially reduced. In addition, other studies have indicated that many offenses in this category never come to police attention, particularly if the value of the stolen goods is small.

In 1979, the average value of goods and property reported stolen as a result of pocket-picking was $190; by purse-snatching, $129; and by shoplifting, $59. Miscellaneous thefts from buildings and thefts from motor vehicles averaged $391 and $299, respectively, and thefts of motor vehicle accessories resulted in average losses of $109 per offense.

As in prior years, a large portion of these offenses, 37 percent, included thefts of motor vehicle parts, accessories and contents. Other major types of thefts which contributed to the large number of these crimes were those from buildings, 16 percent, and stolen bicycles and shoplifting, 11 percent each. The remainder was distributed among pocket-picking, purse-snatching, thefts from coin-operated machines

LARCENY-THEFT FIVE-YEAR TRENDS
1975-1979

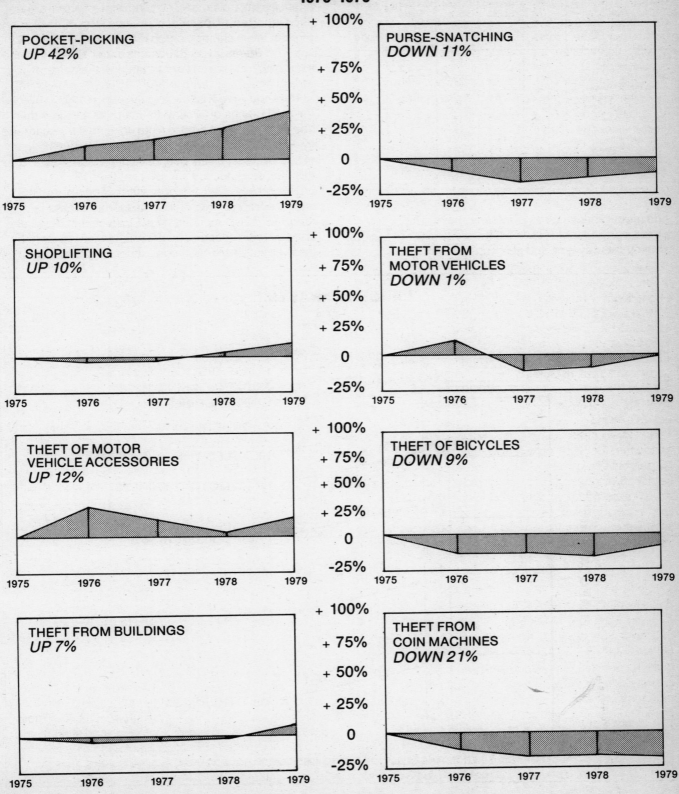

POCKET-PICKING
UP 42%

PURSE-SNATCHING
DOWN 11%

SHOPLIFTING
UP 10%

THEFT FROM MOTOR VEHICLES
DOWN 1%

THEFT OF MOTOR VEHICLE ACCESSORIES
UP 12%

THEFT OF BICYCLES
DOWN 9%

THEFT FROM BUILDINGS
UP 7%

THEFT FROM COIN MACHINES
DOWN 21%

Larceny Analysis by Region, 1979 (in percent)

Type of Larceny-Theft	Total[1]	North-eastern States	North Central States	Southern States	Western States
TOTAL....................	100.0	100.0	100.0	100.0	100.0
Pocket-picking...........	1.1	3.5	.4	.6	.6
Purse-snatching..........	1.4	2.4	1.2	1.3	1.0
Shoplifting..................	11.1	9.3	9.9	10.6	14.6
From motor vehicles (except accessories).	17.2	18.1	13.0	17.5	20.7
Motor vehicle accessories...............	19.3	19.1	19.2	21.7	16.5
Bicycles.....................	10.8	12.3	11.7	8.7	11.3
From buildings............	16.5	18.8	19.0	14.3	14.9
From coin-operated machines..................	.9	.6	.8	1.3	.8
All others...................	21.5	15.8	24.8	24.1	19.6

[1]Because of rounding, percentages may not add to totals.

and miscellaneous types of larceny-thefts. The accompanying table spells out the distribution of larceny-theft by type and geographic region.

Clearances. In 1979, 19 percent of all larceny-thefts brought to the attention of city law enforcement agencies were cleared. The suburban and rural areas each reported 17-percent clearance rates. One of every three of these crimes cleared in the nation's cities and suburban areas involved persons under 18 years of age exclusively. In the rural areas, larceny-theft clearances for this age group represented 20 percent of the total.

Persons Arrested. During the period 1975-1979, the total volume of larceny-theft arrests rose less than one percent. Adult arrests were up eight percent for this five-year period, while those of persons under 18 years of age decreased nine percent. Total 1979 arrests for this offense increased four percent over 1978.

The larceny-theft category not only comprised the largest portion of the total Crime Index offenses reported, it also accounted for 51 percent of the total arrests for Index crimes in 1979. Fifty-eight percent of these arrests were of persons under 18 years of age,

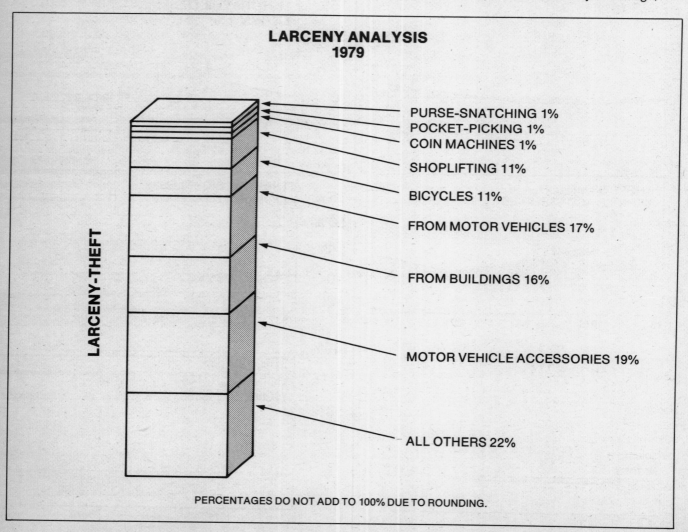

LARCENY ANALYSIS 1979

LARCENY-THEFT

PURSE-SNATCHING 1%
POCKET-PICKING 1%
COIN MACHINES 1%
SHOPLIFTING 11%
BICYCLES 11%
FROM MOTOR VEHICLES 17%
FROM BUILDINGS 16%
MOTOR VEHICLE ACCESSORIES 19%
ALL OTHERS 22%

PERCENTAGES DO NOT ADD TO 100% DUE TO ROUNDING.

and 58 percent of the arrestees were under 21. Arrests of males for larceny-theft violations increased six percent in 1979, and those of females decreased one percent. Females accounted for 30 percent of all larceny-theft arrestees and were arrested more often for this offense than for any other in 1979. Whites accounted for 67 percent of the total larceny-theft arrests and blacks for 30 percent. All other races made up the remaining three percent.

Motor Vehicle Theft

Motor vehicle theft is defined as the theft or attempted theft of a motor vehicle. This is a common everyday crime which is on the rise and has increased 10 percent since 1975.

As a police officer investigating this kind of crime, you should be aware that the perpetrators who usually commit the four basic types of vehicle theft are: 1) the joy-rider, frequently a teenager who commits this relatively minor offense and returns the vehicle; 2) the professional who commits a felony by stealing high-priced cars with the express intent to export them outside the country; 3) the professional who, due to the spiraling costs of new vehicles and their replacement parts, commits a felony by stealing expensive vehicles with the intent of disassembling them and selling the parts for profit; and 4) perhaps the greatest threat to the law enforcement officer, the criminal who steals a vehicle for transportation to or from the scene of a crime he has committed or is about to commit.

Trend. The number of motor vehicle thefts in 1979 jumped 11 percent over 1978, with 1,097,189 offenses recorded.

During the 1978-1979 period, the increases in motor vehicle thefts ranged from 15 percent in cities with populations from 10,000 to 24,999 to six percent in cities with 100,000 to 249,999 inhabitants. Cities 250,000 and over in population and the suburban and rural areas all reported increases of 11 percent in the volume of these offenses.

Geographically, motor vehicle thefts were up in all regions. The greatest increase occurred in the most populous region, the Southern States, which showed a 16-percent upturn. The North Central States recorded a 10-percent rise, and the Northeastern and Western States each reported nine-percent increases. The accompanying chart illustrates that the volume of motor vehicle thefts has risen 10 percent since 1975.

Nature. During 1979, the average value of motor vehicles stolen was $2,692 at the time of theft. Of all motor vehicles reported stolen during the year, 75 percent were automobiles, 13 percent were trucks or buses and 12 percent were other types.

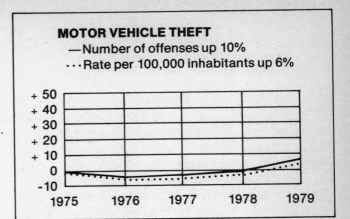

Clearances. Law enforcement agencies in cities cleared 14 percent of the motor vehicle thefts reported in their locales during 1979. Those in the suburban areas cleared 18 percent while rural agencies cleared 34 percent. By geographic location, clearance percentages for motor vehicle theft ranged from 23 percent in the South Atlantic Division to nine percent in both the New England and Middle Atlantic Divisions.

Type of Motor Vehicle Theft, 1979 (in percent)

Region	Total[1]	Autos	Trucks and buses	Other vehicles
Northeastern States...	100.0	88.1	6.1	5.8
North Central States...	100.0	72.1	13.8	14.0
Southern States.........	100.0	67.2	18.5	14.3
Western States...........	100.0	69.1	14.9	15.9
TOTAL....................	100.0	75.1	12.9	12.0

[1]Because of rounding, percentages may not add to totals.

A high proportion of the clearances in all geographic divisions and population groups involved only persons under 18 years of age. In the suburban areas, persons in this age group accounted for 29 percent of the motor vehicle thefts cleared; in the nation's cities, they accounted for 28 percent; and in the rural areas, 25 percent.

Persons Arrested. As in prior years, motor vehicle theft arrests primarily involved the younger segment of the nation's population. During 1979, 69 percent of all persons arrested for motor vehicle theft were under 21 years of age, and those under 18 accounted for 49 percent of the total.

When the total volume of arrests for this offense during 1979 was compared to 1978, a decrease of one percent was observed. Arrests of persons under 18 were down five percent, but adult arrests rose three percent over 1978. During the period 1975-1979, motor vehicle theft arrests increased two percent.

Whites made up 70 percent of the arrestees for motor vehicle theft, blacks 27 percent and all other races accounted for the remainder.

(For additional information please see the article "Stop That Vehicle and Stay Alive," page 32.)

Arson

Arson is defined as any willful or malicious burning, or attempt to burn, with or without intent to defraud, a dwelling, house, structure, public building, motor vehicle, aircraft or personal property of another. Only fires determined through investigation to have been willfully or maliciously set are classified as arsons in these statistics. Fires of suspicious or unknown origins are excluded.

Arson is escalating at a rate second to no other crime against property. Some investigators blame this increase on the fact that there is and has been no federally supported program to fight arson. Others believe that the crime is intimately related to the state of the economy, and that as inflation climbs, so, too, do incidents of arson.

Persons who commit arson can be grouped into seven distinct types: terrorists who seek to gain notoriety for their organization or cause; criminals who attempt to cover up other crimes; businessmen motivated by greed or financial gain, and businessmen pressured to avoid bankruptcy—both groups who buy and burn apartment houses in hopes of collecting on fire insurance claims; vandals who burn for enjoyment and excitement; pyromaniacs who delight in fires for psychological reasons; and persons who destroy others' property out of revenge or hatred.

Unlike the other crime statistics in this report, statistics on arson are for 1979 exclusively. No comparative yearly figures are provided because arson was designated a UCR Index offense only in October 1978, with the formal gathering of statistics beginning shortly thereafter.

Background. In April 1979, an arson data collection form was developed by the UCR staff and distributed to various nationwide agencies interested in the collection, analysis and publication of arson data. The following facts and figures on the crime of arson are gathered from the data forms of these contributing agencies.

Volume. While not all UCR participating agencies were able to respond to the arson data collection request, 8,528 agencies (representing 61 percent of the United States population) submitted six or more monthly arson reports. From the submissions, it was estimated that a total of 77,147 arson offenses were reported during 1979.

Nature. Structures were by far the most frequent targets of arsons in 1979, representing 57 percent of the total reported incidents. Mobile (motor vehicles, trailers, airplanes, boats, etc.) and other property (crops, timber, fences, signs, etc.) accounted for the remaining offenses with 24 and 19 percent, respectively.

Residences accounted for more than half of the structures at which arsons were directed. Seventeen percent of all targeted structural property was uninhabited or abandoned at the time the arson occurred.

The total monetary value of property damaged due to reported arsons during 1979 exceeded one-half billion dollars, and the average loss per incident was $7,465. Industrial/manufacturing structures registered the highest average loss, $49,769 per offense.

Arson, Type of Property, 1979
(8,344 agencies, population 125,237,000)

Property Classification	Number of Offenses	Percent Distribution	Average Damage
TOTAL..	69,100	100.0	$ 7,465
TOTAL STRUCTURE.................................	39,377	57.0	11,765
Single Occupancy Residential...............	15,327	22.2	7,089
Other Residential...............................	7,035	10.2	11,120
Storage..	4,403	6.4	11,712
Industrial/Manufacturing......................	817	1.2	49,769
Other Commercial..............................	5,109	7.4	22,413
Community/Public...............................	4,254	6.2	11,728
Other Structure.................................	2,432	3.5	8,120
TOTAL MOBILE.....................................	16,526	23.9	2,332
Motor Vehicles..................................	15,099	21.9	2,040
Other Mobile....................................	1,427	2.1	5,429
OTHER..	13,197	19.1	1,064

'Because of rounding, percentages may not add to totals.

Clearances. Seventeen percent of all reported arsons were cleared by arrest or exceptional means with the highest clearance rate (32 percent) being recorded for offenses in which community or public structures were involved. Only persons under 18 years of age accounted for 46 percent of the reported arson clearances.

Persons Arrested. While the number of arson offenses reported to law enforcement was first collected by the national UCR program in 1979, the number of arrests for this crime has been reported for many years. During 1979, an estimated 19,800 arson arrests were reported by law enforcement agencies. The volume of arrests rose five percent in 1979 over the 1978 figures and eight percent over those in 1975.

Forty-nine percent of all persons arrested for arson in 1979 were under 18 years of age, and 73 percent were under 25. Seventy-nine percent of the arrestees were white, 19 percent were black and the remainder were of other races. Males made up 89 percent of all persons arrested for this offense.

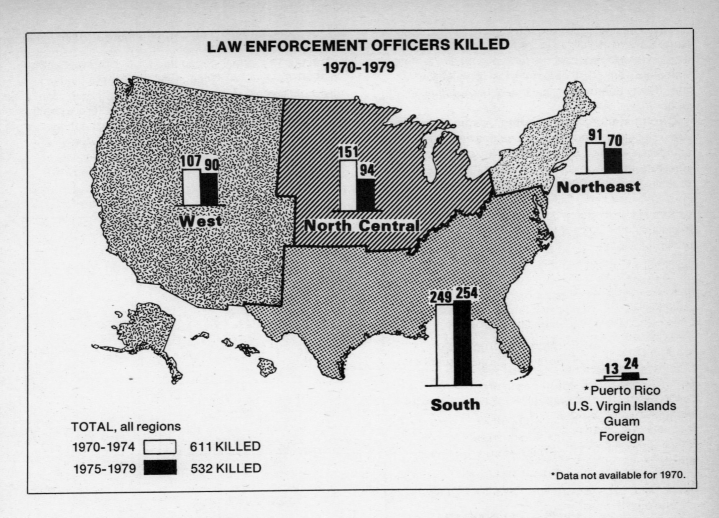

LAW ENFORCEMENT OFFICERS KILLED
1970-1979

West: 107 / 90
North Central: 151 / 94
Northeast: 91 / 70
South: 249 / 254
*Puerto Rico, U.S. Virgin Islands, Guam, Foreign: 13 / 24

TOTAL, all regions
1970-1974 ☐ 611 KILLED
1975-1979 ■ 532 KILLED

*Data not available for 1970.

(For additional information on arson investigation, please see "Arson or Accident?" page 109.)

Officers Killed in the Line of Duty

While the nation has experienced a decline in the number of officers killed in the line of duty in recent years, statistics showed a rise in 1979. In that year, 106 officers were slain, a 14 percent increase over those killed in 1978. During the period 1975 through 1979, more than 500 law enforcement officers were slain and nearly 100,000 more suffered injuries resulting from assaults.

Data from federal, state and local agencies regarding the felonious killings of these officers follow. Officer fatalities resulting from accidents or activities not within the province of official law enforcement duties are excluded from the analysis.

In 1979, 106 local, county, state and federal law enforcement officers were feloniously killed as compared to 93 in 1978. During the 10-year period, 1970-1979, 1,143 officers were slain. It should be noted

Year	Number of Victim Officers	Year	Number of Victim Officers
1970	100	1975	129
1971	129	1976	111
1972	116	1977	93
1973	134	1978	93
1974	132	1979	106
		Total	1,143

that the collection of statistics regarding officers killed in the line of duty was expanded in 1971 to include United States territories (Puerto Rico, the Virgin Islands and Guam). Also, the gathering of data on slain federal officers was begun in 1972. Therefore, 10-year data on officers killed include figures for United States' territories since 1971 and federal officers since 1972.

Geographic Locations. As in previous years, more officers (49) were slain in 1979 in the country's most populous region, the South, than in any other. Twenty-three officers were killed in the Western States, 16 in the North Central States, 13 in the Northeastern States, three in Puerto Rico and two in Guam. Of all the states, California, with 10 officers slain, lost more officers in line-of-duty deaths than any other; Texas followed with eight officers killed.

Circumstances Surrounding Deaths. During the year, 19 officers were slain by persons engaged in the commission of a robbery or during the pursuit of robbery suspects, and seven lost their lives at the scene of burglaries or while pursuing burglary suspects. Twenty-

one officers were killed while attempting arrests for crimes other than robbery or burglary.

Ambush situations accounted for 11 officers' deaths in 1979. Seventeen officers were slain responding to disturbance calls (family quarrels, man-with-gun calls, bar fights, etc.) and 15 were killed while enforcing traffic laws. Nine officers lost their lives while investigating suspicious persons or circumstances, four while handling mentally deranged persons and three while engaged in the handling, transporting or custody of prisoners.

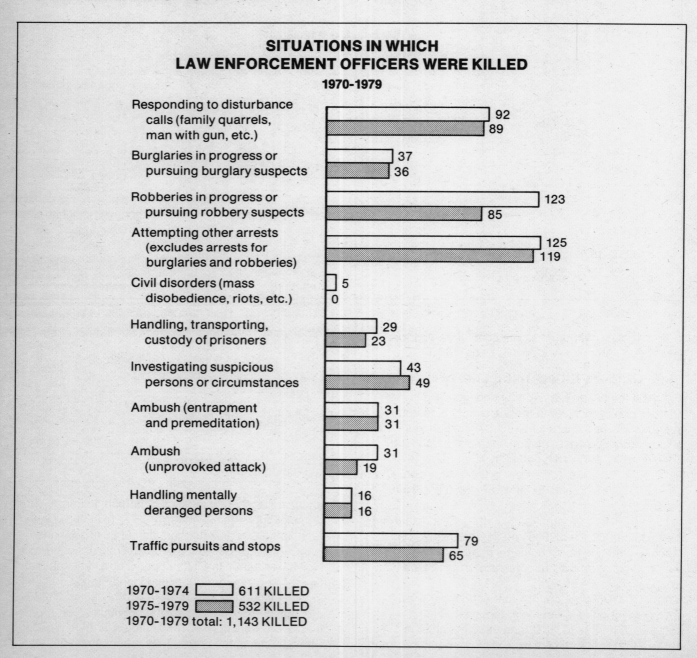

SITUATIONS IN WHICH
LAW ENFORCEMENT OFFICERS WERE KILLED
1970-1979

Situation	1970-1974	1975-1979
Responding to disturbance calls (family quarrels, man with gun, etc.)	92	89
Burglaries in progress or pursuing burglary suspects	37	36
Robberies in progress or pursuing robbery suspects	123	85
Attempting other arrests (excludes arrests for burglaries and robberies)	125	119
Civil disorders (mass disobedience, riots, etc.)	5	0
Handling, transporting, custody of prisoners	29	23
Investigating suspicious persons or circumstances	43	49
Ambush (entrapment and premeditation)	31	31
Ambush (unprovoked attack)	31	19
Handling mentally deranged persons	16	16
Traffic pursuits and stops	79	65

1970-1974 ☐ 611 KILLED
1975-1979 ▨ 532 KILLED
1970-1979 total: 1,143 KILLED

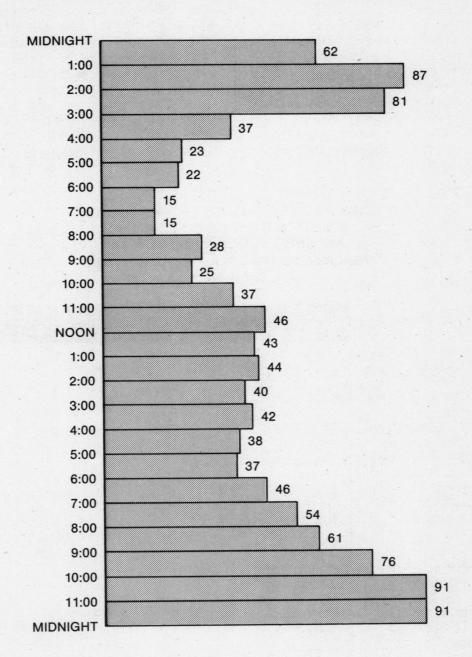

HOUR OF DAY IN WHICH
LAW ENFORCEMENT OFFICERS WERE KILLED
1970-1979

MIDNIGHT	62
1:00	87
2:00	81
3:00	37
4:00	23
5:00	22
6:00	15
7:00	15
8:00	28
9:00	25
10:00	37
11:00	46
NOON	43
1:00	44
2:00	40
3:00	42
4:00	38
5:00	37
6:00	46
7:00	54
8:00	61
9:00	76
10:00	91
11:00	91
MIDNIGHT	

The chart totals 1,141 deaths; the hour of the day in which two officers were killed is not known.

Types of Assignments. Seventy-one of the officers slain in 1979 were on patrol duty, and of those, 68 were assigned to vehicles and three were on foot patrol. The perils inherent in patrol duties are substantiated by the fact that, in recent years, officers assigned in this capacity have consistently been the most frequent victims of the police killer. The patrol officer is often placed in dangerous situations and must react to circumstances as they occur without the benefit of detailed information or planning. He is repeatedly in contact with suspicious or dangerous individuals, each of whom could constitute a threat to his personal safety.

Law enforcement officers assigned in other capacities are confronted with equally tense and dangerous situations, although possibly not with the same regularity as patrol officers. In 1979, 24 officers slain were detectives or on special assignments, and in the highest tradition of the law enforcement profession, 11 officers were murdered off duty while taking appropriate police action in response to a criminal act.

Of the 95 officers who were on duty when slain during 1979, 46 were alone and unassisted when killed. During the period 1970-1979, 42 percent (420) of the on-duty officers killed were alone at the time they were attacked.

Weapons Used. One hundred (94 percent) of the law enforcement officers killed in 1979 were slain with firearms. Seventy-six of these deaths were perpetrated with handguns, 18 with rifles, and six with shotguns. Seventeen officers were felled with their own firearms. Of the six officers not slain with firearms, four were killed with knives, one by a bomb and one by a vehicle.

Forty-nine of the officers who were killed in 1979

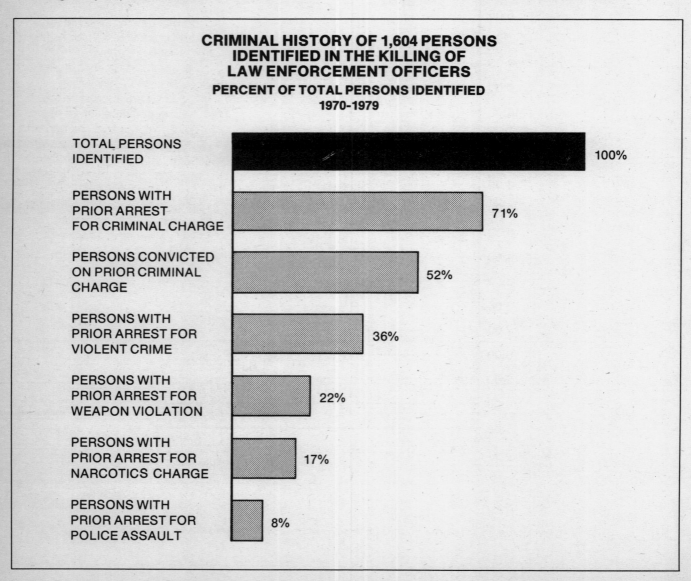

**CRIMINAL HISTORY OF 1,604 PERSONS
IDENTIFIED IN THE KILLING OF
LAW ENFORCEMENT OFFICERS**
PERCENT OF TOTAL PERSONS IDENTIFIED
1970-1979

TOTAL PERSONS IDENTIFIED — 100%

PERSONS WITH PRIOR ARREST FOR CRIMINAL CHARGE — 71%

PERSONS CONVICTED ON PRIOR CRIMINAL CHARGE — 52%

PERSONS WITH PRIOR ARREST FOR VIOLENT CRIME — 36%

PERSONS WITH PRIOR ARREST FOR WEAPON VIOLATION — 22%

PERSONS WITH PRIOR ARREST FOR NARCOTICS CHARGE — 17%

PERSONS WITH PRIOR ARREST FOR POLICE ASSAULT — 8%

attempted to use their service firearms while in contact with their assailants, and 27 of these officers fired their service weapons while attempting to protect themselves. Fifty percent of the officers killed by firearms were within five feet of their assailants at the time they were shot.

Day and Hour of Attack. Although no one day of the week can be singled out as being significantly more hazardous to a law enforcement officer than any other, it can be stated that more officers are slain during nighttime hours than during the daytime. From 1970-1979, 43 percent (488) of the 1,143 officers who lost their lives in the line of duty were killed during the six-hour period, 9 p.m. to 3 a.m.

Officers Killed by Type of Weapon

Type of Weapon	1970-1979 Total number	1970-1979 Per-cent	1970-1974 Number	1970-1974 Per-cent	1975-1979 Number	1975-1979 Per-cent
Handgun	796	69.6	435	71.2	361	67.9
Rifle	150	13.1	73	11.9	77	14.5
Shotgun	132	11.5	75	12.3	57	10.7
Total Firearms	1,078	94.3	583	95.4	495	93.0
Knife	20	1.7	11	1.8	9	1.7
Bomb	9	.8	4	.7	5	.9
Personal Weapons	3	.3	1	.2	2	.4
Other (clubs, etc.)	33	2.9	12	2.0	21	3.9
TOTAL	1,143	100.0	611	100.0	532	100.0

Profile of Victim Officers. Ninety-three (88 percent) of the officers slain during 1979 were white, 10 (nine percent) were black and the remaining three (three percent) were of other races. The average years of service for slain officers was eight. Ten percent of the

Profile of Victim Officers

Law Enforcement Officers	1970-1979	1970-1974	1975-1979
Percent white	89	88	90
Percent black	10	11	9
Percent other race	1	*	1
Average years of service	8	8	8
Percent with 1 year or less of service	12	14	10
Percent with less than 5 years of service	45	48	42
Percent with 5 through 10 years of service	30	27	32
Percent over 10 years of service	25	24	26

*Less than one-half of one percent.
Because of rounding, percentages may not add to totals.

officers killed had one year or less of law enforcement experience; 25 percent had more than one but less than five years of service; 40 percent had five through 10 years of experience; and 26 percent had served as law enforcement officers for more than 10 years.

For the years 1968-1977, the most recent 10-year period for which complete disposition data are available, 1,536 known persons were involved in the killings of 1,094 law enforcement officers. Of these known offenders, 1,280 were arrested and charged with the killings of the officers. The available court disposition data regarding the offenders found guilty of the officers' murders disclosed that 107 were sentenced to death, 407 were sentenced to life imprisonment and 265 received prison terms ranging from one to 2,001 years. Four offenders received probation; five received suspended sentences. The sentences of 14 offenders who were found guilty are unknown.

Motor Vehicle Identification

Because the automobile most often provides transportation for the criminal to and from the scene of his crime, police officers and detectives need a working knowledge of auto identification. The National Auto Theft Bureau (national office: 10330 So. Roberts Rd., Palos Hills, Ill. 60482; divisional offices in Woodbury, N.Y.; Atlanta, Ga; Chicago, Ill.; Dallas, Tex.; and Daly City, Calif.) publishes difficult-to-find information regarding commercial vehicles, domestic and foreign passenger vehicles and motorcycles, as well as boats. Although vehicles are manufactured in many different makes and models each year, some generally applicable I.D. information follows which should assist law enforcement officers in identifying stolen vehicles and vehicles used in the commission of crimes.

PASSENGER VEHICLES

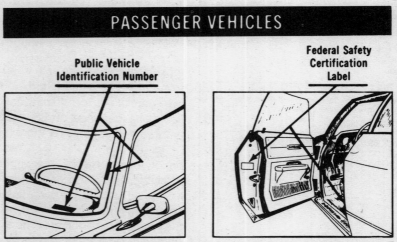

Public Vehicle Identification Number

Federal Safety Certification Label

- Mid 1950's thru 1964 the VIN plates were spot welded to door post. Starting in 1965 they are attached by pop-rivets.
- Vehicles prior to 1956 were identified by the motor number.

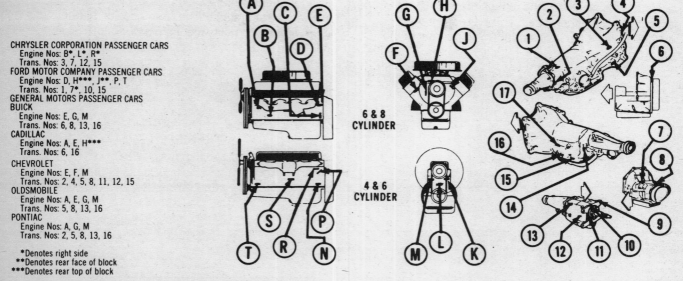

CHRYSLER CORPORATION PASSENGER CARS
Engine Nos: B*, L*, R*
Trans. Nos: 3, 7, 12, 15
FORD MOTOR COMPANY PASSENGER CARS
Engine Nos: D, H***, J**, P, T
Trans. Nos: 1, 7*, 10, 15
GENERAL MOTORS PASSENGER CARS
BUICK
Engine Nos: E, G, M
Trans. Nos: 6, 8, 13, 16
CADILLAC
Engine Nos: A, E, H***
Trans. Nos: 6, 16
CHEVROLET
Engine Nos: E, F, M
Trans. Nos: 2, 4, 5, 8, 11, 12, 15
OLDSMOBILE
Engine Nos: A, E, G, M
Trans. Nos: 5, 8, 13, 16
PONTIAC
Engine Nos: A, G, M
Trans. Nos: 2, 5, 8, 13, 16

*Denotes right side
**Denotes rear face of block
***Denotes rear top of block

6 & 8 CYLINDER

4 & 6 CYLINDER

Imports have an engine number which is not a derivative of the VIN. To determine VIN of an imported vehicle, it will require tracing through your nearest NATB Divisional Office.

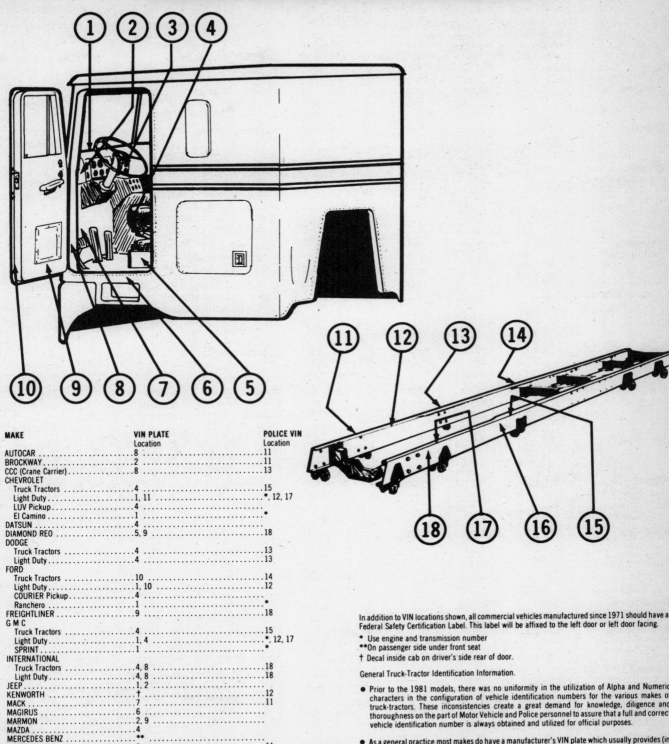

MAKE	VIN PLATE Location	POLICE VIN Location
AUTOCAR	8	11
BROCKWAY	2	11
CCC (Crane Carrier)	8	13
CHEVROLET		
Truck Tractors	4	15
Light Duty	1, 11	*, 12, 17
LUV Pickup	4	
El Camino	1	*
DATSUN	4	
DIAMOND REO	5, 9	18
DODGE		
Truck Tractors	4	13
Light Duty	4	13
FORD		
Truck Tractors	10	14
Light Duty	1, 10	12
COURIER Pickup	4	
Ranchero	1	*
FREIGHTLINER	9	18
G M C		
Truck Tractors	4	15
Light Duty	1, 4	*, 12, 17
SPRINT	1	*
INTERNATIONAL		
Truck Tractors	4, 8	18
Light Duty	4, 8	18
JEEP	1, 2	
KENWORTH	†	12
MACK	7	11
MAGIRUS	6	
MARMON	2, 9	
MAZDA	4	
MERCEDES BENZ	**	
OSHKOSH	9	11
PETERBILT	7	13, 16
PLYMOUTH	4	
VOLVO	3	
WHITE TRUCKS	5, 9	18

In addition to VIN locations shown, all commercial vehicles manufactured since 1971 should have a Federal Safety Certification Label. This label will be affixed to the left door or left door facing.

* Use engine and transmission number
**On passenger side under front seat
† Decal inside cab on driver's side rear of door.

General Truck-Tractor Identification Information.

- Prior to the 1981 models, there was no uniformity in the utilization of Alpha and Numeric characters in the configuration of vehicle identification numbers for the various makes of truck-tractors. These inconsistencies create a great demand for knowledge, diligence and thoroughness on the part of Motor Vehicle and Police personnel to assure that a full and correct vehicle identification number is always obtained and utilized for official purposes.

- As a general practice most makes do have a manufacturer's VIN plate which usually provides (in addition to the vehicle identification number) considerable data as to the year, make, model and construction features. These plates, while not uniformly located, are attached to the cab (door, dash or seat base area). Attachment is usually by screws, brads or rivets. A majority of the manufacturers die stamp a repeat vehicle identification number into the frame rail.

Guide to Controlled Substances

NARCOTICS

Drug	Duration of Effect (Hours)	Dependence Potential Physical	Psychological	Medical Use	Description of Drug	Method of Administration
Codeine	3-6	Moderate	Moderate	Pain relief, cough suppressant	Found in opium but produced from morphine, it appears in tablets, capsules and liquid form.	Oral, injectable
Demerol	3-6	High	High	Pain relief	Tablets: 50 mg., 100 mg. Elixer: banana flavor 16 oz. Injection: 5, 7.5 and 10% solutions.	Oral, injectable
Dilaudid (Hydromorphone)	3-6	High	High	Pain relief	Tablets: 1 mg., 2 mg., 3 mg., 4 mg. Elixir:cough syrup in pint bottles. Suppositories: 3 mg. Injection: 1 mg., 2 mg., 3 mg., 4 mg. Powder: 15-grain vials and ⅛-oz. bottles (derived from opium).	Oral, injectable, per rectum
Dolophine (Methadone)	12-24	High	High	Pain relief, narcotic withdrawal	Tablets: 5 mg., 10 mg. Elixir: pint or gallon. Injection: 1 ml., 20 ml.	Oral, injectable
Heroin (Diacetylmorphine)	3-6	High	High	None	Fine powder off-white to dark brown or in the form of small chunks which may be red or purplish in color. Found in glassine, aluminum foil packets or capsules.	Sniffed, injectable
Methadone	12-24	High	High	Pain relief, narcotic (heroin) withdrawal	Tablets: 5 mg., 10 mg., 40 mg. Injection: 1 ml.	Oral, injectable
Morphine	3-6	High	High	Pain relief	Obtained from a raw opium base; available in white crystalline powder, tablets, capsules or liquid form.	Oral, smoked, sniffed, injectable
Numorphan	3-6	High	High	Pain relief	Tablets: 10 mg. Suppositories: 2 mg., 5 mg. Injection: 1 ml., 1½ ml., 2 ml., 10 ml., 15 ml.	Oral, injectable, per rectum
Opium	3-6	High	High	Pain relief antidiarrheal (as found in Paregoric)	Milky juice from the pod of the unripe poppy plant, *Papaver somniferum*, which thickens upon exposure to air.	Oral, smoked
Percodan	3-6	High	High	Pain relief	Tablets: yellow or pink scored.	Oral

STIMULANTS

Drug	Duration of Effect (Hours)	Dependence Potential Physical	Psychological	Medical Use	Description of Drug	Method of Administration
Benzedrine (Amphetamine)	2-4	None	High	Weight loss	Tablets: scored 5 mg., 10 mg. Capsules: 15 mg.	Oral
Biphetamine	2-4	None	High	Weight loss	Capsules: white 3.75 mg.; black and white or black and green 6.25 mg., black or red and black 10 mg.	Oral
Cocaine	2 (variable)	None	High	Local anesthetic	White crystalline powder extracted from dried coca leaves. Chewing the leaves has a stimulating effect.	Sniffed, injectable
Desoxyn (Methamphetamine)	2-4	None	High	Weight loss	Tablets: white 2.5 mg., 5 mg.; orange 10 mg.; yellow 15 mg.	Oral
Dexedrine (Dextroamphetamine)	2-4	None	High	Weight loss	Tablets: 5 mg. Capsules: 5 mg., 10 mg., 15 mg. Elixir: 16-oz. bottles.	Oral
Didrex	2-4	None	High	Weight loss	Tablets: unscored 25 mg.; scored 50 mg.	Oral

Drug	Duration of Effect (Hours)	Dependence Potential		Medical Use	Description of Drug	Method of Administration
		Physical	Psychological			
Methedrine (*Methamphetamine*)	2-4	None	High	Weight loss	Tablets: white. Powder: white.	Oral, injectable
Preludin	2-4	None	High	Weight loss	Tablets: square scored 25 mg.; round pink 75 mg.	Oral
Ritalin	2-4	None	High	Treatment of mild depression, senility, hyperkinesis	Tablets: pale yellow 5 mg.; pale green 10 mg.; peach 20 mg. Injection: 10 ml., multiple dose vials.	Oral, injectable
Tenuate	2-4	None	High	Weight loss	Tablets: light blue 25 mg.; white capsule shaped 75 mg.	Oral

SEDATIVES-HYPNOTICS
Barbiturates

Drug	Duration of Effect (Hours)	Physical	Psychological	Medical Use	Description of Drug	Method of Administration
Amytal (*Amobarbital*)	1-16	High	High	Sedation, relief of anxiety and tension, preanesthetic medication	Tablets: capsule-shaped, scored, light green 15 mg.; yellow 30 mg.; orange 50 mg.; pink 100 mg. Elixirs: pint or gallon.	Oral
Gemonil (*Methabarbitol*)	1-16	High	High	Control of seizures	Tablets: white 100 mg.	Oral
Mebaral	1-16	High	High	Sedation, anticonvulsant, antispasmodic, relief of tension and anxiety	Tablets: 32 mg., 50 mg., 100 mg., 200 mg.	Oral
Nembutal	1-16	High	High	Sedation	Capsules: yellow 30 mg., 100 mg.; clear with yellow cap 50 mg.; blue 100 mg. Elixir: pint or gallon.	Oral
Seconal	1-16	High	High	Insomnia, sedation	Tablets: 100 mg. Capsules: orange 30 mg., 50 mg., 100 mg. Elixir: pint or gallon. Suppositories: 30 mg., 60 mg., 120 mg., 200 mg. Injection: 50 mg., 100 mg., 250 mg. Powder ½-oz. bottles.	Oral, injectable, per rectum
Tuinal	4- 8	High	High	Sedation	Capsules: blue and orange 50 mg., 100 mg., 200 mg.	Oral

SEDATIVES-HYPNOTICS
Non-barbiturates

Drug	Duration of Effect (Hours)	Physical	Psychological	Medical Use	Description of Drug	Method of Administration
Dalmane	4-8	High	High	Insomnia	Capsules: orange and ivory 15 mg.; red and ivory 30 mg.	Oral
Doriden	4-72	High	High	Sedation	Tablets: white scored 125 mg., 250 mg., 500 mg. Capsules: blue and white 500 mg.	Oral
Equanil (*Meprobamate*)	4-8	High	High	Relief of anxiety and tension, sedation	Tablets: white scored 200 mg., 400 mg., sealed yellow 400 mg. Capsules: 400 mg. Elixir: 200 mg. 4 fl. oz. bottles.	Oral
Miltown (*Meprobamate*)	4-8	High	High	Relief of anxiety, and tension, muscle relaxant, anticonvulsant	Tablets: white scored 400 mg.; white sugar-coated 200 mg.; 400 mg. Capsules: blue topped 400 mg.; yellow topped 200 mg.	Oral
Noctec	4-8	High	High	Sedation, relief of anxiety	Capsules: red 250 mg., 500 mg. Elixir: orange flavored pint or gallon. Syrup: 250mg., 500 mg./tsp. Suppositories: 325 mg., 650 mg., 975 mg., 1.3 gms.	Oral, per rectum
Noludar	4-8	High	High	Insomnia	Tablets: scored and monogrammed 50 mg., 200 mg. Capsules: amethyst and white 300 mg.	Oral

Drug	Duration of Effect (Hours)	Dependence Potential		Medical Use	Description of Drug	Method of Administration
		Physical	Psychological			
Parest (Methaqualone)	6-8	High	High	Insomnia	Capsules: light turquoise blue cap with light-green body 200 mg.; blue cap with light-green body 400 mg.	Oral
Placidyl	4-8	High	High	Insomnia	Capsules: 100 mg., 200 mg., 500 mg., 750 mg.	Oral
Quaalude (Methaqualone)	4-8	High	High	Sedation and insomnia	Tablets: white scored 150 mg., 300 mg.	Oral
Somnafac (Methaqualone)	6-8	High	High	Insomnia	Capsules: two-tone blue 200 mg.; dark blue 400 mg.	Oral
Sopor (Methaqualone)	6-8	High	High	Insomnia, sedation	Tablets: green scored 75 mg.; yellow scored 150 mg.; orange scored 300 mg.	Oral

MAJOR TRANQUILIZERS
Anti-psychotic Agents

Drug	Duration of Effect (Hours)	Physical	Psychological	Medical Use	Description of Drug	Method of Administration
Haldol	24	None	Moderate	Control of psychotic behavior	Tablets: white ½ mg.; yellow 1 mg.; pink 2 mg.; green 5 mg. Injection: 15 cc. and bottles.	Oral, injectable
Mellaril	24	None	Moderate	Control of psychotic behavior, convulsant	Tablets: bright chartreuse 10 mg.; light tan 25 mg.; white 50 mg.; light chartreuse 100 mg.; yellow 150 mg.; pink 200 mg. Injection: 4 oz. or pint.	Oral, injectable
Navane	24	None	Moderate	Control of psychotic behavior	Capsules: 1 mg., 2 mg., 5 mg., 10 mg. Injection: 4-oz. bottles.	Oral, injectable
Stelazine	24	None	Moderate	Relief of anxiety, control of psychotic behavior	Tablets: 1 mg., 2 mg., 5 mg., 10 mg. Injection: 2-oz. bottles.	Oral, injectable
Thorazine	24	None	Moderate	Relief of tension and anxiety, pain relief, control of neurotic and psychotic behavior, nausea, alcohol withdrawal	Tablets: 10 mg., 25 mg., 50 mg., 100 mg., 200 mg. Capsules: 30 mg., 75 mg., 150 mg., 200 mg., 300 mg. Elixir: 4-oz. bottles. Suppositories: 25 mg., 100 mg. Injection: 4 oz., 8 oz., or gallon.	Oral, injectable, per rectum

MINOR TRANQUILIZERS
Anti-anxiety Agents

Drug	Duration of Effect (Hours)	Physical	Psychological	Medical Use	Description of Drug	Method of Administration
Librium	4-8	None	Moderate	Relief of tension and anxiety, alcohol withdrawal	Tablets: 5 mg., 10 mg., 25 mg. Capsules: green and yellow 5 mg.; green and black 10 mg.; green and white 25 mg. Injection: 5 ml.	Oral, injectable
Serax	4-8	None	Moderate	Relief of tension and anxiety, depression, alcohol withdrawal	Tablets: yellow 15 mg. Capsules: pink and white 10 mg., red and white 15 mg., maroon and white 30 mg.	Oral
Valium (Diazepam)	4-8	None	Moderate	Relief of tension and anxiety, depression, alcohol withdrawal, muscle spasm	Tablets: white 2 mg., yellow 5 mg., blue 10 mg. Injection: 2 ml., 10 ml.	Oral, injectable

HALLUCINOGENS

Drug	Duration of Effect (Hours)	Dependence Potential Physical	Dependence Potential Psychological	Medical Use	Description of Drug	Method of Administration
DMT	15-45 minutes	None	Unknown	None	A crystalline powder made chemically or from extracts of a plant grown in the West Indies.	Smoked
LSD	8-12	None	Unknown	Scientific research available through the National Institute of Mental Health, Bethesda, MD	Colorless, odorless, tasteless liquid or powder in tablet or capsule form, and can be produced from the ergot fungus which grows on rye.	Oral
PCP Angel Dust	2-4	None	Unknown	Veterinary anesthetic	Appears in powder, tablet or capsule form.	Oral, smoked, injectable
Peyote— Mescaline	8-12	None	Unknown	None	Peyote, and its active ingredient mescaline, come from a small cactus native to the American Southwest and Mexico, found in button form or as a brown powder in capsule form.	Oral, injectable
Psilocybin	8-12	None	Unknown	None	A Mexican mushroom eaten as is or ground into a brown powder and put into capsules.	Oral
STP— DOM	24	None	Unknown	None	Similar to LSD with the addition of amphetamine; appears in powder, tablet or capsule.	Oral

CANNABIS

Drug	Duration of Effect (Hours)	Dependence Potential Physical	Dependence Potential Psychological	Medical Use	Description of Drug	Method of Administration
Hash Oil	2-4	None	Unknown	None	Black, thick, oil-like liquid made from hashish.	Smoked
Hashish	2-4	None	Unknown	None	Light-green-brown, dark brown or black cakes ¼ to ¾-inch thick.	Oral, smoked
Marijuana	2-4	None	Unknown	None	Dried, ground leaves from *Cannabis sativa* plant.	Smoked, oral

Guide to Drug Abuse

	Possible Effects	Effects of Overdose	Withdrawal Syndrome
Cannabis sativa	Drowsiness; excitation; restlessness; anxiety; euphoria; depression; hallucinations; panic; talkativeness; laughter; relaxed inhibitions; disoriented behavior; increased appetite; distortion of space and time	Fatigue; paranoia	Withdrawal syndrome not reported
Hallucinogens	Euphoria; depression; hallucinations; panic; irrational behavior; tremor; rambling speech; distortion of space and time; central nervous system malfunctions; dilated pupils; high temperature and blood pressure	Psychosis; longer, more intense effects of the drug; extreme anxiety	Withdrawal syndrome not reported
Narcotics	Euphoria; drowsiness; nausea; respiratory depression; constricted pupils; slurred speech; hallucinations; loss of appetite; depressant of central nervous system	Slow and shallow breathing; clammy skin; convulsions; unconsciousness; possible death from respiratory depression (Artificial respiration should be used)	Watery eyes; runny nose; yawning; irritability; tremors; anxiety; panic; confusion; chills and sweating; dilated pupils; insomnia; cramps; diarrhea; nausea and vomiting
Sedative-hypnotics and tranquilizers	Slurred speech; disorientation; drunken-like behavior; excitement or disinhibition; respiratory depression; sedation; general anesthesia (for sedative-hypnotics only); indifference; apathy; drowsiness; motor retardation; (pupil size not relevant)	Drowsiness; respiratory depression; depression of reflexes; lowered blood pressure and body temperature; shock; coma; possible death	Anxiety; convulsions; delirium; insomnia; elevated blood pressure; pulse; respiration; hallucinations; possible death (for sedative-hypnotics only; withdrawal syndromes for tranquilizers are not reported); dangerously high body temperature; psychotic behavior
Stimulants	Increased alertness, excitation and hyperactivity; anxiety; hallucinations; talkativeness; tremor; dizziness; loss of appetite; insomnia; unusually bright shiny eyes with dilated pupils; increased pulse and blood pressure	Agitation; increase in body temperature; hallucinations; convulsions; possible death	Apathy; long periods of sleep; irritability; depression; disorientation

Admissibility of Confessions by Juveniles

The law appropriately recognizes that the conditions under which confessions or statements of confession by juveniles are given should be examined by the court on the question of admissibility.

Before a confession or statement of confession can be received into evidence, the state must make a showing prima facie that the circumstances under which it was obtained were consistent with constitutional requirements. In the search to find the answers to that question, the courts appear to be following the "totality of circumstances" rule.

In applying the "totality of circumstances" rule, the following factors appear to be important:

1. Age. Naturally enough, the court will be more apt to consider a 17-year-old's confession voluntary than a 12-year-old's confession.

2. Presence of parents at the questioning of the juvenile. Adult presence and consent to a juvenile's statement are desired. Evidence showing the presence of the parents at the questioning is perhaps the strongest showing of voluntariness of the statement. Even better is evidence that the parent gave permission for the juvenile to answer the questions.

If the parents are not there, the evidence should show the efforts made by the police to contact the parents. Also, show why parents were not present; e.g. ill, refused to come to the place of questioning, could not be reached by phone, or other methods, etc. A valid explanation of why the parents were not present is necessary.

If the evidence does not show the presence of the parents or attempts to contact the parents, a showing that the juvenile had talked to his parents or another adult prior to the questioning is important.

The presence of parents at the interrogation of the juvenile is an extremely important factor in determining the voluntariness of the statement. Many cases cited allude to this factor.

3. Who was present at the interrogation? The showing of any responsible adult's presence will help establish the voluntariness of the juvenile's statements. Determine if a parent, relative, minister, lawyer, etc., was present when the juvenile's statements were made.

4. Was the juvenile in the custody of persons in authority when his statement was made? More factors indicating voluntariness will have to be shown if he was in the custody of the police or other law enforcement officers. Persons of authority indicate some coercion, intentional or unconscious, in the making of a statement.

5. Who questioned the juvenile? Again, more factors of voluntariness are required if the questioning is done by authorities.

6. Miranda warnings. It is essential that the juvenile be given his Miranda warnings by the police. Welfare workers or probation officers should also give Miranda warnings. The rationale is that they are enough under the control of, and clothed with, authority of law to require they give the warnings. Whether store detectives have to give Miranda warnings will generally depend upon whether they have been commissioned or are acting under some other type of police power. There are no decisions indicating that school authorities have to give Miranda warnings.

To show voluntariness of confessions, the Miranda warnings should be given separately rather than all at once. After each right is given, the juvenile should be asked if he understands that right. If he says no, efforts should be made to explain it to him. Your report should show all this; you must convince the judge that the juvenile did understand his rights. Merely reciting the Miranda warnings is not enough; the evidence must show that these constitutional rights were understood by the juvenile.

Some courts consider the number of times during the interrogation the juvenile is told he does not have to talk. Apparently, the more times the juvenile is reminded of his right to remain silent, the greater the probability of a voluntary statement.

7. Time involved in questioning.

a. What was the duration of the questioning? The longer the interrogation period, the less likely that the statement was voluntary. A relentless and sustained interrogation would seem to negate voluntariness.

b. What time of day did the questioning take place? If the questioning is done during the daylight working hours, this would help indicate voluntariness. On the other hand, a night-time interrogation might point to a coerced statement.

8. Physical state of the juvenile.

a. Was the juvenile under the influence of drugs or alcohol?

b. During the interrogation, was the juvenile sleepy or showing signs of lack of sleep?

c. Did the juvenile go a long time without food before he gave his statement?

In all cases, the courts would most likely rule the confession was involuntary.

9. Emotional state of the juvenile. The courts consider emotional factors like fear, nervousness, excitement as showing lack of voluntariness of the statement. If your witness testifies that the juvenile was calm rational and composed during the questioning and when making statements, this will indicate a voluntary statement.

10. Mental state of the juvenile. The court will want to know the educational background of the juvenile—such things as school attended, grade, whether he is a repeater, how he is doing in school (grades), etc. Although this will rarely be available, an I.Q. rating of the juvenile may be used. It should be noted that a low I.Q. (75-80) does not per se make the confession invalid. I.Q. however, is a factor.

11. Place at which juvenile was questioned. The court will be interested in the place used for questioning. Was it the squad car, a room in the police station, the principal's office at school or on the street? Also to be noted are the conditions of the place where the juvenile was questioned.

12. Past experience of the juvenile with the police and courts? One of the best arguments for voluntariness of the statement is that the juvenile has been confronted by the police before, that he has been given his Miranda warnings previously, and that he has appeared in court on prior occasions. Once it has been shown the juvenile has prior experiences with police and the courts, it will be hard to him to argue he didn't know what he was doing when he made the statements.

13. Conduct of the authorities when questioning. If there is evidence of threats, cajolery, trickery or subterfuge the statement will probably be thrown out. Any offer or promise by the police to the juvenile will invalidate the confession. A showing that the police were callous, angry or abusive will probably bar the confession. We must show that the police were courteous, unemotional, objective and reasonable in their questioning of the juvenile.

14. Failure to bring the juvenile immediately before a juvenile court judge. The question here is what is immediate. Unfortunately, the cases don't really give a guide.

15. Length of detention. If the evidence shows the juvenile has been detained for a long period of time prior to the confession, the court would rule this as a coercive factor in looking at the voluntariness of the confession.

16. Detained incommunicado. Similarly, an incommunicado detention indicates coercion.

17. Sophisticated approach of the juvenile toward the police. For example, if the juvenile offers to deal with the police regarding sentence, this would indicate a sophistication capable of voluntarily giving a statement and understanding the consequences.

18. Juvenile's background. This broad factor covers points like family background (Have other members of the family been involved with the police?), neighborhood, home, parents and siblings, etc.

If from these 18 factors the "totality of circumstances" shows a voluntary waiver of the juvenile's constitutional rights, his statement will be allowed into evidence. Not every case will have evidence of each factor; further, each factor does not have equal weight. These factors can only serve as a guide as to what the court will look for in ruling on the voluntariness of the statement.

One of the leading cases taking into consideration all the circumstances behind a juvenile's confession and most of those discussed above, is a U.S. Supreme Court decision, *Haley v. Ohio,* 332 U.S. 596 (1948).

In this case, Haley, a Negro boy, aged 15, was convicted of murder in the first degree and was sentenced to life imprisonment. His conviction was affirmed by the Ohio appellate courts and he appealed to the U.S. Supreme Court on the basis that admission of his confession at his trial violated the Fourteenth Amendment of the U.S. Constitution.

Relative to the facts of this case, the Supreme Court ruled:

"Taking only the undisputed testimony, we have the following sequence of events. Beginning shortly after midnight, this 15-year-old lad was questioned by the police for about five hours. Five or six of the police officers questioned him in relays of one or two each. During this time no friend or counsel of the boy was present. Around 5 a.m.—after being shown alleged confessions of Lowder and Parks—the boy confessed. A confession was typed in question-and-answer form by the police. At no time was this boy advised of his right to counsel; but the written confession started off with the following statement.

> We want to inform you of your constitutional rights, the law gives you the right to make this statement or not as you see fit. It is made with the understanding that it may be used at a trial in court either for or against you or anyone else involved in this crime with you, of your own free will and accord, you are under no force or duress or compulsion and no promises are being made to you at this time whatsoever.
>
> Do you still desire to make this statement and tell the truth after having had the above clause read to you?
> A. Yes.

"He was put in jail about 6 or 6:30 a.m. on Saturday, the 20th, shortly after the confession was signed. Between then and Tuesday the 23rd, he was held incommunicado. A lawyer retained by his mother tried to see him twice but was refused admission by the police. His mother was not allowed to see him until Thursday, the 25th. But a newspaper photographer was allowed to see him and take his picture in the early morning hours of the 20th, right after he had confessed. He was not taken before a magistrate and formally charged with a crime until the 23rd—three days after the confession was signed.

"The trial court, after a preliminary hearing on the voluntary character of the confession, allowed it to be admitted into evidence over the petitioner's objection that it violated his rights under the Fourteenth Amendment. The court instructed the jury to disregard the confession if it found that he did not make the confession voluntarily and of his free will."

In finding his confession inadmissable because the circumstances would indicate it was involuntarily given, the Court said:

"We do not think the methods used in obtaining this confession can be squared with that due process of law which the Fourteenth Amendment commands.

"What transpired would make us pause for careful inquiry if a mature man were involved. And when, as here, a mere child—an easy victim of the law—is before us, special care in scrutinizing the record must be used. Age 15 is a tender and difficult age for a boy of any race. He cannot be judged by the more exacting standards of maturity. That which would leave a man cold and unimpressed can overawe and overwhelm a lad in his early teens. This is the period of great instability which the crisis of adolescence produces. A 15-year-old lad, questioned through the dead of night by relays of police, is a ready victim of the inquisition. Mature men possibly might stand the ordeal from midnight to 5 a.m. But we cannot believe that a lad of tender years is a match for the police in such a contest. He needs counsel and support if he is not to become the victim first of fear, then of panic. He needs someone on whom to lean, lest the overpowering presence of the law, as he knows it, crush him. No friend stood at the side of this 15-year-old boy as the police, working in relays, questioned him hour after hour, from midnight until dawn. No lawyer stood guard to make sure that the police went so far and no farther, to see to it that they stopped short of the point where he became the victim of coercion. No counsel or friend was called during the critical hours of questioning.

"The age of the defendant, the hours he was grilled, the duration of his quizzing, the fact that he had no friend or counsel to advice him, the callous attitude of the police toward his rights combine to convince us that this was a confession wrung from a child by means which the law should not sanction. Neither man nor child can be allowed to stand condemned by methods which flout constitutional requirements of due process of law.

"But we are told that this boy was advised of his constitutional rights before he signed the confession and that, knowing them, he nevertheless confessed. That assumes, however, that a boy of 15, without aid of counsel, would have a full appreciation of that advice and that on the facts of this record he had a freedom of choice. We cannot indulge those assumptions. Moreover, we cannot give any weight to recitals which merely formalize constitutional requirements. Formulas of respect for constitutional safeguards cannot prevail over the facts of life which contradict them. They may not become a cloak for inquisitorial practices and make an empty form of the due process of law for which free men fought and died to obtain."

Justice Felix Frankfurter, in his concurring opinion, summed up the problem of determining whether a juvenile's confession is voluntary or coerced.

"(W)hether a confession of a lad of 15 is 'voluntary' and as such admissible, or 'coerced' and thus wanting in due process, is not a matter of mathematical determination. Essentially, it invites psychological judgment — a psychological judgment that reflects deep, even if inarticulate, feelings of our society. Judges must divine that feeling as best they can from all the relevant evidence and judgment of such an issue, and with every endeavor to detach themselves from their merely private views."

How to Observe and Describe People

In police work, observation means perception of details pertaining to persons, objects, places and events through the use of the five senses. While sight and hearing are relied upon most often, the senses of smell, taste and touch may occasionally be employed to advantage.

The investigator must be able to observe accurately, to recognize infractions of the law and persons and objects of interest to law enforcement and crime prevention programs. Keen observation is necessary to perceive investigative leads, to evaluate the validity of statements by witnesses and to make accurate reports. Only through practice and experience can the ability to observe accurately be developed.

It is essential that the investigator be aware of influences that tend to impede or otherwise affect observation. He must be able to recognize and compensate for those elements and factors that may detract from his or others' ability to observe effectively.

Events or remarks that are meaningless when seen or overheard by the layman may be of great significance to the trained and experienced investigator. To assist in remembering his observations, the investigator makes extensive use of photographs, sketches, notes and other recording methods.

The investigator diligently observes individuals either to be able to describe them or to identify them from descriptions made by others.

Deliberate observation should proceed methodically from the general to the specific:

First, observe general characteristics, such as sex, race, color of skin, height, build, weight and age;

Second, specific characteristics, such as color of hair and eyes, shape of head and face, distinguishing marks and scars, mannerisms and habits;

Third, changeable characteristics, such as clothing worn, use of cosmetics, hair styling, etc.

When attempting to identify a person from a description, the pattern of observation may be modified or even reversed, particularly if the individual sought has some very noticeable personal characteristic—for example, a man with a limp or a very tall woman.

After noting such a characteristic, further observation of general characteristics (such as height, weight and age) and additional specific characteristics may then complete the identification of the individual as the person being sought.

Description Techniques

The investigator makes descriptions to convey to others either his own observations or the observations of witnesses as reported to him. Such descriptions will usually be written or verbal, but may include signs, gestures, sketches and other means of imparting information. It is essential that the investigator be proficient in both written description—for report writing—and verbal description—for appearances as a witness in legal proceedings.

Every individual has some distinguishing characteristic or combination of characteristics that set him apart from other persons. These distinctive features are the most important part of the description of a person.

It is important that the investigator describe persons so completely and accurately that others will readily be able to recognize the described individuals. Precise description is facilitated by following a pattern that normally proceeds from general characteristics to specific characteristics.

OBSERVING PEOPLE

GENERAL CHARACTERISTICS

Sex	Height
Race	Weight
Build	Age

SPECIFIC CHARACTERISTICS
Color of hair and eyes
Shape of head and face
Mannerisms
Marks and scars

CHANGEABLE CHARACTERISTICS
Clothing
Hair style
Cosmetics

General Characteristics. The following commonly accepted and understood words, terms and methods are recommended for use in describing general characteristics of a person:

Sex. Male or female.

Race. Caucasian, Negroid (Black), American Indian, Mongolian or Malayan.

Height. Exact or estimated. When the height is estimated, this should be clearly indicated. A convenient method of estimating height involves simply comparison with own height. For purposes of simplification, estimated height may be stated in 2-inch blocks, such as 5 feet 8 inches to 5 feet 10 inches, 5 feet 10 inches to 6 feet.

Build (including posture).

General—large, average or small (slight).

Specific—obese (very stout), stout, stocky, medium or slim (slender).

Posture—straight (erect), medium or stooped.

Females—in describing the build of a woman, the investigator should bear in mind that, while the descriptive terms listed above are equally applicable and may be employed, there are basic differences in build and body proportions between the male and the female figures. The female figure tends to be smooth and rounded, while the male's is more angular and muscular. An important part of the description of the build of a female is the appearance of the bust, which should be described as flat, medium or heavy.

Weight. Exact or estimated. If estimated, this should be clearly indicated. As in estimating height, a convenient method for estimating weight is by comparison with the investigator's own weight. Estimates should be stated in 10-pound increments, such as 160 to 170 pounds, 170 to 180 pounds.

Age. Actual or estimated. Estimations should be clearly indicated. For convenience, age may be estimated in multiples of five years. In describing a person's age, it may often be of particular importance to indicate not only the actual age, but also the general age indicated by appearance.

Complexion. Pale, fair, dark, ruddy, sallow (sickly pale) or florid (flushed). Clear, pimpled, blotched, freckled, pockmarked, etc. In the case of a female, the description should include makeup habits, such as none, light, heavy, or other applicable terms or phrases. For blacks, complexion should be described as light brown, medium brown, dark or olive.

Specific Characteristics. In the interest of thoroughness and uniformity, the investigator should pattern both his observation and his description of the specific characteristics of a person along systematic lines, usually beginning with the head and progressing downward.

Head. *Size and shape.* Large, medium or small; long or short; broad or narrow; round, flat in back, flat on top, egg-shaped, high in crown, bulging in back, etc.

Profile. Divide mentally into three parts or sections. Each third is then described in its relationship to the whole and in separate detail. Except in the case of peculiarities, the description of the profile is not as important for identification purposes as is the description of the frontal view of the face.

Face. Round, square, oval, broad or long (as seen from the front).

Hair. Color as blond (light or dark), brown (light or dark), red (light or dark), auburn, black, gray, streaked with gray or white. In the case of bleached, tinted or dyed hair, both the artificial and the natural color should be indicated when possible. Density as thick, medium, thin or sparse. Hairline as low, medium, receding, receding over temples, etc. Baldness should be described as complete, whole top of head, occipital, frontal, receding or the appropriate combination of types. Hair type as straight, wavy, curly or kinky. Hair texture as fine, medium or coarse. Appearance as neat, bushy, unkempt, oily or dry. Hair style as long, medium or short; parted on left, parted on right, parted in center or not parted.

Current descriptive terms of hairstyles which are readily and widely understood should be used as appropriate. Wigs, toupees and hairpieces should be described carefully and in detail. The astute observer can often determine whether a person is wearing a toupee or other hairpiece from such indications as difference in hair texture, color, density, type or appearance. Furthermore, the arrangement of false hair will often be too nearly perfect, and the edges of the hairpiece evident upon close scrutiny.

Forehead. High, medium or low. Slope as receding, medium, vertical, prominent or bulging. Width as wide, medium or narrow. Wrinkles or age lines as none, light, deep, horizontal, curved (up or down) or vertical.

Eyebrows. Color, including any difference from hair color. Slant from center (horizontal, slanted up, slanted down). Line as straight or arched, separated or connected. Texture as heavy, medium or thin. Hair as short, medium or long; plucked; penciled. In describing females, it is often important that both the natural and the artificial appearance and contour of the eyebrows be indicated.

Eyes. Deep-set (sunken), medium or bulging. Separation between them as wide, medium or narrow. Crossed, watery, red or other noticeable peculiarity. Color of iris. Eyelids as normal, drooping, puffy, red, etc. Eyelashes as to color; long, medium or short; straight, curled or drooping. Eyeshadow as none, light, dark or irregular. In describing females, the normal eye makeup habits should be noted as to color, type and extent.

Eyeglasses. Eyeglasses should be described in detail to include style and color of frames, type and color of lenses and method of attachment to face. Contact lenses may prove difficult to observe. However, the careful observer will note such indications of the presence of contact lenses as watery eyes and excessive blinking. Special types of eyeglasses, such as monocles, pince-nez or bifocals, should be carefully noted.

Nose. Length as short, medium or long. Width as thin, medium or thick. Projection as long, medium or short.

Base of the nose as turned up, horizontal or turned downward. The root of the nose (juncture with the forehead) should be described as flat, small, medium or large. The line of the nose should be described as concave, straight, convex (hooked), roman or aquiline. Nostrils should be indicated as medium, wide or narrow; large or small; high or low; round, elongated or flaring. Peculiarities, such as broken, twisted to right or left, turned up, pendulous, hairy, deep-pored, etc., should be carefully noted and reported.

Mouth. Size as small, medium or large (as viewed from front). Expression as stern, sad, (corners drooping), pleasant or smiling. Peculiarities, such as prominent changes made when speaking or laughing, twitching, habitually open, etc., should be indicated.

Lips. Thin, medium or thick (as viewed from front); long, medium or short (as viewed in profile). Position as normal, lower protruding, upper protruding or both protruding. Color. Appearance as smooth, chapped, puffy, loose, compressed, tight (retracted over teeth), moist, dry, etc. Harelip and other peculiarities should be carefully noted. In the case of females, color, type and extent of lipstick should be described. In this connection, the careful investigator will be alert for the use of lipstick to alter or accent the natural appearance of the lips.

Mustache and Beard. Color, including any difference from hair color. Style and configuration, and state of grooming (unshaven).

Teeth. Color; receding, normal or protruding; large, medium or small; stained, decayed, broken, false, gold flared, uneven, missing or gaps between teeth.

Chin. Normal, receding or jutting (as viewed in profile); short, medium or long (as viewed from the front); small, large, pointed, square, dimpled, cleft or double.

Cheeks. Full, bony, angular, fleshy, sunken or flat. Cheekbones as high (prominent), medium or receding. In the case of women, makeup habits should be noted.

Ears. Small, medium or large. Shape as oval, round, triangular, rectangular or other appropriate term. Lobe as descending, square, medium or gulfed. Separation from the head should be described as close, normal or protruding; and setting (based on a line extended horizontally back from the outside corner of the eye, which crosses the normally set ear at the upper third) should be indicated as low, normal or high.

Hearing aids should be described in detail as to type (such as inside the ear, behind the ear, with cord, cordless, etc.), color and ear in which worn.

Neck. Short or long; straight or curved; thin or thick. Adam's apple as large (prominent), medium or small.

Shoulders. Small, medium or heavy; narrow, medium or broad; square or round; level or one side lower.

As seen in profile, straight, stooped, slumped or humped.

Arms. Long, medium or short in comparison to the body (average or medium arms terminate with the heel of the hand about halfway between the hips and the knee when the arms are hanging naturally). Musculature as slight, medium or heavy.

Hands and Fingers. *Hands.* Small, medium or large in relation to the size of the individual. Peculiarities should be noted in detail.

Fingers. Long, medium or short; thin, medium or thick (stubby). Deformities, such as missing fingers, crooked fingers, disfigured nails, etc., should be indicated.

Trunk. *Overall.* Long, medium or short (in relation to rest of body).

Chest. Deep, medium or flat, as seen in profile; broad, medium or narrow, as seen from the front.

Back. Straight, curved, humped, bowed, etc., as viewed in profile; straight or curved, as viewed from rear.

Waist. Small, medium or large.

Abdomen. Flat, medium or protruding.

Hips. Broad, medium or narrow, as seen from the front; small, medium or large, as seen in profile. In this connection, the observer should keep in mind the basic differences between male and female figures as discussed earlier in this section.

Legs. Long, medium or short in comparison to rest of the body (average or medium legs combined with the hips constitute about half the body length); straight, bowed (bandy) or knock-kneed; musculature as slight, medium or heavy.

Feet. Small, medium or large in relation to body size. Deformities and peculiarities, such as pigeon-toed, flat-footed, clubfooted, etc., should be carefully recorded.

Marks and Scars. Such identifying marks as birthmarks, moles, warts, tatoos, and scars should be clearly described as to size, color, location on the body and shape.

Speech. The tone and manner of a person's speech may often be very important aspects of his complete description. His habitual tone should be indicated as low, medium or loud; soft or gruff; or by other descriptive qualities. His manner of speaking should be indicated as cultured, vulgar, clipped, fluent, broken English, with accent (identified whenever possible) or non-English speaking (language specified when possible). Such peculiarities as stuttering, nasal twang. pronounced drawl or a mute condition should be clearly indicated and explained.

Dress. Since a person may change clothing, its value for descriptive purposes is limited. Noticeable habits in manner of dress, such as neatness, carelessness and preferences of style, however, should be indicated. Clothing worn by a person at the time of an offense or when last seen should be described in detail, such as military and civilian, color(s) and condition (clean, soiled, torn, ragged, greasy or bloodstained).

Personal Appearance. Neat or untidy; well-groomed or unkempt; refined or rough.

Mannerisms and Habits. Often the peculiar mannerisms or traits a person exhibits will constitute the major or key parts of his description. The investigator must be alert to record such characteristcs as:

- Feminine traits in men and masculine traits in women
- Peculiarities in walking, moving or talking
- Outward emotional instability, nervousness or indecision
- Type of companions preferred
- Nervous-type repetitive mannerisms, such as scratching the nose, running the hand through the hair, pulling on an ear, hitching up the pants, jingling keys or flipping coins
- Facial tics, muscular twitches and excessive talking with the hands
- Kinds of recreation preferred or hobbies pursued
- Jewelry worn and types of jewelry preferred

Human factors. An individual's perception is largely determined and influenced by his past experiences, physiological and psychological influences and training. The investigator must recognize the implication of these factors and be able to evaluate their effects on the observations of a witness or victim.

Physiological Influences. Defects, both permanent and temporary, in the physical condition of an individual may greatly affect his ability to observe accurately and interpret his observations properly. Such factors as age, disease, injury, underdevelopment and undernourishment must be considered by the investigator whenever appropriate. Pain, hunger, fatigue and unnatural positions of the body may cause a witness to interpret inaccurately observations he would normally place in proper mental perspective.

The following general factors should be considered:

- A person of unusuallly short or tall stature may misinterpret the size of another person. For example, a person six feet tall may appear very tall to an observer who is only 4 feet 10 inches tall, while the same six-footer would likely appear to be of normal height to an observer who is 5 feet 10 inches tall.
- The senses of hearing and touch of a blind person are usually developed far beyond those of a person with normal vision. Thus, a blind person may frequently perceive sounds or note details of objects touched which the normal person may fail to observe.
- The senses of taste and smell are subject to frequent distortion by physical disorders and by external stimuli. The presence of a strong taste or odor may completely conceal the presence of other tastes or odors. Consequently, these two are usually considered the least reliable of the senses as a basis for interpretation.

For example, the presence of strong cooking odors in a room may result in an individual's failing to note the presence of a more subtle odor of importance in a particular case.

Psychological Influences. Temporary or permanent emotional disturbances, such as fear, anger, worry, prejudice or mental instability, may impair the functioning of a person's senses and result in inaccuracies in observation. The investigator must acquire the ability to recognize these influences and make proper allowances for them. For example:

- The victim of a robbery may be in such fear of a weapon used by the perpetrator that his recollection of the incident will be only that of the size of the bore of the weapon and he will be unable to describe the perpetrator accurately. Furthermore, such an individual might be expected to exaggerate the size of the bore.
- A witness of an incident may so dislike a particular person involved as to see only the actions of that person to the exclusion of the actions of other persons involved.
- A witness may be so prejudiced against a class or race of people that his interpretation will be inaccurate even though his senses recorded a true report of what occurred. A case in point is the individual who has formed a dislike for police and similar officials; he may unwittingly permit his prejudice to affect his interpretation of observations of the actions of a night watchman or a security guard.

Training. Specialized training may intensify an individual's power of observation. However, such training may tend to focus the observer's attention on particular characteristics to the detriment or exclusion of others.

Dictionary of Police, Criminal, Gambling and Narcotics Terms/Slang

A's	Amphetamines	Belted	Under the influence of narcotics
ABC sheet / ABC marker	A ruled, professional marker used for horse race bets	Bender	Drug orgy
		Bennies	Benzadrine tablets
Ab	Abcess	Bent	Addicted to drugs
Acapulco gold	High-grade marijuana grown in Mexico	Bernice	Cocaine
		Bhang	Hashish
Acid	LSD-25, lysergic acid diethylamide	Big D	LSD
		Big Harry	Heroin
Acid head	LSD user	Big House	State prison
Acid test	Party at which LSD has been added to the punch	Big John	Policeman
		Big man	Supplier of drugs
Across the board	A bet on a horse, the same amount for win (the horse bet on comes in first), place (the horse bet on comes in second), and show (the horse bet on comes in third)	Bindle	Small amount of narcotics packaged in folded paper or a glassine envelope
		Bing	An isolated cell in a state prison
		Bingle	Supplier of drugs
Ammies	Amyl nitrate	Bingo	To inject drugs
Angel Dust	PCP	Birdseye	A very small amount of narcotics
Apple	A nonaddict	Biscuit	Broken-up methadone tablets
Are you holding?	Have you any narcotics?	Biz	Equipment for injecting drugs
Artillery	Equipment for injecting drugs	Black (stuff)	Opium
Attitude	Sudden hostile feeling	Black acid	LSD
Back-to-back betting	In stud poker, the hold card and the first dealt up-card with the same denomination	Black beauties	Biamphetamines
		Blade	Knife
		Blanca	Heroin
Backer	Someone behind a gambling operation who supplies gamblers with their bankrolls	Blank	Bag of nonnarcotic powder sold as heroin
		Blast	Strong effect from a drug
Bad scene	Unpleasant drug experience	Blast a stick	Smoke a marijuana cigarette
Bad go	Insufficient amount of drugs for money paid	Blast party	Group gathered to smoke marijuana
		Blasted	Under the influence of narcotics or alcohol
Badseed	Peyote		
Bag	$5 and $10 glassine bags of heroin	Blaster	Marijuana smoker
Bagman	Drug supplier; in illegal gambling, person who collects money for those who afford the protection for the operation	Block	Bundle of morphine
		Blow	Cocaine
		Blow a stick	Smoke marijuana cigarette
		Blow away	To kill
Bambi	Mixture of heroin and desoxyn	Blow up	To kill
Bang	An injection	Blue acid	LSD
Bank	Place where controller of a gambling operation turns in the work	Blue angels	Amytal, a barbiturate
		Blue cheer	LSD
		Blue devils	Barbiturates
Banker	A person or syndicate who financially supports an illegal lottery operation	Blue heavens	Sodium amytal tablets or barbiturates
		Blue velvet	Paregoric and pyrobenzomine
Barbs	Barbiturates	Blue water	LSD
Batted out	To be arrested	Blues	Barbiturates
Beans	Amphetamines	Bobo bush	Marijuana
Beard	In gambling, a person whose job is laying off bets for the bookie; also, one who works for the operators who handle hot horses	Bogart a joint	Holding onto a marijuana cigarette rather than passing it to others
		Bolita	A Latin American lottery. The winning two-digit number in bolita is determined by a little ball that drops from a drum
Beat	Out of narcotics		
Beat for the dough	To have a dealer steal money given to him for drugs	Bolita back	The last two digits in a three-digit

	bolita number, e.g., bolita back for the digit 756 is 56
Bolita combination	Bolita lottery based on a combination of numbers
Bolita front	The first two digits in a three-digit bolita number, e.g., bolita front for the digit 756 is 75
Bomber	Large marijuana cigarette
Bombitas	Vial of desoxyn, an amphetamine sometimes taken with heroin for a stronger high
Bond method	Great Britain's premium bond lottery
Bong	Homemade pipe made from cardboard tube, bamboo, glass or other materials
Boo	Marijuana
Boo coo	Large amount of anything
Boogie	To leave an area fast
Book	Short for bookmaker, or the person who takes race and sports bets; to leave an area fast
Bookie	Person who accepts race and sports wagers
Boost	Shoplift
Boostering	Getting rid of stolen property and stealing merchandise
Boot	To feed blood back and forth into the "works" once the heroin is partially injected into the vein to obtain a more lasting effect
Boss/Bossman	Person who controls a gambling operation
Boxman	Person who stands at a gambling table and places all house winnings in a locked box under a slot in the table
Boy	Heroin
Bread	Money
Breakage	Term used at parimutuel tracks denoting the fractions of a cent on each payoff less than a full penny as well as the odd pennies over five or 10 usually kept by the track operators
Brick	Kilogram of marijuana
Brother	A black male police officer
Brown	Amphetamines
Brown dot	LSD
Bug Boy	An apprentice jockey
Bull	Policeman
Bummer	Bad trip or drug experience
Bundle	Twenty-five $5 bags of heroin
Burn	Swindle someone out of drugs or money
Bush	Marijuana
Business	The total play of a bookie or numbers operator
Businessman's Special	DMT
Bust-out game	A crooked gambling game, usually dice or cards, that climaxes in the sudden exit of the owners of the operators
Bust-out man	Someone adept at switching the dice on a craps table
Busted	Arrested
Buster	A dishonest or fixed die
Butter	Marijuana
Buttonman	Soldier in an organized crime family
Buttons	The sections of the peyote cactus
Buy	Purchase of drugs by an undercover officer or informant
Buzz	Drug-induced high
Buzzing	Trying to make a drug purchase
C	Cocaine; in gambling, short for combination
C note	In gambling, a $100 bill
Caballo	Heroin
Cactus	Mescaline, peyote
Can (of marijuana)	Approximately 1½ ounces
Can (of opium)	Usually 3½ or 6⅔ ounces
Canary	Gambling slang meaning an informer
Candy	Cocaine
Canned	To be arrested and put in jail
Cap	Capsule of narcotics
Capman	Supplier of drugs
Carburetor	Pipe for smoking marijuana
Carpet place	High-class gambling establishment
Carrie	Cocaine
Cartwheels	Amphetamines
Cash room	A set location where gambling bets can be placed and results determined
Catcher	Person stationed outside a race track who receives signals from someone inside the track
Catting	Living on rooftops, destitute
Cecil	Cocaine
Ceech	Hashish
Chalk bettor	In horse racing, a gambler who bets on favorites
Charged up	Under the effects of narcotics
Chasing the bag	Looking for the best possible bag of heroin
Cheba cheba	Marijuana
Check cop	A device used for stealing poker chips
Check-up house	In gambling, the place where tally sheets are prepared and money and slips are counted

Cheese eater	Informer
Chicken	Teenage male prostitute
Chicken hawk	Adult male who has sex with teenage male prostitutes
Chief	LSD
Chip	Use heroin in small amounts or occasionally
Chippy	A drug user, but not an addict
Cholly	Cocaine
Christmas trees	Barbiturates
Chuck-a-luck	Gambling game played with several dice and the winning roll is the highest poker hand
Cibas	Barbiturates, specifically, doridens
Clean	Not using drugs
Clipped	To be arrested
Coast to coast	Amphetamines
Coasting	Under the influence of narcotics
Coke	Cocaine
Coke up	Under the influence of cocaine
Cokie	Cocaine addict
Cold deck	Stacked cards, dishonestly introduced into a gambling game
Cold popping	Shooting heroin cold
Cold turkey	Abrupt withdrawal from drugs without medication
Collar	To arrest
Collector	Policy term indicating one who accepts bets from players
Combination	Policy term in numbers games indicating the transposition of numbers within a three digit term—756, 576, 657, etc. For example, when a combination appears on a policy slip, it is usually written 756-C-50¢
Come down	Sick feeling as drug wears off
Come-back money	Money bet at the race track to drive down the odds; insurance to prevent a big hit when book-maker has too many bets on one horse
Commission man	In gambling, one who handles come-back money
Connected	A criminal with ties to organized crime
Connection	Person with a wide acquaintance of public officials willing to make introductions of these officials to persons in control of gambling operations; street peddler of narcotics; source of drug supply
Contact high	Becoming high merely by inter-acting with one who is high
Controller	In gambling, the boss of the collectors. Controllers receive

	the collectors' daily slips
Cook-up	Mix heroin with water and heat for injection
Cooker	Bottletop or spoon used for dissolving heroin in water over heat
Cookie	Cocaine addict
Cop	Finding a source for drugs and making a purchase
Copilots	Amphetamines
Cottons	Bits of cotton saturated with narcotics
Count	Sizeable amount of drugs
Counting rooms	Locked and heavily guarded rooms in gambling establish-ments where winnings from the tables are counted at the end of each shift
County Hotel	A county jail
Cousin	An accommodation arrest, sometimes called a "stand in"
Crack a crib	Burglarize a home
Craps	Dice; a two-dice gambling game
Crash	Fall asleep while using drugs; come down hard and fast from a high or trip
Creep joint	A gambling operation held in different locations each night
Croaker	Unscrupulous doctor who sells drugs or prescriptions to illicit drug users
Croaker joint	Hospital
Cross roader	A gambler who cheats
Crutch	Device used for holding butt of marijuana cigarette
Crystal	Methedrine
Cube head	Frequent user of LSD
Cubes	Dice; morphine; LSD
Cut	To adulterate narcotics with milk sugar, mannite, quinine, etc.; a portion of the gambling money taken in by an operation; the division of cards after the shuffle
Cutting	In gambling, taking a fee or percentage of the amounts wagered while operating a card game
Cutting razor	Razor blade used to separate a lump of cocaine into individual doses
Dabble	Small, irregular drug habit
Daily double	A two-horse parlay on the first and second races only
Day horse	Bolita that is thrown twice a day
Day house	Bolita played in the daytime and daily
Deal	Sell narcotics to addicts
Dealer	Drug pusher

Deck	Small packet of heroin
Dexies	Amphetamines
Dick	A detective; a small packet of narcotics
Dime bag	$10 bag of narcotics
Dirt horse	A tip horse, or one purported to be a sure winner
Dirty	Possessing drugs, liable to arrest if searched
Ditty bops	Adolescents, tough young gang members
Do meth	Shoot speed
DOA	PCP
Doe	Methamphetamine
Dollies	Dolophine, a commercial methadone
Dom	STP
Domino	Purchase drugs
Doo jee	Heroin
Dope	A narcotic, specifically, heroin
Doper	Regular user of drugs
Double the line	Bookie's payoff at double the rate as a bet inducement to a potential customer
Double trouble	Barbiturates
Down with someone	Share a bag of heroin
Downers/Downs	Barbiturates or depressants
Dreamer	Morphine
Dripper	A syringe or eyedropper used for injections
Drop	In a gambling establishment, the place where collectors turn in their day's business; to swallow a drug
Drop a dime	To inform
Dropped	Arrested
Dropper	Medicine dropper used by addicts as a makeshift hypodermic needle
Duige	Heroin
Dummy	Bag of nonnarcotic powder sold as a narcotic
Dumper	In sports gambling, a fixed game
Dust	Cocaine
Dyke	Female homosexual, lesbian
Dynamite	Heroin or other drug of exceptional purity; a cocaine and morphine mixture
Dynamiter	Cocaine addict
Edge work	Marking of cards in a gambling game
Egg	An especially naive gambler or any casino customer
Eighth	Eighth of an ounce of heroin
Entry	In horse racing, all horses owned by one stable or trainer
Emrel	Morphine

Explorers club	A group of LSD users
Eye dropper	Medicine dropper used with hypodermic needle as makeshift syringe for injecting drugs
Eye openers	Amphetamines
Factory	Equipment for injecting drugs
Fade	In gambling, to cover a dice wager
Fading dice	Loaded dice
Fair dice	Honest dice
Fall	Arrest
Favorite	A handicapper's selection for the winner of a horse race
Fed	Federal narcotics agent
Ferry dust	Heroin
Fiend	Morphine addict
Fine stuff	Good marijuana
Fink	An informer, especially one who informs the police of a criminal activity
Fix	Injection of narcotics
Flake	Cocaine
Flash	A quick jolt of sensation in abdomen or across chest from heroin shot
Flash paper	A quick-burning paper with a very low ignition point that burns without leaving residue. Used by bookies
Flash your tin	Police slang for show your badge
Flat	In a lottery, a two-number play. Numbers may be pulled out of order
Flea powder	Poor-quality narcotics
Flip	To trip on acid
Floating	Under the influence of narcotics
Floating casino	A casino that regularly moves its operation to avoid police raids; a casino that operates aboard a converted ship or barge
Four-number play	Any three or four numbers pulled in a lottery drawing
Flower	Marijuana
Fold up	To withdraw from drugs
Footballs	Amphetamines
45-minute psychosis	DMT high
Frame	Handgun
Front man	Person with no criminal record, or a minor one, established as the owner of record for purposes of obtaining a casino license
Front money	Advance payment
Fruit salad	Mixture of pills
Fully	Machine gun
Fuzz	Police
GB's	"Goofballs," i.e., barbiturates, usually Doriden
Gage	Marijuana

Gangster type	Sawed-off shotgun
Ganja	Marijuana
Garbage	Very weak bag of heroin
Gauge	Marijuana
Geed-up	Under the influence of narcotics
Gee-gee	A race horse
Geezer	Small quantity of narcotics
Get high	Smoke marijuana
Get off	Start feeling the effects of a drug
Gig	A three-number play in a lottery. All three numbers must be pulled at the drawing to win; a job
Gig and saddle	A popular double play in gambling. Should a player miss the gig, but two numbers are pulled, the saddle would win. The saddle is sometimes referred to as an insurance play.
Gimmicks	Equipment for injecting drugs, especially heroin
Girl	Cocaine
Glom	To arrest
Glued	Arrested
Go	A deal
Going up	Under the effects of narcotics
Gold	Money.
Gold dust	Cocaine
Gong	Opium pipe
Gong-beater	Smoker of opium
Good fellow	Someone who has killed for organized crime
Good go	A fair quantity of drugs received for payment
Goods	Drugs
Goofballs	Barbiturates
Goofing	Aggressive, drunken behavior caused by barbiturates
Gow head	Narcotics addict
Grass	Marijuana
Grayswirl	LSD
Green	Money
Green hornet	Dexamyl, a barbiturate
Greenie	Amphetamines
Greta	Marijuana
Griefo	Marijuana
Grooving	Under the influence of narcotics
Ground control	Caretaker in LSD session
Gum	Opium
Gun	Hypodermic needle for injecting heroin
Guru	Companion on a trip who has tripped before
H	Heroin
Habit	Addiction to drugs
Hairy	Heroin
Half-load	15 decks of heroin

Hammer	Pen gun, usually a 22 caliber
Hand-to-hand go	Delivery at time of payment
Handbook	A bookie who operates without a fixed location
Hang up	To withdraw from drugs
Happy dust	Cocaine
Hard stuff	Potent drugs such as heroin, cocaine and morphine
Harness	Policeman
Harness bulls	Street detectives
Harry	Heroin
Hash	Hashish
Haven dust	Cocaine
Hay	Hashish or marijuana
Hay head	Marijuana user
Head	Addict
Heads up	LSD
Hearts	Amphetamines
Heat	Police pressure
Heavenly blue	LSD
Heeled	Possession of narcotics or a weapon
Hemp	Marijuana
Herb	Marijuana
High	State of ecstasy; tension-free feeling as a result of injecting drugs
High roller	A gambler who plays for high stakes
Higher than a kite	Under the influence of narcotics
Hikori	Peyote
His stick	Person's specialty in the street or life
Hit	Purchase drugs; to kill; a gambling win
Hit slip	A slip prepared at the bank of a gambling establishment on a winning number
Hit the pit	Drug injection in the elbow
Hit the street	To go out on the street or on patrol
Hitting the stuff	Under the influence of narcotics
Hocus	Morphine
Hog	Addict that requires a maximum drug dosage
Hold out	A device used to cheat at cards
Holding	To have narcotics
Honkte	Suspicious of a certain person
Hooch	Marijuana
Hooked on the needle	Addicted to narcotics, especially heroin
Hooked up	Connected with organized crime
Hop head, hype	Drug addict
Hop joint	A place where opium is smoked
Hoppy	Addict
Horning	To sniff narcotics
Horse	Heroin

Horse degenerate	Person who has a compulsion to bet on horses
Horse room	Bookie's place of business where customers may remain to bet from race to race
Hot/Hot stuff	Stolen property
Hot balling	Heating one of the balls used to determine the winning number in bolita in order to fix the outcome
Hot heroin	Poisoned heroin usually sold to someone suspected of informing and intended to kill him
Hot horse	A horse purported to be a sure winner
Hot load	Overdose, may result in death
Huff	Sniff glue
Hungry croaker	Doctor who sells drugs or prescriptions to support his own addiction
Hustle	Obtain money by devious means
Hype	Narcotics addict
Ice cream habit	Small, irregular drug habit
Idiot pills	Barbiturates, usually Doridens
If bet	A type of parlay betting in horse racing. If horse picked in first race wins, bettor may wager up to half of his first-race winnings on second race
Ill or sick	Having symptoms of withdrawal
I'm flush	I have money
I'm looking	I wish to buy
I'm way down	I need marijuana
In shape	Possession of drugs
In the bag	Officer in uniform
Indian hay	Marijuana
Inside men	In gambling, bookkeepers who use computing machines and other modern equipment for listing all bets and payouts
Instant Zen	LSD
Insurance	A 10-percent addition to a horse bet that will ensure bettor of receiving track odds
Italian policy	Rules and operating methods of the Italian national lottery. Numbers games are all variations of the Italian policy.
J	Marijuana cigarette
Jab	To inject heroin intravenously
Jail plant	Narcotics concealed on a person to be used in jail
Jamaica black	Marijuana
Jelly babies	Amphetamines
Jet fuel	PCP
Jive	Marijuana

Jive sticks	Marijuana cigarettes
John	Client of a prostitute; an especially naive gambler of any casino customer
Joint	A marijuana cigarette; a prison
Jolly beans	Pep pills
Jolt	To inject heroin intravenously
Jones	Heroin habit
Joy pop	An occasional injection
Joy powder	Heroin
Jugged	To be arrested
Juggle	Sell heroin as an addict; to keep one step ahead of game
Junk	Narcotics
Junker/Junkie	Addict
Keef	Hashish
Keister plant	Narcotics secreted in rectum
Key	A kilogram or 2.2 pounds of any drug, expecially marijuana compressed into brick form
Key ticket	Winning ticket in a lottery
Kick a habit	To be detoxified from drugs
Kilo	A kilogram or 2.2 pounds of narcotics
Kiss-off	Last dose of medication, usually referring to clinical detoxification with methadone
Kit	Equipment for injecting drugs, especially heroin
Knocked in	Arrested for possession of marijuana
LA turnabouts	Amphetamines
Lab	Morphine or heroin conversion factory
Lay down	Place where opium is smoked
Lay odds	Line offered to a bettor by a bookie or the racetracks. Used as an inducement by the track or bookie to get the bettor interested in the operation. In theory, the betting risk is proportionate to the odds given
Lay off	Not to bet; a small-time bookmaker who transfers a portion of his bets to a larger operator
Lay on the hop	To smoke opium
Layout	Equipment for injecting drugs; a gambling outfit
Leaf	Cocaine
Leaping	Under the influence of narcotics
Lemonade	A very inferior grade of heroin
Lid	The size of a standard marijuana transaction, i.e., about an ounce
Lid poppers	Amphetamines
Lifer	Person serving a life sentence in prison

Lift the plant	To remove narcotics from hiding
Line	Gambling term referring to the odds to be paid by the bookie; the point spread in some sports gambling games
Lines	Individual doses of cocaine separated into strips using a razor blade
Lipton tea	Poor-quality narcotics
Lit up	Under the influence of narcotics
Little double	Sawed-off shotgun
Load	Bulk sale of heroin, thirty $5 bags; half-load, fifteen $10 bags
Loaded	Under the influence of drugs
Locoweed	Hashish or marijuana
Long run	On the street using drugs for a long time
Lookout	A gambling house employee who sees that the games run smoothly and watches for cheating players or casino personnel
Looking	Searching for narcotics
Lords	Hydromorphone
Love weed	Marijuana
Love wood	Hashish
Lusher	One preferring alcohol to narcotics
M/Morph	Morphine
Mace	Hallucinogenic drugs
Machinery	Equipment for injecting drugs
Mackman	Pimp
Made guy	Someone who has killed for organized crime
Main man	Good friend and partner in crime
Mainline	Intravenous injection of heroin
Mainliner	Addict who injects narcotics intravenously
Maintaining	Remaining coherent while experiencing the effects of drugs
Make a meet	Purchase drugs
Make the turn	To withdraw from drugs
Man	Source of drug supply
(The) man	Police
Manicure/ Manicured tea	Clean and prepare marijuana for rolling into cigarettes
Mark	Gambling slang for a sucker
Marked cards/ Marked paper	Playing cards that are doctored so they may be read from the back
Marker	Paper on which a gambling bet or action is recorded
Mary	Marijuana
Mary Jane	Marijuana
Mary Warner	Marijuana
Matchbox	Usually five to eight cigarettes of marijuana
Mechanic	An experienced and skillful card bettor
Medical hype	A person who has become accidentally addicted during medical treatment for illness or disease, or one who obtains bonafide drugs through doctors or hospitals
Melter	Morphine
Merchandise	Drugs
Mesc	Mescaline, the alkaloid in peyote
Mescal button	Peyote
Meth	Methamphetamine
Methhead	Habitual user of methamphetamine
Mezz	Hashish
Micro-dot	Acid on paper
Mikes	Micrograms (millionths of a gram)
Miss Emma	Morphine
Mob	Group of criminals
Moll buzzer	Pickpocket who steals from women
Money bet	Use of money instead of chips for betting in a game of crap or dice
Monkey juice	PCP
Monkey on back	Using drugs
Monster	Amphetamine
Moon	Peyote; a flat, circular piece of hashish
Morning line	Early horse racing odds
Morpho	Morphine
Mota	Marijuana
Mu	Marijuana
Mud	Opium
Muffler	Silencer for a handgun
Mugger	Strong-armed robber
Muggles	Hashish
Mule	Drug supplier
Murphy game	Con game using sex, drugs, etc., to extract funds
Mushrooms	Psilocybin
Nailed	Arrested
Narc	Narcotics officer
Narco	Narcotics detective
Needle	Hypodermic needle
Needleman	Addict
Nemmies	Nembutal, a barbiturate
Nickel bag	$5 bag of narcotics or marijuana
Night house	Bolita game played at night and nightly
Nimby	Barbiturates
Nose	Silencer for a handgun
Number	The word number appearing in the newspaper referring to a number selected by a player to bet on
Number five	No.5 capsules, referring to capsules containing five milligrams of an illegal substance, usually Benzedrine

Numbers game	A lottery in which money is wagered on the appearance of certain numbers or combination of numbers, e.g., keno, bingo or bolita
O	Opium
OD/Overdose	Overdose of heroin
OZ.	Ounce of any drug
Odds	The ratio of the unfavorable chances to the favorable chances of winning a bet
Off time	Actual starting time of a horse race
Off-track bet	A bet made away from the race-track premises
Office	In gambling, the place where collectors turn in their day's business
On ice	In jail
On the beam	Feeling fine
On the block	On the street
On the bricks	Out of jail
On the nod	Sleepy from narcotics
On the perch	Being high
On the set / On the scene	Place of activity or business
One-armed bandit	Slot machine
Open up	To increase activity in a gambling operation
Operator	One who runs or manages a numbers lottery
Orange	Amphetamines
Out-of-it	A nonaddict
Out of this world	Under the influence of narcotics
Outfit	Equipment for injecting drugs, especially heroin
Overlook	A hit, or win, made and not paid in the numbers game
Package	Morphine
Pago pago	Marijuana
Panama cut	Good grade of marijuana
Panama red	Red marijuana from Panama
Panic	Scarcity of drugs
Paper	Slips or sheets on which gambling bets are placed
Paper bag	Container of drugs
Paper hanger	Forger
Paradise	Cocaine
Parlay	In horse racing, a combination bet that places money won from first bet on the second race
Pass	Transfer of narcotics or money
Passers	Dice designed to favor the shooter
Past posting	Illegal betting on a horse race when the bettor already knows the results
Pay-off man	Person who delivers money won on a bet
Peace	PCP

Peace pill	PCP
Peanuts	Barbiturates
Peddler	Supplier of drugs
Peg	Policeman
Pen	Short for pen gun, usually a 25 caliber; a state prison
Pen yuen	Opium
Pep pills	Amphetamines
Per	Prescription
Percentage dice	A pair of dice, one of which is misspotted
Persuasion	To coerce or pressure someone
Peyote	Mescaline
Phennies	Barbiturates
Pick-up man	Employee of a gambling establishment who picks up the work from a writer and deposits it at a drop designated by the controller. Bankers may also employ pick-up men.
Piece	Share or portion of a gambling operation; one ounce of heroin; a gun; a girl
Pigs	Police
Pill head	Pill addict
Pink ladies / Pinks	Barbiturates
Pit man	Casino employee who supervises a gaming table, corrects errors and watches for cheating
Pitcher	In gambling, a person stationed inside a racetrack who signals a partner outside the track
Place	A right or wrong point bet in the game of craps
Plant	Cache of narcotics
Play round	Small, irregular drug habit
Point spread	In horse racing and sports betting, the number of points given or taken
Points	Gambling terminology on handi-capped bets. Player gives or takes points
Poison act	The Federal Narcotics Act
Poker flat	Apartment used for card games
Policy	Various numbers games or an illegal lottery
Pool selling	Selling tickets on the outcome of a sporting event
Pop	An injection of drugs
Post time	Scheduled starting time of a horse race
Pot	Marijuana
Pot head	Marijuana user
Primo	Heavily opiated marijuana or best-grade marijuana
Product IV	PCP-LSD Combination
Punk	Coward, sissy
Pure	Pure narcotics or a very good grade

Purple haze	LSD
Purple hearts	Phenobarbital
Push	To sell drugs
Pusher	Drug peddler
Q/Queen	Cocaine
Quarter	One-quarter ounce of a drug
Quill	Matchbook cover with powdered drug placed in fold used to inhale narcotics
Quinella	A form of betting similar to the daily double, except players try to pick both the first- and second-place winners in the same race or game
Rainbows	Tuinal, a barbiturate
Rare	Inhalation of cocaine or heroin
Rat	Informer
Reader	Playing cards that are doctored so they may be read from the back
Red bird/Red bullet/Red devil	Seconal, a barbiturate
Reds and blues	Barbiturates
Reefer	Marijuana cigarette
Reentry	Return to normalcy after a drug experience
Relay spot	Place where employees of a gambling operation receive bets by phone and pass them on to the boss. Boss' phone number remains unknown to both bettors and employees
Reverse bet	A horse race bet made with a bookie that involves more than one "if" bet
Rice paper	Water soluble paper that leaves very little residue. Used by bookies
Right	In dice, betting that the player will make his point
Ringer	A horse purported to be a winner, i.e., a sure bet
Ripoff	Swindle
Roach	Butt of a marijuana cigarette
Roach holder	Device for holding a roach
(The) rock	Riker's Island
Roll over	Defendant who turns informer
Rope	Hashish made from hemp
Roper	Person who ropes in, or steers, gamblers to various gambling establishments
Rosco	Handgun
Rough stuff	Marijuana as it comes from the plant
Round robin	A bet with an off-track book that involves the playing of all possible two-or three-race or sports parlays on three or more horses or teams
Routeman	Usually a trusted employee of an

	illegal lottery
Royal blue	LSD
Rumble	Police shakedown or search
Run	Period of addiction
Rundown sheet	Itemized tally of gambling bets, horses, games, teams or numbers played in policy
Runner	A bookmaker or agent
Rush	Warm or ecstatic feeling throughout the body that many addicts report about 15-30 seconds after intra- venous injection of heroin; a tingling sensation in abdomen and genital area
Sacred mushrooms	Psilocybin Psilocybin
Salt shot	Salt and water mixture injected intravenously into an addict who has overdosed on heroin in an effect to revive him.
Satch cotton	Cotton saturated with heroin
Sativa	Marijuana
Sawdust joint	Cheap gambling establishment
Scag	Heroin
Scalper	Bettor who wagers on two opposing teams in order to minimize his losses using a mysterious mathematical formula unknown to bookies
Schmeck	Heroin
Schoolboy	Codeine
Scope	Check the scene out
Score	Buy narcotics or other drugs
Scratch	Money; to take a horse out of a race
Scratch sheet	Daily publication of horse racing information
Screw	Prison guard
Script	Prescription
Seggy	Barbiturates
Seller	Employee of a gambling operation who accepts bets from the players
Shaped dice	Dice whose shapes have been altered so they are no longer perfect cubes
Sharpshooter	Dishonest gambler
Shaving points	In sports betting, a player in collusion with the gambler, who attempts to have his team win by a certain number of points
Shifter	In a card game, one who secretly returns the halves of a cut deck to their original position
Shill	Person who hustles action, or business, for a gambler

Shit	Heroin	Stages	Silencer for a handgun
Shiv	Knife	Stand in	Accommodation arrest, sometimes called "cousin"
Shooter	Hit man		
Shooting gallery	Place where user injects drugs	Stardust	Cocaine
Shooting up	Injecting narcotics	Stash	Cache of narcotics
Short	Car	Stashcan	Container often commercially made with secret compartment for hiding drugs
Short barrel	Sawed-off shotgun		
Shotgun	Putting lighted end of marijuana cigarette into mouth and blowing so that smokes goes into other person's mouth		
		Steam boat	Roach holder
		Steam horse	A tip horse and one purported to be a sure winner
Sick	Withdrawal from narcotics	Steerer	One who steers, or ropes in, gamblers to various gambling establishments
Side games	Casino games of lesser attraction		
Single action	Betting on one digit in a numbers game		
		Stick	Marijuana cigarette; also to stab
Sister	Police slang for a black female officer	Stickman	Employee of a gambling operation who returns the dice to the shooter in any dice game
Sixteenth	Sixteenth of an ounce of heroin		
Skee	Opium	Stiff	A favorite in a horse race that is deliberately held back from winning; a corpse
Skin burner	Good grade of heroin		
Skin game	A dishonest trick		
Skin popping	Drug injected beneath the skin	Stinking	Under the influence of narcotics
Sky out	To flee	Stoned	Being on a high from drugs
Slammer	Jail	Stool/Stool pigeon/Stoolie	An informer, especially one who informs the police of a criminal activity
Sleeping pills	Barbiturates		
Slot	Short for slot machine		
Smack	Heroin	Straight	An addict's feeling of well-being after taking drugs; a person who doesn't take drugs; obtained narcotics
Smoke	Marijuana		
Sniffing/Snorting	Sniffing narcotics through nose		
Snitch	Informer		
Snort	Inhalation of cocaine or heroin	Straw	Marijuana
Snow	Cocaine	Street peddler	A pusher who sells directly to the user
Soapies	Quaaludes, methaqualone		
Space ranger	Someone who uses amphetamines excessively	Strung out	Addicted; more specifically, to be badly in need of drugs
Spaced	Showing the effects of drugs	Stuff	Heroin
Speed	Methedrine	Sucker	An especially naive gambler or any casino customer
Speed ball	Heroin mixed with cocaine		
Speed freak	User of amphetamines	Suey	A liquid solution of opium
Spike	Hypodermic needle	Sugar/Sugar lump	LSD
Spitfire	Machine gun	Sunshine	LSD
Splash	Methamphetamine	Super dropper	Wealthy gambler or sucker who habitually loses large amounts of money
Spoon	Sixteenth of an ounce of heroin		
Sporting game	Betting on athletic events and races		
		Sure-thing man	A gambler who cheats
Spot	In gambling, a fixed location used by a writer for his part of the operation	Swinger	A gambler who is known to play for high stakes
		Swag	Stolen goods
Spot controller	In gambling, a controller who operates without pick-up men and usually takes large bets	Sweet Lucy	Hashish
		Sweets	Amphetamines
		Swingman	Supplier of drugs
Spot you	To pay for drugs first, with delivery later	Switch	The act of changing the cards or dice in a gambling game from honest to crooked or vice versa
Spreading the play	Laying off		
Squad car	Police cruiser	Syndicate acid	STP
Square	A nonaddict; an honest cop	Synthetic marijuana	PCP
Stack	A quantity of marijuana cigarettes		

Tab	Narcotics tablet
Tail trip	Police surveillance of a suspect
Take	Percentage of money bet at the racetrack that goes to the track and the state
Take joint	Crooked gambling establishment
Take off	Use of heroin
Take out of court	To free a prisoner from jail and return him to the street
Taking the odds	To bet the longer, or unfavorable, odds, i.e., 7 to 5
Tally sheet	Numbered gambling sheets used to keep a record of amount bet on each horse or number
Tapes	In gambling, the adding machine tapes upon which the day's business is recorded
Tar	Opium
Taste	Small quantity of narcotics usually given as a reward or favor
Tea	Marijuana
Tea blower/ Tea head	Marijuana user
Tea party	Marijuana party
Tecata	Heroin
10 cents	$10
10-cent pistol	Bag containing "poison"
Texas tea	Hashish
Things	Balloons of heroin
Tighten me up	Take care of me with medication
Time bet	Accepting a bet on the basis that the horse race has not started
Tin	Badge
Tingle	Quick jolt of sensation in abdomen or across chest
Tip sheet	A listing of competitors most likely to win a particular event, e.g., a horse race
To be clean	Not using drugs
To be off	To withdraw from drugs
To chip	Small habit, weekend drug use
To plant	To conceal or hide anything
To the mouth	To swallow narcotic evidence
Todies	Tuinal, a barbiturate
Toke	A puff on a marijuana cigarette
Tommy	Machine gun
Tooies	Barbiturates
Tools	Equipment for injecting narcotics
Toot	Cocaine
Tooter	Device used to sniff cocaine
Tooting spoon	Spoon used to hold individual dose of cocaine for sniffing
Tops	Dice used in a "bust-out" game that makes it impossible for a player to to make his point; flowers of the marijuana plant

Torch up	To light a marijuana cigarette
Torpedo	Hired killer
Toss	To search a person or place
Tout	One who gives information on horse races
Toy	The smallest container of prepared opium
Track odds	Odds established at the racetrack by parimutuel machines
Tracks	Veins collapsed by constant injection; needle scars from drug injections
Tranquility	STP
Trap	Hiding place for narcotics
Travel agent	LSD supplier
Trey	$5 bag of heroin
Trip	Under the influence of LSD
Truck drivers	Amphetamines
Turkey	Bag of nonnarcotic powder sold as a narcotic
Turn on	To introduce a person to drugs and give him his first injection
Turned off	Withdraw from drugs
Turps	Elixir of terpin hydrate with codeine
20 cents	$20
25	LSD (from its original designation, LSD-25)
Twisted	Under the influence of narcotics
Unkie	Morphine
Uppers/Ups	Amphetamines, or stimulants
User	Addict
Vig/Vigorish	The percentage of a win guaranteed to the bookmaker if his bettor wins; illegal interest paid to a loanshark
Viper's weed	Marijuana
Vonce	Butt of marijuana cigarette
Wacked	To "cut" drugs
Wager ticket	A record of bets
Wake up	Morning shot
Wake ups	Amphetamines
Washed up	To withdraw from drugs
Wasted	Under the influence of narcotics
Watcher	Person who oversees a gambling operation for the operator
Wedges	LSD
Weed head	Marijuana or hashish user
Weeds	Marijuana or hashish
Weekend habit	Small, irregular drug habit
Weight	A large quantity of drugs
What's happening?	Do you have any narcotics?
Wheel	Owner or backer of a policy or numbers company
Wheel man	Driver of a bandit vehicle after commission of a crime

White boy/ White girl	Heroin
White horse	Heroin
White lady	Heroin
White lightning	LSD
White stuff	Morphine
Whites	Amphetamines
Windex	Numorphan, a narcotic
Window pane	Square of paper treated with acid
Wire room	Place where betting wagers are accepted over the phone
Wipe it off	To accept no more action on any gambling event, fearing the event is fixed
Wise guy	Street-wise person usually linked with crime families
Work	In illegal gambling, the day's "business"
Works	Hypodermic needle or spike
Writer	Person who takes illegal gambling bets
Writer's code	The gambling system, method and form of recording wager information
Wrong	In a dice game, betting that the player does not make his point
Yellow jackets	Nembutal, a barbiturate
Yen/Yuen	Craving for narcotics
Yen hock	Instrument used in opium smoking
Yen shee	Opium ash
Yen shee suey	Opium wine
Yen sleep	A drowsy, restless state during a drug user's withdrawal period
Yoke	To mug someone
Zip gun	Homemade gun

Handling Prisoners: Security Measures

DO:

● After an arrest, always conduct a thorough search of the prisoner and pat him down before transporting him; also be sure to follow the same procedure before moving him from one lockup to another.

● Wait for assistance or send ahead for assistance when in doubt about moving a prisoner.

● Keep a small split ring on the chain of your handcuffs for easy and fast removal.

● Place the top of the prisoner's head against a wall whenever possible when handcuffing him; and always stand to one side, not directly behind him. Keep his head as low as possible against the wall and his hands behind him with his feet back.

● Remember to double-lock the handcuffs. Once they are on, they will be difficult to remove, even if the prisoner has a hidden key.

● Remember that the shirt tail can be used in the chain of the cuffs to help move the prisoner into a transporting vehicle.

● Always keep in control and perform your duties with dignity.

DO NOT:

● Do not be overconfident.

● Do not abuse your police authority.

● Do not be critical or sarcastic.

● Do not use any unnecessary force when handling a prisoner or making an arrest.

● Do not stand in front of your prisoner; always stand to the side.

● Do not permit your prisoner to stop and talk to anyone and do not grant him permission to use a phone at any time; a phone can be a deadly weapon—both the instrument and the cord.

● Do not allow anyone to touch your prisoner.

● Do not move more than one prisoner at one time without assistance.

● Do not stand with your weapon accessible to the prisoner; always make sure it is away from him, even if it necessitates moving your holster.

● Do not allow your prisoner to remove, throw away or destroy anything he may have on his person.

● Do not bend down to the prisoner if he falls to the floor while being transported. Approach only from the top (head), and look around you in all directions to make sure you are not being set up. Talk to him from a distance and wait for your backup.

NEVER:

● Never underestimate the prisoner.

● Never remove your weapon from the holster unless you intend to use it.

● Never forget that you are in the public eye and that people's opinions of what you are doing may differ from yours. Do not abuse your prisoner unnecessarily, but use your discretion and secure him properly.

Directory of Federal Agencies

BUREAU OF ALCOHOL, TOBACCO AND FIREARMS
Department of the Treasury
1200 Pennsylvania Avenue, NW
Washington, D.C. 20226
(202) 566-7511

Alabama

FOB 1129, Nobel Street
Anniston 36201
(205) 237-2121
FTS: 229-6923

2121 Eighth Avenue North, Room 530
Birmingham 35203
(205) 254-1205
FTS: 229-1205

307 Post Office Building
Florence 35631
(205) 764-4641

P.O. Box 1483
Huntsville 35807
(205) 536-8012

951 Government Street
Mobile 36604
(205) 690-2388
FTS: 534-2338

770 South McDonough Street, Suite 215
Montgomery 36104
(205) 832-7507
FTS: 534-7507

P.O. Box 656
Tuscaloosa 35401
(205) 758-2852
FTS: 229-2935

Alaska

Box 39
Anchorage 99513
(907) 271-5701
FTS: 271-5701

Arizona

522 North Central Avenue, Room 221
Phoenix 85004
(602) 241-3220
FTS: 261-3220

P.O. Box 2510
Tucson 85702
(602) 792-6505
FTS: 762-6505

Arkansas

P.O. Box 1843
Fort Smith 72902
(501) 783-7561

P.O. Box 2461
Little Rock 72201
(501) 378-6181

California

Federal Building
1130 O Street, Room 4005
Fresno 93721
(209) 487-5393
FTS: 467-5393

400 Oceangate, Suite 1130
Long Beach 90802
(213) 548-2494
FTS: 796-2494

P.O. Box 1991, Main Office
Los Angeles 90012
(213) 688-4812
FTS: 798-4816

1515 Clay Street, Room 906
Oakland 94612
(415) 273-7433
FTS: 536-7433

P.O. Box 20126
Riverside 92506
(714) 787-1634
FTS: 796-1634

Downtown Plaza Building
547 L Street
Sacramento 95814
(916) 440-2361
FTS: 448-2361

800 Front Street
San Diego 92188
(714) 293-5608
FTS: 895-5608

525 Market Street, Room 2550
San Francisco 94105
(415) 556-6769
FTS: 556-6769

P.O. Box 12400
Civic Center Station
Santa Ana 92712
(714) 836-2101
FTS: 799-2101

6230 Van Nuys Boulevard, Room 2S11
Van Nuys 91408
(213) 997-3111
FTS: 796-3111

Colorado

P.O. Box 3537
Denver 80294
(303) 837-3421
FTS: 327-3421

Connecticut

135 High Street
Hartford 06101
(203) 244-2770
FTS: 244-3642

150 Court Street
New Haven 06511
(203) 624-7173
FTS: 643-8060

Delaware

Federal Building
Ninth and King Streets
Wilmington 19802
(302) 573-6102
FTS: 487-6102

Florida

4140 Woodcock Drive, Suite 205
Jacksonville 32207
(904) 791-3468
FTS: 946-2228

5205 Northwest 84th Avenue, Suite 108
Miami 33166
(305) 350-4368
FTS: 350-4368

Federal Building
80 North Hughey Avenue
Orlando 32801
(305) 420-6136
FTS: 820-6136

700 Twiggs Street, Room 714
Tampa 33602
(813) 228-2184
FTS: 826-2184

Georgia

3835 Northeast Expressway
Atlanta 30301
(404)455-263?

P.O. Box 33
Augusta 30903
(404) 724-1961
FTS: 251-4122

P.O. Box 669
Columbus 31902
(404) 323-5934
FTS: 247-9785

One West Court Square, Suite 100
Decatur 30030
(404) 242-6146
FTS: 242-6146

P.O. Box 314
Gainesville 30501
(404) 536-3287

P.O. Box 4665
Macon 31208
(912) 238-0232
FTS: 238-0232

P.O. Box 48
Rome 30161
(404) 291-7502

5105 Paulsen Street
Executive Court, Room 211
Savannah 31406

(912) 352-7838
FTS: 248-4251

P.O. Box 1568
Valdosta 31601

(912) 242-8854

Hawaii
300 Ala Moana Boulevard
Honolulu 96850

(808) 546-3196

Idaho
P.O. Box 5833
Boise 83705

(208) 384-1983
FTS: 554-1983

Illinois
230 South Dearborn Street
Chicago 60604

(312) 353-7147
FTS: 353-7147

P.O. Box 3188
Fairview Heights 62208

(618) 398-6650

2115 Butterfield Road, Room 300
Oak Brook 60521

(312) 620-7824
FTS: 353-8444

207 Main Street
Peoria 61602

(309) 671-7111
FTS: 360-7111

P.O. Box 780
Rock Island 61201

(309) 794-9588
FTS: 360-9296

P.O. Box 1028
Springfield 62705

(217) 492-4273
FTS: 955-4273

Indiana
P.O. Box 3144
Evansville 47731

(812) 423-6871
FTS: 335-6271

P.O. Box 5189
Fort Wayne 46805

(219) 424-3166
FTS: 333-9187

151 North Delaware Street
Market Square Center, Room 630
Indianapolis 46204

(317) 269-7464
FTS: 331-7464

Iowa
U.S. Courthouse, Room 400
East First and Walnut Streets
Des Moines 50309

(515) 284-4329
FTS: 862-4329

Kansas
P.O. Box 2834
Wichita 67202

(316) 267-9481
FTS: 752-6229

Kentucky
P.O. Box 1298
Ashland 41101

(606) 928-9522
FTS: 924-5767

P.O. Box 7
Bowling Green 42101

(502) 781-7090
FTS: 352-7265

P.O. Box 1566
Lexington 40501

(606) 233-2771
FTS: 355-2771

600 Federal Plaza
Louisville 40202

(502) 582-5271
FTS: 352-5211

P.O. Box 1062
Paducah 42001

(502) 443-7365
FTS: 352-7365

Louisiana
P.O. Box 3114
Baton Rouge 70821

(504) 387-1070
FTS: 687-0485

Hale Boggs Federal Building, Room 330
New Orleans 70130

(504) 589-2048
FTS: 682-2326

Maine
P.O. Box 342
Downtown Station
Portland 04112

(207) 780-3324
FTS: 833-3324

Maryland
31 Hopkins Plaza, Room 21201
Baltimore 21201

(301) 962-4115
FTS: 922-4115

Presidential Building
Prince Georges Plaza
6525 Bellecrest Road
Hyattsville 20782

(301) 436-8313
FTS: 436-8313

Massachusetts
JFK Post Office, P.O. Box 9115
Boston 02114

(617) 223-3817
FTS: 223-3817

Federal Building, Room 406
436 Dwight Street
Springfield 01103

(413) 781-2439
FTS: 836-9362

Federal Building, Room 216
595 Main Street
Worcester 01601

(617) 752-5525
FTS: 836-5378

Michigan
371 Federal Building
Detroit 48226

(313) 226-7300
FTS: 226-7300

P.O. Box 3458
Flint 48502

(313) 238-7992
FTS: 378-5282

710 Federal Building
110 Michigan Northwest
Grand Rapids 49503

(616) 372-2566
FTS: 372-2566

Minnesota
100 North Sixth Street
Minneapolis 55401

(612) 725-2746
FTS: 725-2746

156 Federal Building
316 North Robert Street
St. Paul 55101

(612) 725-7092
FTS: 725-7092

Mississippi
2301 14th Street
Gulfport 39501

(601) 863-4871
FTS: 499-2650

100 West Capital Street
Jackson 39201

(601) 969-4200
FTS: 490-4200

P.O. Box 8
Meridan 39301

(601) 693-1992

P.O. Box 190
Oxford 38655

(601) 234-3751

Missouri
1150 Grand Avenue, Room 200
Kansas City 64106

(816) 374-3886
FTS: 758-3886

1114 Market Street, Room 611
St. Louis 63101

(314) 425-5560
FTS: 279-5560

300 South Jefferson
Springfield 65806

(417) 866-0691
FTS: 754-2762

Montana
P.O. Drawer 10081
Helena 59601
(406) 449-5338
FTS: 585-5338

Nebraska
P.O. Box 1168
Omaha 68101
(402) 221-3651
FTS: 864-3651

Nevada
300 South Las Vegas Boulevard
Las Vegas 89101
(702) 385-6584
FTS: 598-6584

350 South Center Street
Reno 89501
(702) 784-5251
FTS: 470-5251

New Hampshire
P.O. Box 435
Concord 00301
(603) 225-5881
FTS: 834-4737

New Jersey
U.S. Post Office and Courthouse, Room 211
402 East State Street
Trenton 08608
(609) 695-4445
FTS: 483-2155

2401 Morris Avenue
Union 07083
(201) 645-3000
FTS: 341-6268

New Mexico
P.O. Box 501
Albuquerque 87103
(505) 766-2271
FTS: 474-2271

New York
L.F. O'Brien Federal Building, Suite 411
North Pearl Street and Clinton Avenue
Albany 12207
(518) 472-2851
FTS: 562-2851

Federal Building, Room 217
111 West Huron Street
Buffalo 14202
(716) 846-4048
FTS: 437-4041

P.O. Box 3482
Church Street Station
New York 10008
(212) 264-4658
FTS: 264-4658

P.O. Box 1036
Plattsburgh 12901
(518) 561-6225
FTS: 832-6397

300 Hamilton Avenue, Room 200
White Plains 10601
(914) 761-4250
FTS: 883-7303

North Carolina
P.O. Box 1370
Asheville 28801
(704) 258-2850
FTS: 672-0761

222 South Church Street, Suite 404
Charlotte 28202
(704) 371-6125
FTS: 672-6125

P.O. Box 274
Fayetteville 28302
(919) 483-3030
FTS: 670-7314

P.O. Box 25699
Raleigh 27611
(919) 755-4366
FTS: 672-4366

P.O. Box 3761, Azalea Station
Wilmington 28401
(919) 343-4936
FTS: 671-4936

Federal Office Building, Room 433
251 North Main Street
Winston-Salem 27101
(919) 761-3143
FTS: 670-3143

North Dakota
P.O. Box 2571
Fargo 58102
(701) 237-5748
FTS: 783-5176

Ohio
P.O. Box 1759
Cincinnati 45201
(513) 684-3756
FTS: 684-3756

55 Erieview Plaza, Suite 500
Cleveland 44114
(216) 522-3080
FTS: 293-3080

237 Federal Building
85 Marconi Boulevard
Columbus 43215
(614) 469-6717
FTS: 943-6717

200 West Second Street
Dayton 45402
(513) 774-2851
FTS: 774-2851

Federal Office Building, Room 534
234 Summit Street
Toledo 43604
(419) 259-7520
FTS: 625-7520

P.O. Box 477
Youngstown 44501
(216) 747-8285
FTS: 294-3206

Oklahoma
P.O. Box 129
Muskogee 74401
(918) 687-2354
FTS: 736-2354

200 Northwest Fifth Street
Oklahoma City 73102
(405) 231-4877
FTS: 736-4877

P.O. Box 466
Tulsa 74101
(918) 581-7731
FTS: 736-7731

Oregon
350 Crown Plaza Building
1500 Southwest First Avenue
Portland 97201
(503) 221-2171
FTS: 423-2171

Pennsylvania
P.O. Box 1797
Erie 16507
(814) 454-8383
FTS: 721-2240

P.O. Box 949, Federal Square Station
Harrisburg 17108
(717) 782-2295
FTS: 590-2295

100 West Main Street, Suite 300B
Lansdale 19446
(215) 276-1072

U.S. Custom House, Room 504
Second and Chestnut Streets
Philadelphia 19106
(215) 597-7266
FTS: 597-7266

Federal Building
1000 Liberty Avenue
Pittsburgh 15222
(412) 644-2911
FTS: 722-2911

45 South Front Street
Reading 19602
(215) 372-6233
FTS: 488-2312

Rhode Island
10 Dorrance Street, Room 534
Providence 02903
(401) 528-4366
FTS: 838-4366

South Carolina
Federal Building, Room 503
334 Meeting Street
Charleston 29403
(803) 724-4275
FTS: 677-4275

835 Assembly Street
Columbia 29201
(803) 765-5723
FTS: 677-5723

P.O. Box 1571
Florence 29503
(803) 899-6504
FTS: 677-3373

P.O. Box 10102, Federal Station
Greenville 29603

(803) 232-2292
FTS: 677-9323

South Dakota
P.O. Box 1945
Rapid City 57701

(605) 348-3185
FTS: 782-1413

310 Federal Building
400 Phillips Avenue South
Sioux Falls 57102

(605) 336-6210
FTS: 782-4368

Tennessee
Franklin Building, Suite 315
East Gate Center
Chattanooga 37411

(615) 899-9790
FTS: 328-2348

P.O. Box 336
Greenville 37743

(615) 638-4157

One Northshore Drive, SW, Suite 201
Knoxville 37921

(615) 854-1443
FTS: 854-1351

167 North Main Street, Room 22
Memphis 38134

(901) 521-3489
FTS: 222-3489

4004 Hillsboro Road
Nashville 37215

(615) 251-5412
FTS: 852-5412

Texas
P.O. Box 1609
Austin 78767

(512) 397-5333
FTS: 734-5333

P.O. Box 2047
Brownsville 78520

(512) 546-4561
FTS: 734-8241

P.O. Box 2607
Corpus Christi 78403

(512) 882-3392
FTS: 734-3391

1114 Commerce Street, Room 718
Dallas 75242

(214) 767-2250
FTS: 729-2250

444 Executive Center Boulevard, Suite 233
El Paso 79902

(915) 543-7497
FTS: 572-7497

P.O. Box 17088
Fort Worth 76102

(817) 334-2771
FTS: 334-2771

P.O. Box 600927
Houston 77205

(713) 226-5401
FTS: 527-5405

1205 Texas Avenue, Room 625
Lubbock 79401

(806) 762-7451
FTS: 738-7451

727 East Durango Street, Room A405
San Antonio 78206

(512) 229-6161
FTS: 730-6161

P.O. Box 816
Tyler 75710

(214) 592-2372
FTS: 749-6025

Utah
350 Main Street, Room 445
Salt Lake City 84101

(801) 524-5853
FTS: 588-5853

Vermont
P.O. Box 141
Essex Junction 05452

(802) 879-6567
FTS: 832-6320

Virginia
P.O. Box 683
Bristol 24201

(703) 466-2727
FTS: 937-6047

P.O. Box 897
Danville 24541

(804) 793-6544
FTS: 937-3255

701 West Broad Street, Room 203
Falls Church 22046

(703) 577-2240
FTS: 285-2545

200 Granby Mall
Norfolk 23510

(804) 441-3190
FTS: 827-2190

P.O. Box 10068
Richmond 23240

(804) 771-2871
FTS: 925-2871

P.O. Box 271
Roanoke 24011

(703) 982-6300
FTS: 937-6300

P.O. Box 2868
Winchester 22601

(703) 622-6588

Washington
Federal Building, Room 806
915 Second Avenue
Seattle 98174

(206) 442-4485
FTS: 399-4485

P.O. Box 2202
Spokane 99210

(509) 456-4692
FTS: 439-4692

West Virginia
P.O. Box 4455
Bluefield 24701

(304) 327-3468
FTS: 924-4522

3414 Federal Building
500 Quarrier Street
Charleston 25301

(304) 346-8103
FTS: 924-1268

P.O. Box 1329
Wheeling 26003

(304) 232-4170
FTS: 923-1061

Wisconsin
P.O. Box 92068
Milwaukee 53202

(414) 291-3937
FTS: 362-3939

Wyoming
P.O. Box 67
Cheyenne 82001

(307) 778-2220
FTS: 328-2348

FEDERAL BUREAU OF INVESTIGATION
Department of Justice
10th Street and Pennsylvania Avenue, NW
Washington, D.C. 20535
(202) 324-3000

Alabama
2121 Building, Room 1400
Birmingham 35203

(205) 252-7705

520 Federal Building
Mobile 36602

(205) 438-3674

Alaska
Federal Building
701 C Street, Room E-222
Anchorage 99513

(907) 276-4441

Arizona
2721 North Central Avenue
Phoenix 85004   (602) 279-5511

Arkansas
215 U.S. Post Office Building
Little Rock 72201   (501) 372-7211

California
11000 Wilshire Boulevard
Los Angeles 90024   (213) 272-6161

Federal Building
2800 Cottage Way
Sacramento 95825   (916) 481-9110

Federal Office Building
880 Front Street, Room 6S31
San Diego 92188   (714) 231-1122

450 Golden Gate Avenue
P.O. Box 36015
San Francisco 94102   (415) 552-2155

Colorado
Federal Office Building, Room 18218
Denver 80202   (303) 629-7171

Connecticut
Federal Building
150 Court Street
New Haven 06510   (203) 777-6311

District of Columbia
1900 Half Street, SW
Washington, D.C. 20401   (202) 252-7801

Florida
7820 Arlington Expressway
Oaks V, Fourth Floor
Jacksonville 32211   (904) 721-1211

3801 Biscayne Boulevard
Miami 33137   (305) 573-3333

Federal Office Building, Room 610
Tampa 33602   (813) 228-7661

Georgia
275 Peachtree Street, NE
Atlanta 30303   (404) 521-3900

5401 Paulsen Street
Savannah 31405   (912) 354-9911

Hawaii
Kalanianaole Federal Building
300 Ala Moana Boulevard, Room 4307
Honolulu 96850   (808) 521-1411

Illinois
Everett McKinley Dirksen Building, Room 905
Chicago 60604   (312) 431-1333

535 West Jefferson Street
Springfield 62702   (217) 522-9675

Indiana
575 North Penna Street, Room 679
Indianapolis 46204   (317) 639-3301

Kentucky
Federal Building, Room 502
Louisville 40202   (502) 583-3941

Louisiana
701 Loyola Avenue
New Orleans 70113   (504) 522-4670

Maryland
7142 Ambassador Road
Baltimore 21207   (301) 265-8080

Massachusetts
John F. Kennedy Federal Office Building
Boston 02203   (617) 742-5533

Michigan
Patrick V. McNamara Building
Detroit 48226   (313) 965-2323

Minneapolis
392 Federal Building
Minneapolis 55401   (612) 339-7861

Mississippi
Federal Building
100 West Capitol Street, Room 1553
Jackson 39201   (601) 948-5000

Missouri
U.S. Court House, Room 300
Kansas City 64106   (816) 221-6100

2704 Federal Building
St. Louis 63103   (314) 241-5357

Montana
115 U.S. Court House and Federal
   Office Building
Butte 59701   (406) 792-2304

Nebraska
Federal Building
U.S. Post Office and Court House
215 North 17th Street
Omaha 68102   (402) 348-1210

Nevada
Federal Office Building, Room 2-011
Las Vegas 89101   (702) 385-1281

New Jersey
Gateway 1, Market Street
Newark 07101   (201) 622-5613

New Mexico
301 Grand Avenue, NE
Albuquerque 87102   (505) 247-1555

New York
502 U.S. Post Office and Court House
Albany 12207   (518) 465-7551

111 West Huron Street, Room 1400
Buffalo 14202   (716) 856-7800

26 Federal Plaza
New York 10278   (212) 553-2700

North Carolina
1120 Jefferson Standard Life
   Building
307 Tyron Street
Charlotte 28202   (704) 372-5484

Ohio
400 U.S. Post Office and Court
    House Building
Cincinnati 45202   (513) 421-4310

3005 Federal Office Building
Cleveland 44199   (216) 522-1400

Oklahoma
50 Penn Place, Suite 1600
Oklahoma City 73118   (405) 842-7471

Oregon
Crown Plaza Building
Portland 97201   (503) 224-4181

Pennsylvania
Federal Office Building
600 Arch Street
Philadelphia 19106   (215) 629-0800

1300 Federal Office Building
Pittsburg 15222   (412) 471-2000

Puerto Rico
U.S. Court House and Federal
    Building, Room 526
Hato Rey 00918   (415) 552-2155

South Carolina
1529 Hampton Street
Columbia 29201   (803) 254-3011

Tennessee
1111 Northshore Drive, Room 800
Knoxville 37919   (615) 588-8571

841 Clifford Davis Federal Building
Memphis 38103   (901) 525-7373

Texas
1810 Commerce Street, Room 200
Dallas 75201   (214) 741-1851

202 U.S. Court House Building
El Paso 79901   (915) 533-7451

6015 Federal Building and U.S.
    Court House
Houston 77002   (713) 224-1511

433 Post Office Building
San Antonio 78296   (512) 225-6741

Utah
3203 Federal Building
Salt Lake City 84138   (801) 355-7521

Virginia
300 North Lee Street, Room 500
Alexandria 22314   (703) 683-2680

200 Granby Mall, Room 839
Norfolk 23510   (804) 623-3111

200 West Grace Street
Richmond 23220   (804) 644-2631

Washington
915 Second Avenue   (206) 622-0460
Seattle 98174

Wisconsin
Federal Building and U.S. Court
    House, Room 700
Milwaukee 53202   (414) 276-4684

FEDERAL PRISONS AND COMMUNITY
TREATMENT CENTERS
Federal Bureau of Prisons
Department of Justice
320 First Street, NW
Washington, D.C. 20534
(202) 724-3250

North Central Region
Regional Office:
8800 Northwest 112th Street
K.C.I. Bank Building
Kansas City, Missouri 64153
(816) 243-5680

Illinois
Metropolitan Correctional Center
Chicago, 60605   (312) 353-6819

U.S. Penitentiary
Marion 62959   (618) 964-1441

Indiana
U.S. Penitentiary
Terre Haute 47808   (812) 238-1531

Kansas
U.S. Penitentiary
Leavenworth 66048   (913) 682-8700

Michigan
Federal Correctional Institution
Milan 48160   (313) 439-1571

Minnesota
Federal Correctional Institution
Sandstone 55072   (612) 245-2262

Missouri
U.S. Medical Center for Federal
    Prisoners
Springfield 65802   (417) 862-7041

Wisconsin
Federal Correctional Institution
Oxford 53952   (608) 584-5511

Northeast Region
Regional Office:
Scott Plaza II, Industrial Highway
Philadelphia, Pennsylvania 19113
(215) 596-1871

Connecticut
Federal Correctional Institution
Danbury 06810   (203) 746-2444

New York
Metropolitan Correctional Center
New York 10007   (212) 791-9139

Federal Correctional Institution
Otisville 10963   (914) 386-2456

Federal Correctional Institution
Ray Brook 12946   (518) 891-5400

Pennsylvania
U.S. Penitentiary
Lewisburg 17837   (717) 523-1251

Allenwood Federal Prison Camp
Montgomery 17752   (717) 547-1641

Virginia
Federal Correctional Institution
Petersburg 23803   (804) 733-7881

West Virginia
Federal Correctional Institution
Alderson 24910   (304) 445-2901

Federal Correctional Institution
Morgantown 26505   (304) 296-4416

South Central Region
Regional Office:
3883 Turtle Creek Boulevard
Dallas, Texas 75219
(214) 767-0012

Oklahoma
Federal Correctional Institution
El Reno 73036   (405) 262-4875

Texas
Federal Correctional Institution
Bastrop 78602   (512) 321-3903

Federal Prison Camp
Big Spring 79702   (915) 263-8304

Federal Correctional Institution
Fort Worth 76119   (817) 535-2111

Federal Correctional Institution
La Tuna 88021   (915) 886-3422

Federal Correctional Institution
Seagoville 75159   (214) 767-8471

Federal Correctional Institution
Texarkana 75501   (214) 838-4587

Southeast Region
Regional Office:
523 McDonough Boulevard, NE
Atlanta, Georgia 30315
(404) 221-3528

Alabama
Federal Prison Camp, Maxwell Air Force Base
Montgomery 36112   (205) 293-2784

Federal Correctional Institution
Talladega 35160   (205) 362-0410

Florida
Federal Prison Camp, Eglin Air Force Base
Eglin 32542   (904) 882-5391

Federal Correctional Institution
Miami 33177   (305) 253-4400

Federal Correctional Institution
Tallahassee 32304   (904) 878-2173

Kentucky
Federal Correctional Institution
Ashland 41101   (606) 928-6414

Federal Correctional Institution
Lexington 40507   (606) 255-6812

North Carolina
Federal Correctional Institution
Butner 27509   (919) 575-4541

Tennessee
Federal Correctional Institution
Memphis 38134   (901) 372-2269

Western Region
Regional Office:
330 Primrose Road
Crocker Financial Center Building
Burlingame, California 94010
(415) 347-0721

Arizona
Federal Detention Center
Florence 85232   (602) 868-5862

Federal Prison Camp
Safford 85546   (602) 428-6600

California
Federal Prison Camp
Boron 93516   (714) 762-5161

Federal Correctional Institution
Lompoc 93438   (805) 735-2771

Federal Correctional Institution
Pleasanton 94568   (415) 829-3522

Metropolitan Correctional Center
San Diego 92101   (714) 232-4311

Colorado
Federal Correctional Institution
Englewood 80110   (303) 985-1566

Washington
U.S. Penitentiary, McNeil Island
Steilacoom 98388   (206) 588-5281

Community Treatment Centers

Arizona
850 North Fourth Avenue
Phoenix 85003   (602) 261-4176

California
1720 Chestnut Avenue
Long Beach 90802   (213) 432-2961

205 MacArthur Boulevard
Oakland 94610   (415) 273-7231

Illinois
401 South LaSalle
Chicago 60605 (312) 353-5678

Michigan
1950 Trumbull Avenue
Detroit 48216 (313) 226-7042

Missouri
404 East 10th Street
Kansas City 64106 (816) 374-3946

New York
210 West 55th Street
New York 10019 (212) 826-4728

Texas
3401 Gaston Avenue
Dallas 75246 (214) 767-5248

2320 La Branch Street
Houston 77004 (713) 226-4934

IMMIGRATION AND NATURALIZATION SERVICES
Department of Justice
425 I Street, NW
Washington, D.C. 20220
(202) 633-2000

Alaska
Federal Building, U.S. Courthouse
701 C Street, Room D-229
Anchorage 99513 (907) 271-5029

Arizona
Federal Building
230 North First Avenue
Phoenix 85025 (602) 261-3122

California
300 North Los Angeles Street
Los Angeles 90012 (213) 688-2780

880 Front Street
San Diego 92188 (714) 293-6250

Appraisers Building
630 Sansome Street
San Francisco 94111 (415) 556-2070

Colorado
1787 Federal Office Building
1961 Stout Street
Denver 80202 (303) 837-3526

Connecticut
900 Asylum Avenue
Hartford 06105 (203) 244-2659

District of Columbia
25 E Street, NW
Washington, D.C. 20538 (202) 724-5756

Florida
155 South Miami Avenue
Miami 33130 (305) 350-5344

Georgia
Richard B. Long Federal Building
75 Spring Street, SW
Atlanta 30303 (404) 221-5158

Hawaii
595 Ala Moana Boulevard
Honolulu 96809 (808) 546-8979

Illinois
Dirksen Federal Office Building
219 South Dearborn Street
Chicago 60604 (312) 353-7300

Indiana
102 Federal Building
507 State Street
Hammond 46320 (219) 932-5500

Louisiana
Postal Services Building
1701 Loyola Avenue
New Orleans 70113 (504) 589-6533

Maine
76 Pearl Street
Portland 04112 (207) 780-3352

Maryland
E.A. Garmatz Federal Building
100 South Hanover Street
Baltimore 21201 (301) 962-2010

Massachusetts
John F. Kennedy Federal Building
Boston 02203 (617) 223-2343

Michigan
Federal Building
333 Mount Elliott Street
Detroit 48207 (313) 226-3250

Minnesota
Main Post Office Building
180 East Kellogg Boulevard
St. Paul 55101 (612) 725-7108

Missouri
324 East 11th Street, Suite 1100
Kansas City 64106 (816) 374-3421

Montana
Federal Building
301 South Park, Room 512
Helena 59626 (406) 449-5288

Nebraska
Federal Office Building
106 South 15th Street, Room 1008
Omaha 68102 (402) 221-4651

New Jersey
Federal Building
970 Broad Street
Newark 07102 (201) 645-3350

New York
68 Court Street
Buffalo 14202   (716) 846-4742

26 Federal Plaza
New York 10007   (212) 264-5818

Ohio
Anthony J. Celebrezze Federal Building
1240 East Ninth Street, Room 1917
Cleveland 44199   (216) 522-4770

U.S. Post Office and Courthouse
Fifth and Walnut Streets
Cincinnati 45201   (513) 684-2931

Oregon
Federal Office Building
511 Northwest Broadway
Portland 97209   (503) 221-2271

Pennsylvania
U.S. Courthouse
Independence Mall West
601 Market Street, Room 132
Philadelphia 19106   (215) 597-7305

Puerto Rico
Federal Building (Hato Rey)
GPO Box 5068
San Juan 00936

Rhode Island
Federal Building, U.S. Post Office
Exchange Terrace
Providence 02903   (401) 528-4375

Texas
Federal Building
1100 Commerce Street, Room 6A21
Dallas 75242   (214) 767-0541

343 U.S. Courthouse
El Paso 79984   (915) 543-7600

719 Grimes Avenue
Harlingen 78550   (512) 425-7333

515 Rusk Avenue
Houston 77208   (713) 226-4251

U.S. Federal Building
727 East Durango, Suite A301
San Antonio 78206   (512) 229-6350

Utah
Federal Building
125 South State Street, Room 4103
Salt Lake City 84138   (801) 524-5690

Vermont
Federal Building
P.O. Box 328
St. Albans 05478   (802) 524-6742

Virginia
Bank of Virginia Building
807 North Military Highway
Norfolk 23502   (804) 441-3081

Washington
815 Airport Way South
Seattle 98134   (206) 442-5950

Wisconsin
328-C Federal Building
517 East Wisconsin Avenue
Milwaukee 53202   (414) 291-3565

U.S. COAST GUARD
400 Seventh Street, SW
Washington, D.C. 20950
(202) 426-2158

1st District
150 Causeway Street
Boston, Massachusetts 02114
(617) 223-3611
Maine, Massachusetts, New Hampshire, Rhode Island, eastern
Vermont

2nd District
1430 Olive Street
St. Louis, Missouri 63103
(314) 622-5011
Northern Alabama, Arkansas, Colorado, Illinois, southern Indiana,
Iowa, Kansas, Kentucky, southern Minnesota, northern Mississippi,
Missouri, Nebraska, North Dakota, Oklahoma, southern Ohio,
southwestern Pennsylvania, South Dakota, Tennessee, West Virginia,
western Wisconsin, Wyoming

3rd District
Governors Island, New York 10004
(212) 668-7001
Connecticut, Delaware, New Jersey, southern and eastern New York,
eastern Pennsylvania, western Vermont

5th District
Federal Building
431 Crawford Street
Portsmouth, Virginia 23705
(703) 398-6277
District of Columbia, Maryland, North Carolina, Virginia

7th District
Federal Building
51 Southwest First Avenue
Miami, Florida 33130
(305) 350-5502
Eastern Florida, eastern Georgia, South Carolina, Panama Canal
zone, Puerto Rico, Virgin Islands

8th District
Hale Boggs Building
500 Camp Street
New Orleans, Louisiana 70130
(504) 682-2961
Southern Alabama, western Florida, western Georgia, Louisiana,
southern Mississippi, New Mexico, Texas

9th District
1240 East 9th Street
Cleveland, Ohio 44199
(216) 522-3131
Northeastern Illinois, northern Indiana, Michigan, northern Ohio,
northwestern New York, northwestern Pennsylvania, eastern
Wisconsin

11th District
Union Bank Building
400 Oceangate Boulevard
Long Beach, California 90802
(213) 590-2287
Arizona, southern California, southern Nevada, southern Utah

12th District
630 Sansome Street
San Francisco, California 94126
(415) 556-6074
Northern California, northern Nevada, northern Utah

13th District
Federal Building
915 Second Street
Seattle, Washington 98104
(206) 442-7523
Idaho, Montana, Oregon, Washington

14th District
300 Ala Moana Boulevard
Honolulu, Hawaii 96850
(808) 546-2861
Hawaii, U.S. Pacific Islands, possessions

17th District
P.O. Box 3-5000
Juneau, Alaska 98771
(907) 586-7355
Alaska

OTHER FEDERAL AGENCIES

Department of Justice
Tenth Street and Constitution Avenue, NW
Washington, D.C. 20530
(202) 633-2001

Drug Enforcement Administration
Department of Justice
1405 I Street, NW
Washington, D.C. 20537
(202) 633-1337

Federal Law Enforcement Training Center
Department of the Treasury
Glynco, Georgia 31524
(912) 267-2224

Washington Liaison Office:
1435 G Street, NW
Washington, D.C. 20220
(202) 376-0764

Interpol (National Central Bureau)
Department of Justice
Ninth Street and Pennsylvania Avenue, NW
Washington, D.C. 20530
(202) 633-2867

United States Customs Service
Department of the Treasury
1301 Constitution Avenue, NW
Washington, D.C. 20229
(202) 566-2101

United States Marshals Service
Department of Justice
One Tyson Corner Center
McLean, Virginia 22102
(703) 285-1100

United States Secret Service
Department of the Treasury
1800 G Street, NW
Washington, D.C. 20223
(202) 634-5708

Directory of State Agencies

NATIONAL CRIMINAL JUSTICE COUNCILS
444 North Capitol Street, NW, Suite 305
Washington, DC 20001
(202) 347-4900

Alabama
Alabama Law Enforcement Planning Agency
2863 Fairlane Drive, Executive Park
Building F, Suite 49
Montgomery 36116
(205) 832-6830

Alaska
Alaska Criminal Justice Planning Agency
Department of Law
Pouch KJ
Juneau 99811
(907) 465-3591

American Samoa
Criminal Justice Planning Agency
P. O. Box 7
Pago, Pago 96799
Pago, Pago 633-5222

Arizona
Arizona State Justice Planning Agency
111 West Monroe, Suite 600
Phoenix 85003
(602) 255-5466

Arkansas
Arkansas Crime Commission
Twin City Bank Building, Room 407
North Little Rock 72114
(501) 371-1305/1771

California
Office of Criminal Justice Planning
9719 Lincoln Village Drive, Suite 600
Sacramento 95827
(916) 366-5340

Colorado
Criminal Justice Affairs
1313 Sherman Street, Room 518
Denver 80203
(303) 866-2771

Connecticut
Connecticut Justice Commission
75 Elm Street
Hartford 06115
(203) 566-3020

Delaware
Office of Management, Budget and Planning
Townsend Building
Dover 19901
(302) 736-4271

District of Columbia
Office of Criminal Justice Plans and Analysis
421 8th Street, NW
Washington, D. C. 20004
(202) 727-6537

Florida
Bureau of Criminal Justice Assistance
137 Carlton Building
Tallahassee 32301
(904) 488-6001

Georgia
Criminal Justice Coordinating Council
7 Martin Luther King Jr. Drive, SW
Atlanta 30334
(404) 656-1721

Guam
Guam Criminal Justice Planning Agency
Office of the Governor
P.O. Box 2950
Agana 96910
Guam 772-8781

Hawaii
State Law Enforcement and Juvenile
   Delinquency Planning Agency
250 South King Street, Room 412
Honolulu 96813
(808) 548 4572

Idaho
Law Enforcement Assistance Division
6058 Corporal Lane, State House Mail
Boise 83720
(208) 334-2364

Illinois
Illinois Law Enforcement Commission
120 South Riverside Plaza
Chicago 60606
(312) 454-1560

Indiana
Indiana Criminal Justice Planning Agency
215 North Senate, Graphic Arts Building
Indianapolis 46202
(317) 232-1233

Iowa
Iowa Crime Commission
Lucas State Office Building
Des Moines 50319
(515) 281-3241

Kansas
Governor's Committee on Criminal
   Administration
503 Kansas Avenue
Topeka 66603
(913) 296-3066

Kentucky
Executive Office of Staff Services
Department of Justice
State Office Building Annex
Frankfort 40601
(502) 564-3251

Louisiana
Louisiana Commission on Law Enforcement
   and Administration of Criminal Justice
1885 Wooddale Boulevard, Room 610
Baton Rouge 70806
(504) 925-4436

Maine
Maine Criminal Justice Planning and
   Assistance Agency
4 Wabon Street
Augusta 04330
(207) 289-3361

Maryland
Governor's Commission on Law Enforcement
   and Administration of Justice
One Investment Place, Suite 700
Towson 21204
(301) 321-3636

Massachusetts
Committee on Criminal Justice
100 Cambridge Street
Boston 02202
(617) 727-5497

Michigan
Office of Criminal Justice
Lewis Cass Building
Lansing 48909
(517) 373-6655

Minnesota
Crime Control Planning Board
444 Lafayette Road
St. Paul 55101
(612) 296-3133

Mississippi
Criminal Justice Planning Division
Office of the Governor
Ike Sanford Building
637 North President Street
Jackson 39201
(601) 354-6041

Missouri
Department of Public Safety
Missouri Council on Criminal Justice
P.O. Box 749
Jefferson City 65101
(314) 751-4905

Montana
Board of Crime Control
Scott Hart Building
303 Roberts Avenue
Helena 59620
(406) 449-3604

Nebraska
Nebraska Commission on Law Enforcement
    and Criminal Justice
301 Centennial Mall South
Lincoln 68509
(402) 471-2194

Nevada
Department of Motor Vehicles
430 Jeanell, Capitol Complex
Carson City 89710
(702) 885-4405

New Hampshire
New Hampshire Crime Commission
117 Manchester Street, Pine Inn Plaza
Concord 03301
(603) 271-3601

New Jersey
Law Enforcement Planning Agency
3535 Quaker Bridge Road, CN-083
Trenton 08625
(609) 292-3741

New Mexico
Corrections Department
113 Washington Avenue
Santa Fe 87501
(505) 827-5222

New York
Division of Criminal Justice Services
Executive Park Tower, Stuyvesant Plaza
Albany 12203
(518) 457-6091/4274

North Carolina
Division of Crime Control
P.O. Box 27687
Raleigh 27611
(919) 733-4000

North Dakota
Criminal Justice Training and Statistics
    Division
Attorney General's Office,
State Capitol Building
Bismarck 58505
(701) 224-2594

Northern Marianas
Northern Marianas Criminal Justice Planning
    Agency
Office of the Governor
Saipan 96950

Ohio
Office of Criminal Justice Services
30 East Broad Street
Columbus 43215
(614) 466-7610

Oklahoma
Criminal Justice Services Division—DECA
Lincoln Plaza Building,
4545 North Lincoln Boulevard, Suite 285
Oklahoma City 73105
(405) 521-4545

Oregon
Law Enforcement Council
2001 Front Street, NE
Salem 97310
(503) 378-4347

Pennsylvania
Pennsylvania Commission on Crime and
    Delinquency
P.O. Box 1167, Federal Square Station
Harrisburg 17108
(717) 787-2040

Puerto Rico
Puerto Rico Crime Commission
GPO Box 1256
San Juan 00936
(809) 783-0398

Rhode Island
Rhode Island Governor's Justice Commission
86 Weybosset Street
Providence 02903
(401) 277-2620

South Carolina
Division of Public Safety Programs
Edgar A. Brown State Office Building
1205 Pendleton Street
Columbia 29201
(803) 758-3573

South Dakota
South Dakota State Criminal Justice
    Commission
118 West Capitol
Pierre 57501
(605) 773-3665

Tennessee
Tennessee Law Enforcement Planning
    Agency
James K. Polk Building
505 Deaderick Street
Nashville 37219
(615) 741-3521

Texas
Governor's Office of General Counsel and
    Criminal Justice
P.O. Box 12428, Capitol Station
Austin 78711
(512) 475-4444

Trust Territory of the Pacific Islands
Justice Improvement Commission
Capitol Heights, Rural P.O. Branch
Trust Territory of the Pacific Islands
Saipan, Mariana Islands 96950

U.S. Virgin Islands
Virgin Islands Law Enforcement Planning
    Commission
Box 3807
St. Thomas 00801
(809) 774-6400

Utah
Utah Council on Criminal Justice
    Administration
4501 South 2700 West
Salt Lake City 84119
(801) 965-4587

Vermont
Vermont Commission on the Administration
    of Justice
149 State Street
Montpelier 05602
(802) 828-2351

Virginia
Division of Justice and Crime Prevention
8501 Mayland Drive
Richmond 23229
(804) 281-9276

Washington
Criminal Justice Section
Division of Accounting and Fiscal Services
Office of Financial Management, MS ER-13
400 East Union
Olympia 98504
(206) 754-2802/2803

West Virginia
Criminal Justice and Highway Safety Division
1212 Lewis Street, Suite 321
Charleston 25301
(304) 348-8814

Wisconsin
Wisconsin Council on Criminal Justice
30 West Mifflin, Suite 1000
Madison 53702
(608) 266-3323

Wyoming
Governor's Planning Committee on Criminal
    Administration
Barrett Building
Cheyenne 82002
(307) 777-7716

STATE CRIMINAL INVESTIGATION DEPARTMENTS

Alabama
Department of Public Safety
Bureau of Investigation
500 Dexter Avenue
Montgomery 36192
(205) 832-5061

Alaska
Department of Public Safety
Pouch N
Juneau 99811
(907) 465-4322

Arizona
Department of Public Safety
Criminal Investigations Bureau
P.O. Box 6638
Phoenix 85005
(602) 262-8011

Arkansas
State Police
Criminal Enforcement
P.O. Box 4005
Little Rock 72214
(501) 371-2421

California
Department of Justice
Division of Law Enforcement
3301 C Street
Sacramento 95813
(916) 322-4350

Colorado
Colorado Bureau of Investigation
2002 South Colorado Boulevard
Denver 80222
(303) 759-1100

Connecticut
Department of Public Safety
Division of State Police
100 Washington Street
Hartford 06101
(203) 566-3200

Delaware
Department of Public Safety
Delaware State Police
P.O. Box 430
Dover 19901
(302) 736-5911

Florida
Department of Law Enforcement
P.O. Box 1489
Tallahassee 32302
(904) 488-7880

Georgia
Bureau of Investigation
1001 International Boulevard, Suite 800
Atlanta 30354
(404) 656-2294

Hawaii
Hawaii Department of the Attorney General
415 South Beretania Street
Honolulu 96813
(808) 548-4740

Idaho
Department of Law Enforcement
3311 West State Street
Boise 83731
(208) 334-3628

Illinois
Department of Law Enforcement
Division of Criminal Investigation
2401 West Jefferson Street
Springfield 62706
(217) 782-6053

Indiana
State Police Department
100 North Senate Avenue
Indianapolis 46204
(317) 232-8248

Iowa
Division of Criminal Investigation
Wallace Building
Des Moines 50319
(515) 281-5138

Kansas
Bureau of Investigation
3420 Van Buren
Topeka 66611
(913) 267-5000

Kentucky
Bureau of Kentucky State Police
Department of Justice
State Office Building
Frankfort 40601
(502) 564-3000

Louisiana
Department of Public Safety
P.O. Box 66614
Baton Rouge 70896
(504) 925-6117

Maine
Department of Attorney General
Investigation Division
State House
Augusta 04330
(207) 289-3467

Maryland
State Police
Pikesville 21208
(301) 486-3101

Massachusetts
State Police
1010 Commonwealth Avenue
Boston 02215
(617) 566-4500

Michigan
Department of State Police
714 South Harrison Road
East Lansing 48823
(517) 332-2521

Minnesota
Department of Public Safety
Bureau of Criminal Apprehension
1246 University Avenue
St. Paul 55104
(612) 296-2660

Mississippi
Office of Attorney General
Organized Crime Division
P.O. Box 2
Jackson 39205
(601) 354-7134

Missouri
State Highway Patrol
1510 East Elm Street
Jefferson City 65101
(314) 751-3313

Montana
Law Enforcement Services Division
Criminal Investigation Bureau
303 Roberts Avenue
Helena 59620
(406) 449-3875

Nebraska
State Patrol
Criminal Investigation Division
P.O. Box 94637, State House Station
Lincoln 68509
(402) 477-3951

Nevada
Department of Law Enforcement Assistance
430 Jeanell Street, Capitol Complex
Carson City 89710
(702) 885-4404

New Hampshire
Office of the Department of Safety
James H. Hayes Safety Building
One Hazen Drive
Concord 03301
(603) 271-2791

New Jersey
Department of Law and Public Safety
Division of Criminal Justice
13 Roszel Road
Princeton 08540
(609) 452-9500

New Mexico
State Police
P.O. Box 1628
Santa Fe 87501
(505) 827-5111

New York
State of New York Commission of
   Investigation
270 Broadway
New York 10007
(212) 577-0700

North Carolina
State Bureau of Investigation
State Law Enforcement Complex
3320 Old Garner Road
Raleigh 27626
(919) 779-1400

North Dakota
Bureau of Criminal Investigation
P.O. Box 1054
Bismarck 58505
(701) 224-2990

Ohio
Bureau of Criminal Identification and
   Investigation
P.O. Box 365
London 43140
(614) 466-8204

Oklahoma
State Bureau of Investigation
2132 Northeast 36th Street
Oklahoma City 73136
(405) 427-5421

Oregon
State Police
107 Public Service Building
Salem 97310
(503) 378-3720

Pennsylvania
State Police Headquarters
1800 Elmerton Avenue
Harrisburg 17109
(717) 783-5599

Rhode Island
State Police
P.O. Box 185
North Scituate 02857
(401) 647-3311

South Carolina
State Law Enforcement Division
P.O. Box 21398
Columbia 29221
(803) 758-6000

South Dakota
Division of Criminal Investigation
Attorney General's Office
P.O. Box 1237
Pierre 57501
(605) 773-3331

Tennessee
Bureau of Criminal Identification
Andrew Jackson State Office Building
Nashville 37219
(615) 741-2557

Texas
Department of Public Safety
P.O. Box 4087
Austin 78773
(512) 465-2000

Utah
Department of Public Safety
Bureau of Criminal Identification
300 State Office Building
Salt Lake City 84114
(801) 533-5251

Vermont
State Police Criminal Division
State Department of Public Safety
Montpelier 05602
(802) 828-2144

Virginia
Department of State Police
P.O. Box 27472
Richmond 23261
(804) 323-2000

Washington
State Patrol
General Administration Building
Olympia 98504
(206) 753-6540

West Virginia
Department of Public Safety
725 Jefferson Road
Charleston 25305
(304) 348-2355

Wisconsin
Department of Justice
Division of Criminal Investigation
123 West Washington Avenue
Madison 53702
(608) 266-1671

Wyoming
Division of Criminal Investigation
P.O. Box 1895
Cheyenne 82001
(307) 777-7181

STATE POLICE HEADQUARTERS

Alabama
Department of Public Safety
P.O. Box 1511
Montgomery 36192
(205) 832-5245

Alaska
State Troopers
P.O. Box 6188
Anchorage 99502
(907) 269-5641

Arizona
Department of Public Safety
P.O. Box 6638
Phoenix 85005
(602) 262-8212

Arkansas
Department of Public Safety
State Police
3701 West Roosevelt Road
Little Rock 72214
(501) 371-2491

California
State Highway Patrol
2555 First Avenue
Sacramento 95814
(916) 455-2211

Colorado
State Patrol
4201 East Arkansas Avenue
Denver 80222
(303) 757-9011

Connecticut
Department of Public Safety
Division of State Police
100 Washington Street
Hartford 06101
(203) 566-3200

Delaware
State Police
P.O. Box 430
Dover 19901
(302) 736-5911

Florida
State Highway Patrol
2900 Apalache Parkway
Tallahassee 32301
(904) 488-6517

Georgia
Department of Public Safety
959 East Confederate Avenue, SE
Atlanta 30301
(404) 656-6063

Hawaii
Honolulu Police Department
City and County of Honolulu
415 South Beretania Street
Honolulu 96813

Hawaii County Police Department
P.O. Box 787
Hilo 96720

Maui County Police Department
P.O. Box 1029
Wailuku, Maui 96793

Kauai County Police Department
Lihue, Kauai 96766

Idaho
State Police
P.O. Box 34
Boise 83731
(208) 334-3850

Illinois
Department of Law Enforcement
103 Armory Building
Springfield 62706
(217) 782-7263

Indiana
State Police Department
State Office Building
100 North Senate Avenue
Indianapolis 46204
(317) 232-8248

Iowa
State Patrol
Wallace Building
Des Moines 50319
(515) 281-5824

Kansas
Highway Patrol
Townsite Plaza, Building 2
200 East Sixth Street, Suite 130
Topeka 66603
(913) 296-3801

Kentucky
State Police
State Office Building
Frankfort 40601
(502) 564-4686

Louisiana
State Police
P.O. Box 66614
Baton Rouge 70896
(504) 925-6112

Maine
State Police
36 Hospital Street
Augusta 04330
(207) 289-2155

Maryland
State Police
Pikesville 21208
(301) 486-3101

Massachusetts
State Police
1010 Commonwealth Avenue
Boston 02215
(617) 566-4500

Michigan
State Police
714 South Harrison Road
East Lansing 48823
(517) 332-2521

Minnesota
State Patrol
Transportation Building
John Ireland Boulevard
St. Paul 55155
(612) 482-5901

Mississippi
Department of Public Safety
P.O. Box 958
Jackson 39205
(601) 982-1212

Missouri
State Highway Patrol
1510 East Elm Street
Jefferson City 65101
(314) 751-3313

Montana
Highway Patrol
303 Roberts Avenue
Helena, 59620
(406) 449-3000

Nebraska
State Patrol
South Junction U.S. 77, N-2
Lincoln 68509
(402) 477-3951

Nevada
Highway Patrol
555 Wright Way
Carson City 89711
(702) 885-5300

New Hampshire
State Police
James H. Hayes Safety Building
One Hazen Drive
Concord 03301
(603) 271-3636

New Jersey
Division of State Police
P.O. Box 7068
West Trenton 08625
(609) 882-2000

New Mexico
State Police
P.O. Box 1628
Santa Fe 87501
(505) 827-2551

New York
State Police
Building 22, State Campus
Albany 12226
(518) 457-6811

North Carolina
Highway Patrol
P.O. Box 27687
Raleigh 27611
(919) 733-7952

North Dakota
Highway Patrol
State Capitol Building
Bismarck 58505
(701) 224-2455

Ohio
State Highway Patrol
Columbus 43205
(614) 466-2660

Oklahoma
Highway Patrol
3600 North Eastern Avenue
Oklahoma City 73111
(405) 424-4011

Oregon
State Police
107 Public Service Building
Salem 97310
(503) 378-3720

Pennsylvania
State Police
1800 Elmerton Avenue
Harrisburg 17109
(717) 783-5599

Rhode Island
State Police
P.O. Box 185
North Scituate 02857
(401) 647-3311

South Carolina
State Highway Patrol
P.O. Box 191
Columbia 29202
(803) 758-3315

South Dakota
Department of Public Safety
Division of Highway Patrol
118 West Capitol Avenue
Pierre 57501
(605) 773-3105

Tennessee
Department of Safety
Andrew Jackson State Office Building
Nashville 37219
(615) 741-2101

Texas
Department of Public Safety
5805 North Lamar Boulevard
Austin 78773
(512) 465-2000

Utah
State Highway Patrol
State Office Building
Salt Lake City 84114
(801) 533-4912

Vermont
Department of Public Safety
State Patrol
Montpelier 05602
(802) 828-2136

Virginia
Department of State Police
P.O. Box 27472
Richmond 23261
(804) 323-2000

Washington
State Patrol
General Administration Building
Olympia 98504
(206) 753-6540

West Virginia
State Police
725 Jefferson Road
South Charleston 25309
(304) 348-2355

Wisconsin
Department of Transportation
Division of State Patrol
P.O. Box 7912
Madison 53707
(608) 266-3212

Wyoming
Highway Patrol
P.O. Box 1708
Cheyenne 82001
(307) 777-7301

Canadian Provincial Police

Alberta
Department of the Solicitor General
Law Enforcement Division
Seventh Floor Melton Building
10310 Jasper Avenue
Edmonton T5J 2W4
(403) 427-2746

British Columbia
Department of the Attorney General
Parliament Buildings
Victoria V8V 1X4
(604) 384-4434

Manitoba
Department of the Attorney General
Legislative Building, Room 104
Winnipeg R3C 0V8
(204) 944-3728

New Brunswick
Department of Justice
Box 6000
Fredericton E3B 5H1
(506) 453-2714

Newfoundland
Department of Justice
Confederation Building
St. John's A1C 5T7
(709) 722-5111

Nova Scotia
Department of the Attorney General
P.O. Box 7
Halifax B3J 2L6
(902) 426-6840

Ontario
Ontario Provincial Police
90 Harbour Street
Toronto M7A 2S1
(416) 967-2222

Prince Edward Island
Department of Justice
Box 2000
Charlottetown C1A 7N8
(902) 894-5513

Quebec
Surete du Quebec
1701 Parthenais
Montreal H2L 4K7
(514) 934-2424

Saskatchewan
Department of the Attorney General
Legislative Building
Regina S4S 0B3
(306) 569-3333

Royal Canadian Mounted Police

Headquarters
1200 Alta Vista Drive
Ottawa, Ontario K1A 0R2
(613) 993-1204

A Division
Brunswick Building
400 Cooper Street
Ottawa, Ontario K1A 0R4
(613) 992-6138

B Division
Box 4300, Pleasantville
St. John's, Newfoundland A1C 5S8
(709) 737-5437

C Division
4225 Dorchester Boulevard West
Westmount, Quebec H3Z 2T4
(514) 283-6100

D Division
Box 922, 1091 Portage Avenue
Winnipeg, Manitoba R3C 2T4
(204) 985-5415

E Division
2881 Nanaimo Street
Victoria, British Columbia V8T 4Z8
(604) 566-3244

E Division District-Area 1
1200 West 73rd Avenue
Vancouver, British Columbia V6P 6G6
(604) 542-4417

E Division District-Area 2
Vancouver Island, British Columbia
(604) 556-3371

F Division
Box 2500, Derrick Building
Regina, Saskatchewan S4P 3E1
(306) 569-5477

G Division
Box 5000
Yellowknife, Northwest Territory X0E 1H0
(403) 873-5865

H Division
Box 2286, 3139 Oxford Street
Halifax, Nova Scotia B3J 3E1
(902) 426-3940

J Division
Box 3900, Woodstock Road
Fredericton, New Brunswick E3B 4Z8
(506) 452-3420

K Division
Box 1320, 11140-109th Street
Edmonton, Alberta T5J 2N1
(403) 479-9444

L Division
Box 1360, 450 University Avenue
Charlottetown, Prince Edward
   Island C1A 7N1
(902) 892-2451

M Division
4100 Fourth Avenue
Whitehorse, Yukon Y1A 1H5
(403) 667-5584

N Division
Box 8900
Ottawa, Ontario K1G 3J2
(613) 993-9500

O Division
Box 519, Adelaide P.O.
225 Jarvis Street
Toronto, Ontario M5C 2M3
(416) 369-4754

Depot Division
Box 6500
Regina, Saskatchewan S4P 3J9
(306) 569-5760

STATE MOTOR VEHICLE AGENCIES

Alabama
Department of Revenue
Motor Vehicle and License Tax Division
3030 Eastern Boulevard
Montgomery 36130
(205) 832-6740

Alaska
Department of Public Safety
Motor Vehicle Division
2150 East Dowling Road
Anchorage 99510
(907) 349-4581

Arizona
Department of Transportation
Motor Vehicle Division
1801 West Jefferson Avenue
Phoenix 85001
(602) 261-7531

Arkansas
Department of Finance and Administration
Motor Vehicle Division
Seventh Avenue and Wolfe & Battery Streets
Little Rock 72203
(501) 371-1885

California
Department of Motor Vehicles
2415 First Avenue
Sacramento 95813
(916) 323-4120

Colorado
Department of Revenue
Motor Vehicle Division
140 West Sixth Avenue
Denver 80261
(303) 839-3095

Connecticut
Department of Motor Vehicles
60 State Street
Wethersfield 06109
(203) 566-2640

Delaware
Motor Vehicle Division
Highway Administration Building
Route 113
Dover 19901
(302) 736-4421

District of Columbia
Department of Motor Vehicles
301 C Street, NW
Washington, D.C. 20001
(202) 727-5847

Florida
Division of Motor Vehicles
Neil Kirkman Building
Tallahassee 32301
(904) 488-4127

Georgia
Department of Revenue
Motor Vehicle Unit
Trinity-Washington Building
Atlanta 30334
(404) 488-4127

Hawaii
Department of Finance
415 South Beretania Street
Honolulu 96814
(808) 955-8321

Idaho
Department of Law Enforcement
3311 State Street
Boise 83731
(208) 334-3711

Illinois
Office of Secretary of State
Division of Motor Vehicles
Centennial Building, Room 312
Springfield 62756
(217) 785-3000

Indiana
Bureau of Motor Vehicles
325 State Office Building
Indianapolis 46204
(317) 232-2795

Iowa
Department of Transportation
Wallace State Office Building
Des Moines, Iowa 50319
(515) 281-5818

Kansas
Department of Revenue
Division of Vehicles
State Office Building
Topeka 66626
(913) 296-3621

Kentucky
Motor Vehicle Division
Capitol Annex
Frankfort 40622
(502) 564-3780

Louisiana
Motor Vehicle Division
P.O. Box 66196
Baton Rouge 70896
(504) 925-6281

Maine
Office of Secretary of State
Motor Vehicle Division
Capitol Street, Station 29
Augusta 04333
(207) 289-3556

Maryland
Motor Vehicle Administration
6601 Ritchey Highway, NE
Glen Burnie 21062
(301) 768-7000

Massachusetts
Registry of Motor Vehicles
100 Nashua Street
Boston 02114
(617) 727-3794

Michigan
Department of State
Division of Driver and Vehicle Services
7064 Crowner Drive
Lansing 48918
(517) 322-1460

Minnesota
Motor Vehicle Division
Transportation Building
St. Paul 55155
(612) 296-6911

Mississippi
Motor Vehicle Comptroller
Woolfolk Building
Jackson 39205
(601) 354-7414

Missouri
Motor Vehicle Registration Division
P.O. Box 100
Jefferson City 65105
(314) 751-4509

Montana
Registrar of Motor Vehicles
923 Main Street
Deer Lodge 59722
(406) 846-1423

Nebraska
Department of Motor Vehicles
301 Centennial Mall South
Lincoln 68509
(402) 471-2281

Nevada
Department of Motor Vehicles
Registration Division
Carson City 89701
(702) 885-5370

New Hampshire
Division of Motor Vehicles
James H. Hayes Safety Building
One Hazen Drive
Concord 03301
(603) 271-2484

New Jersey
Division of Motor Vehicles
25 South Montgomery Street
Trenton 08666
(609) 292-5203

New Mexico
Department of Motor Vehicles
Manuel Lujan Sr. Building
Santa Fe 87503
(505) 827-2936

New York
Department of Motor Vehicles
Empire State Plaza
Swan Street Building
Albany 12228
(518) 474-0877

North Carolina
Department of Motor Vehicles
Motor Vehicle Building
1100 New Bern Avenue
Raleigh 27679
(919) 733-7270

North Dakota
Motor Vehicle Department
900 East Boulevard
Bismarck 58505
(701) 224-2725

Ohio
Bureau of Motor Vehicles
4300 Kimberly Parkway
Columbus 43227
(614) 466-2130

Oklahoma
Motor Vehicle Division
2501 Lincoln Boulevard
Oklahoma City 73194
(405) 521-3344

Oregon
Motor Vehicle Division
1905 Lana Avenue, NE
Salem 97314
(503) 378-6935

Pennsylvania
Bureau of Motor Vehicles
Transportation and Safety Building
Harrisburg 17122
(717) 787-3130

Rhode Island
Registry of Motor Vehicles
State Office Building
Providence 02903
(401) 277-3007

South Carolina
Motor Vehicle Division
P.O. Drawer 1498
Columbia 29216
(803) 758-3204

South Dakota
Department of Motor Vehicles
218 West Capital
Pierre 57501
(605) 773-3541

Tennessee
Motor Vehicle Division
500 Deaderick Street
Nashville 37242
(615) 741-2477

Texas
Motor Vehicle Division
40th and Jackson Avenue
Austin 78779
(512) 475-7611

Utah
Motor Vehicle Division
State Fairgrounds
1095 Motor Avenue
Salt Lake City 84116
(801) 533-5312

Vermont
Agency of Transportation
Department of Motor Vehicles
120 State Street
Montpelier 05603
(804) 770-3344

Virginia
Division of Motor Vehicles
2300 West Broad Street
Richmond 23269
(804) 770-3344

Washington
Department of Licensing
P.O. Box 9909
Olympia 98504
(206) 753-6946

West Virginia
Department of Motor Vehicles
1800 Washington Street, East
Charleston 25305
(304) 348-3900

Wisconsin
Division of Motor Vehicles
4802 Sheboygan Avenue
Hill Farms State Office Building
Madison 53707
(608) 266-1466

Wyoming
Motor Vehicle Division
2200 Carey Avenue
Cheyenne 82002
(307) 777-7971

Canadian Motor Vehicle Agencies

Alberta
Registry of Motor Vehicles
10001 Bellamy Hill
Edmonton T5J 3B7
(403) 427-3121

British Columbia
Motor Vehicle Bureau
Parliament Buildings
Victoria V8V 1X4
(604) 387-6841

Manitoba
Motor Vehicle Bureau
1075 Portage Avenue
Winnipeg R3C 0S1
(204) 775-0281

New Brunswick
Motor Vehicle Bureau
Centennial Building
P.O. Box 6000
Fredericton E3B 5H1
(506) 453-2810

Newfoundland
Motor Registration Division
Viking Building, Crosbie Road
St. John's A1C 5T4
(709) 737-2517

Northwest Territory
Registry of Vehicles
Yellowknife X0E 1H0
(403) 873-2951

Nova Scotia
Motor Registration Division
6061 Young Street, Metro Centre
Halifax B3J 2Z3
(902) 424-5851

Ontario
Registry of Motor Vehicles
Department of Transportation and
    Communications
Ferguson Block, Queen's Park
Toronto M7A 2A2
(416) 965-2206

Prince Edward Island
Motor Vehicle Division
P.O. Box 2000
Charlottetown C1A 7N8
(902) 892-5306

Quebec
Motor Vehicle Bureau
880 Saint Foy Road
Quebec City G1S 2K8
(418) 643-5650

Saskatchewan
Motor Vehicle Administration
2260 11th Avenue
Regina S4P 3V7
(306) 565-2345

Yukon
Motor Vehicle Bureau
Whitehorse Y1A 2C6
(403) 667-5315

STATE COORDINATORS OF POISON CONTROL CENTERS
U.S. Department of Health and Human Services
Division of Poison Control
5600 Fishers Lane
Rockville, Maryland 20857
(301) 443-6260

Alabama
Montgomery 36117
(205) 832-3194

Alaska
Juneau 99811
(907) 465-3100

Arizona
Tucson 85734
(602) 626-6016

Arkansas
Little Rock 72201
(501) 661-2397

California
Sacramento 95814
(916) 322-2300

Colorado
Denver 80220
(303) 320-8476

Connecticut
Farmington 06032
(203) 674-3456

Delaware
Wilmington 19899
(302) 655-3389

District of Columbia
Washington, D.C. 20009
(202) 673-6694

Florida
Tallahassee 32301
(904) 487-1566

Georgia
Atlanta 30308
(404) 894-5068

Hawaii
Honolulu 96801
(808) 531-7776

Idaho
Boise 83701
(208) 334-2241

Illinois
Springfield 62761
(217) 785-2080

Indiana
Indianapolis 46206
(317) 633-0332

Iowa
Des Moines 50319
(515) 281-4964

Kansas
Topeka 66620
(913) 862-9360

Kentucky
Frankfort 40601
(502) 564-4935

Louisiana
Baton Rouge 70801
(504) 342-2600

Maine
Portland 04102
1-800/442-6305

Maryland
Baltimore 21201
(301) 528-7604

Massachusetts
Boston 02111
(617) 727-2670

Michigan
Lansing 48909
(517) 373-1406

Minnesota
Minneapolis 55404
(612) 296-5281

Mississippi
Jackson 39205
(601) 354-6650

Missouri
Jefferson City 65102
(314) 751-2713

Montana
Helena 59601
1-800/525-5042

Nebraska
Lincoln 68502
(402) 471-2122

Nevada
Carson City 89710
(702) 885-4750

New Hampshire
Hanover 03755
(603) 643-4000

New Jersey
Trenton 08625
(609) 292-5666

New Mexico
Albuquerque 87131
(505) 843-2551

New York
Albany 12210
(518) 474-3785

North Carolina
Durham 27710
(919) 684-8111

North Dakota
Bismarck 58505
(701) 224-2388

Ohio
Columbus 43216
(614) 466-2544

Oklahoma
Oklahoma City 26307
(405) 271-5454

Oregon
Portland 97201
(503) 225-8968

Pennsylvania
Harrisburg 17120
(717) 787-2307

Rhode Island
Providence 02908
(401) 277-2401

South Carolina
Columbia 29201
(803) 758-5625

South Dakota
Pierre 57501
(605) 773-3361

Tennessee
Nashville 37219
(615) 741-2407

Texas
Austin 78756
(515) 458-7254

Utah
Salt Lake City 84113
(801) 533-6161

Vermont
Burlington 05401
(802) 862-5701

Virginia
Richmond 23219
(804) 786-5188

Washington
Seattle 98115
(206) 522-7478

West Virginia
Charleston 25305
(304) 348-2971

Wisconsin
Madison 53701
(608) 267-7174

Wyoming
Cheyenne 82001
(307) 777-7955

Organizations and Associations

CANINE

North American Police Work Dog Association

410 West Locust
Springfield, Missouri 65803
(202) 889-7768   Richard Warner, President
Founded 1977. Members: 300. Active or retired law enforcement officers and military police who are or were canine handlers, trainers or administrators; associate members are involved with or interested in canine training or law enforcement.Seeks to unite all law enforcement agencies in the training and improvement of police work dogs. Has established a working standard for all police work dogs, handlers and trainers; maintains accreditation program. Sponsors working seminars which allow handlers and their dogs to participate in specific training exercises. Conducts research on the legal ramifications of using police work dogs. Publishes educational materials; plans to publish newsletter and manual. Convention/Meeting: Annually.

United States Police Canine Association

2041 M.L. King Avenue, Suite 201
Washington, DC 20020
(202) 889-7768   R. O. Rogers, President
Founded 1971. Members: 1,400. Full-time paid law enforcement officers, either military, federal, state, county or municipal, who are canine handlers, trainers or administrators (1,700), honorary members (300). Purposes are to unite in a common cause all law enforcement agencies utilizing the services of the canine; to promote friendship and brotherhood among all those interested in the training and utilization of the canine in police work; to coordinate and exchange advanced techniques of training of the police dog; to improve the image of the working police dog to the populace in general through improved public service and the prevention and detection of crime. Conducts semiannual national seminars and several regional mini-seminars. Conducts police dog field trials in obedience, agility, scent and attack work; awards trophies. Provides specialized education. Publications: *Canine Couriers,* bimonthly. Formed by merger of Police K-9 Association and U.S.K.-9 Association. Convention/Meeting: Annual seminar and field trials.

CORRECTIONAL

Alliance of NGOS on Crime Prevention and Criminal Justice

15 Washington Place
New York, New York 10003   Judith F. Weintraub,
(212) 982-5842   Executive Secretary
Founded 1972. Members: 16. International nongovernmental organizations having consultative status with the UN focusing on crime prevention, criminal justice administration or treatment of the offender. Observers are those not having consultative status or not having a major portion of their organizational activity in those areas. Provides for regularized communication with the UN Crime Prevention Branch. Facilitates and provides a structure for NGOs working together on issues of common concern. A major area of activity has been the transfer of imprisoned aliens to their home countries for serving of their sentences. Is presently working for the adoption of a resolution by the UN favoring alternatives to imprisonment. Conducts research on the prevalence of transfer of prisoner treaties internationally. Convention/Meeting: 5-10/y; also holds meeting in conjunction with UN Crime Congress.

Alston Wilkes Society

2215 Devine Street
Columbia, South Carolina 29205   Parker Evatt,
(803) 799-2490   Executive Director
Founded 1962. Members: 6,000. Operates to assist inmates still in prison and those being released or paroled and to aid inmates' families. This society: trains volunteers to visit inmates in prisons, especially those who never have visitors or mail; works with community prerelease centers; operates two residences for released male prisoners and a group home for male status offenders; cooperates in a community residence for women; provides volunteer emergency home placements and other volunteer programs for juveniles; maintains speakers bureau and a film library. Seeks to stimulate public support for progressive prison programs at the state level and for programs of crime prevention. Local chapters assist the society in working with inmates in their localities. Named for the late Rev. Eli Alston Wilkes Jr., a methodist minister who founded the private correctional services agency. Presents awards; children's services; research programs; compiles statistics. Publications: newsletter, quarterly; Annual Report. Formerly South Carolina Therapeutic Association. Convention/Meeting: Annually.

American Association of Correctional Officers

2309 State Street, North Office
Saginaw, Michigan 48602
(517) 799-8208   Dennis Ray Martin, President
Founded 1977. Members: 5,400. Correctional facility officers on the national, state and local levels; sheriffs; other employees in the corrections field or related fields interested in the study and practice of good corrections principles. Promotes the development of innovative services, evaluation and interprofessional cooperation in order to increase the effectiveness of correctional facilities. Seeks to advance high standards of training and the professionalization of corrections personnel, thereby securing public confidence and support. Conducts regional seminars; compiles statistics. Bestows Number One Corrections Officer of the Year Award. Maintains library of over 1,300 books and journals dealing with corrections facilities and personnel, and recent court rulings and legislation affecting the corrections field. Publications: *Keepers Voice Magazine,* bimonthly; *The Corrections Officer* (newsletter), bimonthly; *Through the Key Ring,* bimonthly; also publishes pamphlets and membership brochure. Affiliated with: American Corrections Association. Formerly American Association of Correctional Facility Officers.

American Association of Correctional Psychologists

c/o Robert J. Powitzky
Federal Bureau of Prisons
320 First Street, NW
Washington, DC 20534   Robert J. Powitzky, Ph.D.,
(202) 724-3042   Secretary-Treasurer
Founded 1953. Members: 400. Psychologists engaged in correctional rehabilitative work in prisons, reformatories, juvenile institutions and probation and parole agencies and other aspects of the criminal justice system. Publications: *Journal of Criminal Justice and Behavior,* quarterly; newsletter, quarterly. Convention/Meeting: Annually—in conjunction with American Correctional Association.

American Correctional Association (ACA)

4321 Hartwick Road
College Park, Maryland 20740   Anthony P. Travisono,
(301) 699-7600   Executive Director
Founded 1870. Members: 10,000. Correctional administrators, wardens, superintendents, members of prison and parole boards, probation officers, psychologists, sociologists and other individuals, institutions and associations involved in correctional fields. To improve correctional standards, including selection of personnel; care, super-

vision, education, training, employment, treatment and post-release adjustment of inmates; development of adequate physical facilities. To study causes of crime and juvenile delinquency and methods of crime control and prevention. Compiles statistics; bestows awards. Maintains placement service; conducts research programs. Publications: *Corrections Today,* bimonthly; newsletter, bimonthly; *Directory,* annually; *Proceedings,* annually; also publishes a number of books relating to correctional programs, facilities and standards and counseling guidelines in this area. Formerly National Prison Association; American Prison Association. Convention/Meeting: Annual Congress of Correction.

American Prison Ministry

P.O. Box 5185
Shreveport, Louisiana 71105   Dr. Donald Ned Hicks,
(318) 476-3667   President
Founded 1975. Attempts to educate and inform the public about the penal system and its ramifications. Provides spiritual, mental and physical counseling for convicts and their families. Encourages close personal contact with the prisoners through visits and letters. Has developed a close working relationship with wardens, security staff and judicial personnel to acquaint them with the problems and possible correction of those problems related to prisons. Monitors proposed penal legislation. Sponsors seminars which bring together the general public and leading penologists. Publications: *In-Depth Penal Studies,* bimonthly; *Across the Fence* (newspaper), quarterly; also publishes pamphlets. Convention/Meeting: Annually.

Americans for Human Rights and Social Justice

109 Bent Bridge Road
Greenville, South Carolina 29611   Philip T. Mabry,
(803) 269-1825   National Chairman
Founded 1977. Members: 1,129. Handicapped persons, ex-offenders, prison inmates, senior citizens, lawyers and others interested in human and civil rights. Purpose is to protect the elderly, disabled and socially disadvantaged from discrimination and to advocate for special needs. Seeks to educate public about prison reform. Compiles statistics. Maintains library of 400 volumes, 6,000 documents and brochures and an extensive news article file. Publications: *Action Newsletter,* monthly; *Directory of Information,* annually; also publishes abstract card file on criminal justice and pamphlets. Convention/Meeting: Annually.

Association of Paroling Authorities

Sam Houston University
Criminal Justice Center
Huntsville, Texas 77341
(713) 295-6211   Bill Reed, Secretary
Founded 1960. Members: 225. Chief administrators and members of paroling authorities in the United States, Canada, and U.S. territories. Seeks to develop and promote parole work and programs through conferences and cooperative programs and to secure effective legislation in this field. Gives financial support and leadership to the National Parole Institutes. Publications: newsletter, quarterly. Convention/Meeting: Semiannually.

Association of State Correctional Administrators

Stevens T. Mason Building
Lansing, Michigan 48913
(517) 373-0283   Perry Johnson, President
Members: 58. Administrators of state and federal penal systems. Promotes the exchange of ideas between heads of penal institutions; encourages the improvement of correctional standards; seeks support for advances in correctional operations; stimulates interest among the general public toward the rehabilitation of prisoners; advocates research into antisocial behavior; furnishes information to international agencies interested in correctional programs. Publications: *Correctional Memo,* quarterly. Affiliated with: American Correctional Association and Council of State Governments. Formerly Correctional Administrators Association of America. Convention/Meeting: Annually held with American Correctional Association. Also holds periodic conferences.

Center for Community Justice

918 16th Street, NW, Suite 503
Washington, DC 20006
(202) 296-2565   Linda R. Singer, Executive Director
Founded 1971. Private, nonprofit corporation which designs, develops and implements programs for nonjudicial dispute resolution in prisons, juvenile facilities, schools, mental hospitals and with migrant farm workers. Formerly Center for Correctional Justice. Convention/Meeting: Annual board of directors meeting.

Center for Studies in Criminal Justice

Law School, University of Chicago
1111 East 60th Street
Chicago, Illinois 60637
(312) 753-2438   Franklin Zimring, Director
Founded 1965. Federal and private grants to conduct research in current problems in the administration of justice; to train law students in social science research techniques; and to offer visiting fellowships to distinguished legal scholars. Research projects have included a survey of capital punishment; an analysis of the Illinois jail system; half-way houses for adults and juveniles; juror attitudes on capital punishment; relation between guns, knives and homicide in Chicago; and post-institutional adjustment of 18 men who had been illegally imprisoned for more than 25 years. Has provided legal aid in civil matters to inmates of Cook County Jail and conducted probation officer-case aid project supported by the National Institute of Mental Health. Plans to continue its study of the effectiveness of crime prevention and studies of police problems and other areas of research. Publications: Annual Report; also publishes numerous articles and books.

Connecticut Justice Academy

P.O. Box 384
Haddam, Connecticut 06438
(203) 566-2564   Thomas W. White, Director
Founded 1972. The academy is a joint training facility for three agencies of the state of Connecticut—the Department of Adult Probation, Correction and Children and Youth Services. Since it opened in 1972, the academy has provided programs and support services for the training and education of probation officers, correction officers, youth service workers and family relations staff, judges, public defenders, prosecutors and court clerks. Training programs encompass the job needs of all levels in an organization, from management to line staff. Like its police counterpart, the State and Municipal Police Training Academy in Meriden, the Connecticut Justice Academy was designed to develop and continue the education of competent professionals in the justice area. Located in a refurbished building which formerly served as the Middlesex County Jail, the Justice Academy is an educational facility which offers its member agencies the space and support services needed for staff training.

Correctional Education Association (CEA)

5415 North University
Peoria, Illinois 61614
(309) 691-2200   Tom Baxter, President
Founded 1945. Members: 2,200. Persons connected with or interested in educating people committed by courts to correctional institutions. To promote the cause of education in adult and juvenile correctional institutions; to develop adequate support for correctional education. Publications: *Journal of Correctional Education,* quarterly; also publishes a newsletter. Affiliated with American Correctional Association. Convention/Meeting: Annually.

Correctional Service Federation-U.S.A.

311 South Juniper Street
Philadelphia, Pennsylvania 19107
(215) 732-5990 Rendell A. Davis, President
Founded 1962. Members: 550. Voluntary agencies and bureaus or departments of agencies (20), devoted to rehabilitation of offenders; individuals (530) are nonvoting members. Establishes standards for agencies; produces public information material on crime prevention and rehabilitation of offenders. U.S. National representative of International Prisoners Aid Association. Serves as a clearinghouse for public information about volunteer correctional service agencies. Publications: newsletter, quarterly; also publishes directory. Affiliated with American Correctional Association. Convention/Meeting: Annually—held with American Correctional Association.

Court Employment Project

346 Broadway
New York, New York 10013
(212) 732-0076 Rae Linefsky, Project Director
Founded 1967. To provide counseling and vocational services for court-related clients involved with the New York City criminal courts. Offers such services as individual and group counseling; vocational counseling; career development and job training or academic placement; referral to community social service agencies; and in-house education program. Formerly Manhattan Court Employment Project.

Federal Probation Officers Association

212 U.S. Courthouse
400 South Phillips
Sioux Falls, South Dakota 57102
(605) 336-2980 Charles B. Mandsager, President
Founded 1955. U.S. probation officers, probation officer assistants, and pretrial services officers. Purposes are: to maintain high professional standards; to advocate appropriate economic status for members; to unify members in matters of mutual professional concern; to promote a program of public relations in order to build and maintain an enlightened public interest in the proper administration of probation, parole and other correctional services. Bestows the Richard F. Doyle Award. Publications: newsletter, quarterly; *Bulletin*, semiannually. Affiliated with American Correctional Association. Convention/Meeting: Semiannually.

Fortune Society

229 Park Avenue South
New York, New York 10003
(212) 677-4600 David Rothenberg, Executive Director
Founded 1967. Ex-convicts and other persons interested in penal reform. To create a greater public awareness of the prison system and to understand the problems confronting inmates before, after and during incarceration. Works on a personal level, one-to-one basis, with men and women out of prison; helps to find jobs for ex-convicts. Sends teams of speakers (ex-convicts) to talk to school, church and civic groups and on radio and television to relate first-hand experiences of prison life and to create a greater understanding of the causes of crime in the U. S. Publications: newsletter, monthly.

Friends of the Superior Court

Superior Court, Building B
409 East Street, NW, Room 301
Washington, DC 20001
(202) 727-1788 Frank McGuire, Administrator
Founded 1964. Approximately 180 volunteers from the Washington, DC area. Helps prevent juvenile delinquency and to rehabilitate juvenile and adult offenders in the District of Columbia by providing volunteer services. Volunteers serve as probation aides and tutors and run a summer recreation program. Sponsors volunteer attorney program in which volunteer attorneys represent children in neglect and abuse cases. Publications: newsletter, quarterly. Formerly Friends of the Juvenile Court.

International Conference of Administrators of Residential Centers for Youth

P.O. Box 18
South Kortright, New York 13842 Frederick R. Allen,
(607) 538-3211 SecretaryTreasurer
Founded 1923. Members: 125. Superintendents of training schools and reformatories for delinquent children and youth. Publications: newsletters. Formerly National Conference of Superintendents of Training Schools and Reformatories. Convention/Meeting: Annually.

International Halfway House Association

2525 Victory Parkway, Suite 101
Cincinnati, Ohio 45206
(513) 221-3250 Tom H. Christensen, President
Founded 1965. Members: 750. Agencies and individuals working in residential treatment programs for the socially stigmatized. Programs are in the areas of corrections, alcohol, mental health group homes and drug addiction. Purposes are: to assist members to function more effectively through the exchange of information regarding management and treatment, with the goal of helping the socially handicapped achieve a satisfactory return to the community; to develop and implement a program of public information and education in the field of corrections and other fields of residential treatment programs; to assist social institutions within communities to accept, along with socially handicapped individuals, responsibility for coping with crime, delinquency and related social problems. Operates regional national workshops and institutes. Conducts research programs; compiles statistics. Committees: Affiliation Accreditations and Standards; Agency Assistance; Human Concerns; Publications; Research; Treatment. Publications: newsletter, quarterly; *Directory of Residential Treatment Centers*, annually; also publishes handbooks. Affiliated with American Correctional Association, International Prisoners Aid Association. Convention/Meeting: Annually.

International Juvenile Officers' Association

16220 Wausau Avenue
South Holland, Illinois 60473 Capt. Robert Zeilenga,
(312) 331-4562 Executive Director
Founded 1951. Members: 1,200. Police officers assigned to juvenile divisions. Associate members are accepted from related fields. Purpose is to assist law enforcement agencies to understand working with young people. Cooperates with state associations and universities in establishing training programs and supplying speakers and instructors. Presents Lynn O. Swanson Award, Brice L. Woody Award and Joseph G. Phelan Youth Award. Publications: *Reporter*, bimonthly; *Conference Journal*, annually. Convention/Meeting: Annual training conference.

International Prisoners Aid Association

Department of Sociology
University of Louisville
Louisville, Kentucky 40292
(502) 588-6836 Dr. Badr-El-Din Ali, Executive Director
Members: 68. Agencies (43) and individuals (25) concerned with prisoners aid programs. To improve and broaden prisoners aid services, which include welfare work in the interest of offenders and their reform, crime prevention, social action and legislation and public information concerning sound methods of crime control. Publications: newsletter, 3/y; also publishes *International Directory of Prisoners Aid Agencies*. Formerly National Prisoners Aid Association. Convention/Meeting: Annually.

International Probation Organization

813 Burden Street
Fredericton, New Brunswick,
Canada E3B 4C5
(506) 453-2367 Frank Forestell, General Secretary
Founded 1968. Members: 400. Probation personnel. Purpose is to

foster the concept of the use of probation as an alternative to prison. Organizes probation conference seminars; bestows awards. Publications: *Interpro* (newsletter), quarterly. Convention/Meeting: Annually.

John Howard Association

67 East Madison, Suite 1216
Chicago, Illinois 60603   Michael J. Mahoney,
(312) 263-1901   Executive Director
Founded 1901. Nonprofit, nonsectarian agency supported by private and community funds devoted to prison reform and to the prevention and control of crime and delinquency. Named after John Howard (1726-1790), an 18th-century English prison reformer. Provides professional consultation and survey services in the crime and delinquency field; encourages and develops volunteer programs; monitors criminal justice programs and services. Staffed by professionals in the correctional field reinforced by active citizen leaders. Conducts research projects and publishes findings; conducts public information program to promote community understanding. Publishes newsletter. Convention/Meeting: Annually.

Mothers in Prison Projects

407 South Dearborn Street, Room 875
Chicago, Illinois 60605
(312) 922-2443   Bonita Raterre, Executive Director
Founded 1974. Lawyers, ex-offenders, social workers, interested individuals. Purposes are: to allay the emotional distress of incarcerated mothers and to reduce the possible harmful effects of this separation on their children; to increase the mothers' involvement in making and maintaining satisfactory arrangements for their children's care. Maintains placement service; compiles statistics. Affiliated with Women in Jails and Prison (parent).

National Association of Criminal Justice Planners

1012 14th Street, NW, Suite 403
Washington, DC 20005
(202) 347-2291   Mark A. Cunniff, Executive Director
Founded 1971. Members: 450. Persons involved in criminal justice planning on the state and local levels as well as in police and corrections agencies and the courts. Seeks to improve the technical skills of planners and to institutionalize criminal justice planning. Promotes communication in the areas of criminal justice planning and program development. Conducts research; sponsors workshops. Publications: *News,* 6/y; *News Update,* 6/y; annual directory. Formerly National Association of Urban Criminal Justice Planning Directors. Convention/Meeting: Annually.

National Association of Training Schools and Juvenile Agencies

36 Locksley Lane
Springfield, Illinois 62704   Donald G. Blackburn,
(217) 787-0690   Executive Secretary-Treasurer
Founded 1953. Members: 250. Institutions and agencies for the treatment of children adjudged delinquent; executive and staff personnel of residential centers for delinquent children. Disseminates ideas on the function, philosophy and goals of the juvenile correctional field with emphasis on institutional rehabilitative programs. Promotes evaluative research; fosters progressive legislation; cooperates with other agencies and organizations having kindred interests. Encourages recruitment and retention of qualified personnel and is concerned with training, working conditions, renumeration and other related matters. Bestows awards. Cosponsors National Institute on Crime and Delinquency and the Congress of Corrections. Publications: *Proceedings,* annually. Formed by merger of National Association of Training Schools and National Conference of Juvenile Agencies. Convention/Meeting: Annually.

National Clearinghouse for Justice Planning and Architecture

505 East Green Street, Suite 200
Champaigne, Illinois 61820
(217) 333-0312   James Taylor, Director
Founded 1970. A part of the Department of Architecture at the University of Illinois, the clearinghouse provides planning assistance to state and local jurisdictions in the development of correctional facilities and programs and to determine if corrections construction projects meet the advanced practices criteria of Part E of the Omnibus Safe Streets and Crime Control Act of 1968. Sponsors annual symposium on criminal justice planning. Conducts training seminars on correctional facility planning and research pertaining to design standards. Compiles statistics on prison and jail populations. Maintains 10,000 volume library on all aspects of criminal justice. Publications: *Clearinghouse Transfer,* irregularly; also publishes special issues on design and planning.

National Criminal Justice Councils

444 North Capitol Street, NW, Suite 305
Washington, DC 20001
(202) 347-4900   R. Thomas Parker, Executive Director
Founded 1974. Members: 57. State and territorial directors of state planning agencies. Allows directors to develop unified state views on substantive issues related to direction, management and implementation of the Crime Control program in accordance with the Crime Control Act of 1977. Informs governors, congress, state planning agency supervisory boards and other groups of demonstrated needs and accomplishments within the states related to crime and justice. Is concerned with improving state administration of the Crime Control program by exchanging information and personnel among the states and also by ensuring the availability of quality training and technical assistance. Attempts to determine and effectively express collective views of the administrators on pending and recently enabled legislation and activity which encompasses the entire scope of criminal justice. Publications: *Bellringer,* quarterly; bulletin, irregularly. Convention/meeting: Annually.

National Correctional Recreational Association

c/o Robert Young
M.T.C.M.
Moberly, Missouri 65270
(816) 263-3778   Robert Young, Secretary-Treasurer
Founded 1966. Members: 170. Correctional recreation personnel, professional physical education educators and students of correctional education or recreation. Works to elevate professionalism in the field and toward the recognition of correctional recreation as a separate area of correctional concern. Members seek to raise inmate morale by providing healthy activity which may help engender socially acceptable attitudes and conduct among the men and to arouse the interest of the inmates in recreation to an extent that they will continue this type of activity following their releases from prison. Sponsors prison postal weightlifting contest for inmates in the U.S. and Canada (contest sanctioned by the Amateur Athletic Union of the U.S.); horseshoe meets and track meets. Conducts national surveys on qualifications and duties. Publications: *Grapevine,* quarterly. Affiliated with American Correctional Association. Formerly National Corrections Recreation Association. Convention: Annually.

National Jail Association

c/o D.C. Department Of Corrections
614 H Street, NW, Suite 1114
Washington, DC 20001
(202) 727-4000   Charles M. Rodgers, Executive Director
Founded 1939. Members: 450. Sheriffs, police chiefs and other law enforcement officers; prison wardens, jail wardens, jail employees; architects, engineers, judges, newspapermen, educators and others interested in raising standards of correctional institutions. Conducts

specialized education; maintains speakers bureau on jails and detention. Holds quarterly regional jail forums sponsored by sheriffs departments and other local or state agencies. Presents annual awards for outstanding jailer and jail matron. Publications: *National Jail Association Newsletter*, quarterly; Convention/Meeting: Annually—held with Congress of Correction.

National Jail Managers Association

c/o Paul E. Bailey
200 East Carson Avenue
Las Vegas, Nevada 89101   Paul E. Bailey, Secretary-Treasurer
Founded 1973. Members: 400. Sheriffs, chiefs of police and persons wholly or partially engaged in jail work, and public employees involved with inspection and training of jail staff; honorary members and others who attend the national conference. Purposes are to encourage exchange of information on jail management techniques and general jail information, to assure professionalization of jail personnel and to encourage research. Conducts jail management training seminars. Bestows awards. Publications: newsletter, monthly. Convention/Meeting: Annually.

National Juvenile Detention Association

The Old Stone Church
91 Public Square
Cleveland, Ohio 44113
(216) 241-7503   Martin C. Kelly, Executive Director
Founded 1971. Members: 650. Juvenile detention home personnel. Coordinates lines of communication among juvenile detention facilities; conducts training institutes; provides education and consultation to detention facilities and units of government. Bestows annual Don Hammergren Meritorious Award to the individual making the most outstanding contribution to the field of juvenile dentention, and individual merit awards to the outstanding line staff person in each detention center. Publications: *Counterpoint*, bimonthly; also publishes *Directory of Juvenile Detention Homes*. Convention/Meeting: Seminannually.

National Moratorium on Prison Construction

324 C Street, SE
Washington, DC 20003
(202) 547-3633   Michael A. Kroll, Coordinator
Founded 1974. Members: 6,000. Funded by the Unitarian Universalist Service Committee. Engages in public education, lobbying and direct action to stop construction of new prisons and jails; encourages monitoring and collecting of data on prison construction and incarceration; coordinates efforts in the U.S. to reduce use of incarceration and to seek systematic alternatives to imprisonment. Maintains small collection of literature relevant to penology and alternatives to incarceration. Publications: *Jericho* (newsletter), quarterly.

National Prison Project

1346 Connecticut Avenue, NW, Suite 1031
Washington, DC 20036
(202) 331-0500   Alvin J. Bronstein, Executive Director
Founded 1972. Project of the American Civil Liberties Union established to provide litigation and education programs aimed at improving prison conditions and developing alternatives to incarceration. Engages in prisoners' rights litigation. Maintains library. Publishes self-help manual and directory, and reports on the penal system and prisoners' rights. Formed by merger of Penal Reform Institute and ACLU Prisoners' Rights Project.

National Yokefellow Prison Ministry

112 Old Trail North
Shamokin Dam, Pennsylvania 17876
(717) 743-7832   Newman R. Gaugler, President
Founded 1969. Members: 178. To help serve the religious needs of residents in correctional and penal institutions; bridge the gulf between persons confined and those in the outside community; demonstrate a continuing concern for offenders against society by promoting employment aid; promote, support and cooperate in the establishment and operation of local community-sponsored halfway house facilities; participate in programs designed to improve correctional methods; bear concern for the decisions made by those who are responsible for the policies and procedures of rehabilitative efforts. Program is administered regionally by directors and at the local level by volunteers, "committeed Christians (who) become involved in the lives of offenders against society both during incarceration and upon release from the penal institution." Publications: *Prison Ministry "Yoke News"*, quarterly; *National Yokefellow Prison Ministry Directory*, annually. Convention/Meeting: Semiannually.

North American Association of Wardens and Superintendents

Clemens Unit
Box 77, Route 1
Brazoria, Texas 77422
(713) 798-2188   Lester Beaird, Executive Officer
Founded 1870. Members: 200. Wardens, superintendents and heads of detention, penal, and correctional institutions (male and female). To focus national attention on the problems and programs of correctional institutions. To promote better management of institutions and the care, custody, and treatment of committed offenders. Conducts research into causes of antisocial behavior. Will survey or investigate any correctional system or facility upon the request of the governor or acting official. Publications: *The Grapevine*, bimonthly. Affiliated with American Correctional Association (parent). Formerly Wardens Association of America, (1980) American Association of Wardens and Superintendents. Convention/Meeting: Annually—held with American Correctional Association.

Offender Aid and Restoration

The Old Albemarle Jail
409 East High Street
Charlottesville, Virginia 22901
(804) 295-6196   Fahy G. Mullaney, Executive Director
Founded 1969. Volunteers who work one-to-one with jail inmates to teach them practical skills and provide counseling and emotional support while they are in jail and after their release. Volunteers are citizens from all walks of life, including teachers, businessmen and former prisoners who are carefully trained before they are matched with an inmate. OAR operates 23 programs in eight states and plans to expand. Since its founding, 9,000 citizen volunteers have been involved in helping 22,000 prisoners and ex-prisoners. Conducts National Citizens Involvement Project to train and educate selected sheriffs and civic leaders in the use of volunteers in the jail. Conducts pilot projects in alternatives to jail. Maintains library of 400 volumes; presents awards. Publications: *OAR News*, quarterly.

Ohio Penal Racing Association

c/o L.F. Campbell
Ohio State Reformatory
Box 788
Mansfield, Ohio 44901
(419) 526-2000   L.F. "Jerry" Campbell, Director
Founded 1965. Members: 50. A club within the Ohio State Reformatory whose members are inmates. Services, maintains and helps set up a late model stock car for racing. Three members of the club are allowed to go to races in the Mansfield area, with OPRA director, Jerry Campbell, acting as driver of the High Wall Special. The members of the club make up the pit crew and are completely unsupervised during the race. Sponsors Model Car Contests and a slot car track; maintains a library of periodicals on stock car racing. Convention/Meeting: Weekly.

Older Adult Offender Project

A special three-year project of the Alston Wilkes Society (see separate entry) to assist inmates 45 years or older, both in prison and upon the release. Although the project was completed in 1970, its work is bein carried on by the Alston Wilkes Society.

Osborne Association

105 East 22nd Street, Room 811
New York, New York 10010
(212) 673-6633   Joseph M. Callan, Executive Director
Founded 1932. Members: 500. Organization of professional personnel and interested laymen. Named in honor of Thomas Mott Osborne (1859-1926), American prison reformer and founder of Mutual Welfare League. Provides consultative and advisory services to criminal justice agencies; participates in work of local, national and international criminal justice organizations; implements demonstration programs to decrease population of correctional institutions and jails; and assists probationers, parolees and discharged prisoners by providing supportive services, including employment, and in some cases, lodging, meals, clothing and cash relief. Affiliated with Correctional Service Federation, U.S.A. and American Correctional Association. Convention/Meeting: Annually.

Parole and Probation Compact Administrators Association

Box 267
Jefferson City, Missouri 65101
(314) 751-2441   Victor Townsley, President
Founded 1945. Members: 100. State agency officials administer regulations necessary to the operation of the interstate agreement, which permits states to send parolees and probationers to other states for supervision. Works for uniform laws and interstate agreements to improve prisoners' prospects for rehabilitation. Formerly Association of Administrators of the Interstate Compact for the Supervision of Parolees and Probationers. Convention/Meeting: Annually.

Prisoner's Union

1315 18th Street
San Francisco, California 94107
(415) 648-2880   Roney Nunes, President
Founded 1971. Members: 25,000. Convicts and ex-convicts who have organized to collectively bargain with the prisons, support convict-initiated prison change and seek redress for convict grievances; end economic exploitation by gaining the right to a prevailing wage for all work done in prison; establish a uniform and equitable sentencing procedure; restore civil and human rights to convicts and ex-convicts. Publications: *Journal,* bimonthly.

Private Concerns

477 Madison Avenue
New York, New York 10022   Albert P. Sirota, President
Founded 1974. Seeks to find jobs for paroled New York State convicts with private companies that will make use of skills learned in prison. These skills include welding, woodworking, sewing machine operation, machine-shop work, sheet-metal trades, auto mechanics, pressing, spray painting and building maintenance. Goal is to place 25 parolees a month in jobs. Has sought to change traditional policy prohibiting individuals convicted of felonies from serving in the armed forces.

Quaker Center for Prisoner Support Activities

12024 Tulip Grove Drive
Bowie, Maryland 20715
(301) 262-0223   William H. Conway, Secretary
Founded 1976. Members: 48. Coalition of Quaker groups and others interested in developing and sustaining prisoner support groups in the U.S. and Canada. Gives individual and group support and action in all aspects of criminal justice and prison environment; maintains referral service for resources available to discuss prohibition of, and alternatives to, prisons; conducts nonviolent training workshops for prisons. Convention/Meeting: Annually.

Rehabilitation Research Foundation

Box 266
Canton, Missouri 63435   Dr. Earl-Clayton Grandstaff Sr.,
(314) 874-8791   Executive Officer
Founded 1958. Plans, funds and evaluates innovative programs in the areas of prison reform, offender resocialization and mental health. Acts as consultant to governments (national, state, local and foreign) and private agencies and societies. Holds seminars and retreats. Sponsors charitable program; operates hall of fame; bestows awards and grants; maintains library. Convention/Meeting: Annually.

Social Issues Research Associates

2490 Channing Way, No. 513
Berkeley, California 94704
(415) 548-4680   Margo N. Robison, Secretary-Treasurer
Founded 1970. Professional researchers and social observers with experience and training in the management of research projects and personnel, familiarity with social control agency operations and a wide-ranging consultative practice. To increase understanding of the criminal justice system including causes and prevention of crime, detection of persons accused of crimes, functions of the courts and the law and rehabilitation of offenders. Designs and executes research; reviews specialized literature; critiques research designs; develops data systems for analysis of agency records and documents; offers technical assistance concerning research aspects of ongoing projects; holds conferences and training workshops. Has provided services to federal, state and local agencies; national and regional associations; public interest law firms; and individual attorneys, authors and legislators. Maintains library of 3,000 published and unpublished reports on correctional and drug-abuse treatment programs, journal articles and books. Publishes monographs, abstracts and papers. Formerly Criminological Research Association.

Society of Dismas

4234 Munger Avenue
P.O. Box 10626
Dallas, Texas 75207
(214) 823-9743   Brother Ron Smith, Coordinator
Founded 1978. Members: 93. Persons dedicated to improving the lot of men and women who have served sentences under the criminal justice system and who need assistance in readjusting to society. (Dismas is the legendary name of the "good thief" in Christian theology who died on a cross at Christ's right hand.) Operates halfway houses for parolees and those discharged from penal institutions. Funds rehabilitation programs, finances alcohol and drug abuse programs and offers additional education. The organization is ecumenical and spiritually oriented and begins its program of prayer, spiritual exercises, devotions, personal counseling and work aids while persons are still in prison. The program is continued in the halfway houses and in society through encouragement and supportive action. Offers job placement within the community but also plans to own and operate small enterprises such as a used-clothing store and leased service station which can offer temporary employment until more suitable jobs can be found.

Seventh Step Foundation

2644 Colerain Avenue
Cincinnati, Ohio 45214
(513) 681-5880   Ray White, Director
Founded 1973. Ex-offenders and nonoffenders united to help motivate inmates and former inmates of penal or correctional institutions. Operates through local groups, which work in harmony with professional and social agencies on a five-part program: prerelease, to offer counseling and group meetings to people inside prison; post-

release, to hold meetings for released prisoners; employment, to help ex-convicts find jobs; juvenile, to work with the potential felon who is under 20 years old; public information, to inform the public about crime and what is needed to prevent it and to reduce the tendency to relapse into criminal behavior.

Stop the Olympic Prison

324 C Street, SE
Washington, DC 20003
(202) 547-3633   Michael A. Kroll, Coordinator
An ad hoc coalition supported by the Unitarian Universalist Service Committee National Moratorium on Prison Construction and more than 50 other religious organizations, churches, prison groups, sports groups, service organizations, individual athletes and private citizens who are concerned with federal government plans to convert the Olympic Village in Lake Placid, New York, into a prison for youthful offenders. Desires a more constructive use of the complex. Suggested uses include: a training center for amateur sports; a low-cost public housing center; a youth hostel.

VIP Division

200 Washington Square Plaza
Royal Oak, Michigan 48067   Judge Keith J. Leenhouts,
(313) 398-8550   Executive Director
Founded 1969. A division of the National Council on Crime and Delinquency (see separate entry). Purpose is to stimulate the development of effective citizen participation in court rehabilitative programs. VIP stands for volunteers in probation, prevention, prosecution, prisons and parole. Sponsors National Education Training Program for professionals and nonprofessionals. Publications: *VIP Examiner* (newspaper), quarterly; also publishes books. Formerly Volunteers in Probation. Convention/Meeting: Annually.

Volunteer Prison League

Volunteers of America
340 West 85th Street
New York, New York 10024   Gen. F. McMahon,
(212) 873-2600   Commander-In-Chief
Founded 1896. Members: 23,780. Offers counseling to aid prisoners overcome personal and family problems; gives material assistance to inmates' families; provides job placement service for discharged prisoners and parolees; establishes and maintains pre- and post-release centers and halfway houses to help reestablish discharged prisoners and parolees in constructive employment. Affiliated with Volunteers of America (sponsor). Convention/Meeting: Annually.

Women's Prison Association

110 Second Avenue
New York, New York 10003
(212) 674-1163   Susan K. Ginsberg, President
Founded 1844. Not a membership organization. A service agency helping women who have been in conflict with the law. Sponsors Hopper Home, a halfway house in New York City. Offers individual and group counseling, work placement and job development and referrals to other resources. Administers The Learning Center, a program for academic and vocational training for former women prisoners. Sponsors specialized parental education and court diversion programs. Publications: *A Study in Neglect: A Report on Women Prisoners.*

World Correctional Service Center

2849 West 71st Street
Chicago, Illinois 60629
(312) 925-6591   Harry H. Woodward Jr., President
Founded 1969. Members: 1,000. Individuals having an interest in criminal justice. Acts as information clearinghouse. Sponsors workshops, seminars and conferences on issues. Distributes literature.

CRIME AND CRIMINAL JUSTICE

Academy of Criminal Justice Sciences

John Jay College of Criminal Justice
444 West 56th Street
New York, New York 10019
(212) 247-1600   Dr. Harry W. More Jr., President
Founded 1963. Individuals, including teachers, administrators, researchers, students and practitioners, involved in the professional advancement of the criminal justice system through education. Purposes are to foster excellence in education and research in the field of criminal justice in institutions of higher education; to encourage understanding and cooperation among those engaged in teaching and research in criminal justice agencies and related fields; to provide a forum for the exchange of information among persons involved with education and research in the criminal justice field; to serve as a clearinghouse for the collection and dissemination of information related to, or produced by, criminal justice education and/or research programs; to foster the highest ethical and personal standards in criminal justice educational programs as well as in operational agencies and allied fields. Presents numerous awards to individuals for outstanding contributions. Publications: *Journal of Criminal Justice,* quarterly; *Directory,* annually. Formerly International Association of Police Professors. Convention/Meeting: Annually.

American Association of Criminology

P.O. Box 1115
North Marshfield, Massachusetts 02059
(617) 837-0052   Wayne A. Forester, Secretary
Founded 1953. Members: 2,000. Representatives from the entire field of criminology, including criminologists, police officers, lawyers, parole and prison personnel, psychologists, educators, superintendents of identification bureaus, principals of detective agencies, polygraph examiners, security officers, questioned document examiners, etc. Offers extensive consulting services to members, including arson investigation, firearms investigation, medico-legal pharmacology, forensic psychiatry, ciphers and codes, fraud detection and prevention, polygraph and lie detection equipment and others. Presents awards. Through its educational services division, the American Institute of Criminology, AAC offers courses to members in various fields of criminology. Has sponsored institutes on socio-pathic disorganization, narcotics and drug abuse, suicide and the dynamics of police-riot confrontation. Sponsors professional police-criminological fraternity, Lambda Epsilon Chi. Publications: *The American Criminologist* monthly; also publishes a directory, *Leaders in Practical Criminology in America.* Member: International Society of Criminology. Convention/Meeting: Annually.

American Criminal Justice Association—
Lambda Alpha Epsilon

P.O. Box 61047
Sacramento, California 95860   Karan K. Campbell, Executive
(916) 484-6553   Secretary-Treasurer
Founded 1937. Members: 3,500. Persons employed in an area concerned with the administration of criminal justice; persons honorably retired from a career in criminal justice; persons enrolled in a program of study in this field at a college or university, and persons approved by the Executive Board of Grand Chapter, involved in volunteer work directly related to the administration of criminal justice. Dedicated to the furtherance of professional standards of criminal justice; the fostering of assistance and understanding of the problems and objectives of those agencies devoted to the administration of criminal justice. Conducts annual seminars, workshops and competitive activities. Presents Key Awards for recognition of outstanding scholastic attainment in criminal justice. Sponsors scholastic research paper competition; compiles statistics. Sponsors competitions. Publications: journal, quarterly; newsletter, quarterly.

American Society of Criminology

1314 Kinnear Road, Suite 212
Columbus, Ohio 43212
(614) 422-9207   Charles H. McCaghy, Treasurer
Founded 1941. Members: 2,500. Professional and academic criminologists, students of criminology, universities, psychiatrists, psychologists, sociologists. To develop criminology as a science and
academic discipline; to aid in the construction of criminological cur-
ricula in accredited universities; to upgrade the practitioner in criminological fields (police, prisons, probation, parole, delinquency workers). Presents Vollmer, Block, Sutherland and Sellin-Glueck Awards
annually. Conducts research programs; sponsors competitions. Provides placement service at annual convention. Publications: *The
Criminologist Newsletter,* 6/y; *Criminology: An Interdisciplinary Journal,* quarterly; *Member Directory,* annually; also publishes proceedings of annual meeting and Sage publications. Affiliated with American Association for the Advancement of Science. Convention/
Meeting: Annually.

CB Radio Patrol

American Law Enforcement Officers Association
1100 125th Street, NE
North Miami, Florida 33161
(305) 891-1700   Robert Ferguson, President
Founded 1976. Members: 30,000. Fraternal association of CB radio
operators united to promote safety and discourage crime by means
of a volunteer community radio patrol. Bestows awards. Publications:
Police Times, monthly. Formerly: (1978) CB Radio Posse. Conven-
tion/Meeting: Biennially.

Canadian Association for the Prevention of Crime

55 Parkdale
Ottawa, Ontario, Canada K1Y 1E5
(613) 728-1865   W.T. McGrath, Executive Director
Founded 1919. Members: 1,600. A national citizens' organization to
promote cooperation and participation among individuals, groups and
disciplines concerning the problems of crime and its consequences as
related to people of all ages, without limitation. Concerned with
prevention, sources of crime, diversion, concepts of crime, law enforcement, pretrial practice, trial and adjudication, correctional services,
dispositional alternatives and community reintegration. Publications:
Bulletin, 5/y; *Annual Report; Canadian Journal of Criminology,* quarterly. Formerly Canadian Congress on the Prevention of Crime. Con-
vention/Meeting: Biennially.

Center for Studies in Criminology and Criminal Law

3718 Locust Street
Philadelphia, Pennsylvania 19104
(215) 243-7411   Marvin E. Wolfgang, Director
Founded 1960. Housed at the University of Pennsylvania. The center
operates with foundation and federal, as well as university support.
Research is conducted in the areas of crime, delinquency, police,
judicial systems, prisons, social control and social deviance. Also
trains graduate students toward the M.A. and Ph.D. degrees. Operates statistical services; awards grants.

Citizens Committee for Victim Assistance

53 West Jackson Street
Chicago, Illinois 60604
(312) 786-0500   Ms. Marty Goddard, Executive Director
Founded 1974. Organization concerned with victim treatment and
public education in the areas of sexual assault and child abuse. Goals
are to encourage interagency coordination for improved services to
victims of crime; to assist in the training of personnel of public and
private agencies which deal with victims of crime; to inform the public
of the services available to assist victims of crime. Sponsors seminars,
training and training materials for public and private agency professionals on sexual assault and child abuse. Compiles statistics.

Publishes educational booklet, *What You Need to Know About Rape;*
has also developed an evidence collection kit for sexual assault
examination which is currently being used in hospitals.

International Center for Comparative Criminology

Universite De Montreal C.P. 6128
Montreal, PQ, Canada H3C 3J7
(514) 343-7065   Denis Szabo, Director
Founded 1969. Established by agreement between the International
Society for Criminology (which acts as consultant to the UN and
UNESCO) and the University of Montreal. Main objectives of the
Center are the initiation of comparative research studies and the
training of professional personnel and research workers in the field of
criminal justice; the dissemination of cross-cultural experience and
resources; and the exchange of information in research and penal
reform in different countries and the Third World. The Center is
currently undertaking studies in the adaptation of traditional systems
of criminal justice to the demands of modern industrial societies;
exchanges and comparison of projects and ideas of multidisciplinary
character in the field of criminal justice; organization of refresher
courses for practitioners to enable them to evaluate the experiences
of many countries with a view to initiating reforms in their own
systems. Plans to arrange for professors and research workers from
different countries to come to the center for periods varying from a few
weeks to a year, while North American research workers will go from
the center to other countries.

London Club

P.O. Box 4527
Topeka, Kansas 66604   Dennis A. Baranski, Chairman
Founded 1975. Members: 1,000. Criminologists, members of the
press, investigative freelancers, educators and interested individuals.
Goals are to accumulate data; to apply theories and to draw conclusions concerning unsolved crimes (such as Jack the Ripper and
Whitechapel cases), controversial trial verdicts (such as Sam Sheppard and Lizzie Borden murder cases) and theories involving alleged
criminal conspiracies both past and present (such as Lincoln and
Kennedy assassinations). Seeks to become a mass private sector for
research into unsolved crime by bringing together experts on many
levels of criminal investigation; foster international communications
among members and serve as a forum for their investigative data.
Bestows annual Award of Merit for the best essay in criminal research
submitted for publication in the London Club Journal. Publishes
register and journal. Convention/Meeting: Annually.

National Association of Citizens Crime Commissions

1336 Hickory Avenue
Waukegan, Illinois 60085
(312) 623-4416   Phyllis B. Stevenson, Executive Director
Founded 1952. Members: 25. Crime commissions not affiliated with
local, state or federal governments. To facilitate exchange of mutually
helpful information between member commissions. To inform the
public on dangers of organized crime and effective methods of
controlling it; to arouse public interest in clean government; to encourage formation of citizens' crime commissions where needed.
Convention/Meeting: Annually.

National Association on Volunteers in Criminal Justice

Box 6365
University, Alabama 35486
(205) 348-6738   John Stoeckel, Executive Director
Founded 1976. Members: 300. Individuals interested in the criminal
justice volunteer movement. Purposes are to increase the quality and
quantity of voluntary action; to improve technical assistance, education, and training of volunteers; to become the recognized authority on
volunteers in criminal justice; to develop a relationship with other
national organizations with similar concerns and goals; to provide a
strong power base and advocacy agency; to enhance the image of
volunteer action. Sponsors seminars and workshops at annual forum.

Acts as information clearinghouse. Bestows awards. Formerly (1976) National Forum on Volunteers in Criminal Justice, (1980) Compassion. Convention/Meeting: Annual forum.

National Council on Crime and Delinquency

Continental Plaza
411 Hackensack Avenue
Hackensack, New Jersey 07601
(201) 488-0400   Milton G. Rector, President
Founded 1907. Members: 30,000. Social workers, correction experts and others interested in community programs, juvenile and family courts, detention services and the prevention, control and treatment of crime and delinquency. Sponsors professional training institutes. Maintains library of 6,000 volumes, information files of 25,000 items. Maintains four centers: Research Centers in, San Francisco, California, and Hackensack, New Jersey; Information Center and Training Center, Hackensack, New Jersey. Presents Awards. Cosponsors National Institute on Crime and Delinquency annually. Publications: *Criminal Justice Newsletter*, biweekly; *Crime and Delinquency*, quarterly; *Criminal Justice Abstracts*, quarterly; *Youth Forum and Concerned Corporate Citizen*, quarterly; *Journal of Research in Crime and Delinquency*, semiannually; also books, standard acts, pamphlets, forms and training materials. Convention/Meeting: Annually.

National Crime Prevention Association

985 National Press Building
Washington, DC 20045
(202) 347-2230   Wilbur Rykert, President
Founded 1976. Members: 400. Businesses, nonprofit organizations, law enforcement agencies, government officials, crime prevention educators and individuals interested in crime prevention. Serves as an information exchange, seeking to reduce opportunities for crime. Acts as a reference source for members' specific crime prevention problems. Endorses development of performance standards for security devices and services. Provides educational and advisory services; conducts seminars.

National Crime Prevention Institute

School of Police Administration
University of Louisville, Shelby Campus
Louisville, Kentucky 40292
(502) 588-6987   Norman Bryant, Acting Director
Founded 1971. To train police officers and criminal justice planners in crime prevention for the establishment of crime prevention bureaus within police departments and to provide information and technical assistance to these bureaus. Conducts seminars and schools in the areas of crime prevention theory and practice, crime prevention administration and security for private industry. Maintains library.

National Forum on Criminal Justice

c/o Center For Legal Studies
Sangamon State University
Springfield, Illinois 62708   Edward J. Schoenbaum,
(217) 782-9558   Executive Secretary
Founded 1952. Not a membership organization. Conducts annual national interdisciplinary forum in the field of criminal and juvenile justice to promote professional growth, encourage research, disseminate information on new knowledge and techniques. Forum includes workshops, delivery of papers and general sessions of interest to all disciplines operating in the various programs relating to the administration of justice. Sponsored by 16 national and two regional organizations. Formerly National Institute on Crime and Delinquency. Convention/Meeting: Annually.

Search Group Inc.

1620 35th Avenue, Suite 200
Sacramento, California 95822
(916) 392-2550   Steve E. Kolodney, Executive Director
Founded 1969. Members: 57. Gubernatorial appointees from each state and territory and four federal appointees. To develop and test prototype systems which may have multistate utility for the application of advanced technology to the administration of criminal justice; to assist the Law Enforcement Assistance Administration (LEAA) in developing appropriate plans for the interstate or national implementation of these prototypes; to create a recognized source of technological expertise related to the problems of the criminal justice system which can provide assistance in the application of technology to state or federal government; and to foster communication and liaison between LEAA and the governors of several states. Maintains 1200 library volumes on criminal justice related subjects. Publications: *Interface*, quarterly; *Report*, annually; also publishes newsletter, proceedings, technical reports and memorandums. Formerly Project Search. Convention/Meeting: Biennially.

Society for the Prevention of Crime

30 East 39th Street
New York, New York 10017
(212) 986-6910   Marjorie Singer, Secretary
Founded 1877. Members: 8. Awards Charles Parkhurst Scholarship to law schools for studies in crime prevention, currently granted to Columbia School of Law. Convention/Meeting: Annually.

FORENSIC

American Academy of Forensic Sciences

225 South Academy Boulevard
Colorado Springs, Colorado 80910   Margaret M. Hibbard,
(303) 596-6006   Executive Director
Founded 1948. Members: 2,100. Publications: *Journal of Forensic Sciences*, quarterly; newsletter, quarterly. Convention/Meeting: Annually.

American Society of Forensic Odontology

4605 Elm Avenue
Ashtabula, Ohio 44004
(216) 992-3146   Curtis Mertz, President
Founded 1969. Members: 150. Dentists and others interested in the study of teeth for identification purposes, particularly in relation to malpractice, child abuse and bite mark identification. Publications: *International Journal of Forensic Odontology*, 3/y.

Canadian Society of Forensic Science

171 Nepean Street, Suite 303
Ottawa, Ontario, Canada K2P 0B4   JoAnne Cottingham,
(613) 235-7112   Executive Secretary
Publications: *Canadian Society of Forensic Science Journal*, quarterly. Formerly: (1952) Canadian Forensic Society. Convention/Meeting: Annually.

INVESTIGATION AND IDENTIFICATION

Association of Federal Investigators

815 15th Street, NW, Suite 824
Washington, DC 20005
(202) 347-5500   Louis T. Williams, Director
Founded 1957. Members: 2,500. Professional society of federal investigators; persons currently or formerly engaged in investigations, enforcement, security and related activities for the federal government. Has established professional standards of work, education and conduct. Serves as a vehicle for exchange of ideas and broadening of professional contacts. Publications: *AFI Report*, quarterly; directory, biennially. Formerly Association of Former Civil Service Investigators. Convention/Meeting: Annual awards meeting; also holds biennial seminar.

Association of Former Intelligence Officers

6723 Whittier Avenue, Suite 303A
McLean, Virginia 22101
(703) 790-0320　　　　　　　　John F. Blake, President
Founded 1975. Members: 3,000. Individuals who have served honorably in any agency or department involved in U.S. Intelligence; individuals of good character who support the position that the U.S. needs an adequate intelligence capability. Purpose is to foster a full understanding of the role of intelligence in America. Provides research assistance to writers and scholars in the field; provides speakers for schools and professional and civic groups. Maintains library. Publications: *Periscope* (newsletter), bimonthly; directory of members, annually. Formerly Association of Retired Intelligence Officers. Convention/Meetings: Annually.

International Association for Identification

P.O. Box 139
Utica, New York 13503
(315) 732-2897　　　　Walter G. Hoetzer, Secretary-Treasurer
Founded 1915. Members: 2,400. Police officials, identification personnel and others engaged in identification, investigation and scientific crime detection work. To improve methods of fingerprinting and other scientific identification techniques used in criminal and civil investigations; to work for mandatory fingerprinting of all persons. Bestows annual award for outstanding contribution to science of identification. Maintains 200-volume library. Publications: *Identification News*, monthly; roster of members, annually. Convention/Meeting: Annually.

International Association of Arson Investigators, Inc.

25 Newton Street, Box 600
Marlboro, Massachusetts 01752　　　　　Robert E. May,
(617) 481-5977　　　　　　　　　　Executive Secretary
Founded 1949. Members: 5,500. Publications: *The Fire and Arson Investigator*, quarterly; *I.A.A.I. Directory*, annually. Convention/Meeting: Semiannually.

International Association of Credit Card Investigators

P.O. Box 813
Novato, California 94947
(415) 897-8800　　　　Eve Wydajewski, Executive Secretary
Founded 1968. Members: 1,500. Includes special agents, investigators and investigation supervisors whose primary duties are to investigate criminal violations of credit card laws and to prosecute offenders; law enforcement officers, prosecutors or related public officials engaged in the investigation, apprehension and prosecution of credit card offenders. Primary purposes are to aid in the establishment of effective credit card security programs, to suppress fraudulent use of credit cards and to detect and cause the apprehension of credit card thieves.

International Association of Voice Identification

714 South Harrison Road
East Lansing, Michigan 48823
(517) 332-2521　　　　　　　Malcolm E. Hall, President
Founded 1972. Members: 54. Purposes are to establish voice identification as a scientific means of identification; to promote its acceptance in all courts as a scientific means of identification and ensure its continued acceptance as such; to ensure that all persons of the world using voice identification are trained with qualified instructors and acceptable instructional material and equipment; to investigate all new methods and constantly attempt to improve the voice identification as it is established; to assure that each member is of the highest integrity. Provides specialized training in voice identification by aural-spectrographic means. Training includes schools, seminars and a minimum two-year apprenticeship followed by a written and practical examination. Conducts research. Publications: newsletter, monthly. Convention/Meeting: Annually.

National Military Intelligence Association

1606 Laurel Lane, Route 10
Annapolis, Minnesota 21401　　Col. Charles F. Thomann, Ret.
(301) 757-2345　　　　　　　　　　Executive Director
Founded 1974. Members: 2,000. Active duty and retired military and civilian intelligence professionals and interested U.S. citizens. Purposes are to enhance the military intelligence profession and to assure that through knowledge, dedication, the judicious practice of the craft, and the promotion of public understanding, the security of the U.S. will not be jeopardized by a lack of intelligence resources and military intelligence specialists. Informs members of relevant legislation and actions; acts as a medium for the exchange of ideas and knowledge between the intelligence branches of the armed services; interacts with other intelligence organizations on matters of importance to the profession; provides a focal point where members of the intelligence profession of all the services may meet professionally and socially; acts as unofficial spokesman of military intelligence to the public as appropriate. Sponsors a Merit Scholarship program for members' children who are entering college; bestows awards to outstanding intelligence units of the Army, Navy and Air Force.

Security and Intelligence Fund

499 South Capitol Street, SW
Suite 500
Washington, DC 20002　　　Brig.-Gen. Robert C. Richardson,
(202) 484-1676　　　　　　　　　　Secretary-Treasurer
Founded 1978. Members: 25,000. Contributors to SIF activities in support of the Federal Bureau of Investigation and the Central Intelligence Agency of the U.S. Works in coordination with, but has with no formal relationship to, the American Security Council Education Foundation; disseminates information; and gives congressional advice on policies, legislation and activities that affect the capabilities of the FBI and CIA. Maintains extensive files on FBI and CIA operations and news stories. Publications: *Estimate of the Situation*, quarterly.

Society of Former Special Agents of the Federal Bureau of Investigation

2754 Graybar Building
420 Lexington Avenue
New York, New York 10017　　　　　Frances M. Keogh,
(212) 687-6222　　　　　　　　　　Executive Secretary
Founded 1937. Members: 7,700. Persons who have served at least one year as a special agent of the FBI. Maintains National Executive Services Committee to help members obtain employment, a foundation to aid needy members and children of deceased members and a scholarship program. Publications: *Grapevine*, monthly; also publishes directory. Convention/Meeting: Annually.

Society of Professional Investigators

85-04 Queens Midtown Expressway
Elmhurst, New York 11373
(212) 335-3257　　　　　　William Rowland, Secretary
Founded 1955. Members: 300. Persons with at least five years investigative experience for an official federal, state or local government agency or for a quasi-official agency formed for law enforcement or related activities. To advance knowledge of the science and technology of professional investigation, law enforcement, and police science; to maintain high standards and ethics; to promote efficiency of the investigator in the services he performs. Seeks to preserve the memory of services rendered by the investigative profession in the crusade against crime, racketeering, and corruption in government. Grants annual award for outstanding law enforcement achievement. Maintains library of books and studies on law enforcement. Operates placement service for members and speakers bureau. Publications: *Bulletin*, annually; *Roster*, triennially. Convention/Meeting: Annual awards dinner; also holds monthly meetings in New York City, except during summer.

POLICE

Afro-American Police League

One South Cottage Gover
Chicago, Illinois 60619
(312) 873-0200   Renault Robinson, President
Founded 1968. Members: 2,000. Police officers of Afro-American descent. Serves as national headquarters for the National Black Police Association (see separate entry). To improve the relationship between citizens of the black community and police departments; to improve the relationship between black policemen and white policemen; to educate the public about police departments; to aid police departments in planning successful law enforcement programs in the black community. Maintains speakers bureau. Conducts professional training seminars; presents National Law and Social Justice Leadership Award annually to the individual in public service who has done most to improve the relationship between the community and police department. Has initiated referral program for matters of police brutality and legal services; also conducts research on subjects such as police malfeasance and law and order legislation. Maintains 200-volume library on police science, law enforcement and statistics. Publications: *Black Watch,* weekly; *Bulletin on Special Events,* monthly; *Grapevine,* quarterly. Formerly Afro-American Patrolmen's League. Convention/Meeting: Annually.

Airborne Law Enforcement Association, Inc.

524 Belmar Drive
Birmingham, Alabama 35215   Robert F. Brooks, President
Founded 1968. Members: 600. Law enforcement officers who use both fixed and rotary-wing aircraft and are engaged full time in airborne law enforcement. Publications: *Airborne Law Enforcement Association Newsletter,* monthly. Convention/Meeting: Annually.

American Academy for Professional Law Enforcement

c/o T. Kenneth Moran
444 West 56th Street, Suite 2312
New York, New York 10019   T. Kenneth Moran, Ph.D.,
(212) 765-1364   Executive Director
Founded 1974. Members: 1,600. Police officials and academicians with college degrees who are united to promote professional standards and ethical practice in police services. Sponsors seminars and provides consultation on police services. Publications: *Police Studies,* quarterly; *Annual Proceedings; Workshop Proceedings,* annually; also publishes newsletter, *Rape: The Violent Crime Corruption and Its Management* and plans to publish journal. Formed by merger of Academy of Police Science (founded 1958) and Law Enforcement Association on Professional Standards, Education and Ethical Practice (founded 1970). Convention/Meeting: Annually.

American Federation of Police

1100 NE 125th Street
North Miami, Florida 33161
(305) 891-1700   Gerald Arenberg, Executive Director
Founded 1966. Members: 50,000. Governmental and private law enforcement officers (paid, part time, or volunteer) united in purpose for the prevention of crime and the apprehension of criminals. Offers insurance benefits and training programs to members. Maintains placement service. Issues 24 types of service and bravery awards. Publications: *Police Times Magazine,* monthly; membership newsletter and in-service training bulletins. Formerly United States Federation of Police. Convention/Meeting: Biennially, even years.

American Law Enforcement Officers Association

2000 P Street, NW
Washington, DC 20036   Dr. L.L. Higgins,
(202) 293-9088   Executive Vice President
Founded 1976. Members: 55,000. Men and women concerned with the practice of criminal justice by either enforcement of the laws or provision of technical and clerical support services (includes federal state, county, municipal, town and village law enforcement agencies; also includes special security organizations and guard services). Established as a fraternal organization to offer services and benefits to individual members; inspire cooperation and a close working relationship among all law enforcement personnel; close the ranks in law enforcement that have been split by influences which would engage in dissension and strife; protect life and property; prevent crime; arrest those who break the law, assist in their successful prosecution and, if guilty, in their ultimate imprisonment. Maintains lodge system on national, regional, state and local bases; opposes unions.

Associated Public Safety Communications Officers

Box 669
New Smyrna Beach, Florida 32069   Ernest J. Landreville,
(904) 428-8700   Executive Director
Founded 1935. Members: 3,700. Publications: *The APCO Bulletin,* monthly. Convention/Meeting: Annually.

Canadian Association of Police Chiefs

116 Albert Street, Suite 1002
Ottawa, Ontario, Canada K1P 5G3
(613) 233-1106   J.W. Paul Laurin, Director
Founded 1905. Members: 566. Membership is composed of heads and deputy heads of federal, provincial, municipal, national harbor and railway police forces; heads and deputy heads of other law enforcement agencies; law enforcement officials who have rendered distinguished service in law enforcement. The association's foremost objectives are to encourage and develop cooperation of all Canadian police organizations, to create and develop the highest standards of efficiency in law enforcement; and to promote and maintain a high standard of ethics, integrity, honor and conduct in the profession of law enforcement. Publications: *The Canadian Police Chief,* quarterly; also publishes information bulletins when required on police operational matters. Convention/Meeting: Annually.

Committee on Uniform Crime Records

c/o International Association of Chiefs of Police
11 Firstfield Road
Gaithersburg, Maryland 20760
(301) 948-0922   William T. Dean, Staff Liaison
Founded 1930. Members: 17. A committee of the International Association of Chiefs of Police. Is official liaison between the IACP and FBI in all matters relating to the gathering and publishing of crime statistics in the United States. Evaluates methods used by police agencies in maintaining records and making reports relative to law enforcement; provides IACP with information and recommendations pertaining to maintenance of uniform crime reports by its members and other police agencies in the U.S. and abroad. Has developed standard crime classifications and reporting and accounting methods. Convention/Meeting: Annually.

Federation of Postal Security Police

Box 1804
Pittsburgh, Pennsylvania 15230   Eugene J. Lewis, President
Members: 1,100. Publications: *Federal News,* quarterly. Convention/Meeting: Biennially, even years.

Friends of the FBI

1735 DeSales Street, NW, Suite 500
Washington, DC 20036
(202) 785-3830   J.A. Parker, President
Founded 1971. Conducts educational and research programs and disseminates knowledge about the FBI and all other law enforcement organizations in the U.S. Distributes literature to opinion molders,

political leaders, university personnel and business leaders in the U.S. and other countries. Exchanges publications and information. Sponsors conferences, seminars and meetings. Commissions surveys. Publications: newsletter; also publishes scholarly studies, pamphlets and reprints.

International Association of Chiefs of Police

11 Firstfield Road
Gaithersburg, Maryland 20760
(301) 948-0922   Norman Darwick, Director
Founded 1893. Members: 12,000. Police executives (commissioners, superintendents, chiefs and directors of national, state, provincial and municipal departments, assistant and deputy chiefs, division or district heads). Provides consultation and research services in all phases of police activity. Sponsors Institute for Police Management. Raises funds to improve performance standards of law enforcement management through research, surveys and consulting services. Presents Parade Policeman of the Year Award annually. Maintains a library of approximately 5,000 volumes on criminology and law enforcement. Publications: *Police Chief*, monthly; *Journal of Police Science and Administration*, quarterly; *Directory of IACP Members*, annually. *IACP Police Buyers' Guide*, annually. Convention/Meeting: Annually.

International Association of Women Police

P.O. Box 1978
Sun City, Arizona 85372
(602) 974-5092   Maurine E. Barkdoll, Executive Director
Founded 1915. Members: 600. Full-time women law enforcement officers authorized to make arrests under authority of the penal code of the county, state, province or country in which they reside. To further the education and training of women police and to employ women in law enforcement; to encourage the general improvement of police service. Presents Policewoman of the Year Award. Publications: *Bulletin*, quarterly; membership directory, biennially; newsletter; also publishes *Women in Law Enforcement* (brochure). Formerly International Policewomen's Association. Convention/Meeting: Annually.

International Conference of Police Chaplains, Inc.

401 Marquette Avenue, NW
Albuquerque, New Mexico 87102
(505) 766-7086   Donald R. Jacobs, President
Founded 1973. Members: 350. Promotes professionalism among police chaplains in law enforcement agencies. Publications: *Report*, quarterly; *Directory of Police Chaplains*, annually; *Chaplains Handbook*, irregularly. Convention/Meeting: Annually.

International Federation of Senior Police Officers

Postfach 480127
Feldkamp 4
D-4400 Munster, West Germany   G. Kratz, Secretary General
Founded 1950. Police officers and their associations in 64 countries. Considers problems of traffic police; social and preventive action of the police, especially regarding young people; police and human rights; study of an international code of police ethics; police relations with the public; protection of police officers in times of war and occupation. Publications: *International Police Information*, 2-4/y; also publishes directory, Congress proceedings and monographs. Convention/Meeting: Triennial International Congress of Traffic Police; semiannual meetings.

International Footprint Association

1095 Market Street, Room 206
San Francisco, California 94103   Walter J. Vervais,
(415) 431-3324   Secretary-Treasurer
Founded 1929. Members: 7,500. Law enforcement officers and citizens of all professions and businesses. To bring together on a social basis conscientious law enforcement personnel and other interested

parties to improve knowledge of law enforcement problems. Convention/Meeting: Annually.

International Law Enforcement Stress Association

P.O. Box 415   Edward C. Donovan,
Canton, Massachusetts 02021   Executive Officer
Founded 1978. Members: 450. Individuals in all branches of law enforcement from all over the world, as well as doctors, psychiatrists, psychologists, social workers, counselors and others interested in the reduction and treatment of police stress. Objectives are to complement professional training in the area of police stress; to offer a variety of training programs and educational experiences related to countering the hazard of law enforcement stress; and to coordinate and exchange new counseling techniques and treatment modalities used in the diagnosis and treatment of stress. Publications: newsletter, bimonthly; *Police Stress*, quarterly.

International Union of Police Associations

422 First Street, SE
Washington, D.C. 20003
(202) 546-0010   Edward J. Kiernan
Founded: 1978. Members: 175 locals; 75,000 individuals. Members are individual police local unions in the U.S. and Canada. Establishment of the union came about when certain members, who wanted to affiliate with the AFL-CIO, split away from the International Conference of Police Associations. Publications: *The Law Officer*, monthly. Convention/Meeting: Annually.

Justice System Training Association

Box 356
Appleton, Wisconsin 54912
(414) 731-8893   Kevin Parsons, Director
Founded 1974. Members: 400. Defensive tactics and physical training instructors from criminal justice agencies. Purposes are to make available to the law enforcement community the expertise of those knowledgeable in the area of police self-defense; disseminate information regarding new developments in the field and innovative programs; cooperate with professional law enforcement organizations in production of practical training aids; and foster professionalism of the law enforcement community by training police self-defense instructors in the use of humane, effective and reliable self-defense techniques. Awards national certification to qualified Police Self-Defense Instructors (PSDI). Maintains speakers bureau and a 10,000 volume library. Sponsors regional seminars and conducts research. Publications: *PSDI Memorandum in Law and Order Magazine*, monthly; also publishes monographs. Formerly Law Enforcement Liaison Division. Convention/Meeting: Annual national PSDI training seminar.

National Association of Police Community Relations Officers

144 West Colfax, Room 302
Denver, Colorado 80202   Edna Berry, Secretary
Founded 1969. Members: 200. Law enforcement officers, college professors, criminal justice personnel. Purpose is to promote professionalism of law enforcement officers through the development of more positive orientation, attitudes and skills regarding police-public cooperation. Acts as consultant; gives technical assistance; conducts needs assessments, training and research. Maintains library. Publications: newsletter, quarterly; semiannual report; annual report. Convention/Meeting: Annually.

National Black Police Association

Lock Box 49122
Chicago, Illinois 60649
(312) 873-0220   Renault A. Robinson, Executive Officer
Founded 1972. Members: 15,000. Black police officers, both male and female. Publications: *Grapevine*; newsletter, monthly. Affiliated with Afro-American Police League (see separate entry). Convention/Meeting: Annually.

National Police and Fire Fighters Association

1100 125th Street, NE
North Miami, Florida 33161   Gerald S. Arenberg,
(305) 891-1700   Executive Vice President
Founded 1961. Members: 41,000. A fraternal association of full-time/part-time law enforcement officers, full-time/part-time and volunteer fire fighters of all ranks, and charter citizen members. Pays benefits for death in line of duty; maintains burial assistance fund. Provides extension service training through the American Police Academy in arson investigation, and basic private guard and private detectives training. Publications: *Police Times,* monthly. Formerly National Detectives and Special Police Association. Convention/Meeting: Biennially.

National Police Officers Association of America

609 West Main Street, Third Floor
Louisville, Kentucky 40202
(502) 845-4141   Frank J. Schira, Executive Director
Founded 1955. Members: 32,000. Professional and fraternal benefit organization of full-time police officers of federal, state, county and local police departments. Issues awards for police work, including good arrests, bravery, merit and valor. Publications: *Enforcement Journal, Official Police Review,* quarterly. Convention/Meeting: Biennially.

National Sheriffs' Association

1250 Connecticut Avenue, Suite 320
Washington, DC 20036
(202) 872-0422   Ferris E. Lucas, Executive Director
Founded 1940. Members: 65,000. Sheriffs, deputy sheriffs, and municipal, state and federal law enforcement officers, and all others professionally involved with criminal justice. Sponsors Junior Deputy Sheriffs League. Provides consulting service to local peace officers. Publications: *National Sheriff,* bimonthly; also publishes monographs and guidelines. Convention/Meeting: Annually.

Police Executive Research Forum

1909 K Street, NW, Suite 400
Washington, DC 20006
(202) 466-7820   Gary P. Hayes, Executive Director
Founded 1975. Members: 71. General members (58) are executive heads of large public police agencies with at least four years of college; associate members (13) are executives other than department heads, executives of national law enforcement agencies and former members who no longer qualify for general membership. Seeks to improve delivery of police services through the professionalization of police executives and officers. Stresses cooperation with other professionals and organizations in the criminal justice system. Seeks to stimulate public understanding and discussion of important criminal justice issues. Encourages development of new knowledge through research and experimentation and disseminates research information. Publications: *Police Collective Bargaining Agreements: A National Management Survey,* annually; *Survey of Departmental Research and Special Projects,* annually; *Survey of Police Operational and Administrative Practices,* annually; also publishes *Burglary Investigation Decision Model Replication* and brochure. Convention/Meeting: Annually.

Police Marksman Association

305 South Lawrence Street
Montgomery, Alabama 36104
(205) 262-5761   Charles L. Dees, President
Founded 1976. Members: 15,000. Organization of policemen dedicated to the highest interest of competitive shooting and police firearms training. Its purposes are to promote police competitive shootings as a training and a sport to provide shooting education and instruction and to organize incentive and recreational programs. Publications: *Police Marksman,* quarterly and bimonthly.

Public Safety Personnel Research Institute, Inc.

501 Grandview Drive, No. 207
South San Francisco, California 94080
(415) 877-0735   Wayne W. Schmidt, President
Founded 1974. Staff: 2. Conducts research on personnel practices in police and fire departments, compiles court decisions on arbitration, disciplinary procedures, pension rights and discriminatory hiring practices. Sponsors periodic seminars for fire and police chiefs. Publications: *Fire and Police Personnel Reporter,* monthly.

POLYGRAPH

American Polygraph Association

P.O. Box 1061
Severna Park, Maryland 21146
(301) 779-5530   Lynn P. Marcy, Executive Director
Founded 1966. Members: 1,700. Law enforcement officers, attorneys, private investigators, government agency personnel and others. Members must have completed a course of formal instruction in polygraph instrumentation and techniques totaling at least 252 hours of classroom instruction at a civilian, military or governmental school accredited by APA; hold at least a bachelor's degree; have administered at least 200 polygraph examinations within a three-year period following completion of formal instruction and have demonstrated proficiency in the conduct of polygraph examinations to the satisfaction of the APA membership committee. Promotes research on instrumentation and techniques; seeks to improve qualifications of polygraph examiners; works to create an improved public image of the polygraph (sometimes referred to as a lie detector) and its users. Maintains speakers bureau, placement service, museum and biographical archives. Bestows awards. Publications: newsletter, bimonthly; *Journal,* quarterly; *Polygraph Law Reporter,* quarterly, *State Laws,* quarterly; *Roster,* annually; also publishes *Truth and Science, a Bibliography.* Formed by merger of Academy of Scientific Interrogation, American Academy of Polygraph Examiners and National Board of Polygraph Examiners. Convention: Annually.

American Association of Police Polygraphists

c/o Raymond Inglin
Los Angeles Police Department
150 North Los Angeles Street
Austin, Texas 78765
(213) 664-6305   Raymond Inglin, President
Founded 1977. Members: 683. Individuals currently affiliated with a public criminal justice agency or military service in the profession of polygraphy (operation of the polygraph or lie detector), and former polygraphists who remain active in the field. Purposes are to encourage cooperation among members; increase polygraph proficiency; promote and maintain highest standards of ethics; upgrade the profession and provide a forum for the exchange of information. Sponsors seminars; compiles statistics; bestows awards for outstanding contributions to polygraphy. Publications: *Journal,* quarterly; *Membership Roster,* annually. Convention/Meeting: Annually.

National Association of Extradition Officials

506 Toluca Park Drive
Burbank, California 91505
(213) 845-1912   Elvyn Holt, Archivist
Founded 1964. Members: 46 states. Extradition officials (one representative from each state) who are concerned with carrying out the provisions of the Uniform Extradition Act. Publications: *Law Report,* annually. Convention Meeting: Annually.

National Rifle Association of America

1600 Rhode Island Avenue, NW
Washington, DC 20036   Harlon B. Carter,
(202) 828-6000   Executive Vice President

Founded 1871. Members: 1,800,000. Target shooters, hunters, gun collectors, gunsmiths, police officers and others interested in firearms. Promotes rifle, pistol and shotgun shooting; hunting; gun collecting; hunter and home firearms safety; conservation, etc. Encourages civilian marksmanship in areas of national defense. Maintains national records of shooting competitions; sponsors teams to compete in the Olympic Games and other world championships. Collects, tabulates and compiles information on hunting casualties in the U.S. and Canada. Maintains comprehensive collection of antique to modern firearms. Publications: *The American Hunter,* monthly; *The American Rifleman,* monthly; *Uniform Hunter Casualty Report,* semiannually; *Conservation Yearbook; Hunting Annual.* Convention/Meeting: Annually.

Police Insignia Collector's Association
c/o James Fahy
15 Pond Place
Cos Cob, Connecticut 06807
(203) 661-3927   James J. Fahy, Secretary
Founded 1973. Members: 700. Individuals interested in the lawful collection and preservation of police memorabilia (shoulder patches, badges, hats, uniforms). To assist collectors in obtaining police items and to provide a medium of trading information among members. Publications: newsletter, bimonthly; also publishes annual membership list.

MISCELLANEOUS

American Association of Motor Vehicle Administrators
1201 Connecticut Avenue, NW
Washington, DC 20036
(202) 296-1955   Donald J. Bardell, Executive Director
Founded 1933. Members: 100. Membership composed of state and provincial councils responsible for the administration and enforcement of motor vehicle and traffic laws in the U.S. and Canada. Publications: *AAMVA Bulletin,* monthly; *D.L. Newsletter;* bimonthly. Convention/Meeting: Annually.

Americans for Effective Law Enforcement
501 Grandview Drive, Suite 209
South San Francisco, California 94080   Wayne W. Schmidt,
(415) 877-0731   Executive Director
Founded 1966. Members: 5,000. Nonpolitical organization seeking to arouse public concern with the nation's crime problems. Aims are to explore the needs for effective enforcement of criminal law, inform the public about them, and help the police, prosecutors and the courts to promote a more effective and fairer administration of criminal law. Aids the victims of crime through litigation on their behalf. Drafts model legislation and constitutional amendments to aid in effective law enforcement and public protection. AELE will reject, support and withhold voting membership from advocates of racial bias or other unconstitutional concepts. Compiles statistics. Law Enforcement Legal Defense Center assists police administrators in defense of civil suits alleging police misconduct. Maintains library of 800 volumes. Publications: *Liability Reporter,* monthly; *Jail & Prison Law Bulletin,* monthly; *Defense Manual,* quarterly; *Police Plaintiff,* quarterly. Also publishes *Amicus Curiae Briefs.*

Evidence Photographers International Council
24 East Main Street
Norwich, New York 13815
(607) 344-6833   Casey Jones, President
Founded 1967. Members: 700. Members are photographers working with law enforcement agencies and the courts. Works to improve forensic photography. Publications: *Journal of Evidence Photography,* quarterly. Convention/Meeting: Annually.

International Narcotic Enforcement Officers Association
112 State Street, Suite 1310
Albany, New York 12207
(518) 463-6232   John J. Bellizzi, Executive Director
Founded 1960. Members: 7,500. Narcotics enforcement officers, government employees and others concerned with narcotics control. Seeks ways to improve international, national narcotics addiction and drug abuse. Provides a forum for exchange of ideas and conducts seminars, conferences and study groups. Maintains collection of pamphlets and reprints of articles on narcotics enforcement. Publications: *International Drug Report,* monthly; *Conference Proceedings,* annually; *Directory,* annually. Formerly National Narcotic Enforcement Officers Association. Convention/Meeting: Annually.

Justice System Training Association
Box 356
Appleton, Wisconsin 54912
(414) 731-8893   Kevin Parsons, Director
Founded 1974. Members: 3,400. Trainers of defense tactics and physical-training instructors from law enforcement, correctional and security agencies. Publications: *Law and Order,* monthly. Formerly Law Enforcement Liaison Division of the U.S. Karate Association. Convention/Meeting: Annually.

The Magazine Rack

Explanation of symbols: **(A)** *Annually;* **(SA)** *Semiannually;* **(Q)** *Quarterly;* **(BM)** *Bimonthly;* **(M)** *Monthly;* **(SM)** *Semimonthly;* **(BW)** *Biweekly;* **(W)** *Weekly;* **(I)** *Irregularly. Note: Additional publications related to law enforcement can be found in the Organizations and Associations Section.*

APA Newsletter (BM)
American Polygraph Association
P.O. Box 1061
Severna Park, Maryland 21146
(301) 647-0936
Established 1963; circulation: 3,750

Accident Reporter, The (BM)
University of North Carolina
Highway Safety Research Center
Trailer 13, CTP, 197-A
Chapel Hill, North Carolina 27514
(919) 933-2202
Established 1971; circulation: 5,000

**American Correctional Association Directory;
State and Federal Correctional
Institutions (A)**
American Correctional Association
Woodridge Station
4321 Hartwick Road
College Park, Maryland 20740
(301) 864-1070
Established 1940

American Criminal Law Review (Q)
Georgetown University Law Center
600 New Jersey Avenue, NW
Washington, D.C. 20001
(202) 331-2200
Established 1962; circulation: 12,000

American Criminologist (M)
American Association of Criminology
Box 1115
North Marshfield, Massachusetts 02059
(617) 837-0052
Established 1953; circulation: 2,500

American Journal of Correction (BM)
American Correctional
    Association/Craftsman Press
2117 West River Road North
Minneapolis, Minnesota 55411
(612) 522-4356
Established 1920; circulation: 10,040

American Journal of Criminal Law (3/Y)
University of Texas, School of Law
2500 Red River
Austin, Texas 78705
(512) 471-5151
Established 1972; circulation: 900

Annual Report
Public Information Officer
Office of the Director
Federal Bureau of Prisons
320 First Street, NW
Washington, D.C. 20537
(202) 724-3198

**Annual Report 1979-1980: Solicitor
General of Canada**
Solicitor General of Canada
340 Laurier Avenue, West
Ottawa, Ontario, Canada KIA 0P8
(613) 996-1061
Established 1966; circulation: 7,600

Bank Security Report (M)
Warren, Gorham & Lamont, Inc.
210 South Street
Boston, Massachusetts 02111
(617) 423-2020
Established 1971; circulation: 2,600

CAPC, Annual Report of
Canadian Association for the Prevention of Crime
55 Parkdale Avenue
Ottawa, Ontario, Canada K1Y 1E5
(613) 725-3715
Circulation: 2,000

CAPC Bulletin (5/Y)
Canadian Association for the Prevention of Crime
55 Parkdale Avenue
Ottawa, Ontario, Canada K1Y 1E5
(613) 725-3715
Established 1971; circulation: 2,000

**Canada Corrections Association,
Delinquency and Crime Division,
Annual Report**
Canadian Council on Social Development
55 Parkdale Avenue
Ottawa, Ontario, Canada K1Y 1E5
(613) 728-1865

Canadian Criminal Cases (W)
Canada Law Book Ltd.
240 Edwards Street
Aurora, Ontario, Canada L4G 3S9
(416) 859-3880
Established 1892

Canadian Journal of Criminology (Q)
Canadian Association for the Prevention of Crime
55 Parkdale Avenue
Ottawa, Ontario, Canada K1Y 1E5
(613) 725-3715
Established 1958; circulation: 1,600

Canadian Police Chief (Q)
Canadian Association of Chiefs of Police, Inc.
606 Bathurst Avenue
Ottawa, Ontario, Canada K1P 5G3
(613) 233-1106
Established 1967; circulation: 1,300

Combat Handguns (BM)
Harris Publications, Inc.
79 Madison Avenue
New York, New York 10016
(212) 686-4121
Established 1980; circulation: 150,000

Constables Review (M)
Montreal Policemen's Brotherhood, Inc.
480 Gilford Street
Montreal, Quebec, Canada H2J 1N3
(514) 849-6012
Established 1946; circulation: 5,000

Corporate Security (M)
Man and Manager, Inc.
817 Broadway
New York, New York 10003
(212) 673-4700
Established 1971

Corrections (Q)
Criminal Justice Publications, Inc.
116 West 32nd Street
New York, New York 10001
(212) 947-2700
Established 1974; circulation: 6,500

Corrections Digest (BW)
Washington Crime News Services
7620 Little River Turnpike
Annandale, Virginia 22003
(703) 941-6600
Established: 1969

Corrections Magazine (BM)
Correctional Information Service
116 West 32nd Street
New York, New York 10017
(212) 947-2700
Established 1974; circulation: 9,000

Corrections Today (BM)
American Correctional Association
4321 Hartwick Road, L-208
College Park, Maryland 20740
(301) 864-1070
Established 1920; circulation: 11,900

Counter Spy (4-5/Y)
Box 647 Ben Franklin Station
Washington, D.C. 20044
Established 1971; circulation: 6,000

Court Review (BM)
(Municipal Court Review)
American Judges Association
Box 1399
Holyoke, Massachusetts 01040
(413) 534-1506
Established 1961; circulation: 2,100

Crime & Delinquency (Q)
National Council on Crime and Delinquency
411 Hackensack Avenue
Hackensack, New Jersey 07601
(201) 488-0400
Established 1955; circulation: 8,000

Crime and Justice (Q)
P.O. Box 27, Station A
Hull, Quebec, Canada J8Y 6M7
(819) 827-0717
Established 1976; circulation: 800

Crime & Social Justice: Issues in Criminology
Crime and Social Justice
P.O. Box 40601
San Francisco, California 94140
Established 1974; circulation: 3,000

Crime and Traffic Enforcement Statistics Annual
Statistics Canada
R.H. Coats Building, Tunneys Pasture
Ottawa, Ontario, Canada K1A 0T6
(613) 995-0855
Established 1962; circulation: 2,000

Crime Control Digest (W)
Washington Crime News Services
7620 Little River Turnpike
Annandale, Virginia 22003
(703) 941-6600
Established 1967

Crime in the US (A)
Federal Bureau of Investigation
Justice Department
Washington, D.C. 20535
(202) 324-2614
Established 1930; circulation: 50,000

Criminal Justice and Behavior (Q)
Sage Publications, Inc.
275 South Beverly Drive
Beverly Hills, California 90212
(213) 274-8004
Established 1974; circulation: 750

Criminal Justice and the Public (M)
Grafton Publications, Inc.
667 Madison Avenue
New York, New York 10021
(212) 832-3170
Established 1974

Criminal Justice Newsletter (BW)
National Council on Crime and Delinquency
411 Hackensack Avenue
Hackensack, New Jersey 07601
(201) 488-0400
Established 1970; circulation: 1,700

Criminal Justice Periodical Index (3/Y)
University Microfilms International,
    Serials Indexing
300 North Zeeb Road
Ann Arbor, Michigan 48106
(313) 761-4700
Established 1975

Criminal Law Bulletin (BM)
Warren, Gorham & Lamont, Inc.
210 South Street
Boston, Massachusetts 02111
(617) 423-2020
Established 1964; circulation: 4,500

Criminal Reports (SM)
The Carswell Company Limited
2330 Midland Avenue
Agincourt, Ontario, Canada M1S 1P7
(416) 291-8421
Established 1978; circulation: 1,800

Criminal Victimization in the U.S. Trends
U.S. Bureau of Justice Statistics
633 Indiana Avenue, NW
Washington, D.C. 20531
(301) 492-9148
Established 1973

Criminology (Q)
Sage Publications, Inc.
275 South Beverly Drive
Beverly Hills, California 90212
(213) 274-8004
Established 1963; circulation: 2,500

Drug Enforcement (Q)
(BNDD Bulletin)
Drug Enforcement Administration
U.S. Department of Justice
1405 I Street, NW
Washington, D.C. 20537
(202) 633-1230
Established 1968; circulation: 55,000

FBI Law Enforcement Bulletin (M)
Federal Bureau of Investigation
Department of Justice
Washington, D.C. 20535
(202) 324-3000
Established 1932

Federal Prisons (A)
Bureau of Prisons, Department of Justice
Washington, D.C. 20534
(202) 724-3198
Established 1930

Fortune News (BM)
Fortune Society
229 Park Avenue South
New York, New York 10003
(212) 677-4600
Established 1967; circulation: 33,000

Guns & Ammo (M)
Petersen Publishing Company
8490 Sunset Boulevard
Los Angeles, California 90069
(213) 657-5100
Established 1956; circulation: 475,000

Homicide Statistics (A)
Statistics Canada
Ottawa, Ontario, Canada K1A 0T6
(613) 992-3151

IACP Law Enforcement Legal Review (M)
International Association of Chiefs of Police, Inc.
Gaithersburg, Maryland 20760
(301) 948-0922
Established 1972; circulation: 400

IACP Legal Points (M)
International Association of Chiefs of Police, Inc.
11 Firstfield Road
Gaithersburg, Maryland 20760
(301) 948-0922
Established 1972; circulation: 7,500

Identification News (M)
International Association for Identification
P.O. Box 139
Utica, New York 13503
(315) 732-2897
Established 1956; circulation: 2,500

Inside Out (M)
N. Y. C. Department of Correction
100 Centre Street
New York, New York 10013
(212) 374-4440
Circulation: 5,000

International Association of Personnel in Employment Security News (M)
Box 173
Frankfort, Kentucky 40601
(502) 223-4459
Established 1940; circulation: 24,500

International Drug Report (M)
International Narcotic Enforcement Officers
    Association
112 State Street
Albany, New York 12207
(518) 463-6232
Established 1960; circulation: 10,000

International Review of Criminal Policy (I)
United Nations Department of Social Affairs
United Nations
New York, New York 10017
(212) 754-1234
Established 1952

Intersearch (BW)
International Terrorist Research Center, Inc.
P.O. Box 26804
El Paso, Texas 79926
(915) 592-5238
Established 1978; circulation: 3,000

Journal of Correctional Education (Q)
Correctional Education Association
2633 West Moss Avenue
Peoria, Illinois 61604
(309) 676-5165
Established 1948; circulation: 1,600

Journal of Criminal Justice (BM)
Pergamon Press, Inc.
Maxwell House, Fairview Park
Elmsford, New York 10523
(914) 592-7700
Established 1973; circulation: 1,250

Journal of Criminal Law and Criminology (Q)
The Williams and Wilkins Company
428 East Preston Street
Baltimore, Maryland 21202
(301) 528-4000

Journal of Forensic Sciences (Q)
American Society of Testing and Materials
1916 Race Street
Philadelphia, Pennsylvania 19103
(215) 299-5400
Established 1956; circulation: 3,400

Journal of Police Science and Administration (Q)
International Association of Chiefs of Police, Inc.
11 Firstfield Road
Gaithersburg, Maryland 20760
(301) 948-0922
Established 1972; circulation: 2,700

Journal of Polygraph Science, The (BM)
National Training Center of Lie Detection, Inc.
57 West 57th Street
New York, New York 10019
(212) 755-5241
Established 1966; circulation: 4,200

Journal of Research in Crime and Delinquency (SA)
National Council on Crime and Delinquency
411 Hackensack Avenue
Hackensack, New Jersey 07604
(201) 488-0400
Established 1964; circulation: 1,700

Justice - Directory of Services (A)
Canadian Association for the Prevention of Crime
55 Parkdale Avenue
Ottawa, Ontario, Canada K1Y 1E5
(613) 725-3715
Established 1980; circulation: 1,000

Justice System Journal, The (I)
Institute for Court Management
1624 Market Street, Suite 210
Denver, Colorado 80202
(303) 534-3063
Established 1974; circulation: 850

Juvenile and Adult Correctional Departments, Institutions, Agencies and Paroling Authorities: United States and Canada
American Correctional Association
4321 Hartwick Road, Suite L-208
College Park, Maryland 20740
(301) 699-7600
Established 1940; circulation: 7,000

Juvenile Justice Digest (SM)
Washington Crime News Services
7620 Little River Turnpike
Annandale, Virginia 22003
(703) 941-6600
Established 1973

LEAA, Annual Report of
Superintendent of Documents
U.S. Government Printing Office
Washington, D.C. 20402
(202) 783-3238

LEAA Grants and Contracts
U.S. Department of Justice
Office of Law Enforcement Assistant
U.S. Govt. Printing Office
Washington, D.C. 20402
(202) 783-3238
Established 1968

LEAA Newsletter (10/Y)
Superintendent of Documents
U.S. Govt. Printing Office
Washington, D.C. 20402
(202) 783-3238

Law and Order (M)
5526 North Elston Avenue
Chicago, Illinois 60630
(312) 792-1838
Established 1952; circulation: 25,000

Law Enforcement Communications (BM)
United Business Publications, Inc.
475 Park Avenue South
New York, New York 10016
(212) 725-2300
Established 1974; circulation: 25,000

Law Enforcement Journal (M)
P.O. Box 2039
Martinez, California 94553
(415) 228-0260
Established 1961; circulation: 10,000

Law Enforcement News (SM)
444 West 56th Street
New York, New York 10019
(212) 489-3592
Established 1975; circulation: 10,000

Law Enforcement Report (Q)
Planning Section of the Chief Postal
    Inspector's Office
U.S. Postal Service
Washington, D.C. 20260
(202) 245-5497
Established 1962; circulation: 7,600

Narcotics Control Digest (BW)
Washington Crime News Services
7620 Little River Turnpike
Annandale, Virginia 22003
(703) 941-6600
Established 1971

National Directory of Law Enforcement Administrators and Correctional Institutions (A)
National Police Chiefs and Sheriffs
    Information Bureau
152 West Wis Avenue
Box 92007, Suite 727
Milwaukee, Wisconsin 53203
(414) 272-3853
Established 1964; circulation: 9,000

National Jail and Adult Detention Directory (A)
American Correctional Association
4321 Hartwick Road, Suite L-208
College Park, Maryland 20740
(301) 699-7600
Established 1979; circulation: 3,000

National Prisoner Statistics Bulletin; Executions (A)
Bureau of Prisons; U.S. Department of Justice
National Prisoner Statistics Program
H.O.L.C. Building, Room 136
101 Indiana Avenue, NW
Washington, D.C. 20534
(202) 724-3198
Established 1949; circulation: 4,000

National Prisoner Statistics Bulletin; Prisoners in State and Federal Institutions for Adult Felons (A)
Bureau of Prisons; U.S. Department of Justice
National Prisoner Statistics Program
H.O.L.C. Building, Room 136
101 Indiana Avenue, NW
Washington, D.C. 20534
(202) 633-2000
Established 1950; circulation: 3,000

National Sheriff (BM)
National Sheriffs' Association
1250 Connecticut Avenue, Suite 320
Washington, D.C. 20036
(202) 872-0422
Established 1940; circulation: 47,800

Organized Crime Digest (M)
Washington Crime News Services
7620 Little River Turnpike
Annandale, Virginia 22003
(703) 941-6600
Established 1980

Peace Officer, The (BM)
Dale Corporation
30500 Van Dyke, Suite 600
Warren, Michigan 48093
(313) 573-0200
Established 1958; circulation: 10,000

Peace Officer Law Report (M)
Department of Justice Accounting POLR
1315 Fifth Street
Sacramento, California 95814
(916) 322-4088
Established 1971; circulation: 4,000

Point Blank (M)
Citizens Committee for the Right to Keep and
    Bear Arms
1601 SE 114th Street
Bellevue, Washington 98004
(206) 454-4911
Established 1971; circulation: 200,000

Police Chief, The (M)
International Association of Chiefs of Police, Inc.
11 Firstfield Road
Gaithersburg, Maryland 20760
(301) 948-0922
Established 1934; circulation: 22,000

Police Command (M)
American Federation of Police
1100 NE 125th Street
North Miami, Florida 33161
(305) 891-1700
Established 1978; circulation: 33,000

Police Digest (A)
Digest Publications, Inc.
2234 West Irving Park Road
Chicago, Illinois 60618
(312) 478-1275
Established 1938; circulation: 12,000

Police Labor Review (M)
International Association of Chiefs of Police, Inc.
11 Firstfield Road
Gaithersburg, Maryland 20760
(301) 948-0922
Established 1974; circulation: 412

Police Law Reporter (Q)
International Association of Chiefs of Police, Inc.
11 Firstfield Road
Gaithersburg, Maryland 20760
(301) 948-0922
Established 1974; circulation: 200

Police Product News (M)
Dyna Graphics, Inc.
P.O. Box 847
Carlsbad, California 92008
(714) 438-3286
Established 1976; circulation: 52,000

Police Studies (Q)
John Jay Press
444 West 56th Street
New York, New York 10019
(212) 489-3515
Established 1978; circulation: 400

Police Times (M)
American Federation of Police
1100 NE 125th Street
North Miami, Florida 33161
(305) 891-1700
Established 1961; circulation: 80,000

Police Yearbook (A)
Davis Publishing Company, Inc.
250 Potrero Street
Santa Cruz, California 95061
(408) 423-4968
Established 1960; circulation: 2,500

Police Yearbook, The (A)
(International Association of Chiefs of Police,
Proceedings of Annual Conference)
11 Firstfield Road
Gaithersburg, Maryland 20760
(301) 948-0922
Established 1893; circulation: 11,100

Polygraph (Q)
APA Publications
P.O. Box 1061
Severna Park, Maryland 21146
Established 1972; circulation: 2,000

Prison Law Monitor (11/Y)
P.O. Box 3104
Washington, D.C. 20009
(202) 387-7249
Established 1978; circulation: 3,000

Prisoners Union Journal (BM)
(The Outlaw), Pioneers Union
1315 18th Street
San Francisco, California 94107
(415) 648-2880
Established 1971; circulation: 4,000

Prosecutor (BM)
National District Attorneys Association
666 North Lake Shore Drive, Suite 1432
Chicago, Illinois 60611
(312) 944-4610
Established 1965; circulation: 7,800

RCMP Quarterly (Q)
Royal Canadian Mounted Police
1200 Alta Vista Drive
Ottawa, Ontario, Canada K1A 0R2
(613) 993-3800
Established 1933; circulation: 22,500

**Report of the Attorney General on
Administration of the Foreign Agents
Registration Act (A)**
U.S. Department of Justice
Attorney General
U.S. Govt. Printing Office
Washington, D.C. 20402
(202) 783-3238
Established 1945

Research Relating to Juvenile Delinquents
U.S. Govt. Printing Office
Division of Public Documents
Washington, D.C. 20402
(202) 275-2035

Reserve Law (M)
2440 Freedom Drive
San Antonio, Texas 78217
(512) 344-7072
Established 1970; circulation: 10,000

Royal Canadian Mounted Police Report (A)
Royal Canadian Mounted Police
1200 Alta Vista Drive
Ottawa, Ontario, Canada K1A 0R2
(613) 993-3800

Royal Canadian Mounted Police Quarterly (Q)
Royal Canadian Mounted Police
MPS Building, 5th Floor, Quarterly Section
1200 Alta Vista Drive
Ottawa, Ontario, Canada K1A 0R2
(613) 993-3800
Established 1933; circulation: 20,000

Safety Management (M)
National Foreman's Institute
24 Rope Ferry Road
Waterford, Connecticut 06836
(203) 442-4365
Established 1976

Scarlet and Gold (A)
675 West Hastings Street, #813
Vancouver, B.C., Canada V6B 1N2
(604) 685-7729
Established 1919; circulation: 3,000

Security Distributing and Marketing (M)
Security World Publication Company, Inc.
2639 South La Cienega Boulevard
Los Angeles, California 90034
(213) 836-5000
Established 1970; circulation: 17,600

Security Management (M)
American Society for Industrial Security
2000 K Street, NW, Suite 651
Washington, D.C. 20006
(202) 331-7887
Established 1956; circulation: 17,000

Security Systems Digest (BW)
Washington Crime News Services
7620 Little River Turnpike
Annandale, Virginia 22003
(703) 941-6600
Established 1969

Security World Magazine (M)
5670 Wilshire Boulevard, Suite 2170
Los Angeles, California 90036
(213) 933-9525
Established 1966; circulation: 40,000

Selected Biography of White Collar Crime, A
Department of Justice
Enforcement Law Assistance Administration
Washington, D.C. 20531
(202) 724-3198
Established 1977

Sheriffs of the United States Annual Directory
National Sheriffs' Association
1250 Connecticut Avenue, Suite 209
Washington, D.C. 20036
(202) 872-0422
Established 1940; circulation: 3,500

State Peace Officers Journal (BM)
North American Publishing Company
P.O. Box 13155
Houston, Texas 77019
(713) 526-6425
Established 1969; circulation: 4,000

**Systems, Technology and Science for Law
Enforcement and Security (M)**
(STS Newsletter)
Lomond Publications, Inc.
P.O. Box 56
Mt. Airy, Maryland 21771
(301) 829-1496
Established 1969; circulation: 700

Time & Tide (Washington D.C.)
Department of Corrections
Reformatory Division
Washington, D.C. 20537
(202) 655-4000

Today's Policeman (Q)
Towerhigh Publications, Inc.
P.O. Box 594
Kansas City, Missouri 64141
(816) 221-7075
Established 1960; circulation: 15,000

Training Aids Digest (M)
Washington Crime News Services
7620 Little River Turnpike
Annandale, Virginia 22003
(703) 941-6600
Established 1976

Training Key (BW)
International Association of Chiefs of Police, Inc.
11 Firstfield Road
Gaithersburg, Maryland 20760
(301) 948-0922
Established 1964; circulation: 40,000

Truthseekers, The (M)
1680 North Vine Street, Suite 400
Hollywood, California 90028
(213) 466-3283
Established 1970; circulation: 2,500

**Uniform Crime Reports for the United
States (A)**
Superintendent of Documents
U.S. Govt. Printing Office
Washington, D.C. 20402
(202) 783-3238

U.S. Bureau of Prisons, Director (A)
U.S. Department of Justice, Bureau of Prisons
320 First Street, NW
Washington, D.C. 20534
(202) 724-3198
Established 1968

U.S. Bureau of Prisons, Federal Prisons (A)
Bureau of Prisons
320 First Street, NW
Washington, D.C. 20534
(202) 724-3198
Established 1930

U.S. Bureau of Prisons, National Prisoner Statistics Executions (A)
Bureau of Prisons
320 First Street, NW
Washington, D.C. 20534
(202) 724-3198

U.S. Bureau of Prisons, National Prisoner Statistics, Personnel in State and Federal Institutions (A)
Bureau of Prisons
320 First Street, NW
Washington, D.C. 20534
(202) 724-3198

U.S. Bureau of Prisons, National Prisoner Statistics, Prisoners in State and Federal Institutions
Bureau of Prisons
320 First Street, NW
Washington, D.C. 20534
(202) 724-3198

U.S. Department of Health, Education and Welfare, Juvenile Court Statistics (A)
U.S. Department of Health, Education
   and Welfare
National Center for Social Statistics
Washington, D.C. 20201
(202) 655-4000

U.S. Department of Justice and the Courts of the United States, Register (A)
Department of Justice
Washington, D.C. 20534
(202) 724-3198
Established 1871

Victimless Crime
National Criminal Justice Reference Service
Department of Justice
Washington, D.C. 20534
(202) 724-3198
Established 1977

Victimology, An International Journal (Q)
Visage Press, Inc.
P.O. Box 39045
Washington, D.C. 20016
(703) 549-7694
Established 1975; circulation: 2,700

World Association of Detectives, Membership Directory (A)
World Association of Detectives
P.O. Box 5068
San Mateo, California 94402
(415) 341-0060

World Association of Detectives, Newsletter (M)
World Association of Detectives
P.O. Box 5068
San Mateo, California 94402
(415) 341-0060
Established 1925; circulation: 500

Law Enforcement Bookshelf

The books that appear in the Law Enforcement Bookshelf are arranged for easy reference according to the following categories:

Ammunition
Anarchy
Arrest (*see* also Searches and Seizures)
Arson (*see* also Fire Investigation)
Assassination
Bail
Ballistics
Bombs
Capital Punishment
Child Abuse
Combat
Confession (Law)
Counterfeits and Counterfeiting
Crime and Criminals
Crime and Criminals—Addresses, Essays, Lectures
Crime and Criminals—Bibliography
Crime and Criminals—Biography
Crime and Criminals—Data Processing
Crime and Criminals—Identification
Crime and Criminals—Study and Teaching
Crime and Criminals—United States
Crime and Criminals—West
Crime Prevention
Crimes Without Victims
Criminal Courts
Criminal Investigation
Criminal Justice, Administration of—
Criminal Justice, Administration of—Bibliography
Criminal Law
Criminal Law—Study and Teaching
Criminal Procedure
Criminal Psychology
Criminal Statistics
Delinquents
Detectives
Drug Abuse and Crime
Drugs and Youth
Embezzlement
Euthanasia
Evidence, Criminal
Evidence, Expert
Evidence, Law
Explosives
Female Offenders
Fingerprints
Fire Investigation
Firearms (*see* Pistols, Revolvers, Rifles, Shotguns)
Firearms—Laws and Regulations

Forensic Hypnotism (*see* Hypnosis and Crime)
Fraud
Fugitives
Gangs
Governmental Investigations
Gunshot Wounds
Hand-To-Hand Fighting (*see* also Self-Defense)
Handguns
Hijacking of Aircraft
Homicide
Homicide Investigation
Hostages (*see* Terrorism)
Hypnosis and Crime
Identification
Informers
Investigations
Judo
Juvenile Courts
Juvenile Delinquency
Kidnapping
Law Enforcement
Law Enforcement Officers
Lie Detectors
Medical Jurisprudence
Murder
Narcotics Laws
Offenses Against the Person
Organized Crime
Pistols
Poisoning
Police
Police—Data Processing

Police—Equipment and Supplies
Police—Examinations, Questions
Police—Handbooks, Manuals
Police—Records and Correspondence
Police—Study and Teaching
Police—Vocational Guidance
Police Administration
Police Communications Systems
Police Corruption
Police Dogs
Police Patrol
Police Power
Police Questioning
Police Services for Juveniles
Police Stress
Police Training
Policewomen
Rape
Report Writing
Revolvers
Rifles
Riot Control
Robbery
Searches and Seizures (*see* also Arrest)
Self-Defense
Sexual Assaults (*see* Child Abuse, Rape)
Sheriffs
Shotguns
State Police
Terrorism
Traffic Courts
Traffic Police
United States—Immigration Border Patrol
White Collar Crimes
Witnesses

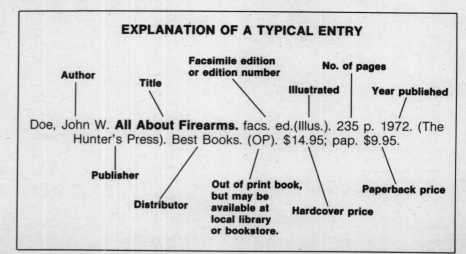

EXPLANATION OF A TYPICAL ENTRY

Author
Title
Facsimile edition or edition number
No. of pages
Illustrated
Year published

Doe, John W. **All About Firearms.** facs. ed. (Illus.). 235 p. 1972. (The Hunter's Press). Best Books. (OP). $14.95; pap. $9.95.

Publisher
Distributor
Out of print book, but may be available at local library or bookstore.
Hardcover price
Paperback price

AMMUNITION

Central Intelligence Agency. **CIA Ammunition and Explosives Supply Catalog.** (Illus.). 1975. pap. Paladin Press. $7.95.

—**CIA Explosives for Sabotage Manual.** (Illus.). 1975. pap. Paladin Press. $5.95.

Guns and Ammo Magazine Editors, ed. **Guns and Ammo Annual, 1981.** (Illus.). 320p. 1980. pap. Petersen Publishing. $6.95.

Labbett, Peter. **Military Small Arms Ammunition of the World, 1945-1980.** (Illus.). 160p. 1980. Presidio Press. $18.95.

Matunas, Edward. **American Ammunition and Ballistics.** (Illus.). 1979. Winchester Press. $12.50.

Parkerson, Codman. **A Brief History of Bullet Moulds.** Pioneer Press. $1.75.

Sears and Roebuck Ammunition Catalog. (Illus.). pap. Sand Pond. $1.50.

Steindler, R.A. **Reloader's Guide.** 3rd ed. (Illus.). 1975. softbound. Stoeger. $7.95.

Suydam, Charles R. **U.S. Cartridges and Their Handguns: 1795-1975.** (Illus.). 1978. Beinfeld. (OP) $14.95; pap. $9.95.

Warner, Ken. **Handloader's Digest Bullet and Powder Update.** 1980. pap. DBI Books. $4.95.

Williams, Mason. **The Law Enforcement Book of Weapons, Ammunition and Training Procedures: Handguns, Rifles and Shotguns.** (Illus.). 1977. C.C. Thomas. $35.75.

ANARCHY

Gibbons, Don. **The Criminological Enterprise: Theories and Perspectives.** 1979. pap. Prentice-Hall. $8.95.

New York State Joint Legislative Committee Investigating Seditious Activities— Revolutionary Radicalism. 8 vols. 1971. Repr. of 1920 ed. Da Capo Press. $250.

ARREST

Asch, Sidney H. **Police Authority and the Rights of the Individual.** 2nd ed. 1968. pap. Arc Books. (OP) $1.45.

Bassiouni, M. Cherif. **Citizen's Arrest: The Law of Arrest, Search and Seizure for Private Citizens and Private Police.** (Illus.). 1977. C.C. Thomas. $15.25; pap. $10.25.

Berry, Calvin W. **Arrest, Search and Seizure.** 1973. Michie Co. $25.

Cramer, J.Shane. **The Law of Arrest, Search and Seizure.** 3rd ed. 1980. Saunders. $12.95.

Gardner, Thomas J. & Manian, Victor. **Principles of Cases of the Law of Arrest, Search and Seizure.** Clevendon, Ardelle, ed. (Illus.). 1974. pap. McGraw-Hill. $14.95; Instructor's manual $3.

LaFave, Wayne R. **Arrest: The Decision to Take a Suspect into Custody.** 1965. pap. Little, Brown. $5.95.

Markle, A. **The Law of Arrest and Search and Seizure.** (Illus.). 1974. C.C. Thomas. $19.

Vallow, Herbert P. **Police Arrest and Search.** (Illus.). 1962. C.C. Thomas. (OP) $5.75.

Varon, Joseph A. **Searches, Seizures and Immunities.** 2 vols. rev. ed. 1974. Bobbs-Merrill. $60.

Waddington, Lawrence C. **Arrest, Search, and Seizure.** 1974. Glencoe. $10.95.

ARSON

Barracato, John & Michelmore, Peter. **Arson!** 1976. W.W. Norton. $8.95.

Battle, Brendan P. & Weston, Paul B. **Arson Detection and Investigation.** 1978. Arco. $9.95.

Borg, Nicholas & David, Leonard. **Arson: A Multi-Dimensional Problem.** 1976. Society Fire Protect. $2.50.

Carroll. **Physical and Technical Aspects of Fire and Arson Investigation.** (Illus.). 1979. C.C. Thomas. $29.50.

Carter, Robert E. **Arson Investigation.** 1978. Glencoe. $13.95.

The Fire Fighter's Responsibility in Arson Detection. rev. ed. 1971. pap. Natl. Fire Protection Assn. $1.50.

Fitch, Richard D. & Porter, Edward A. **Accidental or Incendiary.** 1975. C.C. Thomas. $11.25.

French, Harvey M. **The Anatomy of Arson.** (Illus.). 1979. Arco. $12.50.

Huron, Benjamin S. **Elements of Arson Investigation.** (Illus.). 1963. Fire Engine. Book Dept. Tech. Pub. Co. $5.00.

Macdonald, John M. **Bombers and Firesetters.** 1977. C.C. Thomas. $17.25.

Madison, Arnold. **Arson!** (Illus.). 1978. Watts. $5.90.

Provencher, R.G. **Arson.** 1976. Society Fire Protect. $3.25.

ASSASSINATION

Camellion, Richard. **Assassination: Theory and Practice.** 1977. pap. Paladin Enterprises. $8.

Havens, Murray C., et al. **Assassination and Terrorism: Their Modern Dimensions.** Orig. Title: The Politics of Assassination. Prentice-Hall. 200p. 1975. pap. Sterling Swift. $5.95.

McKinley, James. **Assassination in America.** (Illus.). 1977. Harper & Row. $11.95.

Miller, Tom. **The Assassination Please Almanac.** (Illus.). 1977. pap. Contemporary Books. $5.95.

Paine, Lauran. **Assassins' World.** (Illus.). 212p. 1975. Taplinger. $9.50.

BAIL

Beeley, Arthur. **Bail System in Chicago.** 1965. Repr. of 1927 ed. U. of Chicago Press. $8.

De Haas, Elsa. **Antiquities of Bail: Origin and Historical Development in Criminal Cases to the Year 1275.** Repr. of 1940 ed. AMS Press. $17.50.

Goldkamp, John S. **Two Classes of Accused: A Study of Bail and Dentention in American Justice.** (Illus.). 1979. Ballinger Pub. $22.50.

Gould Editorial Staff. **Bailments Law of New York.** 1962. pap. Gould. $1.50.

Murphy, John J. **Arrest by Computer: The Controversy Over Bail and Extradition.** 1975. Lexington Books. $15.95.

Nimenos, Nimas. **How to Become a Professional Bondsman.** 1978. pap. Golden State Industries. $3.95.

Thomas, Wayne. **Bail Reform in America.** 1977. U. of Calif. Press. $14.

Wice. **Freedom for Sale.** 1974. Lexington Books. $18.95.

BALLISTICS

Matunas, Edward. **American Ammunition and Ballistics.** (Illus.). 1979. Winchester Press. $12.50.

McShane. **Exterior Ballistics.** Swallow. $2.

Wilber, Charles G. **Ballistic Science for the Law Enforcement Officer.** (Illus.). 1977. C.C. Thomas. $30.

—**Forensic Biology for the Law Enforcement Officer.** 1974. C.C. Thomas $24.25.

Williams, M. **Practical Handgun Ballistics.** 1980. C.C. Thomas. $17.50.

BOMBS

Brodie, Thomas G. **Bombs and Bombings: A Handbook to Detection, Disposal and Investigations for Police and Fire Departments.** 1980. C.C. Thomas. $15.75.

Lenz, Robert R. **Explosives and Bomb Disposal Guide.** 1976. C.C. Thomas. $14.50.

Macdonald, John M. **Bombers and Firesetters.** 1977. C.C. Thomas. $17.25.

Pike, Earl A. **Protection Against Bombs and Incendiaries: For Business, Industrial and Educational Institutions.** (Illus.). 1973. C.C. Thomas. $8.25.

Stoffel, Joseph. **Explosives and Homemade Bombs.** 2nd ed. (Illus.). 1977. C.C. Thomas. $23.75.

CAPITAL PUNISHMENT

Arteaga, Dan. **The Death Penalty Versus Thou Shalt Not Kill.** 1980. Vantage Press. $8.95.

Bedau, Hugo A. **The Courts, the Constitution, and Capital Punishment.** 1977. Lexington Books. $17.95.

Bedau, Hugo A., ed. **Death Penalty in America: An Anthology.** 2nd ed. 1968. Aldine. $21.95.

Bedau, Hugo A. & Pierce, Chester M., eds. **Capital Punishment in the United States.** 1976. Ams Press. $27.50.

Berns, Walter. **For Capital Punishment: Crime and the Morality of the Death Penalty.** 1979. Basic Books. $11.95.

Black, Charles L., Jr. **Capital Punishment: The Inevitability of Caprice and Mistake.** 1974. W.W. Norton. $6.95; pap. $2.95.

Bowers, William J. **Executions in America.** 1974. Lexington Books. (OP) $20.00.

Burns, Creighton L. **Tait Case.** 1962. pap. Intl. Scholarly Book Services. $6.50.

Calvert, E. Roy. **Capital Punishment in the Twentieth Century.** 5th rev. ed. 1973. Repr. Patterson Smith. $13.50.

—**Capital Punishment Dilemma 1950-1977: A Subject Bibliography.** 1979. Whitston Pub. $18.50.

Carrington, Frank G. **Neither Cruel nor Unusual: The Case for Capital Punishment.** 1978. Arlington House. $9.95.

Folgelson, Robert M., ed. **Capital Punishment: Nineteenth-Century Arguments.** facs. ed. 1974. Arno Press. $12.00.

Gettinger, Stephen H. **Sentenced to Die: The People, the Crimes and the Controversy.** 1979. Macmillan. $9.95.

Glover, Jonathan. **Causing Death and Saving Lives.** 1977. pap. Penguin Books. $3.95.

Heline, Theodore. **Capital Punishment: Trends Toward Abolition.** 1965. pap. New Age Press. $1.00.

Horwitz, Elinor L. **Capital Punishment, U.S.A.** (Illus.). 1973. Lippincott. $8.95.

James, Antony. **Capital Punishment.** 1977. pap. Belmont-Tower. $1.75.

Jayewardene, C.H. **Penalty of Death: The Canadian Experiment.** (Illus.). 1977. Lexington Books. $13.95.

Josephson, Barney R. **Humane Reciprocity: The Moral Necessity of the Capital Penalty.** 1979. pap. Ann Arbor. $1.50.

Lawes, Lewis E. **Man's Judgment of Death: An Analysis of the Operation and Effect of Capital Punishment Based on Facts, Not On Sentiment.** 1969. Repr. of 1924 ed. Patterson Smith. $8.00.

Lewis, C.S., et al. **Essays on the Death Penalty.** 2nd ed. Ingram, T. Robert, ed. 1978. pap. St. Thomas. $1.95.

Lewis, Clive S., et al. **Essays on the Death Penalty.** 1963. pap. Pacific Meridian. $1.95.

Loeb, Robert. **Crime and Capital Punishment.** (Illus.). 1978. Watts, Franklin, Inc. $4.90.

McCafferty, James A., ed. **Capital Punishment.** 1972. text ed. Lieber-Atherton. $9.95.

Mackey, Philip E., ed. **Voices Against Death: American Opposition to Capital Punishment, 1787-1975.** 1977. pap. B. Franklin. $7.95.

—**Voices Against Death: Classic Appeals Against the Death Penalty in America, 1787-1974.** (Illus.). 1976. B. Franklin. $17.95.

Meador, Roy. **Capital Revenge: Fifty-Four Votes Against Life.** 1975. Dorrance. (OP) $6.95.

Meltsner, Michael. **Cruel and Unusual.** 1974. pap. Morrow. (OP) $3.95.

—**Cruel and Unusual: The Supreme Court and Capital Punishment.** 1973. Random House. $10.95.

O'Sullivan, John L. **Report in Favor of the Abolition of the Punishment of Death by Law, Made to Legislature of the State of New York April 14, 1841.** facsimile ed. 1974. Repr. of 1841 ed. Arno Press. $13.00.

Prettyman, Barrett, Jr. **Death and the Supreme Court.** 1968. pap. Harcourt Brace Jovanovich. $2.95.

Roucek, Joseph S. **Capital Punishment.** Rahmas, D. Steve, ed. 1975. SamHar Press. $2.75; pap. $1.50.

Sellin, Thorsten. **The Penalty of Death.** (Illus.). 1980. Sage. $18.00; pap. $8.95.

Shin, Kilman. **Death Penalty and Crime: Empirical Studies.** 1978. Center for Economic Analysis, George Mason Univ. $18.00.

Stevens, Leonard A. **The Death Penalty: The Case of Life vs Death in the United States, the 8th Amendment.** 1978. Coward, McCann & Geoghegan. $6.58.

Von Mittermaier, Carl J. **Capital Punishment.** Moir, John M., ed. 1980. Repr. of 1865 ed. Hyperion Press. $22.50.

Yallop, David A. **To Encourage the Others.** 1974. St. Martin's Press. (OP) $6.95.

CHILD ABUSE

The Abused and Neglected Child: Multi-Disciplinary Court Practice, 1979. (Litigation & Administrative Practice Course Handbook Ser. 1978-79. Vol. 104). Practicing Law Inst. $20.00.

Bakan, David. **Slaughter of the Innocents: A Study of the Battered Child Phenomenon.** (Social & Behavioral Science Ser.). 1971. Jossey-Bass. $11.95.

Boardman, et al. **The Neglected-Battered Child Syndrome: Role Reversal in Parents.** 49p. 1963. pap. Child Welfare League of America. $2.75.

Bourne, Richard & Newberger, Eli H., eds. **Critical Perspectives on Child Abuse.** (Illus.). 1978. Lexington Books. $18.95.

Brazier, Shelley, ed. **Fourth National Congress on Child Abuse and Neglect.** 560p. 1980. PSG Pub. $30.

Burgess, Ann W., et al. **Sexual Assault of Children and Adolescents.** 1978. Lexington Books. $21.95; pap. $9.95.

Burns, Alice, et al. **Child Abuse and Neglect in Suffolk County.** 1973. pap. Edmond Pub. Co. $2.00.

Burt, Marvin R. & Balyeat, Ralph R. **A Comprehensive Emergency Services System for Neglected and Abused Children.** 1977. Vantage Press. $5.95.

Burt, Robert A. & Wald, Michael. **Standards Relating to Abuse and Neglect.** 1977. Ballinger Publishing. softcover $7.95; casebound $16.50.

Cameron, I.M. & Rae, L. John. **Atlas of the Battered Child Syndrome.** (Illus.). 160p. 1975. Churchill Livingstone. $35.00.

Carter, Jan, ed. **The Maltreated Child.** 1976. Technomic. $11.50.

Chase, Naomi F. **A Child Is Being Beaten: Violence Against Children, An American Tragedy.** 1976. pap. McGraw-Hill. $3.95.

Christiansen, James. **Educational and Psychological Problems of Abused Chidren.** 125p. 1980. Century Twenty One. $10.00.

Coigney, Virginia. **Children Are People Too: How We Fail Our Children and How We Can Love Them.** 1975. Morrow. $6.95.

Collins, Marilyn C. **Child Abuser: A Study of Child Abusers in Self-Help Group Therapy.** 140p. 1978. pap. PSG Publishing. $9.50.

Costs, Joseph H. & Nelson, Gordon K. **Child Abuse and Neglect: Legislation, Reporting and Prevention.** 1978. Lexington Books. $25.95.

DeCourcy, Peter & DeCourcy, Judith. **A Silent Tragedy: Child Abuse in the Community.** 231p. 1973. Alfred Publishing. $13.95.

Dolan, Jr. **Child Abuse.** (gr. 7 up). 1980. Watts, Franklin, Inc. $7.90.

Ebeling, Nancy & Hill, Deborah, eds. **Child Abuse-Intervention and Treatment.** 198p. 1975. PSG Publishing. $15.00.

Ellerstein, Norman S. **Child Abuse and Neglect: A Medical Reference.** 350p. 1981. Wiley, John & Sons. $35.00.

Elmer, Elizabeth. **Children in Jeopardy: A Study of Abused Minors and Their Families.** 1967. pap. U. of Pittsburgh Press. $4.95.

—**Fragile Families, Troubled Children: The Aftermath of Infant Trauma.** 1977. U. of Pittsburgh Press. $8.95.

Erickson, Edsel L., et al. **Child Abuse and Neglect: A Guidebook for Educators and Community Leaders.** 1979. Learning Publications. $9.95; pap. $6.95.

Farson, Richard. **Birthrights.** 1978. pap. Penguin Books. $2.50.

Finkelhor, David. **Sexually Victimized Children.** 1979. Free Press. $13.95.

Fontana, Vincent J. **Maltreated Child: The Maltreatment Syndrome in Children - A Medical, Legal and Social Guide.** 4th ed. (Illus.). 192p. 1976. C.C. Thomas. $16.00.

—**Somewhere a Child Is Crying: Maltreatment-Causes and Prevention.** 1976. pap. NAL. $2.50.

—**Somewhere a Child Is Crying: The Battered Child.** 360p. 1973. Macmillan. $9.95.

Fosson, Abe R. & Kaak, Otto H. **Child Abuse and Neglect Case Studies.** 1977. Medical Examination Publishing Co. spiral bdg. $12.00.

Franklin, Alfred. **Concerning Child Abuse.** (Illus.). 209p. 1975. Churchill Livingstone. $22.00.

Franklin, Alfred W., ed. **The Challenge of Child Abuse.** 1978. Grune & Stratton. $28.50.

—**Child Abuse: Prediction, Prevention and Follow-Up.** 1978. pap. Churchill Livingstone. $18.50.

Freeman, M.D. **Violence in Home: A Socio-Legal Study.** 1979. (Pub. by Saxon Hse England.) Lexington Books. $18.95.

Frude, Neil, ed. **Psychological Approaches to Child Abuse.** 200p. 1981. Rowman & Littlefield. $19.50.

Garbarino, James & Gilliam, Gwen. **Understanding Abusive Families.** 288p. 1980. Lexington Books. $19.95.

Garbarino, James & Stocking, S. Holly. **Protecting Children from Abuse and Neglect: Developing and Maintaining Effective Support Systems for Families.** 1980. Jossey-Bass. $13.95.

Garland, Roberta, ed. **Readings in Child Abuse.** (Illus., Orig.). 1979. pap. Special Learning Corp. $9.95.

Geiser, Robert L. **Hidden Victims: The Sexual Abuse of Children.** 1979. Beacon Press. $10.95.

—**Hidden Victims: The Sexual Abuse of Children.** 204p. 1980. pap. Beacon Press. $5.95.

Geoke, John C. **Factors Related to the Alienation of the Male Married Offender.** 130p. 1980. Century Twenty One. $9.00.

Gerbner, George, et al, eds. **Child Abuse: An Agenda for Action.** (Illus.). 352p. 1980. Oxford University Press. $14.95; pap. $7.95.

Gil, David G. **Violence Against Children: Physical Child Abuse in the United States.** (Illus.). 1970. Harvard University Press. $8.50; pap. $3.50.

Gil, David G., ed. **Child Abuse and Violence.** 1978. AMS Press. $24.50; pap. $11.95.

Giovannoni, Jeanne M. & Becerra, Rosina. **Defining Child Abuse.** (Illus.). 1979. Free Press. $15.95.

Giovannoni, Jeanne M., et al. **Child Abuse and Neglect: An Examination from the Perspective of Child Development Knowledge.** 1978. pap. R & E Research Associates. $10.00.

Green, Arthur. **Child Maltreatment: A Handbook for Mental Health Professionals and Child Care Workers.** 300p. 1980. Aronson, Jason. $25.00.

Hafen, Brent Q., ed. **Child Maltreatment: Developing a Community Team Approach.** 1981. PSG Publishing. price not set.

Hallett, Christine & Stevenson, Olive. **Child Abuse.** 1980. Allen Unwin. $17.95; pap. $7.95.

Halperin, Michael. **Helping Maltreated Children: School and Community Involvement.** 1979. pap. Mosby. $8.95.

Hampton, Sandra J. & Hultquist, Lee. **Whatever Happened to Judy?** 1980. pap. Logos International. $4.95.

Helfer, Ray E. & Kempe, C. Henry, eds. **The Battered Child.** 2nd ed. 1978. pap. U. of Chicago Press. $6.95.

—**Child Abuse and Neglect: The Family and the Community.** 1976. Ballinger Publishing. $25.00; pap. $9.95.

Herbruck, Christine. **Breaking the Cycle of Child Abuse.** 1979. pap. Winston Press. $4.95.

Herrmann, Kenneth J. **I Hope My Daddy Dies, Mister.** 108p. 1975. Dorrance. $4.95.

Hunner, Robert J., ed. **Exploring the Relationship Between Child Abuse and Delinquency.** Date not set. Allanheld, Osmun & Co. $19.50.

Hyde, Margaret O. **Cry Softly: The Story of Child Abuse.** 1980. Westminster Press. $8.95.

International Congress on Child Abuse and Neglect, 2nd, London, September 1978. Selected Papers, Vol. 3. Kempe, C.H., et al, eds. 1100p. 1980. Pergamon Press. $113.00.

International Congress on Child Abuse and Neglect, 2nd, London 1978. Abstracts of the Second International Congress on Child Abuse and Neglect. Franklin, A. White, ed. 1979. Pergamon Press. $26.00.

Jordan, Bill. **Poor Parents: Social Policy and the Cycle of Deprivation.** 1974. Routledge & Kegan. $14.50; pap. $5.50.

Justice, Rita & Justice, Blair. **The Abusing Family.** 1976. Human Sciences Press. $16.95; pap. $7.95.

Kadushin, Alfred & Martin, Judith A. **Child Abuse: An Interactional Event.** (Illus.). 360p. 1981. Columbia University Press. $25.00.

Kalisch, Beatrice J. **Child Abuse and Neglect: An Annotated Bibliography.** 1978. Greenwood Press. $27.50.

Kalmar, Roberta. **Child Abuse: Perspectives on Diagnosis, Treatment and Prevention.** 1977. pap. Kendall-Hunt. $5.95.

Kempe, C. Henry & Helfer, Ray E. **The Battered Child.** (Illus.). 1980. University of Chicago Press. $20.00.

Kempe, C. Henry & Helfer, Ray E., eds. **Helping the Battered Child and His Family.** (Illus.). 320p. 1972. Lippincott. $14.00; pap. $9.35.

Kempe, Ruth S. & Kempe, C. Henry. **Child Abuse.** 1978. Harvard University Press. $7.95; pap. $3.95.

Kertzman, Don. **Dependency, Frustration, Tolerance, and Impulse Control in Child Abusers.** 150p. 1980. Century Twenty One. $10.00.

Kline, Donald F., ed. **Child Abuse and Neglect: A Primer for School Personnel.** 1977. pap. Council for Exceptional Children. $4.00.

Kroth, Jerome A. **Child Sexual Abuse: Analysis of a Family Therapy Approach.** (Illus.). 216p. 1979. C.C. Thomas. $17.50.

Lieber, L. & Wheat, Patte. **Hope for the Children: A Personal History of Parent's Anonymous.** 1979. pap. Winston Press. $6.95.

Lyndecker. **Children in Chains.** 1981. Everest House. price not set.

Martin, Harold P., ed. **The Abused Child: A Multidisciplinary Approach to Developmental Issues and Treatment.** 1976. Ballinger Publishing. $18.00.

Martin, J.P., ed. **Violence and the Family.** 1978. Wiley-Interscience. $34.50.

Nagi, Saad Z. **Child Maltreatment in the United States.** 1977. Columbia University Press. $12.50.

NSPCC. **At Risk: An Account of the Work of the Battered Child Research Department.** (Orig.). 1976. pap. Routledge & Kegan. $12.50.

Nystrom, Carolyn. **Forgive Me If I'm Frayed Around the Edges.** (Illus., Orig.) 1977. pap. Moody Press. $1.50.

O'Brien, Shirley. **Child Abuse: A Crying Shame.** 184p. 1980. Brigham Young University Press. $15.95.

Pelcovitz, David A. **Child Abuse As Viewed by Suburban Elementary School Teachers.** 120p. 1980. Century Twenty One. $10.00.

Pelton. **Social Context of Child Abuse and Neglect.** 1980. Human Sciences Press. $22.95.

Polansky, Norman A., et al. **Roots of Futility.** 1972. Jossey-Bass. $15.95.

—**Child Neglect: Understanding and Reaching the Parent.** 1972. pap. Child Welfare League of America. $4.75.

Renvoize, Jean. **Children in Danger.** 1975. Routledge & Kegan. $12.50.

Roberts, Albert R., ed. **Childhood Deprivation.** 232p. 1974. C.C. Thomas. $12.50.

Rodriguez, Alejandro. **Handbook of Child Abuse and Neglect.** 1977. spiral bdg. Medical Examination Publishing Co., $12.00.

Rosenblatt, Gary C. **Parental Expectations and Attitudes About Childrearing in High Risk Vs. Low Risk Child Abusing Families.** 145p. 1980. Century Twenty One. $10.00.

Rush, Florence. **The Best Kept Secret: Sexual Abuse of Children.** 296p. 1980. Prentice-Hall. $11.95.

Sanford, Linda T. **Silent Children: A Parent's Guide to the Prevention of Child Abuse.** 312p. 1980. Doubleday. $12.95.

Schmitt, Barton E. **Child Protection Handbook: A Multidisciplinary Approach to Managing Child Abuse and Neglect.** 435p. 1980. Garland Publishing. $29.50.

Seaberg, James R. **Physical Child Abuse: An Expanded Analysis.** 145p. 1980. Century Twenty One. $10.00.

Shapiro, Deborah. **Parents and Protectors: A Study in Child Abuse.** 1979. pap. Child Welfare League of America. $5.45.

Smith, S.M. **Battered Child Syndrome.** 1976. Butterworths. $28.95.

Smith, Selwyn. **The Maltreatment of Children: A Comprehensive Guide to the Battered Baby Syndrome.** 1978. University Park. $22.50.

SPR Charter. **Outrage!** 1978. Guild of Tutors. $9.95; pap. $6.95.

Sussman, Alan & Cohen, Stephan. **Reporting Child Abuse and Neglect: Guidelines for Legislation.** 288p. 1975. Ballinger Publishing. $18.50.

Thomas, M. Angele, ed. **Children Alone: What Can Be Done About Abuse and Neglect.** 1977. pap. Council for Exceptional Children. $7.50.

Volpe, Richard, et al eds. **Maltreatment of the School-Aged Child.** 1980. Lexington Books. price not set.

Walters, David R. **Physical and Sexual Abuse of Children: Causes and Treatment.** 192p. 1976. Indiana University Press. $10.95; pap. $4.95.

Wayne, Julianne & Avery, Nancy C. **Child Abuse: Prevention and Treatment Through Social Group Work.** (Orig.). 1979. Charles River Books. $12.00; pap. $5.75.

Wells, Dorothy P. & Carroll, Charles R., eds. **Child Abuse: An Annotated Bibliography.** 458p. 1980. Scarecrow Press. $20.00.

Wheat, Patte. **By Sanction of the Victim.** 1978. pap. Timely Books. $4.50.

Williams, Gertrude & Money, John. **Traumatic Abuse and Neglect of Children.** 1980. Johns Hopkins. $30.00.

Young, Leontine. **Wednesday's Children.** 1971. pap. McGraw-Hill. $3.50.

—**Wednesday's Children: A Study of Child Neglect and Abuse.** 1979. Repr. of 1964 ed. Greenwood Press. $17.00.

COMBAT

Draeger, Donn F. **Classical Budo.** (Illus.). 1973. Weatherhill. $12.95.

—**Classical Bujutsu.** (Illus.). 1973. Weatherhill. $10.00.

Harris, M. **Lethal Unarmed Combat.** Wehman Brothers, Inc. $6.95.

Leather, E. Hartley. **Combat Without Weapons.** (Illus.). pap. Paladin Enterprises. $3.00.

Logan & Petra. **Martial Arts Handbook.** Wehman Brothers, Inc. $12.95.

Maslak, Paul. **Strategy in Unarmed Combat.** 1977. Wehman Brothers, Inc. $10.00.

CONFESSION (LAW)

Gould Staff. **Confession and Admissions.** Gould $8.50.

Inbau, Fred E. and Reid, John E. **Criminal Interrogation and Confessions.** 2nd ed. 1967. Williams and Wilkins. $17.00.

Medalie, Richard J. **Escobedo to Miranda.** 1966. Lerner Law Book Co. (OP). $7.50.

Milner, Neal A. **Court and Local Law Enforcement: The Impact of Miranda.** 1971. Sage. $17.50.

Reik, Theodor. **Compulsions to Confess: On the Psycho Analysis of Crime and Punishment.** Repr. of 1959 ed. Books for Libs. $30.00.

Rogge, O. John. **Why Men Confess.** 1971 Repr. of 1959 ed. Da Capo Press. $22.50.

Schafer, William J., 3rd. **Confessions and Statements.** 1968. C. C. Thomas. (OP). $5.75.

Sobel, Nathan R. **Confession Standards.** 1966. pap. Gould. $6.50.

Stephens, Otis H., Jr. **The Supreme Court and Confessions of Guilt.** 1973. University of Tennessee Press. $11.50.

Tobias, Marc W. and Petersen. R. David. **Pre-Trial Criminal Procedure: A Survey of Constitutional Rights.** (Illus.) 1972. C. C. Thomas. $21.50.

Zagel, James. **Confessions and Interrogations After Miranda: A Comprehensive Guideline of the Law.** 5th ed. National District Attorney's Association. $3.00.

COUNTERFEITS AND COUNTERFEITING

Baudin, Robert. **Confessions of a Promiscuous Counterfeiter.** 1979. Harcourt Brace Jovanovich. $9.95.

Becker the Counterfeiter. (Illus.). 1979. Obol International. $20.00.

Dilliston, William H. **Bank Note Reporters and Counterfeit Detectors 1826-1866.** 1949. pap. American Numismatic Society. $3.50.

Hancock, Virgil and Spanbauer, Larry. **The Standard Catalog of United States Counterfeit Coins.** 1979. S.J. Durst. deluxe ed. $37.50; $30.00.

Harsche, Bert. **Detecting Altered Coins.** 5th ed. (Illus.) pap. House of Collectibles. (OP). $1.00.

Landress, M. M. and Dobler, Bruce. **I Made It Myself.** 1973. Grosset and Dunlap. (OP) $6.95.

Low, Lyman H. **Observations on the Practice of Counterfeiting Coins and Medals.** 1979. Repr. of 1895 ed. S. J. Durst. $2.00.

CRIME AND CRIMINALS

Abadinsky, Howard. **Social Service in Criminal Justice: Theory and Practice.** (Illus.) 1979. ref. Prentice-Hall. $14.95.

Abrahamsen, David. **Crime and the Human Mind.** 1969. Repr. of 1944 ed. Patterson Smith. $12.00.

Adams, Virginia. **Crime.** 1976. Time-Life Books. $8.95.

Adler, J. A. **Elsevier's Dictionary of Criminal Science.** 1960. Elsevier-North Holland Pub. $83.00.

Ancel, Marc. **Social Defense: A Modern Approach to Criminal Problems.** 1966. Schocken Books. $6.95.

Andreano, Ralph and Siegfried, John J., eds. **The Economics of Crime.** 1979. Halsted Press. $19.50; pap. $8.95.

Arana, Belen F. **Crime, Suicide or Natural Death?** Carlton Press. (OP). $4.95.

Arnold, Peter. **Crime and Youth: A Practical Guide to Crime Prevention.** 1976. Messner, Julian. $7.29.

Aschaffenburg, Gustav. **Crime and Its Repression.** Albrecht, Adalbert, tr. 1968. Repr. of 1913 ed. Patterson Smith. $17.00.

Athens, Lonnie. **Violent Criminal Acts and Actors: A Symbolic Interactionist Study.** 1979. Routledge and Kegan. $11.50.

Aubry, Arthur S., Jr. and Caputo, Rudolph R. **Criminal Interrogation.** 2nd ed. 1975. C. C. Thomas. $17.00.

Baldwin, John and Bottoms, A. E. **The Urban Criminal.** 1979. pap. Methuen Inc. (Pub. by Tavistock England). $10.95.

Bard, Morton and Sangrey, Dawn. **The Crime Victim's Book.** 1979. Basic. $11.95.

Barkas, J. L. **Victims.** 1978. Scribner's. $10.95.

Barlow, **Introduction to Criminology.** 2nd ed. 1981. Little, Brown and Co. teachers manual, free. $16.95.

Barnes, Harry E. and Teeters, N. K. **New Horizons in Criminology.** 3rd ed. 1959. Prentice-Hall. (OP). $12.50.

Bartol, Curt R. **Criminal Behavior: A Psychosocial Approach.** (Illus.) 1980. Prentice-Hall. $16.95.

Barzini, Luigi. **From Caesar to the Mafia.** 1971. Open Court. (OP). $8.95.

Barzun, Jacques, ed. **Burke and Hare: the Resurrection Men: A Collection of Contemporary Documents Including Broadsides, Occasional Verses, Illustrations, Polemics, and a Complete Transcript of the Testimony at the Trial.** (Illus.) 1974. Scarecrow Press. (OP) $15.00.

Bates, Sanford. **Prisons and Beyond.** facs. ed. Repr. of 1936 ed. Books for Libs. $22.00.

Becker, Gary S. and Landes, William M., eds. **Essays in the Economics of Crime and Punishment.** 1974. National Bureau of Economic Research $12.50; pap. $5.00.

Becker, Howard S., ed. **Other Side: Perspectives on Deviance.** 1964. Free Press. $8.95; pap. $4.95.

Bersani, Carl A. **Crime and Delinquency: A Reader in Selected Areas.** (Illus.) 1970. pap. Macmillan. $10.95.

Bloomfield, Louis M. and FitzGerald, Gerald F. **Crimes Against International Protected Persons: Prevention and Punishment—an Analysis of the UN Convention.** 1975. Praeger. $24.95.

Blumer, Herbert & Hauset, Philip M. **Movies, Delinquency, and Crime.** 1933. Norwood Editions. $17.50.

Bonger, William. **Criminality and Economic Conditions.** 1969. Indiana University Press. (OP). $2.50.

—**Race and Crime.** Hordyk, Margaret M., tr. 1969. Patterson Smith. $8.00; pap. $3.75.

Bottomley, A. Keith. **Criminology in Focus: Past Trends and Future Prospects.** 1979. Barnes & Noble. $21.00

Bottoms, A.E. & McClintock, F.H. **Criminals Coming of Age: A Study of Institutional Adaptation in the Treatment of Adolescent Offenders.** 1973. Heinemann Ed. $20.95.

Braithwaite, John. **Inequality, Crime and Public Policy.** (Illus.). 1979. Routledge & Kegan. $32.50.

Brasol, Boris. **Elements of Crime: Psycho-Social Interpretation.** 2nd ed. 1969. Repr. of 1931 ed. Patterson Smith. $15.00.

Burkhart, Kathryn W. **Women in Prison.** (Illus.). 1973. Doubleday. (OP). $10.00.

Burkhart, Kathryn. **Women in Prison.** 1976. pap. Popular Library. $1.75.

Byrnes, Thomas. **Professional Criminals.** (Illus.). 1976. pap. Chelsea House (OP). $7.95.

Caldwell, Robert G. **Criminology.** 2nd ed. 1965. Ronald Press. $16.95.

Camps, Frances E. **Camps on Crime.** (Illus.). 1973. David & Charles. (OP). $4.95.

Carey, Mary & Sherman, George. **A Compendium of Bunk or How to Spot a Con Artist: A Handbook for Fraud Investigators, Bankers and Other Custodians of the Public Trust.** 1976. C.C. Thomas. $13.50; pap. $8.75.

Carper, Jean. **Not with a Gun: The True Story of a Multi-Million Dollar Robbery of Home Owners in Washington, D.C. Which Led to an Indictment of a U.S. Congressman.** 1973. Grossman. (OP). $6.95.

Carpozi, George, Jr. **Great Crimes of the Century No. One.** 1979. pap. Manor Books. $1.95.

—**Great Crimes of the Century No. Two.** 1979. pap. Manor Books. $1.95.

Chang, Dae H., ed. **Comparative Criminology: A Cross-Cultural Perspective.** 2 vols. 1976. Carolina Academic Press. $35.00 set.

—**Crime and Delinquency.** 1977. Schenkman. $5.95.

Child, Richard W. **Battling the Criminal.** 1979. Repr. of 1925. ed. R. West. $25.00.

Clouser, John W. & Fisher, David. **The Most Wanted Man in America.** 1975. Stein & Day. $25.00; pap. $1.95.

Cohen, Bruce J., ed. **Crime in America: Perspectives on Criminal and Delinquent Behavior.** 1977. pap. Peacock Pubs. $11.95.

Cohn, Alvin W. **Crime and Justice Administration.** 1976. Lippincott. $11.95.

Conconi, Charles & House, Toni. **The Washington Sting.** 1979. Coward, McCann & Geoghegan. $10.95.

Conklin, John E. **The Impact of Crime.** 1975. pap. Macmillan. $7.50.

Conklin, John E., ed. **The Crime Establishment: Organized Crime and American Society.** (Illus.). 1973. Prentice-Hall. $7.95; pap. $2.95.

Conrad, John P. **Crime and Its Correction: An International Survey of Attitudes and Practices.** 1976. University of California Press. $16.50.

Could You Kill. pap. Harper & Row. (OP). $1.32.

Cressey, Donald R. & Ward, David A., eds. **Delinquency, Crime and Social Process.** 1969. Harper & Row.

Darrow, Clarence. **Crime, Its Cause and Treatment.** 1972. Repr. of 1922 ed. Patterson Smith. $14.00.

David, Pedro R., ed. **The World of the Burglar: Five Criminal Lives.** 1974. University of New Mexico Press. $10.00; pap. $5.95.

Davidson, Bill. **Indict and Convict: The Inside Story of a Prosecutor and His Staff in Action.** 1973. pap. Ace Books. (OP). $.95.

Demaris, Ovid. **The Lucky Luciano Story.** (Illus.). 1974. pap. Belmont-Tower. (OP). $1.25.

Denfeld, Duane. **Streetwise Criminology.** 1974. Schenkman. (OP). $8.95; pap. $5.95.

—**Streetwise Criminology.** 1974. pap. General Learning Press. (OP). $5.95.

De Quiros, C. Bernaldo. **Modern Theories of Criminality.** 1911. Agathon Press. $8.50.

Dessaur, C. I. **Foundations of Theory-Formation in Criminology: A Methodological Analysis.** 1971. Mouton. $16.75.

De Vore, R. William & Jackson, John S., eds. **Carnahan Conference on Crime Countermeasures, 1978: Proceedings.** 1978. ORES Pubns. microfiche, $22.50; pap. $3.50.

Ditton, Jason. **Controlology: Beyond the New Criminology.** (Illus.). 1979. Humanities Press. $22.50.

Di Tullio, Benigno. **Horizons in Clinical Criminology.** 1969. pap. Rothman. $15.00.

Dorf, Robert C. **The Crime Victim's Handbook.** Hopkinson & Blake. (OP). $7.95.

Doshay, Lewis J. **Boy Sex Offender and His Later Career.** 1969. Repr. of 1943 ed. Patterson Smith. $10.00.

Downes, David & Rock, Paul, eds. **Deviant Interpretations: Problems in Criminological Theory.** 1979. Barnes & Noble. $18.50.

Drabek, Thomas E. & Sykes, Gresham. **Law and the Lawless: A Reader in Criminology.** 1969. Random House. (OP). $6.96.

Drahms, August. **Criminal, His Personnel and Environment: A Scientific Study.** 1971. Repr. of 1900 ed. Patterson Smith. $14.00.

Drapkin, Israel & Viano, Emilio, eds. **Victimology: A New Focus-Exploiters and Exploited.** 1975. Lexington Books. $17.95.

—**Victimology: A New Focus-Violence and Its Victims.** 1975. Lexington Books. $16.95.

Eissler, Kurt R., ed. **Searchlights on Delinquency.** 1967. International Universities Press. $30.00.

Ellis, Havelock. **Criminal.** 5th rev. ed. (Illus.). 1973. Repr. of 1914 ed. Patterson Smith $15.00.

—**Criminal.** Repr. of 1890 ed. AMS Press. $12.50.

—**The Criminal.** 1977. Repr. of 1916 ed. Longwood Press. $25.00.

Elwood, Roger. **Salvation Behind Bars.** 1977. pap. Belmont Tower. $1.50.

Farr, Robert. **The Electronic Criminals.** McGraw-Hill. (OP). $9.95.

Farson, Daniel. **Jack the Ripper.** (Illus.). 1972. International Pubns. Service. $12.50.

Feldman, M. Philip. **Criminal Behaviour: A Psychological Analysis.** 1977. Wiley, John & Sons, Inc. $63.50.

Felstead, Sidney T. **Famous Criminals and Their Trials.** Repr. of 1926. ed. Ridgeway Books. $20.00.

Ferri, Enrico. **Criminal Sociology.** 1967. Repr. of 1917 ed. Agathon. $18.50.

—**Criminal Sociology.** 1900. Quality Lib. $20.00.

Field, Xenia. **Under Lock and Key.** 1970. International Pubns. Service. (OP). $7.50.

Flynn, Edith E. & Conrad, John P., eds. **The New and the Old Criminology.** 1978. Praeger. $23.95

Fox, Vernon. **Introduction to Criminology.** (Illus.). 1975. Prentice-Hall. $15.95.

Foxe, Arthur N. **Advanced Studies in Criminology.** 1972. Tunbridge. (OP). $4.75.

Fraser, Gordon. **Modern Transportation and International Crime.** (Illus.). 1970. C.C. Thomas. (OP). $7.00.

Galliher, John F. & McCartney, James. **Criminology: Power, Crime and Criminal Law.** 1977. Dorsey. $14.95.

Garcia, Ector. **Portraits of Crime.** (Illus.). 1977. pap. Condor Pub. Company. $2.25.

Gardiner, John & Mulkey, Michael, eds. **Crime and Criminal Justice.** 1974. pap. Policy Studies. $3.00.

Gardiner, John A.& Mulkey, Michael A., eds. **Crime and Criminal Justice: Issues in Public Policy Analysis.** 1977. Heath. $6.95.

Garfield, Brian, ed. **I, Witness.** 1978. Times Books. $9.95.

Garofalo, Raffaele. **Criminology.** Millar, Robert W., tr. 1968. Repr. of 1914 ed. Patterson Smith. $20.00.

Geis, Gilbert & Bloch, Herbert A. **Man, Crime and Society: The Forms of Criminal Behavior.** 2nd ed. 1962. Random House. $13.95.

Gelb, Barbara. **On the Track of Murder: Behind the Scenes with a Homicide Commando Squad.** 1975. Morrow. (OP). $8.95.

Georges, Daniel E. **The Geography of Crime and Violence: A Spatial and Ecological Perspective.** Natoli, Salvatore, ed. 1978. Assn. Am. Geographers. $3.50.

Gibbens, Trevor C. & Ahrenfeldt, Robert H. **Cultural Factors in Delinquency.** 1966. Lippincott. (OP). $6.00; pap. $2.75.

Gibbons, Don C. **Society, Crime and Criminal Careers.** 3rd ed. (Illus.). 1977. Prentice-Hall. $17.95.

Gibbs, Jack P. **Crime, Punishment and Deterrence.** 1975. Elsevier-North Holland Pub. Co. $13.95.

Gillin, John L. **Criminology and Penology.** 3rd. ed. (Illus). 1972. Repr. of 1945 ed. Greenwood Press. $40.00.

—**Criminology and Penology.** 1926. Norwood Editions. $20.00.

—**Taming the Criminal: Adventures in Penology.** (Illus). 1969. Repr. of 1931 ed. Patterson Smith. $12.00.

Glaser, Daniel, ed. **Handbook of Criminology.** 1974. Rand McNally & Co. $45.00.

Glass, Bill & Bauer, Fred. **Free at Last.** 1976. Word Books. $5.95.

Glueck, Sheldon S. **Crime and Correction.** 1952. Kraus Reprint. $20.00.

Glueck, Sheldon S. & Glueck, Eleanor T., eds. **Preventing Crime, a Symposium.** 1936. Kraus Reprint. $25.00.

Goldsmith, Jack & Goldsmith, Sharon. **Crime and the Elderly.** (Illus). 1976. Lexington Books. $18.50.

Gooderson, Richard. **Alibi.** 1977. Heinemann Ed. $39.95.

Goodman, Jonathan, ed. **The Trial of Ian Brady and Myra Hindley.** (Illus). 1973. David & Charles. $14.50.

Greenland Criminal Code. 1970. Rothman. $5.95.

Grex, Leo. **Mystery Stranger Than Fiction.** 1980. St. Martin. $10.95.

Grunhut, Max. **Penal Reform: A Comparative Study.** 1972. Rep. of 1948 ed. Patterson Smith. $18.00.

Guenther, Anthony L., ed. **Criminal Behavior and Social Systems.** 2nd ed. 1976. Rand McNally & Co. $10.95.

Gurr, Ted R. **Rogues, Rebels and Reformers: A Political History of Urban Crime and Conflict.** (Illus). 1976. Sage. $18.00; pap. $8.95.

Gurr, Ted & Grabosky. **The Politics of Crime and Conflict: A Comparative History of Four Cities.** 1977. Sage. $37.50.

Guttmacher, Manfred S. **Mind of the Murderer.** 1973. Repr. of 1960 ed. Books for Libs. $14.00.

—**Mind of the Murderer.** 1973. Repr. of 1960 ed. Arno Press. $17.00.

Hall, Arthur C. **Crime in Its Relations to Social Progress.** 1968. Repr. of 1902 ed. AMS Press. $27.50.

Hall, James P. **Peacekeeping in America: A Developmental Study of American Law Enforcement: Philosophy and Systems.** 1978. pap. Kendall-Hunt. $8.95.

Halleck,Seymour & Bromberg, Walter. **Psychiatric Aspects of Criminology.** 1968. pap. C.C. Thomas. $9.50.

Harmachea, Carroll R. **Sourcebook in Criminalistics.** (Illus). 1973. Reston, (OP). $11.50.

Harries, Keith D. **Crime and the Environment.** (Illus). 1979. C.C. Thomas. $14.00.

—**The Geography of Crime and Justice.** (Illus). 1974. McGraw-Hill. (OP). $7.95; pap. $4.95.

Hartjen, Clayton. **Crime and Criminalization.** 1978. Praeger. $8.00; pap. $6.95.

Hartjen, Clayton A. **Crime and Criminalization.** 2nd ed. 1978. Holt, Rinehart & Winston. $7.50.

—**Crime and Criminalization** 1978. Repr. of 1974 ed. Krieger. $11.95.

Haskell, Martin R. & Yablonsky, Lewis. **Criminology: Crime and Criminality.** 1977. Rand McNally & Co. $16.50; pap. $12.50.

—**Crime and Delinquency.** 3rd ed. 1978. Rand McNally & Co. $17.50.

Haycraft, Howard. **Murder for Pleasure.** 1941. Biblo & Tannen Booksellers & Pubs. $13.50.

Heaps, Willard. A. **Assassination: A Special Kind of Murder.** 1969. Hawthorn. (OP). $5.95.

Hirsch, Richard. **Crimes That Shook the World.** facs. ed. 1949. Books for Libs. $19.00.

Hood, Roger & Sparks, Richard. **Key Issues in Criminology.** (Illus). McGraw-Hill. $4.95; pap. $3.95.

Horgan, J.J. **Criminal Investigation.** 1974. McGraw-Hill. $15.50.

Hudson, Joe & Galaway, Burton. **Considering the Victim: Readings in Restitution and Victim Compensation.** 1975. C.C. Thomas. $34.00.

Ianni, Francis A. & Ianni, Elizabeth R. **A Family Business: Kinship and Social Control in Organized Crime.** 1973. pap. NAL (OP). pap. $1.50.

—**A Family Business: Kinship and Social Control in Organized Crime.** 1972. Russell Sage. $8.50.

Inciardi, J.A. **Reflections on Crime.** 1978. pap. Holt, Rinehart & Winston. $6.95.

Inciardi, James A. **Careers in Crime.** 1975. pap. Rand McNally & Co. $8.50.

Inciardi, James A. & Hass, Kenneth C. **Crime and the Criminal Justice Process.** 1978. pap. Kendall-Hunt. $10.95.

Inciardi, James A., et al. **Historical Approaches to Crime: Research Strategies and Issues.** (Illus). 1977. Sage $18.00; pap. $8.95.

Ingersoll, Robert G. **Crimes Against Criminals.** rev. ed. 1974. Gordon Press. $59.95.

Ives, George. **History of Penal Methods: Criminals, Witches and Lunatics.** 1970. Repr. of 1914 ed. Patterson Smith. $15.00.

Jackson, Bruce. **In the Life: Versions of the Criminal Experience.** 1974. pap. NAL. (OP). $1.95.

Jacobs, Jerry. **Getting By: Illustrations of Marginal Living.** 1972. pap. Little, Brown & Co. (OP). $4.95.

Jeffery, C.R. **Biology and Crime.** (Illus). 1979. Sage $12.95; pap. $6.50.

Joey & Fischer, Dave. **Killer: Autobiography of a Hit Man for the Mafia.** 1973. Playboy. (OP). $8.95.

Johnson, Elmer H. **Crime, Correction, and Society.** 4th ed. 1978. Dorsey. $15.95.

Johnson, Ray D. & McCormick, Mona. **Too Dangerous to Be at Large.** 1975. Times Books. $6.95.

Johnston, Norman, et al. **Sociology of Punishment and Correction.** 2nd ed. 1970. pap. Wiley, John & Sons, Inc. $18.50.

Kahn, Joan. **Edge of the Chair.** 1967. Harper & Row. $13.50.

Kaplan, Lawrence J. & Kessler, Dennis. **An Economic Analysis of Crime: Selected Readings.** (Illus). 1976. C.C. Thomas. $20.25; pap. $16.50.

Keane, Christopher. **The Hunter: Tales of a Different Papa.** 1976. Arbor House. $8.95.

Kiester, Edwin, Jr. **Crimes with No Victims: How Legislating Morality Defeats the Cause of Justice.** 1972. American Jewish Committee. $1.00.

Kinton, J. **Criminology Tomorrow.** 1974. pap. Social Science & Sociological Resources. $5.95.

Kinton, J., ed. **Criminology, Law Enforcement and Offender Treatment: A Sourcebook for the 1970's.** 1980. Social Science & Sociological Resources.

Kirk, Paul L & Bradford, Lowell W. **The Crime Laboratory: Organization and Operation.** 132p. 1972. C.C. Thomas. $7.75.

Klare, H.J., ed. **Changing Concepts of Crime and Its Treatment.** 1967. Pergamon. (OP). $13.25.

Klare, H.J. & Haxby, D., eds. **Frontiers of Criminology.** 1967. Pergamon. $17.50.

Klasner, Lily. **My Girlhood Among Outlaws.** Ball, Eve, ed. 1972. pap. University of Arizona Press. $7.50.

Klockars, Carl B. **The Professional Fence.** 1974. pap. Free Press. $8.95.

Knudten, Richard D. **Crime, Criminology, and Contemporary Society.** 1970. pap. Dorsey. (OP). $6.95.

Krisberg, Barry. **Crime and Privilege.** 1975. Prentice-Hall. $8.95; pap. $3.45.

Larson, John A., et al. **Lying and Its Detection, a Study of Deception and Deception Tests.** 1969. Repr. of 1932 ed. Patterson Smith. $17.50.

Lemert, Edwin M. & Dill, Forrest. **Offenders in the Community.** 1978. Lexington Books. $18.95.

Leonard, V.A. **Police Crime Prevention.** 1972. C.C. Thomas. $12.50.

—**The Police, The Judiciary, and the Criminal.** (Illus). 320p. 1975. C.C. Thomas $17.50.

Leopold, Nathan F., Jr. **Life Plus Ninety-Nine Years.** 1974. Repr. of 1958 ed. Greenwood Press. $22.25.

Lepera, Patsy A. & Goodman, Walter. **Memoirs of a Scam Man: The Life and Deals of Patsy Anthony Lepera.** 1974. Farrer, Straus, & Giroux. (OP). $7.95.

Letkemann, Peter. **Crime As Work.** (Illus.) 1973. pap. Prentice-Hall. $2.95.

Levine, Felice J. & Tapp, June L. **The Psychology of Criminal Identification: The Gap from Wade to Kirby.** 1973. pap. American Bar Association. $2.00.

Lipman, Ira. **How to Protect Yourself from Crime.** (Illus.). 1975. Atheneum. (OP). $9.95.

Lombroso, Cesare. **Crime, Its Causes and Remedies.** Horton, Henry P., tr. 1968. Repr. of 1911 ed. Patterson Smith. $22.50.

—**The Physiology and Psychology of Crime.** (Illus.). 1980. American Institute for Psychological Research. $49.85.

Lombroso-Ferrero, Gina & Savitz, Leonard D. **Criminal Man: According to the Classification of Cesare Lombroso.** (Illus). 1972. Patterson Smith. $14.00; pap. $4.50.

Lunden, Walter A. **Crimes and Criminals.** facs. ed. 1967. pap. Iowa State University Press. $11.25.

Lustgarten, Edgar. **The Illustrated Story of Crime.** (Illus.). 1976. Follett. (OP). $7.95.

—**The Illustrated Story of Crime** (Illus.). 1977. pap. Barnes & Noble. $4.95.

MacDonald, Arthur. **Criminological Literature.** Repr. of 1890 ed. AMS Press. (OP). $10.00.

—**Criminology.** Repr. of 1893 ed. AMS Press. $34.50.

Mack, John A. & Kerner, Hans-Jurgen. **The Crime Industry.** 1979. Lexington Books. $17.50.

McCabe, Sarah & Sutcliffe, Frank. **Defining Crime.** 1978. pap. Biblio Distribution Center. $6.00.

McDade, Thomas M. **Annals of Murder: A Bibliography of Books and Pamphlets on American Murders from Colonial Times to 1900.** (Illus.). 1961. Patterson Smith. (OP). $20.00.

McKnight, Gerald. **Computer Crime: How a New Breed of Criminals Is Making off with Millions.** 1974. Walker & Co. (OP). $6.95.

McPheters, Lee R. & Stronge, William B. **The Economics of Crime and Law Enforcement.** (Illus.). 1976. C.C. Thomas. $22.75.

Maiken, Peter. **Ripoff: How to Spot It, How to Avoid It.** 1979. Andrews & McMeel. $12.95; pap. $5.95.

Maine, Charles E. **World's Strangest Crimes.** 1970. pap. Pocket Books. $0.75.

Malinowski, Bromislaw. **Crime and Custom in Savage Society.** 1976. pap. Littlefield. $2.50.

Mannheim, Hermann. **Comparative Criminology: A Text Book,** 2 vols. 1970. Repr. of 1965 ed. Routledge & Kegan. $22.00 each.

Marland, Nigel. **An International Pattern of Murder.** 1978. State Mutual Book & Periodical Service. $9.95.

Marsh, Thomas O. **Roots of Crime.** 1980. Nellen Publishing. $10.00.

Martin, J.P. & Webster, D. **Social Consequences of Conviction.** (Illus.). 1971. Humanities Press. $20.95.

Maurer, David W. **The American Confidence Man.** 1974. C.C. Thomas. $15.25; pap. $8.00.

Mays, John B. **Crime and Its Treatment.** 2nd ed. Craft, Maurice, ed. 1975. pap. Longman. (OP). $4.50.

Megargee, Edwin I., et al. **Classifying Criminal Offenders: A New System Based on the MMPI.** 1980. Sage. $18.00.

Meier, Robert F., ed. **Theoretical Concerns in Criminology: Contemporary Views.** 1977. Sage. $12.95; pap. $6.50.

Merklin, Lewis, Jr. **They Chose Honor: The Problem of Conscience in Custody.** 1974. Harper & Row. $8.95.

Messinger, Sheldon L. & Bittner, Egon, eds. **Criminology Review Yearbook.** Vol. 1 (Illus.). 1979. Sage. $35.00.

Michael, Jerome & Adler, Mortimer J. **Crime Law and Social Science.** 1971. Repr. of 1933 ed. Patterson Smith. $15.00.

Miller, Gale. **Odd Jobs: The World of Deviant Work.** 1978. Prentice-Hall. $12.95; pap. $4.95.

Morley, Jackson & Hyde, H. Montgomery, eds. **Crimes and Punishment.** 20 vols. (Illus.). 1976. Symphonette Press. (OP). $109.50.

Morris, Norval & Hawkins, Gordon. **Honest Politicians Guide to Crime Control.** 1970. U. of Chicago Press. $12.50.

Mueller, Gerhard O. **Essays in Criminal Science.** 1960. Rothman. $10.00.

Nelson, A.T. & Smith, Howard E. **Car Clouting: The Crime, the Criminal and the Police.** (Illus.). 1958. C.C. Thomas. $6.00.

Nettler, Gwynn. **Explaining Crime.** (Illus.). 1977. McGraw-Hill. $8.95; pap. $10.95.

Newman, Graeme, ed. **Crime and Deviance: A Comparative Perspective.** (Sage Annual Reviews of Studies in Deviance: Vol 4). (Illus.). 1980. Sage. $20.00; pap. $9.95.

Niederhoffer, A. & Blumberg, A.S. **The Ambivalent Force.** 2nd ed. 1976. pap. Holt, Rinehart & Winston. (Dryden Press.) $7.95.

Nietzel, Michael. **Crime and Its Modification: A Social Learning Perspective.** (Illus.). 1979. Pergamon Press. $30.00; pap. $9.75.

O'Brien, Kevin P. & Sullivan, Robert C. **Criminalistics: Theory and Practice.** 3rd ed. 1980. Holbrook. $16.95.

O'Brien, William J. **Crime-Punishment—Parole.** Vantage. (OP) $3.50.

Olson, Sheldon R. **Issues in the Sociology of Criminal Justice.** 1975. pap. Bobbs-Merrill. $2.25.

Parsons, Philip A. **Responsibility for Crime: An Investigation of the Nature and Causes of Crime and a Means of Its Prevention.** 1968. Repr. of 1909 ed. AMS Press. $16.50.

Pelfrey, William V. **The Evolution of Criminology.** 1980. pap. Anderson Pub. Co. $8.95.

Pepinsky, Harold E. **Crime and Conflict.** 1976. Academic Press. $25.00.

Phillip, Alban M. **Prison-Breakers: A Book of Escapes from Captivity.** (Illus.). 1971. Repr. of 1927 ed. Gale Research Co. $14.00.

Phillipson, Michael. **Sociological Aspects of Crime and Delinquency.** 1971. pap. Routledge & Kegan. $2.75.

—**Understanding Crime and Delinquency: A Sociological Introduction.** 1974. Aldine. $7.50; pap. $2.95.

Pinkerton, Allan. **Criminal Reminiscences and Detective Sketches.** 1879. Repr. Somerset Publishing. $19.00.

Platnick, Kenneth B. **Great Mysteries of History.** 1973. pap. Harper & Row. $1.95.

Powis, David. **The Signs of Crime: A Field of Manual for Police.** 1978. pap. John Jay Press. pap. $5.95.

Prins, Herschel. **Criminal Behaviour: An Introduction to Its Causes and Treatment.** 1974. pap. Beekman Pubs. $6.95.

Pyle, Gerald F., et al. **The Spatial Dynamics of Crime.** (Illus.). 1974. University of Chicago, Dept. of Geography, Research Papers. $8.00.

Quinney, Richard. **Crime and Justice in Society.** 1969. pap. Little, Brown & Co. (OP) $6.95.

—**Problem of Crime.** (Illus.). 1970. pap. Harper & Row. (OP). $5.95.

—**Class, State, and Crime: On the Theory and Practice of Criminal Justice.** 1977. Longman. $8.95; pap. $4.95.

Quinney, Richard & Wildeman, John. **The Problem of Crime: A Critical Introduction to Criminology.** 2nd ed. 1977. pap. Harper & Row. $11.50.

Radzinowicz, Leon. **Ideology and Crime.** 1966. Columbia University Press. $13.50.

Radzinowicz, Leon & Wolfgang, Marvin E., eds. **Crime and Justice.** 3 vols. 1977. Basic Books. set $72.00.

—**Crime and Justice, Vol. 1: The Criminal in Society.** 1977. pap. Basic Books. $9.95.

—**Crime and Justice, Vol. 2: The Criminal in the Arms of the Law.** 1977. pap. Basic Books. $7.95.

—**Crime and Justice, Vol. 3: The Criminal in Confinement.** 1977. pap. Basic Books. $7.95.

Radzinowicz, Sir Leon. **The Growth of Crime: The International Experience.** 1977. Basic Books. $11.95.

Rao, S. Venugopal. **Crime in Our Society.** 1980. Advent Books. $15.00.

Reckless, Walter C. **American Criminology: New Directions.** (Illus.). 1973. Prentice-Hall. (OP). $12.95.

—**The Crime Problem.** 4th ed. 1967. Prentice-Hall. (OP). $9.10.

Reid, S.T. **Crime and Criminology.** 1979. Holt, Rinehart & Winston. $14.95.

Rennie, Ysabel. **The Search for Criminal Man.** 1978. Lexington Books. $20.95.

Reppetto, Thomas A. **Residential Crime.** 1974. Ballinger Publishing. $16.50.

Rhodes, Robert P. **The Insoluble Problems of Crime.** 1977. Wiley, John & Sons, Inc. $10.95.

Riedel, Marc & Thornberry, Terrence P., eds. **Crime and Delinquency: Dimensions of Deviance.** (Illus.). 1974. Praeger. (OP). $16.50.

Roebuck, Julian B. **Criminal Typology: The Legalistic, Physical—Constitutional—Hereditary—Psychological—Psychiatric and Sociological Approaches.** 1971. C.C. Thomas. (OP). $13.50.

Rogers, A.J. **Economics of Crime.** 1973. pap. Holt, Rinehart & Winston. $3.95.

Rottenberg, Simon, ed. **Economics of Crime and Punishment.** 1973. American Enterprise Institute for Public Policy Research. $8.50; pap. $4.00.

Roucek, Joseph S., ed. **Sociology of Crime.** Repr. of 1961 ed. Greenwood Press. $23.95.

Rusche, Georg & Kirchheimer, Otto. **Punishment and Social Structure.** Finkelstein, M.I. & Kirchheimer, Otto, trs. (Illus.). 1968. Repr. of 1939 ed. Russell. $23.00.

Saferstein, Richard. **Criminalistics: An Introduction to Forensic Science.** (Illus.).

1981. Prentice-Hall. $18.95.

Sagarin, Edward, ed. **Criminology: New Concerns.** (Illus.). 1979. Sage. $18.95; pap. $9.95.

Saleilles, Raymond. **Individualization of Punishment.** Jastrow, Rachel S., tr. 1968. Repr. of 1911 ed. Patterson Smith. $17.50.

Sandhu, Harjit S. **Modern Corrections: The Offenders, Therapies and Community Reintegration.** (Illus.). 1978. C.C. Thomas. $14.00. pap. $11.50.

Savitz, Leonard D. **Dilemmas in Criminology.** 1967. pap. McGraw-Hill. $6.95.

Schacter, Stanley. **Emotion, Obesity and Crime.** 1971. Academic Press. $19.50.

Schafer, Stephen. **Introduction to Criminology.** 1976. Reston. $13.95.

—**Readings in Contemporary Criminology.** 1976. pap. Reston. $9.50.

—**Theories in Criminology.** 1969. Random House. (OP). $9.95.

Scott, John & Miller, Nicholas, eds. **Crime and the Responsible Community.** 160p. 1980. pap. Eerdmans. $6.95.

Sellin, Thorsten, ed. **Police and the Crime Problem.** 1971. Repr. of 1929 ed. Arno Press. $15.00.

Selmier, Dean & Kram, Mark. **Blow Away.** 1979. Viking Press. $9.95.

Shaw, George B. **Crime of Imprisonment.** Repr. of 1946 ed. Greenwood Press. $11.00.

Sheley, Joseph F. **Understanding Crime.** 1979. pap. Wadsworth Publishing. $10.95.

Short, James F., Jr., **Delinquency, Crime, and Society.** 1976. University of Chicago Press. (OP). $15.00.

—**Delinquency, Crime and Society.** 1978. pap. University of Chicago Press. $5.95.

Silver, I., intro. by. **Challenge of Crime in a Free Society.** pap. Avon. (OP). $2.45.

Simon, Rita J. **Women and Crime.** 1975. Lexington Books. $14.50.

Skogan, Wesley G. & Klecka, William R. **Setups: The Fear of Crime.** 1977. pap. American Enterprise Institute for Public Policy Research. $3.50.

Smith, A.B. **Crime and Justice.** (Dryden Press). 1973. Holt, Reinhart & Winston. $9.95.

Stebbins, Robert A. **Commitment to Deviance: The Nonprofessional Criminal in the Community.** 1971. Greenwood Press. $12.75; pap. $4.95.

Stirling, Nora. **Your Money or Your Life.** 1974. Bobbs-Merrill. (OP). $7.95.

Sutherland, Edwin H. **On Analyzing Crime.** Schuessler, Karl, ed. 1973. University of Chicago Press. $15.00.

—**On Analyzing Crime.** Schuessler, Karl, ed. 1974. pap. University of Chicago Press. $2.95.

Sutherland, Edwin H. & Cressey, Donald R. **Criminology.** 10th ed. 1978. Lippincott. $14.95.

Sykes, Gresham M. **Crime and Society.** 2nd ed. Peter Smith. $7.50.

—**Crime and Society.** 2nd ed. 1967. pap. Random House. $3.95.

Sylvester, Sawyer F. **The Heritage of Modern Criminology.** (Illus.). 1972. Schenkman. (OP). $5.95; pap. $3.95.

Sylvester, Sawyer F., Jr. **Heritage of Modern Criminology.** 1972. General Learn Press. (OP). $8.95; pap. $4.25.

Sylvester, Sawyer F., Jr. & Sagarin, Edward, eds. **Politics and Crime.** 1974. (Illus.). Praeger. (OP). $12.50.

Szabo, Denis & Katzenelson, Susan, eds. **Offenders and Corrections.** 1978. Praeger. $21.95.

Tabori, Paul. **Crime and the Occult.** 1974. Taplinger. $8.95.

Taft, Donald R. & England, R. W., Jr. **Criminology.** 4th ed. 1964. Macmillan. $14.95.

Talbitzer, W.M. **Too Much Blood.** 1979. Vantage Press. $8.95.

Tappan, Paul W. **Crime, Justice and Correction.** 1960. McGraw-Hill. $14.95.

Taylor Ian, et al. **Critical Criminology.** 1975. Routledge & Kegan. $21.00; pap. $8.95.

—**The New Criminology: For a Social Theory of Deviance.** 1973. Routledge & Kegan. $19.95.

Thomas, William I., et al. **Old World Traits Transplanted.** 1975. pap. Patterson Smith. $4.75.

Thompson, Thomas. **Serpentine.** 1979. Doubleday. $12.95.

Top Investigative Journalists. The World's Greatest Rip-Offs. Rose, Colin, ed. 1978. Sterling. $7.95; bdg. $8.39.

Tulchin, Simon H. **Intelligence and Crime: A Study of Penitentiary and Reformatory Offenders.** 1974. pap. University of Chicago Press. $7.00.

Vetter, Harold J. & Wright, Jack, Jr. **Introduction to Criminology.** (Illus.). 1977. C.C. Thomas. $17.50.

Von Hentig, Hans. **The Criminal and His Victim: Studies in the Sociobiology of Crime.** 1979. pap. Schocken Books. $8.95.

Wade, John. **A Treatise on the Police and Crimes of the Metropolis.** 1972. Repr. of 1829 ed. Patterson Smith. $15.00.

Walker, Nigel. **Behavior and Misbehavior: Explanations and Non-Explanations.** 1977. Basic Books. $12.95.

Warden, Bob & Groves, Martha, eds. **Murder Most Foul: And Other Great Crime Stories from the World Press.** 1979. Swallow. $15.00.

Warner, Sam B. **Crime and Criminal Statistics in Boston.** 1974. Repr. Arno Press. $11.00.

Weisser, Michael. **Crime and Punishment in Early Modern Europe.** 1979. Humanities Press. $22.00.

Weppner, Robert S., ed. **Street Ethnography: Selected Studies of Crime and Drug Use in Natural Settings.** 1977. Sage. $18.50; pap. $8.95.

Whibley, Charles. **Book of Scoundrels.** Repr. of 1912 ed. Arno Press. $15.00.

White, Bertha R. **Crimes and Penalties.** 2nd ed. 1970. Oceana. $5.95.

Wickman, Paul M. & Whitten, Philip. **Readings in Criminology.** 1978. pap. Heath. $8.95.

Wiles, Paul, ed. **The Sociology of Crime: The New Criminologies.** 1977. Barnes & Noble. $14.00.

Williams, Vergil L. **Dictionary of American Penology: An Introductory Guide.** 1979. Greenwood Press. $29.95.

Willwerth, James. **Jones: Portrait of a Mugger.** 1974. M. Evans. $7.95.

Wilmer, M.A. **Crime and Information Theory.** 1970. Edinburgh Univ. (OP). $8.75.

Wilson & Brown, J.W. **Crime and the Community.** 1973. U. of Queensland Press. $9.00; pap. $6.00.

Wilson, James Q. **Thinking About Crime.** 1977. pap. Random House. $1.95.

Wilson, Patrick. **Children Who Kill.** 1974. Transatlantic Arts, Inc. $12.00.

Wines, Frederick H. **Punishment and Reformation: A Study of the Penitentiary System.** 1975. Repr. of 1919 ed. AMS Press. $30.00.

Winslow. **Crime in a Free Society.** 3rd ed. 1977. pap. Dickenson. $12.95.

Winslow, Robert W. & Winslow, Virginia. **Deviant Reality: Alternative World Views.** 1974. pap.

Allyn. (OP). $5.95.

Wolfgang, Marvin. **Patterns in Criminal Homicide.** 1975. Patterson Smith. $14.00.

Wolfgang, Marvin E. & Ferracuti, F. **Subculture of Violence: Towards an Integrated Theory in Criminology.** 1967. pap. Barnes & Noble. (OP). $8.50.

Wolfgang, Marvin E., et al. **Sociology of Crime and Delinquency.** 2nd ed. 1970. Wiley, John & Sons, Inc. pap. $15.95.

—**Criminology Evaluation.** 1978. Elsevier-North Holland Publishing Co. $27.50.

—**Criminology Index: Research and Theory in Criminology in the United States, 1945-1972.** 2 vols. Vols. 1 & 2. 1975. Elsevier-North Holland Publishing Co. Set. $70.00.

Woodson, Robert L., ed. **Black Perspectives on Crime and the Criminal Justice System.** 1977. G.K. Hall. $15.00.

Wootton, Barbara. **Crime and Penal Policy.** 1978. Allen Unwin. $16.50; pap. $8.95.

Zenk, Gordon K. **Project SEARCH: The Struggle for Control of Criminal Information in America.** (Illus.). 1979. Greenwood Press. $16.95.

Ziegenhagen, Eduard A. **Victims, Crime and Social Control.** 1977. Praeger. $17.50.

CRIME AND CRIMINALS— ADDRESSES, ESSAYS, LECTURES

Anderson, Robert. **Criminals and Crime: Some Facts and Suggestions.** 1976. Repr. of 1907 ed. Scholarly Press. (OP) $12.00.

Barnett, Randy E. & Hagel, John, eds. **Assessing the Criminals: Restitution, Retribution and the Legal Process.** 1977. Ballinger Pub. $18.50.

Bender, David L. & McCuen, Gary E., eds. **Crime and Criminals: Opposing Viewpoints.** 1977. Greenhaven. $11.95; pap. $5.00.

Bloch, Herbert A. **Crime in America.** 1961. Philosophical Library. $6.00.

Chang, et al. **The Fundamentals of Criminal Justice: A Syllabus and Workbook.** 1977. Paladin House. $12.95.

Cull, John G. & Hardy, Richard E. **Fundamentals of Criminal Behavior and Correctional Systems.** (Illus.). 1973. C.C. Thomas. $15.00.

Douglas Jack D., ed. **Crime and Justice in American Society.** 1971. pap. Bobbs-Merrill. $5.65.

Dressler, David. **Readings in Criminology and Penology.** 2nd ed. 1972. pap. Columbia University Press. $11.00.

Eldefonso, Edward. **Readings in Criminal Justice.** 1973. Glencoe. $7.95.

Hawes, Joseph, ed. **Law and Order in American History.** 1979. Kennikat. $15.00.

Henshel, Richard L. & Silverman, Robert A. **Perception in Criminology.** 1975. Columbia University Press. $22.50; pap. $5.00.

Kelly, Delos H., ed. **Criminal Behavior: Readings in Criminology.** 1980. St. Martin's Press. $16.95; pap. $9.95.

Mannheim, Hermann. **Group Problems in Crime and Punishment.** 2nd ed. 1972. Patterson Smith. $14.00.

Mednick, Sarnoff A. and Shoham, Shlomo, eds., **New Paths in Criminology.** 1979. Lexington Books. $20.95.

Morland, Nigel, ed. **The Criminologist.** (Illus.). 1972. Open Court. $17.50.

Oatman, Eric F., ed. **Crime and Society.** 1979. Wilson. $5.75.

Quincy, H. Keith. **The Seamy Side of Government: Essays on Punishment and Coercion.** 1979. pap. University Press of America. $7.25.

Radzinowicz, Sir Leon & Wolfgang, Marvin E., eds. **Crime and Justice.** 3 vols. 2nd rev. ed. 1977. Basic Books. Vol. 1. $25.00; Vol. 2. $25.00; Vol. 3. $19.50; Set. $72.00; Vol. 1. pap. $9.95; Vol. 2. pap. $7.95; Vol. 3 pap. $7.95.

Reasons, Charles E., ed. **The Criminologist: Crime and the Criminal.** 1974. pap. Goodyear. $8.95.

Schafer, Stephen & Knudten, Richard D., eds. **Criminological Theory.** 1977. Lexington Books. $21.00.

Silver, Isidore. **A National Strategy to Reduce Crime.** 1975. pap. Avon. (OP). $2.65.

Stewart, Leland & Clarke, Wentworth. **Crime.** (Illus.). 1971. pap. John Day. (OP). $2.95.

Thornberry, Terrence P. & Sagarin, Edward, eds. **Images of Crime: Offenders and Victims.** (Illus.). 1974. Praeger. $17.95.

Voss, Harwin L. & Petersen, David M., eds. **Ecology, Crime and Delinquency.** 1971. pap. Prentice-Hall. $5.95.

Wilson, James Q. **Thinking About Crime.** 1975. Basic Books. $12.50.

CRIME AND CRIMINALS— BIBLIOGRAPHY

Cumming, John. **Contribution Towards a Bibliography Dealing with Crime and Cognate Subjects.** 3rd ed. 1970. Repr. of 1935 ed. Patterson Smith. $8.50.

Davis, Bruce L., compiled by. **Criminological Bibliographies: Uniform Citations to Bibliographies, Indexes, and Review Articles of the Literature of Crime Study in the United States.** 1978. Greenwood Press. $17.50.

Hewitt, William H. **Bibliography of Police Administration, Public Safety and Criminology.** 1967. C.C. Thomas. (OP). $13.75.

Kinton, J. **Criminology and Criminal Justice in America: A Guide to the Literature.** 1978. Social Science & Sociological Resources. $3.95.

Kinton, Jack. **Criminology, Law Enforcement and Offender Treatment.** rev. ed. 1980. Social Science & Sociological Resources.

Kuhlman, Augustus F. **Guide to Material on Crime and Criminal Justice.** 1969. Repr. of 1929 ed. Patterson Smith. $22.50.

Prostano, Emanuel T. & Piccirillo, Martin L. **Law Enforcement: A Selective Bibliography.** 1974. Libraries Unlimited. $13.50.

Radzinowicz, Leon & Hood, Roger. **Criminology and the Administration of Criminal Justice: A Bibliography.** 1976. Greenwood Press. $32.50.

CRIME AND CRIMINALS— BIOGRAPHY

Altman, Larry. **The Call of the Cricket.** 1978. pap. Celestial Arts. $4.95.

Asinov, Eliot. **The Fox Is Crazy Too.** 1979. pap. Pocket Books. $2.25.

Atkins, Susan & Slosser, Bob. **Child of Satan, Child of God.** (Illus.). 1978. pap. Bantam Books. $1.95.

Berkman, Alexander. **Prison Memoirs of an Anarchist.** (Illus.). 1970. Frontier Press Calif. $8.50; pap. $3.50.

Brannon, W.T. **The Con Game and "Yellow Kid" Weil: The Autobiography of the Famous Con Artist.** (Illus.). Peter Smith. $6.75.

Franke, David. **The Torture Doctor: The Incredible but True Story of Herman W. Mudgett, the Most Fiendish Killer in the Annals of American Crime.** 1975. Hawthorn. (OP). $8.95.

Irving, Henry B. **A Book of Remarkable Criminals.** 1975. Repr. of 1918 ed. Hyperion Press. $15.00.

MacClure, Victor. **She Stands Accused: Being a Series of Accounts of the Lives and Deeds of Notorious Women Murderesses.** (Illus.). 1975. Repr. of 1935 ed. Hyperion Press. $14.00.

Martin, John B., as told to. **My Life in Crime: The Autobiography of a Professional Criminal.** Repr. of 1952 ed. Greenwood Press. $12.00.

Mendoza, Fay. **Portrait of a Con Man.** Vantage Press. (OP). $4.50.

Messick, Hank & Goldblatt, Burt. **Gangs and Gangsters.** 1974. pap. Ballantine. $2.00.

Messick, Hank & Nellis, Joseph L. **The Private Lives of Public Enemies.** 1973. Wyden Books. (OP). $6.95.

Nadeau, Remi. **The Real Joaquin Murietta.** Trans-Anglo Books. $10.00.

Nash, Jay R. **Bloodletters and Badmen: A Narrative Encyclopedia of American Criminals from the Pilgrims to the Present.** (Illus.). 1973. M. Evans. $16.95; pap. $7.95.

Rice, Robert. **The Business of Crime.** 1974. Repr. of 1956 ed. Greenwood Press. $14.75.

Rudensky, Morris R. & Riley, Don. **Gonif: Red Rudensky.** 1970. Piper. $7.95.

Sereny, Gitta. **The Case of Mary Bell.** 1973. McGraw-Hill. $7.95.

Wells, Charles K. **Life and Adventures of Polk Wells, the Notorious Outlaw.** facsimile ed. Repr. of 1907 ed. Arno Press. $19.00.

Wells, Charles K. **Life and Adventures of Polk Wells, the Notorious Outlaw.** (facs. ed.). Repr. of 1907 ed. Books for Libs. $19.00.

Williams, Roger, ed. **Super Crooks: A Rogue's Gallery of Famous Hustlers, Swindlers and Thieves.** (Illus.). 1973. Playboy. (OP). $8.95; pap. $1.50.

Willwerth, James. **Jones: Portrait of a Mugger.** 1976. pap. Fawcett World. (OP). $1.75.

—**Jones: Portrait of a Mugger.** 252p. 1974. M. Evans. $7.95.

Wolf, George & DiMona, Joseph. **Frank Costello: Prime Minister of the Underworld.** (Illus.). 1974. Morrow. (OP). $7.95.

Zimmerman, Isidore & Bond, Francis. **Punishment Without Crime.** 1973. pap. Manor Books. $1.25.

CRIME AND CRIMINALS—DATA PROCESSING

Marchand, Donald A. **The Politics of Privacy. Computers and Criminal Justice Records: Controlling the Social Cost of Technological Change.** 433p. 1980. Information Resources. $34.95.

Zenk, Gordon K. **Project SEARCH: The Struggle for Control of Criminal Information in America.** 1979. Greenwood Pres. $16.95.

CRIME AND CRIMINALS—IDENTIFICATION

Abbott, John R. **Footwear Evidence: The Examination, Identification and Comparison of Footwear Impressions.** (Illus.). 1964. pap. C.C. Thomas. $6.25.

Allison, Harrison C. **Personal Identification.** (Illus.). 1973. Holbrook. (OP). $15.95.

Bertillon, Alphonse. **Alphonse Bertillon's Instruction for Taking Descriptions for the Indentification of Criminals.** 1977. Repr. of 1889 ed. AMS Press. $19.00.

Block, Eugene. **Voiceprinting.** 1975. McKay. $9.95.

Borchard, Edwin M. **Convicting the Innocent: Errors of Criminal Justice.** 1970. Repr. of 1932 ed. Da Capo. $22.50.

Leonard, V.A. **Criminal Investigation and Identification.** (Illus.). 1971. C.C. Thomas. $9.25.

Moenssens, Andre. **Fingerprints and the Law.** Orig. Title: Fingerprint Identification and the Law. 1969. Chilton. (OP). $6.50.

Ringel, William E. **Identification and Police Line-Ups.** 1968. pap. Gould. $5.00.

Wall, Patrick M. **Eye-Witness Identification in Criminal Cases.** 1975. C.C. Thomas. $12.00.

Zavala, Albert & Paley, James J., eds. **Personal Appearance Identification.** (Illus.). 1972. pap. C.C. Thomas. $20.00.

CRIME AND CRIMINALS—STUDY AND TEACHING

McCall, George J. **Observing the Law: Field Methods in The Study of Crime and the Criminal Justice System.** (Illus.). 1978. Free Press. $15.95.

McLean, R.J. **Education For Crime Prevention and Control.** (Illus.). 168p. 1975. C.C. Thomas. $12.50.

Pitler, Robert M. **New York Criminal Practice under the CPL.** 1972. with 1976 suppl. Boardman. $50.00.

CRIME AND CRIMINALS—UNITED STATES

Abrahamsen, David. **Who Are the Guilty? Study of Education and Crime.** 1972. Repr. of 1952 ed. Greenwood Press. $16.25.

Albini, Joseph L. **American Mafia: Genesis of a Legend.** 1971. Irvington. $17.95; pap. $8.95.

Allen, Francis A. **Borderland of Criminal Justice: Essays in Law and Criminology.** 1964. University of Chicago Press. $7.50.

Allen, John. **Assault with a Deadly Weapon: Autobiography of a Street Criminal.** Kelly, Diane H. & Heymann, Philip, eds. 1977. Pantheon. $8.95.

—**Assault with a Deadly Weapon: The Autobiography of a Street Criminal.** Kelly, Dianne H. & Heyma, K., eds. 1978. pap. McGraw-Hill. $3.95.

American Friends Service Committee. **Struggle for Justice: A Report on Crime and Punishment in America.** 1971. Hill & Wang. $4.50; pap. $4.95.

Angelella, Michael. **Trail of Blood: A True Story.** 1979. Bobbs Merrill. $10.00.

Asbury, Herbert. **The French Quarter:** (Illus.). 1979. pap. Mockingbird Books. $2.25.

—**The Barbary Coast: An Informal History of the San Francisco Underworld.** (Illus.). 1968. pap. Putnam. (OP). $2.25.

—**Great Illusion: An Informal History of Prohibition.** (Illus.). 1968. Repr. of 1950 ed. Greenwood Press. $16.50.

—**Suckers Progress: An Informal History of Gambling in America from the Colonies to Canfield.** (Illus.). 1969. Repr. of 1938 ed. Patterson Smith. $17.50.

Balbus, Isaac D. **Dialectics of Legal Repression: Black Rebels Before the American Criminal Courts.** 1973. Russell Sage. $11.50.

Barnes, Harry E. **Repression of Crime. Studies in Historical Penology.** 1969. Repr. of 1926 ed. Patterson Smith. $14.00.

Bartholomew, Ed. **Jesse Evans.** 1955. Peter Wolff. (OP). $20.00.

—**Kill or Be Killed.** 1953. Peter Wolff. (OP). $20.00.

Beach, Walter G. **Oriental Crime in California.** (Illus.). 1972. Repr. of 1972 ed. AMS Press. $13.50.

Beeley, Arthur. **Bail System in Chicago.** 1965. Repr. of 1927 ed. University of Chicago Press. $8.00.

Bell, Arthur. **Kings Don't Mean a Thing.** 1979. pap. Berkley Publishing. $2.25.

—**Kings Don't Mean a Thing: The John Knight Murder Case.** 1978. Morrow. $8.95.

Betenson, Lula P. & Flack, Dora. **Butch Cassidy, My Brother.** 1976. pap. Penguin Books. $2.50.

Boyer, Brian. **Prince of Thieves: Memoirs of the World's Greatest Forger.** 1975. Dial. $8.95.

Braley, Malcom. **False Starts: A Memoir of San Quentin and Other Prisons.** 1976. Little, Brown & Co. (OP). $8.95.

Breslin, Jimmy & Schaap, Dick. **Forty-Four Caliber.** 1978. Viking Press. $9.95.

Burns, Robert E. **I Am a Fugitive from a Georgia Chain Gang.** 1972. Repr. of 1932 ed. Gale Research Co. $12.00.

Campbell, Helen. **Darkness and Daylight: Or, Lights and Shadows of New York Life: A Pictorial Record of Personal Experiences by Day and Night in the Great Metropolis with Hundreds of Thrilling Anecdotes and Incidents.** 1969. Repr. of 1895 ed. Gale Research Co. $20.00.

Carpozi, George, Jr. **Son of Sam: The 44 Caliber Killer.** 1977. pap. Manor Books. $2.25.

Chandler, Peleg W. **American Criminal Trials.** 2 vols. 1970. Repr. of 1844 ed. AMS Press. Set. $42.50.

Chang, Dae & Armstrong, Warren B., eds. **The Prison: Voices from the Inside.** 1972. Schenkman. $8.95; pap. $5.95.

Charles, St. **Narcotics Menace.** Borden. $3.00.

Chessman, Caryl. **Cell Twenty Four Fifty Five, Death Row.** Repr. of 1954 ed. Greenwood Press. $15.00.

Cho, Y.H. **Public Policy and Urban Crime.** 1974. Ballinger Pub. $17.50.

Christian, Charles. **Brief Treatise on the Police of the City of New York.** 1970. Repr. of 1812 ed. Arno Press. $10.00.

Clark, Ramsey. **Crime in America.** 1971. Simon & Schuster. (OP). $2.95.

—**Crime in America.** 1971. pap. Pocket Books. (OP). $1.95.

—**Crime in America: Its Nature, Causes, Control and Correction.** 1970. Simon & Schuster. (OP). $8.95.

Clark, Ramsey, ed. **Crime and Justice.** (Illus.). 1974. Arno Press. $35.00.

Clayton, Merle. **Union Station Massacre: The Shootout That Started the F.B.I.'s War on Crime.** (Illus.). 1975. Bobbs-Merrill. (OP). $8.95.

—**Union Station Massacre.** 1977. pap. Nordon Publishing. $1.50.

Clemmer, Donald. **The Prison Community.** 1958. pap. Irvington. $8.95.

Clinton, Henry L. **Extraordinary Cases.** Repr. of 1896 ed. Books for Libraries. $16.00.

Coblentz, Stanton A. **Villians and Vigilantes.** (Illus.). 1961. pap. A.S. Barnes. (OP). $1.95.

Cohen, Bruce J., ed. **Crime in America: Perspectives on Criminal and Delinquent Behavior.** 2nd ed. 1977. pap. Peacock Pubs. $9.95.

Conklin, John. **Illegal but Not Criminal: Business Crime in America.** 1977. Prentice-Hall. $8.95; pap. $3.95.

Conrad, John P. & Dinitz, Simon. **In Fear of Each Other: Studies of Dangerousness in America.** 1977. Lexington Books. $14.00.

Cooper, David. **The Manson Murders: A Philosophical Inquiry.** French, Peter A., ed. 1974. Schenkman. (OP). $5.95; pap. $3.95.

Count-van Manen, Gloria. **Crime and Suicide in the Nation's Capital: Toward Macro-Historical Perspectives.** 1977. Praeger. $22.95.

Crichton, Kyle S. **Law and Order LTD: The Rousing Life of Elfego Baca of New Mexico.** (Illus.). 1974. Repr. Arno Press. $14.00.

—**Criminology in America: The 20th Century.** 1975. Social Science and Social Resources. (OP). $6.95; pap. $4.95.

Curtis, Lynn A. **Criminal Violence.** (Illus.). 1974. Lexington Books. (OP). $17.00.

—**Violence, Race, and Culture.** 1977. pap. Heath. $6.95.

Curvin, Robert & Porter, Bruce. **Blackout Looting: New York City July 13, 1977.** 1979. pap. Halsted Press. $6.95.

De Wolf, L. Harold. **What Americans Should Do About Crime** (Illus.). 1976. pap. Harper & Row. $3.95.

Dillon, Richard. **The Hatchett Men.** 1972. pap. Ballantine. (OP). $1.65.

Duke, Thomas S. **Celebrated Criminal Cases of America.** (Illus.). Patterson Smith. $22.50.

Elliott, J. F. & Sardino, Thomas J. **Crime Control Team: An Experiment in Municipal Police Department Management and Operations.** (Illus.). 1971. C.C. Thomas. $14.75.

Feeley, Malcolm M. **The Process Is The Punishment: Handling Cases in a Lower Court.** 1979. Russell Sage. $10.00.

Floherty, John J. **Behind the Silver Shield.** rev. ed. (Illus.). 1957. Lippincott. (OP). $5.50.

Fox, James A. **Forecasting Crime Data.** 1978. Lexington Books. $14.95.

Fraenkel, Jack R. **Crime and Criminals: What Should We Do About Them.** 1970. Prentice-Hall. $8.04; pap. $3.48.

Gaddis, Thomas. **Birdman of Alcatraz.** rev. ed. 1979. pap. Comstock Editions. $2.50.

Gardiner, John A. **Politics of Corruption: Organized Crime in an American City.** 1970. Russell Sage. $5.95.

Geraway, William R. **There's 50,000 Dollars on My Head.** 1976. Exposition Press. $7.50.

Gervassi, John & Browning, Frank. **Crime in America.** 1979. Putnam. $8.95.

Glaser, Daniel. **Adult Crime and Social Policy.** 1972. Prentice-Hall. (OP). $5.95; pap. $3.95.

Glueck, Sheldon S. **Crime and Justice.** 1945. Kraus Reprint. $18.00.

Glueck, Sheldon S. & Glueck, Eleanor T. **After-Conduct of Discharged Offenders.** 1945. Kraus Reprint. $12.00.

—**Criminal Careers in Retrospect.** 1943. Kraus Reprint. $18.00.

—**Five Hundred Criminal Careers.** 1930. Kraus Reprint. $14.00.

—**Later Criminal Careers.** 1937. Kraus Reprint. $14.00.

Godwin, John. **Murder, U.S.A.** 1979. pap. Ballantine Books. $2.50.

Goldstein, Jeffrey H. **Aggression and Crimes of Violence.** Lana, Robert & Rosnow, Ralph, eds. (Illus.). 1975. Oxford University Press. $10.95; pap. $3.50.

Graham, Fred P. **The Due Process Revolution: The Warren Court's Impact on Criminal Law.** 1971. pap. Hayden Book Co. $6.95.

Greenberg, Douglas. **Crime and Law Enforcement in the Colony of New York, 1691-1776.** (Illus.). 1976. Cornell University Press. $16.50.

Halperin, Morton H. & Borosage, Robert. **The Lawless State: The Crimes of the U.S. Intelligence Agencies.** 1976. pap. Penguin Books. $3.95.

Harries, Keith D. **The Geography of Crime and Justice.** (Illus.). 1974. McGraw-Hill. (OP) $7.95; pap. $4.95.

Hernon, Peter. **A Terrible Thunder: The Story of the New Orleans Sniper.** 1978. Doubleday. $10.00.

Hindelang, Michael I. **Criminal Victimization in Eight American Cities. A Descriptive Analysis of Common Theft and Assault.** 1976. Ballinger Publishing. $25.00.

Hoffman, Paul. **Courthouse.** 1979. Hawthorn. $12.50.

Hohimer, Frank. **The Home Invaders.** 1976. pap. Playboy. (OP). $1.75.

—**The Home Invaders: Confessions of a Cat Burglar.** (Illus.). 1975. Chicago Review. $8.75.

Hooton, Earnest A. **American Criminal: An Anthropological Study.** Repr. of 1939 ed. Grennwood Press. $46.00.

Hurwitz, Stephan & Christiansen, Karl O. **Criminology.** 400p. 1981. Fairleigh Dickinson University Press. $30.00.

Ianni, Francis J. **Black Mafia.** 1975. pap. Pocket Books. $1.95.

Ianni, Francis & Reese, Elizabeth. **Crime Society: Organized Crime and Corruption in America.** 1976. NAL. $5.95.

Inciardi, J.A. **Reflections on Crime.** 1978. pap. Holt, Rinehart & Winston. $6.95.

Inciardi, James A. & Seigal, Harvey A. **Crime: Emerging Issues.** 1977. pap. Praeger. $5.50.

Inciardi, James A. & Pottieger, Anne E., eds. **Violent Crime: Historical and Contemporary Issues.** 1978. Sage. $12.50; pap. $6.50.

Jackson, Bruce. **Outside the Law: A Thief's Primer.** Orig. Title: Thief's Primer: Life of an American Character. 1972. pap. Transaction Books. $3.95.

Jacob, H. **Crime and Justice in Urban America.** 1980. pap. Prentice-Hall. $7.95.

Joey & Fisher, Dave. **Joey Kills.** 1975. pap. Pocket Books. (OP). $1.75.

Kefauver, Estes. **Crime in America.** Shalett, Sidney, ed. (Illus.). 1968. Repr. of 1951 ed. Greenwood Press. $21.50.

Keylin, Arleen & DeMirijan, Arto, Jr., eds. **Crime: As Reported by the New York Times.** (Illus.). 1976. Arno Press. $12.98.

Kidner, John. **Crimaldi-Contract Killer.** 1976. Acropolis Books. $8.95.

Kinton, Jack. **Criminology Tomorrow.** 1974. pap. Social Science & Sociological Resources. $5.95.

Kohn, Aaron, ed. **The Kohn Report: Crime and Politics in Chicago: a Preliminary Report of an Interrupted Investigation.** fac. ed. 1974. Repr. of 1953 ed. Arno Press. $10.00.

Kunstler, William M. **And Justice for All.** 1963. Oceana. $8.50.

La Fountaine, George. **The Scott-Dunlap Ring.** 1978. Coward, McCann & Geoghegan. $8.95.

Landesco, John. **Organized Crime in Chicago.** 2nd ed. 1979. pap. University of Chicago Press. $11.00.

Lawes, Lewis E. **Twenty Thousand Years in Sing Sing.** facs. ed. 1974. Repr. of 1932 ed. Arno Press. $25.00.

Leonard, Joe. **In Hot Pursuit** (Illus.). 1977. Greatlakes Liv. $9.95.

Lesberg, Sandy, ed. **A Picture History of Crime.** (Illus.). 1976. Bobbs-Merrill. (OP). $14.95.

Levine, Gary. **Anatomy of a Gangster: The Life and Times of Jack "Legs" Diamond.** 1979. A.S. Barnes. $12.00.

Lewin, Stephen, ed. **Crime and Its Prevention.** 1968. Wilson. $5.75.

Loth, David. **Crime in Suburbs.** 1970. pap. Belmont-Tower Books. $0.95.

Luttrell, Mark. **Behind Prison Walls.** 1975. Broadman. $2.95.

MacBrayne, Lewis & Ramsey, James P. **One More Chance: An Experiment with Human Salvage.** Repr. of 1916 ed. AMS Press. $18.00.

Mass, Peter. **Valachi Papers.** (Illus.). 1968. Putnam. (OP). $7.95.

McCaghy, Charles H. **Crime in American Society.** (Illus.). 1980. Macmillan. $16.95.

McLennan, Barbara N., ed. **Crime in Urban Society.** (Illus.). 1970. Dunellan Pub. Co. (OP). $8.95; pap. $3.95.

McMillan, George. **The Making of an Assassin: The Life of James Earl Ray.** 1976. Little, Brown & Co. $8.95.

McTeer, Ed. **High Sheriff to the Low Country.** Beaufort Book Co. $6.95.

Magee, Doug. **Slow Coming Dark: Interviews on Death Row.** (Illus.). 1980. Pilgrim Press. $10.95.

Messick, Hank. **Syndicate in the Sun.** 1968. Macmillan. (OP). $5.95.

Mid-West Debate Bureau. **Control of Crime.** 1967. pap. Mid-West. (OP). $3.00.

Millspaugh, Arthur Chester. **Crime Control by the National Government.** 1972. Repr. Da Capo. $27.50.

Monkkonen, Eric H. **The Dangerous Class: Crime and Poverty in Columbus, Ohio, 1860-1885.** 1975. Harvard University Press. $16.00.

Moore, William H. **The Kefauver Committee and the Politics of Crime 1950-1952.** 1974. University of Missouri Press. $15.00.

Moquin, Wayne & Van Doren, Charles. **The American Way of Crime: A Documentary History.** 1976. Praeger. $12.95.

Nash, J. Robert. **Bloodletters and Badmen, Vol. I.** 1975. pap. Warner Books. $2.50.

—**Bloodletters and Badmen, Vol. 2.** 1975. pap. Warner Books. $2.50.

—**Bloodletters and Badmen, Vol. 3.** 1975. pap. Warner Books. $2.50.

Nash, Jay R. **Bloodletters and Badmen: A Narrative Encyclopedia of American Criminals from the Pilgrims to the Present.** 1973. pap. M. Evans. $7.95.

National Council On Crime And Delinquency. **Correction in the United States.** 1967. pap. Kraus Reprint. (OP). $6.00.

Ness, Eliot & Fraley, Oscar. **Untouchables.** 1957. Simon & Schuster. $3.95.

Oatman, Eric F., ed. **Crime and Society.** 1979. Wilson. $5.75.

O'Brien, John T., ed. **Crime and Justice in America.** (Illus.). 1979. Pergamon Press. $35.00.

Osborne, Thomas M. **Society and Prisons.** 1975. Patterson Smith. $11.00.

Oswald, Russell G. **Attica: My Story.** Campbell, Rodney, ed. 1972. Doubleday. $7.95.

Packer, Peter. **Death of the Other Self.** 1979. pap. Belmont-Tower. $1.75.

Palmer, Stuart. **Prevention of Crime.** 1973. Human Sciences Press. (OP) $12.95.

Pasley, Fred. **Al Capone: The Biography of a Self-Made Man.** facs. ed. Repr. of 1930 ed. Books for Libraries. $22.00.

Patrick, Clarence H., ed. **Police, Crime, and Society.** 1972. C.C. Thomas. $14.50.

Peterson, Robert W., ed. **Crime and the American Response.** (Illus.). 1973. Facts on File. $10.95.

Peterson, Virgil W. **Barbarians in Our Midst.** 1952. Peter Wolff. (OP). $10.00.

Philips, David A. **The Great Texas Murder Trials: A Compelling Account of the Sensational T. Cullen Davis Case.** 1979. Macmillan. $9.95.

Plate, Thomas. **Crime Pays!** 1977. pap. Ballantine. (OP). $1.75.

—**Crime Pays!** 1975. Simon & Schuster. $8.95.

Quinney, Richard. **Criminology: Analysis and Critique of Crime in America.** 1975. Little, Brown & Co. $12.50.

—**Criminology.** 2nd ed. 1979. Little, Brown & Co. $15.00.

Reasons, Charles E. & Kuykendall, Jack L., eds. **Race, Crime and Justice.** 1971. pap. Goodyear. (OP). $8.95.

Reckless, Walter C. **American Criminology: New Directions.** (Illus.). 1973. Prentice-Hall. (OP). $12.95.

Rettig, Richard P., et al. **Manny: A Criminal-Addict's Story.** 1977. pap. Houghton Mifflin. $8.50.

Reynolds, Quentin. **Courtroom.** facs. ed. 1950. Arno Press. $20.50.

Roesch, Roberta & De La Roche, Harry. **Anyone's Son: A True Story.** (Illus.). 1979. Andrews & McMeel. $9.95.

Rogers, James T. **Four Tough Cases of the F.B.I.** 1969. Holt, Rinehart & Winston. (OP). $3.50.

Rosenberg, J. Mitchell. **Our Crime Riddled Society.** 1978. pap. University Press of America. $11.50.

Rumney, Jay & Murphy, Joseph P. **Probation and Social Adjustment.** 1968. Repr. of 1952 ed. Greenwood Press. $15.00.

Ruth, H., et al. **Challenge of Crime in a Free Society.** 1971. Repr. of 1968 ed. Da Capo. $15.00.

Savitz, Leonard D. & Johnson, Norman. **Crime in Society.** 1978. pap. Wiley, John & Sons. $18.95.

Schultz, D. O. & Scott, S.K. **The Subversive.** 1973. C.C. Thomas. $7.50.

Schur, Edwin M. **Our Criminal Society: The Social and Legal Sources of Crime in America.** 1969. pap. Prentice-Hall. $3.25.

Sellin, Torsten. **Research Memorandum on Crime in the Depression.** 1971. Repr. of 1937 ed. Arno Press. $12.00.

Semmes, Raphael. **Crime and Punishment in Early Maryland.** 1970. Repr. of 1938 ed. Patterson Smith. $14.00.

Senate Committee On The District of Columbia. **Crime and Law Enforcement in the District of Columbia: Hearings and Report.** 1971. Repr. of 1952 ed. Arno Press. $45.00.

Shalloo, J.P., ed. **Crime in the United States.** facs. ed. 1974. Repr. of 1941 ed. Arno Press. $14.00.

Shaw, Clifford R. **Natural History of a Delinquent Career.** (Illus.). 1968. Repr. of 1931 ed. Greenwood Press. $16.75.

Shaw, Clifford R., et al. **Brothers in Crime.** 1967. University of Chicago Press. $12.50.

Short, James F., Jr., ed. **Modern Criminals.** rev, 2nd. ed. 1973. Transaction Books. $9.95; pap. $4.95.

Silberman, Charles. **Criminal Violence-Criminal Justice: Criminals, Police, Courts and Prisons in America.** 1978. Random House. $15.00.

Skolnick, Jerome H., et al, eds. **Crime and Justice in America.** 1977. pap. Publishers, Inc. $6.95.

Slovenko, Ralph. **Crime, Law and Corrections.** (Illus.). 1966. C.C. Thomas. $26.50.

Southern California Research Council. **Crime, Police and the Judiciary in Southern California.** Rpt. No. 20. 1972. pap. Economics

Research Center. (OP). $4.00.

Sullivan, Edward D. **Rattling the Cup on Chicago Crime.** facs. ed. Repr. of 1929 ed. Books for Libraries. $16.00.

Supreme Court Holding a Criminal Term No. 14056: The United States vs. Charles J. Guiteau. 2 vols. Repr. of 1882 ed. Arno Press. Set. $106.00.

Sutherland, Edwin H., ed. **Professional Thief.** 1937. University of Chicago Press. $9.50.

—**Professional Thief.** 1956. pap. University of Chicago Press. $2.95.

Sutton, Charles. **New York Tombs, Its Secrets and Its Mysteries.** Mix, James B. & Mackeever, Samuel A., eds. (Illus.). 1973. Repr. of 1874 ed. Patterson Smith. $18.50.

Sutton, Willie & Linn, Ed. **Where the Money Was.** (Illus.). 1976. Viking Press. (OP). $10.00.

Sutton, Willie & Linn. Edward. **Where the Money Was.** 1977. pap. Ballantine Books. $1.95.

Swisher, Carl B., ed. **Selected Papers of Homer Cummings.** (Illus.). 1972. Repr. of 1939 ed. Da Capo. $29.50.

Tannenbaum, Frank. **Crime and the Community.** 1938. Columbia University Press. (OP). $15.00.

—**Wall Shadows: A Study in American Prisons.** 1975. Repr. of 1922 ed. AMS Press. $12.50.

Toplin, Robert B. **Unchallenged Violence: An American Ordeal.** 1975. Greenwood Press. $16.00.

Train, Arthur. **Courts and Criminals.** facs. ed. 1974. Repr. of 1928 ed. Arno Press. $17.00.

—**The Prisoner at the Bar: Sidelights on the Administration of Criminal Justice.** 1974. Repr. Arno Press. $20.00.

Trainer, Orvel, et al. **Deathroads: The Story of the Donut Shop Murders.** 1979. Pruett. $14.95.

Trenerry, Walter N. **Murder in Minnesota: A Collection of True Cases.** (Illus.). 1962. Minnesota Historical Society. $4.95.

True Story of Bonnie and Clyde (the Fugitives). Fortune, Jan, ed. pap. NAL $0.75.

Truzzi, Marcello & Petersen, David M., eds. **Criminal Life: Views from the Inside.** 1972. Prentice-Hall. pap. $8.95.

U.S. Senate Special Committee to Investigate Organized Crime in Interstate Commerce. **Reports on Crime Investigations: Vol. 6 of the Senate Reports, 82nd Congress, 1st Session, Reports Nos. 141, 307, 725.** 1951. Arno Press. $12.00.

Van Cise, Philip S. **Fighting the Underworld.** (Illus.). 1968. Repr. of 1936 ed. Greenwood Press. $20.00.

Van Every, Edward. **Sins of New York.** (Illus.). Repr. of 1930 ed. Arno Press. $20.00.

Vollmer, August. **Police and Modern Society.** 1969. Repr. of 1936 ed. Consortium Press. (OP). $15.00.

—**Police and Modern Society.** 273p. 1971. Patterson Smith. $10.00; pap. $4.25.

Warren, John H., Jr. **Thirty Years Battle with Crime: Or, the Crying Shame of New York, As Seen Under the Broad Glare of an Old Detective's Lantern.** (Rise of Urban America). 1970. Repr. of 1875 ed. Arno Press. $19.00.

Wellman, Manly W. **Dead and Gone.** 1955. University of North Carolina Press. $7.50.

West, Don. **Sacrifice Unto Me.** 1974. pap. Pyramid Publications. (OP). $1.25.

Willard, Josiah F. **World of Graft.** 1969. Repr. of 1901 ed. Consortium Press. (OP). $14.00.

Wilson, James Q. **Thinking About Crime.** 1975. Basic Books. $12.50.

—**Thinking About Crime.** 1977. pap. Random House. $1.95.

Winslow, Robert W. **Crime in a Free Society.** 3rd ed. 1977. pap. Dickenson. $12.95.

Wolff, Geoffrey. **Black Sun: The Brief Transit and

Violent Eclipse of Harry Crosby.** 1976. Random House. $12.95.

Yazijian, H. & Blumenthal, S. **Government by Gunplay: Assassination Conspiracy Theories from Dallas to Today.** 1976. pap. NAL. $1.50.

CRIME AND CRIMINALS—WEST

Adams, Ramon F. **Six-Guns & Saddle Leather.** 1954. Peter Wolff. (OP). $45.00.

—**Six-Guns and Saddle Leather: A Bibliography of Books and Pamphlets on Western Outlaws and Gunmen.** rev. ed. (Illus.). 1969. University of Oklahoma Press. (OP). $30.00.

Beidler, John X. **X. Beidler: Vigilante.** Sanders, Helen F. & Bertsche, William H., Jr., eds. (Illus.). 1969. Repr. of 1957 ed. University of Oklahoma Press. $4.95.

Breihan, Carl W. **Great Gunfighters of the West.** (Illus.). 1971. Naylor. (OP). $7.95.

—**Great Gunfighters of the West.** 1977. pap. NAL. $1.50.

Brownlee, Richard S. **Gray Ghosts of the Confederacy: Guerrilla Warfare in the West 1861-65.** (Illus.). 1958. Louisiana State University Press. $15.00.

Cook, D.J. **Hands Up: Or Twenty Years of Detective Life in the Mountains and on the Plains.** (Illus.). 1971. pap. University of Oklahoma Press. $4.95.

Coolidge, Dane. **Fighting Men of the West.** facs. ed. (Illus.). 1968. Repr. of 1932 ed. Books for Libraries. $19.50.

Dimsdale, Thomas J. **Vigilantes of Montana.** 1968. Repr. of 1953. ed. University of Oklahoma Press. $7.95; pap. $4.95.

Drago, Harry S. **Great Range Wars: Violence on the Grasslands.** (Illus.). 1970. Dodd, Mead & Co. $8.50.

Durham, George & Wantland, Clyde. **Taming the Nueces Strip: The Story of McNelly's Rangers.** (Illus.). 1962. University of Texas Press. $8.95.

Gard, Wayne. **Frontier Justice.** (Illus.). 1968. Repr. of 1949. ed. University of Oklahoma Press. (OP). $7.95.

Garrett, Pat F. **Authentic Life of Billy, the Kid.** 1967. University of Oklahoma Press. $6.95; pap. $3.95.

Hanna, David. **Harvest of Horror: Mass Murder in Houston.** 1975. pap. Belmont-Tower. (OP). $1.25.

Hardin, John W. **Life of John Wesley Hardin As Written by Himself.** (Illus.). 1966. Repr. of 1961 ed. University of Oklahoma Press. $3.95; pap. $2.95

Hayes, Jess. **Sheriff Thompson's Day: Turbulence in the Arizona Territory.** (Illus.). 1968. University of Arizona Press. (OP). $4.95.

Hendricks, George. **Badman of the West.** rev. ed. (Illus.). 1970. Naylor. (OP). $8.95.

Horan, James D. **Authentic Wild West: The Gunfighters.** 1976. Crown. $12.95.

Lyon, Peter. **Wild Wild West.** (Illus.). 1969. Funk & Wagnalls. (OP). $5.95.

Martin, Charles L. **Sketch of Sam Bass, the Bandit.** (Illus.). 1968. Repr. of 1956 ed. University of Oklahoma Press. $4.95.

Mercer, A.S. **Banditti of the Plains.** (Illus.). 1968. pap. University of Oklahoma Press. $3.95.

Metz, Leon. **The Shooters.** 1976. Mangan Books. $14.95.

Miller, Nyle H. & Snell, Joseph W. **Great Gunfighters of the Kansas Cowtowns, 1867-1886.** (Illus.). 1967. pap. University of Nebraska Press. $4.50.

Myers, John M. **Doc Holliday.** 1973. pap. University of Nebraska Press. $3.95.

Peltier, Jerome, ed. **Banditti of the Rockies.** 1964. Ross & Haines Old Books Co. $6.00.

Preece, Harold. **Dalton Gang.** 1963. Hastings House Publishers. (OP) $5.95.

Ray, Grace E. **Wily Women of the West.** (Illus.). 1972. Naylor. (OP). $7.95.

Reese, John W. **Flaming Feuds of Colorado County, Texas.** (Illus.). 1962. A. Jones. $12.00.

Rennert, Vincent P. **Western Outlaws.** (Illus.). 1968. Macmillan. $4.95.

Rockwell, Wilson, ed. **Memoirs of a Lawman.** Swallow Press. $12.00.

Rosa, Joseph G. **Gunfighter: Man or Myth.** (Illus.). 1973. Repr. of 1969 ed. University of Oklahoma Press. $9.95.

Shirley, Glenn. **Law West of Fort Smith: A History of Frontier Justice in the Indian Territory, 1834-1896.** 1969. pap. University of Nebraska Press. $4.25.

Sonnichsen, C.L. **I'll Die Before I'll Run: The Story of the Great Feuds of Texas.** 1961. Devin-Adair Co. $10.00.

—**Outlaw: Bill Mitchell, Alias Baldy Russell: His Life and Times.** Swallow Press. $4.95.

Surge, Frank. **Western Outlaws.** (Illus.). 1969. Lerner Pubns. $4.95.

Tilghman, Zoe. **Marshal of the Last Frontier.** (Illus.). 1964. A.H. Clark. $9.50.

Trachtman, Paul. **The Gunfighters.** (Illus.). 1974. Time-Life Books. $10.95.

Walters, Lorenzo D. **Tombstone's Yesterday: Bad Men of Arizona.** 2nd ed. (Illus.). 1968. Repr. of 1928 ed. Rio Grande Press. (OP). $7.50.

CRIME PREVENTION

Agarwal, R.S. **Prevention of Crime.** 1977. Humanities Press. $6.50.

Akers, Ronald L. & Sagarin, Edward, eds. **Crime Prevention and Social Control.** 1974. Praeger. (OP). $13.50.

Arnold, Peter. **How to Protect Your Child Against Crime.** 1977. pap. Assn. Press. $5.95.

—**Lady Beware.** 1974. Doubleday. (OP). $5.95.

—**Lady Beware.** (Illus.). 1975. pap. Doubleday. (OP). $2.50.

Astor, Saul D. **Loss Prevention: Controls and Concepts.** 1978. Security World. $13.95.

Bennett, Vivo & Clagett, Cricket. **One Thousand One Ways to Avoid Getting Mugged, Murdered, Robbed, Raped or Ripped off.** 1977. Van Nos Reinhold. $9.95.

Bunting, James. **The Protection of Property Against Crime** 1975. International Pubns. Service. $8.50.

Carter, R.L. **Theft in the Market.** 1975. Transatlantic Arts Inc. $4.25.

Clifford, William. **Crime Control in Japan.** 1976. Lexington Books. $18.00.

Coffey, Alan R. **The Prevention of Crime and Delinquency.** (Illus.). 1975. Prentice-Hall. $14.95.

Darrow, Frank M. **Stop Crime Soon As Possible.** 1975. pap. Darrow. $3.00.

Greenbank, Anthony. **Survival in the City.** (Illus.). 1975. Harper & Row. (OP). $12.95; pap. $6.95.

Harvard Civil Rights Civil Liberties Law Review Staff. **Preventive Detention: An Empirical Analysis.** 1971. pap. American Bar Foundation. $2.50.

Henke, Shirley & Mann, Stephanie. **Alternative to Fear: A Citizen's Manual for Crime Prevention through Neighborhood Involvement.** (Illus.). 1975. pap. Lex-Cal-Tex Press. $2.95.

Huff, C. Ronald. **Issues in Contemporary Corrections: Social Control and Conflict.** 1977. Sage. $12.95; pap. $6.50.

Hunter, George. **How to Defend Yourself, Your Family and Your Home.** 1970. pap. Univ. Pub. & Dist. (OP). $0.95.

—**How to Defend Yourself, Your Family and Your Home.** 1967. McKay, David, Co. (OP). $7.95.

Jeffery, C. Ray. **Crime Prevention Through Environmental Design.** 1977. Sage. $20.00; pap. $9.95.

Kingsbury, A.A. **Introduction to Security and Crime Prevention Surveys.** 1973. C.C. Thomas. $15.00; pap. $10.95.

Koepsell-Girard & Assoc. Inc. **Crime Prevention Handbook.** 1976. MTI Teleprograms. $2.95.

Leonard V.A. **Police Crime Prevention.** 1972. C.C. Thomas. $13.75.

McLean, Robert Joe. **Education for Crime Prevention and Control.** (Illus.). 168p. 1975. C.C. Thomas. $12.50.

Marsh, Thomas O. **Roots of Crime.** 1980. Nellen Publishing. $10.00.

Morris, Norval & Hawkins, Gordon. **The Honest Politician's Guide to Crime Control.** 1972. pap. University of Chicago Press. $3.95.

Morris, Norval & Hawkins, Gordon J. **Letter to the President on Crime Control.** pap. University of Chicago Press. $1.95.

Nelson, Ralph. **Home Security Manual.** 1977. pap. Rucker Press. $1.95.

New York State & Crime Commission. **Crime and the Community.** facs. ed. 1974. Repr. of 1930 ed. Arno Press. $17.00.

Newman, Oscar. **Defensible Space: Crime Prevention Through Urban Design.** (Illus.). 1973. pap. Macmillan. $3.95.

—**Defensible Space: Crime Prevention Through Urban Design.** (Illus.). 1972. Macmillan. $9.95.

Palmer, Stuart. **Prevention of Crime.** 1973. Behavioral Pubns. (OP). $12.95.

Parsons, Philip A. **Responsibility for Crime: An Investigation of the Nature and Causes of Crime and a Means of Its Prevention.** 1968. Repr. of 1909 ed. AMS Press. $16.50.

Perry, Philip M. **Security for Schools and Centers.** 1976. pap. Creative Book Co. $3.30.

Post, Richard S., ed. **Combating Crime Against Small Business.** 1972. C.C. Thomas. $8.75.

Protect Your Business Against Crime: A Guide for the Small Businessman. (Illus.). 1974. pap. Drake Pubs. (OP). $4.95.

Pursuit, Dan G., et al, eds. **Police Programs for Preventing Crime and Delinquency.** (Illus.). 1972. C.C. Thomas. $22.25; pap. $13.75.

Quincy, H. Keith. **The Seamy Side of Government: Essays on Punishment and Coercion.** 1979. pap. University Press of America. $7.25.

Rankin, Guy R. **The Professional Handbook for Patrol and Security Guards.** 1977. Exposition Press. $5.00.

Rowe, Richard & Mallman, Joyce. **Total Self-Protection: The Handbook of Crime Prevention.** (Illus.). 1979. Morrow. $12.95; pap. $6.95.

Ruth, Henry. **Research Priorities for Crime Reduction Efforts.** 1977. pap. Urban Institute. $3.50.

Samuel, Dorothy T. **Safe Passage on City Streets.** 1975. Abingdon. (OP). $3.95.

Silver, Isidore. **The Crime Control Establishment.** 1974. pap. Prentice-Hall. (OP). $2.45.

Sorrentino, Anthony. **Organizing Against Crime: Redeveloping the Neighborhood.** 1977. Human Sciences Press. $19.95.

Stratton, John R. & Terry, Robert M. **Prevention of Delinquency: Problems and Programs.** 1968. Macmillan. $6.95.

Strobl, W. **Crime Prevention Through Physical Security.** 1978. Dekker, Marcel, Inc. $35.00.

Trojanowicz, John M. & Moss, Forrest M. **Community Based Crime Prevention.** 1975. pap. Goodyear. (OP). $7.95.

Vestermark, S.D., Jr. & Blauvelt, Peter D. **Controlling Crime in the School: A Complete Security Handbook for Administrators.** (Illus.). 1978. Prentice-Hall. $24.95.

Washnis, George J. **Citizen Involvement in Crime Prevention.** 1976. Lexington Books. $15.95.

Whisenand, Paul M. **Crime Prevention.** 1977. Holbrook. $16.50.

Wines, Frederick H. **Punishment and Reformation: A Study of the Penitentiary System.** 1975. Repr. of 1919 ed. AMS Press. $30.00.

Woods, Arthur. **Crime Prevention.** 1971. Repr. of 1918 ed. Arno Press. $12.00.

—**Crime Prevention.** 1975. Repr. of 1918 ed. AMS Press. $9.50.

Zimring, Franklin E. & Hawkins, Gordon. **Deterrence: The Legal Threat in Crime Control.** 1973. University of Chicago Press. $13.50.

Zimring, Franklin E. & Hawkins, Gordon J. **Deterrence: The Legal Threat in Crime Control.** 1976. pap. University of Chicago Press. $5.95.

CRIMES WITHOUT VICTIMS

Geis, Gilbert L. **Victimless Crimes: Not the Law's Business?** 1976. pap. St. Martin's Press. $3.95.

Rich, Robert M. **Crimes Without Victims: Deviance and the Criminal Law.** 1978. University Press of America. $9.25.

Schur, Edwin M. & Bedau, Hugo A. **Victimless Crimes: Two Sides of a Controversy.** 1974. pap. Prentice-Hall. $3.45.

CRIMINAL COURTS

Eisenstein, James & Jacob, Herbert. **Felony Justice: An Organizational Analysis of Criminal Courts.** 1977. Little, Brown & Co. $11.95; pap. text ed. $7.95.

Levin, Martin A. **Urban Politics and the Criminal Courts.** 1979. University of Chicago Press. $20.00; pap. $6.95.

Lewis, Merlin, et al. **An Introduction to the Courts and Judicial Process.** (Illus.). 1978. Prentice-Hall. $16.95.

Nardulli, Peter F., ed. **The Study of Criminal Courts: Political Perspectives.** 1979. Ballinger Publishing. $22.50.

Nimmer, Raymond T. **The Nature of System Change: Reform Impact in the Criminal Courts.** Sikes, Bette, ed. American Bar Foundation. $10.00; pap. $5.00.

Robertson, John A. **Rough Justice: Perspectives on Lower Criminal Courts.** 1974. pap. Little, Brown & Co. $8.95.

Rovner-Piecznik, Roberta. **The Criminal Court.** (Illus.). 1978. Lexington Books. $13.50.

Silva, John W., ed. **An Introduction to Crime and Justice.** 1973. Mss Information Corp. $15.00.

Ulmer, S.S. ed. **Courts, Law and Judicial Processes.** 1981. pap. Free Press. $12.95.

United States Task Force on the Administration of Justice. **Task Force Report: The Courts.** (Illus.). 1978. Repr. of 1967 ed. Greenwood Press. $22.00.

Utz, Pamela J. **Settling the Facts.** 1978. Lexington Books. $17.95.

Whitebread, Charles. **Standards Relating to Transfer Between Courts.** (Juvenile Justice Standards Projects Ser.) 1977. Ballinger Publishing. pap. $5.95; casebound. $12.50.

CRIMINAL INVESTIGATION

Ackroyd, James J. **The Investigator: A Practical Guide to Private Detection.**

1975. Transatlantic Arts Inc. (OP).$8.25

Akin, Richard H. **The Private Investigator's Basic Manual.** 208p. 1979. C.C. Thomas. $16.25.

Arons, Harry. **Hypnosis in Criminal Investigation.** pap. Borden. $9.00

Asch, Sidney H. **Police Authority and the Rights of the Individual.** 2nd ed. 1968. pap. Arc Books. (OP.) $1.45.

Bequai, August. **Computer Crime.** 1978. Lexington Books. $16.95

Block, Eugene B. **Science Vs. Crime and Men's Rights** (Illus). 1980. Cragmont Publications. $9.95; pap. $6.95.

Bozza, Charles M. **Criminal Investigation.** Nelson-Hall. $20.95

Chilmidos, R.S. **Auto Theft Investigation.** Legal Book Corporation. $12.50.

Criminal Investigation. (Public Service Technology Ser.). 1980. Merrill, Charles E. $16.95.

Criminal Investigation and Presentation of Evidence. 1976. West Publishing. $12.95.

Cunliffe, Frederick & Piazza, Peter B. **Criminalistics and Scientific Investigation.** (Illus.). 1980. Prentice-Hall. $16.95.

Curry, A. S. **Methods of Forensic Science.** Vol. 4. 1965. Wiley, John & Sons. (OP). $19.95.

Dash, Samuel, et al. **Eavesdroppers.** (Illus.). 1970. Repr. of 1959 ed. Da Capo. $17.50.

DeLadurantey, Joseph C. & Sullivan, Daniel R. **Criminal Investigation Standards.** (Illus.). 1979. Harper & Row. inst. manual free. $17.50.

Dienstein, William. **Technics for the Crime Investigator.** 2nd ed. 1974. C.C. Thomas. $12.00.

Ferguson, Robert J., Jr. **Scientific Informer.** (Illus.) 1974. C.C. Thomas. $12.00

Fitzgerald, Maurice J. **Handbook of Criminal Investigation.** 1951. Arco. $5.00.

Fricke, Charles W. **Criminal Investigation and the Law.** 7th ed. Payton, George T., ed. 1974. Legal Book Corporation. $14.00.

Given, Bruce, et al. **Tire Tracks and Tread Marks.** (Illus.) 1977. Gulf Publishing. $10.95.

Goddard, K. **Crime Scene Investigation.** 1977. Reston. $12.50.

Graham, Daniel. **The Use of X-ray Techniques in Forensic Investigations.** (Illus.). 1973. So Longman. (OP). $13.50.

Greenwood, Peter W., et al. **The Criminal Investigation Process.** 1977. pap. Heath. $6.95.

—**The Criminal Investigation Process.** 1977. Lexington Books. $15.00

Gugas, Chris. **The Silent Witness: A Polygraphist's Casebook.** 1979. Prentice-Hall. $9.95.

Hall, Jay C. **Inside the Crime Lab.** 1973. Prentice-Hall. $7.95.

Harris, Raymond I. **Outline of Death Investigation.** (Illus.). 1973. C.C. Thomas. (OP). $12.75.

Heffron, Floyd N. **Evidence for the Patrolman.** (Illus.). 1972. C.C. Thomas. $10.00.

Horgan, J. J. **Criminal Investigation.** 1973. McGraw-Hill. $15.50.

Inbau, Fred E., et al. **Scientific Police Investigation.** (Illus.). 1972. Chilton. (OP). $6.95.

Kenney, John P. & More, Harry W., Jr. **Pri974. Wiley, John & Sons. $22.95.**

Kirk, Paul L. & Bradford, Lowell W. **Crime Laboratory: Organization and Operation.** (Illus.). 1972. C.C. Thomas. $7.75.

Kirshnan, S.S. **An Introduction to Modern Criminal Investigation: With Basic Laboratory Techniques.** (Illus.). 1978. C.C. Thomas. $28.25; pap. $21.75.

Lee, Peter G. **Interpol.** 1976. Stein & Day. $25.00.

Leonard, V.A. **Criminal Investigation and Identification.** (Illus.). 1971. C.C. Thomas. $9.25.

—**Police Detective Function.** 1970. C.C. Thomas. $8.25.

Loth, David. **Crime Lab.** 1966. Simon & Schuster. $4.95.

Lucas, Norman. **The Laboratory Detectives: How Science Traps the Criminals.** 1972. Taplinger. $7.95.

Markle, Arnold. **Criminal Investigation and Presentation of Evidence.** 1976. West Publishing. $12.95.

Morland, Nigel. **Science in Crime Detection.** (Illus.). 1960. Emerson. (OP). $5.95.

Morland, Nigel, ed. **The Criminologist.** (Illus.) 1972. Open Court. $17.50.

Mulhearn, Henry. **Crime Investigation.** 1976. Gould. $7.50.

Mulhearn, Henry. J. **Police Science Fundamentals.** 1973 ed. pap. Gould. $7.50.

Murray, Joseph A. **Police Administration and Criminal Investigation.** 3rd ed. 1968. Arco. $12.50; pap $10.00.

Nash, Donald J. **Individual Identification and the Law Enforcement Officer.** (Illus.). 1978. C.C. Thomas. $16.00.

Nelson, John. **Preliminary Investigation and Police Reporting: A Complete Guide to Police Written Communication.** 1970. Glencoe. $14.95.

O'Hara, Charles E. **Fundamentals of Criminal Investigation.** 4th ed. (Illus.). 1978. C.C. Thomas. $22.50.

O'Hara, Charles E. and Osterburg, James W. **An Introduction to Criminalistics: The Application of the Physical Sciences to the Detection of Crime.** rev. ed. 1972. Repr. of 1949 ed. Indiana University Press. $17.50.

Osterburg, James W. **Crime Laboratory: Case Studies of Scientific Criminal Investigation.** (Illus.). 1968. Indiana University Press. $12.50; pap $8.95.

Photographic Surveillance Techniques for Law Enforcement Agencies. pap. Eastman Kodak. $1.00.

Reik, Theodor. **Compulsions to Confess: On the Psycho Analysis of Crime and Punishment.** Repr. of 1959 ed. Arno Press. $30.00.

Ringel, William E. **Identification and Police Line-Ups.** 1968. pap. Gould. $5.00.

Rudman, Jack. **Criminal Investigation.** (ACT Proficiency Examination Program: PEP-9) pap. Natl. Learning. $9.95.

—**Criminal Investigation.** (College Proficiency Examination Ser.: CPEP-30) 1977. pap. National Learning Corporation. $9.95.

—**Criminal Investigator.** (Career Examination Ser.: C-1229). pap. National Learning Corporation. $8.00.

—**Criminal Law Investigator.** (Career Examination Ser.: C-969.) pap. National Learning Corporation. $8.00.

—**Detective Investigator.** (Career Examination Ser.: C-1247). pap. National Learning. $10.00.

—**Investigator.** (Career Examination Ser.: C-377). pap. National Learning. $8.00.

Saferstein, Richard. **Criminalistics: An Introduction to Forensic Science** (Illus.) 1977. Prentice-Hall. $17.95.

—**Criminalistics: An Introduction to Forensic Science.** 2nd ed. 1981. Prentice-Hall. $18.59.

Salottolo, Lawrence. **Criminal Science Quizzer.** 1972. Arco. (OP). $8.00; pap. $5.00.

Sanders, William B. **Detective Work: A Study of Criminal Investigations.** (Illus.). 1977. Free Press. $12.95.

—**Detective Work: A Study of Criminal Investigations** (Illus.). 1979. pap. Free Press. $6.95.

Schultz, Donald & Scheer, Samuel. **Crime Scene Investigation** (Illus.). 1977. Prentice-Hall. $14.95.

Schultz, Donald O. **Criminal Investigation Techniques.** 1978. Gulf Publishing. $12.95.

Scott, James D. **Investigative Methods.** (Illus.). 1978. Reston. $13.95.

Shaffer, Ron & Klose, Kevin. **Surpisel Surprise.** 1979. pap. Avon Books. $2.25.

Soderman, Harry & O'Connell, John J. **Modern Criminal Investigation.** 5th ed. O'Hara, Charles E., ed. (Illus.). 1962. Crowell. $10.00.

Sowle, Claude R., ed. **Police Power and Individual Freedom: The Quest for Balance.** 1962. Aldine. (OP). $11.50.

Stone, Alfred R. & Deluca, Stuart M. **Investigating Crimes: An Introduction.** (Illus.). 1980. Houghton Mifflin. inst. manual $1.00; $18.95; pap. $1.00.

Stuckey, Gilbert. B. **Evidence for the Law Enforcement Officer.** Cleverdon, Ardelle, ed. (Illus.). 1974. McGraw-Hill. $14.95.

Swanson, C.R. et al. **Criminal Investigation.** 1981. Good year. $18.95.

Svensson, Arne. **Techniques of Crime Scene Investigation.** 1965. Elsevier North Holland Publishing. $19.95.

Thorwarld, Jurgen. **Century of the Detective.** (Illus.). 1965. Harcourt Brace Jovanovich. $12.50.

—**Crime and Science: The New Frontier in Criminology.** 1969. pap. Harcourt Brace Jovanovich. (OP). $5.95.

Tiffany, Lawrence P., et al. **Detection of Crime: Stopping and Questioning, Search and Seizure, and Encouragement and Entrapment.** 1967. pap. Little, Brown & Co. (OP). $4.95.

Tobias, Marc W. & Petersen, R. David. **Field Manual of Criminal Law and Police Procedure.** (Illus.). 1975. pap. C.C. Thomas $15.25.

Walls, H.J. **Forensic Science: An Introduction to Scientific Crime Detection.** 2nd ed. (Illus.). 1974. Praeger. (OP). $13.95.

Ward, Richard A. **Introduction to Criminal Investigation.** 1975. Addison-Wesley Publishing Co. $12.95.

Wells, Kenneth M. & Weston, Paul B. **Criminal Evidence for Police.** 2nd ed. (Illus.). 1976. Prentice-Hall. $16.95.

Weston, Paul B. & Wells, Kenneth M. **Criminal Investigation: Basic Perspectives.** 1980. 3rd ed. (Illus.). 1980. Prentice-Hall. $17.95.

—**Elements of Criminal Investigation.** (Illus.). 1971. Prentice Hall. (OP). $3.50.

Whited, Charles. **Chiodo: Undercover Cop.** 1974. pap. Playboy. $1.50.

Wilber, Charles G. **Forensic Biology for the Law Enforcement Officer.** 1974. C.C. Thomas $24.25.

Winks, Robin W., ed. **Historian As Detective: Essays on Evidence.** 1970. pap. Harper & Row. $6.50.

CRIMINAL JUSTICE, ADMINISTRATION OF

Adams, Gary B., et al. **Juvenile Justice Management.** (Illus). 660p. 1973. C.C. Thomas. $25.00.

Adams, Thomas. F. **Introduction to the Administration of Criminal Justice: An Overview of the Justice System and Its Components** 2nd ed. (Illus.). 1980. Prentice-Hall. $14.95.

—**Law Enforcmement: An Introduction to the Police Role in the Criminal Justice System.** 2nd ed. (Illus.) 1973. Prentice-Hall. $16.95.

Adams, Thomas F., et al. **Criminal Justice: Organization and Management.** (Illus.). 416p. 1974. Goodyear. $19.95.

Adelson, Daniel & Sarbin, Theodore R., eds. **Challenge to the Criminal Justice System: The Perspectives of Community Psychology.** 166p. 1979. Human Sciences Press. $14.95.

Agee, Vicki L. **Treatment of the Violent Incorrigible Adolescent.** (Illus.) 1979. Lexington Books. $16.95.

Allen, Francis A. **The Borderland of Criminal Justice.** 152p. 1974. pap. University of Chicago Press. $2.45.

Alpert, Geoffrey P. **Legal Rights of Prisoners.** 280p. 1980. Sage. $20.00; pap. $9.95.

American Bar Association. **ABA Standards for Criminal Justice.** 4 vols. 1980 write for info. Little, Brown & Co.

—**American Bar Association on Standards for Criminal Justice.** 4 vols. 2nd ed. 2325p. 1980. write for info. Little, Brown & Co.

American Friends Service Committee. **Struggle for Justice: A Report on Crime and Punishment in America.** 1971. Hill & Wang. $4.50; pap. $4.95.

Atkins, Burton & Pogrebin, Mark. **Invisible Justice System: Discretion and the Law.** 1978. Anderson Publishing Company. $14.95.

Baker, Ralph & Meyer, Fred, Jr. **The Criminal Justice Game.** 1980. pap. Duxbury Press. $8.95.

Baker, Ralph & Meyer, Fred, eds. **Evaluating Alternative Law-Enforcement Policies.** (Illus.) 240p. 1979. Lexington Books. $18.95.

Balbus, Issac D. **The Dialectics of Legal Repression: Black Rebels Before the American Criminal Courts.** new ed. 270p. 1977. Transaction Books. $4.95.

Baldwin, John & McConville, Michael J. **Negotiated Justice: Pressure to Plead Guilty.** 1977. (Pub. by Martin Robertson England). Biblio Distribution Center $12.50.

Baldwin, John & Bottomley, A. Keith, eds. **Criminal Justice: Selected Readings.** 1978. (Pub. by Martin Robertson England). Biblio Distribution Center $19.50; pap. $10.95.

Ball, Howard. **Courts and Politics: The Federal Judicial System.** 1980. Prentice-Hall. $9.95.

Ballinger, Tom. **Clean Slate.** 1978. Crown. $14.95; pap. $8.95.

Beccaria, Cesare. **On Crimes and Punishments.** Paolucci, Henry, tr. 1963. pap. Bobbs-Merrill. $3.50.

Becker, Gary S. & Landes, William M., eds. **Essays in the Economics of Crime and Punishment.** 1974. National Bureau of Economic Research. $12.50; pap. $5.00.

Becker, Harold K. & Hjellemo, Einar O. **Justice in Modern Sweden: A Description of the Components of the Swedish Criminal Justice System.** (Illus.). 160p. 1976. C.C. Thomas. $16.25.

Beckman, Erik. **The Criminal Justice Dictionary.** 1979. Pierian. $14.95; pap. $8.50.

Bedford, Sybille. **Faces of Justice.** 1963. pap. Simon & Schuster. $1.95.

Bender, David L. ed. **Criminal Justice: Opposing, Viewpoints.** 1981. Greenhaven Press. $8.95; pap. $3.95.

Bennett-Sandler, Georgette, et al. **Law Enforcement and Criminal Justice: An Introduction.** (Illus.). 1979. pap. Houghton Mifflin. $14.95.

Bent, Alan E. & Rossum, Ralph A. **Police, Criminal Justice, and the Community.** 384p. 1976. Harper & Row. $16.95.

Bequai, August. **Computer Crime.** 1978. Lexington Books. $16.95.

Berkley, George E., et al. **Introduction to Criminal Justice: Police, Courts, Corrections.** 1976. instr's manual free. Holbrook. $16.95.

Berkman, Ronald. **Opening the Gates: the Rise of the Prisoners Movement.** 224p. 1979. Lexington Books. $21.00.

Blonien, Rodney & Greenfield, Joel I. **California Law Manual for the Administration of Justice.** 1979. pap. West Publishing. $18.95.

Blumberg, Abraham S. **Criminal Justice.** 1967. pap. New Viewpoints. $4.95.

—**Criminal Justice: Issues and Ironies.** 2nd ed. Watts, Franklin, Inc. $15.00; pap. $9.95.

Bohigian, Haig E. **The Foundations and Mathematical Models of Operations Research with Extensions to the Criminal Justice System.** (Illus.). XXIII, 282p. (Orig.). 1972. Gazette Press. $10.95.

Bond, James E. **Plea Bargaining and Guilty Pleas.** 1975. looseleaf with 1978 rev. pages & supplement. Boardman. $37.50.

Bopp, William J. & Schultz, Donald O. **Principles of American Law Enforcement and Criminal Justice.** (Illus.). 596p. 1975. C.C. Thomas. $15.25.

Brantingham, Patricia L. & Blomberg, Tom G., eds. **Courts & Diversion:**

Policy and Operations Studies. (Illus.). 1979. Sage. $12.95; pap. $6.50.

Briggs, Dennie. **In Place of Prison** 155p. 1976. pap. International Pubns. Service. $7.50.

Buckle, Suzann R. & Buckle, Leonard G. **Bargaining for Justice: Case Disposition and Reform in the Criminal Courts.** 1977. Praeger. $18.50.

Butler, Alan. **The Law Enforcement Process.** (Illus.). 300p. 1976. Alfred Publishing. $9.95.

Caldwell, Robert G. **Foundations of Law Enforcement & Criminal Justice.** Nardini, William, ed. 1977. $16.40. Bobbs—Merrill.

Calvin, Allen D., ed. **Challenges and Alternatives to the American Criminal Justice System.** 1979. pap. University Micofilms International. $10.00.

Carlson, Ronald L. **Criminal Justice Procedure for Police.** 2nd ed. 1978. $13.95 Anderson Publishing co.

Carney, Louis P. **Introduction to Correctional Science.** 2nd ed. (Illus.). 1978. $14.50, McGraw-Hill.

Carrington, Frank & Lambie, William. **The Defenseless Society.** 160p. (Orig.). 1976. pap. $1.95. Green Hill.

Carter, Lief H. **The Limits of Order.** 1974. $18.95. Lexington Books.

Casper, J. **American Criminal Justice: The Defendant's Prospective.** 1972. pap. $3.45. Prentice-Hall.

Cederblom, J. B. & Blizek, William L., eds. **Justice and Punishment.** 1977. $16.50. Ballinger Publishing.

Chambliss, William J. **Criminal Law in Action** 480p. 1975. $16.50. Wiley, John & Sons.

Chamelin, Neil C., et al. **Introduction to Criminal Justice.** 2nd ed. (Illus.). 1979. $15.95. Prentice-Hall.

Chang. Dae H. **Introduction to Criminal Justice Theory and Application.** (Orig.). 1979 pap. $13.95. Kendall-Hunt.

Chappell, Duncan & Monahan, John, eds. **Violence and Criminal Justice.** 1977. pap. $6.95. Health.

—**Violence and Criminal Justice.** 1975. $15.95. Lexington Books.

Cho. Y. H. **Public Policy and Urban Crime.** 1974. $17.50. Ballinger Publishing.

Clark, Ramsey, ed. **Crime and Justice.** (Illus.) 1974 (Copub. by The New York Times). Arno Press. $35.00

Clark, Robert S. **Fundamentals of Criminal Jusitce Research** (Illus.). 1977. $17.95 Lexington Books.

—**Criminal Justice System: An Analytical Approach.** Date not set. Allyn and Bacon. Price not set.

Clarke, R. V. & Hough, J. M., eds. **The Effectiveness of Policing.** 184p. 1980. $18.95. (Pub. by Gower Pub Co England). Lexington Books. $18.95.

Cleveland Foundation. **Criminal Justice in Cleveland.** Round, Roscoe & Frankfurter, Felix, eds. (Illus.). 1968. Repr. of 1922 ed. $24.00. Patterson Smith. $24.00

Co-Op East Law Outlines: Criminal Justice Administration. 44p. 1975. Sterling Swift. $3.50.

Coffey, Alan & Renner, Vernon. **Criminal Justice As a System: Readings.** (Illus.). 320p. 1974. pap. Prentice-Hall. $12.95.

Coffey, Alan R. **Juvenile Justice As a System: Law Enforcement to Rehabilitation.** 1974. Prentice-Hall. $11.95

Cohen, Fred **Standards Relating to Dispositional Procedures.** 1977. Ballinger Publishing. softcover $5.95; casebound, $12.50.

Cohen, Henry. **Brutal Justice: The Ordeal of an American City.** 1980. John Jay Press. $10.00.

Cohn, Alfred & Udolf, Roy. **Criminal Justice System and Its Psychology.** 1979. Van Nos Reinhold. $17.95.

Cohn, Alvin W. **Criminal Justice Planning and Development.** 1977. Sage. $12.95; pap. $6.50.

Cole, George. **Criminal Justice: Law and Politics.** 2nd ed. 1976. pap. Duxbury Press. $8.50.

Cole, George F. **The American System of Criminal Justice.** 2nd ed. (Illus.). 1979. Duxbury Press. $15.95.

—**Politics and the Administration of Justice.** 234p. 1973. pap. Sage. $8.95.

Committee for Economic Development. **Reducing Crime and Assuring Justice.** (Illus.). 86p. 1972. pap. Committee for Economic Development. $2.50; pap. $1.50.

Congressional Quarterly Staff. **Crime and Justice: Trends and Directions.** 1978. pap. Congressional Quarterly. $6.95.

Conklin, John E. **Robbery and the Criminal Justice System.** 250p. 1972. pap. Lippincott. $2.75.

Conrad, John P., ed. **The Evolution of Criminal Justice: A Guide for Practical Criminologists.** 1978. Sage. $12.95; pap. $6.50.

Cortes, Carlos E., ed. **The Mexican American and the Law.** 1974. Arno Press. Repr. $20.00.

Council of State Governments. **The Handbook of Interstate Crime Control.** 1977. Repr. of 1966 ed. Greenwood Press. $15.50.

Crelinsten, Ronald D. & Szabo, Denis. **Hostage-Taking: Theory and Practice.** (Illus.). 1979. Lexington Books. $15.95.

Crelinsten, Ronald D., et al, eds. **Terrorism and Criminal Justice.** (Illus.). 1978. Lexington Books. $15.95.

Cressey, Donald R., ed. **Crime and Criminal Justice.** (Orig.) 1971. New Viewpoints. $6.95; pap. $2.45.

Criminal Courts in New York State. facsimile ed. 1974. Repr. of 1909 ed. Arno Press. $35.00.

Criminal Justice in America. 46 vols. 1974. Arno Press. Set. $890.00.

Criminal Justice System. 1976. pap. American Enterprise Institute for Public Policy Research. $2.00.

Cromwell, Paul F., Jr., ed. **Jails and Justice.** (Illus.). 336p. 1975. C.C. Thomas. $19.00; C.C. Thomas. $13.50.

Culver, Dorothy C. **Bibliography of Crime and Criminal Justice: 1927-1931.** 1969. Repr. of 1934 ed. Patterson Smith. $16.50.

Datesman, Susan K., ed. **Women, Crime and Justice.** Scarpitti, Frank R. (Illus., Orig.). 1980. pap. Oxford University Press. $5.95.

Daudistel, Howard, et al. **Criminal Justice: Situations and Decisions.** 1979. inst. manual avail. Holt, Rinehart and Winston. $13.95.

Davidson, William, et al. **Evaluation Strategies in Criminal Justice.** Pergamon Press. $25.00.

Dawson, Robert O. **Standards Relating to Adjudication.** 1977. softcover $5.95; Ballinger Publishing. casebound $12.50.

DeWolf, L. Harold. **Crime and Justice in America: A Paradox in Conscience.** 288p. 1975. Harper Row. $15.00.

Dodge, Calvert R., ed. **A World Without Prisons.** 304p. 1979. Lexington Books. $23.95.

Duffee, David & Fitch, Robert. **An Introduction to Corrections: A Policy and Systems Approach.** 384p. 1976. Goodyear. $19.95.

Duffee, David, et al. **Criminal Justice: Organization, Structure and Analysis.** 1978. Prentice-Hall. $16.95.

Eldefonso, Edward. **Issues in Corrections: A Book of Readings.** 320p. 1974. pap. Glencoe. $7.95.

Falkin, Gregory R. **Reducing Delinquency.** (Illus.). 240p. 1979. Lexington Books. $20.95.

Fay, John. **Approaches to Criminal Justice Training.** 264p. (Orig.). 1979. pap. University of Georgia, Institute of Government. $12.00.

Feeley, Malcolm M. **The Process Is the Punishment: Handling Cases in a Lower Criminal Court.** (Illus.). 1979. Russell Sage. $12.95.

Feeley, Malcolm & Sarat, Austin. **The Policy Dilemma: Federal Crime Policy and the Law Enforcement Assistance Administration.** 1980. University of Minnesota Press. $17.50; pap. $7.95.

Fehr, Will. **The Law and Gary Gilmore.** 1979. pap. Anthelion Press. $2.95.

Felkenes, George T. **Criminal Justice System: Its Function and Personnel.** (Illus.). 336p. 1974. Prentice-Hall. $16.95.

Field Research Corporation. **Public Opinion of Criminal Justice in California: A Survey Conducted by Field Research Corporation.** new ed. 156p. 1975. pap. University of California, Institute of Government Studies. $7.00.

Fishman, Robert. **Criminal Recidivism in New York City: An Evaluation of the Impact of Rehabilitation and Diversion Services.** 1977. Praeger. $19.95.

Fitzgerald, Edward T. & Hughes, Robert E. **Effective Written Communication in Criminal Justice.** 1978. Benjamin-Cummings. $10.50.

Folgelson, Robert M., ed. **Administration of Justice in the United States.** facsimile ed. 1974. Repr. of 1910 ed. Arno Press. $13.00.

Foserr, C.A., et al. **Introduction to the Administration of Justice.** 2nd ed. 1979. Wiley, John & Sons. $17.50.

Foundations of Criminal Justice. 43 vols. in 47. Repr. of 1933 ed. Set. write for info. AMS Press.

Foust, Cleon H. & Webster, D. Robert, eds. **An Anatomy of Criminal Justice: A System Overview.** 352p. 1980. Lexington Books. $25.95.

Fox, Vernon. **Introduction to Criminology.** (Illus.). 416p. 1976. Prentice-Hall. $16.95.

Freed, Daniel J. & Terrell, Timothy P. **Standards Relating to Interim Status: The Release, Control, & Detention of Accused Juvenile Offenders Between Arrest and Disposition.** 1977. Ballinger Publishing. softcover $7.95; casebound $16.50.

Galaway, Burt & Hudson, Joe, eds. **Offender Restitution in Theory and Action.** 1978. Lexington Books. $17.95.

Galaway, Burton & Hudson, Hamilton C. **Perspectives on Crime Victims.** (Illus.). 1980. pap. Mosby. $12.00.

Galloway, John, ed. **Criminal Justice and the Burger Court.** 1978. Facts on File. $17.50.

Gardiner, John & Mulkey, Michael, eds. **Crime and Criminal Justice.** 1974. pap. Policy Studies. $3.00.

Gardiner, John A. & Mulkey, Michael A., eds. **Crime and Criminal Justice: Issues in Public Policy Analysis.** 1977. pap. Heath. $6.95.

Germann, A.C., et al. **Introduction to Law Enforcement and Criminal Justice.** rev. ed. (Illus.). 400p. 1978. C.C. Thomas. $11.75.

Gibbons, Don C., et al. **Criminal Justice Planning: An Introduction.** (Illus.). 192p. 1977. Prentice-Hall. $14.95.

Glueck, S., ed. **Roscoe Pound and Criminal Justice.** 1965. Oceana. $12.50.

Goldfarb, Ronald L. & Singer, Linda R. **After Conviction.** 1973. Simon & Schuster. $19.95.

Goldstein, Herman. **Policing a Free Society.** 1977. Ballinger Publishing. $16.50; pap. $8.95.

Gorecki, Jan. **A Theory of Criminal Justice.** 1979. Columbia University Press. $15.00.

Gottfredson, Don M., et al. **Guidelines for Parole and Sentencing.** 1978. Lexington Books. $20.95.

Gottfredson, Michael R. & Gottfredson, Don M. **Decision-Making in Criminal Justice: Toward the Rational Exercise of Discretion.** 1980. Ballinger Publishing. $22.50.

Gray, Charles M. **The Costs of Crime.** 1979. Sage. $20.00; pap. $9.95.

Gray, Virginia & Williams, Bruce. **The Organizational Politics of Criminal Justice: Policy in Context.** 1980. Lexington Books. price not set.

Greenberg, David F. **Corrections and Punishment.** (Illus.). 1977. Sage. $20.00; pap. $9.95.

Greenwood, Peter R., et al. **Prosecution of Adult Felony Defendants: A Policy Perspective.** (Illus.). 1976. Lexington Books. $13.50.

Grygier, Tadeusz. **Social Protection Code: A New Model of Criminal Justice.** 1977. Rothman. $11.50.

Gurr, Ted R. **Rogues, Rebels and Reformers: A Political History of Urban Crime and Conflict.** (Illus.). 1976. Sage. $18.00; pap. $8.95.

Hall, James P. **Peacekeeping in America: A Developmental Study of American Law Enforcement: Philosophy and Systems.** 1978. pap. Kendall-Hunt. $8.95.

Handman, H.I. **The Rights of Convicts.** 128p. 1975. Oceana. $5.95.

Harries, Keith D. & Brunn, Stanley D. **The Geography of Laws and Justice: Spatial Perspectives on the Criminal Justice System.** 1978. Praeger. $19.95.

Hartjen, Clayton A. **Crime and Criminalization.** 2nd ed. 1978. pap. Holt, Rinehart & Winston. $7.50.

Hawes, Joseph, ed. **Law and Order in American History.** 1979. Kennikat. $15.00.

Heineke, J.M., ed. **Economic Models of Criminal Behavior.** Elsevier-North Holland Publishing Co. $44.00.

Hemphill, Charles F. **Criminal Procedure: The Administration of Justice.** (Illus.). 1978. instructor's manual free. Goodyear. $19.95.

Heyd, Uriel. **Studies in Old Ottoman Criminal Law.** Menage, V.I., ed. 1973. Oxford University Press. $19.95.

Hills, Stuart L. **Crime, Power, and Morality: The Criminal Law Process in America.** 1971. Harper & Row. $8.50.

Hoffman, Paul. **Courthouse.** 1979. Dutton, E.P. $12.50.

Holten, N. Gary & Jones, Melvin E. **The System of Criminal Justice.** 1978. tchr's manual free. Little, Brown & Co. $15.95.

Hoover, Larry T. & Lund, Dennis W. **Guidelines for Criminal Justice Programs in Community and Junior Colleges.** 1977. American Association of Community and Junior Colleges. $3.00.

Horoszowski, Pawel. **Economic Special-Opportunity Conduct and Crime.** Lexington Books. date not set. price not set.

Huckabee, Harlow. **Lawyers, Psychiatrists and Criminal Law: Cooperation or Chaos?** 184p. 1980. write for info. C.C. Thomas.

Hudson, Joe & Galaway, Burt, eds. **Victims, Offenders, and Alternative Sanctions.** 1980. Lexington Books. price not set.

Humphrey, John A. & Milakovich, Michael. **Administration of Justice: Law Enforcement Courts and Corrections.** 1980. Human Sciences Press. $26.95; pap. $12.95.

Iacovetta, Ronald & Chang, Dae H., eds. **Critical Issues in Criminal Justice.** (Illus.). 1979. Carolina Academic Press. $24.00; pap. $12.95.

Illinois Association For Criminal Justice. **Illinois Crime Survey.** Wigmore, John H., ed. 1968. Repr. of 1929 ed. Patterson Smith. $35.00.

Inciardi, J. A., **Reflections on Crime.** 1978. pap. Holt, Rinehart & Winston. $6.95.

Irvine, Lynn M., Jr. & Brelje, Terry B., eds. **Law, Psychiatry and the Mentally Disordered Offender.** Vol. I. 164p. 1972. C.C. Thomas. $12.50.

—**Law, Psychiatry and the Mentally Disordered Offender.** Vol. 2. 148p. 1973. C.C. Thomas. $12.50.

Jackson, Bruce & Christian, Diane. **Death Row.** (Illus.). 1980. Beacon Press. $13.95.

Jacob, Herbert, ed. **The Potential for Reform of Criminal Justice.** 1974. Sage. $20.00; pap. $9.95.

Jeffery, C.R. **Crime Prevention Through Environmental Design.** rev. ed. 1977. Sage. $20.00; pap. $9.95.

Jones, David A. **Crime Without Punishment.** 1979. Lexington Books. $21.95.

Kalmanoff, Alan. **Criminal Justice: Enforcement and Administration.** 1976. Little, Brown & Co. resource materials & tests free. $14.95.

Kamins, Barry. **The Social Studies Student Investigates the Criminal Justice System.** (Illus.). 1978. Rosen Press. $7.97.

Kennedy, Daniel B. **The Dysfunctional Alliance Emotion and Reason in Justice Administration.** 1977. pap. Anderson Publishing Co. $10.75.

Kerper, Hazel B. & Israel, Jerold H. **Introduction to the Criminal Justice System.** 2nd ed. (Illus.). (Study guide pap.) 1979. West Publishing. $15.95; pap. $5.95.

Kilbane, Marjorie & Claire, Patricia. **Police, Courts, and the Ghetto.** new ed. Burnes, Alan J., (Illus.). 61p. (Orig.). (gr. 6-10). 1969. pap. Pendulum Press. $0.95.

Kittrie, Nicholas N. & Susman, Jackwell, eds. **Legality, Morality, and Ethics in Criminal Justice.** 1978. Praeger. $21.95.

Klein, Irving. **Constitutional Law for Criminal Justice Professionals.** 1980. Duxbury Press. $15.95.

Klein, John F. **Let's Make a Deal.** (Illus.). 1976. Lexington Books. $16.95.

Klein, Malcolm W. & Teilmann, Katherine S., eds. **Handbook of Criminal Justice Evaluation.** (Illus.). 693p. 1980. Sage. $39.95.

Klonoski, James R. & Mendelsohn, Robert I., eds. **The Politics of Local Justice.** 355p. 1970. pap. Little, Brown & Co. $5.95.

Klotter, John C. & Rosenfeld, Joseph. **Criminal Justice Instructional Techniques.** (Illus.). 216p. 1979. C.C. Thomas. $15.50; pap Student Workbook, 80p. $6.00

Krantz, Sheldon. **Law of Corrections and Prisoners' Rights, 1977 Supplement: Cases & Materials.** 1973. pap. West Publishing. $5.95.

Kratcoski, Peter C. & Walker, Donald B. **Criminal Justice in America: Process and Issues.** 1978. Scott, Foresman. $15.95.

LaPatra, Jack. **Analyzing the Criminal Justice System.** (Illus.). 1978. Lexington Books. $16.95.

LeGrande, James L. **The Basic Processes of Criminal Justice.** 288p. 1973. Glencoe. $9.95.

Leistner, G. **Abbreviations Guide to French Forms in Justice and Administration.** 2nd ed 101p. (Eng. Fr. & Ger). 1975. (Pub. by Vlg. Dokumentation). French & European Pubns., Inc. $27.50.

Levine, James P., et al. **Criminal Justice: A Public Policy Approach.** 591p. 1980. instructor's manual avail. Harcourt Brace Jovanovich. $15.95.

Lewis, Merlin, et al. **An Introduction to the Courts and Judicial Process.** (Illus.). 1978. Prentice-Hall. $16.95.

Lineberry, William P., ed. **Justice in America.** 200p. 1972. Wilson. $5.75.

Littrell, W. Boyd. **Bureaucratic Justice: Police, Prosecutors, and the Construction of Crime.** (Illus.). 1979. Sage. $18.00; pap. $8.95.

Long, Elton, et al. **American Minorities: The Justice Issue.** (Illus.). 256p. 1975. pap. Prentice-Hall. $8.95.

McCall, George J. **Observing the Law: Field Methods in the Study of Crime and the Criminal Justice System.** (Illus.). 1978. Free Press. $15.95.

McDonald, W.F., ed. **Criminal Justice and the Victim.** 1976. Sage. $20.00; pap. $9.95.

McIntyre, Donald M., et al. **Criminal Justice in the United States.** 1974. pap. American Bar Foundation. $2.00.

McIntyre, Donald M., Jr., ed. **Law Enforcement in the Metropolis: A Working Paper on the Criminal Law System in Detroit.** 1967. American Bar Foundation. $7.00.

MacLachlan, Colin M. **Criminal Justice in Eighteenth Century Mexico: A Study of the Tribunal of the Acordada.** 1975. University of California Press. $16.50.

McLean, R.J. **Education for Crime Prevention and Control.** (Illus.). 168p. 1975. C.C. Thomas. $12.50.

Madigan, Kathleen E. & Sullivan, William J. **Crime and Community in Biblical Perspective.** 128p. 1980. pap. Judson. $9.50.

Malinchak, Alan A. **Crime and Gerontology.** (Illus.). 1980. Prentice-Hall. $14.95; pap. $12.95.

Manning, Peter K. **Police Work.** 1979. pap. MIT Press. $8.95.

Marchand, Donald A. **The Politics of Privacy, Computers, and Criminal Justice Records: Controlling the Social Costs of Technological Change.** xvi. 433p. 1980. Information Resources Press. $34.95.

Martin, J.A. & Astone, N.A. **Criminal Justice Vocabulary.** 1980. C.C. Thomas. $16.95.

Mather, Lynn M. **Plea Bargaining or Trial? The Process of Criminal Case Disposition.** (Illus.). 1979. Lexington Books. $16.95.

Mathias, William, et al. **Foundations of Criminal Justice.** (Illus.). 1980. Prentice-Hall. $16.95.

Meyer, Fred & Baker, Ralph, eds. **Determinants of Law Enforcement Policies.** 240p. 1979. Lexington Books. $18.95.

Meyer, W., et al, eds. **Justice in America.** 1972. Gordon. $24.00.

Miller, Kent S. **The Criminal Justice and Mental Health Systems: Conflict and Collusion.** 144p. 1980. Oelgeschlager. $17.50.

Mills, James. **On the Edge.** 1976. pap. Ballantine Books. $1.75.

Milner, Neal A. **Court and Local Law Enforcement: The Impact of Miranda.** 1971. Sage. $17.50.

Misner, Gordon E. **Criminal Justice: Its Transdisciplinary Nature.** 1981. pap. Mosby. $14.95.

Moley, Raymond. **Our Criminal Courts.** facsimile ed. 1974. Repr. of 1930 ed. Arno Press. $17.00.

—**Politics and Criminal Prosecution.** 256p. 1974. Arno Press. Repr. $13.00.

Moore, Richter H., Jr. & Marks, Thomas C. **Readings in Criminal Justice.** 1976. pap. Bobbs-Merrill. $10.15.

Moran, Michael. **Standards Relating to Appeals and Collateral Review.** 1977. Ballinger Publishing. softcover $5.95; casebound $12.50.

More, Harry W. **Criminal Justice Management: A Text and Readings.** 1977. pap. West Publishing. $12.95.

More, Harry W., ed. **Principles and Procedures in the Administration of Justice.** 456p. 1975. (Pub. by Wiley-Interscience). Wiley, John & Sons. $18.95.

More, Harry W., Jr., ed. **Contemporary Criminal Justice.** 2nd ed. 304p. 1977. Justice Systems Development, Inc. $8.95.

Morris, Madelyn N., ed. **Youth, Law and Justice: Program Guide.** 131p. (gr. 9-12). 1980. pap. Microfilming Corp. $9.95.

Morris, Norval & Hawkins, Gordon. **Honest Politicians Guide to Crime Control.** 1970. University of Chicago Press. $12.50.

Morris, Norval & Hawkins, Gordon J. **Letter to the President on Crime Control.** 1977. University of Chicago Press. $1.95

Morris, Norval & Tony, Michael, eds. **Crime and Justice: An Annual Review of Research.** Vol. I. 1979. University of Chicago Press. $14.00.

Morse, Wayne L. & Beattie, Roanld H. **Survey of the Administration of Criminal Justice in Oregon: Final Report on 1771 Felony Cases in Multnomah County Report Number One.** facsimile ed. 1974. Repr. of 1932 ed. Arno Press. $16.00.

Munro, Jim L. **Classes, Conflict and Control: Studies in Criminal Justice Management.** 1976. pap. Anderson Publishing Company. $14.95.

Nagel, Stuart S., ed. **Modeling the Criminal Justice System.** 1977. Sage. $20.00; pap. $9.95.

Nardulli, Peter F. **The Courtroom Elite: An Organizational Perspective on Criminal Justice.** Ballinger Publishing. $16.50.

National Conference on Bail and Criminal Justice, May 27-29, 1964 and May, 1964-Apr. 1965. **Proceedings and Interim Report: Proceedings.** facsimile ed. Fogelson, Robert M., ed. 1974. Arno Press. Repr. $22.00.

Neil. **Interpersonal Communications for Criminal Justice Personnel.** 216p. 1980. Allyn. $13.95.

Neubauer, David W. **America's Courts and the Criminal Justice System.** (Illus.). 1979. Duxbury Press. $14.95.

Newman, Donald J. **Introduction to Criminal Justice.** 2nd ed. 1978. Harper & Row. $18.50.

Newman, Graeme R., ed. **Crime and Justice in America: Seventeen Seventy-Six to Nineteen Seventy-Six.** American Academy of Political and Social Science. Repr. $5.50.

Nimmer, Raymond T. **Two Million Unnecessary Arrests: Removing a Social Service Concern from the Criminal Justice System.** 202p. 1971. American Bar Foundation. $10.00; pap. $5.00.

Oatman, Eric F., ed. **Crime and Society.** 1979. Wilson. $5.75.

O'Brien, John T., ed. **Crime and Justice in America.** (Illus.). 1979. Pergamon Press. $35.00.

Olson, Sheldon R. **Issues in the Sociology of Criminal Justice.** 58p. 1975. pap. Bobbs-Merrill. $2.25.

O'Neill, Michael E. & Martensen, Kai R. **Criminal Justice Group Training: A Facilitator's Handbook.** 290p. 1975. pap. University Associates. $15.00.

O'Neill, Michael E., et al. **Criminal Justice Planning: A Practical Approach.** 260p. 1976. Justice Systems Development, Inc. $13.95.

Owens, Charles E. & Bell, Jimmy, eds. **Blacks and Criminal Justice.** 1977. Lexington Books. $16.00.

Patterson, David W., ed. **Crime and Criminal Justice.** 149p. 1974. pap. Mss. Information Corp. $4.75.

Pease, Ken & McWilliams, William. **Community Service by Order.** 200p. 1980. pap. (Pub. by Scottish Academic Press Scotland). Columbia University Press. $12.50.

Peoples, Edward E. **Readings in Criminal Justice: An Introduction to the System.** (Illus.). 1978. pap. Goodyear. $10.95.

Perrine, Garrith D. **Administration of Justice: Principles and Procedures.** (Illus.). 300p. 1980. West Publishing. $14.95.

Phelps, Thomas R., et al. **Introduction to Criminal Justice.** 1979. inst. manual write for info. Goodyear. $16.95.

Pound, Roscoe. **Criminal Justice in America.** xiv, 226p. 1975. pap. Da Capo. $3.45.

—**Criminal Justice in America.** 224p. 1972. Repr. of 1930 ed. Da Capo. $17.50.

Prassel, Frank R. **Introduction to Criminal Justice.** 260p. 1975. instructor's manual free. Harper & Row. $18.50.

Pursley, Robert. **Introduction to Criminal Justice.** 1977. Glencoe. $14.95.

Quinney, Richard, ed. **Criminal Justice in America: A Critical Understanding.** new ed. (Orig.). 1974. pap. Little, Brown & Co. $6.95.

Radzinowicz, Sir Leon & Wolfgang, Marvin E., eds. **Crime and Justice.** Basic Books. 3 vols. 2nd, rev. ed. 1977. Vol. 1. $25.00; Vol. 2. $25.00; Vol. 3. $19.50; Set. $72.00; Vol. 1. pap. $9.95; Vol. 2. pap. $7.95; Vol. 3. pap. $7.95.

Rank, Richard. **Criminal Justice Systems of the Latin-American Nations: A Bibliography of the Primary and Secondary Literature.** xxxiii, 540p. 1974. Rothman. $45.00.

Readings in Criminal Justice, 1977-78. (Illus.). 1976. write for info. Dushkin Publishing.

Readings in Criminal Justice 78-79. (Illus.). 1978. pap. Dushkin Publishing. $5.75.

Reid, Sue T. **Crime and Criminology.** 2nd ed. 1979. inst. manual avail. Holt, Rinehart & Winston. $14.95.

Remington, et al. **Criminal Justice Administration.** 1969. Michie. $19.00.

Reynolds, Helen. **Cops and Dollars: The Economics of Criminal Law and Justice.** (Illus.). 256p. 1981. pap. C.C. Thomas. $14.75.

Robbins, Ira P. **Comparative Post-Conviction Remedies.** 128p. 1980. Lexington Books. $13.95.

Roberts, Charles C. **Tangled Justice: Some Reasons for a Change of Policy in Africa.** Repr. of 1937 ed. Negro University Press. $9.25.

Robertson, John A. **Rough Justice: Perspectives on Lower Criminal Courts.** 1974. pap. Little, Brown & Co. $8.95.

Robin, Gerald D. **Introduction to the Criminal Justice System: Principles, Procedures, Practice.** (Illus.). 1980. instrs. manual avail. Harper & Row. $17.50.

Rossum, R.A. **The Politics of the Criminal Justice System: An Organizational Analysis.** Vol. 6. 1978. Dekker, Marcel. $17.75.

Rudman, Jack. **Introduction to Criminal Justice.** (ACT Proficiency Examination Program. PEP-8). National Learning Corp. $14.95; pap. $9.95.

—**Introduction to Criminal Justice.** (College Proficiency Examination Ser: CPEP-29). 1977. National Learning Corp. $14.95; pap. $9.95.

Rush, George E. **Dictionary of Criminal Justice.** 1977. pap. Holbrook. $9.50.

Ryan, Mick. **Radical Alternatives to Prison and the Penal Lobby.** 1975. Praeger. $14.95.

Saks, Michael J. & Baron, Charles H., eds. **The Use-Nonuse-Misuse of Social Research in the Courts.** 1980. Abt Associates. $26.00.

Sales, Bruce D., ed. **The Criminal Justice System.** (Illus.). 268p. 1977. Plenum Publishing. $19.50.

Savitz, Leonard D. **Dilemmas in Criminology.** 1967. pap. McGraw-Hall. $6.95.

Schultz, Donald O. **Critical Issues in Criminal Justice.** (Illus.). 304p. 1975. C.C. Thomas. $18.00.

Schultz, Jon S. & Thames, Jon P., eds. **Criminal Justice Systems Review.** 1974. W.S. Hein. $37.50.

Scott, Joseph E. & Dinitz, Simon, eds. **Criminal Justice Planning.** 1977. Praeger. $19.95.

Seiter, Richard P. **Evaluation Research As a Feedback Mechanism for Criminal Justice Policy Making: A Critical Analysis.** 1978. pap. R&E Research Associates. $10.00.

Senna, Joseph J. & Siegel, Larry J. **Introduction to Criminal Justice.** (Illus.). 1978. West Publishing. $16.95.

—**Introduction to Criminal Justice.** 2nd ed. (Illus.). 656p. 1981. West Publishing. $16.95.

Senna, Joseph J., et al. **Study Guide for Senna and Siegel's Introduction to Criminal Justice.** 1978. pap. West Publishing. $6.95.

Shanahan & Whisenand. **Criminal Justice Planning.** 444p. 1980. Allyn & Bacon. $15.95.

Silberman, Charles. **Criminal Violence-Criminal Justice: Criminals, Police, Courts and Prisons in America.** 1978. Random House. $15.00.

Silberman, Charles E. **Criminal Violence, Criminal Justice.** 1980. pap. Random House. $3.95.

Silving, Helen. **Criminal Justice.** 2 vols. 1971. W.S. Hein. Set. $75.00.

Simon, Rita J. **Women and Crime.** 1978. pap. Heath. $5.95.

Singer & Statsky. **The Criminal Process: Sentencing and Criminal Commitment.** 1974. Michie. softcover $12.00.

Singer, Richard G. **Just Deserts: Sentencing Based on Equality and Desert.** 1979. Ballinger Publishing. $17.50.

Skoler, Daniel L. **Organizing the Non-System.** (Illus.). 1977. Lexington Books. $18.50.

Skolnick, Jerome H. **Justice Without Trial: Law Enforcement in Democratic Society.** 2nd ed. 320p. 1975. pap. Wiley, John & Sons. $8.95.

Smith, Alexander B. & Berlin, Louis. **Treating the Criminal Offender.** 2nd ed. 368p. 1981. Prentice-Hall. $15.95.

Smith, Alexander B. & Pollack, Harriet. **Criminal Justice: An Overview.** 2nd ed. 1979. pap. Holt, Rinehart & Winston. $8.95.

Smith, Alexander B. & Pollack, Harriet. **Some Sins Are Not Crimes: A Plea for Reform of the Criminal Law.** 224p. 1975. New Viewpoints. $12.50; pap. $5.95.

Smith, Barbara L. **Social Problems and the Criminal Justice System: Legal Aspects of Counseling.** 1979. Challenge Press. $15.00.

Snortum, John R. & Hadar, Ilana, eds. **Criminal Justice: Allies and Adversaries.** 1978. pap. Palisades Publishing. $7.50.

Sparks, Richard F., et al. **Surveying Victims: A Study of the Measurement of Criminal Victimization, Perceptions of Crime and Attitudes to Criminal Justice.** 1978. (Pub. by Wiley-Interscience). Wiley, John & Sons. $43.95.

Steadman, Henry J. **Beating a Rap? Defendants Found Incompetent to Stand Trial.** 1979. University of Chicago Press. $13.00.

Stuckey, Gilbert B. **Procedures in the Justice System.** new ed. 288p. 1976. Merrill. $14.95.; instructor's manual. $3.95.

—**Procedures in the Justice System.** 2nd ed. 280p. 1980. Merrill. $15.95; instructor's manual. $3.95.

Sutherland, Edwin H. & Cressey, Donald R. **Criminology.** 10th ed. 1978. Harper & Row. $19.50.

Swigert, Victoria & Farrell, Ronald A. **Murder, Inequality, and the Law: Differential Treatment and the Legal Process.** 1976. Lexington Books. $14.95.

Szabo, Denis. **Criminology and Crime Policy.** 256p. 1979. Lexington Books. $25.95.

Szabo, T. **Unification and Differentiation in Socialist Criminal Justice.** 1978. (Pub. by Kaido Hungary). Heyden & Son, Inc. $26.50.

Talarico, Susette, ed. **Research in Criminal Justice: Approaches, Problems and Policy.** 384p. (Orig.). 1980. pap. Anderson Publishing Co. $14.95.

Toch, Hans. **Psychology of Crime and Criminal Justice.** 1979. Holt, Rinehart & Winston. $15.95.

Tompkins, Dorothy C. **Administration of Criminal Justice, Nineteen Forty-Nine-Nineteen Fifty-Six: A Selected Bibliography.** 1970. Repr. of 1956 ed. Patterson Smith. $16.50.

Train, Arthur. **Courts and Criminals.** facsimile ed. 1974. Repr. of 1928 ed. Arno Press. $17.00.

—**The Prisoner at the Bar: Sidelights on the Administration of Criminal Justice.** 1974. Arno Press. Repr. $20.00.

Trojanowicz, Robert & Dixon, Samuel. **Criminal Justice and the Community.** (Illus.). 464p. 1974. Prentice-Hall. $16.95.

Uhlman, Thomas M. **Racial Justice: Black Judges and Defendants in an Urban Trial Court.** 144p. 1979. Lexington Books. $14.50.

United States Task Force on the Administration of Justice. **Task Force Report: The Courts.** (Illus.). 1978. Repr. of 1967 ed. Greenwood Press. $22.00.

University of Chicago Law Review Staff. **Criminal Justice in Extremis: Administration of Justice During the April 1968 Chicago Disorder.** 163p. 1969. American Bar Foundation. Repr. $3.00.

Uviller, H. Richard. **Processes of Criminal Justice: Adjudication.** 2nd ed. 1979. pap. West Publishing. $13.95.

—**The Processes of Criminal Justice: Investigation and Adjudication.** 2nd ed. 1979. West Publishing. $23.95.

—**Processes of Criminal Justice Investigation.** 2nd ed. 1979. pap. West Publishing. $12.95.

VanDine, Stephen, et al. **Restraining the Wicked: The Incapacitation of the Dangerous Criminal.** (Illus.). 1979. Lexington Books. $14.50.

Waddington, Lawrence C. **Arrest, Search and Seizure.** 320p. 1974. Glencoe. $12.95.

Waldron, Ronald J., et al. **The Criminal Justice System: An Introduction.** 2nd ed. (Illus.). 1980. Houghton Mifflin. $16.95; inst. manual $0.65.; study guide $5.95.

—**The Criminal Justice System: An Introduction.** (Illus.) 480p. 1976. pap. Houghton Mifflin. (op) $15.75; instructors manual $1.25.

Walker, Nigel. **Punishment, Danger and Stigma: The Morality of Criminal Justice.** 224p. 1980. Barnes & Noble. $22.50.

Walker, Samuel E. **Popular Justice: A History of American Criminal Justice.** 1980. Oxford University Press. $12.95; pap. $4.95.

Warner, Sam B. & Cabot, Henry B. **Judges and Law Reform.** 1974. Repr. Arno Press. $15.00.

Warren, W.C., et al. **Criminal Law and Its Administration: The Ditchley Papers.** 1971. Repr. of 1966 ed. Da Capo. $12.50.

Way, H. Frank. **Criminal Justice and the American Constitution.** 1980. Duxbury Press. $17.95.

Webb, G.L. **Conviction and Sentencing: Deception and Racial Discrimination.** 1979. Coker Books. $4.95.

Weinreb, Lloyd L. **Denial of Justice: Criminal Process in the United States.** 1979. pap. Free Press. $5.95.

Weston, Paul B. **Supervision in the Administration of Justice: Police, Corrections, Courts.** 2nd ed. (Illus.). 224p. 1978. C.C. Thomas. $13.25.

Weston, Paul B. & Wells, Kenneth. **Criminal Justice Introduction and Guidelines: A Revision of Law Enforcement and Criminal Justice.** 1976. instructor's manual free. Goodyear. $20.95.

Weston, Paul B. & Wells, Kenneth M. **Administration of Justice.** 3rd ed. (Illus.). 1977. Prentice-Hall. $16.95.

Whitebread, Charles H., 2nd, ed. **Mass Production Justice and the Constitutional Ideal.** xxv, 236p. 1970. University Press of Virginia. $7.50.

Wickwar, Hardy. **The Place of Criminal Justice in Developmental Planning.** 130p. 1977. NYU Press. $12.50.

Williams, D.G. & Weir, J.A. **Compensation for Personal Injuries and Death: Recent Proposals for Reform: The Accountability of the Police.** 1979. pap. Kluwer Boston. $7.90.

Wills, Antoinette. **Crime and Punishment in Revolutionary Paris.** (Illus.). 248p. 1981. Greenwood Press. $27.50.

Wilson, James Q. **Thinking About Crime.** 1977. pap. Random House. $1.95.

—**Thinking About Crime.** 1975. Basic Books. $12.50.

Wolfgang, Martin E., ed. **Prison: Present and Possible.** 1979. Lexington Books. $17.95.

Worton, Stanley N. **Law Enforcement and Justice.** (gr. 10 up). 1977. pap. Hayden Book Co. $4.50.

Wright, Burton & Fox, Vernon. **Criminal Justice and the Social Sciences.** (Illus.). 1978. Holt, Rinehart & Winston. $13.50.

Wright, Jack & Lewis, Peter. **Modern Criminal Justice.** 1977. McGraw-Hill. $14.95.

Wright, Kevin N., ed. **Crime and Criminal Justice in a Declining Economy.** 128p. 1981. Oelgeschlager, Gunn & Hain. $20.00.

Wrobleski, Henry M. & Hess, Karen M. **Introduction to Law Enforcement and Criminal Justice.** 1979. West Publishing. $17.95.

Wylie, Max. **Four Hundred Miles from Harlem: Courts, Crime, and Correction.** 228p. 1972. Macmillan. $6.95.

Young Rifai, Marlene A., ed. **Justice and Older Americans.** (Illus.). 1977. Lexington Books. $18.95.

Zarr, Melvyn. **The Bill of Rights and the Police.** Sloan, Irving J., ed. 125p. 1980. Oceana. $5.95.

Zimring, Franklin E. & Frase, Richard S. **The Criminal Justice System.** 1038p. 1980. Little, Brown & Co. $24.00.

CRIMINAL JUSTICE, ADMINISTRATION OF— BIBLIOGRAPHY

Culver, Dorothy C., ed. **Bibliography of Crime and Criminal Justice: Nineteen Thirty-Two to Nineteen Thirty-Seven.** 1969. Repr. of 1939 ed. Patterson Smith. $16.50.

Kinton, J. **Criminology and Criminal Justice in America: A Guide to the Literature.** 1978. Social Science & Sociological Resources. $3.95.

Kuhlman, Augustus F. **Guide to Material on Crime and Criminal Justice.** (Added author index prepared by Dorothy C. Culver). 1969. Repr. of 1929 ed. Patterson Smith. $22.50.

Prostano, Emanuel T. & Piccirillo, Martin L. **Law Enforcement: A Selective Bibliography.** 1974. Libraries Unlimited. $13.50.

Radzinowicz, Leon & Hood Roger. **Criminology and the Administration of Criminal Justice: A Bibliography.** (Orig.). 1976. Greenwood Press. $32.50.

Tompkins, Dorothy C. **Sources for the Study of the Administration of Criminal Justice, 1938-1948: A Selected Bibliography.** 1970. Repr. of 1949 ed. Patterson Smith. $15.00.

CRIMINAL LAW

Ancel, Marc. **Social Defense: A Modern Approach to Criminal Problems.** 1966. Schocken Books. $6.95.

Bailey, F. Lee & Rothblatt, Henry B. **Handling Misdemeanor Cases.** new ed. 1976. Lawyers Co-Operative Publishing Co. $45.00.

Berry, Calvin W. **Criminal Practice in Municipal and County Courts.** 1964. Michie. $25.00.

Brandstatter, A.F. & Hyman, A.A. **Fundamentals of Law Enforcement.** 1972. Glencoe. $14.95.

Brickey, Kathleen F. **Kentucky Criminal Law: A Treatise on Criminal Law Under the New Kentucky Penal Code.** 1974. Banks-Baldwin. $45.00.

Canudo, Eugene R. **Criminal Law of New York.** 660p. (Supplemented annually). 1978. looseleaf. Gould. $15.00.

Carr, James G. **Criminal Law Review.** 1979. Boardman. $39.50.

Chadman, Charles E. **A Treatise on Criminal Law and Criminal Procedure.** 1976. Repr. of 1906 ed. AMS Press. $64.00.

Chambliss, William J. **Crime and the Legal Process.** (Sociology Ser.) 1968. McGraw-Hill. $11.50; pap. $10.95.

Chamelin, Neil C. & Evans, Kenneth R. **Criminal Law for Policemen.** 2nd ed. 288p. 1976. Prentice-Hall. $15.95.

Clift, Raymond E. **Guide to Modern Police Thinking.** 3rd ed. 1970. Anderson Publishing Co. $9.50.

Co-Op East Law Outlines: Criminal Law. (Orig.). 1976. Sterling Swift. $3.50.

Cohen, Fred. **Criminal Law Digest.** 1970. Warren, Gorham & Lamont. $44.50.

Connecticut Penal Code. 200p. looseleaf. Gould $10.00.

Criminal Law of Kentucky Annotated. 1978. Banks-Baldwin. $35.00.

Criminal Law Reporter Editorial Staff. **Criminal Law Revolution and Its Aftermath, the 1977-80 Supplement.** 1981. pap. Bureau of National Affairs. $10.00.

Criminal Laws of California. 500p. (Supplemented annually). looseleaf. Gould. $15.00.

Criminal Procedure Law (N.Y.) (Supplemented annually). 1976. Gould. looseleaf $5.95; pap. $5.50.

Dahl, Richard C. & Dix, George E., eds. **Crime Law and Justice Annual, 1972.** 1972. W.S. Hein. $34.50.

Dix, George E. & Sharlot, M. Michael. **Cases and Materials on Criminal Law.** 2nd ed. 1979. West Publishing. $18.95.

Eldefonso, Edward & Coffey, Alan R. **Criminal Law: History, Philosophy, and Enforcement.** (Illus.). 304p. 1980. Harper & Row. $17.50.

Evans, Ken & Chamelin, Neil C. **Criminal Law for Police Officers.** 3rd ed. 352p. 1981. Prentice-Hall. $15.95.

Felkenes, George T. & Becker, Harold K. **Law Enforcement: A Selected Bibliography.** 2nd ed. 1977. Scarecrow Press. $14.00.

Foote, Caleb & Levy, Robert J. **Criminal Law: Cases and Materials.** 950p. 1981. Little, Brown & Co.

Fricke, Charles W. **California Criminal Law.** 11th ed. Alarcon, Arthur L., ed. 1977. Legal Book Corporation. $16.00.

—**Criminal Investigation and the Law.** 7th ed. Payton, George T., ed. 1974. Legal Book Corp. $14.00.

—**Five Thousand Criminal Definitions Terms and Phrases.** 5th ed. 1968. Legal Book Corporation. $6.00.

Friedland, M.L. **Cases and Materials on Criminal Law and Procedure.** 5th ed. 1978. University of Toronto Press. $50.00; $30.00.

Gammage, Allen Z. & Hemphill, Charles F., Jr. **Basic Criminal Law.** 2nd ed. 1979. McGraw-Hill. $13.95; study guide $6.95; instructor's manual & key; $3.00.

Garofalo, Raffaele. **Criminology.** Millar, Robert W., tr. 1968. Repr. of 1914 ed. Patterson Smith. $20.00.

Glueck, Sheldon S. **Mental Disorder and the Criminal Law.** 1925. Kraus Reprint. $24.00.

Goldman, Lawrence S. **New York Criminal Law Handbook.** 500p. Date not set. Dist. by Shepard's Inc. McGraw-Hill. $60.00.

Goldstein, Joseph, et al. **Criminal Law: Theory and Process.** 2nd ed. (Illus.). 1974. Free Press. $30.25.

Gould Editorial Staff. **Penal Law of New York: Spanish Edition.** 1980. Gould. looseleaf. $10.00.

Gould Editorial Staff. **Crime Codes of Pennsylvania.** 250p. (Supplemented annually). 1978. Gould. looseleaf. $12.00.

—**Crimes Code of Pennsylvania.** 400p. Gould. $13.00.

—**Criminal Justice Code of New Jersey.** 150p. Gould. looseleaf. $10.50.

—**Criminal Law Digest of Pennsylvania.** Gould. looseleaf. $10.00.

—**Criminal Laws of Florida.** (Annual). 1979. Gould. $8.50.

—**Criminal Laws of Illinois.** (Annual). 1979. Gould. $8.50.

—**Criminal Laws of Massachusetts.** (Supplemented annually). looseleaf. Gould. $13.50.

—**Criminal Laws of Michigan.** 300p. Gould. looseleaf. $10.50.

—**Criminal Laws of Ohio.** (Annual). Gould. looseleaf. $10.50.

Gould Editorial Staff, ed. **Penal Code of Michigan.** 2nd ed. 350p. 1980. Gould. $10.50.

Grimes, William A. **Criminal Law Outline.** 1979. pap. National Judicial College. $5.00.

Gross, Hyman. **A Theory of Criminal Justice.** 1979. Oxford University Press. $19.95; pap. $6.95.

Hall, Arthur C. **Crime in Its Relations to Social Progress.** 1968. Repr. of 1902 ed. AMS Press. $27.50.

Hall, Jerome. **General Principles of Criminal Law.** 2nd ed. 1960. Michie. $16.00.

Harvard Civil Rights Civil Liberties Law Review Staff. **Preventive Detention: An Empirical Analysis.** 108p. 1971. pap. American Bar Foundation. $2.50.

Hood, Roger & Sparks, Richard. **Key Issues in Criminology.** (Illus. Orig.). 1970. pap. McGraw-Hill. $3.95.

Hortwitz, Morton, et al, eds. **Reform of Criminal Law in Pennsylvania: Selected Enquiries 1787-1819.** 1972. Arno Press. $23.00.

Huckabee, Harlow. **Lawyer, Psychiatrists and Criminal Law: Cooperation or Chaos?** 184p. 1980. write for info. C.C. Thomas.

Hunt, Derald D. **California Criminal Law Manual.** 5th ed. 1980. write for info. Burgess.

—**California Criminal Law Manual.** 4th ed. 1976. pap. Burgess. $9.95.

Hutnick, M.B. **Criminal Law and Court Procedures.** 176p. 1974. Delmar. $8.00; instructor's guide. $1.45.

Idaho State Department of Education and Northwest Regional Educational Laboratory. **Understanding Contracts and Legal Documents and Understanding Criminal Law.** (Illus.). 1980. pap. McGraw-Hill. $4.00.

Imwinkelried, Edward J., et al. **Criminal Evidence.** 1979. pap. West Publishing. $16.95.

Inbau, Fred E., et al. **Criminal Law for the Layman.** 2nd ed. 1978. Chilton. $10.95; pap. $7.95.

Johnson, Philip E. **Criminal Law, Cases, Materials and Text on the Substantive Criminal Law in Its Procedural Context.** 2nd ed. 1000p. 1980. write for info. West Publishing.

Josephson, Michael. **Criminal Law.** Center for Creative Educational Services. $8.95.

Kadish, Sanford H. & Paulsen, Monrad G. **Criminal Law and Its Process.** 3rd ed. 1975. write for info. suppl. Little, Brown & Co. $27.00.

Kerper, Hazel B. & Kerper, Janeen. **Legal Rights of the Convicted.** 1974. West Publishing. $16.95.

LaFave, Wayne R. **Principles of Criminal Law.** abr. ed. 1978. West Publishing. $17.95.

Livingston, Edward. **Complete Works on Criminal Jurisprudence: Consisting of Systems of Penal Law for the State of Louisiana and for the United States of America, with Introductory Reports to the Same.** 2 vols. (With an intro. by Salmon P. Chase). 1968. Repr. of 1873 ed. Patterson Smith. Set. $35.00.

Loewy, Arnold H. **Criminal Law in a Nutshell.** 1980. pap. West Publishing. $6.95.

McClain, Emlin. **A Treatise on the Criminal Law As Now Administered in the United States.** 2 vols. Incl. Vol. 1. Criminal Law - United States. Vol. 2. Criminal Procedure 1578p. 1974. Repr. of 1897 ed. AMS Press. Set. $94.50.

McIntyre, Donald M., et al. **Criminal Justice in the United States.** 1974. pap. American Bar Foundation. $2.00.

McKenna, George G. **Introduction to Criminal Law: New York Edition.** 1977. pap. Kendall-Hunt. $9.95.

Marks, Edward & Paperno, Lloyd I. **Criminal Law in New York Under the Revised Penal Law.** Acme Law Book Co. $35.00.

Maryland Crimes and Offenses and Related Matters. 2 vols. 1979. Michie. $40.00.

Murrell, David E. **Kentucky Criminal Practice: A Treatise on Criminal Practice and Procedure.** 1975. Banks-Baldwin. $45.00.

Neier, Arych. **Crime and Punishment: A Radical Solution.** 256p. 1976. Stein & Day. $25.00; pap. $5.95.

Newman, Jason, et al. **Street Law.** (Illus.). (gr. 9-12). 1975. pap. West Publishing. $5.50; tchr's manual $5.50.

Orland, Leonard. **Prisons: Houses of Darkness.** 1975. Free Press. $12.50.

Pantaleoni, C.A. & Bigler, James C. **California Criminal Law: A Guide for Policemen.** 1969. Prentice-Hall. $15.95.

Penal Law of New York. (Supplemented annually). Gould. looseleaf. $5.75; pap. $4.50.

Pistole, Jesse R. **Criminal Law for Peace Officers.** 480p. 1976. Reston. $15.95.

Reynolds, Helen. **Cops and Dollars: The Economics of Criminal Law and Justice.** (Illus.). 256p. 1981. pap. C.C. Thomas. $14.75.

Roche, Philip. **Criminal Mind: A Study of Communication Between the Criminal Law and Psychiatry.** 1976. Repr. of 1958 ed. Greenwood Press. $19.00.

Schroeder, Oliver C. & Katz, Lewis R. **Schroeder-Katz Ohio Criminal Law and Practice: A Guide to Ohio's New Criminal Law and Criminal Procedure Under the Rules.** 2 vols. 1974. Banks-Baldwin. Set. $110.00.

Schur, Edwin M. & Bedau, Hugo A. **Victimless Crimes: Two Sides of a Controversy.** 160p. 1974. pap. Prentice-Hall. $3.45.

Senna, Joseph J. & Siegel, Larry J. **Introduction to Criminal Justice.** (Illus.). 1978. West Publishing. $16.95.

Senna, Joseph J., et al. **Study Guide for Senna and Siegel's Introduction to Criminal Justice.** 1978. pap. West Publishing. $6.95.

Shannon, Mary L., et al. **The Map Abstract of Criminal Justice Information: Alabama.** (Illus.) 112p. 1976. pap. University of Alabama Press. $5.00.

Silving, Helen. **Criminal Justice.** 2 vols. 1971.

W.S. Hein. Set. $75.00.

Smith, Alexander B. & Pollack, Harriet. **Some Sins Are Not Crimes: A Plea for Reform of the Criminal Law.** 224p. 1975. New Viewpoints. $12.50; pap. $5.95.

Smith, Eugene. **Criminal Law in the United States.** Repr. of 1910 ed. Irvington. $23.00.

Snee, Joseph M. & Pye, Kenneth A. **Status of Forces Agreements and Criminal Jurisdiction.** 1957. Oceana. $12.50.

Symmes, ed. **Ewbank's Indiana Criminal Law.** 2 vols. 1956. Michie. with 1979; suppl. $75.00; suppl. $35.00.

Tobias, Marc W. & Petersen, R. David. **Field Manual of Criminal Law and Police Procedure.** (Illus.). 212p. 1975. pap. C.C. Thomas. $15.25.

Torcia, Charles E., ed. **Wharton's Criminal Law.** 4 vols. 14th ed. 1978. Lawyers Co-operative Publishing Co. $150.00.

Underhill's Criminal Evidence. 3 vols. Set. Michie. with 1978 suppl. $95.00; 1978. suppl. $50.00.

Waite, John B. **Criminal Law in Action.** 1974. Repr. Arno Press. $18.00.

Weinreb, Lloyd L. **Criminal Law, Cases, Comment and Questions.** 3rd ed. 787p. 1980. Foundation Press. write for info.

Wells, Ken & Weston, Paul. **Criminal Law.** (Illus.). 1978. Goodyear. $18.95.

Wells, Paul W. **Basic Law: For the Law Enforcement Officer.** (Illus.). 305p. 1976. Saunders, W.B. $9.75.

Wise, E. M. & Mueller, G.O. **Studies in Comparative Criminal Law.** (Illus.). 338p. 1975. C.C. Thomas. $24.25.

Wootton, Barbara. **Crime and Penal Policy.** 1978. Allen & Unwin. $16.50; pap. $7.95.

Young, R.B. **Criminal Law: Codes and Cases.** 1972. McGraw-Hill. $12.92: instructor's manual $2.50.

CRIMINAL LAW—STUDY AND TEACHING

Criminal Law New York Questions and Answers. 1979 ed. 250p. 1978. Gould. $8.50.

Salottolo, Lawrence. **Criminal Law: Handbook for Law Enforcement Officers.** 416p. (Orig.). 1975. pap. Arco. $12.00.

CRIMINAL PROCEDURE

Bailey, F. Lee & Rothblatt, Henry B. **Complete Manual of Criminal Forms.** 2 vols. 2nd ed. 1974. Lawyers Co-Operative Publishing Co. $80.00.

—**Fundamentals of Criminal Advocacy.** 1974. Lawyers Co-Operative Publishing Co. $18.00.

—**Investigation and Preparation of Criminal Cases.** 1 vol. 1970. Lawyers Co-Operative Publishing Co. $45.00.

—**Successful Techniques for Criminal Trials.** 1971. Lawyers Co-Operative Publishing Co. $45.00.

Del Carmen, Rolando. **Criminal Procedure and Evidence.** 190p. 1979. pap. Harcourt Brace Jovanovich. instructor's manual avail. $7.95.

Dowling, Jerry L. **Teaching Materials on Criminal Procedure.** 1976. West Publishing. $17.95.

Felkenes, George T. & Becker, Harold K. **Law Enforcement: A Selected Bibliography.** 2nd ed. 1977. Scarecrow Press. text ed. $14.00.

Ferdico, John M. **Criminal Procedure for the Law Enforcement Officer.** 2nd ed. (Illus.). 1979. West Publishing. $17.95.

Fricke, Charles W. & Alarcon, Arthur L. **California Criminal Procedure.** 8th ed. 1974. Legal Book Corp. $16.00.

Friedland, M.L. **Cases and Materials on Criminal Law and Procedure.** 5th ed. 1978. University of Toronto Press. text ed. $30.00.

George, B. James, Jr. **Criminal Procedure Sourcebook: Including Nineteen Seventy-Nine Supplement.** 1979. Practising Law Institute. Set. $60.00; suppl alone $25.00.

Gibbens, T.C., et al. **Medical Remands in the Criminal Court.** 1977. Oxford University Press. $22.00.

Glueck, Sheldon S. **Crime and Justice.** 1945. Kraus Reprint. $18.00.

Goldstein, Abraham S. & Orland, Leonard. **Criminal Procedure, Cases and Materials on the Administration of Criminal Law: 1978 Supplement.** 1974. Little, Brown & Co. $25.50.

Gould Editorial Staff. **Criminal Procedure Law of New York Quizzer, 1978-79.** 1978. Gould. looseleaf $5.50.

Harding, Arthur L., ed. **Fundamental Law in Criminal Prosecutions.** 1959. Southern Methodist University Press. $4.00.

Hemphill, Charles F. **Criminal Procedure: The Administration of Justice.** (Illus.). 1978. Goodyear. instructor's manual free. $19.95.

Herman, Michele G. **Federal Rules of Criminal Procedure.** 2nd ed. 1980. write for info. Boardman.

Hermann, Michele G., ed. **Federal Rules of Criminal Procedure.** 1975. looseleaf with 1978 rev. pages. Boardman. $25.00.

Hewitt, William H. **Administration of Criminal Justice in New York.** 1967. Lawyers Co-Operative Publishing Co. $11.50.

Inbau, Fred E., et al. **Cases and Comments on Criminal Procedure.** 2nd ed. write for info. Foundation Press.

Israel, Jerold H. & LaFave, Wayne R. **Criminal Procedure in a Nutshell: Constitutional Limitations.** 1980. pap. text ed. West Publishing. $6.95.

Johnson, Philip E. **Elements of Criminal Due Process.** 1975. pap. West Publishing. $11.95.

Jones, David A. **Law of Criminal Procedure: An Analysis and Critique.** 600p. 1981. Little, Brown & Co. teachers manual free. $17.95.

Kamisar, Yale, et al. **Criminal Procedure.** 1st ed. 1977. Center for Creative Educational Services. $12.95.

—**Modern Criminal Procedure: Cases, Comments and Questions.** 5th ed. 1600p. 1980. West Publishing. $25.95.

Katz, Lewis R. **The Justice Imperative: An Introduction to Criminal Justice.** Piaget, Candice, ed. (Illus.). 375p. 1980. Anderson Publishing Co. instrs' guide avail. $16.95.

Kiraly. **Criminal Procedure: Truth and Probability.** 1979. (Pub. by Kaido Hungary). Heyden & Son. $21.00.

Kittrie, Nicholas N. & Zenoff, Elyce H. **Criminal Sanctions, Sentencing and Corrections: Law, Policy and Practice.** 1981. Foundation Press. price not set.

Leonard, V.A. **The Police, the Judiciary, and the Criminal.** 2nd ed. (Illus.). 320p. 1975. C.C. Thomas. $17.50.

Lewis, Merlin, et al. **An Introduction to the Courts and Judicial Process.** (Illus.). 1978. Prentice-Hall. $16.95.

Miller, Frank W. **Prosecution: The Decision to Charge a Suspect with a Crime.** 366p. 1970. pap. Little, Brown & Co. $5.95.

Mueller, Gerhard OW. & Le Poole-Griffiths, Fre. **Comparative Criminal Procedure.** 1969. NYU Press. $12.00.

Newman, Donald J. **Introduction to Criminal Justice.** 2nd ed. Harper & Row. $18.50.

O'Brien & Sullivan. **Criminalistics: Theory and Practice.** 3rd ed. 384p. 1980. Allyn & Bacon. $16.95.

Orfield, Lester B. **Criminal Procedure from Arrest to Appeal.** 614p. 1972. Repr. of 1947 ed. Greenwood Press. $29.50.

—**Criminal Procedure Under the Federal Rules.** 7 vols. 1968. Lawyers Co-Operative Publishing Co. Set. $262.50.

Paperno, Lloyd J. & Goldstein, Arthur. **Criminal Procedure in New York.** 2 pts. Incl. Pt. 1. Practice & Forms. rev. ed; Pt. 2. Criminal Evidence. Acme Law. $35.00 each.

Petersen, R. David. **The Police Officer in Court.** (Illus.). 192p. 1975. C.C. Thomas. $12.50.

Pinkerton, Alan. **Thirty Years a Detective: A Thorough and Comprehensive Expose of Criminal Practices of All Grades and Classes.** (Illus.). 1975. Repr. of 1884 ed. Patterson Smith. $16.00.

Pound, Roscoe. **Criminal Justice in America.** 224p. 1972. Repr. of 1930 ed. Da Capo. $17.50.

Puttkammer, Ernst W. **Administration of Criminal Law.** 1953. University of Chicago Press. $7.50.

Saltzberg, Stephen A. **American Criminal Procedure: Cases and Commentary.** 1253p. 1980. West Publishing. $22.95.

—**Introduction to American Criminal Procedure.** abr. ed. 689p. 1980. pap. West Publishing. $13.95.

Schroeder, Oliver C. & Katz, Lewis R. **Schroeder-Katz Ohio Criminal Law and Practice: A Guide to Ohio's New Criminal Law and Criminal Procedure Under the Rules.** 2 vols. 1974. Banks-Baldwin. Set. $110.00.

Stuckey, Gilbert B. **Procedures in the Justice System.** 2nd ed. 280p. 1980. Merrill. $15.95; instructor's manual $3.95.

Subin, Harry I. **Criminal Justice in Metropolitan Court.** 234p. 1973. Repr. of 1966 ed. Da Capo. $17.50.

Szabo, Denis. **Criminology and Crime Policy.** 256p. 1979. Lexington Books. $25.95.

Tobias, Marc W. & Petersen, R. David. **Pre-Trial Criminal Procedure: A Survey of Constitutional Rights.** (Illus.). 448p. 1972. C.C. Thomas. $21.50.

Torcia, Charles E. **Wharton's Criminal Procedure.** 4 vols. 12th ed. 1976. Lawyers Co-Operative Publishing Co. $150.00.

Uhlman, Thomas M. **Racial Justice: Black Judges and Defendants in an Urban Trial Court.** 144p. 1979. Lexington Books. $14.50.

United States Task Force on the Administration of Justice. **Task Force Report: The Courts.** (Illus.). 1978. Repr. of 1967 ed. Greenwood Press. $22.00.

Waite, John B. **Criminal Law in Action.** 1974. Repr. Arno Press. $18.00.

Weinreb, Lloyd L. **Denial of Justice: Criminal Process in the United States.** 1977. Free Press. $12.95.

Wells, Kenneth M. & Weston, Paul B. **Criminal Procedure and Trial Practice.** (Illus.). 1977. Prentice-Hall. $15.95.

Wells, Paul W. **Basic Law: For the Law Enforcement Officer.** 305p. 1976. Saunders, W.B. $9.75.

Wright, G.R. & Marlo, J. **Police Officer and Criminal Justice.** 197. McGraw-Hill. $12.90.

Zarr, Melvyn. **Bill of Rights and the Police.** rev. ed. 1970. Oceana. $4.95.

—**The Bill of Rights and the Police.** Sloan, Irving J., ed. 125p. 1980. Oceana. $5.95.

CRIMINAL PSYCHOLOGY

Abrahamsen, David. **Crime and the Human Mind.** 1969. Repr. of 1944 ed. Patterson Smith. $12.00.

—**The Murdering Mind.** 1973. Harper & Row. $6.95.

—**The Murdering Mind.** 1975. Harper & Row. (OP). $2.95.

—**Psychology of Crime.** 1960. Columbia University Press. $15.00.

Alexander, Franz & Healy, William. **Roots of Crime: Psychoanalytic Studies.** 1969. Repr. of 1935 ed. Patterson Smith. $12.50.

Aschaffenburg, Gustav. **Crime and Its Repression.** Albrecht, Adalbert, tr. 1968. Repr. of 1913 ed. Patterson Smith. $17.50.

Bermant, Gordon, et. al. **Psychology and the Law.** 1976. Lexington Books. $19.95.

Blumer, Herbert & Hauser, Philip M. **Movies, Delinquency—Crime.** Repr. of 1933 ed. Arno Press. $11.00.

Brodsky, Stanley L. **Psychologists in the Criminal Justice System.** 1974. pap. University of Illinois Press. pap $3.45.

Clemmer, Donald. **The Prison Community.** 1958. pap. Irvington. $8.95.

Clinard, Marshall B. & Meier, Robert F. **Sociology of Deviant Behavior.** 5th ed. 1979. Holt, Rinehart & Winston. $15.95.

Cooke, Gerald. **The Role of the Forensic Psychologist.** 432p. 1980. C.C. Thomas. $26.50.

Cortes, Juan B. & Gatti, Florence M. **Delinquency and Crime, a Biopsychosocial Approach: Empirical, Theoretical, and Practical Aspects of Criminal Behavior.** 1972. Academic Press. $25.75.

Craig, Parker L., Jr. **Legal Psychology: Eyewitness Testimony-Jury Behavior.** 184p. 1980. C.C. Thomas. $20.75.

Dudycha, George J. **Psychology for Law Enforcement Officers.** (Illus.). 1973. C.C. Thomas. $13.75.

Ellis, Albert & Gullo, John M. **Murder and Assassination.** 1971. Lyle Stuart. $10.00.

Ericson, Richard V. **Criminal Reactions: The Labelling Perspective.** 1976. Lexington Books. $16.50

Feldman, M. Philip. **Criminal Behaviour: A Psychological Analysis.** 1977. (Pub. by Wiley Interscience). Wiley, John & Sons. $26.50.

Ferdinand, Theodore N. **Typologies of Delinquency: A Critical Analysis.** Peter Smith. (OP). $5.50.

Geis, Gilbert & Bloch, Herbert A. **Man, Crime and Society: The Forms of Criminal Behavior.** 2nd ed. 1962. Random House. $13.95.

Glover, Edward. **The Roots of Crime: Selected Papers on Psychoanalysis,** Vol. 2. 1960. International Universities Press. $20. pap. $5.95.

Glueck, Sheldon S. & Glueck, Eleanor T., eds. **Preventing Crime, a Symposium.** 1936. Kraus Reprint. $25.00.

Goodwin, John C. **Insanity and the Criminal.** 1979. Repr. of 1924 ed. R. West. $30.00.

Gordon, Robert. **Forensic Psychology.** 1977. Nelson-Hall. $6.95.

Green, Edward J. **Psychology for Law Enforcement.** 1976. Wiley, John & Sons. $13.95; pap. $7.95.

Gross, Hans. **Criminal Psychology: A Manual for Judges, Practitioners and Student.** Kallen, Horace M., tr. 1968. Repr. of 1911 ed. Patterson Smith. $20.00.

Halleck, Seymour L. & Bromberg, Walter. **Psychiatric Aspects of Criminology.** 1968. C.C. Thomas. $9.50.

Halleck, Seymour L. **Psychiatry and the Dilemmas of Crime.** 1967. Irvington. (OP). $22.50

—**Psychiatry and the Dilemmas of Crime: A Study of Causes, Punishment & Treatment.** 1971. pap. University of California Press. $6.95.

Hardy, Richard E. & Cull, John G., eds. **Applied Psychology in Law Enforcement and Corrections.** (Illus.) 1973. C.C. Thomas. $11.50.

Hentig, Hans Von. **The Criminal and His Victim: Studies in the Sociobiology of Crime.** 1967. Repr. of 1948 ed. Shoe String Press. $19.50.

Jeffery, Clarence R. **Criminal Responsibility and Mental Disease.** 1967. C.C. Thomas. $12.75.

Laune, Ferris F. **Predicting Criminality.** 1974. Repr. of 1936 ed. Greenwood Press. $10.00.

Letkemann, Peter. **Crime As Work.** (Illus.). 1973. pap. Prentice-Hall. $2.95.

Lindner, Robert M. **Rebel Without a Cause.** 1944 Grune. $22.75.

Locklin, Gerald. **The Criminal Mentality.** 1976. pap. SBD: Small Press Distribution. $2.50.

McCraney, William L., ed. **Readings in Criminal Psychology.** 1972. Mss Information Corp. $13.00.

MacDonald, John M. **Homicidal Threats.** (Illus.). 1968. C.C. Thomas. $7.50.

—**Psychiatry and the Criminal: A Guide to Psychiatric Examinations for the Criminal Courts.** 3rd ed. (Illus.) 1976. C.C. Thomas. $36.25.

Matza, D. **Delinquency and Drift.** 1964. pap. Wiley. $7.25.

Mednick, Sarnoff A. & Christiansen, K.O., eds. **Social and Biological Bases of Asocial Behavior.** 1976. Halsted Press. $22.95.

—**Biosocial Bases of Criminal Behavior.** 1977. Halsted Press. $22.95.

Menninger, Karl. **Crime of Punishment.** 1968. Viking Press. $8.95; 1977. pap. Penguin Books. $2.95.

Meyer, C. Kenneth, et al. **A Social-Psychological Analysis of Police Assailants.** 1978. University of Oklahoma Bureau of Government Research. $3.00.

Monroe, Russell R. **Brain Dysfunction in Aggressive Criminals.** (Illus.) 1978. Lexington Books. $17.95.

Morgan, Patricia. **Delinquent Fantasies.** 1979. Transatlantic Arts Inc. $16.50.

Muensterberg, Hugo. **On the Witness Stand: Essays on Psychology and Crime.** Moss, Richard, ed. Repr. of 1923 ed. AMS Press. $18.00.

Nice, Richard W. **Criminal Psychology.** 1962. Philosophical Library. $6.00.

Palmer, Stuart. **Psychology of Murder.** Orig. Title: Study of Murder. pap. Apollo Editions. (OP). $1.95.

Pfohl, Stephen J. **Predicting Dangerousness.** (Illus.). 1978. Lexington Books. $19.50.

Rada, Richard T., ed. **Clinical Aspects of the Rapist.** 1977. Grune & Stratton. $18.50.

Rappeport, Jonas R. **Clinical Evaluation of the Dangerousness of the Mentally Ill.** 1967. C.C. Thomas. (OP). $6.50.

Reik, Theodor. **Compulsions to Confess: On the Psycho Analysis of Crime and Punishment.** Repr. of 1959 ed. Books for Libraries. $25.50.

Reinhardt, James M. **The Final Echo.** 1971. pap. Johnsen (OP) $1.95.

—**Nothing Left but Murder.** pap. Johnsen. (OP). $2.95.

—**Psychology of Strange Killers.** 1962. C.C. Thomas. (OP). $7.00.

Reiser, Martin. **Practical Psychology for Police Officers.** 1973. C.C. Thomas. $10.50.

Rennie, Ysabel. **The Search for Criminal Man.** 1978. Lexington Books. $19.95.

Resnik, H. L. & Wolfgang, Marvin E., eds. **Sexual Behaviors: Social, Clinical and Legal Aspects.** 1972. Little, Brown & Co. (OP). $15.00.

Revere, Virginia. **Psychology for Law Enforcement Officers.** Nelson-Hall. $22.95.

Roebuck, Julian B. **Criminal Typology: The Legalistic, Physical—Constitutional—Hereditary—Psychological—Psychiatric and Sociological Approaches.** 1971. C.C. Thomas. (OP). $13.50.

Rogers, Joseph W. **Why Are You Not a Criminal.** 1977. Prentice-Hall. (OP) $9.95; pap. $3.95.

Samuel, Dorothy T. **Safe Passage on City Streets.** 1975. Abingdon Press. (OP). $3.95.

Sheldon, William. **Varieties of Delinquent Youth.** 2 Vols. 1970. Repr. of 1949 ed. Hafner Press. Set $33.00.

Slovenko, Ralph. **Crime Law and Corrections.** (Illus.). 1966. C.C. Thomas. $26.50.

Taylor, William & Braswell, Michael. **Issues in Police and Criminal Psychology.** 1978. University Press of America. $10.00.

Thornberry, Terence P. & Jacoby, Joseph E. **The Criminally Insane: A Community Follow-Up of Mentally Ill Offenders.** (Illus.). 1978. University of Chicago Press. $19.00.

Toch, Hans. **Legal and Criminal Psychology.** 1961. Holt, Rinehart & Winston. (OP). $13.95.

—**Psychology of Crime and Criminal Justice.** 1979. Holt, Rinehart & Winston. $14.95.

Wertham, Frederic. **Show of Violence.** Repr of 1949 ed. Greenwood Press. $14.00; pap. $5.95.

Wille, Warren S. **Citizens Who Commit Murder: A Psychiatric Study.** (Illus.). 1975. Green, Warren H. $12.50.

Yochelson, Samuel & Samenow, Stanton E. **The Criminal Personality.** Vol. 1. 1976. Aronson. $35.00.

—**The Criminal Personality, Vol. II: The Treatment Process.** 1977. Aronson. $25.00.

Zilboorg, Gregory. **Psychology of the Criminal Act and Punishment.** (Illus.). 1968. Repr. of 1954 ed. Greenwood Press. $11.25.

CRIMINAL STATISTICS

Clinard. M.B. **Cities with Little Crime.** 1978. Cambridge University Press. $17.95; pap. $6.95.

Committee on National Statistics. **National Research Council Surveying Crime.** Penick, Bettye, ed. 1976. pap. National Academy of Sciences. $11.00.

Glueck, Sheldon S. & Glueck, Eleanor T. **Five Hundred Criminal Careers.** 1930. Kraus Reprint. $14.00.

—**Juvenile Delinquents Grown Up.** 1940. Kraus Reprint. $19.00

—**Later Criminal Careers.** 1937. Kraus Reprint. $14.00.

—**One Thousand Juvenile Delinquents.** 1934. Kraus Reprint. $14.00

Greenberg, David F. **Mathematical Criminology.** (Illus.). 1979. Rutgers University Press. $19.50.

Griffin, John I. **Statistics Essential for Police Efficiency.** 1972. C.C. Thomas. $11.00.

Hanawalt, Barbara A. **Crime and Conflict in English Communities, Thirteen Hundred to Thirteen Forty-Eight.** 1979. Harvard University Press. $20.00.

Heumann, Milton. **Plea Bargaining: The Experiences of Prosecutors, Judges, and Defense Attorneys** (Illus.). 1978. University of Chicago Press. $15.00.

Illinois Association For Criminal Justice. **Illinois Crime Survey.** Wigmore, John H., ed. 1968. Repr. of 1929 ed. Patterson Smith. $35.00.

Morse, Wayne L. & Beattie, Ronald H. **Survey of the Administration of Criminal Justice in Oregon: Final Report on 1771 Felony Cases in Multnomah County Report Number One.** facs. ed. 1974. Repr. of 1932 ed. Arno Press. $16.00.

Robinson, Louis N. **History and Organization of Criminal Statistics in the United States.** 1969. Repr. of 1911 ed. Patterson Smith. $6.50.

Robison, Sophia. **Can Delinquency Be Measured?** 1973. Repr. of 1936 ed. Kraus Reprint. $25.00.

Robison, Sophia Moses. **Can Delinquency Be Measured?** (Illus.) 1972. Repr. of 1936 ed. Patterson Smith. $13.00.

Ross, Marvin. **Economic Opportunity and Crime.** 1977. pap. Renouf U.S.A., Inc. $12.20.

Walker, Nigel. **Crimes, Courts and Figures: An Introduction to Criminal Statistics.** Peter Smith. (OP) $5.25.

Warner, Sam B. **Crime and Criminal Statistics in Boston.** 1974. Repr. Arno Press. $11.00.

Whitten, Woodrow C. **Criminal Syndicalism and the Law in California: 1919-1927.** (Illus.). 1969. pap. American Philisophical Society $1.00.

Wilson, Orlando W. **Police Records: Their Installation and Use.** 1942. Pub. Admin. (OP). $6.50.

DELINQUENTS

Alexander, Franz & Healy, William. **Roots of Crime: Psychoanalytic Studies.** 1969. Repr. of 1935 ed. Patterson Smith. $12.50.

Becker, Howard S., ed. **Other Side: Perspectives on Deviance.** 1964. Free Press. $8.95; pap. $4.95.

Chang, Dae H., ed. **Crime and Delinquency.** 1977. pap. Schenkman. $5.95.

Cooley, Edwin J. **Problem of Delinquency: The Study and Treatment of the Individual Delinquent,** 1927. Norwood Editions. $17.50.

Dubin, Harry N. **Collegefields: From Delinquency to Freedom.** 1980. Irvington. $16.95. pap. $8.95.

Empry, La Mar T. **American Delinquency: Its Meaning and Construction.** 1978. Dorsey Press. $16.95.

Ferdinand. **Typologies of Delinquency.** pap. Philadelphia Book Co. $3.95.

Gibbons, Don C. **Delinquent Behavior.** 3rd ed. (Illus.). 1980. Prentice-Hall. $16.95.

Glueck, S. & Glueck, E. **Of Delinquency and Crime: A Panorama of Years of Search and Research.** 1974. C.C. Thomas. $16.25.

Glueck, Sheldon & Glueck, Eleanor, eds. **Identification of Pre-Delinquents.** 1972. Stratton Intercon. $7.75.

Glueck, Sheldon S. & Glueck, Eleanor T., eds. **Preventing Crime, a Symposium.** 1936. Kraus Reprint. $25.00.

Gold, Martin. **Status Forces in Delinquent Boys.** (Illus.) 1963. pap. University of Michigan, Institute for Social Research. $5.00.

Healy, William & Bonner, Augusta F. **Delinquents and Criminals: Their Making and Unmaking, Studies in Two American Cities.** 1969. Repr. of 1926 ed. Patterson Smith. $12.00.

Healy, William & Bronner, Augusta F. **Delinquents & Criminals: Their Making & Unmaking.** 1969. Repr. of 1926 ed. AMS Press. $10.00.

Henderson, Charles R. **Introduction to the Study of the Dependent, Defective, and Delinquent Classes.** 1901. Repr. Norwood Editions. (OP). $15.00.

Hirschi, Travis. **Causes of Delinquency.** 1969. University of California Press. $16.00; pap. $4.95.

Jensen, Gary F. & Rojek, Dean G. **Delinquency: A Sociological View.** 1980. Heath. $15.95.

Kvaraceus. **Dynamics of Delinquency.** 1966. pap. Merrill. $4.95.

Kvaraceus, William C. **Prevention and Control of Delinquency: The School Counselor's Role.** 1970. pap. Houghton Mifflin. $2.40.

Legal Norms of Delinquency: A Comparative Study. 1969. pap. Rothman, Fred B., & Co. $4.00.

McCord, William & McCord, J. **Psychopathy and Delinquency.** (Illus.). 1956. Grune & Stratton $22.00.

Reed, John P. & Baali, Fuad. **Faces of Delinquency.** (Illus.). 1972. pap. Prentice-Hall. $6.95.

Ribes-Inesta, E. & Bandura, A., eds. **Analysis of Delinquency and Aggression.** 1976. Halsted Press. $14.95.

Rosen, Laurence. **The Delinquent and Non-Delinquent in a High Delinquent Area.** 1978. pap. R & E Research Associates. $10.00.

Savitz, Leonard D. **Delinquency and Migration.** 1975. pap. R & E Research Associates. $9.00.

Shields, Robert W. **Cure of Delinquents: The Treatment of Maladjustment.** 1971. International Universities Press. $12.00.

Slawson, John. **Delinquent Boy: A Socio-Psychological Study.** (Illus.). 1975 Repr. of 1926 ed. Russell & Russell. $22.00.

Strasburg, Paul A. **Violent Delinquents.** (Illus.). 1978. Sovereign Books. $16.95; pap. $8.95.

Voss, Harwin L., ed. **Society, Delinquency, & Delinquent Behavior.** 1970. pap. Little, Brown & Co. (OP) $8.95.

West, D.J. **Who Becomes Delinquent?** 1973. Crane-Russak Co. (OP) $14.75.

Wolfgang, Marvin E., et al. **Delinquency in a Birth Cohort.** 1979. University of Chicago Press. $11.00.

DETECTIVES

Ackroyd, James J. **The Investigator: A Practical Guide to Private Detection.** 1975. Transatlantic Arts Inc. (OP). $8.25.

Armes, Jay J. **Jay J. Armes, Investigator: The World's Most Successful Private Eye.** Nolan, Frederick, ed. (Illus.). 1976. Macmillan. $8.95.

Block, Judy R. **The World's First Police Detective.** (Illus.). 1978. Silver Burdett Co. $6.99.

Cook, D.J. **Hands Up: Or Twenty Years of Detective Life in the Mountains and on the Plains.** (Illus.). 1971. pap. University of Oklahoma Press. $4.95.

Cummings, Richard. **Be Your Own Detective.** 1980. Mckay, David, Co. $7.95.

Edwards, Samuel. **The Vidocq Dossier: The Story of the World's First Detective.** 1977. Houghton Miffline. $7.95.

Gelb, Barbara. **On the Track of Murder.** 1976. pap. Ballantine Books. $1.95.

Henderson, Bruce & Summerlin, Sam. **The Super Sleuths: The World's Greatest Real Life Detectives and Their Toughest Cases.** (Illus.). 1976. Macmillan. (OP). $8.95.

Leonard, V. A. **Police Detective Function.** 1970. C.C. Thomas. $8.25.

McConnell, Jean. **The Detectives.** 1976. David & Charles. $5.50.

Millimaki, Robert H. **The Making of a Detective.** 1976. Lippincott. $8.95.

Nolan, Frederick, ed. **Jay J. Armes: Investigator.** 1977. Avon Books. $1.95.

Otash, Fred. **Investigation Hollywood: Memoirs of Hollywood's Top Private Detective.** (Illus.). 1976. Contemporary Books. (OP). $9.95.

Pearce, William W. & Hoffer, William. **Caught in the Act: The True Adventures of a Divorce Detective.** 1976. Stein & Day. $25.00; pap. $1.95.

Penzler, Otto. **The Great Detectives.** 1978. Little, Brown & Co. $9.95.

Petacco, Arrigo. **Joe Petrosino.** Markmann, Charles Lam., tr. (Illus.). 1974. Macmillan. $5.95.

Pileggi, Nicholas. **Blye, Private Eye: The Real World of the Private Detective.** 1976. Playboy. (OP). $8.50.

Pinkerton, Allan. **Criminal Reminiscences and Detective Sketches.** 1878. Arno Press. $25.00.

—**Professional Thieves and the Detective** Repr. of 1881 ed. AMS Press. $35.00.

Regency International Directory of the Inquiry Agents, Private Detectives, Debt Collecting Agencies. 12th ed. 1978. pap. International Pubns. Service. $30.00.

Ripley, H.A. **How Good a Detective Are You?** 1977. pap. Harper & Row. $1.95.

Rudman, Jack. **Civil Service Examination Passbook: Senior Detective Investigator.** pap. National Learning Corp. $10.00.

Ruehlmann, William. **Saint with a Gun: The Unlawful American Private Eye.** 1974. NYU Press. $8.95.

Sander, William B. **Detective Work: A Study of Criminal Investigations.** (Illus.). 1978. Lippincott. $12.50; pap. $7.95.

Seedman, Albert A. & Hellman, Peter. **Chief!** (Illus.). 1975. pap. Avon. $1.95.

Smyth, Frank & Ludwig, Myles. **The Detectives: Crime and Detection in Fact and Fiction.** (Illus.). 1978. Lippincott. $12.50. pap. $7.95.

Turner, David R. **Detective Investigator.** 1975. pap. Arco. $6.00.

Von Block, B.W. **Super-Detective.** 1972. Playboy. (OP). $7.95; pap. $1.25.

DRUG ABUSE AND CRIME

Baridon, Philip. **Addiction, Crime and Social Policy.** 1976. Lexington Books. (OP). $14.00.

Cohrssen, John J. **The Organization of the United Nations to Deal with Drug Abuse.** (Illus.). 88p. 1973. pap. Drug Abuse Council. $1.25.

Danaceau, Paul. **Methadone Maintenance: The Experience of Four Programs.** 1973. Drug Abuse Council. $1.25.

Engel, Madeline H. **The Drug Scene: A Sociological Perspective.** (Illus.). 1974. pap. Hayden Book Co. $4.95.

Haberman, Paul W. & Baden, Michael M. **Alcohol, Other Drugs and Violent Death.** 1978. Oxford U. Press. $13.95.

Hayes, Billy & Hoffer, William. **Midnight Express.** 1978. pap. Popular Lib. $2.50.

Helmer, John & Vietorisz, Thomas. **Drug Use, the Labor Market and Class Conflict.** 1974. Drug Abuse Council. $1.25.

Rudman, Jack. **(Career Examination Ser.: C-1767). Coordinator of Drug Abuse Educational Programs.** 1976. pap. Natl. Learning. $10.00.

Street, Leroy. **I was a Drug Addict.** 1973. Repr. of 1953 ed. Arlington House. (OP). $7.95.

Weston, Paul & Cole, Robert. **Case Studies of Drug Abuse and Criminal Behavior.** 1973. pap. Goodyear. (OP). $7.50.

DRUGS AND YOUTH

Berry, James. **Heroin Was My Best Friend.** 1974. pap. Macmillan. $.95.

Beschner & Friedman, eds. **Youth Drug Abuse: Problems, Issues, and Treatment.** 1979. Lexington Books. $26.50.

Cohen, Michael J., ed **Drugs and the Special Child.** 1979. Halsted Press. $18.95.

Coles, Robert, et al. **Drugs and Youth.** 1971. Liveright $8.95; pap. $3.95.

Hardy, Richard E. & Cull, John G. **Climbing Ghetto Walls: Disadvantagement, Delinquency and Rehabilitation.** (Illus.). 1973. C.C. Thomas. $11.50.

—**Problems of Adolescents: Social and Psychological Approach.** (Illus.). 1974. C.C. Thomas. $18.75.

Harms, E., ed. **Drugs and Youth: The Challenge of Today.** 1973. Pergamon Press. $17.60.

Hemsing, Esther D., ed. **Children and Drugs.** (Illus.) 1972. pap. Association for Childhood Education International. $1.25.

Hendin, Herbert. **Age of Sensation** 1977. pap. McGraw Hill. $3.95.

Hyde, Margaret O. **Mind Drugs.** 3rd ed. 1974. McGraw Hill. $6.95.

Johnson, Bruce D. **Marihuana Users and Drug Subcultures.** (Illus.). 1973. Wiley. (OP). $16.75.

Johnston, Lloyd. **Drugs and American Youth.** 1973. University of Michigan Institute for Social Research. $10.00; pap. $6.50.

Leech, Kenneth & Jordan, Brenda. **Drugs for Young People: Their Use and Misuse.** 2nd ed. 1974. pap. Pergamon Press. $3.25.

—**Youthquake: The Growth of a Counter-Culture Through Two Decades.** 1977. pap. Littlefield, Adams & Co. $3.95.

Leinwand, Gerald, ed., **Drugs.** 1970. pap. Washington Square Press. (OP). $.95.

Lieberman, Florence, et al. **Before Addiction: How to Help Youth.** 1973. Human Sciences Press. $14.95.

—**Before Addiction: How to Help Youth.** 1973. Human Sciences Press. $14.95.

Light, Patricia K. **Let the Children Speak.** 1975. Lexington Books. $13.50.

Livingston, Gary. **Exiles End.** 1976. Repr. of 1973 ed. Sagarin Press. $4.95.

Moore, Harvey A. **Drug Users and Emergent Organizations.** 1977. pap. Univ. Presses of Florida. $4.50

Moses, Donald A. & Burger, Robert E. **Are You Driving Your Children to Drink: Coping with Teenage Alcohol and Drug Abuse.** 1975. Van Nos Reinhold. (OP). $8.95.

Scarpitti, Frank R. & Datesman, Susan K., eds. **Drugs and the Youth Culture.** (Illus.). 1980. Sage. $20.00; pap. $9.95.

Tessler, Diane J. **Drugs, Kids and Schools: Practical Strategies for Educators and Other Concerned Adults.** 1980. pap. Goodyear. $8.95.

Thompson, Thomas. **Richie.** 1974. pap. Bantam Books. $1.95.

—**Richie.** pap. Dell. $2.50.

Travers, Milton. **Each Other's Victims.** pap. Pocket Books. $1.25.

Watson, Tom. **What Can I Do?** 1974. pap. Logos International. (OP). $1.25.

EMBEZZLEMENT

Cressey, Donald R. **Other People's Money: A Study in the Social Psychology of Embezzlement.** 1971. pap. Wadsworth Publishing. $4.95.

—**Other People's Money: A Study in the Social Psychology of Embezzlement.** 1973. Repr. of

1953. ed. Patterson Smith. $8.00.

Hall, Jerome. **Theft, Law and Society.** 2nd ed. 1952. Bobbs-Merrill. $13.50.

Pratt, Lester A. **Bank Frauds: Their Detection and Prevention.** 2nd ed. 1965. Ronald Press. $19.95.

EUTHANASIA

Barnard, Christian. **Good Life Good Death: A Doctor's Case for Euthanasia and Suicide.** 120p. 1980. Prentice-Hall. $7.95.

Downing, A. B., ed. **Euthanasia and the Right to Death: The Case for Voluntary Euthanasia.** 1970. Humanities Press. $14.00.

Elliott, Neil. **The Gods of Life.** 192p. 1974. Macmillan. $7.95.

Grisez, Germain & Boyle, Joseph M. **Life and Death with Liberty and Justice: A Contribution to the Euthanasia Debate.** 1979. University of Notre Dame Press. $20.00.

Kluge, Eike-Henner W. **The Ethics of Deliberate Death.** 1980. Kennikat. $17.50.

Kohl, Marvin, **The Morality of Killing: Euthanasia, Abortion and Transplants.** 1974. Humanities Press. $10.50.

Kohl, Marvin. ed. **Beneficent Euthenasia** 255p. 1975. Prometheus Books. $10.95.

Maguire, Daniel C. **Death by Choice.** 236p. 1975. pap. Schocken Books. $4.95.

Mannes, Marya. **Last Rights.** 1975. pap. NAL. $1.50.

May, William & Westley, Richard. **Catholic Perspectives: The Right to Die.** 1980. pap. Thomas More. $3.95.

—**The Right to Die.** 112p. 1980. pap. Thomas More. $3.95.

Mitchell, Paige. **Act of Love.** 1976. Knopf. $8.95.

Munk, William. **Euthanasia: Or, Medical Treatment in Aid of an Easy Death.** Kastenbaum, Robert, ed. 1977. Repr. of 1887 ed. Arno Press. $14.00.

Robison, Wade L. & Pritchard, Michael S., eds. **Medical Responsibility: Paternalism, Informed Consent, and Euthanasia.** 1979. Humana Press. $19.50.

Russell, O. Ruth. **Freedom to Die: Moral and Legal Aspects of Euthanasia.** rev. ed. 1977. Human Sciences Press. $19.95.

Schaeffer, Francis A. & Koop, C. Everett. **Whatever Happened to the Human Race?** 1979. Revell, Fleming H., Co. $13.95; study guide $2.95.

Swinyard, Chester A. **Decision Making and the Defective Newborn.** (Illus.). 672p. 1978. C.C. Thomas. $31.25.

Thielicke, Helmut. **The Doctor As Judge of Who Shall Live and Who Shall Die.** 48p. (Orig.). 1976. pap. Fortress Press. $1.00.

Triche, Charles W. & Triche, Diane S. **Euthanasia Controversy, 1812-1974: A Bibliography with Select Annotations.** ix, 242p. 1975. Whitston Publishing. $18.00.

Van Den Berg, Jan H. **Medical Ethics and Medical Power.** (Illus.). 1978. Norton, W.W., & Co. $7.95.

Wertenbaker, Lael T. **Death of a Man.** 192p. 1974. pap. Beacon Press. $4.95.

Wertham, Frederick. **German Euthanasia: A Sign for Cain.** 1977. Hayes. $1.25.

Wilson, Jerry B. **Death by Decision: The Medical, Moral, and Legal Dilemmas of Euthanasia.** 1975. Westminster Press. $7.50.

EVIDENCE, CRIMINAL

Ansley, Norman. **Legal Admissibility of the Polygraph.** (Illus.). 348p. 1975. C.C. Thomas. $43.00.

Bridges, Burtis C. **Practical Fingerprinting.** 2nd ed. O'Hara, Charles E., ed. (Illus.). Funk & Wagnalls. (OP). $7.95.

Chafee, Zechariah, Jr., et al. **Third Degree.** Repr. of 1931 ed. Arno Press. $12.00.

Conway, James V.P. **Evidential Documents.** (Illus.). 288p. 1978. C.C. Thomas. $13.50.

Crown, David A. **The Forensic Examination of Paints and Pigments.** 276p. 1968. C.C. Thomas. $18.00.

Ferguson, Robert J., Jr. & Miller, Allan L. **Polygraph for the Defense.** 1974. C.C. Thomas. $18.75.

—**The Polygraph in Court.** 1973. pap. C.C. Thomas. $19.00.

Fricke, Charles W. & Alarcon, Arthur L. **California Criminal Evidence.** 9th ed. 1978. Legal Book Corp. $16.00.

Gard, Spencer A. **Jones on Evidence, Civil and Criminal.** 4 vols. 6th ed. 1972. Lawyers Co-Operative Publishing Co. $150.00.

Gladfelter, Irl A. **Dental Evidence: A Handbook for Police.** (Illus.). 208p. 1975. C.C. Thomas. $24.00.

Heffron, Floyd N. **Evidence for the Patrolman.** (Illus.). 1972. C.C. Thomas. $10.00.

Imwinkelried, Edward J., et al. **Criminal Evidence.** 1979. pap. West Publishing. $16.95.

Inbau, Fred E., et al. **Evidence Law for the Police.** 1972. Chilton. (OP). $5.95.

Kaplan, Eugene J. **Evidence: A Law Enforcement Officer's Guide.** 374p. 1979. C.C. Thomas. $19.75.

Katsaris, Kenneth, ed. **Evidence and Procedure in the Administration of Justice.** 1975. Wiley, John & Sons. $17.95.

Klotter, John C. **Criminal Evidence.** 500p. 1980. Anderson Publishing Co. $18.95.

Klotter, John C. & Meier, Carl L. **Criminal Evidence for Police.** 2nd ed. 1975. Anderson Publishing Co. $16.95.

Moenssens, Andre. **Fingerprints and the Law.** Orig. Title: Fingerprint Identification and the Law. 1969. Chilton. (OP). $6.50.

Munster, Joe H. & Larkin, Murl A. **Military Evidence.** 2nd ed. 1978. with 1979 suppl. Bobbs-Merrill Law. $35.00; 1979 suppl. Michie $5.00.

Ringel, William E. **Identification and Police Line-Ups.** 1968. pap. Gould. $5.00.

Schloss, Joseph D. **Evidence and Its Legal Aspects.** 1976. Merrill. $14.95.

Stuckey, G. B. **Evidence for the Law Enforcement Officer.** (Illus.). 3rd ed. 1978. McGraw-Hill. $14.95; instructor's manual & key $3.00; $5.95.

Torcia, Charles E. **Wharton's Criminal Evidence.** 4 vols. 13th ed. 1972. Lawyers Co-Operative Publishing Co. $150.00.

Waddington, Lawrence C. **Criminal Evidence.** 1978. Glencoe. $13.95.

Waltz, Jon R. **Criminal Evidence.** 1975. Nelson Hall. $19.95; pap. $12.95.

Weston, Paul B. & Wells, Kenneth M. **Criminal Evidence for Police.** 2nd ed. (Illus.). 352p. 1976. Prentice-Hall. $16.95.

Williams, John B. **California Criminal Evidence.** Gourley, G. Douglas, ed. 1969. pap. Glencoe. (OP). $6.95.

EVIDENCE, EXPERT

Beresford, H. Richard. **Legal Aspects of Neurologic Practice.** 1975. Davis Co. $22.00.

Cederbaums, Juris G. & Arnold, Selma, eds. **Scientific and Expert Evidence in Criminal Advocacy.** 1975. Practising Law Institute. $20.00.

Haring, J. Vreeland. **Hand of Hauptmann: The Handwriting Expert Tells the Story of the Lindberg Case.** (Illus.). 1937. Patterson Smith. $10.00.

Kraft, Melvin D., ed. **Using Experts in Civil Cases.** 1977. Practising Law Institute. $30.00.

McCracken, Daniel D. **Public Policy and the Expert: Ethical Problems of the Witness.** 1971. pap. Council on Religion & International Affairs. $2.00.

Robinson, Daniel N. **Psychology and Law: Can Justice Survive the Social Sciences.** 1980. Oxford University Press. $14.95; pap. $5.95.

Saudek, Robert. **Anonymous Letters.** (Illus.). 1976. Repr. of 1933 ed. AMS Press. $14.00.

EVIDENCE, LAW

Baldus, David C. & Cole, James W. **Statistical Proof of Discrimination.** (Illus.). 1980. McGraw-Hill. $50.00.

Bocchino, Anthony J. & Tanford, J. Alexander. **North Carolina Trial Evidence Manual.** 1976. with 1978 suppl. Michie. $20; Suppl. $7.50.

Brownlee, Gardner E. **Trial Judge's Guide: Objections to Evidence.** 1974. National Judicial College. $15.00.

California Evidence Code. 1979. pap. Legal Book Corp. $4.00.

Canudo, Eugene R. **Evidence (N.Y.).** 1980. Gould. $9.50.

Clark, Miles, ed. **California Evidence Code.** 1980. Parker & Son. $7.00.

Cleary, Edward W. & Graham, Michael H. **Handbook of Illinois Evidence.** 1979. Little, Brown & Co. $50.00.

Co-Op East Law Outlines: Evidence. 1975. Sterling Swift. $6.50.

Conway, James V. **Evidential Documents.** (Illus.). 288 p. 1978. C.C. Thomas. $13.50.

Cotchett, Joseph W. & Elkind, Arnold B. **Federal Courtroom Evidence.** 1975. incl. 1979 suppl. Parker & Sun. $29.50.

Cowen, Zelman & Carter, P.B. **Essays on the Law of Evidence.** 1973. Repr. of 1956 ed. Greenwood Press. $16.50.

Criminal Investigation and Presentation of Evidence. 1976. West Publishing Co. $12.95.

Donigan, Robert L. & Fisher, Edward C. **Evidence Handbook.** 3rd rev. ed. 1975. Northwestern University Traffic Institute. $18.00.

Evidence. Lerner Law. (OP). $5.00.

Faber, Stuart J. **Faber's Evidence Courtroom Book.** 1979. pap. Good Life Press. $36.50.

Felkenes, George T. **Rules of Evidence.** 224p. 1974. pap. Delmar. $8.40.

Ferguson, Robert W. & Stokke, Allan H. **Legal Aspects of Evidence.** 139p. 1979. pap. Harcourt Brace Jovanovich. Instructor's manual avail. $7.95.

Fisch, Edith L. **Fisch on New York Evidence.** 2nd ed. 1977. Lond Publications. $25.00.

Friend, Charles E. **The Law of Evidence in Virginia.** 1977. Michie $40.00.

Gard, Spencer A. **Jones on Evidence, Civil and Criminal.** 4 vols. 6th ed. 1972. Lawyers Co-Operative Publishing Co. $150.00.

Gould Staff Editors. **Evidence Code-Federal.** 1980. Gould. $8.50.

—**Evidence Law of New York Quizzer 1979.** 1978. Gould. $7.50.

—**Evidence Law of New York Quizzer 1981.** 1981. Gould. $7.50.

Greenleaf, Simon. **A Treatise on the Law of Evidence.** 3 vols. 1972. Repr. of 1850 ed. Arno Press. Set $90.00.

Haight, Fulton & Cotchett, Joseph W. **California Courtroom Evidence.** 1979. Parker & Son. $27.50.

Hardberger, Phillip D. **Texas Courtroom Evidence.** 1978. Parker & Son. $42.00.

Inbau, Fred E., et al. **Evidence Law for the Police.** 1972. Chilton. (OP). $5.95.

Imwinkelreid, Edward J. **Evidentiary Foundations.** 1980. pap. Bobbs-Merrill. $12.50.

Josephson, Michael. **Evidence.** Center for Creative Educational Services. $8.95.

Junkerman, Helen B. **The Death of a DC-6B: "Julian Frank" Case.** 1972. Boardman. (OP). $10.00.

Kaplan, Eugene J. **Evidence: A Law Enforcement Officer's Guide.** 374p. 1979. C.C. Thomas. $19.75.

LaPlante, Joseph A. & Tait, Colin C. **Handbook of Connecticut Evidence.** 1976. Little, Brown & Co. $40.00.

Larson, John A., et al. **Lying and Its Detection, a Study of Deception and Deception Tests.** 1969. Repr. of 1932 ed. Patterson Smith. $17.50.

Leach, W. Barton & Liacos, Paul J. **Handbook of Massachusetts Evidence.** 4th ed. 1967. Little, Brown & Co. $20.00.

Lilly, Graham C. **An Introduction to the Law of Evidence.** 1978. West Publisning. $9.95.

Livingston, Edward. **Complete Works on Criminal Jurisprudence: Consisting of Systems of Penal Law for the State of Louisiana and for the United States of America.** with Introductory Reports to the Same. 2 vols. 1968. Repr. of 1873 ed. Patterson Smith. Set. $35.00.

Louisell, David W. & Mueller, Christopher B. **Federal Evidence, vol. 5.** 1978. Lawyers Co-Operative Publishing Co. $247.50.

Louisell, David W. & Kaplan, John. **Cases and Materials on Evidence.** 980p. 1981. Foundation Press. write for info.

Markle, Arnold. **Criminal Investigation and Presentation of Evidence.** 1976. West Publishing. $12.95.

McCormick, Charles T., et al. **Cases and Materials on Evidence.** 1250p. 1980. West Publishing. write for info.

Morgan, Edmund M., ed. **Some Problems of Proof Under the Anglo-American System of Litigation.** 1976. Repr. of 1956 ed. Greenwood Press. $14.00.

Paine, Donald F. **Tennessee Law of Evidence.** 1974. with 1976 suppl. Bobbs-Merrill. $30.00.

Pugh. **Louisiana Law of Evidence.** 1974. with 1978 suppl. Bobbs-Merrill. $50.00; suppl. $19.50.

Redden, Kenneth R. & Saltzburg, Stephen A. **Federal Rules of Evidence Manual.** 2nd ed. 1977. with 1979. suppl. Michie. $50.00; suppl. $20.00.

Reiser, Walter A., Jr. **Federal Rules of Evidence: Special Supplement.** 1975. Little, Brown & Co.

Roady, Thomas G., Jr. & Covington, Robert N., eds. **Essays on Procedure and Evidence.** 1961. Vanderbilt University Press. $8.95.

Rothstein, Paul F. **The New Federal Rules of Evidence, Annotated, with Analysis.** 100p. 1975. pap. Bureau of National Affairs. $4.00.

Rothstein, Paul F., ed. **Federal Rules of Evidence.** rev. ed. 1977. Boardman. $17.50.

—**Evidence in a Nutshell, State and Federal Rules.** 2nd ed. 401p. 1981. pap. West Publishing. $6.95.

Sandifer, D.V. **Evidence Before International Tribunals.** Repr. of 1939 ed. Kraus Reprint. $23.00.

Sandifer, Durward V. **Evidence Before International Tribunals.** rev. ed. (Illus.). 500p. 1975. University Press of Virginia. $27.50.

Saltzburg, Stephen A. & Redden, Kenneth R. **Federal Rules of Evidence Manual.** 2nd ed. 1977. with 1979 suppl. Michie. $50.00; suppl. $20.00.

Schlesinger, Steven. **Exclusionary Injustice: The Problem of Illegally Obtained Evidence, Vol. 3.** 1977. Dekker, Marel. $14.75.

Select Committee on Police. **Reports from the Select Committee on Police and Minutes of Evidence, Vol. 36.** 1971. Repr. of 1853 ed. Arno Press. $19.00.

Sinclair, Kent, Jr. **Federal Rules of Evidence at a Glance—Trial Objections at a Glance.** 1978. Practising Law Institute. $6.00.

Stephens, Harold M. **Administrative Tribunals and the Rules of Evidence.** 1933. Johnson Reprint. $15.50.

Thayer, James B. **Preliminary Treatise on Evidence at Common Law.** Repr. of 1898 ed. Kelley. $22.50.

—**Preliminary Treatise on Evidence at Common Law.** 636p. 1970. Repr. of 1898 ed. Rothman. $22.50.

Weston, Paul & Wells, Kenneth. **Fundamentals of Evidence.** 96p. 1972. Prentice-Hall. $6.95.

Wigmore, John H. **Evidence.** 10 vols. 3rd ed. 1940. Little, Brown & Co. $400.00. Incl. McNaughton Revision of Volume 8. McNaughton, John T. 1961. $35.00. Chadbourn Revision of Volume 3. 2 vols. Chadbourn, James H. 1970. $50.00 Supplement 1980. Reiser, Walter A., Jr. Chadbourn Revision of Volume 4. Chadbourn, James H. 1972. $50.00.

EXPLOSIVES

Brodie, Thomas G. **Bombs and Bombings: A Handbook to Detection, Disposal and Investigation for Police and Fire Departments.** 1980. C.C. Thomas. $15.75.

Brunswig, Heinrich. **Explosives: A Synoptic and Critical Treatment of the Literature of the Subject As Gathered from Various Sources.** Monroe, Charles E. & Kibler, Alton L., trs. 1980. Gordon Press. $69.95.

Clark, George B. & Raese, Jon W. **Industrial High Explosives: Composition and Calculations for Engineers.** (Illus.). 1980. pap. Colorado School of Mines. $10.00.

Cook, Melvin A. **Science of High Explosives.** 456p. 1970. Repr. of 1958 ed. Krieger. $33.50.

—**The Science of High Explosives.** 1958. American Chemical Society. (OP). $33.50.

Davis, Tenny L. **Chemistry of Powder and Explosives.** 1972. pap. Angriff Press. $10.00.

De Barry Barnett, Edward. **Explosives.** 1980. Gordon Press. $64.95.

Fordham, S. **High Explosives and Propellants.** (Illus.). 1966. Pergamon Press. $22.00; pap. $12.50.

Gregory, C.E. **Explosives for Engineers: A Primer of Australasian Industrial Practice.** 2nd ed. 1966. University of Queensland Press. $10.75.

—**Explosives for North American Engineers.** (Illus.). 2nd ed. 1973. Trans Tech. $29.50.

Haines, Gail K. **Explosives.** (Illus.). 1976. Morrow. $5.75.

Holzmann, R. T. **Chemical Rockets and Flame and Explosives Technology.** 1969. Dekker, Marcel. $59.50.

James, Ronald W. **Propellants and Explosives.** (Illus.). 1975. Noyes Data Corp. (OP). $36.00.

Johansson, C.H. & Persson, P.A. **Tectonics of High Explosives.** 1970. Academic Press. (OP). $19.00.

Leet, Lewis D. **Vibrations from Blasting Rock.** 1960. Harvard University Press. $10.00.

Lenz, Robert R. **Explosives and Bomb Disposal Guide.** (Illus.). 1973. C.C. Thomas. $14.50.

Marshall, Arthur. **Explosives: Their History, Manufacture, Properties and Tests.** 3 vols. 1977. Gordon Press. $375.95.

Meidl, James H. **Flammable Hazardous Materials.** 2nd ed. 1978. Glencoe. $14.95.

—**Hazardous Materials Handbook.** 1972. pap. Glencoe. $7.95.

Meyer, Rudolph. **Explosives.** 1977. $38.90.

Rudman, Jack. **Supervising Demolition Inspector.** (Career Examination Ser.: C-777) pap. National Learning Corp. $10.00.

—**Senior Demolition Inspector.** (Career Examination Ser.: C-1475) pap. National Learning Corp. $8.00.

Separation Distances of Ammonium Nitrate and Blasting Agents from Explosives or Blasting Agents. 1968. pap. National Fire Protection Association. $2.00.

Stoffel, Joseph. **Explosives and Homemade Bombs.** 2nd ed. (Illus.). 1972. C.C. Thomas. $23.75.

Urbanski, T. **Chemistry and Technology of Explosives.** Vol. 2. Pergamon Press. (OP). $35.00.

Van Gelder, et al. **History of the Explosives Industry in America.** (Illus.). 1972. Repr. of 1927 ed. Arno Press. $56.00.

FEMALE OFFENDERS

Adler, Freda & Simon, Rita J. **The Criminology of Deviant Women.** (Illus.). 1979. pap. Houghton Mifflin. $8.50.

Adler, R. **Sisters in Crime: The Rise of the New Female Criminal.** 1975. McGraw-Hill. $9.95; pap. $3.95.

Bowker, Lee H. **Women, Crime, and the Criminal Justice System.** (Illus.). 1978. Lexington Books. $22.95.

Brodsky, Annette M. **The Female Offender.** 1975. Sage. $4.95.

Bronner, Augusta F. **A Comparative Study of the Intelligence of Delinquent Girls.** Repr. of 1914 ed. AMS Press. $17.50.

Burkhart, Kathryn. **Women in Prison.** 1976. pap. Popular Library. $1.75.

Chapman, Jane R. **Economic Realities and Female Crime: Program Choices and Economic Rehabilitation.** 1980. write for info. Lexington Books.

Cowie, John, et al. **Delinquency in Girls.** 1968. Humanities Press. (OP). $8.75.

Crites, Laura, ed. **The Female Offender: A Total Look at Women in the Criminal Justice System.** 1977. Lexington Books. $19.95.

Crosbie, John. **The Incredible Mrs. Chadwick.** 1975. McGraw-Hill. (OP). $7.95.

Datesman, Susan K., ed. **Women, Crime and Justice.** Scarpitti, Frank R. (Illus. Orig.). 1980. pap. Oxford University Press. $5.95.

Deming, Richard. **Women: The New Criminals.** 1977. Elsevier-Nelson. $7.95.

Earnest, Marion R. **Criminal Self-Conceptions in the Penal Community of Female Offenders: An Empirical Study.** 1978. pap. R&E Research Associates. $9.00.

Feinman, Clarice. **Women in the Criminal Justice System.** (Illus.) 1980. Praeger. $18.95; pap. $8.95.

Fernald, Mabel R., et al. **Study of Women Delinquents in New York State.** 1968. Repr. of 1920 ed. Patterson Smith. $18.00.

Gabel, Katherine & Bartleson, Henrietta. **Legal Rights for Women Prisoners.** Date not set. price not set. Lexington Books.

Giallombardo, Rose. **The Social World of Imprisoned Girls: A Comparative Study of Institutions for Juvenile Delinquents.** 1974. Wiley, John & Sons. $22.95.

Glueck, S. & Glueck, Eleanor. **Five Hundred Delinquent Women.** Repr. of 1934 ed. Kraus Reprint. $24.00.

Hartman, Mary S. **Victorian Murderesses: A True Story History of 13 Respectable French and English Women Accused of Unspeakable Crimes.** 1976. Schocken Books. $15.00.

Victorian Murderesses: A True History of Thirteen Respectable French and English Women Accused of Unspeakable Crimes. (Illus.). 1979. pap. Schocken Books. $6.95.

Heffernam, Esther. **Making It in Prison: The Square, the Cool and the Life.** 1972. Wiley, John & Sons. (OP). $12.25.

Jenkins, Elizabeth. **Six Criminal Women.** facs. ed. 1949. Arno Press. $18.00.

Jones, Ann. **Women Who Kill.** 1980. Holt, Rinehart & Winston. $15.95.

Jurjevich. Ratibor-Ray M. **No Water in My Cup.** 1968. Libra. $5.00.

Konopka, Gisela. **Adolescent Girl in Conflict.** 1966. pap. Prentice-Hall. $2.95.

—**Young Girls: A Portrait of Adolescence.** Prentice-Hall. $8.95; pap. $3.45.

Lampman, Henry P. **The Wire Womb: Life in a Girls' Penal Institution.** 1973. Nelson-Hall. $9.95.

Lombroso, Cesar & Ferrero, William. **The Female Offender.** (Illus.). 1980. Repr. of 1895 ed. Rothman. $32.50.

Lytton, Constance. **Prisons and Prisoners: Experiences of a Suffragette.** 1977. Repr. of 1914 ed. Charles River Books. $25.00.

McCarthy, Belinda R. **Easy Time: The Experiences of Female Inmates on Temporary Release.** 1979. Lexington Books. $21.50.

MacClure, Victor. **She Stands Accused: Being a Series of Accounts of the Lives and Deeds of Notorious Women Murderesses.** (Illus.). 1975. Repr. of 1935 ed. Hyperion Press. $14.00.

McNulty, Faith. **The Burning Bed: The True Story of a Wife Who Killed.** 1980. Harcourt Brace Jovanovich. $12.95.

Meyer, Henry J., et al. **Girls At Vocational High.** 1965. Russell Sage. $6.50.

Mitchell, Arlene E. **Informal Inmate Social Structure in Prisons for Women: A Comparative Study.** 1975. pap. R&E Research Associates. (OP). $8.00.

Pollak, Otto. **The Criminality of Women.** 1961. pap. A.S. Barnes. $3.95.

Simon, Rita J. **Women and Crime.** 1978. pap. Heath. $5.95.

Smart, Carol. **Women, Crime and Criminology: A Feminist Critique.** 1976. Routledge & Kegan. $12.75.

—**Women, Crime and Criminology: A Feminist Critique.** 1978. pap. Routledge & Kegan. $6.95.

Smith, Pauline. **The End of the Line.** 1970. A.S. Barnes. (OP). $5.95.

Spaulding, Edith R. **Experimental Study of Psychopathic Delinquent Women.** (Illus.). 1969. Repr. of 1923 ed. Patterson Smith. $15.00.

Stanton, Ann M. **When Mothers Go to Jail.** 1980. Lexington Books. $22.95.

Sullivan, Katharine. **Girls on Parole.** 243p. 1973. Repr. of 1956 ed. Greenwood Press. $13.00.

Thomas, William I. **Unadjusted Girl, with Cases and Standpoint for Behavior Analysis.** 1969. Repr. of 1923 ed. Patterson Smith. $12.00.

Totman, Jane. **The Murderess: A Psychosocial Study of Criminal Homicide.** 1978. pap. R & E Research Association. $10.00.

Vedder, Clyde B. & Somerville, Dora B. **The Delinquent Girl.** 2nd ed. 1975. C.C. Thomas. $18.50.

FINGERPRINTS

Battley, Harry. **Single Finger Prints: A New & Practical Method of Classifying & Filing Single Finger Prints & Fragmentary Impressions.** (Illus.). 1931. Elliots Books. $37.50.

Boy Scouts Of America. **Fingerprinting.** (Illus.). 36p. (gr. 6-12). 1964. pap. BSA. $.55.

Bridges, Burtis C. **Practical Fingerprinting.** 2nd ed. O'Hara, Charles E., ed. (Illus.). Funk & Wagnalls. $7.95.

Field, Annita T. **Fingerprint Handbook.** (Illus.). 196p. 1976. C.C. Thomas. $12.00.

Galton, Francis. **Finger Prints.** 2nd ed. 1966. Repr. of 1892 ed. Da Capo. $12.50.

Herschel, William J. **The Origin of Fingerprinting.** (Illus.). 178p. 1974. Repr. of 1916 ed. AMS Press. $18.00.

Kolb, Patricia A. **H.I.T. A Manual for the Classification, Filing, & Retrieval of Palmprints.** (Illus.). 112p. 1979. spiral bdg. C.C. Thomas. $15.25.

Millimaki, Robert H. **Fingerprint Detective** (gr. 4-7). 1973. Lippincott. $8.95.

Olsen, Robert D., Sr. **Scott's Fingerprint Mechanics.** (Illus.). 480p. 1978. C.C. Thomas. $30.00.

Rudman, Jack. **Fingerprint Technician.** (Career Examination Ser.: C-255). pap. Natl Learning Corp. $8.00.

Fingerprint Technician Trainee (Career Examination Ser.: C-286). pap. Natl Learning Corp. $8.00.

—**Senior Fingerprint Technician.** (Career Examination Ser.: C-2073). 1977. pap. Natl Learning Corp. $10.00.

Wertelecki, Windimir & Plato, Chris C., eds. **Dermatoglyphics-Fifty Years Later.** 766p. 1980. A R Liss. $76.00.

Wilton, George W. **Fingerprints: History, Law & Romance.** 1971 Repr. of 1938 ed. Gale Research Co. $15.00.

FIRE INVESTIGATION

Aircraft Fire Investigators Manual. 1972. pap. National Fire Protection Association. $2.00.

Berrin, Elliott R. **Investigative Photography.** Date not set. Society of Fire Protection Engineers. $3.25.

Carroll, John R. **Physical and Technical Aspects of Fire and Arson Investigation.** (Illus.). 1979. C.C. Thomas. $32.50.

Dennett, M.F. **Fire Investigation: A Practical Guide for Fire Students and Officers, Insurance Investigators, Loss Adjustors, and Police Officers.** (Illus.). 1980. Pergamon Press. $15.01; pap. $8.51.

Fire Reporting Field Incident Manual. 1973. pap. National Fire Protection Association. $2.00.

Fitch, Richard D. & Porter, Edward A. **Accidental or Incendiary.** 1975. C.C. Thomas. $12.50.

IFSTA Committee. **Fire Service Instructor Training.** 4th ed. (Illus.). 1981. pap. International Fire Service Training Association. $7.00.

—**Fire Service Rescue Practices.** 5th ed. 1981. pap. International Fire Service Training Association. price not set.

Kirk, P.L. **Fire Investigation.** 1969. Wiley, John & Sons. $17.95.

Roblee, C. & McKechnie, A. **Investigations of Fires.** 1981. Prentice-Hall $13.95.

Tuck, Charles A., Jr. **Analysis of Three Multiple Fatality Penal Institution Fires.** 1978. pap. National Fire Protection Association. $35.00.

Tuck, Charles A., Jr. ed. **Fire Incident Data Coding Guide.** 1977. pap. National Fire Protection Association. $3.50.

FIREARMS—LAWS AND REGULATIONS

Davidson, Bill R. **To Keep and Bear Arms.** 2nd ed. 1979. Sycamore Island Books. $12.95.

Dolan, Edward F., Jr. **Gun Control: A Decision for Americans.** (Illus.). 1978. Watts, Franklin, Inc. $4.90.

Gottlieb, Alan B. **The Gun Owner's Political Action Manual.** 1976. pap. Green Hill. $1.95.

The Gun. 1976. pap. Bantam. (OP). $1.50.

Gun Control. 1976. pap. American Enterprise for Public Policy Research. $2.00.

Gun Control Means People Control. 1974. Independent American. $1.75.

Kates, Don B., Jr. **Restricting Handguns: The Liberal Skeptics Speak Out.** 1979. North River Press. $9.95; pap. $6.95.

Kennet, Lee & Anderson, James L. **The Gun in America: The Origins of a National Dilemma.** (Illus.). 1975. Greenwood Press. $14.95.

Kennett, Lee & Anderson, James L. **The Gun in America: The Origins of a National Dilemma.** (Illus.). pap. Greenwood Press. $3.95.

Krema, Vaclav. **Identification and Registration of Firearms.** (Illus.). 1971. C.C. Thomas. $18.50.

Kukla, Robert J. **Gun Control: A Written Record of Efforts to Eliminate the Private Possession of Firearms in America.** Orig. Title: Other Side of Gun Control. 1973. pap. Stackpole Books. $4.95.

Sherrill, Robert. **The Saturday Night Special.** 1975. pap Penguin Books. (OP). $2.75.

—**The Saturday Night Special.** 1973. Charterhouse. (OP). $8.95.

FRAUD

Anderson, Kent, ed. **Television Fraud: The History and Implications of the Quiz Show Scandals.** Greenwood Press. $18.95.

Bane, Charles A. **The Electrical Equipment Conspiracies: The Treble Damage Actions.** (Illus.). 1973. Federal Legal Pubns. $17.50.

Blum, Richard H. **Deceivers and Deceived: Observations on Confidence Men and Their Victims, Informants and Their Quarry, Political and Industrial Spies and Ordinary Citizens.** (Illus.). 1972. C. C. Thomas $18.25.

Bromberg, A. R. **Securities Law: Fraud, SEC 10b-5.** 1967. McGraw-Hill. $160.00.

Carey, Mary & Sherman, George. **A Compendium of Bunk or How to Spot a Con Artist.** 216 p. 1976. C. C. Thomas. $13.50 pap. $8.75.

Cartwright, Joe & Patterson, Jerry. **Been Taken Lately? The Comprehensive Consumer Fraud Digest.** 1976. pap. Grove Press (OP). $1.95.

Comstock, Anthony. **Frauds Exposed; or, How People Are Deceived and Robbed, and Youth Corrupted.** (Illus.). 1969. Repr. of 1880 ed. Patterson Smith. $18.00.

Conklin, John. **Illegal but Not Criminal: Business Crime in America.** 1977. pap. Prentice-Hall. $3.95.

Cornell, James. **Fakes, Frauds and Phonies.** (Illus.) 1974. pap. Scholastic Book Services (OP). $0.75.

Curtis, Bob. **Security Control: External Theft.** 1971. Lebhar Friedman. $18.95.

—**Security Control: External Theft.** 1971. Lebhar Friedman. $18.95.

Dallos, Robert E. & Soble, Ronald. **The Impossible Dream.** 1975. pap. NAL. $1.95.

Elliott, Robert K. and Willingham, John. **Management Fraud: Deterents and Detection.** (Illus.) 1980. Petrocelli. $25.00.

Elliott, Robert K. and Willingham, John J. **Management Fraud: Detection and Deterrence.** 1980. McGraw-Hill. $25.00.

Evans, D. Morier. **Facts, Failures, and Frauds Revelations, Financial, Mercantile, Criminal.** Repr. of 1859 ed. Kelley. $25.00.

Feld, Lipman G. **Bad Checks and Fraudulent Identity.** 1978. pap. National Association of Credit Management. $6.50.

Friedman, Paul. **And If Defeated Allege Fraud: Stories.** 1971. Univ. of Illinois Press. $3.95.

Glick, Rush G. & Newsom, Robert S. **Fraud Investigation: Fundamentals for Police.** (Illus.). 1974. C. C. Thomas. $16.25.

Haldane, R. A. **With Intent to Deceive: Frauds Famous and Infamous.** 1972. British Book Center. (OP). $7.95.

Harding, T. Swann. **The Popular Practice of Fraud.** 1976. Repr. of 1935 ed. Arno. $21.00.

How to Reduce Business Losses from Employee Theft and Customer Fraud. 1978. Almar Press. $3.00.

Hull, Burling. **The Billion Dollar Bait.** (Illus.). pap. Volcanda Educational Publications. $6.50.

Hutchinson, Robert A. **Vesco.** 1976. pap. Avon. (OP). $1.95.

Kahn, E. J., Jr. **Fraud: The United States Postal Inspection Service and Some of the Fools and Knaves It Has Known.** 1973. Harper & Row. (OP). $10.00.

Klein, John F. & Montague, Arthur. **Check-Forgers.** 1978. Lexington Books. $15.95.

Kwitny, Jonathan. **Fountain Pen Conspiracy.** 1973. Knopf. $10.95.

Moger, Art. **Pros and Cons.** 1975. pap. Fawcett World. (OP). $0.95.

Nash, Jay R. **Hustlers and Con Men.** (Illus.). 1976. M. Evans. $14.95.

Oughton, Frederick. **Fraud and White Collar Crime.** 1971. Merrimack Bk. Serv. $8.95.

Roberts, Murray B. **King of Con Men.** (Illus.). 1976. International Pubns. Service. (OP). $11.45.

Robinson, Kenneth M. **The Great American Mail-Fraud Trial: U.S.A. Vs. Glenn W. Turner, F. Lee Bailey.** 1976. Nash Publishing. (OP). $8.95.

Russell, Harold. **Foozles and Frauds.** 1977. Institute of Internal Auditors. $16.00.

Soble, Ronald & Dallos, Robert E. **Impossible Dream.** 1975. Nal. $1.95.

Steele, Eric H. **Fraud, Dispute and the Consumer: Responding to Consumer Complaints.** 1975. pap. American Bar Foundation. (OP). $1.00.

Verplanck, Gulian C. **An Essay on the Doctrine of Contracts.** 244p. 1972. Repr. of 1825 ed. Arno Press. $10.00.

FUGITIVES

Bradbury, John M. **The Fugitives.** 1958. pap. College & Univ. Press. $3.95.

Mahlerman, Herman. **The Fugitive.** Pageant-Poseidon. (OP). $5.00.

GANGS

Asbury, Herbert. **Gangs of New York: An Informal History of the Under World.** (Illus.). 1971. pap. Putnam. (OP). $3.25.

Bernstein, Saul. **Youth on the Streets.** 1964. Assn Press. (OP). $3.95.

Block, Herbert A. & Niederhoffer, Arthur. **Gang: A Study in Adolescent Behavior.** 1958. Philosophical Library. $6.00.

—**The Gang.** 1976. Repr. of 1958 ed. Greenwood Press. $15.75.

Cartwright, Desmond S., et al. eds. **Gang Delinquency.** 1975. pap. Brooks-Cole. (OP). $5.95.

Cloward, Richard A. & Ohlin, Lloyd E. **Delinquency and Opportunity: A Theory of Delinquent Gangs.** 1966. Free Press. $12.95; pap. $4.50.

Ellison, Harlan. **Memos from Purgatory.** 1975. pap. BJ Pub Group. $1.50.

Gale, William. **The Compound.** 1978. pap. Ballantine Books. $1.95.

Green, Janet. **The Six.** 1978. Hastings. $6.95.

Hanna, David. **Vito Genovese.** (Illus.) 1974. pap. Belmont-Tower. (OP). 95¢.

Haskins, James. **Street Gangs: Yesterday & Today.** (Illus.). 1974. Hastings. $7.95.

—**Street Gangs: Yesterday and Today.** (Illus.) pap. Hastings. $4.95.

Hoenig, Gary. **Reaper: The Inside Story of a Gang Leader.** 1975. Bobbs-Merrill. $6.95.

Keiser, R. L. **Vice Lords: Warriors of the Streets.** 1969. pap. Holt, Rinehart & Winston. $4.95.

Klein, Malcolm W. & Myerhoff, Barbara G., eds. **Juvenile Gangs In Context: Theory, Research and Action.** 1967. pap. Prentice-Hall. (OP). $4.95.

Krisberg, Barry A. **The Gang and the Community.** 1975. pap. R & E Research Associates. $9.00.

Liebow, Elliot. **Tally's Corner.** 1967. Little, Brown & Co. (OP) $7.95 pap. $2.95.

Maas, Peter. **Valachi Papers.** 1969. pap. Bantam. (OP). $1.75.

McLean, Gordon. **Terror in the Streets.** (Illus.) 1977. pap. Bethany Fell. $1.95.

McPhaul, Jack. **Johnny Torrio: First of the Gang Lords.** (Illus.). 1970. Arlington House. (OP). $8.95.

Meskil, Paul. **Don Carlo: Boss of Bosses.** 1973. pap. Popular Library. (OP). $1.25.

Moore, Joan, et al. **Homeboys: Gangs, Drugs and Prison in the Barrios of Los Angeles.** (Illus.). 1979. Temple University Press. $15.00; pap. $7.95.

Short, James F., Jr. & Strodtbeck, Frank L. **Group Process and Gang Delinquency.** 1965. University of Chicago Press. $10.50.

Thrasher, Frederic M. **Gang: A Study of One Thousand Three Hundred Thirteen Gangs in Chicago.** abr. ed. Short, James F., Jr., ed. 1963. University of Chicago Press. $14.00.

—**Gang: A Study of One Thousand Three Hundred Thirteen Gangs in Chicago.** Short, James F., Jr., ed. 1963. pap. University of Chicago Press. $7.00.

Whyte, William F. **Street Corner Society: The Social Structure of an Italian Slum.** rev. ed. (Illus.). 1955. University of Chicago Press. $15.00; pap. $4.95.

Yablonsky, Lewis. **Violent Gang.** rev. ed. 1971, pap. Penguin Books. (OP). $1.95.

Zieger, Henry. **Sam the Plumber.** 1972. pap. NAL. (OP). $0.95.

GOVERNMENTAL INVESTIGATIONS

Barth, Alan. **Government by Investigation.** Repr. of 1955 ed. Kelly. $13.50.

Burton, Frank & Carlen, Pat. **Official Discourse: On Discourse Analysis, Government Publications, Ideology and the State International Library of Sociology.** (Illus.). 1979. Routledge & Kegan $20.00.

Clokie, Hugh M. & Robinson, J. William. **Royal Commissions of Inquiry: The Significance of Investigation in British Politics.** 1969. Repr. of 1937 ed. Octagon Books. $13.00.

Dimock, Marshall E. **Congressional Investigating Committees.** Repr. of 1929 ed. AMS Press. $12.50.

Dorman, Michael. **Witch Hunt.** 192p. (gr. 7 up). 1976. Delacorte. $8.95.

Eberling, Ernest J. **Congressional Investigations: A Study of the Origin and Development of the Power of Congress to Investigate and Punish for Contempt.** 1972. Octagon Books. $21.00.

Hatton, Henry, ed. **Uncle Sam Is Watching You.** 1971. Public Affairs Press. $6.00.

Lipsky, Michael & Olsen, David J. **Commission Politics: The Processing of Racial Crisis in America.** 500p. 1977. Transaction Books. $14.95.

McGeary, M. Nelson. **Development of Congressional Investigative Power.** 1966. Octagon Books. $12.00.

Marcy, Carl. **Presidential Commissions.** 156p. 1973. Repr. of 1945 ed. Da Capo. $17.50.

Packer, Herbert L. **Ex-Communist Witnesses: Four Studies in Fact Finding.** 1962. Stanford University Press. $12.50.

Platt, Anthony M., ed. **Politics of Riot Commissions.** 1971. pap. Macmillan. $3.95.

Popper, Frank. **President's Commissions.** 74p. 1973. Repr. of 1970 ed. pap. Kraus Reprint. $5.00.

Report of the Seventh Session of WMO Executive Committee Inter-Governmental Panel on the First GARP Global Experiments. 132p. 1980. pap. Unipub. $25.00.

Schlesinger, Arthur M., Jr. & Bruns, Roger, eds. **Congress Investigates: A Documented History, 1792-1974** abr. ed. 1975. (Pub by Chelsea House). Bowker. $19.25.

—**Congress Investigates: A Documented History, 1792-1974,** 5 vols. 1980. pap. Chelsea House. $85.00.

Wraith, R. E. & Lamb, G. B. **Public Inquiries As an Instrument of Government.** 1971. Allen & Unwin. $25.00.

GUNSHOT WOUNDS

Fatteh, Abdullah. **Medicolegal Investigation of Gunshot Wounds.** (Illus.). 1976. Lippincott. $23.75.

Swan, Kenneth G. & Swan, Roy C. **Gunshot Wounds: Pathophysiology and Management.** (Illus.). 1980. PSG Pub. $27.50.

Wilber, Charles G. **Medicolegal Investigation of the President John F. Kennedy Murder.** (Illus.) 1978. C. C. Thomas. $17.50.

HAND-TO-HAND FIGHTING

Applegate, Rex. **Riot Control: Material and Technique.** (Illus.) 320p. Date not set. Paladin Enterprises. $15.95.

Baltazzi, Evan S. **A Stick for Self-Protection: Stick-Foot Fighting for Men and Women.** (Illus.) Evanel Associates. $10.00.

Birkenhead, **Fifty Famous Fights in Fact and Fiction.** 1932. Repr. R. West $20.00.

Campbell, Sid, et al. **Two Thousand One Martial Arts Questions, Kung Fu, Karate, Tae Kwon Do, Kenpo Students Should Know.** (Illus.). 1980 pap. Dimond Pubs. $8.95.

Cassidy, William L. **The Basic Manual of Knife Fighting.** 1978 pap. Paladin Enterprises. $4.00.

Cheong Cheng Leong & Draeger, Donn F. **Phoenix-Eye Fist: A Shaolin Fighting Art of South China.** (Illus.). 1977. pap. Weatherhill. $7.95.

Cooper, Jeff. **Principles of Personal Defense.** Brown, Robert K. & Lund, Peter C., eds. 1972. pap. Paladin Press. $4.00.

Corcoran, John & Farkas, Emil. **The Complete Martial Arts Catalogue.** 1977. Simon & Schuster. $10.95; pap. $5.95.

Diagram Group. **Enjoying Combat Sports.** (Illus.). 1977. pap. Paddington. $3.95.

Draeger, Don. **Budo: Classical.** 1975. Wehman Brothers, Inc. $10.00.

—**Bujutso & Budo: Modern.** 1974. Wehman Brothers, Inc. $15.00.

—**Bujutso: Classical.** 1973. Wehman Brothers, Inc. $10.00.

Draeger, Don F. **Modern Bujutsu and Budo.** (Illus.). 1947. Weatherhill. $16.50.

—**The Weapons and Fighting Arts of the Indonesian Archyselage.** (Illus.). Wehman Brothers, Inc. $12.50.

Draeger, Don F. & Smith, Robert W. **Asian Fighting Arts.** (Illus.). 1969. Wehman Brothers, Inc. $16.50.

—**Asian Fighting Arts.** 1974. pap. Berkley Publishing. $1.95.

—**Comprehensive Asian Fighting Arts.** (Illus.) 1981. pap. Kodansha. $11.95.

Draeger, Don F., et al. **Pentjak-Silat: The Indonesian Fighting Art.** (Illus.). 150p. 1970. Kodansha. $8.95.

Echanis, Michael D. **Knife Self-Defense for Combat.** 1977. pap. Ohara Publications. $5.95.

Fairbairn, W. E. **Get Tough.** (Illus.). 1974. Repr. Paladin Press. $12.95.

Gilbey, J. F. **Fighting Arts of World.** Wehman Brothers, Inc. $6.50.

Gilbey, John F. **Secret Fighting Arts of the World.** (Illus.) 1963. C. E. Tuttle. $8.50.

James, C. **Great Fights in Literature.** 1939. Repr. R. West. $40.00.

Khim, P'Ng C. & Draeger, Donn F. **Shaolin: An Introduction to Lohan Fighting Techniques.** (Illus.). 1979. C.E. Tuttle. $19.50.

Kiong & Draeger. **Shantung Black Tiger.** 1976. Wehman Brothers, Inc. $6.95.

Laiken, Deidre S. **Mind - Body - Spirit: The Martial Arts and Oriental Medicine.** 1978. Messner. $7.79.

Lee, Jae M. & Wayt, David H. **Hapkido: The Korean Art of Self Defense.** (Illus.). 1977. pap. Arco. $3.95.

Mashiro, N. **Black Medicine: The Dark Art of Death.** 1978. pap. Paladin Enterprises. $8.00.

Maslak, Paul. **Strategy in Unarmed Combat.** 1977. Wehman Brothers, Inc. $10.00.

Neff, Fred. **Everybody's Book of Self-Defense.** (Adult & Young Adult Ser). (Illus.). 1978. Lerner Publishing. $12.95; pap. $7.95.

Random, Michel. **Martial Arts.** (Octopus Book). (Illus.). 1978. Mayflower Books. $25.00.

Ribner, Susan & Chin, Richard. **The Martial Arts.** (Illus.). 1978. Harper & Row. $8.95.

Schultz, D.O. & Slepecky, M. **Police Unarmed Defense Tactics.** 102p. 1973. C.C.Thomas. $5.25.

Smith, Robert W. & Draeger, Donn F. **Asian Fighting Arts.** (Illus.). 1969. Kodansha. $16.50.

Steele, David E. **Secrets of Modern Knife Fighting.** (Illus.). 1975. Phoenix Assocs. $15.95; pap. $9.95.

Steiner, Bradley J. **Manuals on Mayhem: An Annotated Bibliography of Books on Combat Martial Arts and Self-Defense.** 1979. pap. Loompanics Unlimited. $6.00.

Tegner, Bruce. **Bruce Tegner's Complete Book of Aikido and Holds and Locks.** 1974. pap. Bantam Books. (OP). $1.25.

Tjoa Khek Kiorg, et al. **Shantung Black Tiger: A Fighting Art of North China.** (Illus.). 1976. pap. Weatherhill. $7.95.

Walston, Gerald. **The Legal Implications of Self-Defense: A Reference Text for the Martial Arts.** 1979. Vantage Press. $6.95.

Winderbaum, Larry, et al. **The Martial Arts Encyclopedia.** Brown, Roger G., ed. 1978. Inscape Corp. $19.50.

Yamada, Yoshimitsu. **Aikido Complete.** (Illus.). 128p. 1974. pap. Citadel Press. $4.95.

Zarrilli, Philip B., ed. **Martial Arts in Actor Training.** Date not set. Drama Book Specialists. price not set; pap. price not set.

HANDGUNS

Bristow, Allen P. **The Search for an Effective Police Handgun.** (Illus.). 256p. 1973. C.C. Thomas. $20.00.

Grennell, Dean A., ed. **Law Enforcement Handgun Digest.** 2nd rev. ed. (DBI Bks). 1976. pap. Follett. $6.95.

Hertzberg, Robert. **The Modern Handgun.** 1977. Arco. $4.95; pap. $2.50.

Koller, Harry. **How to Shoot: A Complete Guide to the Use of Sporting Firearms—Rifles, Shotguns and Handguns—on the Range and in the Field.** rev. ed. Elman, Robert, et al, eds. (Illus.). 1976. Doubleday. $9.95.

Lewis, Jack. **Law Enforcement Handgun Digest.** 3rd ed. 288p. 1980. pap. DBI Books. $8.95.

Nonte, George C. **Handgun Competition.** (Illus.). 1978. Winchester Press. $12.95.

—**Handloading for Handgunners.** 1978. pap. DBI Books. $7.95.

Nonte, George C., Jr. **Combat Handguns.** Jurras, Lee F., ed. (Illus.). 1980. Stackpole Books. $17.95.

Skillen, Charles R., & Williams, Mason. **American Police Handgun Training.** (Illus.). 216p. 1977. C.C. Thomas. $13.00.

Weston, Paul B. **The New Handbook of Handgunning.** (Illus.). 96p. 1980. write for info. C.C. Thomas.

Williams, Mason. **The Defensive Use of the Handgun: For the Novice.** (Illus.). 240p. 1978. C.C. Thomas. $12.75; pap. $7.75.

Williams, Mason. **The Law Enforcement Book of Weapons Ammunition and Training Procedures: Handguns, Rifles and Shotguns.** (Illus.). 544p. 1977. C.C. Thomas. $35.75.

Wood, J.B. **Troubleshooting Your Handgun.** 1978. pap. DBI Books $5.95.

HIJACKING OF AIRCRAFT

Agrawala, S.K. **Aircraft Hijacking and International Law.** 1973. Oceana. (OP) $10.00.

Barker, Ralph. **Not Here, but in Another Place.** (Illus.). 352p. 1980. St. Martins Press. $12.95.

Clyne, Peter. **Anatomy of Skyjacking.** 1974. Transatlantic Arts Inc. (OP). $9.95.

Haas, William & Blair, Ed. **Odyssey of Terror.** (Illus.). 1977. Broadman. $7.95.

Hubbard, David G. **Skyjacker: His Flights of Fancy.** Alexandre, Clement, ed. 1971. Macmillan. $5.95; pap. $1.95.

Joyner, Nancy D. **Aerial Hijacking As an International Crime.** 352p. 1974. Oceana. $21.00.

Moore, Kenneth C. **Airport, Aircraft and Airline Security.** (Illus.). 1976. Butterworths. $18.50.

Sato, Bunsei. **Hijack: 144 Lives in the Balance.** (Illus.). 1975. Japan Pubns. (OP) $8.95.

HOMICIDE

Adelson, Lester. **The Pathology of Homicide: A Vade Mecum for Pathologist, Prosecutor and Defense Counsel.** (Illus.). 992p. 1974. C.C. Thomas. $50.00.

Allen, Nancy. **Homicide: Perspectives on Prevention.** 1979. Human Sciences Press. $15.95; pap. $8.95.

Bailey, F. Lee & Rothblatt, Henry B. **Crimes of Violence: Rape and Other Sex Crimes.** (Criminal Law Library). 1973. Lawyers Co-Operative Publishing Co. $45.00.

Bensing, Robert C. & Schroeder, Oliver, Jr. **Homicide in an Urban Community.** (Illus.). 1960. C.C. Thomas. pap. $8.75.

Biggs, John, Jr. **The Guilty Mind: Psychiatry and the Law of Homicide.** (Isaac Ray Award Lectures Ser.). 248p. (Orig.). 1967. pap. Johns Hopkins. $2.95.

Brearley, H.C. **Homicide in the United States.** (Criminology, Law Enforcement, & Social Problems Ser.: No. 36). 1969. Repr. of 1932 ed. Patterson Smith. $10.00.

Bromberg, Walter. **The Mold of Murder: A Psychiatric Study of Homicide.** 230p. Repr. of 1961 ed. Greenwood Press. $11.25.

Chimbos, Peter D. **Marital Violence: A Study of Interspouse Homicide.** 1978. pap. R & E Research Associates. $12.00.

Danto, Bruce, et al, eds. **Homicide and Survivors.** (Thanatology Service Ser.). 225p. 1980. pap. Highly Specialized Promotions. $9.95.

Devine, Philip E. **The Ethics of Homicide.** 1978. Cornell University Press. $15.00.

Dieckmann, Edward A., Sr. **Practical Homicide Investigation.** 96p. 1961. C.C. Thomas. $5.25.

Gelb, Barbara. **On the Track of Murder.** 1976. pap. Ballantine Books. $1.95.

Henry, Andrew F. & Short, James F., Jr. **Suicide and Homicide: Some Economic, Sociological and Psychological Aspects of Aggression.** Kastenbaum, Robert, ed. (Death & Dying Ser.). (Illus.). 1977. Repr. of 1954 ed. Arno Press. $15.00.

Hughes, Daniel J. **Homicide: Investigative Techniques.** (Illus.). 376p. 1974. C.C. Thomas. $21.50.

Lester, David & Lester, Gene. **Crime of Passion: Murder and the Murderer.** 1975. Nelson-Hall. $14.95.

Macdonald, John M. **Homicidal Threats.** (Illus.). 136p. 1968. C.C. Thomas. $8.25.

—**Murderer and His Victim.** 1961. C.C. Thomas. (OP) $10.50.

Moreland, Roy. **Law of Homicide.** 1952. Bobbs-Merrill. (OP) $10.00.

Palmer, Stuart. **The Violent Society.** 1972. College & University. Press. $6.50; pap. $2.95.

Palmer, Stuart, ed. **Homicide and Suicide.** Date not set. L'oer-Atherton. $9.95; pap. $3.95.

Richardson, Lewis F. **Statistics of Deadly Quarrels.** Wright, Quincy & Lienau, C.C., eds. (Illus.). 1960. Boxwood Press. $24.00.

Snyder, LeMoyne. **Homicide Investigation: Practical Information for Coroners, Police Officers and Other Investigators.** 3rd ed. (Illus.). 416p. 1977. C.C. Thomas. $24.75.

Sullivan, Shaun J. **Killing in Defense of Private Property: The Development of a Roman**

Catholic Moral Teaching, Thirteenth to Eighteenth Centuries. (American Academy of Religion. Dissertation Ser.). (Illus.). 1976. pap. Scholars Press. $7.50.

Sylvester, Sawyer F., et al. **Prison Homicide.** (Sociomedical Science Ser.). 1977. Halsted Press. $12.00.

Thakur, Upendra. **Introduction to Homicide in India: Ancient and Early Medieval Period.** 1978. South Asia Books. $9.50.

Totman, Jane. **The Murderess: A Psychosocial Study of Criminal Homicide.** 1978. pap. R & E Research Associates. $10.00.

HOMICIDE INVESTIGATION

Bailey, F. Lee & Rothblatt, Henry B. **Crimes of Violence: Homicide and Assault.** 543p. 1973. Lawyers Co-Operative Publishing Co. $45.00.

Dieckmann, Edward A. **Practical Homicide Investigation.** 96p. 1961. C.C. Thomas. $5.25.

Gelb, Barbara. **On the Track of Murder.** 1976. pap. Ballantine Books. $1.95.

Lundsgaarde, Henry. **Murder in Space City: A Cultural Analysis of Houston Homicidal Patterns.** (Illus.). 1977. Oxford University Press. $12.95.

Snyder, LeMoyne. **Homicide Investigation: Practical Information for Coroners, Police Officers, and Other Investigators.** 3rd ed. (Illus.). 416p. 1977. C.C. $24.75.

HYPNOSIS AND CRIME

Arons, Harry. **Hypnosis in Criminal Investigation.** pap. Borden. $9.00.

Bryan, William J., Jr. **Chosen Ones.** 1970. Vantage Press. (OP) $12.75.

Hibbard, Whitney & Worring, Raymond. **Forensic Hypnosis: The Practical Application of Hypnosis in Criminal Investigations.** (Illus.). 400p. 1981. text ed. C.C. Thomas. $32.75.

Monoghan, Frank J. **Hypnosis in Criminal Investigation.** (Orig.). 1980. pap. Kendall-Hunt. $6.95.

Reiser, Martin. **Handbook of Investigative Hypnosis.** 1980. LEHI Publishing Co. $24.95.

IDENTIFICATION

Alexander, Harold L.V. **Classifying Palm-Prints: A Complete System of Coding, Filing and Searching Palmprints.** (Illus.). 136p. 1973. C.C. Thomas. $15.25.

Allison, Harrison C. **Personal Identification.** (Illus.). 1973. Holbrook. (OP). $15.95.

Bates, Billy Prior. **I.S.Q.D. (Identification System for Questioned Documents).** (Illus.). 112p. 1970. C.C. Thomas. $9.75.

—**Typewriting Identification. (I.S.Q.T.): Identification System for Questioned Typewriting.** (Illus.). 112p. 1971. C.C. Thomas. $10.00.

Clifford, Brian & Bull, Ray. **The Psychology of Person Identification.** 1978. Routledge & Kegan. $20.00.

Kolb, Patricia A. **H.I.T. A Manual for the Classification, Filing and Retrieval of Palmprints.** (Illus.). 112p. 1979. C.C. Thomas. $15.25.

Nash, Donald J. **Individual Identification and The Law Enforcement Officer.** (Illus.). 176p. 1978. C.C. Thomas. $16.00.

Rudman, Jack. **Identification Officer.** (Career Examination Ser.: C-1986). pap. National Learning Corp. $8.00.

—**Identification Specialist.** (Career Examination Ser.: C-2294). 1977. pap. National Learning Corp. $8.00.
—**Senior Identification Clerk.** (Career Examination Ser.: C-2293). pap. National Learning Corp. $10.00.
—**Senior Identification Officer.** (Career Examinations Ser.: C-1987). pap. National Learning Corp. $10.00.
—**Senior Identification Specialist.** (Career Examination Ser.: C-2512). pap. National Learning Corp. $10.00.
—**Supervising Identification Specialist.** (Career Examination Ser.: C-2513). pap. National Learning Corp. $10.00.
Sobel, Nathan R. **Eye-Witness Identification.** 1972. 1978 supplement incl. Boardman. $20.00.
Sopher, Irvin M. **Forensic Dentistry.** (Illus.). 176p. 1976. C.C. Thomas. $18.75.
Wall, Patrick M. **Eye-Witness Identification in Criminal Cases.** 248p. 1975. C.C. Thomas. $12.00.
Warfel, Geroge H. **Identification Technologies: Computer, Optical, and Chemical Aids to Personal ID.** (Illus.). 200p. 1979. C.C. Thomas. $18.50.
Zavals, Albert & Paley, James J., eds. **Personal Appearance Identification.** (Illus.). 352p. 1972. pap. C.C. Thomas. $20.00.

INFORMERS

Harney, Malachi L. & Cross, John C. **Informer in Law Enforcement.** 2nd ed. 1968. C.C. Thomas. (OP) $7.50.
Hoffman, Paul & Pecznick, Ira. **To Drop a Dime.** 1977. pap. BJ Publishing Group. $1.95.
—**To Drop a Dime: The Mafia Hitman's Uncensored Story.** 1976. Putnam. (OP). $8.95.

INVESTIGATIONS

Akin, Richard H. **The Private Investigator's Basic Manual.** 208p. 1979. C.C. Thomas. $16.25.
Arco Editorial Board. **Investigator-Inspector.** 4th ed. 1979. pap. Arco. $10.00.
Arther, Richard O. **The Scientific Investigator.** (Illus.). 248p. 1976. C.C. Thomas. $14.50.
Barefoot, J. Kirk. **Undercover Investigation.** (Illus.). 100p. 1975. C.C. Thomas. $13.50.
Bequai, August. **Computer Crime.** 1978. Lexington Books. $16.95.
Block, Eugene B. **Science vs. Crime and Men's Rights.** (Illus.). 1980. Cragmont Publishing. $9.95; pap. $6.95.
Bozza, Charles M. **Criminal Investigation.** (Nelson-Hall Law Enforcement Ser.). 1977. Nelson-Hall. $20.95.
Cawley, Donald F., et al. **Managing Criminal Investigations.** Date not set. Lexington Books. price not set.
Chafee, Zechariah, Jr., et al. **Third Degree.** (Mass Violence in America Ser.). Repr. of 1931 ed. Arno Press. $12.00.
Chilimidos, R.S. **Auto Theft Investigation.** 1971. Legal Book Corp. $12.50.
Criminal Investigation. (Public Service Technology Ser.). 496p. 1980. Merrill. $16.95.
Cunliffe, Frederick & Piazza, Peter B. **Criminalistics and Scientific Investigation.** (Ser. in Criminal Justice). (Illus.). 1980. Prentice-Hall. $16.95.
Dash, Samuel, et al. **Eavesdroppers.** (Civil Liberties in American History Ser.). (Illus.). 1970. Repr. of 1959 ed. Da Capo. $17.50.
Davies, Geoffrey, ed. **Forensic Science.** (ACS Symposium Ser.: No. 13). 1975. American Chemical Society. $20.75.

DeLadurantey, Joseph C. & Sullivan, Daniel R. **Criminal Investigation Standards.** (Illus.). 1979. Harper & Row. inst manual free. $17.50.
Dellheim, S.D. **Forensic Handbook.** new ed. (Illus.). 1978. pap. Scott Protective Resources. $3.95.
De Vore, R. William, ed. **Carnahan Conference on Crime Countermeasures: Proceedings 1979.** Jackson, J.S. (Illus. Orig.). 1979. ORES Pubns. microfiche. $22.50; pap. $3.50.
Dienstein, William. **Technics for the Crime Investigator.** 2nd ed. 196p. 1974. C.C. Thomas. $12.00.
Dowling, Jerry L. **Criminal Investigation.** (HBJ Criminal Justice Ser.). 219p. 1979. pap. Harcourt Brace Jovanovich. instructor's manual avail. $7.95.
Ferguson, Robert J., Jr. **Scientific Informer.** (Illus.). 248p. 1971. C.C. Thomas. $12.00.
Fitzgerald, Maurice J. **Handbook of Criminal Investigation.** 1951. Arco. $5.00.
Fricke, Charles W. **Criminal Investigation and the Law.** 7th ed. Payton, George T., ed. 1974. Legal Book Corp. $14.00.
Given, Bruce, et al. **Tire Tracks and Tread Marks.** (Illus.). 1977. Gulf Publishing. $10.95.
Goddard, K. **Crime Scene Investigation.** 1977. Reston. students manual avail. $12.50.
Golec, Anthony M. **Techniques of Legal Investigation.** (Illus.). 280p. 1976. C.C. Thomas. $18.75.
Granet, Irving. **Strength of Materials for Engineering Technology.** 2nd ed. (Illus.). 448p. 1979. Reston. instrs. manual avail. $19.95.
Greenwood, Peter W., et al. **The Criminal Investigation Process.** 1977. Lexington Books. $15.00.
—**The Criminal Investigation Process** 1977. pap. Heath. $6.95.
Gugas, Chris. **The Silent Witness: A Polygraphist's Casebook.** 1979. Prentice-Hall. $9.95.
Hall, Jay C. **Inside the Crime Lab.** 288p. 1973. Prentice-Hall. $7.95.
Heffron, Floyd N. **Evidence for the Patrolman.** (Police Science Ser.). (Illus.). 192p. 1972. C.C. Thomas. $10.00.
Hicks, Randolph D., II. **Undercover Operations and Persuasion.** 104p. 1973. C.C. Thomas. $7.75.
Howington, Jon. **Laboratory Manual for Introductory Criminal Investigation.** pap. University Press of America. $8.75.
Kaplan, Abraham. **The Conduct of Inquiry.** 1964. pap. Harper & Row. $12.95.
Kenney, John P. & More, Harry W., Jr. **Principles of Investigation.** (Illus.). 1979. West Publishing. $17.95; workbook. $5.50.
Kind, Stuart & Overman, Michael. **Science Against Crime.** 160p. 1972. Doubleday. $7.95.
Kirk, Paul L. & Bradford, Lowell W. **Crime Laboratory: Organization and Operation.** (Illus.). 132p. 1972. C.C. Thomas. $7.75.
Kirk, Paul L., et al. **Crime Investigation.** 2nd ed. 1974. Wiley, John & Sons. $22.95.
Krishnan, S.S. **An Introduction to Modern Criminal Investigation: With Basic Laboratory Techniques.** (Illus.). 440p. 1978. C.C. Thomas. $28.25; pap. $21.75.
Lee, Peter G. **Interpol.** 224p. 1976. Stein & Day. $25.00.
Leonard, V.A. **Criminal Investigation and Identification.** (Illus.). 160p. 1971. C.C. Thomas. $9.25.
—**Police Detective Function.** 124 p. 1970. C.C. Thomas. $8.25.
Loth, David. **Crime Lab.** 1966. Simon & Schuster. $4.95.

Lucas, Norman. **The Laboratory Detectives: How Science Traps the Criminals.** 205p. 1972. Taplinger. $7.95.
Markle, Arnold. **Criminal Investigation and Presentation of Evidence.** 1976. West Publishing. $12.95.
Mettler, George B. **Criminal Investigation.** 1977. Holbrook. instructor's manual free. $16.50.
Morland, Nigel, ed. **The Criminologist.** (Illus.). 318p. 1972. Open Court. $17.50.
Mulhearn, Henry. **Crime Investigation.** 1976. pap. Gould. $7.50.
—**Police Science Fundamentals** 220 p. 1973. Pap. Gould. $7.50.
Murray, Joseph A. **Police Administration and Criminal Investigation.** 3rd ed. (Orig.). 1968. Arco. $12.50; pap. $10.00.
Murray, R.C. & Tedrow, John C. **Forensic Geology: Earth Sciences and Criminal Investigation.** 1975. Rutgers University Press. $15.00.
Nash, Donald J. **Individual Identification and the Law Enforcement Officer.** (Illus.). 176p. 1978. C.C. Thomas. $16.00.
Nelson, John. **Preliminary Investigation and Police Reporting: A Complete Guide to Police Written Communication.** 1970. Glencoe. $14.95.
O'Hara, Charles E. **Fundamentals of Criminal Investigation.** 4th ed. (Illus.). 1000p. 1978. C.C. Thomas. $22.50.
O'Hara, Charles E. & Osterburg, James W. **An Introduction to Criminalistics: The Application of the Physical Sciences to the Detection of Crime.** rev. ed. 728p. 1972. Repr. of 1949 ed. Indiana University Press. $17.50.
Osterburg, James W. **Crime Laboratory: Case Studies of Scientific Criminal Investigation.** (Illus.). 1968. Indiana University Press. $12.50; pap. $8.95.
Plutchik, Robert. **Fundamentos De Investigacion Experimental.** rev. ed. 1975. pap. Harper & Row. $7.25.
Reik, Theodor. **Compulsions to Confess: On the Psycho Analysis of Crime and Punishment.** Repr. of 1959 ed. Arno Press. $30.00.
Rhodes, Gerald. **Committees of Inquiry.** 224p. 1975. Crane-Russak Co. $21.50.
Ringel, William E. **Identification and Police Line-Ups.** (Orig.). 1968. pap. Gould. $5.00.
Rudman, Jack. **Chief Special Investigator.** (Career Examination Ser.: C-1591). pap. National Learning Corp. $12.00.
—**Complaint Investigator.** (Career Examination Ser.: C-1863). pap. National Learning Corp. $8.00.
—**Criminal Investigation.** (ACT Proficiency Examination Program: PEP-9). pap. National Learning Corp. $9.95.
—**Criminal Investigation.** (College Proficiency Examination Ser.: CPEP-30). 1977. pap. National Learning Corp. $9.95.
—**Criminal Investigator.** (Career Examination Ser.: C-1229). pap. National Learning Corp. $8.00.
—**Criminal Law Investigator.** (Career Examination Ser.: C-969). pap. National Learning Corp. $8.00.
—**Detective Investigator.** (Career Examination Ser.: C-1247). pap. National Learning Corp. $10.00.
—**Hospital Case Investigator.** (Career Examination Ser.: C-1889). pap. National Learning Corp. $8.00.
—**Investigator.** (Career Examination Ser: C-377). pap. Natl Learning. $8.00.
—**Principal Investigator.** (Career Examination Ser.: C-1791). pap. National Learning Corp. $10.00.

—**Principal Special Investigator.** (Career Examination Ser.: C-1590). pap. National Learning Corp. $10.00.

—**Private Investigator.** (Career Examination Ser.: C-2462). pap. National Learning Corp. $10.00.

—**Senior Special Investigator.** (Career Examinaton Ser.: C-1589). pap. National Learning Corp. $8.00.

—**Special Investigator.** (Career Examination Ser.: C-1588). pap. National Learning Corp. $8.00.

—**Supervising Investigator.** (Career Examination Ser.: C-2106). 1977. pap. National Learning Corp. $10.00.

Saferstein, Richard. **Criminalistics: An Introduction to Forensic Science.** (Illus.). 1977. Prentice-Hall. $17.95.

—**Criminalistics: An Introduction to Forensic Science.** 2nd ed. 1981. Prentice-Hall. $18.95.

Salottolo, Lawrence. **Criminal Science Handbook.** 160p. 1972. Arco. $8.00; pap. $5.00.

Sanders, William B. **Detective Work: A Study of Criminal Investigations.** (Illus.). 1977. Free Press. $12.95.

—**Detective Work: A Study of Criminal Investigations.** (Illus.). 1979. pap. Free Press. $6.95.

Schultz, Donald & Scheer, Samuel. **Crime Scene Investigation.** (Illus.). 1977. Prentice-Hall. $14.95.

Schultz, Donald O. **Criminal Investigation Techniques.** 1978. Gulf Publishing. $12.95.

Scott, James D. **Investigative Methods.** (Illus.). 1978. ref. ed. instrs'. manual available. Reston. $13.95.

Shaffer, Ron & Klose, Kevin. **Surprise! Surprise.** 1979. pap. Avon. $2.25.

Soderman, Harry & O'Connell, John J. **Modern Criminal Investigation.** 5th ed. O'Hara. Charles E., ed. (Funk & W Bk.). (Illus.). 1962. T. Y. Crowell. $10.00.

Stone, Alfred R. & Deluca, Stuart M. **Investigating Crimes: An Introduction.** (Illus.). 1980. Houghton Mifflin. $18.95; inst. manual $1.00.

Stuckey, Gilbert B. **Evidence for the Law Enforcement Officer.** 2nd ed. (illus.). 448p. 1974. McGraw-Hill. $14.95. instructor's guide. $3.00.

Svensson, Arne. **Techniques of Crime Scene Investigation.** 1965. Elsevier-North Holland Publishing Co. $19.95.

Swanson, C.R., et al. **Criminal Investigation.** 2nd ed. Territo, Leonard, tr. 1980. Goodyear. price not set.

Thorwald, Jurgen. **Century of the Detective.** (Helen & Kurt Wolff Bk.). (Illus.). 1965. Harcourt Brace Jovanovich. $12.50.

Tobias, Marc W. & Petersen, R. David. **Field Manual of Criminal Law and Police Procedure.** (Illus.). 212p. 1975. pap. C.C. Thomas. $15.25.

Turner, David R. **Detective Investigator.** 160p. (Orig.). 1975. pap. Arco. $6.00.

U.S. Army. **Basic Criminal Investigations.** (Illus.). 1977. pap. Paladin Enterprises. $4.00.

Ward, Richard A. **Introduction to Criminal Investigation.** 368p. 1975. Addison-Wesley Publishing Co. $12.95.

Wells, Kenneth M. & Weston, Paul B. **Criminal Evidence for Police.** 2nd ed. (Illus.). 352p. 1976. Prentice-Hall. $16.95.

Weston, Paul B. & Wells, Kenneth M. **Criminal Investigation: Basic Perspectives.** 3rd ed. (Illus.). 1980. Prentice-Hall. $17.95.

Wilber, Charles G. **Forensic Biology for the Law Enforcement Officer.** (Illus.). 392p. 1974. C.C. Thomas. $24.25.

—**Forensic Toxicology for the Law Enforcement Officer.** (Illus.). 310p. 1980. C.C. Thomas. $27.50.

Winks, Robin W., ed. **Historian As Detective: Essays on Evidence.** 1970. pap. Harper & Row. $6.50.

Zeiger, Henry A., ed. **Inquest.** 1970. pap. Belmont-Tower Books. (OP). $0.95.

JUDO

AAU Official Judo Rules 1978-80. (Illus.). 1978. softcover. Amateur Athlete Union of the United States Publications. $3.50.

Bartlett, E.G. **Basic Judo.** Wehman Brothers, Inc. $2.95.

—**Basic Judo.** (Illus.). 1975. pap. Arco. $2.95.

Bartlett, Eric G. **Judo and Self-Defense.** (Illus.). 1971. pap. Arc Books. (OP). $1.45.

Bruce, Jeannette. **Judo: A Gentle Beginning.** (Illus.). 160p. (gr. 3 up). 1975. TY Crowell. $7.95.

Butler, Pat. **Judo Complete.** (Illus.). 1971. (Pub. by Faber & Faber); Merrimack Book Service. $7.95; pap. $4.95.

Butler, Pat & Butler, Karen. **Judo and Self-Defence for Women and Girls.** (Illus.). 1968. (Pub. by Faber & Faber). Merrimack Book Service. $7.95.

Campbell, B. **Championship Judo.** Wehman Brothers, Inc. $6.95.

Dominy. **Judo: Beginner to Black Belt.** Wehman Brothers, Inc. $6.95.

Dominy, Eric. **Judo: Basic Principles.** (Illus.). 1975. Sterling. (OP) $4.95.

—**Judo: Self-Taught.** (Illus.). 208p. 1976. pap. Barnes & Noble. $1.95.

—**Judo Techniques and Tactics.** (Illus.). 1969. pap. Dover. $2.50.

—**Judo Techniques and Tactics: Contest Judo.** (Illus.). Peter Smith. $6.75.

—**Teach Yourself Judo.** (Illus.). 1962. Emerson. $7.95.

Draeger, Donn F. & Otaki, Tadao. **Kodokan Judo.** (Illus.). 1981. G.E. Tuttle. price not set.

—**A Complete Guide to Kodokan Randori No Kata.** (Illus.). 1981. C.E. Tuttle. $30.00.

—**Judo Formal Techniques.** (Illus.). 1976. C.E. Tuttle. (OP). $15.00.

Feldenkrais, Moshe. **Higher Judo.** (Illus.). 1952. Warne. (OP). $2.95.

—**Judo.** (Illus.). 1944. Warne. $4.95.

Feldenkrais, Moshe. **Judo.** (Illus.). 1944. Warne. $4.95.

Freudenberg, Karl. **Natural Weapons: A Manual of Karate, Judo, and Jujitsu Techniques.** (Illus., Orig.). 1962. pap. A.S. Barnes. $3.95.

Frommer, Harvey. **The Martial Arts: Judo and Karate.** (Illus.). 1978. Atheneum. $7.95.

Gardner, Ruth. **Judo for the Gentle Woman.** (Illus.). 1971. pap. C.E. Tuttle. $3.25.

Geesink, A. **Go-Kyo: Principles of Judo.** Wehman Brothers, Inc. $8.95.

—**My Championship Judo.** (Illus.). 1973. Arco. (OP) $8.95.

Glass, George. **Competitive Judo: Throwing Techniques and Weight Control.** (Illus., Orig.). 1977. pap. (Pub. by Faber & Faber). Merrimack Book Service. $3.95.

—**Your Book of Judo.** (Illus.). 1978. (Pub. by Faber & Faber). Merrimack Book Service. $5.95.

Gleason, G.R. **Better Judo.** rev. ed. (Illus.). 1978. Sportshelf & Soccer Associates. $14.50.

Gleeson, G.E. **Better Judo.** (Illus.). 96p. 1972. International Publishing Service. $8.50.

—**Judo As a Sport.** (Illus.). 1971. International Publications Service. (OP) $5.25.

Gleeson, Geoff. **All About Judo.** (Illus.). 1975. Charles River Books. $6.95.

Gleeson, Geoff. **All About Judo.** (Illus.). 1979. Sterling. $10.95; pap. $5.95.

Goodbody, John. **Judo: How to Become a Champ.** (Illus.). 1976. pap. Transatlantic Arts Inc. $4.75.

Harrington, Anthony P. **Every Boy's Judo.** (Illus.). (gr. 7 up). Emerson. $7.95.

—**Every Boy's Judo.** (Illus.). 1971. pap. NAL. $0.95.

—**Every Girl's Judo.** (Illus.). (gr. 7 up). Emerson. $7.95.

—**Science of Judo.** (Illus.). Emerson. $6.95.

Harrison, E.J. **Junior Judo.** rev. ed. (gr. 4 up). 1965. Sterling. $5.95.

Illustrated Kodokan Judo. (Illus.). Wehman Brothers, Inc. $37.00.

Inokuma, Isao & Sato, Noguyuki. **Best Judo.** (Illus.). 1979. Kodansha. $19.95.

James, Stuart. **The Complete Beginner's Guide to Judo.** (gr. 6-12). 1978. Doubleday. $6.95.

Judo. 1976. pap. British Book Center. $2.50.

Kim, Daeshik & Shin, Kyung Sun. **Judo.** 2nd ed. 1977. pap. Wm. C. Brown. $3.25.

Klinger, Hubert. **Judo Self-Taught.** pap. Wehman Brothers, Inc. $1.95.

Kobayashi, K. **Sport of Judo.** Wehman Brothers, Inc. $5.75.

Kobayashi, Kiyoshi & Sharp, Harold E. **Sport of Judo.** (Illus.). (gr. 9 up). 1957. pap. C.E. Tuttle. $6.95.

Kodokan. **Illustrated Kodokan Judo.** (Illus.). 1955. Japan Publishers. $22.50.

Kotani, Sumuyuki. **Kodokan Judo Revised.** 1968. Wehman Brothers, Inc. $7.95.

Kozuki, Russell. **Blackbelt Techniques in the Martial Arts.** 1976. Sterling. (OP). 4.95; $4.89.

Kudo, K. **Judo in Action.** 2 vols. Wehman Brothers, Inc. $4.50 ea.

Kudo, Kazuzo. **Judo in Action: Grappling Techniques.** (Illus.). 1967. pap. Japan Pubns. $4.50.

—**Judo in Action: Throwing Techniques.** (Illus.). pap. Japan Pubns. $4.50.

Lawson-Wood, D. & Lawson-Wood, J. **Judo Revival Points, Athletes' Points and Posture.** (Illus.). 1975. British Book Center. (OP). $3.95.

LeBell, Gene & Coughran, L. C. **Handbook of Judo.** 192p. 1963. pap. Cornerstone Library. $1.95.

Longhurst, Percy. **Ju-Jutsu and Judo.** (Illus.). 64p. 1980. softcover. Paladin Enterprises. $6.00.

Nakabayashi, Sadaki, et al. **Fundamentals of Judo.** (Illus.). 1964. Ronald Press. (OP). $7.95.

Neff, Fred. **Fred Neff's Manual of Throws for Sport Judo and Self-Defense.** (Illus.). 56p. (gr. 5 up). 1976. Lerner Pubns. $4.95.

Nishioka, Hayward. **Foot Throws.** Wehman Brothers, Inc. $3.25.

—**The Judo Textbook.** (Illus.). 1979. pap. Ohara Pubns. $5.95.

Ohashi, Takumi. **A Guide to Judo Grappling Techniques.** (Illus.). 1958. C.E. Tuttle. (OP). $2.50.

Okano, I. & Sato, T. **Vital Judo.** Wehman Brothers, Inc. $14.95.

Okano, Isai. **Vital Judo: Grappling Techniques.** Wehman Brothers, Inc. $14.95.

Okano, Isao & Sato, Tetsuya. **Vital Judo: Throwing Techinques.** (Illus.). 1973. Japan Pubns. (OP). $12.00.

Reay, Tony & Hobbs, Geoffrey. **The Illustrated Guide to Judo.** 1979. pap. Van Nos Reinhold. $9.95.

Rhee, J. **Tan-Gun and to-San.** Wehman Brothers, Inc. $4.95.

Robert, Hank. **Ketsugo.** pap. Key Books. $1.00.

Science of Judo. Wehman Brothers, Inc. $6.25.

So, Doshin. **What Is Shorinji Kempo.** Wehman Brothers, Inc. $4.50.

Starbrook, Dave. **Judo Starbrook Style: Champion's Method.** (Illus.). 1978. Beekman Pubs. $14.95.

Stewart, Paul. **Sports Illustrated Judo.** (Illus.). 1976. Lippincott. $4.95; pap. $2.95.

Takagaki, S. **Techniques of Judo.** Wehman Brothers, Inc. $6.25.

Takagaki, Shinzo & Sharp, Harold E. **Techniques of Judo.** (Illus.). 1956. pap. C.E. Tuttle. $6.25.

Tegner, Bruce. **Bruce Tegner's Complete Book of Judo.** rev. ed. (Illus.). 224p. 1980. Thor. $6.95.

—**Bruce Tegner's Complete Book of Jukado Self Defense: Jiu Jitsu Modernized.** (Illus.). 1968. Thor. $6.95.

—**Judo: Sport Techniques for Physical Fitness and Tournament.** (Illus.). 144p. 1976. pap. Thor. $2.95.

—**Karate and Judo Exercises: Physical Conditioning for the Oriental Sport Fighting Arts.** (Illus.). 127p. (Orig.). 1972. pap. Thor. $2.95.

Wall, Bob. **Who's Who in the Martial Arts and Directory of Black Belts.** (Illus.). 275p. (Orig.). 1975. pap. R.A. Wall. $7.95.

Watanabe, Jiichi & Avakian, Lindy. **Secrets of Judo.** (Illus.). 1959. C.E. Tuttle. $7.50.

JUVENILE COURTS

Altman, Michael L. **Standards Relating to Juvenile Records and Information Systems.** 1977. Ballinger Publishing. casebound $16.50; softcover $7.95.

Autin, Diana. **Young People and the Law.** 4th ed. Youth Liberation, ed. (Illus.). 1978. Youth Liberation Press. $2.50.

Besharov, Douglas J. **Juvenile Justice Advocacy: Practice in a Unique Court.** 1974. Practising Law Institute. $20.00.

Bing, Stephen & Brown, Larry. **Standards Relating to Monitoring.** 1977. Ballinger Publishing. casebound $12.50; softcover $5.95.

Bittner, Egon & Krantz, Sheldon. **Standards Relating to Police Handling of Juvenile Problems.** 1977. Ballinger Publishing. final casebound $16.50; softcover $7.95.

Bliss, Dennis C. **The Effects of the Juvenile Justice System on Self-Concept.** 1977. soft bdg. R&E Research Associates. $8.00.

Blomberg, Thomas G. **Social Control and the Proliferation of Juvenile Court Services.** 1978. pap. R&E Research Associates. $10.00.

—**Juvenile Court Reform: Widening The Social Control Net.** 256p. 1981. Oelgeschlager, Gunn & Hain. $20.00.

Bremner, Robert H. **The Juvenile Court: An Original Anthology.** 1974. Arno Press. $19.00.

Buckle, Leonard & Buckle, Suzann. **Standards Relating to Planning for Juvenile Justice.** 1977. Ballinger Publishing. final casebound $12.50; softcover $5.95.

Carlin, Angela G. & Schwartz, Richard W., eds. **Merrick-Rippner Ohio Probate Law: Practice and Forms, Including Juvenile Law Practice and Forms.** 3rd rev. ed. 1978. Banks-Baldwin. $95.00

Coffey, Alan R. **Juvenile Corrections: Treatment and Rehabilitation.** (Illus.). 320p. 1975. Prentice-Hall. $15.95.

Cohen, Fred. **Standards Relating to Dispositional Procedures.** 1977. Ballinger Publishing. casebound $12.50; softcover $5.95.

Cox, Steven M. & Conrad, John J. **Juvenile Justice: A Guide to Practice and Theory.** 1978. Wm. C. Brown. $12.95; instructor's resource manual $1.00.

Dawson, Robert O. **Standards Relating to Adjudication.** 1977. Ballinger Publishing. casebound $12.50; softcover $5.95.

Eldefonso, Edward & Coffey, Alan. **Process and Impact of the Juvenile Justice System.** 1976. pap. Glencoe. $9.95.

Emerson, Robert M. **Judging Delinquents: Context and Process in Juvenile Court.** 1969. Aldine Publishing. $14.50.

Empey, LaMar T. **The Future of Childhood and Juvenile Justice.** 1980. University Press of Virginia. $20.00.

Faust, Frederic L. & Brantingham, Paul J. **Juvenile Justice Philosophy: Readings, Cases and Comments.** 2nd ed. 1978. pap. West Publishing. $15.95.

Flammang, C.J. **Police Juvenile Enforcement.** 284p. 1972. C.C. Thomas. $16.50.

Flicker, Barbara. **Standards for Juvenile Justice: A Summary and Analysis.** 1977. Ballinger Publishing. casebound $16.50; softcover $7.95.

Freed, Daniel J. & Terrell, Timothy P. **Standards Relating to Interim Status: The Release, Control, and Detention of Accused Juvenile Offenders Between Arrest and Disposition.** 1977. Ballinger Publishing. casebound $16.50; softcover $7.95.

Friday, Paul C. & Stewart, V. Lorne, eds. **Youth Crime and Juvenile Justice: International Perspectives.** 1977. Praeger. $18.95.

Gittler, Josephine. **Standards Relating to Juvenile Probation Function: Intake and Predisposition Investigative Services.** 1977. Ballinger Publishing. casebound $16.50; $7.95.

Gough, Aidan. **Standards Relating to Non-Criminal Misbehavior.** 1977. Ballinger Publishing. casebound $14.00; softcover $6.95.

Hart, Hastings H. **Juvenile Court Laws in the United States.** Repr. of 1910 ed. Irvington. $21.00.

Heaps, Willard A. **Juvenile Justice.** 1974. Houghton Mifflin. $7.95.

Hopson, D., Jr., et al. **Juvenile Offender and the Law: A Symposium.** 1968. Repr. Da Capo. $17.50.

Hurley, Timothy D., compiled by. **Origin of the Illinois Juvenile Court Law: Juvenile Courts and What They Have Accomplished.** 3rd ed. Repr. of 1907 ed. AMS Press. $19.00.

Hyde, Margaret O. **Juvenile Justice and Injustice.** (gr. 7 up). 1977. Watts, Franklin, Inc. $6.90.

International Penal and Prison Commission. Children's Courts in the United States. Repr. of 1904 ed. AMS Press. $15.00.

Kenney, John P. & Pursuit, Dan G. **Police Work with Juveniles and the Administration of Juvenile Justice.** (Illus.). 496p. 1978. C.C. Thomas. $15.25.

Klein, M.W. **The Juvenile Justice System.** 1976. Sage. $20.00; pap. $9.95.

Knight, James M. **The Juvenile Courts Functions and Relevant Theory.** 1978. pap. R&E Research Associates. $8.00.

Krisberg, Barry & Austin, James, eds. **The Children of Ishmael: Critical Perspectives on Juvenile Delinquency.** 1978. pap. Mayfield Publishing. $10.95.

Lindsey, Ben B. & Borough, Rube. **The Dangerous Life.** 468p. 1974. Repr. Arno Press. $22.00.

Lindsey, Ben B. & O'Higgins, Harvey J. **The Beast.** (Illus.). 1970. Repr. of 1910 ed. University of Wash. Press. $11.50.

Lou, Herbert H. **Juvenile Courts in the United States.** 297p. 1972. Repr. of 1927 ed. Arno Press. $16.00.

McCarthy, Francis B. & Carr, James G. **Juvenile Law and Its Processes: Cases and Materials.** 700p. 1980. Bobbs-Merrill. $21.00.

McCreedy, Kenneth R. **Juvenile Justice: System and Procedures.** 1975. pap. Delmar. $8.80; instructor's guide $1.45.

Moran, Michael. **Standards Relating to Appeals and Collateral Review.** 1977. Ballinger Publishing. casebound $12.50; softcover $5.95.

Nyquist, Ola. **Juvenile Justice.** (Illus.). 302p. 1975. Repr. of 1960 ed. Greenwood Press. $19.75.

Parsloe, Phyllida. **Juvenile Justice in Britain and the United States: The Balance of Needs and Rights.** 1978. Routledge & Kegan. $18.50.

Platt, Anthony M. **The Child Savers.** 1977. pap. University of Chicago Press. $4.95.

Polier, Justine W. **Everyone's Children, Nobody's Child: A Judge Looks at Underprivileged Children in the United States.** facsimile ed. 370p. 1974. Repr. of 1941 ed. Arno Press. $21.00.

Riekes, Linda & Ackerly, Sally M. **Juvenile Problems and Law.** 2nd ed. (Illus.). 52p. (gr. 4-6). 1980. pap. write for info. West Publishing.

—**Juvenile Problems and Law.** (Illus.). (gr. 7-8). 1975. West Publishing. pap. $3.25; teacher's manual $3.25.

Rosenheim, Margaret K., ed. **Pursuing Justice for the Child.** (Illus.). 1976. University of Chicago Press. $15.00.

—**Pursuing Justice for the Child.** (Illus.). 1978. pap. Univ. of Chicago Press. $5.95.

Rubin, H. Ted. **Juvenile Justice: Policy Practice & Law.** new ed. 1979. pap. Goodyear. $10.95.

Rubin, Sol. **Law of Juvenile Justice: With a New Model Juvenile Court Act.** 1976. Oceana. $5.95.

Rubin, Ted. **Standards Relating to Court Organization and Administration.** 1977. Ballinger Publishing. casebound $12.50; softcover $5.95.

Rutherford, Andrew & Cohen, Fred. **Standards Relating to Corrections Administration.** 1977. Ballinger Publishing. casebound $16.50; softcover $7.95.

Ryerson, Ellen. **The Best-Laid Plans: America's Juvenile Court Experiment.** 1978. pap. Hill & Wang. $4.95.

—**The Best Laid Plans: America's Juvenile Court Experiment.** 1978. pap. Hill & Wang. $4.95.

Schlossman, Steven L. **Love and the American Delinquent: The Theory and Practice of "Progressive" Juvenile Justice, 1825-1920.** (Illus.). 1977. University of Chicago Press. $15.00.

Simonsen, Clifford E. & Gordon, Marshall S. **Juvenile Justice in America.** 1979. write for info. Glencoe.

Singer, Linda R. **Standards Relating to Dispositions.** 1977. Ballinger Publishing. casebound $16.50; softcover $7.95.

Sprowls, James T. **Discretion and Lawlessness: Compliance in Juvenile Court.** 144p. 1980. pap. Lexington Books. $14.95.

Stapleton, W. Vaughan & Teitelbaum, Lee E. **In Defense of Youth: A Study of the Role of Counsel in American Juvenile Courts.** 1972. Russell Sage. $10.00.

Stewart, V. Lorne, ed. **The Changing Faces of Juvenile Justice.** 1978. NYU Press. $10.95.

Streib, Victor L. **Juvenile Justice in America.** 1978. Kennikat. $13.95.

Teitelbaum, Lee E. & Gough, Aidan, eds. **Beyond Control: Status Offenders in the Juvenile Court.** 1977. Ballinger Publishing. $17.50; pap. $7.95.

Turner, Kenneth A. **Juvenile Justice: Juvenile Court Problems, Procedures and Practices in Tennessee.** 1969. Michie. $20.00.

Twentieth Century Fund. **Confronting Youth Crime Report of the Twentieth Century Fund Task Force on Sentencing Policy Toward Young Offenders.** (Illus.). Holmes & Meier. $14.95; pap. $5.75.

United States Children's Bureau. **Standards for Specialized Courts Dealing with Children.** 1978. Repr. of 1954 ed. Greenwood Press. $13.50.

U.S. Children's Bureau. **Juvenile Courts at Work.** 323p. 1975. Repr. of 1925 ed. AMS Press. $24.50.

U.S. Senate, Juvenile Court of the District of Columbia. **Message from the President of the United States Transmitting a Letter from the Judge of the Juvenile Court of the District of Columbia: A Report Covering the Work of the Juvenile Court During the Period from July 1, 1906 to June 30, 1926.** 174p. 1974. Repr. Arno Press. $12.00.

Van Waters, Miriam. **Youth in Conflict.** 1970. Repr. of 1925 ed. AMS Press. $22.50.

Virtue, Maxine B. **Family Cases in Court: Four Case Studies Dealing with Judicial Administration.** 1956. Duke. $14.75.

Wheeler, Gerald R. **Counterdeterrence: A Report on Juvenile Sentencing and Effects of Prisonization.** 1978. Nelson-Hall. $14.95.

Whinery, Leo H., et al. **Predictive Sentencing: An Empirical Evaluation.** 1976. Lexington Books. $19.95.

Whitebread, Charles. **Standards Relating to Transfer Between Courts.** 1977. Ballinger Publishing. casebound $12.50; softcover $5.95.

Wies, Louis B. **A Guide to Juvenile Court.** 1977. pap. Lawyers & Judges. $8.50.

Young, Pauline V. **Social Treatment in Probation and Delinquency.** 2nd ed. 1969. Repr. of 1952 ed. Patterson Smith. $20.00.

JUVENILE DELINQUENCY

Abbott, Grace, ed. **Child and State: Select Documents.** 2 Vols. (Illus.). 1968. Repr. of 1938 ed. Greenwood Press. Set. $53.75.

Abstracts on Crime and Juvenile Delinquency 1977: An Index to the Microform Collection. 79p. 1978. Microfilming Corp. $15.00.

Abstracts on Crime and Juvenile Delinquency, 1976: An Index to the Microform Collection. 82p. 1978. Microfliming Corp. $15.00.

Adams, Gary B., et al. **Juvenile Justice Management.** (Illus.). 660p. 1973. C.C. Thomas. $25.00.

Addams, Jane, et al. **Child, the Clinic, and the Court.** 1971. Repr. Johnson Reprint. $10.00.

Agee, Vicki L. **Treatment of the Violent Incorrigible Adolescent.** (Illus.). 1979. Lexington Books. $16.95.

Aichhorn, August. **Delinquency and Child Guidance: Selected Papers of August Aichhorn.** Fleischmann, Otto, et al, eds. 1967. International Universities Press. $15.00.

Alissi, Albert S. **Boys in Little Italy: A Comparison of Their Individual Value Orientations, Family Patterns, and Peer Group Associations.** 1978. R&E Research Associates. softcover $10.00.

Altieri de Barreto, Carmen G. **El Lexico De la Delincuencia En Puerto Rico.** pap. University of Puerto Rico Press. $1.85.

An Annotated Bibliography of Works on Juvenile Delinquency in America and Britain in the Nineteenth Century. 1980. Folcroft. $25.00.

Arnold, William R. **Juveniles on Parole: A Sociological Perspective.** 1970. Philadelphia Book Co. $6.95.

Bakal, Yitzhak & Polsky, Howard W. **Reforming Corrections for Juvenile Offenders.** new ed. 1979. Lexington Books. $16.95.

Bartollas, Clemens & Miller, Stuart J. **The Juvenile Offender: Control, Correction and Treatment.** 1978. Allyn & Bacon. $16.50.

Beard, Belle B. **Juvenile Probation: An Analysis of the Case Records of Five Hundred Children Studies at the Judge Baker Guidance Clinic and Placed on Probation in the Juvenile Court of Boston.** 1969. Repr. of 1934 ed. Patterson Smith. $10.00.

Belkin, Alison. **The Criminal Child.** 1978. pap. Kendall-Hunt. $6.95.

Bloch, Herbert & Niederhoffer, Arthur. **Gang: A Study in Adolescent Behavior.** 1958. Philosophical Library. $6.00.

Bloch, Herbert A. & Niederhoffer, Arthur. **The Gang: A Study in Adolescent Behavior.** 1976. Repr. of 1958 ed. Greenwood Press. $15.75.

Blumer, Herbert & Hauset, Philip M. **Movies, Delinquency, and Crime.** 1933. Norwood Editions. $17.50.

Bovet, Lucien. **Psychiatric Aspects of Juvenile Delinquency, a Study.** Repr. of 1951 ed. Greenwood Press. $8.00.

Boyle, Hugh. **Delinquency and Crime.** new ed. (Illus.). 61p. (Orig.). 1970. pap. Pendulum Press. $0.95.

Breckinridge, Sophonisba P. & Abbott, Edith. **Delinquent Child and the Home.** 1970. Repr. of 1912 ed. Arno Press. $17.00.

Burgess, Ernest W. **Ernest W. Burgess on Community, Family and Delinquency.** Cottrell, Leonard S., Jr., et al, eds. (Illus.). 1977. pap. University of Chicago Press. $4.45.

—**On Community, Family and Delinquency.** Cottrell, Leonard S., Jr., et al, eds. 1974. University of Chicago Press. $15.00.

Cain, Arthur H. **Young People and Crime.** 1969. TY Crowell. $5.95.

Carpenter, Mary. **Juvenile Delinquents, Their Condition and Treatment.** (With essay by Katharine Lenroot & index added). 1970. Repr. of 1853 ed. Patterson Smith. $12.50.

—**Reformatory Schools for the Children of the Perishing and Dangerous Classes and for Juvenile Offenders.** 1970. Repr. of 1851 ed. Patterson Smith. $12.00.

Carter, Robert M. & Klein, Malcolm. **Back on the Street: The Diversion of Juvenile Offenders.** (Illus.). 400p. 1976. pap. Prentice-Hall. $11.95.

Cavan, Ruth S. **Juvenile Delinquency.** 3rd ed. (Illus.). 1975. pap. Harper & Row. $14.95.

Cavan, Ruth S., ed. **Readings in Juvenile Delinquency.** 3rd ed. 1975. pap. Harper & Row. $14.50.

Cavan, Ruth S. & Ferdinand, Theodore N. **Juvenile Delinquency.** 1981. Harper & Row. $17.50.

Cloward, Richard A. & Ohlin, Lloyd E. **Delinquency and Opportunity: A Theory of Delinquent Gangs.** 1966. Free Press. $12.95; pap. $4.50.

Coates, Robert B. & Miller, Alden D. **Diversity in a Youth Correctional System: Handling Delinquents in Massachusetts.** 1979. Ballinger Publishing. $16.50.

Coffey, Alan R. **Juvenile Justice As a System: Law Enforcement to Rehabilitation.** 1974. Prentice-Hall. $11.95.

—**The Prevention of Crime and Delinquency.** (Illus.). 400p. 1975. Prentice-Hall. $15.95.

Cohen, A.K. **Delinquent Boys.** 1955. Free Press. $15.95; pap. $4.95.

Cottle, Thomas J. **Children in Jail.** 1977. Beacon Press. $9.95; pap. $4.95.

Cromwell, Paul F., Jr., et al. **Introduction to Juvenile Delinquency: Text and Readings.** 1978. pap. West Publishing. $11.50.

Crow, Lester D. & Crow, Alice. **Our Teen-Age Boys and Girls.** facs. ed. 1945. Arno Press. $16.50.

Cull, John G. & Hardy, Richard E. **Problems of Runaway Youth.** 184p. 1976. pap. C.C. Thomas. $15.25.

Deutsch, Albert. **Our Rejected Children.** 316p. 1974. Repr. of 1950 ed. Arno Press. $19.00.

Donohue, John K. **Baffling Eyes of Youth.** 251p. 1974. Repr. of 1957 ed. Greenwood Press. $13.75.

Doshay, Lewis J. **Boy Sex Offender and His Later Career.** 1969. Repr. of 1943 ed. Patterson Smith. $10.00.

Drucker, Saul & Hexter, Maurice-Beck. **Children Astray.** 450p. 1974. Repr. of 1923 ed. Arno Press. $25.00.

Eldefonso, Edward. **Law Enforcement and the Youthful Offender.** 3rd ed. 1978. Wiley, John & Sons. Teacher's manual avail. $18.95.

Elliott, Desmond & Voss, Harwin L. **Delinquency and Dropout.** 224p. 1974. Lexington Books. $19.95.

Empey, LaMar T. & Lubeck, Stephen G. **Explaining Delinquency: Construction, Test and Reformulation of a Sociological Theory.** 1971. Lexington Books. $16.95.

Ericson, Richard V. **Young Offenders and Their Social Work.** 248p. 1976. (Pub. by Saxon House.) Lexington Books. $21.50.

Fabricant, Michael. **Deinstitutionalizing Delinquent Youth.** 222p. 1980. Schenkman Publishing Co. $15.50; pap. $8.95.

Falkin, Gregory R. **Reducing Delinquency.** (Illus.). 240p. 1979. Lexington Books. $20.95.

Ferdinand, Theodore N., ed. **Juvenile Delinquency: Little Brother Grows up.** (Illus.). 1977. Sage. $12.95; pap. $6.50.

Ferracuti, Franco, et al. **Delinquents and Nondelinquents in the Puerto Rican Slum Culture.** 1975. Ohio State University Press. $15.00.

Finestone, Harold. **Victims of Change: Juvenile Delinquents in American Society.** (Illus.). 256p. 1976. Greenwood Press. $16.00.

Flammang, C.J. **Police Juvenile Enforcement.** 284p. 1972. C.C. Thomas. $16.50.

Frankenstein, C. **Varieties of Juvenile Delinquency.** 1970. Gordon & Breach Science Pubs. $34.00.

Friday, Paul C. & Stewart, V. Lorne, eds. **Youth Crime and Juvenile Justice: International Perspectives.** 1977. Praeger. $18.95.

Friedlander, Kate. **Psychoanalytical Approach to Juvenile Delinquency: Theory, Case Studies, Treatment.** 1960. International Universities Press. $15.00.

Fyvel, T.R. **Troublemakers: Rebellious Youth in an Affluent Society.** 1964. pap. Schocken Books. $2.25.

Gale, William. **The Compound.** 1978. pap. Ballantine Books. $1.95.

Garabedian, Peter G. & Gibbons, Don C., eds. **Becoming Delinquent: Young Offenders and the Correctional Process.** (Illus.). 1970. Aldine Publishing. $13.50.

Gardiner, Muriel. **The Deadly Innocents: Portraits of Children Who Kill.** 192p. 1976.

Basic Books. $13.95.

Giallombardo, Rose, ed. **Juvenile Delinquency: A Book of Readings.** 3rd ed. 1976. pap. Wiley, John & Sons. $14.95.

Gibbons, Don C. **Delinquent Behavior.** 2nd ed. (Illus.). 1976. Prentice-Hall. $16.95.

Glueck, Sheldon & Glueck, Eleanor. **Delinquents in the Making.** 1952. Harper & Row. $7.95.

—**Of Delinquency and Crime: A Panorama of Years of Search and Research.** 384p. 1974. C.C. Thomas. $16.25.

—**Toward a Typology of Juvenile Offenders: Implications for Therapy and Prevention.** 1970. Grune & Stratton. $23.50.

Glueck, Sheldon & Glueck, Eleanor T. **Delinquents and Nondelinquents in Perspective.** 1968. Harvard University Press. $14.00.

Glueck, Sheldon S., & Glueck, Eleanor T. **Juvenile Delinquents Grown Up.** 1940. Kraus Reprint. $19.00.

—**One Thousand Juvenile Delinquents.** 1934. Kraus Reprint. $14.00.

—**Physique and Delinquency.** 1956. Kraus Reprint. $28.00.

Gold, Martin. **Status Forces in Delinquent Boys.** 229p. 1963. pap. University of Michigan, Institute for Social Research. $5.00.

Goldberg, Harriet L. **Child Offenders: A Study in Diagnosis and Treatment.** 1969. Repr. of 1948 ed. Patterson Smith. $10.00.

Goldberg, Jacob A. & Goldberg, Rosamond W. **Girls on the City Streets: A Study of 1400 Cases of Rape.** 384p. 1974. Repr. of 1935 ed. Arno Press. $22.00.

Goshen, Charles E. **Society and the Youthful Offender.** (Illus.). 192p. 1974. C.C. Thomas. $14.50.

Griffin, Brenda S. & Griffin, Charles T. **Juvenile Delinquency in Perspective.** (Illus.). 1978. Harper & Row. $18.50.

Grimm, Fred. **No Time for Fairy Tales.** 158p. 1980. pap. Impact Books. $3.95.

Hackler, James C. **The Prevention of Youthful Crime: The Great Stumble Foward.** 1979. pap. Methuen Inc. $10.90.

Hahn, Paul H. **The Juvenile Offender and the Law.** 2nd ed. 1978. Anderson Publishing Co. $16.95.

Hardy, Richard E. & Cull, John G., eds. **Climbing Ghetto Walls: Disadvantagement, Delinquency and Rehabilitation.** (Illus.). 210p. 1973. C.C. Thomas. $11.50.

—**Fundamentals of Juvenile Criminal Behavior and Drug Abuse.** 276p. 1975. C.C. Thomas. $16.50.

—**Problems of Adolescents: Social and Psychological Approach.** (Illus.). 296p. 1974. C.C. Thomas. $18.75.

—**Psychological and Vocational Rehabilitation of the Youthful Delinquent.** (Illus.). 264p. 1974. C.C. Thomas. $14.50.

Hart, Hastings H. **Preventive Treatment of Neglected Children with Special Papers by Leading Authorities.** 1971. Repr. of 1910 ed. Arno Press. $20.00.

Haskell, Martin R. & Yablonsky, Lewis. **Juvenile Delinquency.** 2nd ed. 1978. pap. Rand McNally & Co. instructor's manual free. $12.50.

Hawes, Joseph M. **Children in Urban Society: Juvenile Delinquency in Nineteenth-Century America.** 1971. Oxford University Press. $13.95.

Healy, William. **Individual Delinquent, a Text-Book of Diagnosis and Prognosis for All Concerned in Understanding Offenders.** (Illus.). 1969. Repr.of 1915 ed. Patterson Smith. $25.00.

Healy, William & Bonner, Augusta F. **Delinquents**

and **Criminals, Their Making and Unmaking. Studies in Two American Cities.** (With an intro added). 1969. Repr. of 1926 ed. Patterson Smith. $12.00.

Healy, William & Bronner, Augusta F. **Delinquents and Criminals, Their Making and Unmaking.** (No. 470). 1969. Repr. of 1926. ed AMS Press. $10.00.

—**New Light on Delinquency and Its Treatment.** Repr. of 1936 ed. Greenwood Press. $11.00.

Hirschi, Travis. **Causes of Delinquency.** 1969. University of California Press. $16.00; pap. $4.95.

Hirschi, Travis & Selvin, Hanan C. **Principles of Survey Analysis.** Orig. Title: Delinquency Research. 304p. 1973. pap. Free Press. $4.95.

Hoenig, Gary. **Reaper: The Inside Story of a Gang Leader.** 192p. 1975. Bobbs-Merrill. $6.95.

Hyde, Margaret O. **Juvenile Justice and Injustice.** (gr. 7 up). 1977. Watts, Franklin, Inc. $6.90.

Index to Abstracts on Crime and Juvenile Delinquency: 1968-1975. 201p. Microfilming Corp. $25.00.

Johnson, R. E. **Juvenile Delinquency and Its Origins.** (Illus.). 1979. Cambridge University Press. $17.95; pap. $5.95.

Jones, Vernon F. **Adolescents with Behavior Problems: Strategies for Teaching, Counseling and Parent Involvement.** 353p. 1979. Allyn & Bacon. $15.95.

Kamm, Ernest, et al. **Juvenile Law and Procedure in California.** 2nd ed. (California Handbook Ser.). 1971. pap. Glencoe. $7.95.

Khanna, J.L. **New Treatment Approaches to Juvenile Delinquency.** (Illus.). 164p. 1975. C.C. Thomas. $15.25.

Konopka, Gisela. **Young Girls: A Portrait of Adolescence.** Prentice-Hall. $8.95; pap. $3.45.

Kornhauser, Ruth R. **Social Sources of Delinquency: An Appraisal of Analytic Models.** (Illus.). 1978. University of Chicago Press. $16.00.

Kratcoski, P. & Kratcoski, L. **Juvenile Delinquency.** 1979. Prentice-Hall. $15.95.

Kvaraceus, William & Miller, Walter B. **Delinquent Behavior.** 2 vols. in 1. 1976. Repr. of 1959 ed.Greenwood Press. $28.25.

Lander, Bernard. **Towards an Understanding of Juvenile Delinquency.** Repr. of 1954 ed. AMS Press. $11.50.

Lerman, Paul. **Community Treatment and Social Control: A Critical Analysis of Juvenile Correctional Policy.** 1977. pap. University of Chicago Press. $4.95.

Levine, Phyllis. **Delinquency Proneness: A Comparison of Delinquent Tendencies in Minors Under Court Supervision.** 1978. pap. R&E Research Associates. $8.00.

Lewis, Dorothy O. & Balla, David A. **Delinquency and Psychopathology.** 1976. Grune & Stratton. $25.50.

Liu, Jin-An. **Sino-American Juvenile Justice System.** 340p. Date not set. pap. Carrollton Press. $27.50.

McClintock, F. H. & Bottoms, A. E. **Criminals Coming of Age.** 1973. Heinemann Educational Books. $20.95.

McPartland, James M. & McDill, Edward L., eds. **Violence in Schools: Perspectives, Programs and Positions.** 1977. Lexington Books. $16.95.

Malmquist, Carl. **Handbook of Adolescence.** 1978. Aronson. $40.00.

Mannheim, Hermann. **Juvenile Delinquency in an English Middletown.** (Illus., With intro. added). 1970. Repr. of 1948 ed. Patterson Smith. $9.00.

Marohn, Richard C., et al. **Juvenile Delinquents:**

Psychodynamic Assessment and Hospital Treatment. 256p. 1980. Brunner-Mazel. $17.50.

Martinez, Emanuel J. **Aggression and Criminality of Adolescence.** 1979. Exposition Press. $7.50.

Matza, D. **Deliquency and Drift.** 1964. pap. Wiley, John & Sons. $8.50.

Mennel, Robert M. **Thorns and Thistles: Juvenile Delinquents in the United States, 1825-1940.** 259p. 1973. pap. University Press of New England. $12.50.

Merrill, Maud A. **Problems of Child Delinquency.** Carmichael, Leonard, ed. (Illus.). 403p. 1972. Repr. of 1947 ed. Greenwood Press. $22.50.

Meyer, Henry J., et al. **Girls at Vocational High: An Experiment in Social Work Intervention.** 1965. Russell Sage. $6.50.

Moore, Joan, et al. **Homeboys: Gangs,Drugs and Prison in the Barrios of Los Angeles.** (Illus.). 1979. Temple University Press. $15.00; pap. $7.95.

Morrison, William D. **Juvenile Offenders.** Repr. of 1897 ed. AMS Press. $10.00.

—**Juvenile Offenders.** 1975. Patterson Smith. $12.50.

Mueller, Gerhard O., et al. **Delinquency and Puberty Examination of a Juvenile Delinquency Fad.** (Illus.). 123p. (Orig.). 1971. pap. Rotham. $6.50.

Murray, Charles A. & Cox, Louis A., Jr. **Beyond Probation: Juvenile Corrections and the Chronic Delinquent.** (Illus.). 1979. Sage. $18.00; pap. $8.95.

Offer, Daniel, et al. **The Psychological World of the Juvenile Delinquent.** 1979. Basic Books. $15.00.

Palmer, Ted & Lewis,Roy V. **An Evaluation of Juvenile Diversion.** 304p. 1980. Oelgeschlager. $22.50.

Parizeau, Alice. **Parenting and Delinquent Youth.** 208p. 1980. Lexington Books. $22.95.

Peirce, Bradford K. **Half Century with Juvenile Delinquents, or the New York House of Refuge and Its Times.** (Illus., With intro. added). 1969. Repr. of 1896 ed. Patterson Smith. $15.00.

Perez, Joseph F. **Family Roots of Adolescent Delinquency.** 1978. Van Nos Reinhold. $14.95.

Phelps, Thomas R. **Juvenile Delinquency: A Contemporary View.** 300p. 1976. Goodyear. $19.95.

Phillipson, Michael. **Understanding Crime and Delinquency: A Sociological Introduction.** 204p. 1974. Beresford Book Service. $9.95.

Pickett,RobertS. **House of Refuge: Origins of Juvenile Reform in New York State, 1815-1857.** (Illus.). 1969. Syracuse University Press. $9.50.

Platt, Anthony M. **The Child Savers.** 1977. pap. University of Chicago Press. $4.95.

—**The Child Savers: The Invention of Delinquency.** 2nd enl. ed. 1980. Repr. of 1969 ed. University of Chicago Press. $12.50.

Powers, Edwin & Witmer, Helen. **Experiment in the Prevention of Delinquency: The Cambridge - Somerville Youth Study.** 1972. Repr. of 1951 ed. Patterson Smith. $18.50.

Ramos, Nancy P., ed. **Delinquent Youth and Learning Disabilities.** 1978. pap. Academic Therapy Pubns. $4.00.

Reckless, Walter C. & Dinitz, Simon. **The Prevention of Juvenile Delinquency: An Experiment.** 1972. Ohio State University Press. $12.00.

Redl, Fritz & Wineman, David. **Children Who Hate: The Disorganization and Breakdown of Behavior Controls.** 1965. pap. Free Press. $4.95.

KIDNAPPING

LAW ENFORCEMENT

Armstrong, T.R. & Cinnamon, Kenneth M. **Power and Authority in Law Enforcement.** 208p. 1976. C.C. Thomas. $17.25.

Baker, Ralph & Meyer, Fred, eds. **Evaluating Alternative Law-Enforcement Policies.** (Illus.). 240p. 1979. Lexington Books. $18.95.

Bard, M. & Shellow, Robert. **Issues in Law Enforcement: Essays and Case Studies.** (Illus.). 1976. Reston. (OP.) $9.95.

Beall, James R. & Downing, Robert E. **Helicopter Utilization in Municipal Law Enforcement: Administrative Considerations.** (Illus.). 96p. 1973. C.C. Thomas. $9.75.

Beckman, Erik. **Law Enforcement in a Democratic Society: An Introduction.** 1980. Nelson-Hall. $20.95.

Bent, Alan E. **The Politics of Law Enforcement.** 1977. pap. text ed. Heath. $6.95.

Berney, Donald W. **American Government for Law Enforcement Training.** 1976. Nelson-Hall. $19.95.

Bopp, William J. & Schultz, Donald O. **Principles of American Law Enforcement and Criminal Justice.** (Illus.). 596p. 1975. C.C. Thomas. $15.25.

Brounstein, Sidney H. & Kamrass, Murray, eds. **Operations Research in Law Enforcement and Social Security.** (Illus.). 1976. Lexington Books. $21.00.

Caldwell, Robert G. **Foundations of Law Enforcement and Criminal Justice.** Nardini, William, ed. 1977. Bobbs-Merrill. $16.40.

Cawley, Donald F. & Miron, H. Jerome. **Managing Patrol Operations.** 1980. write for info. Lexington Books.

Chambliss, William J. **Criminal Law in Action.** 480p. 1975. text ed. Wiley, John & Sons. $16.50.

Clifford, William. **Crime Control in Japan.** 224p. 1976. Lexington Books. $18.95.

Coleman, Joseph. **Your Career in Law Enforcement.** 1979. pap. Arco. $3.50.

Cope, Jeff & Goddard, Kenneth. **Weaponless Control: For Law Enforcement and Security Personnel.** (Illus.). 302p. 1979. C.C. Thomas. $19.50.

Cronkhite, Clyde L. **Automation and Law Enforcement.** (Illus.). 160p. 1974. C.C. Thomas. $13.50; pap. $8.75.

Davidson, Phillip L. **SWAT (Special Weapons and Tactics).** (Illus.). 1979. C.C. Thomas. $13.75.

Edelhertz, Herbert & Rogovin, Charles, eds. **A National Strategy for White-Collar-Crime Enforcement.** 1980. Lexington Books. price not set.

Eldefonso, Edward. **Law Enforcement and the Youthful Offender.** 3rd ed. Wiley, John & Sons. Teachers' manual avail. $18.95.

Farmer, Richard & Kowalewski, Victor. **Law Enforcement and Community Relations.** 160p. 1976. instrs'. manual avail. Reston. $11.50.

Felkenes, George T. & Becker, Harold K. **Law Enforcement: A Selected Bibliography.** 2nd ed. 1977. Scarecrow Press. $14.00.

Ferdico, John M. **Criminal Procedure for the Law Enforcement Officer.** 2nd ed. (Illus.). 1979. West Publishing. $17.95.

Folley. **American Law Enforcement: Police, Courts, and Corrections.** 3rd ed. 512p. 1980. Allyn & Bacon. $16.95.

Galaway, Burton & Hudson, Hamilton C. **Perspectives on Crime Victims.** (Illus.). 1980. pap. Mosby. $12.00.

Gardner, Harry. **Blacks with Badges.** Lawrence, Joseph, ed. 1980. pap. Crescent Pubns. $4.95.

Germann, A.C., Day, Frank D. & Gallati, Robert R.J. **Introduction to Law Enforcement and Criminal Justice.** (Illus.). 400p. 1978. $11.75.

Greenberg, Douglas. **Crime and Law Enforcement in the Colony of New York, 1691-1776.** (Illus.). 1976. Cornell University Press. $19.50.

Hall, James P. **Peacekeeping in America: A Developmental Study of American Law Enforcement: Philosophy and Systems.** 1978. pap. Kendall-Hall. $8.95.

Hardy, Richard E. & Cull, John G. **Applied Psychology in Law Enforcement and Corrections.** (Illus.). 248p. 1973. C.C. Thomas. $12.75.

Hazard, Geoffrey C., Jr. **Ethics in the Practice of Law.** 177p. 1980. pap. Yale University Press. $5.95.

Hess, Karen M. & Wrobleski, Henry M. **For the Record: Report Writing in Law Enforcement.** 1978. pap. Wiley, John & Sons. $6.95.

Hibbard, Jack & Fried, Bryan A. **Weaponless Defense: A Law Enforcement Guide to Non-Violent Control.** (Illus.). 184p. 1980. pap. C.C. Thomas. $14.75.

Kinton, J., ed. **Criminology, Law Enforcement and Offender Treatment: A Sourcebook.** rev. ed. 1980. write for info. Social Science & Sociological Resources.

Kirkham, George L. & Wollan, Laurin A., Jr. **Introduction to Law Enforcement.** (Illus.). 1980. Harper & Row. instrs'. manual free. $17.50.

Kowalewski, Victor & Farmer, Richard. **Law Enforcement and Community Relations.** 160p. 1976. Reston. $11.50.

Lee, Dick & Pratt, Colin. **Operation Julie.** 1980. St. Martin's Press. $10.95.

Leonard, V.A. **Fundamentals of Law Enforcement: Problems and Issues.** (Illus.). 350p. 1980. West Publishing. $15.50.

Martin, Carol A. **Law Enforcement and Community Relations: A Selected Biography.** 1980. pap. Vance Bibliographies. $7.50.

McDonald, Phyllis. **Law Enforcement Education in the Middle Grades: Police-Student Relations.** 96p. 1978. pap. National Education Assn. $4.50.

McPheters, Lee R. & Stronge, William B. **The Economics of Crime and Law Enforcement.** (Illus.). 520p. 1976. C.C. Thomas. $25.00.

Martin, Julian A. **Law Enforcement Vocabulary.** 262p. 1973. C.C. Thomas. $13.75.

Meyer, Fred & Baker, Ralph, eds. **Determinants of Law Enforcement Policies.** 240p. 1979. Lexington Books. $18.95.

—**Law Enforcement and Police Policy.** 1979. pap. Policy Studies Organization. $5.00; pap. $3.00.

Miles, John G., Jr., et al. **The Law Officer's Pocket Manual: 1979-80 Edition.** 1980. spiral bd. Bureau of National Affairs. $4.00.

More, Harry W., Jr. **Critical Issues in Law Enforcement.** 2nd ed. 1975. Anderson Publishing Co. $8.95.

Olson, Bruce T. **Pattern of American Law Enforcement: Research by Questionnaire.** 1968. Michigan State Univ., Institute for Community Development & Services. $2.50.

Pace, Denny F. & Styles, Jimmie C. **Organized Crime: Concepts and Control.** (Illus.). 352p. 1974. ref. ed. Prentice-Hall. $16.95.

Palmquist, Al & Hovelsrud, Joyce. **The Real Centurions.** 2nd ed. Orig. Title: Holy Smokies. 173p. 1979. pap. Landmark Books. $2.25.

Petersen, David M., ed. **Police Work: Strategies and Outcomes in Law Enforcement.** (Illus.). 1979. Sage. $12.95; pap. $6.50.

Powis, David. **The Signs of Crime: A Field Manual for Police.** (Illus.). 1978. pap. John Jay Press. $5.95.

Prostano, Emanuel T. & Piccirillo, Martin L. **Law Enforcement: A Selective Bibliography.** 1974. Libraries Unlimited. $13.50.

Punch, Maurice. **Policing the Inner City: A Study of Amsterdam's Warmoesstraat.** 231p. 1979. (Archon). Shoe String Press. $17.50.

Radzinowicz, Sir Leon & King, Joan. **The Growth of Crime: The International Experience.** 1977. Basic Books. $11.95.

Reith, Charles. **The Blind Eye of History: A Study of the Origins of the Present Police Era.** 1975. Patterson Smith. $11.00; pap. $4.50.

Revere, Robert B. & Tesman, Solomon. **American History for the Law Enforcement Professions.** Nelson Hall. (OP.) $14.00.

Scanlon, Robert, ed. **Law Enforcement Bible.** 1978. pap. Stoeger. $7.95.

—**Law Enforcement Bible II.** 1981. pap. Stoeger. $10.95.

Seymour, Whiteney H., Jr. **United States Attorney: An Inside View of "Justice" in America Under the Nixon Administration.** 1975. Morrow. (OP.) $8.95.

Skolnick, Jerome H. **Justice Without Trial: Law Enforcement in Democratic Society.** 2nd ed. 320p. 1975. pap. Wiley, John & Sons. $8.95.

Snarr, Richard W. & Craft, Larry N. **Student Programmed Learning Guide & Introduction to Law Enforcement & Criminal Justice.** 1976. pap. C. C. Thomas. (OP.) $14.95.

Steiner, Bradley. **The Techniques and Psychology of Disarming for Law Enforcement Personnel.** (Illus.). 248p. 1980. write for info. C C. Thomas.

Stinchcomb, James. **Opportunities in Law Enforcement and Related Careers.** rev. ed. (Illus.). (gr.. 8 up.). 1976. National Textbook Co. $6.60; pap. $4.95.

Tegner, Bruce. **Defense Tactics for Law Enforcement: Weaponless Defense and Control and Baton Techniques.** rev. ed. (Illus.). 1978. pap. Thor. $4.95.

Ulmer, S.S., ed. **Courts, Law and Judicial Processes.** 1981. pap. Free Pres. $12.95.

Wadman, Robert C. & Svet, Don. **Rules and Regulations for State and Local Law Enforcement Agencies.** 108p. 1975. pap. C. C. Thomas. $5.75.

Wadman, Robert C., et al. **Law Enforcement Supervision: A Case Study Approach.** 1975. pap. West Publishing. $9.50.

Weinreb, Lloyd L. **Denial of Justice: Criminal Process in the United States.** 1977. Free Press. $12.95.

Williams, E. W. **Modern Law Enforcement and Police Science.** (Illus.). 408p. 1967. C. C. Thomas. $19.75.

Williams, Mason. **The Law Enforcement Book of Weapons, Ammunitions and Training Procedures: Handguns, Rifles and Shotguns.** (Illus.). 544p. 1977. C. C. Thomas. $35.75.

Woodson, Robert. **Mediating Structures and Law Enforcement.** 150p. 1980. Ballinger Publishing. $16.50.

Worton, Stanley N. **Law Enforcement and Justice.** (gr. 10 up.) 1977. pap. Hayden Book Co. $4.50.

Wrobleski, Henry M. & Hess, Karen M. **Introduction to Law Enforcement and Criminal Justice.** (Illus.). 1979. West Publishing. $17.95.

Zeichner, Irving B., ed. **Law Enforcement Reference Manual: 1981 Edition.** 1980. New Jersey Law Journal. $19.50.

—**Law Enforcement Desk Reference.** 1976. New Jersey Law Journal. (OP.) $16.50.

LAW ENFORCEMENT OFFICERS

Adams, Ramon F., compiled by. **The Adams One-Fifty.** (Illus.). 100p. 1976. Jenkins. $17.50.

Ahern, James F. **Police in Trouble: Our Frightening Crisis in Law Enforcement.** 256p. 1971. Dutton, E. P. $9.95.

Becker, Harold K. & Felkenes, George T. **Law Enforcement: A Selected Bibliography.** 2nd. ed. 1977. Scarecrow Press. $14.00.

Blalock, Joyce. **Civil Liability of Law Enforcement Officers.** 1974. C. C. Thomas. (OP). $10.50.

Bopp, William J. & Schultz, Donald. O. **Principles of American Law Enforcement and Criminal Justice.** (Illus.). 596p. 1975. C. C. Thomas. $15.25.

—**A Short History of American Law Enforcement.** (Illus.). 192p. 1977. pap. C. C. Thomas. $7.25.

Boyd, Gerald W. **The Will to Live—Five Steps to Officer Survival.** (Illus.). 124p. 1980. C. C. Thomas. $12.50.

Caldwell, Harry. **Basic Law Enforcement.** 1972. Goodyear. (OP). $8.95.

Chambliss, William J. **Crime and the Legal Process.** 1968. McGraw-Hill. $11.50; pap. $10.95.

Cohen, Stanley. **Law Enforcement Guide to United States Supreme Court Decisions.** (Illus.). 232p. 1972. text ed. C. C. Thomas. $15.25.

Crime and Law Enforcement in the District of Columbia: Hearings and Report. 1971. Repr. of 1952 ed. Arno. Press. $45.00.

Cronkhite, C. L. **Automation and Law Enforcement.** (Illus.). 160p. 1974. C. C. Thomas. $13.50; pap. $8.75.

Curran, James T., et al, eds. **Police and Law Enforcement, Nineteen Seventy-Three to Nineteen Seventy-Five.** 2 vols. (Orig.) 1973. AMS Press. Set. lib. bdg. $60.00; Vol. 1. lib. bdg. $30.00; Vol. 2. lib. bdg. $30.00; Vol. 1. pap. $8.95; Vol. 2. pap. $8.95.

Curry, Jesse E. & King, Glen D. **Race Tensions and the Police.** 1962. C. C. Thomas. (OP). $5.50.

Didactic System Staff. **Handling Conflict in Law Enforcement Management: Conflict Among Peers.** 1978. Didactic Systems Inc. pap. $24.90; pap. $21.50 two or more; leader's guide. $0.50.

—**Handling Conflict in Law Enforcement Management: Superior Subordinate Conflict.** 1978. Didactic Systems Inc. pap. $24.90; pap. $21.50 two or more; leader's guide (AA) 50¢.

Eisenhower, Milton S. **Rule of Law: An Alternative to Violence.** (Illus.). Aurora Pubs. $7.95; pap. $3.95.

Edelfonso, Edward, et al. **Principles of Law Enforcement.** 2nd. ed. 480p. 1974. Wiley, John & Sons. $18.95.

Felkenes, George T. **Criminal Justice System: Its Function and Personnel.** (Illus.). 336p. 1974. Prentice-Hall. $16.95.

Fox, Vernon. **Introduction to Criminology.** 416p. 1976. Prentice-Hall. $16.95.

Fraenkel, Jack R. **Crime and Criminals: What Should We Do About Them.** (gr. 10-12). 1977. Prentice-Hall. $8.04; pap. $3.48.

Gammage, Allen Z. **Your Future in Law Enforcement.** (gr. 7 up). 1974. Rosen Press. $5.97.

Gardner, Harry. **Blacks with Badges.** Lawrence, Joseph, ed. 1980 pap. Crescent Pubns. $4.95.

Germann, A. C., et al. **Introduction to Law Enforcement and Criminal Justice.** rev. ed. (Illus.). 400p. 1978. C. C. Thomas. $11.75.

Hanna, Donald G. & Kleberg, John R. **Law Handbook for Ohio Law Enforcement Officers.** 1979. pap. Stipes. $3.40.

Hardy, Richard E. & Cull, John G., eds. **Applied Psychology in Law Enforcement and Corrections.** (Illus.). 248p. 1973. C. C. Thomas. $12.75.

Iannone, N. F. **Principles of Police Patrol.** 1974. McGraw-Hill. $13.95; instructor's manual $3.00.

Jackson, R. M. **Enforcing the Law.** Peter Smith. (OP) $5.50.

Jordan, Philip. D. **Frontier Law and Order: Ten Essays.** (Illus.). 1970. University of Nebraska Press. $10.95.

Journal Of Urban Law Editors. **Riot in the Cities.** Moran, Michael C. & Chikota, Richard A., eds. 1970. Fairleigh Dickinson. $20.00.

Killinger, George G. & Cromwell, Paul F., Jr. **Issues in Law Enforcement.** 1975. pap. Holbrook. (OP). $7.95.

Kuhn, Charles L. **The Police Officer's Memorandum Book.** (Illus.). 80p. 1964. pap. C. C. Thomas. $5.00.

Leonard, V. A. **The Police, the Judiciary, and the Criminal.** 2nd ed. (Illus.). 320p. 1975. C. C. Thomas. $17.50.

Lewin, Stephen, ed. **Crime and It's Prevention.** 1968. Wilson. $5.75.

Martin, Julian A. **Law Enforcement Vocabulary.** 262p. 1973. C C. Thomas. $13.75.

Mather, Frederick C. **Public Order in the Age of the Chartists.** (Illus.). Repr. of 1959 ed. Kelley. $15.00.

Miles, John, G., et al. **Law Officer's Pocket Manual 1979-1980 Edition.** 1980. Bureau of National Affairs. $4.00.

Millspaugh, Arthur Chester. **Crime Control by the National Government.** 306p. 1972. Repr. of 1937 ed. Da Capo. $27.50.

Milner, Neal A. **Court and Local Law Enforcement: The Impact of Miranda.** 1971. Sage. $17.50.

Neal, Harry E. **Six Against Crime: Treasury Agencies in Action.** (Illus.). 1959. (OP). $3.95.

Osborn, Albert S. **Questioned Documents.** rev. 2nd ed. (Illus.). 760p. 1973. Patterson Smith. $28.00.

Pace, Denny F. **Handbook of Vice Control.** (Illus.). 1971. Prentice-Hall. (OP). $5.50; pap. $2.95.

Prassel, Frank R. **The Western Peace Officer: The Legacy of Law and Order.** 304p. 1972. University of Oklahoma Press. $13.95.

Rektor, Bela. **Federal Law Enforcement Agencies.** 1974. Danubian Press. (OP) $12.50.

Rieder, Robert J. **Law Enforcement Information Systems.** (Illus.). 272p. 1972. C. C. Thomas. $14.25.

Seitzinger, Jack M. & Kelley, Thomas M. **Police Terminology: Programmed Manual for Criminal Justice Personnel.** (Illus.). 152p. 1974. pap. C. C. Thomas. $10.25.

Silver, Isidore. **The Crime Control Establishment.** 1974. Prentice-Hall. (OP). $2.45.

South Carolina General Assembly Joint Committee to Investigate Law Enforcement Report. facsimile ed. 1974. Repr. of 1937. ed. Arno Press. $47.00.

Spackman, Robert R., Jr. & Vincent, William F. **Physical Fitness in Law Enforcement: A Guide to More Efficient Service.** (Illus.). 1969. pap. Southern Illinois. $1.95.

Steiner, Bradley J. **The Techniques and Psychology of Disarming for Law Enforcement Personnel.** (Illus.). 248p. 1980. C. C. Thomas. write for info.

Swisher, Carl S., ed. **Selected Papers of Homer Cummings.** (Illus.). 1972. Repr. of 1939 ed. Da Capo. $29.50.

Towler, Juby E. **Police Role in Racial Conflicts.** (Illus.). 1969. C. C. Thomas. (OP). $5.75.

Trojanowicz, Robert & Dixon, Samuel. **Criminal Justice and the Community.** (Illus.). 464p. 1974. ref. ed. Prentice-Hall. $16.95.

Wadman, Robert C. & Svet, Don. **Rules and Regulations for State and Local Law Enforcement Agencies.** 108p. 1975. pap. C. C. Thomas. $5.75.

Waters, **Introduction to Law Enforcement.** 1974. Merrill. (OP). $12.95.

Whisenand, Paul M. **Police Supervision: Theory and Practice.** 2nd ed. (Illus.). 576p. 1976. Prentice-Hall. $16.95.

Wickersham Commission — National Commission On Law Observance And Enforcement. **Wickersham Commission, National Commission on Law Observance and Enforcement: Complete Reports, Including the Mooney-Billings Report.** 14 Vols. (Illus.). 1968. Repr. of 1931 ed. Patterson Smith. $200.00.

Wicks, Robert J. & Josephs, Ernest H., Jr. **Practical Psychology of Leadership for Criminal Justice Officers.** 128p. 1973. pap. C C. Thomas. $7.25.

Wilson, Jerry. **Police Report: A View of Law Enforcement:** 1975. Little, Brown & Co. (OP). $9.95.

LIE DETECTORS

Abrams, Stanley. **Polygraph Handbook for Attorneys.** (Illus.). 1977. Lexington Books. $18.95.

Ansley, Norman, ed. **Legal Admissibility of the Polygraph.** (Illus.). 348p. 1975. C. C. Thomas. $43.00.

Ferguson, Robert J., Jr. **The Polygraph in Private Industry.** (Illus.). 352p. 1966. pap. C. C. Thomas. $22.75.

Ferguson, Robert J., Jr. & Miller, Allan L. **Polygraph for the Defense.** 312p. 1974. C. C. Thomas. $18.75.

Ferguson, Robert T., Jr. & Miller, Allan L. **The Polygraph in Court.** (Illus.). 372p. 1973. pap. C. C. Thomas. $19.00.

Lykken, David T. A. **A Tremor in the Blood: Uses and Abuses of the Lie Detector.** 320p. 1980. McGraw-Hill. $14.95.

Matte, James. A. **The Art and Science of the Polygraph Technique.** (Illus.). 304p. 1980. C. C. Thomas. write for info.

Reid, John E. & Inbau, Fred E. **Truth and Deception.** 2nd. ed. (Illus.). 1977. Williams & Wilkins. $36.00.

MEDICAL JURISPRUDENCE

Adelson, Lester. **The Pathology of Homicide: A Vade Mecum for Pathologist, Prosecutor and Defense Counsel.** (Illus.). 992p. 1974. C. C. Thomas. $50.00.

Averbach, Albert. **Handling Accident Cases: 1963-73.** 7 vols. in 8 bks. 1973. Lawyers Co-Operative Publishing Co. Set $80.00; $35.00 ea.

Blassingame, Wyatt. **Science Catches the Criminal.** (Illus.). 192p. 1975. Dodd, Mead & Co. $5.95.

Brown, Kent L. **Medical Problems and the Law.** (Illus.). 296p. 1971. C. C. Thomas. $17.50.

Burns, Chester R., ed. **Legacies in Law & Medicine.** 1977. Neale Watson Academic Pubns. $12.95.

Clifford, Brian & Bull, Ray. **The Psychology of Person Identification.** 1978. Routledge & Kegan. $20.00.

Douthwaite, Graham. **Jury Instructions on Medical Issues.** 2nd ed. 1980. A Smith Co. $37.50.

Fatteh, Abdullah. **Medicolegal Investigation of Gunshot Wounds.** (Illus.). 1976. Lippincott. $23.75.

Gibbens, T. C., et al. **Medical Remands in the Criminal Court.** (Maudaley Monographs). 1977. Oxford Univesity Press. $22.00.

Horsley & Carlova. **Testifying in Court: The Advanced Course, A Comprehensive Guidebook Especially Written for Doctors.** 1972. Van Nos Reinhold. $7.95.

Jeffery, C. R. **Biology & Crime.** (Illus.). 1979. Sage. $12.95; pap. $6.50.

Nash, Donald J. **Individual Identification and the Law Enforcement Officer.** (Illus.). 176p. 1978. C. C. Thomas. $16.00.

Siegal, Lewis J. **Forensic Medicine: Courtroom Applications to Legal Principles.** 1963. Grune & Stratton. $37.50.

Tennenhouse, Dan J. **Attorneys Medical Deskbook.** new ed. 1975. Lawyers Co-Operative Publishing Co. $47.50.

University of Miami Law Center & School of Medicine. **Medicine for Attorneys-Orthopedics.** 225p. 1970. Trans-Media Publishing Co. $10.00.

Wadlington, Walter J., et al. **Cases and Materials on Law and Medicine.** 1100p. 1980. Foundation Press. write for info.

Waters, John F. **Crime Labs: The Science of Forensic Medicine.** (Illus.). (gr. 7 up). 1979. Watts, Franklin, Inc. $5.45.

MURDER

Abrahamsen, David. **The Murdering Mind.** 256p. 1973. Harper & Row. $6.95.
—**The Murdering Mind.** 1975. pap. Harper & Row. (OP). $2.95.

Allen, William. **Starkweather.** 1977. pap. Avon Books. $1.75.

Armbrister, Trevor. **Act of Vengeance: The Yablonski Murders and Their Aftermath.** (Illus.). 1975. Sat Rev Pr. (Dutton). (OP). $2.75.

Barnes, Margaret A. **Murder in Coweta County.** 1977. pap. Pocket Books. $1.95.

Bensing, Robert C. & Schroeder, Oliver, Jr. **Homicide in an Urban Community.** (Illus.). 1960. C. C. Thomas. (OP). $8.75.

Borowitz, Albert I. **The Woman Who Murdered Black Satin: The Bermondsey Horro.** 255p. 1980. Ohio State University Press. $15.00.

Bradlee, Ben, Jr. **The Ambush Murders: The True Account of the Killing of Two California Policemen.** (Illus.). 1979. Dodd, Mead & Co. $12.95.

Brearley, H. C. **Homicide in the United States.** 1969. Repr. of 1932 ed. Patterson Smith. $10.00.

Buchanan, Edna. **Carr: Three Years of Murder.** 1979. Dutton, E. P. $10.95.

Bugliosi, Vincent & Gentry, Curt. **Helter Skelter.** (Illus.). 704p. 1975. pap. Bantam Books. $2.50.
—**Helter Skelter: The True Story of the Manson Murders.** (Illus.). 502p. 1972. Norton, W. W. & Co. $15.00.

Bugliosi, Vincent & Hurwitz, Ken. **Till Death Us Do Part: A True Murder Mystery.** 1979. pap. Bantam Books. $2.75.
—**Till Death Us Do Part: A True Murder Mystery.** 1978. Norton, W.W. & Co. $10.95.

Capote, Truman. **In Cold Blood.** 1966. Random House. $10.95.
—**In Cold Blood.** 1971. pap. NAL. $2.25.

Cheney, Margaret. **The Coed Killer.** 240p. 1976. Walker & Co. $8.95.

Critchley, T. A. & James, P. D. **The Maul & the Pear Tree: the Ratcliff Highway Murders 1811.** 1971. Crane-Russak Co. (OP). $9.95.

Crump, David & Jacobs, George. **Capital Murder.** (Illus.). 1977. Texian Press. $11.95.

Daley, Robert. **To Kill A Cop.** 1976. Crown. (OP). $8.95.

Damio, Ward. **Urge to Kill.** (Illus., Orig.). 1974. pap. Pinnacle Books. (OP). $1.50.

Derleth, August. **Wisconsin Murders.** 1968. Arkham House Publishers. (OP). $5.00.

Donoghue, Mary A. **Assassination: Murder in Politics.** (Illus.). 192p. (Orig.). 1975. pap. Major Books. $1.25.

Elwin, Verrier. **Maria Murder and Suicide.** (Illus.). 1977. Oxford University Press. $9.75.

Foucault, Michel I. **Pierre Riviere, Having Slaughtered My Mother, My Sister & My Brother: A Case of Parricide in the Nineteenth Century.** 1975. Pantheon Books. (OP). $10.00.

Frank, Gerold. **Boston Strangler.** 1971. pap. NAL. $1.50.

Franke, David. **The Torture Doctor: The Incredible but True Story of Herman W. Mudgett, the Most Fiendish Killer in the Annals of American Crime.** 1975. Hawthorn. (OP). $8.95.

Gaddis, Thomas E. **Killer.** 1970. Macmillan. $7.95.

Gardiner, Muriel. **The Deadly Innocents: Portraits of Children Who Kill.** 192p. 1976. Basic Books. $13.95.

Gaute, J. H. & Odell, Robin. **The Murderer's Who's Who.** (Illus.). 1979. Methuen Inc. $17.95.

Giese, Donald J. **Carol Thompson Murder Case.** 1969. pap. Llewellyn Pubns. $1.00

Gorder, Eric, ed. **Murder My Love: The Great Crimes of Passion.** 1974. Playboy. (OP). $7.95; pap. $.95.

Hartman, Mary S. **Victorian Murderesses: A True History of Thirteen Respectable French and English Women Accused of Unspeakable Crimes.** (Illus.). 1979. pap. Schocken Books. $6.95.
—**Victorian Murderesses: A True History of Thirteen Respectable French and English Women Accused of Unspeakable Crimes.** (Illus.). 1976. Schocken Books. $15.00.

Higdon, Hal. **Crime of the Century: The Leopold and Loeb Case.** (Illus.). 1975. Putnam. (OP). $10.00.

Hirsch, Richard. **Crimes That Shook the World.** fasc. ed. 1949. Arno. Press. $19.00.

Jayewardene, C.H. **Penalty of Death: The Canadian Experiment.** (Illus.) 1977. Lexington Books. $13.95.

Jones, Ann. **Women Who Kill.** 420p. 1980. Holt, Rinehart & Winston. $15.95.

Kelly, Tom. **Murders: The Capital's Famous Murder Stories.** 1976. Washingtonian Books. (OP). $6.95; pap. $3.95.

Keyes, Edward. **The Michigan Murders.** 1978. pap. Pocket Books. $2.50.

Kunstler, William M. **The Hall-Mills Murder Case: The Minister and the Choir Singer.** 350p. 1980. pap. Rutgers University Press. $6.95.

Kutash, Irwin L., et al. **Violence: Perspectives on Murder and Aggression.** (Illus.). 1978. Jossey-Bass. 25.00.

Kwitney, Johnathan. **The Mullendore Murder Case.** 336p. (Illus.). 1974. Farrar, Straus & Giroux. $11.95.

Lester, David & Lester, Gene. **Crime of Passion:**

Murder and the Murderer. 1975. Nelson-Hall. $14.95.

Levitt, Leonard. **The Healer: A True Story of Medicine and Murder.** 276p. 1980. Viking Press. $12.95.

Lunde, Donald T. **Murder and Madness.** 1976. San Francisco Book Co. (OP). $7.95.

Lunde, Donald T. **Murder and Madness.** 1979. pap. Norton, W.W. & Co. $3.95.
—**Murder and Madness.** 1976. pap. San Francisco Book Co. $4.95.

Lundsgaarde, Henry. **Murder in Space City: A Cultural Analysis of Houston Homicidal Patterns.** (Illus.). 1977. Oxford University Press. $12.95.

McComas, J. Francis. **Graveside Companion.** 1962. Astor-Honor. $8.95.

MacDonald, John M. **Murderer and His Victim.** 1961. C.C. Thomas. (OP). $10.50.

Mars, Florence. **Witness in Philadelphia.** 1977. Louisiana State University Press. $10.00.

Meyer, Gerald. **The Memphis Murders.** 1974. Seabury Press. (OP). $7.95.

Miller, Gene. **Invitation to a Lynching.** (Illus.). 1975. Doubleday. (OP). $8.95.

Moore, Billy. **From Darkness to Light.** 1980. Carlton Press. $4.95.

Olsen, Jack. **The Man with the Candy: The Story of the Houston Mass Murders.** 256p. 1974. S&S. $7.95.
—**The Man with the Candy.** 1975. pap. Pocket Books. $1.75.

Palmer, Stuart. **Psychology of Murder.** Orig. Title: Study of Murder. pap. Apollo Editions. (OP). $1.95.

Pearson, Edmund. **Murder at Smutty Nose and Other Murders.** Repr. of 1926 ed. Arden Library. $25.00

Phillips, Steven. **No Heroes, No Villains: The Story of a Murder.** 1978. pap. Random House. $2.45.

Reinhardt, James M. **Nothing Left but Murder.** pap. Johnsen. (OP). $2.95.
—**Psychology of Strange Killers.** 1962. C.C. Thomas. (OP). $7.00.

Ruotolo, Andrew K. **Once Upon a Murder.** (Illus.). 1979. Grosset & Dunlap. $10.00.

Schmidt, J.E. **Police Medical Dictionary.** 256p. 1968. C.C. Thomas. $18.50.

Simpson, Keith. **Forty Years of Murder.** (Illus.). Scribner. $12.95.

Sparrow, Gerald. **Women Who Murder.** 1971. pap. Belmont-Tower Books. (OP). $.95.

Swigert, Victoria & Farrell, Ronald A. **Murder, Inequality, and the Law: Differential Treatment and the Legal Process.** 1976. Lexington Books. $14.95.

Tallberg, Martin. **Don Bolles: An Investigation into His Murder.** 1978. pap. Popular Library. $1.95.

Trenerry, Walter N. **Murder in Minnesota: A Collection of True Cases.** (Illus.). 1962. Minnesota Historical Society. $4.95.

Trilling, Diana. **A Respectable Murder.** 1980. Harcourt Brace Jovanovich. $12.95.

Turkus, Burton B. **Murder, Inc.** 448p. 1975. pap. Manor Books. $2.25.

Wallace, William S. **Murders and Mysteries: A Canadian Series.** 333p. 1975. Repr. of 1931 ed. Hyperion Press. $16.50.

Wellman, Manly W. **Dead and Gone.** 1955. University of North Carolina Press. $7.50.

Wertham, Frederic. **Show of Violence.** Repr. of 1949 ed. pap. Greenwood Press. $5.95.

West, Donald J. **Murder Followed by Suicide.** 1965. Harvard University Press. $9.00.

Whittington, Stephen N. **The Psychology of Murder and of Murderers.** (Illus.). 1980. American Institute for Psychological Research. deluxe ed. $39.85.

Wille, Warren S. **Citizens Who Commit Murder: A Psychiatric Study.** (Illus.). 280p. 1975. Green. $12.50.

Wolfgang, Marvin E. & Ferracuti, F. **Subculture of Violence: Towards an Integrated Theory in Criminology.** (Orig.). 1967. pap. Barnes & Noble. (OP). $8.50.

NARCOTICS LAWS

Bailey, F. Lee & Rothblatt, Henry B. **Handling Narcotic and Drug Cases.** 652p. 1972. Lawyers Co-Operative Publishing Co. $45.00.

Blum, Richard H., et al. **Drug Dealers - Taking Action: Options for International Response.** 1973. Jossey-Bass. $15.95.

Bogomolny, R. L., et al. **A Handbook on the 1970 Federal Drug Act: Shifting the Perspective.** (Illus.). 192p. 1975. C.C. Thomas. $17.25.

Damgaard, John A. **The Student and the Courts: Campus Profile.** 1971. Exposition Press. (OP). $4.00.

Danaceau, Paul. **Pot Luck in Texas: Changing a Marijuana Law.** 1974. Drug Abuse Council. $1.25.

Eldridge, William B. **Narcotics and the Law.** 2nd ed. 1967. University of Chicago Press. $10.00.

Harney, Malachi L. & Cross, John C. **The Narcotic Officers Notebook.** 2nd ed. (Illus.). 396p. 1975. C.C. Thomas. $19.00.

Levine, Harvey R. **Legal Dimensions of Drug Abuse in the United States.** 208p. 1974. C.C. Thomas. $12.50.

Levine, Samuel M. **Narcotics and Drug Abuse.** 1973. pap. Anderson Publishing Co. $12.00.

Lindesmith, Alfred R. **Addict and the Law.** (Illus.). 1965. Indiana University Press. $12.50.

Maurer, David W. & Vogel, Victor H. **Narcotics and Narcotic Addiction.** (Illus.). 496p. 1973. C.C. Thomas. $20.00.

Messick, Hank. **Of Grass and Snow.** (Illus.). 1979. Prentice-Hall. $9.95.

Rudman, Jack. **Narcotics Security Assistant.** (Career Examination Ser.: C-1378). pap. National Learning Corp. $10.00.

Ware, Mitchell. **Operational Handbook for Narcotic Law Enforcement Officers.** 128p. 1975. C.C. Thomas. $16.00.

OFFENSES AGAINST THE PERSON

Bailey, F. Lee & Rothblatt, Henry B. **Crimes of Violence: Homicide and Assault.** 543p. 1973. Lawyers Co-Operative Publishing Co. $45.00.

—**Crimes of Violence: Rape and Other Sex Crimes.** 1973. Lawyers Co-Operative Publishing Co. $45.00.

Chappell, Duncan & Monahan, John. **Violence and Criminal Justice.** 1975. Lexington Books. $15.95.

—**Violence and Criminal Justice.** 1977. pap. Heath. $6.95.

Block, Richard. **Violent Crime.** (Illus.). 1977. Lexington Books. $14.50.

Fanon, Frantz. **Wretched of the Earth.** Farrington, Constance, tr. 1965. pap. Grove Press. $2.45.

Hunter, George. **How to Defend Yourself, Your Family and Your Home.** 1967. McKay, David, Co. (OP). $7.95.

—**How to Defend Yourself, Your Family and Your Home.** 1970. pap. Univ Pub & Dist. (OP). $.95.

Meyers, David W. **Human Body and the Law.** 1970. Edinburgh Univ. (OP). $8.75.

National Commission on the Causes & Prevention of Violence. **Violent Crime.** 1970. pap. Braziller. $2.50.

Schur, Edwin M. **Crimes Without Victims - Deviant Behavior and Public Policy: Abortion, Homosexuality, Drug Addiction.** (Orig.). 1965. pap. Prentice-Hall. $3.95.

ORGANIZED CRIME

Abadinsky, Howard. **Organized Crime.** 400p. 1980. Allyn & Bacon. $13.95.

Bequai, August. **Organized Crime.** 1979. Lexington Books. $16.95.

Chambliss, William J. **On the Take: From Petty Crooks to Presidents.** Indiana University Press. $10.95.

Cook, Fred J. **Mob, Inc.** (gr. 7 up) 1977. Watts, Franklin, Inc. $6.90.

Duke, Harry. **Neutral Territory: The True Story of the Rackets in Atlantic City.** 1977. Dorrance & Co. $5.00.

Graham, Fred. **The Alias Program.** (Illus.). 1977. Little, Brown & Co. $8.95.

Homer, Frederic D. **Guns and Garlic: Myths and Realities of Organized Crime.** 240p. 1974. Purdue University Press. $7.95; pap. $3.50.

Ianni, Francis A. **Black Mafia.** 1974. Simon & Schuster. $9.95.

Ianni, Francis A. & Ianni, Elizabeth R. **A Family Business: Kinship and Social Control in Organized Crime.** 1972. Russell Sage. $8.50.

Ianni, Francis J. **Black Mafia.** 1975. pap. Pocket Books. $1.95.

Iorizzo, Luciano J., ed. **An Inquiry into Organized Crime.** 1970. American Italian Historical Assn. $2.50.

Landesco, John. **Organized Crime in Chicago.** 2nd ed. 1979. pap. University of Chicago Press. $11.00.

McIntosh, Mary. **The Organization of Crime.** 1977. pap. Verry, Lawrence, Co. $4.00.

Nelli, Humbert S. **The Business of Crime: Italians and Syndicate Crime in the United States.** (Illus.). 304p. 1976. Oxford University Press. $14.95.

Pace, Denny F. & Styles, Jimmie C. **Organized Crime: Concepts and Control.** (Illus.). 352p. 1974. Prentice-Hall. $16.95.

Philcox, Norman W. **An Introduction to Organized Crime.** 108p. 1978. C.C. Thomas. $8.75.

Pitkin, Thomas M. & Cordasco, Francesco. **The Black Hand: A Chapter in Ethnic Crime.** (Illus.). 1977. Rowman & Littlefield. $12.50.

—**The Black Hand: A Chapter in Ethnic Crime.** (Illus.). 1977. pap. Littlefield. $4.95.

Turkus, Burton. **Murder, Inc.** 448p. 1975. pap. Manor Books. $2.25.

Villano, Anthony & Astor, Gerald. **Brick Agent.** 1978. pap. Ballantine Books. $1.95.

Waller, Leslie. **The Mob: The Story of Organized Crime in America.** 160p. (gr. 7 up) 1973. Delacorte Press. $5.95.

Wendland, Michael F. **The Arizona Project: How a Team of Investigative Reporters Got Revenge on Deadline.** 1978. Andrews & McMeel. $9.95.

PISTOLS

Archer, Denis, ed. **Jane's Pocket Book of Pistols and Submachine Guns.** 1977. Macmillan. pap $6.95.

Askins, Charles. **Askins on Pistols and Revolvers.** Bryant, Ted & Askins, Bill, eds. 144p. 1980; pap. $8.95. National Rifle Assn. $25.00.

Belford & Dunlap. **Mauser Self Loading Pistol.** Borden. $13.50.

Best, Charles W. **Cast Iron Toy Pistols, Eighteen Seventy to Nineteen Forty; A Collector's Guide.** (Illus.) 220p. (Orig.). 1973. Best Antiques. $15.00.

Blair, Claude. **Pistols of the World.** (Illus.). 1969. Viking Press. (OP). $30.00.

Chamberlain, Peter & Gander, Terry. **Allied Pistols, Rifles and Grenades.** 1976. pap. Arco. $3.95.

—**Axis Pistols, Rifles, and Grenades.** 1977. pap. Arco. $4.95.

Cooper, Jeff. **Cooper on Handguns.** (Illus.). 1974. pap. Petersen Publishing. (OP). $5.95.

Datig, Fred. A. **Luger Pistol.** rev. ed. Borden. $9.50.

Dixon, Norman. **Georgian Pistols: The Art and Craft of the Flintlock Pistol, 1715-1840.** 184p. 1972. George Shumway Publisher. casebound $22.50.

Dunlap, H.J. **American, British and Continental Pepperbox Firearms.** (Illus.). 1967. Repr. of 1964 ed. Pacific Books. $19.95.

Dyke, S.E. **Thoughts on the American Flintlock Pistol.** (Illus.) 52p. 1974. pap. George Shumway Publisher. $6.50.

Grennell, Dean. A. **Pistol and Revolver Digest.** (DBI Bks). (Illus., Orig.) 1976. pap. DBI Books. $7.95.

Grennell, Dean A., ed. **Pistol and Revolver Digest.** 2nd ed. (Illus.) 1979. pap. DBI Books. $7.95.

Hogg, I.V. **Military Pistols and Revolvers.** (Illus.). 1970. Arco. $3.50; pap. $1.95.

Holland, Claude V. **The Military Four.** Holland Bks. $4.95; pap. $2.98.

Horlacher, R., ed. **The Famous Automatic Pistols of Europe.** Seaton, L. & Steindler, R.A., trs. from Ger. (Illus.). 1976. Jolex. pap. $6.95.

Kirkland, Turner. **Southern Derringers of the Mississippi Valley.** Pioneer Press. $2.00.

Klay, Frank. **The Samuel E. Dyke Collection of Kentucky Pistols.** 30p. Date not set. Gun Room Press. $1.75.

Koch, R.W. **The FP-45 Liberato Pistol, 1942-1945.** (Illus. Orig.) 1977. Research. $10.00.

Lachuk, John & Guns & Ammo Editors. **Wonderful World of the Twenty-Two.** (Illus.). 1972. pap. Petersen Publishing. (OP). $3.95.

Leithe. **Japanese Hand Guns.** Borden. $9.95.

Millard, J.T. **A Handbook on the Primary Identification of Revolvers and Semi-Automatic Pistols.** (Illus.). 168p. 1974. C.C. Thomas. $13.50; pap. $10.25.

Mitchell, Jack. **The Gun Digest Book of Pistolsmithing.** 288p. 1980. pap. DBI Books. $8.95.

Neal, Robert J. & Jinks, Roy G. **Smith and Wesson, 1857-1945,** rev. ed. 400p. 1975. A.S. Barnes. $25.00.

Nonte, George C. **The Pistol Guide.** 256p. 1980. pap. Stoeger. $7.95.

Nonte, George C., Jr. **Combat Handguns.** Jurras, Lee F., ed. (Illus.) 1980. Stackpole Books. $17.95.

—**Pistolsmithing.** (Illus.). 560p. 1974. Stackpole. $15.95.

Nonte, George C., Jr. & Jurras, Lee E. **Handgun Hunting.** (Illus.). 1975. Winchester Press. $8.95.

North & North. **Simeon North: First Official Pistol Maker of the United States.** Repr. Gun Room Press. $7.95.

Olsen, John, compiled by. **The Famous Automatic Pistols of Europe.** (Illus.). 1975. Relex. (OP) $9.95; pap. $6.95.

Pender. **Mauser Pocket Pistols: 1910-1946.** Borden. $14.50.

Pollard, H.B. **Automatic Pistols.** (Illus.) Repr. of 1921 ed. 1970. We Inc. (OP) $6.00.

Reese, Michael. **Collector's Guide to Luger Values.** 1972. pap. Pelican. $1.95.

Sawyer, Charles W. **United States Single Shot Martial Pistols.** 1971. Paladin Enterprises. $5.00.

Scott, Robert F., ed. **1982 Shooter's Bible.** No. 73. (Illus.). 1981. pap. Stoeger. $10.95.

Van Der Mark, Kist & Van Der Sloot, Puype. **Dutch Muskets and Pistols.** new ed. (Illus.). 160p. 1974. Shumway Publishers. $25.00.

Wallack, L.R. **American Pistol and Revolver Design and Performance.** 1978. Winchester Press. $13.95.

Whittington, Robert D. **German Pistols and Holsters 1943-1945: Military — Police — NSDAP.** (Illus.). Gun Room Press. $15.00.

Wilkerson, Frederick. **British and American Flintlocks.** 1972. Transatlantic Arts Inc. $2.95.

Wilkinson, F.J. **Flintlock Pistols.** (Illus.). 1976. pap. Hippocrene Books. $2.95.

Williams, Mason. **The Sporting Use of the Handgun.** (Illus.). 288p. 1979. C. C. Thomas. $14.75.

Wilson, R.K. & Hogg, Ian. **Textbook of Automatic Pistols,** rev. ed. (Illus.) 1975. Stackpole Books. (OP.) $17.95.

POISONING

Curry, Alan. **Poison Detection in Human Organs.** (Illus.). 376p. 1976. C.C. Thomas. $27.25.

Wilber, Charles G. **Forensic Toxicology for the Law Enforcement Officer.** (Illus.). 310p. 1980. C.C. Thomas $27.50.

POLICE

Adams, Herbert B. **Norman Constables in America.** 1976. Repr. of 1883 ed. AMS Press. $11.50.

Adams, Thomas F. **Law Enforcement: An Introduction to the Police Role in the Criminal Justice System.** 2nd ed. (Illus.). 1973. ref. ed. Prentice-Hall. $16.95.

Adams, Thomas F., et al. **Criminal Justice: Readings.** 1971. pap. Goodyear. (OP). $7.95.

Adams, Thomas F., et al. **Criminal Justice: Organization and Management.** (Illus.). 416p. 1974. Goodyear. $19.95.

Ahern, James F. **Police in Trouble: Our Frightening Crisis in Law Enforcement.** 256p. 1971. Dutton, E. P. $9.95.

Akers, Ronald L. & Sagarin, Edward, eds. **Crime Prevention and Social Control.** 1974. Praeger. (OP). $13.50.

American Academy of Political & Social Science, Philadelphia. **The Police and the Crime Problem.** Sellin, Thorsten, ed. Repr. of 1929 ed. AMS Press. $24.50.

Anastor, Herb. **Rookie Leadfoot.** 1973. Dorrance. (OP). $4.95.

Answer Book to Study Guide. (Monticello Bks.) 1970. pap. Jefferson Pubns. $2.00.

Armstrong, T. R. & Cinnamon, Kenneth M. **Power and Authority in Law Enforcement.** 208p. 1976. C.C. Thomas. $17.25.

Asch, Sidney H. **Police Authority and the Rights of the Individual.** 2nd ed. 1968. pap. Arc Books. (OP). $1.45.

—**Police Authority and the Rights of the Individual.** 2nd ed. 1968. Arco. (OP). $4.95.

Aubry, Arthur S., Jr. **Officer in the Small Department.** (Illus.). 1961. C.C. Thomas. (OP). $10.50.

Aziz, Harry. **Police Procedures and Defensive Tactics Training Manual.** Halet, Sydney S., ed. (Illus.). 1979. Japan Pubns. $19.95.

Baldwin, Roger. **Inside a Cop: The Tensions in the Public and Private Lives of the Police.** (Illus.). 1977. pap. Boxwood Press. $3.95.

Banton, Michael. **Policeman in the Community.** 1965. Basic Books. $10.00.

Basinger, Louis F. **The Techniques of Observation and Learning Retention: a Handbook for The Policeman and The Lawyer.** (Illus.). 88p. 1973. pap. C.C. Thomas. $5.00.

Bayley, David. H. **Forces of Order: Police Behavior in Japan and the United States.** 1976. University of California Press. $15.50; pap. $3.95.

Bayley, David H., ed. **Police and Society.** 1977. Sage. $18.95; pap. $9.95.

Becker, Harold K. **Issues in Police Administration.** 1970. Scarecrow Press. $9.50.

Becker, Harold K. & Whitestone, Jack E. **Police of America: A Personal View, Introduction and Commentary.** (Illus.). 108p. 1979. C.C. Thomas. $9.75.

Bent, Alan E. **The Politics of Law Enforcement.** 1977. pap. Heath. $6.95.

Bent, Alan E. & Rossum, Ralph A. **Police, Criminal Justice, and the Community.** 384p. 1976. Harper & Row. $16.95.

Berenbaum, Esai. **Municipal Public Safety: A Guide for the Implementation of Consolidated Police-Fire Services.** (Illus.). 104p. 1977. C.C. Thomas.

Berger, Melvin. **Police Lab.** (Illus.). 1976. John Day. $8.79.

Berkley, George. **The Democratic Policeman.** 256p. 1974. pap. Beacon Press. $4.95.

Bittner, Egon. **The Functions of the Police in Modern Society.** 144p. 1975. Repr. Aronson. $17.50.

—**The Functions of the Police in Modern Society.** 1979. Oelgeschlager. $16.50; pap. $7.95.

Black, Donald. **The Manners and Customs of the Police.** 1980. Academic Press. price not set.

Block, Eugene B. **Science vs. Crime.** (Illus.). 208p. 1980. pap. Cragmont Pubns. $6.95.

Bolz, Frank & Hershey, Edward. **Hostage Cop.** 1980. Rawson Wade. $11.95.

Bopp, William J. **Police Personnel Administration.** 1974. Holbrook. (OP). $13.95.

—**Police Rebellion: A Quest for Blue Power.** 1971. C.C. Thomas. (OP) $10.75.

Bopp, William J. O. W. O. W. **Wilson and the Search for a Police Profession.** 1977. Kennikat Press. $12.50; pap. $7.95.

Bopp, William J. & Schultz, Donald O. **Principles of American Law Enforcement and Criminal Justice.** (Illus.). 596p. 1975. C.C. Thomas. $15.25.

—**A Short History of American Law Enforcement.** (Illus.). 192p. 1977. pap. C.C. Thomas. $7.25.

Bordua, David J., ed. **Police: Six Sociological Essays.** 1967. Krieger. (OP). $9.00.

—**Police: Six Sociological Essays.** 1967. pap. Wiley, John & Sons., $9.95.

Bouza, Anthony J. **Police Intelligence: The Operations of an Investigative Unit.** 200p. 1976. AMS Press $18.50.

Bramstedt, Ernest K. **Dictatorship and Political Police: The Technique of Control by Fear.**

1976. Repr. of 1945 ed. AMS Press. $17.50.

Brandstatter, A. F. & Hyman, A. A. **Fundamentals of Law Enforcement.** 1972. Glencoe. $14.95.

Bristow, Allen P. **Effective Police Manpower Utilization.** (Illus.). 1969. C.C. Thomas. (OP). $6.75.

—**Police Disaster Operations.** (Illus.). 240p. 1972. C.C. Thomas. $18.50; pap. $18.50.

Brooks, Pierce R. **Officer Down Code Three.** 1975. MTI Teleprograms. $8.95.

Brown, John & Howse, Graham, eds. **The Police and the Community.** 112p. 1975. (Pub. by Saxon Hse). Lexington Books. $15.00.

Cahalane, Cornelius F. **Policeman.** 1970. Repr. of 1923. ed. Arno. Press. $17.00.

Chapman, et al. **Introduction and Methodology to the Study of Police Assaults in the South Central United States.** 30p. 1974. pap. University of Oklahoma Bureau of Government Research. $1.00.

Chapman, Samuel G., et al. **A Descriptive Profile of the Assault Incident.** 1974. pap. University of Oklahoma Bureau of Government Research. $4.50.

—**Civil Litigation and the Police: A Method of Communication.** 168p. 1976. C.C. Thomas. $13.75.

Clark, Donald E. & Chapman, Samuel G. **Forward Step: Educational Backgrounds for Police.** (Illus.). 1966. C.C. Thomas. (OP). $5.50.

Clark, Ramsey. **Crime in America: Its Nature, Causes, Control and Correction.** 1970. Simon & Schuster. (OP). $8.95.

Clark, Robert S. **Police-Community Relations: An Analytic Perspective.** 1978. New Viewpoints. $9.95.

Clarke, R. V. & Hough, J. M., eds. **The Effectiveness of Policing.** 184p. 1980. (Pub. by Gower Publishing Co., England). Lexington Books. $18.95.

Clarke, R. V. G. &. Hough, J. M., eds. **The Effectivness of Policing.** 184p. 1980. (Pub. by Gower Publishing Co., England). Lexington Books. $18.95.

Clift, Raymond E. **Guide to Modern Police Thinking.** 3rd ed. 1970. Anderson Publishing Co. $9.50.

Cohn, Alvin W. **The Future of Policing.** 1978. Sage. $20.00; pap. $9.95.

Colbach, Edward M. & Fosterling, Charles D. **Police Social Work.** 168p. 1976. C. C. Thomas. $13.50.

Cooper, John L. **The Police and the Ghetto.** 1980. Kennikat Press. $13.50.

Cooper, Lynn & Platt, Anthony. **Policing America.** 224p. 1974. pap. Prentice-Hall $2.95.

Cope, Jeff & Goddard Kenneth. **Weaponless Control.** (Illus.). 302p. 1979. C.C. Thomas. $19.50.

Cramer, James. **Uniforms of the World's Police: With Brief Data on Organizations, Systems, and Weapons.** (Illus.). 216p. 1968. C. C. Thomas. $23.75.

Cromwell, Paul F., Jr. & Keefer, George. **Readings on Police-Community Relations.** 2nd ed. 1978. pap. West Publishing. $12.95.

Curran, James T., et al, eds. **Police and Law Enforcement, 1973-1975.** 2 vols. (Orig.). 1973. AMS Press. Set. $60.00; Vol. 1. $30.00; Vol. 2. $30.00; Vol. 1. pap. $8.95; Vol. 2. pap. $8.95.

Davidson, Bill. **Collura: Actor with a Gun.** 1977. Simon & Schuster. $7.95.

Davidson, Phillip L. **SWAT (Special Weapons and Tactics).** (Illus.). 148p. 1979. C.C. Thomas. $13.75.

Drabek, Thomas E. **Laboratory Simulation of a Police Communications System Under Stress.** 1970. pap. Ohio State Univ., College of Administrative Science. $4.50.

Droge, Edward F., Jr. **The Patrolman: A Cop's Story.** (Orig.). 1973. pap. NAL. (OP) $1.25.

Dudycha, George J. **Psychology for Law Enforcement Officers.** (Illus.). 416p. 1976. C. C. Thomas. $15.25.

Earle, Howard H. **Police Recruit Training: Stress Vs. Non-stress: A Revolution in Law Enforcement Career Programs.** (Illus.). 240p. 1973. C. C. Thomas. $16.25; pap. $11.25.

—**Student-Instructor Guide on Police-Community Relations.** 1972. pap. C. C. Thomas. (OP). $10.75.

—**Police-Community Relations: Crisis in Our Time.** (Illus.). 224 p. 1976. C. C. Thomas. $16.25.

Educational Research Council of America. **Police Team.** rev. ed. Ferris, Theodore N. & Marchak, John P., eds. (Illus.). 1976. pap. Changing Times Education Service. $2.25.

Egan, Frederick. **Plainclothesman.** (Illus.). 1959. Arco. (OP). $5.00.

Eldefonso, Edward. **Readings in Criminal Justice.** 512p. 1973. Glencoe. $7.95.

Eldridge, Benjamin P. & Watts, William B. **Our Rival, the Rascal: A Faithful Portrayal of the Conflict Between the Criminals of This Age and the Defenders of Society, the Police.** (Illus., With intro. added). 1973. Repr. of 1897 ed. Patterson Smith. $14.00.

Elliott, J. F. **The New Police.** 88p. 1973. C. C. Thomas. $8.25.

Elliott, J. F. & Sardino, Thomas J. **Crime Control Team: An Experiment in Municipal Police Department Management and Operations.** (Illus.). 140p. 1971. C. C. Thomas. $16.25.

Evans, Peter. **The Police Revolution.** 1974. Allen & Unwin. $14.95.

Fink, Joseph & Sealy, Lloyd G. **The Community and the Police: Conflict or Cooperation?** 240p. 1974. (Pub. by Wiley-Interscience). Wiley. $17.95.

Flammang, C. J. **The Police and the Underprotected Child.** 324p. 1970. C. C. Thomas. $15.25.

Flynt, Josiah. **Notes of an Itinerant Policeman.** 1972. Repr. of 1900 ed. Arno. Press. $18.00.

—**World of Graft.** facs. ed. 1901. Arno Press. $16.00.

Fogelson, Robert M. **Big-City Police: An Urban Institute Study.** 1979. Harvard University Press. $17.50; pap. $7.95.

Fogelson, Robert M., ed. **Police in America.** 35 Bks. 1971. Repr. Arno Press. Set. $628.00.

Folsor, DeFrancias. **Our Police: A History of the Baltimore Police from the First Watchman to the Latest Appointee.** (Illus.). Date not set Repr. of 1888 ed. Patterson Smith. $17.50.

Fosdick, Raymond B. **American Police Systems.** (With intro. added). 1969. Patterson Smith. $15.00; pap. $5.00.

—**European Police Systems.** (With intro. added). 1969. Patterson Smith. $15.00; pap. $5.00.

Freed, Leonard. **Police Work.** 1981. Simon & Schuster. $19.95; pap, $9.95.

Friend, Charles E. **Police Rights: Civil Remedies for Law Enforcement Officers.** 1979. Michie. $14.50.

Friendlander, C. P. & Mitchell, E. **Police: Servants or Masters.** 1974. Transatlantic Arts Inc. (OP). $8.75.

Frost, Thomas M. **Forward Look in Police Education.** (Illus.). 1959. C.C. Thomas. (OP). $8.75.

Fuld, Leonhard Felix, **Police Administration: A Critical Study of Police Organizations in the United States and Abroad.** (Illus.). 583p. (With intro. added). 1971. Repr. of 1909 ed. Patterson Smith. $16.50.

Gammage, Allen Z. **Police Training in the United States.** 1963. C. C. Thomas. (OP). $12.75.

Garner, Gerald W. **The Police Role in Alcohol-Related Crises.** 168p. 1979. C. C. Thomas. $14.00.

—**Police Supervision: A Common Sense Approach.** 264p. 1981. C. C. Thomas. $19.75.

Geary, David P. **Community Relations and the Administration of Justice.** 1975. Wiley, John & Sons. (OP). $10.95.

Goldsmith, Jack & Goldsmith, Sharon S., eds. **The Police Community: Dimensions of an Occupational Subculture.** 1974. Palisades Publishing. $8.95; pap. $5.95.

Goldstein, Arnold P., et al. **Police Crisis Intervention.** 175p. Pergamon Press. $15.00; pap. $6.95.

Goldstein, Herman. **Policing a Free Society.** 1977. Ballinger Publishing. $16.50; pap. $8.95.

Gould Editorial Staff. **Law Digest of New York.** (Supplemented annually). Gould. $7.50.

Gourley, G. Douglas. **Effective Municipal Police Organization.** 1970. pap. Glenco. $3.95.

Graper, Elmer D. **American Police Administration: A Handbook on Police Organization and Methods of Administration in American Cities.** (With intro. added). 1969. Repr. of 1921 ed. Patterson Smith. $15.00.

Green, Edward J. **Psychology for Law Enforcement.** 167p. 1976. Wiley, John & Sons. $13.95; pap. text ed. $8.95.

Greenwood, Colin. **Police Tactics in Armed Operations.** (Illus.). 325p. 1979. Paladin Enterprises. $19.95.

Griffin, Gerald R. **A Study of Relationships Between Level of College Education and Police Patrolmen's Performance.** 120p. 1980. Century Twenty One. $9.00.

Griffin, John I. **Statistics Essential for Police Efficiency.** (Illus.). 248p. 1972. C.C. Thomas. $11.00.

Hahn, Harlan, ed. **Police in Urban Society.** 1971. Sage. (OP). $10.95.

Hale. **Police Community Relations.** 208p. 1974. Delmar. pap. $8.00; instructor's guide. $1.45.

Hale, Charles D. & Wilson, Wesley R. **Personal Characteristics of Assaulted & Non-Assaulted Officers.** pap. University of Oklahoma Bureau of Government Research. $4.50.

Halpern, Stephen. **Police — Association and Department Leaders.** 1974. Lexington Books. $13.95.

Hansen, David A. **An Analysis of Police Concepts and Programs.** (Illus.). 144p. 1972. C.C. Thomas. $11.25.

—**Police Ethics.** (Illus.). 96p. 1973. pap. C.C. Thomas. $4.75.

Harris, Richard N. **The Police Academy: An Inside View.** 202p. 1973. (Pub. by Wiley). Krieger. $14.95.

Hart, Hastings H. **Plans for City Police Jails and Village Lockups.** (Illus.). Repr. of 1932 ed. Irvington. $23.50.

Hauser, Thomas. **The Trial of Patrolman Thomas Shea.** 273p. 1980. Viking Press. $11.95.

Haynes, William D. **Stress Related Disorders in Policemen.** 1978. pap. R & E Research Associates. $8.00.

Heller, Denise L. **An Analysis of Police Assailants in Albuquerque.** 23p. 1974. pap. University of Oklahoma Bureau of Government Research. $1.50.

Henderson, Bruce. **Ghetto Cops.** (Illus.). 224p. (Orig.). 1975. pap. Major Books. $1.25.

Henderson, George. **Police Human Relations.** (Illus.). 368p. 1981. C.C. Thomas. $22.75.

Hewitt, William H. **New Directions in Police Personnel Administration.** 128p. 1975. Lexington Books. $14.50.

Holcomb, Richard L. **Police and the Public.** (Illus.). 1975. pap. C.C. Thomas. $3.25.

Hopkins, Ernest J. **Our Lawless Police.** 379p. 1972. Repr. of 1931 ed. Da Capo. $27.50.

Ingleton, Roy D. **Police of the World.** (Illus.). 1979. Scribner. $12.95.

International Association of Chiefs of Police **Police Unions.** 1971. Repr. of 1944 ed. Arno Press. $9.00.

James, Charles S. **Frontier of Municipal Safety.** 1955. Pub. Admin. (OP). $4.00.

—**Police and Fire Integration in the Small City.** 1955. Pub. Admin. (OP). $2.00.

James, Pat & Nelson, Martha. **Police Wife: How to Live with the Law and Like It.** 144p. 1975. C.C. Thomas. $14.50.

Johnson, David R. **Policing the Urban Underworld: The Impact of Crime on the Development of the American Police, 1800-1887.** 1979. Temple University Press. $15.00.

Kennedy, Daniel B. & Kennedy, Bruce. **Applied Sociology for Police.** 1972. C.C. Thomas. $7.75; pap. $4.50.

Kenney, John P. **California Police.** (Illus.). 1964. C.C. Thomas. (OP). $6.50.

—**Police Administration.** rev. ed. (Illus.). 376p. 1975. C.C. Thomas. $16.00.

Kenney, John P. & Williams, John B. **Police Operations: Policies and Procedures.** 2nd ed. (Illus.). 224p. 1973. C.C. Thomas. $10.25.

Kieselborst, Daniel C. **A Theoretical Perspective of Violence Against Police.** 1974. pap. University of Oklahoma Bureau of Government Research. $3.00.

Killinger, George G. & Cromwell, Paul F., Jr. **Issues in Law Enforcement.** 1975. pap. Holbrook. (OP). $7.95.

Kinnane, Adrian. **Policing.** 1979. Nelson-Hall. $14.95.

Kinton, Jack, ed. **American Police Roles in the Seventies: Professionalism.** new ed. 1980. Social Science & Sociological Resources. $11.95; pap. $8.95.

Kinton, Jack F., ed. **The American Police's New World: A Reader.** 1975. American Society Press. (OP). $9.95; pap. $5.95.

—**Police Roles in the Seventies, Vol. 1.** 1975. Social Science & Sociological Resources. $10.95; pap. $6.95.

—**Police Roles in the Seventies, Vol. 2.** 1978. Social Science & Sociological Resources. $10.95; pap. $4.95.

Klotter, John C. & Kanovitz, Jacqueline R. **Constitutional Law for Police: With 1979 Supplement.** 3rd ed. 1977. Anderson Publishing Co. $18.95.

Kornblum, Allan N. **The Moral Hazards: Police Strategies for Honesty and Ethical Behavior.** 224p. 1976. Lexington Books. $21.95.

Kroes, William H. **Society's Victim — the Policeman: An Analysis of Job Stress in Policing.** (Illus.). 144p. 1977. C.C. Thomas. $12.50.

Larson, Richard C. **Police Deployment.** (Illus). 1978. Lexington Books. $22.00.

Leinwand, Gerald, ed. **Police.** (Orig.). 1972. pap. Pocket Books (OP). $0.95.

Leonard, V.A. **Police Communications System.** 96p. 1970. C.C. Thomas. $7.50.

—**Police Crime Prevention.** (Illus.). 210p. 1972. C.C. Thomas. $13.75.

—**Police Enterprise: Its Organization and Management.** (Illus.). 104p. 1969. C.C. Thomas. $7.50.

—**Police Pre-Disaster Preparation.** (Illus.). 344p. 1973. C.C. Thomas. $14.00.

Lipsky, Michael, ed. **Police Encounters.** 144p. 1973. pap. Transaction Books. $3.95.

Livingston, Hazel. **Officer on the Witness Stand.** 1967. pap. Legal Book Corp. $1.50.

Los Angeles Public Library. **Catalog of the Police Library of the Los Angeles Public Library, First Supplement.** 1980. G K Hall. $220.00.

Lundman, Richard J. **Police and Policing.** 216p. 1980. pap. Holt, Rinehart & Winston. $8.95.

Lundman, Richard J., ed. **Police Behavior: A Sociological Perspective.** (Orig.). 1980. pap. Oxford University Press. $5.95.

McCabe, Clinton. **Our Police: A History of the Cincinnati Police Force, from the Earliest Period Until the Present Day.** Repr. of 1890 ed. AMS Press. (OP). $16.00.

McDavid, James C. **Police Cooperation and Performance: The Greater St. Louis Interlocal Experience.** (Illus.). 1979. pap. Pennsylvania State University Press. $4.50.

McDowell, Charles D. **Police in the Community.** 400p. 1975. Anderson Publishing Co. $13.95.

McEvoy, Donald W. **The Police and Their Many Publics.** 154p. 1976. Scarecrow Press. $8.00.

Macnamara, Donal E. & Reidei, Marc, eds. **Police: Perspectives, Problems, Prospects.** (Illus.). 150p. 1974. Praeger. $17.95.

Maitland, Frederic. **Justice and Police.** Repr. of 1885 ed. AMS Press. $15.00.

Manning & Vanmaanen. **Policing: A View from the Street.** 1978. pap. Goodyear. $13.95.

Manning, Peter K. **Police Work.** 1979. pap. MIT Press. $8.95.

—**Police Work: The Social Organization of Policing.** 1977. MIT Press. $19.95.

Marchiafava, Louis J. **The Houston Police, 1878-1948.** (Illus.). 119p. (Orig.). 1977. pap. Rice University Studies. $4.25.

Mawby, Rob. **Policing the City.** 1979. Renouf USA. $27.00.

Meyer, C. Kenneth, et al. **An Analysis of Officer Characteristics and Police Assaults Among Selected South Central Cities.** 1974. pap. University of Oklahoma Bureau of Government Research. $1.00.

Meyer, Fred & Baker, Ralph, eds. **Law Enforcement and Police Policy.** 1979. Policy Studies Organization. $5.00; pap. $3.00.

Michie Editorial Staff, ed. **Police, Crimes and Offenses and Motor Vehicle Laws of Virginia.** 1975. Michie. (OP). $30.00.

Moose, George, ed. **Police Forces in History, Vol. 2.** 1975. Sage. (OP). $12.50; pap. $6.00.

More, Harry W., Jr. **The American Police: Text and Readings.** 1976. pap. West Publishers. (OP). $6.95.

Morris, Jack. **The Deadly Routine.** (Illus.). 210p. 1980. wkbk. Palmer Publishing Co. $8.95.

Morrison, Patton N. & Hale, Charles D. **Perceptions of the Police Organization: A Sociometric Analysis.** 26p. 1974. pap. University of Oklahoma Bureau of Government Research. $1.50.

Morrison, Patton N. & Meyer, C. Kenneth. **A Microanalysis of Assaults on Police in Austin, Texas.** 1974. pap. University of Oklahoma Bureau of Government Research. $1.50.

Mosse, George L., ed. **Police Forces in History.** 1975. Sage. $17.50; pap. $8.95.

Muir, William K., Jr. **Police: Streetcorner Politicians.** (Illus.). 1977. University of Chicago Press. $15.00; pap. $6.95.

Munro, Jim L. **Administrative Behavior and Police Organization.** 1974. Anderson Publishing Co. $10.95.

Murray, Joseph A. **Police Administration and Criminal Investigation.** 3rd ed. (Orig.). 1968. Arco. $12.50; pap. $10.00.

—**Police Officer.** 8th ed. 288p. 1981. Arco. $12.00; pap. $6.95.

Mylonas, Anastassios D. **Perception of Police**

Power: A Study in Four Cities. (Illus.). 131p. (Orig.). 1974. pap. Rothman. $7.50.

National Commission On Law Observance And Enforcement. **Report on the Police, No. 14, June 26, 1931.** 1971. Repr. of 1931 ed. Arno Press. $9.00.

National Police Convention. **Official Proceedings of the National Police Convention.** 1971. Repr. of 1871 ed. Arno Press. $9.00.

Niederhoffer, Arthur. **Behind the Shield: The Police in Urban Society.** 1969. Doubleday. $2.95.

Niederhoffer, Arthur & Blumberg, Abraham S. **The Ambivalent Force.** 2nd ed. 1976. pap. Holt, Rinehart & Winston. $10.95.

Niederhoffer, Arthur & Niederhoffer, Elaine. **The Police Family.** 1978. Lexington Books. $15.95.

Norrgard, David L. **Regional Law Enforcement: A Study of Intergovernmental Cooperation and Coordination.** 1969. pap. Pub. Admin. (OP). $3.00.

O'Leary, Lawrence R. **The Selection and Promotion of the Successful Police Officer.** (Illus.). 200p. 1979. C.C. Thomas. $19.25.

Olmos, Ralph A. **An Introduction to Police-Community Relations: A Guide for the Pre-Service Student and Practicing Police Officer.** 128p. 1974. C.C. Thomas. $8.75.

Ostrom, Elinor. **Decision-Related Research on the Organization of Service Delivery Systems in Metropolitan Areas Police Protection.** 1979. codebook. Inter-University Consortium for Political & Social Research. $26.00.

Ostrom, Elinor & Parks, Roger B. **Patterns of Metropolitan Policing.** 1978. Ballinger Publishing. $18.50.

Parker, Alfred E. **The Berkeley Police Story.** 1972. (Illus.). 308p. C.C. Thomas. $12.50.

Parsons, Kevin. **Techniques of Vigilance: A Textbook for Police Self-Defense.** (Illus.). 1980. C.E. Tuttle. $35.00.

Patrick, Clarence H., ed. **Police, Crime, and Society.** 320p. 1972. C.C. Thomas. $14.50.

Patterson, Frank M. **Police Report Writing for in-Service Officers.** 156p. 1977. C.C. Thomas. $13.50.

Payton, George T. **Patrol Procedure.** 4th ed. (Illus.). 1977. Legal Book Corp. $15.00.

Peirson, Gwynne. **Police Operations.** 182p. 1976. Nelson-Hall. $16.95.

Pell, Arthur R. **Police Leadership.** (Illus.). 152p. 1967. C.C. Thomas. $4.25.

Perry. **Police in the Metropolis.** 1975. pap. Merrill. $8.50.

Petersen, David M., ed. **Police Work: Strategies and Outcomes in Law Enforcement.** (Illus.). 1979. Sage. $12.95; pap. $6.50.

Petersen, R. David. **The Police Officer in Court.** 192p. 1975. C.C. Thomas. $12.50.

Platt, Tony, et al. **The Iron Fist and the Velvet Glove: An Analysis of the U.S. Police.** 2nd ed. (Illus.). 1977. pap. Center for the Study of Crime and Social Justice. $3.50.

Polakoff, Keith I. **Police Parties in American History.** 550p. 1981 pap. Wiley, John & Sons. $14.95.

Police Foundation. **The Police.** Staufenberger, Richard A., ed. 1980. price not set prof. reference. Ballinger Publishing.

Potholm, C.P. & Morgan, R.E., eds. **Focus on Police: The Police in American Society.** 1976. Halsted Press. $18.50; pap. $6.95.

Potholm, Christian, P. & Morgan, Richard E., eds. **Focus on Police: Police in American Society.** 1976. Schenkman. $16.95; pap. $6.95.

President's Commission On Law Enforcement And Administration Of Justice. **Task Force Report: The Police.** 1971. Repr. of 1967 ed.

Arno Press. $17.00.

Price, Barbara R. **Police Professionalism.** 1977. Lexington Books. $14.50.

Proceedings of the Annual Conventions of the International Association of Chiefs of Police, 1893-1930. 5 Vols. 1971. Repr. of 1893 ed. Arno Press. $250.00.

Pursuit, Dan G., et al, eds. **Police Programs for Preventing Crime and Delinquency.** (Illus.). 512p. 1972. C.C. Thomas. $22.25; pap. $13.75.

Radano, Gene. **Stories Cops Only Tell Each Other.** 1975. pap. Stein & Day. $1.95.

Radelet, Louis. **The Police and the Community.** 1977. Glencoe. $14.95.

Reasons, Charles E., ed. **The Criminologist: Crime and the Criminal.** 1974. pap. Goodyear. (OP). $8.95.

Regens, James L., et al. **An Analysis of Assaults on Police Officers in Forty-Six South Central Cities.** 23p. 1974. pap. University of Oklahoma Bureau of Government Research. $1.50.

Reiser, Martin. **The Police Department Psychologist.** 136p. 1972. C.C. Thomas. $8.75.

—**Practical Psychology for Police Officers.** 196p. 1973. C.C. Thomas. $11.50.

Reiss, Albert J., Jr. **Police and the Public.** (Illus.). 1971. Yale University Press. $17.00; pap. $3.95.

Reith, Charles. **The Blind Eye of History: A Study of the Origins of the Present Police Era.** 1975. Patterson Smith. $11.00; pap. $4.50.

Reppetto, Thomas A. **The Blue Parade.** 1978. Free Press. $12.95.

Richardson, James. **New York Police: Colonial Times to 1901.** 1970. Oxford University Press. (OP). $10.95.

Richardson, James F. **Urban Police in the United States: A Brief History.** 225p. 1974. Kennikat Press. $12.50.

Rider, Eugene F. **Early Years of the Denver Police.** Carlton. (OP). $6.00.

Rickes, Linda & Ackerly, Sally M. **Youth Attitudes and Police.** (Illus.). 1975. West Publishing. tchr's manual $3.25; pap. $3.25.

Roberg, Roy R., ed. **The Changing Police Role: New Dimensions and New Issues.** 308p. 1976. pap. Justice Systems Development. $8.95.

Roe, George M., ed. **Our Police: A History of the Cincinnati Police Force, from the Earliest Period Until the Present Day.** Repr. of 1890 ed. AMS Press. $37.50.

Roucek, Joseph S., ed. **Sociology of Crime.** Repr. of 1961 ed. Greenwood Press. $23.75.

Rubenstein, Jonathan. **City Police.** 1980. pap. Farrar, Straus & Giroux. $8.95.

Rubenstein, Jonathan. **City Police.** 1973. Farrar, Straus & Giroux. $12.95.

—**City Police.** 480p. 1975. pap. Ballantine Books. $1.95.

Ruchelman, Leonard. **Police Politics: A Comparative Study of Three Cities.** 134p. 1974. Ballinger Publishing. $16.50.

Ruchelman, Leonard, ed. **Who Rules the Police?** 288p. 1973. NYU Press. $12.50.

Rudman, Jack. **Police Cadet.** (Career Examination Ser.: C-594). pap. National Learning Corp. $8.00.

Russell, Francis. **A City in Terror: 1919-The Boston Police Strike.** 1975. Viking Press. (OP). $10.00.

Salerno, Charles. **Police at the Bargaining Table.** 272p. 1981. C.C. Thomas. $17.75.

Salottolo, A. Lawrence. **Modern Police Service Encyclopedia.** 2nd ed. (Illus.). 1970. pap. Arco. $8.00.

San Diego Police Dept. **Police Tactics in Hazardous Situations.** 1976. pap. West Publishing (OP). $4.95.

Schaffer, Evelyn B. **Community Policing.** 1980. (Pub. by Croom Helm Ltd. England). Biblio Distribution Center. $25.00.

Schlossberg, Harry & Freeman, Lucy. **Psychologist with a Gun.** 1974. Coward, McCann & Geoghegan. (OP) $6.95.

Schultz, D.O. & Norton, L.A. **Police Operational Intelligence.** rev. ed. 244p. 1973. C.C. Thomas. $13.50.

Schultz, Donald O. & Slepecky, Michael. **Police Unarmed Defense Tactics.** (Illus.). 102p. 1973. pap. C.C. Thomas. $5.25.

Schwartz, Stephen. **Police Emergency Squad No. 1.** (Illus.). 1974. Walker & Co. (OP) $6.95.

Schwarz, John I., **Police Roadblock Operations.** (Illus.). 96p. 1962. C.C. Thomas. $5.75.

Sellin, Thorsten, ed. **Police and the Crime Problem.** 1971. Repr. of 1929 ed. Arno Press. $15.00.

Sepe, John, et al. **Cop Team.** (Orig.). 1975. pap. Pinnacle Books. (OP) $1.50.

Shane, Paul G. **Police and People: A Five Country Comparison.** (Illus.). 1980. pap. Mosby. $9.95.

Sheppard, David I. & Glickman, Albert S. **Police Careers: Constructing Career Paths for Tomorrow's Police Force.** (Illus.). 164p. 1973. C.C. Thomas. $10.25.

Sherman, Lawrence W. & National Advisory Commission on Higher Education for Police Officers. **The Quality of Police Education: A Critical Review with Recommendations for Improving Programs in Higher Education.** (Illus.). 1978. Jossey-Bass. $14.95.

Sherman, Lawrence W. & Lambert, Richard D., eds. **Police and Violence.** 1980. American Academy of Political & Social Science. $7.00; pap. $6.00.

Shoup, Donald C. & Mehay, Stephen L. **Program Budgeting for Urban Police Services: With Special Reference to Los Angeles.** 1972. Irvington. $27.50.

Siegel, Arthur I., Federman, Phillip J., and Schultz, Douglas G. **Professional Police - Human Relations Training.** 192p. 1970. C.C. Thomas. $9.75.

Sikes, Melvin P. **The Administration of Injustice.** 1975. pap. Harper & Row. $4.95.

Siljander, Raymond P. **Fundamentals of Physical Surveillance: A Guide for Uniformed and Plainclothes Personnel.** (Illus.). 288p. 1978. C.C. Thomas. $18.75.

—**Applied Police and Fire Photography.** (Illus.). 336p. 1976. C.C. Thomas. $23.75.

—**Applied Surveillance Photography.** (Illus.). 120p. 1975. C.C. Thomas. $13.50.

Skolnick, Jerome H. **Justice Without Trial: Law Enforcement in Democratic Society.** 2nd ed. 320p. 1975. pap. Wiley, John & Sons. $8.95.

Skolnick, Jerome H. & Gray, Thomas C. **Police in America.** (Illus.). 300p. 1975. pap. Little, Brown & Co. $8.95.

Smith, Bruce. **Police Systems in the United States.** rev. & enl. ed. Smith, Bruce, Jr., ed. Harper & Row. $9.95.

Smith, Bruce, ed. **New Goals in Police Management.** 1971. Repr. of 1954 ed. Arno Press. $9.00.

Smith, Ralph L. **The Tarnished Badge.** facsimile ed. 1974. Repr. of 1965 ed. Arno Press. $17.00.

Snibbe, J.R. & Snibbe, H.M. **The Urban Policeman in Transition.** (Illus.). 628p. 1973. C.C. Thomas. $21.00; pap. $15.25.

Sokol, Ronald P. **Law Abiding Policeman.** rev. 2nd ed. 1969. softbound. Michie. $3.95.

Southern California Research Council. **Crime, Police and the Judiciary in Southern California, Rpt. No. 20.** 1972. pap. Economics Research Center. (OP) $4.00.

Spielberger, Charles D. **Police Selection and Evaluation: Issues and Techniques.** 1979. Praeger. $24.50.

Sprogle, Howard O. **Philadelphia Police, Past and Present.** Repr. of 1887 ed. AMS Press. $35.00.

—**The Philadelphia Police: Past and Present.** (Illus.). Date not set. Repr. of 1887 ed. Patterson Smith. $17.50.

Stahl, O. Glenn & Staufenberger, Richard A. **Police Personnel Administration.** 1976. pap. Duxbury Press. $5.95.

Stead, Philip J., ed. **Pioneers in Policing.** (Illus.). 1978. Patterson Smith. $15.00; pap. $6.75.

Steadman, Robert F., ed. **The Police and the Community.** 112p. 1972. Johns Hopkins. $9.00; pap. $2.45.

Steinberg, J. Leonard & McEvoy, Donald, eds. **The Police and the Behavioral Sciences.** 176p. 1974. C.C. Thomas. $11.25.

Strecher, Victor G. **Environment of Law Enforcement: A Community Relations Guide.** 1971. Prentice-Hall. (OP) $5.50; pap. $3.50.

Sullivan, John L. **Introduction to Police Science.** 3rd ed. (Illus.). 1976. McGraw-Hill. $14.50; instructor's manual & key $3.50.

Sulnick, Robert H. **Civil Litigation and the Police: A Method of Communiction.** 168p. 1976. C.C. Thomas. $13.75.

Sumrall, Raymond O., et al. **The Map Abstract of Trends in Calls for Police Service: Birmingham, Alabama, 1975-1976.** 104p. 1978. spiral bdg. University of Alabama Press. $9.75.

—**Map Abstract of Crime and Requests for Police Services: Birmingham Alabama, 1975.** 75p. 1976. pap. University of Alabama Press. $5.00.

Sutor, Andrew P. **Police Operations-Tactical Approaches to Crimes in Progress.** 1976. West Publishing. $12.50.

Swanson, Cheryl & Hale, Charles D. **A Question of Height Revisited: Assaults on Police.** 12p. 1974. pap. University of Oklahoma Bureau of Government Research. $1.00.

Taylor, William & Braswell, Michael. **Issues in Police and Criminal Psychology.** 1978. pap. University Press of America. $10.00.

Territo, Leonard, et al. **The Police Personnel Selection Process.** (Illus.). 1977. pap. Bobbs-Merrill. $9.65.

Toch, Hans. **Agents of Change.** 1974. Halsted Press. $17.95; pap. $5.95.

Toch, Hans & Grant, Douglas J. **Agents of Change: A Study in Police Reform.** 1975 Schenkman. (OP) $16.25; pap. $6.25.

Training of Law Enforcement Personnel. 1971. Adult Education Assn. of the U.S.A. (OP) $2.00.

Treger, Harvey. **The Police-Social Work Team.** (Illus.). 308p. 1975 pap. C.C. Thomas. $18.00.

Turner, David R. **Police Administrative Aide.** 1974. pap. Arco. $5.00.

Twentieth Century Fund, Inc. **Law Enforcement: The Federal Role, Report of the Twentieth Century Fund Task Force on the Law Enforcement Assistance Administration.** 1976. McGraw-Hill. $6.95; pap. text ed. $3.95.

Unsinger, Peter C. & Kuykendall, Jack L. **Community Police Administration.** 475p. 1975. Nelson-Hall. $18.95.

—**Urban Police: Selected Surveys.** 1971. Repr. of 1946 ed. Arno Press. $18.00.

Vernon, Bob. **L.A. Cop - Peacemaker in Blue.** 1977. Impact Books. $4.95; pap. $2.50.

Viano, Emilio C. & Reiman, Jeffrey H., eds. **The Police in Society.** 208p. 1975. Lexington Books. $19.95.

Vickers, Robert H. **The Powers and Duties of Police Officers and Coroners.** 275p. 1975. Repr. of 1889 ed. AMS Press. $18.00.

Vollmer, August. **The Police and Modern Society.** 273p. 1971. Patterson Smith. $10.00; pap. $4.25.

Walker, Samuel. **A Critical History of Police Reform.** 1977. Lexington Books. $19.95.

Wasby, Stephen L. **Small Town Police and the Supreme Court: Hearing the Word.** 1976. Lexington Books. $19.95.

Weiner, Norman L. **The Roles of the Police in Urban Society: Conflicts and Consequences.** 1976. pap. Bobbs-Merrill. $3.35.

Weisbord, M., et al. **Improving Police Department Management Through Problem Solving Task Forces: A Case in Organization Development.** 1974. Addison-Wesley Publishing Co. $6.95.

Weistart, John C., ed. **Police Practices.** 168p. 1974. Oceana. $10.00.

Wells, Paul W. **Basic Law: For the Law Enforcement Officer.** (Illus.). 305p. 1976. Saunders. $9.75.

Westley, William A. **Violence and the Police: A Sociological Study of Law, Custom and Morality.** 1970. MIT Press. $12.50; pap. $4.95.

What Can a Police Officer Do: A Comparative Study: USA - German Federal Republic - Israel - Italy. (Illus.). xiii, 272p. (Orig.). 1974. pap. Rothman. $10.00.

Whitehouse, Jack E. **A Police Biography.** 2 vols. 1980. Set. AMS Press. $75.00.

Whittemore, L.H. **The Super Cops.** 1973. pap. Bantam Books (OP) $1.50.

Whittingham, Richard. **Joe D: On the Street with a Chicago Homicide Cop.** 288p. 1980 pap. Argus Communications. $5.95.

Wicks, Robert J. & Josephs, Ernest H. Jr. **Practical Psychology of Leadership for Criminal Justice Officers.** 128p. 1973. C.C. Thomas. $7.25.

Williams, E. W. **Modern Law Enforcement and Police Science.** (Illus.). 408p. 1967. C.C. Thomas. $19.75.

Williams, Marden E. **The Portsmouth Police Story.** 1973. Exposition Press. (OP) $6.00.

Willwerth, James. **Badge of Madness: The True Story of a Psychotic Cop.** 252p. 1977. M Evans. $8.95.

Wilson, James Q. **Varieties of Police Behavior: The Management of Law and Order in Eight Communities.** 1970. pap. Atheneum. (OP) $3.95.

—**Varieties of Police Behavior: The Management of Law and Order in Eight Communities.** 1968. Harvard University Press. $16.50; pap. $5.95.

Wilson, O.W. **Police Planning.** 2nd ed. (Illus.). 562p. 1977. C.C. Thomas. $19.75.

—**Police Records: Their Installation and Use.** 1942. Pub. Admin. (OP) $6.50.

Wintersmith, Robert. **Police and the Black Community.** 1974. Lexington Books. $16.95.

Wolf, John B. **Police Intelligence System.** 1978. pap. John Jay Press. $3.00.

Wolfe, Joan L. & Heaphy, John F., eds. **Readings in Productivity and Policing.** (Illus.). 1976. Lexington Books. $14.95.

Woods, Arthur. **Crime Prevention.** xxii, 124p. 1975. Repr. of 1918 ed. AMS Press. $9.50.

—**Policeman and Public.** 1971. Repr. of 1919 ed. Arno Press. $11.00.

—**Policeman and Public.** (Illus.). 1975. Repr. of 1912 ed. Patterson Smith. $7.50.

Wynne, G. Ray. **Police Transportation Management.** (Illus.). 1965. pap. Auto Book Press. $8.50.

Zarr, Melvyn. **Bill of Rights and the Police.** rev. ed. 1970. Oceana. $4.95.

POLICE—DATA PROCESSING

Colton, Kent W. **IRP, Vol III: Police Computer Technology.** 1978. Lexington Books. $22.95.

Murphy, John J. **Arrest by Computer: The Controversy Over Bail and Extradition.** 160p. 1975. Lexington Books. $15.95.

POLICE—EQUIPMENT AND SUPPLIES

Ayoob, Massad F. **Fundamentals of Modern Police Impact Weapons.** (Illus.). 168p. 1978. C.C. Thomas. $15.50.

Beall, James R. & Downing, Robert E. **Helicopter Utilization in Municipal Law Enforcement: Administrative Considerations.** (Illus.). 96p. 1973. C.C. Thomas. $9.75.

Bristow, Allen P. **The Search for an Effective Police Handgun.** (Illus.). 256p. 1973. C.C. Thomas. $20.00.

Chapman, Samuel G. & Peck, Gail. **Dogs in Police Work in Oklahoma.** 1978. University of Oklahoma Bureau of Government Research. $4.00.

Hansen, David A. & Kolbmann, John J. **Closed Circuit Television for Police.** 1970. C.C. Thomas. $8.75.

Kubota, Takayuki & McCaul, Paul F. **Baton Techniques and Training.** (Illus.). 320p. 1974. C.C. Thomas. $13.75.

Leonard, V.A. **The New Police Technology.** 1980. C.C. Thomas. $29.75.

Lewis, Jack. **Law Enforcement Handgun Digest.** 3rd ed. 288p. 1980. pap. Follett. $8.95.

Roberts, Willis J. & Bristow, Allen P. **Introduction to Modern Police Firearms.** Gourley, Douglas, ed. (Illus.). 1969. Glencoe. $10.95.

Robinson, Roger H. **The Police Shotgun Manual.** (Illus.). 168p. 1973. C.C. Thomas. $13.50.

Williams, Mason. **The Law Enforcement Book of Weapons, Ammunition and Training Procedures: Handguns, Rifles and Shotguns.** (Illus.). 544p. 1977. C.C. Thomas. $35.75.

POLICE—EXAMINATIONS, QUESTIONS, ETC.

Arco Editorial Board. **Lieutenant, P. D.** 6th ed. 1973. pap. Arco. $8.00.

—**Captain, Police Department.** 4th ed. (Orig.). 1967. pap. Arco. $10.00.

—**Correction Captain—Deputy Warden.** 4th ed. (Orig.). 1974. pap. Arco. $8.00.

—**Correction Officer.** 5th ed. 1975. Arco. (OP). $6.00.

—**Court Officer.** 5th ed. 1974. Arco. $7.50; pap. $8.00.

—**Patrol Inspector.** 4th ed. 1977. pap. Arco. $8.00.

—**Police Officer: Patrolman, P.D.** 7th ed. 1975. Arco. $10.00; pap. $6.00.

—**Police Promotion Course: Police Science Advancement.** 1972. pap. Arco. (OP) $10.00.

—**Police Science Advancement.** 2nd ed. 736p. 1979. pap. Arco. $15.00.

—**Probation And Parole Officer.** 3rd ed. 1978. pap. Arco. $8.00.

—**State Trooper.** 6th ed. 1978. pap. Arco. $8.00.

—**Transit Patrolman.** 4th ed. 1969. pap. Arco. (OP). $5.00.

—**Transit Sergeant-Lieutenant.** 3rd ed. (Orig.). 1967. pap. Arco. $4.00.

Eastman, George D. & Eastman, Esther M. **Municipal Police Administration.** 7th ed. 1971. International City Management Assn. (OP). $18.00.

Fricke, Charles W. **Five Thousand Criminal Definitions Terms and Phrases.** 5th ed. 1968. Legal Book Corp. $6.00.

Fricke, Charles W. & Payton, George T. **One Thousand Police Questions and Answers.** 7th ed. 1978. Legal Book Corp. $7.50.

Gocke, B. W. & Payton, George T. **Police Sergeants Manual.** 5th ed. 1972. Legal Book Corp. $14.00.

Koch, Harry W. **Facts and Strategy for Police Promotional Examinations.** 1973. Ken-Books. (OP). $5.00.

—**Police and Other Law Enforcement Examinations.** 1975. Ken-Books. $5.00.

Murray, Joseph. **Sergeant, P. D.** 6th ed. (Orig.). 1972. pap. Arco. $10.00.

Pomerance, Rocky & Legrande, James. **Police Officer Examination Test.** 1975. pap. Monarch Press. $4.95.

Rudman, Jack. **Bridge and Tunnel Officer.** (Career Examination Ser.: C-95). pap. National Learning Corp. $8.00.

—**Campus Security Officer Trainee.** (Career Examination Ser.: C-2081). 1977. pap. National Learning Corp. $8.00.

—**Capital Police Officer.** (Career Examination Ser.: C-2264). 1977. pap. National Learning Corp. $8.00.

—**Captain, Police Department.** (Career Examination Ser.: C-121). pap. National Learning Corp. $12.00.

—**Chief of Police.** (Career Examination Ser.: C-2148). 1976. pap. National Learning Corp. $12.00.

—**Commissioner of Police.** (Career Examination Ser.: C-1200). pap. National Learning Corp. $10.00.

—**Housing Sergeant.** (Career Examination Ser.: C-344). pap. National Learning Corp. $10.00.

—**Lieutenant, Police Department.** (Career Examination Ser.: C-442). pap. National Learning Corp. $10.00.

—**Patrolman - Police Department.** (Career Examination Ser.: C-576). pap. National Learning Corp. $8.00.

—**Patrolman - Policewoman.** (Career Examination Ser.: C-1922). pap. National Learning Corp. $8.00.

—**Patrolman Examinations - All States.** (Career Examination Ser.: C-575). pap. National Learning Corp. $8.00.

—**Police Administration and Supervision.** (Career Examination Ser.: CS-32). National Learning Corp. $16.00.

—**Police Administrative Aide.** (Career Examination Ser.: C-640). pap. National Learning Corp. $8.00.

—**Police Captain.** (Career Examination Ser.: C-2803). 1980. pap. National Learning Corp. $14.00.

—**Police Chief.** (Career Examination Ser.: C-2754). 1980. pap. National Learning Corp. $14.00.

—**Police Clerk.** (Career Examination Ser.: C-639). pap. National Learning Corp. $8.00.

—**Police Lieutenant.** (Career Examination Ser.: C-2802). 1980. pap. National Learning Corp. $12.00.

—**Police Officer.** (Career Examination Ser.: C-1939). 1977. pap. National Learning Corp. $8.00.

—**Police Officer - Nassau County Police Dept. (NCPD).** (Career Examination Ser.: C-1755). pap. National Learning Corp. $8.00.

—**Police Officer - New York Police Dept. (NYPD).** (Career Examination Ser.: C-1739). 1977. pap. National Learning Corp. $8.00.

—**Police Officer - Suffolk County Police Dept. (SCPD).** (Career Examination Ser.: C-1741). 1977. pap. National Learning Corp. $8.00.

—**Police Officer - Los Angeles Police Dept. (LAPD).** (Career Examination Ser.: C-2441). pap. National Learning Corp. $8.00.

—**Police Patrolman.** (Career Examination Ser.: C-595). pap. National Learning Corp. $8.00.

—**Police Promotion Course.** (1 Vol.) (Career Examination Ser.: CS-18). pap. National Learning Corp. $10.00.

—**Police Trainee.** (Career Examination Ser.: C-597). pap. National Learning Corp. $8.00.

—**Senior Capital Police Officer.** (Career Examination Ser.: C-2070). 1977. pap. National Learning Corp. $10.00.

—**Senior Fingerprint Technician.** (Career Examination Ser.: C-2073). 1977. pap. National Learning Corp. $10.00.

—**Senior Police Administrative Aide.** (Career Examination Ser.: C-1020). pap. National Learning Corp. $10.00.

—**Sergeant - Police Department.** (Career Examination Ser.: C-733). pap. National Learning Corp. $10.00.

—**Transit Captain.** (Career Examination Ser.: C-819). pap. National Learning Corp. $12.00.

—**Transit Lieutenant.** (Career Examination Ser.: C-820). pap. National Learning Corp. $10.00.

—**Transit Patrolman.** (Career Examination Ser.: C-821). pap. National Learning Corp. $8.00.

—**Transit Sergeant.** (Career Examination Ser.: C-822). pap. National Learning Corp. $10.00.

—**United States Park Police Officer.** (Career Examination Ser.: C-1989). pap. National Learning Corp. $8.00.

—**Urban Park Officer.** (Career Examination Ser.: C-1995). pap. National Learning Corp. $8.00.

Salottolo, Lawrence. **Criminal Science Handbook.** 1972. Arco. $8.00; pap. $5.00.

—**Guard-Patrolman.** 7th ed. 1975. pap. Arco. (OP). $5.00.

Turner, David R. **Police Administrative Aide.** 1974. pap. Arco. $5.00.

—**Detective Investigator.** 160p. (Orig.). 1975. pap. Arco. $6.00.

Turner, David R. **Guard-Patrolman.** 7th ed. 1975. pap. Arco. $6.00.

POLICE—HANDBOOKS, MANUALS, ETC.

Agosta, Roy. **Manual of Basic Police Firearms Instructions and Safe Handling Practices.** (Illus.). 116p. 1974. pap. C.C. Thomas. $8.75.

Allen Smith Co. Editorial Staff. **Ohio Police Officers' Manual.** 5th ed. 1979. A Smith Co. $9.00.

Basinger, Louis F. **The Techniques of Observation and Learning Retention: A Handbook for the Policeman and the Lawyer.** (Illus.). 88p. 1973. pap. C.C. Thomas. $5.00.

Berenbaum, Esai. **Municipal Public Safety: A Guide for the Implementation of Consolidated Police-Fire Services.** (Illus.) 104p. 1977. C.C. Thomas. $13.75.

Boyd, G.W. **The Will to Live: Five Steps to Officer Survival.** 1980. C.C. Thomas. $12.50.

Cappel, Robert P. **S. W. A. T. Team Manual.** (Illus.). 134p. 1979. pap. Paladin Enterprises. $10.00.

Chamelin, Neil C. & Evans, Kenneth R. **Criminal Law for Policemen.** 2nd ed. 288p. 1976. Ref. Ed. Prentice-Hall. $15.95.

Doane, Gerald G. **Hostage Negotiator's Manual.** (Illus.) pap. Police Press. $13.95.

Fricke, Charles. **Five Thousand Criminal Definitions Terms and Phrases.** 5th ed. 1968. Legal Book Corp. $6.00.

Gammage, Allen Z. & Hemphill, Charles F., Jr. **Basic Criminal Law.** 2nd ed. 1979. McGraw-Hill. $13.95; study guide $6.95; instructor's manual & key $3.00.

Gallagher, Richard & Remsberg, Charles. **Hostage Negotiation for Police: Officer Reference.** 1977. MTI Tele programs. $1.95.

Hansen, David A. & Culley, Thomas R. **Police Leader: A Handbook.** (Illus.). 128p. 1971. C.C. Thomas. $9.00.

Hendel, Ralph E. **Police Lieutenant's-Captain's Handbook.** Vol. 3. 1976. pap. Davis Publishing Co. $6.00.

—**Police Sergeant's Handbook,** Vol. 3. 1976. pap. Davis Publishing Co. $6.00.

Inbau, Fred E. & Aspen, Marvin E. **Criminal Law for the Police.** 1969. Chilton Book Co. (OP) $5.50.

Kenney, John P. & Williams, John B. **Police Operations: Policies and Procedures.** 2nd ed. (Illus.). 224p. 1973. C.C. Thomas. $10.25.

Klotter, John C. **Legal Guide for Police.** 1977. pap. Anderson Publishing Co. $6.95.

—**Techniques for Police Instructors.** 180p. 1978. C.C. Thomas. $11.50.

Klotter, John C. & Kanovitz, Jacqueline R. **Constitutional Law for Police With 1979 Supplement.** 3rd ed. 1977. Anderson Publishing Co. $18.95.

Miles, John G., Jr., et al. **The Law Officer's Pocket Manual: 1979-80 Edition.** 1980. spiral bd. Bureau of National Affairs. $4.00.

Moyer, Frank A. **Police Guide to Bomb Search Techniques.** (Illus.) 198p. (Orig.) 1980. pap. Paladin Enterprises. $12.95.

Pistole, Jesse R. **Criminal Law for Peace Officers.** 480p. 1976. Reston. $15.95.

Powis, David. **The Signs of Crime: A Field of Manual for Police.** 1978. pap. John Jay Press. $5.95.

—**Public Employee Safety Manual: Police Department.** 20p. 1974. pap. National Safety Council. $3.35.

Roth, Jordan & Downey, Robert. **Officer Survival: Arrest and Control.** (Illus.). 1976. pap. Davis Publishing Co. $8.00.

Salottolo, Lawrence. **Criminal Law: Handbook for Law Enforcement Officers.** 416 p. (Orig.) 1975. pap. Arco. $12.00.

—**Criminal Science Handbook.** 160p. 1972. Arco. $8.00; pap. $5.00.

Schmidt, J.E. **Police Medical Dictionary.** 256p. 1968. C.C. Thomas. $18.50.

Schultz, D. O. & Slepecky, M. **Police Unarmed Defense Tactics.** 102p. 1973. C.C. Thomas. $5.25.

Seitzinger, Jack M. & Kelley, Thomas M. **Police Terminology: Programmed Manual for Criminal Justice Personnel.** (Illus.) 152p. 1974. pap. C.C. Thomas. $10.25.

Spring Hill Center. **Police-Minority Community Relations: the Control and Structuring of Police Discretion.** Hoel, Donna & Ziegenhagen, John, eds. 1978. pap. Spring Hill Center. $2.50.

Tierney, Kevin. **Courtroom Testimony: A Policeman's Guide.** (Funk & W Bk.) 1970. T.Y. Crowell. $7.95.

Tobias, Marc Weber & Petersen, R. David. **A Field Manual of Criminal Law and Police Procedure.** (Illus) 212p. 1975. pap. C.C. Thomas. $15.25.

Wade, Richard C., ed. **Metropolitan Police Manuals 1871-1913: Rules and Regulations for the Government of the Richmond County Police Force, of the State of New York. New York, 1871.** Incl. Patrolman's Manual. (Philadelphia) 1913. 330p. 1974. Repr. Arno Press. $17.00.

Wright, G.R. & Marlo, J. **Police Officer and Criminal Justice.** 1970. McGraw-Hill. $12.90.

Yount, August M., Jr. **Vehicle Stops Manual.** 1976. pap. Stipes. $3.80.

POLICE—RECORDS AND CORRESPONDENCE

Cunningham, Donald H., ed. **A Reading Approach to Professional Police Writing.** (Illus.). 152p. 1972. C.C. Thomas. $11.00.

Dienstein, William. **How to Write a Narrative Investigation Report.** 128p. 1975. C.C. Thomas. $10.25.

Gammage, Allen Z. **Basic Police Report Writing.** 2nd ed. (Illus.). 344p. 1978. C.C. Thomas. $15.25.

—**Study Guide for Basic Police Report Writing.** (Illus.). 288p. 1975 pap. C.C. Thomas. $12.75.

Griffin, John I. **Statistics Essential for Police Efficiency.** (Illus.). 248p. 1972. C.C. Thomas. $11.00.

Hanna, Donald G. & Kleberg, John R. **A Police Records System for the Small Department.** 2nd ed. (Illus.). 125p. 1974. C.C. Thomas. $11.50.

Hewitt, William H. **Police Records Administration.** 1967. Lawyers Co-Operative Publishing Co. (OP). $24.95.

Kakonis, Tom E. & Hanzek, Donald. **A Practical Guide to Police Report Writing.** 1978. McGraw-Hill. pap. $7.50; teacher manual & key $3.00.

Kuhn, Charles L. **The Police Officer's Memorandum Book.** 80p. 1964 pap. C.C. Thomas. $5.00.

Leonard, V.A. **The Police Records System.** (Illus.). 104p. 1977. C.C. Thomas. $9.75.

Levie, Robert C. & Ballard, Lou E. **Writing Effective Reports on Police Investigations: Concepts, Procedures, Samples.** 1978. Allyn & Bacon. $15.95.

Nelson, John. **Preliminary Investigation and Police Reporting: A Complete Guide to Police Written Communication.** 1970. Glencoe. $14.95.

Patterson, Frank M. **Police Report Writing for In-Service Officers.** 156p. 1977. C.C. Thomas. $13.50.

Patterson, Frank M & Smith, Patrick D. **Manual of Police Report Writing.** 88p. 1977. C.C. Thomas. $8.75.

Ross, Alec & Plant, David. **Writing Police Reports: a Practical Guide.** 1977. pap. MTI Tele. $4.95.

Squires, Harry A. **Guide to Police Report Writing.** (Illus.). 104p. 1976 pap. C.C. Thomas $5.00.

POLICE—STUDY AND TEACHING

Adams, Thomas F., et al. **Criminal Justice: Organization and Management.** (Illus.). 416p. 1974. Goodyear. $19.95.

Chandler, George F., et al. **The Policeman's Art: As Taught in the New York State School for Police.** Repr. of 1922 ed. AMS Press. $15.00.

Earle, Howard H. **Police Recruit Training: Stress Vs. Non-stress: A Revolution in Law Enforcement Career Programs.** (Illus.). 240p. 1973. C.C. Thomas. $16.25; pap. $11.25.

Hansen, David A. & Culley, Thomas R. **The Police Training Officer.** (Illus.). 244p. 1973. C.C. Thomas. $12.00.

Harrison, Leonard H. **How to Teach Police Subjects: Theory and Practice.** 2nd ed. (Illus.). 132p. 1977. C.C. Thomas. $14.50.

Klotter, John C. **Techniques for Police Instructors.** 180p. 1978. C.C. Thomas. $11.50.

Peel, John D. **The Training, Licensing and Guidance of Private Security Officers.** 288p. 1973. C.C. Thomas. $13.50.

Phillips, James M. **The Nunchaku and Police Training.** 2nd ed. (Illus. Orig.). pap. J.M. Phillips. $3.95.

Police Foundation. **Progress in Policing: Essays on Change.** 1980. Ballinger Publishing. $19.50.

Saunders, Charles B., Jr. **Upgrading the American Police: Education and Training for Better Law Enforcement.** 1970. Brookings. $9.95.

Vandall, Frank J. **Police Training for Tough Calls.** 1976. pap. Center for Research in Social Change. $5.00.

Williams, Mason. **The Law Enforcement Book of Weapons, Ammunition and Training Procedures: Handguns, Rifles and Shotguns.** (Illus.). 544p. 1977. C.C. Thomas. $35.75.

POLICE—VOCATIONAL GUIDANCE

Gammage, Allen Z. **Your Future in Law Enforcement.** (gr. 7 up). 1974. Rosen Press. $5.97.

Goldreich, Gloria & Goldreich, Esther. **What Can She Be? A Police Officer.** (Illus.). 48p. (gr. K-5). 1975. Lothrop. $6.00.

Leonard, V.A. **Police Science for the Young American.** (Illus.). 80p. 1968. C.C. Thomas. $6.00.

Liston, Robert A. **Your Career in Law Enforcement.** rev. ed. (Illus.). 192p. (gr. 7 up). 1973. Messner. $7.79.

O'Leary, Lawrence R. **The Selection and Promotion of The Successful Police Officer.** (Illus.). 200p. 1979. C.C. Thomas. $19.25.

Ray, Jo A. **Careers with a Police Department.** (Illus.). 36p. (gr. k-5). 1973. Lerner Publications. $4.95.

Reuter, Margaret. **Careers in a Police Department.** (Illus.). (gr. 3-6). 1977. Raintree Publishers. $7.95.

Sheppard, David I. & Glickman, Albert S. **Police Careers: Constructing Career Paths for Tomorrow's Police Force.** (Illus.). 164p. 1973. C.C. Thomas. $10.25.

Turner, David R. **Law Enforcement Positions:** 3rd ed. (Orig.). 1975. pap. Arco. $6.00.

POLICE ADMINISTRATION

Bopp, William J.O.W.O.W. **Wilson and the Search for a Police Profession.** 1977.Kennikat Press. $12.50; pap. $7.95.

Booth, Weldon L. **Police Management of Traffic Accident Prevention Programs.** (Illus.). 360p. 1980. C.C. Thomas. $29.50.

Bouza, Anthony V. **Police Administration: Organization and Performance.** 1978. Pergamon Press. $16.50.

Carte, Gene E. & Carte, Elaine A. **Police Reform in the United States: The Era of August Vollmer, 1905-1932.** 390p. 1976. University of California Press. $12.50.

Leonard, V. A. **Police Patrol Organization.** (Illus.). 116p. 1970. C. C. Thomas. $8.00.

McCreedy, Kenneth R. **Theory and Methods of Police Patrol.** 240p. 1974. Delmar. pap. $8.40; instructor's guide $1.45.

Payton, George T. **Patrol Procedure.** 5th ed. 1977. Legal Book Corp. $15.00.

Rudman, Jack. **Patrolman - Police Department.** (Career Examination Ser.: C-576). pap. National Learning Corp. $8.00.

—**Police Patrolman.** (Career Examination Ser.: C-595). pap. National Learning Corp. $8.00.

Schultz, Donald O. **Police Pursuit Driving Handbook.** 1979. pap. Gulf Publishing $5.95.

Schwarz, J.I. **Police Roadblock Operations.** 96p. 1962. C. C. Thomas. $5.75.

Shanahan, Donald T. **Patrol Administration: Management by Objectives.** 2nd ed. 1978. pap. Allyn & Bacon. $17.50.

Siljander, Raymond P. **Fundamentals of Physical Surveillance: A Guide for Uniformed and Plainclothes Personnel.** (Illus.). 288p. 1978. C. C. Thomas. $18.75.

Turner, David R. **Guard-Patrolman.** 7th ed. 1975. pap. Arco. $6.00.

Whisenand, Paul M. **Patrol Operations.** 1971. ref. ed. pap. Prentice-Hall. $7.50.

POLICE POWER

Armstrong, Terry R. & Cinnamon, Kenneth M. **Power and Authority in Law Enforcement.** 208p. 1976. C. C. Thomas. $17.25.

Bloch, Peter B. **Equality of Distribution of Police Services: A Case Study of Washington, D.C.** 27p. 1974. pap. Urban Institute. $1.50.

Klotter, John C. **Legal Guide for Police.** 1977. pap. Anderson Publishing Co. $6.95.

Tiedeman, C. G. **Treatise on the Limitations of Police Power in the United States.** 1971. Repr. of 1886 ed. Da Capo. $42.50.

Tiedeman, Christopher G. **A Treatise on State and Federal Control of Persons and Property in the United States.** 2 vols. 2nd ed. 1975. Repr. of 1980 ed. AMS Press. Set $68.50.

POLICE QUESTIONING

Aubry, Arthur S., Jr. & Caputo, Rudolph R. **Criminal Interrogation.** 3rd ed. 464p. 1977. C. C. Thomas. $18.75.

Bristow, Allen P. **Field Interrogation.** (Illus.). 168p. 1980. C. C. Thomas. $9.75.

Inbau, Fred E. & Reid, John E. **Criminal Interrogation and Confessions.** 2nd ed. 1967. Williams & Wilkins. $17.00.

Kamisar, Yale. **Police Interrogation and Confessions: Essays in Law and Policy.** 1980. University of Michigan Press. $17.50.

Van Meter, C. H. **Principles of Police Interrogation.** (Illus.). 148p. 1973. C. C. Thomas. $10.00.

Wicks, Robert J. and Josephs, Ernest H. Jr. **Techniques in Interviewing for Law Enforcement and Corrections Personnel: A Programmed Text.** 152p. 1977. C. C. Thomas. $9.25.

POLICE SERVICES FOR JUVENILES

Bittner, Egon & Krantz, Sheldon. **Standards Relating to Police Handling of Juvenile Problems.** 1977. Ballinger Publishing. final casebound $16.50; softcover $7.95.

Flammang, C. J. **Police and the Underprotected Child.** 324p. 1970. C. C. Thomas. $15.25.

—**Police Juvenile Enforcement.** 284p. 1972. C. C. Thomas. $16.50.

Holman, Mary. **Police Officer and the Child.** (Illus.). 1962. C. C. Thomas. $5.50.

Kenney, John P. & Pursuit, Dan G. **Police Work with Juveniles and the Administration of Juvenile Justice.** 5th ed. (Illus.). 496p. 1978. C. C. Thomas. $15.25.

POLICE STRESS

Baldwin, Roger. **Inside a Cop: The Tensions in the Public and Private Lives of the Police.** (Illus.). 1977. pap. Boxwood Press. $3.95.

Earle, Howard H. **Police Recruit Training: Stress vs. Non-stress: A Revolution in Law Enforcement Career Programs.** (Illus.). 240p. 1973. C. C. Thomas. $16.25; pap. $11.25.

Ellison, Katherine, and Buckhout, Robert. **Police Stress.** 1981. Harper & Row. $11.95.

Haynes, William D. **Stress Related Disorders in Policemen.** 1978. pap. R & E Research Associates. $8.00.

Kroes, William H. **Society's Victim—the Policeman: An Analysis of Job Stress in Policing.** (Illus.). 144p. 1977. C. C. Thomas. $12.50.

Monahan, Lynn H. & Farmer, Richard E. **Stress and the Police: A Manual for Prevention.** 1981. pap. Palisades Publishing. $7.95.

Reiser, Martin. **The Police Department Psychologist.** 136p. 1972. C. C. Thomas. $8.75.

—**Practical Psychology for Police Officers.** 196p. 1973. C. C. Thomas. $11.50.

Selye, Hans. **The Stress of Life.** 2nd ed. 1978. McGraw-Hill. pap. $4.95.

POLICE TRAINING

Agosta, Roy. **Manual of Basic Police Firearms Instructions and Safe Handling Practices.** (Illus.). 116p. 1974. C. C. Thomas. $8.75.

Auten, James H. **Training in the Small Department.** 144p. 1973. C. C. Thomas. $7.50.

Adams, Thomas F., et al. **Criminal Justice: Organization and Management.** (Illus.). 416p. 1974. Goodyear. $19.95.

Chandler, George F., et al. **The Policeman's Art: As Taught in the New York State School for Police.** Repr. of 1922 ed. AMS Press. $15.00.

Earle, Howard H. **Police Recruit Training: Stress Vs. Non-stress: A Revolution in Law Enforcement Career Programs.** (Illus.). 240p. 1973. C. C. Thomas. $16.25; pap. $11.25.

Hansen, David A. & Culley, Thomas R. **The Police Training Officer.** (Illus.). 244p. 1973. C. C. Thomas. $12.00.

Harris, Richard N. **The Police Academy: An Inside View.** 202p. 1973. (Pub. by Wiley). Krieger. $14.95.

Harrison, Leonard H. **How to Teach Police Subjects: Theory and Practice.** 2nd ed. (Illus.). 132p. 1977. C. C. Thomas. $14.50.

King, Glen D. **First-Line Supervisor's Manual.** 160p. 1976. C. C. Thomas. $9.75.

Klotter, John C. **Techniques for Police Instructions.** 180p. 1978. C. C. Thomas. $11.50.

Klotter, John C. & Rosenfeld, Joseph. **Criminal Justice Instructional Techniques.** (Illus.). 216p. 1979. C. C. Thomas. $15.50.

—**Student Workbook for Criminal Justice Instructional Techniques.** 80p. 1979. pap. C. C. Thomas. $6.00.

Peel, John D. **The Training, Licensing and Guidance of Private Security Officers.** 288p. 1973. C. C. Thomas. $13.50.

Phillips, James M. **The Nunchaku and Police Training.** 2nd ed. (Illus., Orig.). pap. J. M. Phillips. $3.95.

Saunders, Charles B., Jr. **Upgrading the American Police: Education and Training for Better Law Enforcement.** 1970. Brookings. $9.95.

Vandall, Frank J. **Police Training for Tough Calls.** 1976. pap. Center for Research in Social Change. $5.00.

Williams, Mason. **The Law Enforcement Book of Weapons, Ammunition and Training Procedures: Handguns, Rifles and Shotguns.** (Illus.). 544p. 1977. C. C. Thomas. $35.75.

POLICEWOMEN

Albrecht, Mary E. & Stern, Barbara L. **The Making of a Woman Cop.** new ed. 288p. 1976. Morrow. $8.95.

Allen, Mary S. **Pioneer Policewomen.** Heyneman, Julie H., ed. Repr. of 1925 ed. AMS Press. $23.50.

Arco Editorial Board. **Policewoman.** 5th ed. 1976. pap. Arco. $6.00.

Feinman, Clarice. **Women in the Criminal Justice System.** (Illus.). 1980. Praeger. $18.95; pap. $8.95.

Fleming, Alice. **New on the Beat: Woman Power in the Police Force.** 1975. Coward, McCann & Geoghegan. (OP). $7.95.

Fooner, Michael. **Women in Policing: Fighting Crime Around the World.** (Illus.). (gr. 5 up). 1976. Coward, McCann & Geoghegan. $5.59.

Goldreich, Gloria & Goldreich, Esther. **What Can She Be? A Police Officer.** (Illus.). 48p. (gr. k-5). 1975. Lothrop. $6.00.

Hamilton, Mary E. **Policewoman: Her Service and Ideals.** 1971. Repr. of 1924 ed. Arno Press. $14.00.

Higgins, Lois L. **Policewoman's Manual.** (Illus.). 196p. 1972. C. C. Thomas. $10.25.

Horne, P. **Women in Law Enforcement.** 2nd ed. 1980. C. C. Thomas. $15.50; pap. $10.50.

Martin, Susan E. **Breaking and Entering: Policewoman on Patrol.** 275p. 1980. University of California Press. $12.95.

Muro, Diane P. **Woman on Patrol.** 128p. 1976. Judson Press. $6.95; pap. $2.95.

Owings, Chloe. **Women Police, a Study of the Development and Status of the Women Police Movement.** 1969. Repr. of 1925 ed. Patterson Smith. $12.00.

Rudman, Jack. **Policewoman.** (Career Examination Ser.: C-598). pap. National Learning Corp. $8.00.

Schnabel, Martha. **Officer Mama.** (Illus.). 1973. Naylor. (OP). $7.95.

Uhnak, Dorothy. **Policewoman.** pap. Pocket Books. $1.95.

—**Policewoman.** 1964. Simon & Schuster. $4.50.

RAPE

Addams, Jane & Wells, Ida B. **Lynching and Rape: An Exchange of Views.** Aptheker, Bettina, ed. 1977. American Institute for Marxist Studies. $1.25.

Barnes, Dorothy L. **Rape: A Bibliography 1965-1975.** 1977. Whitston Publishing. $15.00.

Bode, Janet. **Fighting Back: How to Cope with the Medical, Emotional, Legal Consequences of Rape.** 1978. Macmillan. $8.95.

Booher, Dianna D. **Rape: What Would You Do If . . .?** 192p. 1981. Messner, Julian. price not set.

Cizankas, Victor I. & Hanna, Donald G. **Modern Police Management Organization.** (Illus.). 256p. 1977. Prentice-Hall. $14.95.

Cohen, Robert, et al. **Working with Police Agencies.** 1976. Human Sciences Press. $16.95.

Colton, Kent W. **IRP, VOL. III: Police Computer Technology.** 1978. Lexington Books. $22.95.

Davis, Edward M. **Staff One: Perspectives on Effective Police Management.** (Illus.). 1978. Prentice-Hall. $14.95; pap. $10.95.

Eastman, George D. & Chapman, Samuel G. **Short of Merger: Countywide Police Resource Pooling.** (Illus.). 1976. Lexington Books. $16.95.

Enloe, Cynthia. **Police, Military, and Ethnicity.** 1980. Transaction Books. $14.95.

Fabreau, Donald F. & Gillespie, Joseph E. **Modern Police Administration.** (Illus.). 1978. Prentice-Hall. $15.95.

Felkenes, George T., ed. **Effective Police Supervision: A Behavioral Approach.** 1977. pap. Justice Systems Development. $8.95.

Gaines, Larry K. & Ricks, Truett A. **Managing the Police Organization: Selected Readings.** (Illus.). 1978. pap. West Publishing. $13.95.

Garmire, Bernard L., ed. **Local Government Police Management.** (Illus.). 1977. International City Management Assn. $25.00.

Gocke, B.W. & Payton, George T. **Police Sergeants Manual.** 5th ed. 1972. Legal Book Corp. $14.00.

Hale, Charles D. **Fundamentals of Police Administration.** 1977. Holbrook Press. instructor's manual free. $15.95.

Hanna, Donald G. & Gentel, William D. **A Guide to Primary Police Management Concepts.** (Illus.). 208p. 1971. C.C. Thomas. $12.50.

Hansen, David A. & Culley, Thomas R. **The Police Leader: A Handbook.** (Illus.). 128p. 1971. C.C. Thomas. $9.00.

Jansen, Frances O. & Johns, Ruth. **Management and Supervision of Small Jails.** (Illus.). 360p. 1978. C.C. Thomas. $22.25.

Kenney, John P. **Police Administration.** (Illus.). 376p. 1975. C.C. Thomas. $16.00.

King, Glen D. **First-Line Supervisor's Manual.** 160p. 1976. C.C. Thomas. $9.75.

Klotter, John C. **Legal Guide for Police.** 1977. pap. Anderson Publishing Co. $6.95.

Kornblum, Allan N. **The Moral Hazards: Police Strategies for Honesty and Ethical Behavior.** 224p. 1976. Lexington Books. $21.95.

Krantz, Sheldon, et al. **Police Policymaking: The Boston Experience.** 1979. Lexington Books. $25.95.

Leonard, V.A. **Police Personnel Administration.** 144p. 1970. C.C. Thomas. $9.75.

Lynch, Ronald G. **The Police Manager: Professional Leadership Skills.** 2nd ed. 1978. Allyn & Bacon. $17.50.

More, Harry W., Jr. **Effective Police Administration: A Behavioral Approach.** 2nd ed. (Illus.). 1979. West Publishing. $18.50.

Mulhearn, Henry J. **Police Supervision.** 1976 pap. Gould. $7.50.

Munro, Jim L. **Administrative Behavior and Police Organization.** 1974. Anderson Publishing Co. $10.95.

Pelissero, John. **Recruitment and Selection Practices in Oklahoma Police Departments.** 47p. 1978. University of Oklahoma Bureau of Government Research. $3.00.

Roberg, Roy R. **Police Management and Organizational Behavior: A Contingency Approach.** (Illus.). 1979. West Publishing. $18.50.

Schultz, Donald O., ed. **Modern Police Administration.** 1979. Gulf Publishing. $12.95.

Schwartz, Alfred I., et al. **Employing Civilians for Police Work.** 1975. pap. Urban Institute. $3.50.

Sheehan, Robert & Cordner, Gary W. **Introduction to Police Administration: A Systems and Behavioral Approach with Case Studies.** (Illus.). 1979. instr's guide with tests. Addison-Wesley Publishing Co. $15.95; instr's guide with tests. $2.50.

Souryal, Sam. **Police Administration and Management.** 1977. West Publishing. $17.50.

Tansik & Elliot. **Managing Police Organizations.** (Illus.). 250p. 1981. pap. Duxbury Press. $9.95.

Tielsch, George & Whisenand, Paul M. **The Assessment Center Approach in the Selection of Police Personnel.** (Orig.). pap. Davis Publishing Co. $9.50.

Truitt, John. **Dynamics of Police Administration.** 1978. pap. Anderson Publishing Co. $8.95.

Unsinger, Peter C. & Kuykendall, Jack L. **Community Police Administration.** 475p. 1975. Nelson-Hall. $18.95.

Ward, Richard H. & McCormack, Robert. **An Anti-Corruption Manual for Administrators in Law Enforcement.** 1979. pap. John Jay Press. $4.95.

Whisenand, P. **The Effective Police Manager.** 1981. Prentice-Hall. $16.95.

Whisenand, Paul M. & Ferguson, R. Fred. **The Managing of Police Organizations.** 2nd ed. (Illus.). 1978. Prentice-Hall. $17.95.

Wilson, O.W. & McLaren, Roy C. **Police Administration.** 4th ed. 1977. McGraw-Hill. $19.95.

POLICE COMMUNICATIONS SYSTEMS

Burton, Alan. **Police Telecommunications.** (Illus.) 452p. 1973. C.C. Thomas. $18.00.

Felkenes, George T. & Whisenand, Paul M. **Police Patrol Operations.** 300p. 1972. pap. McCutchan. $6.95.

Leon, George & Sands, Leo G. **Dial 911: Modern Emergency Communications Networks.** (Illus.). 128p. 1975 pap. Hayden Book Co. $3.95.

Leonard, V.A. **The New Police Technology: Impact of the Computer and Automation on Police Staff and Line Performance.** (Illus.). 384p. 1980. C.C. Thomas. $29.75.

—**The Police Communications System.** 96p. 1970 C.C. Thomas. $7.50.

Rieder, Robert J. **Law Enforcement Information Systems.** (Illus.). 272p. 1972. C.C. Thomas. $14.25.

Rudman, Jack. **Police Dispatcher.** (Career Examinations Ser.: C-2256). 1977 pap. National Learning Corp. $8.00.

Tobias, Marc W. **Police Communications.** (Illus.). 650p. 1974. C.C. Thomas. $35.00; pap. $25.00.

POLICE CORRUPTION

Armstrong, Michael, frwd., by. **The Knapp Commission Report on Police Corruption.** 1973. Braziller. $10.00; pap. $5.95.

Barker, Thomas & Roebuck, Julian. **An Empirical Typology of Police Corruption: A Study in Organizational Deviance.** 80p. 1973. C.C. Thomas. $8.75.

Beigel, Herbert & Beigel, Allan. **Beneath the Badge: A Story of Police Corruption.** 1977. Harper & Row. $15.00.

Bollens, John C. & Schmandt, Henry J. **Political Corruption: Power, Money, and Sex.** 1979. Palisades Publishing. $9.95.

Douglas, Jack D. & Johnson, John M., eds. **Official Deviance: Readings in Malfeasance, Misfeasance and Other Forms of Corruption.** 1977. pap. Harper & Row. $8.50.

Duchaine, Nina. **The Literature of Police Corruption. A Selected, Annotated Bibliography, Vol. II.** 1979. John Jay Press. $10.00.

Sherman, Lawrence W. **Scandal and Reform: Controlling Police Corruption.** 1978. University of California Press. $15.75.

Simpson, Antony E. **The Literature of Police Corruption: Vol. I, a Guide to Bibliography and Theory.** 1977. John Jay Press. $10.00.

Smith, Ralph L. **The Tarnished Badge.** facsimile ed. 1974. Repr. of 1965 ed. Arno Press. $17.00.

Special Grand Jury, Commonwealth of Pennsylvania. **Investigation of Vice, Crime and Law Enforcement.** facsimile ed. 1974. Repr. of 1939 ed. Arno Press. $15.00.

POLICE DOGS

Chapman, Samuel G. **Dogs in Police Work: A Summary of Experience in Great Britain and the United States.** (Illus.). 1960. pap. Pub. Admin. $3.00.

Chapman, Samuel G. & Peck, Gail. **Dogs in Police Work in Oklahoma.** 1978. University of Oklahoma Bureau of Government Research. $4.00.

Handel, Leo H. **Dog Named Duke: True Stories of German Shepherds at Work with the Law.** (Illus.). (gr. 7-9). 1966. Lippincott. $8.95.

Rapp, Jay. **How to Train Dogs for Police Work.** 1979. Denlingers. $14.95; pap. $9.95.

Watson, Sam D., Jr. **Dogs for Police Service: Programming and Training.** (Illus.). 100p. 1972. C.C. Thomas. $8.25.

POLICE PATROL

Adams, T. **Police Patrol: Tactics and Techniques.** 1971 ref. ed. Prentice-Hall. $15.95.

Applegate, Rex. **Scouting and Patrolling.** (Illus.). 117p. 1980. Paladin Enterprises. $15.95.

Bristow, Allen P. **Field Interrogation.** 2nd ed. (Illus.). 168p. 1972. C. C. Thomas. $9.75.

Cawley, Donald F. & Miron, H. Jerome. **Managing Patrol Operations.** 1980. write for info. Lexington Books.

Chapman, Samuel G. **Police Patrol Readings.** 2nd ed. 788p. 1972. pap. C. C. Thomas. $21.50.

Clowers, Norman L. **Patrolman Patterns, Problems, and Procedures.** 308p. 1971. C. C. Thomas. $12.00.

Colton, Kent W. **IRP, Vol. III: Police Computer Technology.** 1978. Lexington Books. $22.95.

Elliott, J. F. **Interception Patrol: An Examination of the Theory of Random Patrol As a Municipal Police Tactic.** (Illus.). 88p. 1973. C. C. Thomas. $6.00.

Felkenes, George T. & Whisenand, Paul M. **Police Patrol Operations.** 300p. 1972. pap. McCutchan. $6.95.

Folley, Vern L. **Police Patrol Techniques and Tactics.** 192p. 1974. C. C. Thomas. $12.50.

Gourley, G. Douglas. **Patrol Administration.** 2nd ed. (Illus.). 400p. 1974. C. C. Thomas. $15.25.

Hale, Charles D. **Police Patrol: Operations and Management.** 300p. 1981. Wiley, John & Sons. $13.95.

Holcomb, Richard L. **Police Patrol.** (Illus.). 128p. 1971. C. C. Thomas. $5.75.

Larson, Richard C. **Urban Police Patrol Analysis.** 256p. 1972. MIT Press. $16.50.

Brownmiller, Susan. **Against Our Will.** 544p. 1976. pap. Bantam Books. $2.95.

—**Against Our Will.** 480p. 1975. Simon & Schuster. $12.95.

Burgess, Ann W. & Holmstrom, Lynda L. **Rape; Crisis and Recovery.** (Illus.). 350p. 1979. pap. R.J. Brady. $13.95.

—**Rape: Victims of Crisis.** 250p. 1974. R.J. Brady. $9.95; pap. $7.95.

Chappell, Duncan, et al. **Forcible Rape. The Crime, the Victim, and the Criminal.** 1977. Columbia University Press. $20.00; pap. $9.00.

de River, J. Paul. **Crime and the Sexual Psychopath.** (Illus.). 384p. 1958. C.C. Thomas. $8.75.

Eyman, Joy S. **How to Convict a Rapist.** 288p. 1980. Stein & Day. $9.95.

Feidl, Hubert S. & Bienen, Leigh B. **Jurors and Rape: A Study in Psychology and Law.** (Illus.). 1980. Lexington Books. price not set.

Gilder, George. **Visible Man.** 1978. Basic Books. $10.95.

Goldberg, Jacob A. & Goldberg, Rosamond W. **Girls on the City Streets: A Study of 1400 Cases of Rape.** 384p. 1974. Repr. of 1935 ed. Arno Press. $22.00.

Griffin, Susan. **Rape: The Power of Consciousness.** 1979. pap. Harper & Row. $3.95.

Groth, A. N. **Men Who Rape: The Psychology of the Offender.** 245p. 1979. Plenum Publishing. $15.00.

Halpern, S. **Rape: Helping the Victim.** 1978. Medical Economics Co. Book Division. $14.95.

Hilberman, Elaine. **The Rape Victim.** 1976. Basic Books. $8.95.

—**The Rape Victim.** 1976. American Psychiatric Assn. $7.95; pap. $5.00.

Holmstrom, Lynda L. & Burgess, Ann W. **The Victim of Rape: Institutional Reactions.** 1978. (Pub. by Wiley-Interscience). Wiley, John & Sons. $17.95.

Horos, Carol V. **Rape: The Private Crime, a Social Horror.** Tucker, Tarvez, ed. (Illus.). 130p. 1974. Tobey Publishing. $5.95; pap. $2.95.

—**Rape.** rev. ed. 208p. 1981. pap. Dell. $2.50.

Hursch, Carolyn J. **The Trouble with Rape: A Psychologist's Report on the Legal, Medical, Social, and Psychological Problems.** (Illus.). 1977. Nelson-Hall. $9.95; pap. $5.95.

Hyde, Margaret O. **Speak Out on Rape.** 160p. (Orig.). (gr. 7-12). 1975. McGraw-Hill. $6.95.

Katz, Sedelle & Mazur, Mary Ann. **Understanding the Rape Victim: A Synthesis of Research Findings.** 1979. (Pub. by Wiley-Interscience). Wiley, John & Sons. $22.95.

Kemmer, Elizabeth J. **Rape and Rape Related Issues: An Annotated Bibliography.** 1977. Garland Publishing. $22.00.

McCahill, Thomas W. & Meyer, Linda C. **The Aftermath of Rape.** (Illus.). 288p. 1979. Lexington Books. $21.95.

McCombie, S. L., ed. **The Rape Crisis Intervention Handbook: A Guide to Victim Care.** (Illus.). 250p. 1980. Plenum Publishing. $19.50.

Macdonald, John M. **Rape: Offenders and Their Victims.** 352p. 1979. C.C. Thomas. $19.25.

Medea, Andrea & Thompson, Kathleen. **Against Rape.** 1974. pap. Farrar, Straus & Giroux. $8.95.

Mills, Patrick. **Rape Intervention Resource Manual.** (Illus.). 300p. 1977. C.C. Thomas. $18.75.

Nass, Deanna. **The Rape Victim.** 1977. pap. Kendall-Hunt. $5.95.

Pekkanen, John. **Victims: An Account of a Rape.** 288p. 1976. Dial Press. $8.95.

—**Victims: An Account of a Rape.** 1977. pap. Popular Library. $1.95.

Qureshi, Donna I. **Rape: Social Facts from England and America.** 293p. 1979. write for info. pap. Stipes.

Rada, Richard T., ed. **Clinical Aspects of the Rapist.** 1977. Grune & Stratton. $24.25.

—**Rape: Preventing It; Coping with the Legal, Medical, and Emotional Aftermath.** (gr. 7 up). 1979. Watts, Franklin, Inc. $5.90.

Reston, James. **The Innocence of Joan Little.** 1977. Times Books. $12.50.

Richards, Dell-Fitzgerald. **The Rape Journal.** 1974. Diana Press. $.75.

Roucek, Joseph S. **Sexual Attack and the Crime of Rape.** rev. ed. Rahmas, D. Steve, ed. 32p. 1980. SamHar Press. $2.75 incl. catalog cards; pap. $1.50 vinyl laminated covers.

Russell, Diana E. **Politics of Rape.** 1975. pap. Stein & Day. $6.95.

Sanders, William B. **Rape and Woman's Identity.** (Illus.). 184p. 1980. Sage. $18.00; pap. $8.95.

Sanford, Linda Tschihart & Fetter, Ann. **In Defense of Ourselves.** 1979. Doubleday. $5.95.

Scacco, Anthony M., Jr. **Rape in Prison.** 144p. 1975. C.C. Thomas. $13.50.

Schneider, Harriet R. **I Was a Victim.** 1978. Vantage Press. $5.95.

Schultz, LeRoy G. **Rape Victimology.** 424p. 1975. C.C. Thomas. $35.50.

Smart, Carol. **Women, Crime and Criminology: A Feminist Critique.** 1978. pap. Routledge & Kegan. $6.95.

Smith, A. Robert & Giles, James V. **An American Rape: A True Account of the Giles-Johnson Case.** (Illus.). 300p. 1975. New Republic Book. $10.00; pap. $4.95.

Smith, James. **Rapists Beware.** 1979. Green. $15.00.

Smith, James. A. **Rapist Beware.** (Illus.). 1980. pap. Macmillan. $6.95.

Storaska, Frederic. **How to Say No to a Rapist — and Survive.** 224p. 1976. pap. Warner Books. $1.95.

—**How to Say No to a Rapist and Survive.** 1975. Random House. $9.95.

Walker, Marcia J. & Brodsky, Stanley L. **Sexual Assault: The Victim and the Rapist.** (Illus.). 208p. 1976. Lexington Books. $17.95.

Walker, Marcia J. & Brodsky, Stanley L., eds. **Sexual Assault.** 1978. pap. Heath. $6.95.

Warner, Carmen G. **Rape and Sexual Assault: Management and Intervention.** (Illus.). 364p. 1980. Aspen Systems. $22.50.

Wilson, Cassandra & Connell, Noreen. **Rape: The First Sourcebook for Women.** (Orig.). 1974. pap. NAL. $3.95.

Wilson, Paul R. **The Other Side of Rape.** 1978. University of Queensland Press. $14.50; pap. $7.25.

REPORT WRITING

Agnos, T.J. & Schatt, S. **The Practical Law Enforcement Guide to Writing Field Reports, Grant Proposals, Memos, and Resumes.** 1980. pap. C.C. Thomas. write for info.

Cox, C. Robinson. **Criminal Justice: Improving Police Report Writing.** 1977. pap. Interstate. $8.95; student manual, instructor's manual. $1.75.

Cunningham, Donald H., ed. **A Reading Approach to Professional Police Writing.** (Illus.) 152p. 1972. C.C. Thomas. $11.00.

Dienstein, William. **How to Write a Narrative Investigation Report.** 128p. C.C. Thomas. $10.25.

Gammage, Allen Z. **Basic Police Report Writing** 2nd ed. 344 p. 1978. C.C. Thomas. $15.25.

—**Study Guide for Basic Police Report Writing** (Illus.) 288p. 1975. C.C. Thomas. $12.75.

Hess, Karen M. & Wrobleski, Henry M. **For the Record: Report Writing in Law Enforcement.** 1978. pap. Wiley, John & Sons. $6.95.

Kakonis, Tom E. & Hanzek, Donald A. **Practical Guide to Police Report Writing.** 1978. McGraw-Hill. teacher manual & key. $3.00; pap. $7.50.

Levie, Robert C. & Ballard, Lou E. **Writing Effective Reports on Police Investigations: Concepts, Procedures, Samples.** 1978. Allyn & Bacon. $15.95.

Nelson, John. **Preliminary Investigation and Police Reporting: A Complete Guide to Police Written Communication.** 1970. Glencoe. $14.95.

Patterson, Frank M. **Police Report Writing for In-Service Officers.** 156p. 1977. C.C. Thomas. $13.50.

Patterson, Frank M. & Smith, Patrick D. **Manual of Police Report Writing.** 88p. 1977. C. C. Thomas. $8.75.

Ross, Alec & Plant, David. **Writing Police Report and Practical Guide.** pap. 1977. MTI Teleprograms. $4.95.

Squires, Harry. **A Guide to Police Report Writing.** (Illus.). 104p. 1976. pap. C.C. Thomas. $5.00.

REVOLVERS

Askins, Charles. **Askins on Pistols and Revolvers.** Bryant, Ted & Askins, Bill, eds. 144p. 1980. National Rifle Association. $25.00; pap. $8.95.

Chamberlain, W. H. & Taylerson, A. W. **Adams' Revolvers.** 1978. (Dis. by Arco) Barrie & Jenkins. $29.95.

Grennel, Dean A., ed. **Pistol and Revolver Digest.** 2nd ed. (Illus.) 1979. pap. DBI Books. $7.95.

Hertzberg, Robert. **The Modern Handgun.** 1977. Arco $4.95; pap. $2.50.

Hogg, I. V. **Military Pistols and Revolvers.** (Illus.). 1970. Arco. $3.50; pap. $1.95.

James, Garry, ed. **Guns of the Gunfighters.** (Illus.). 1975. pap. Petersen Publication. (OP). $4.95.

Millard, J. T. **A. Handbook on the Primary Identification of Revolvers and Semi-Automatic Pistols** (Illus.) 168p. 1974. C.C. Thomas. $13.50; pap. $10.25.

Neal, Robert J. & Jinks, Roy G. **Smith and Wesson, 1857-1945.** rev. ed. 400p. 1975. A.S. Barnes. $25.00.

Nonte, George C. **Pistol and Revolver Guide.** 3rd ed. 1975. softbound. Stoeger. (OP) $6.95.

—**The Revolver Guide.** (Illus.). 1980. pap. Stoeger. $8.95.

Report of Board on Test of Revolvers and Automatic Pistols 1907. (Illus.). Sand Pond. $3.00

Rywell, Martin. **American Nickel-Plated Revolver (1870-1890).** Pioneer Press. (OP). $1.25.

Scott, Robert F., ed. **1982 Shooter's Bible.** No. 73 (Illus.). 1981. pap. Stoeger. $10.95.

William, Mason. **The Sporting Use of the Handgun.** (Illus.). 288p. 1979. CC. Thomas. $14.95.

RIFLES

Archer, Denis. **Jane's Pocket Book of Rifles and Light Machine Guns.** 1977. pap. Macmillan. $6.95.

Barnes, Duncan. **History of Winchester Firearms 1866 to 1980.** rev. ed (Illus). 272p. 1980. Winchester Press. $21.95.

Beard, Ross E., Jr. **Carbine: The Story of David Marshall Williams.** 1977. Sandlapper Store. $12.50; ltd. ed, signed $25.00.

Behn, Jack. **Fourty-Five - Seventy Rifles.** Repr. of 1956 ed. Gun Room Press. $7.95.

Buchele, William & Shumway, George. **Recreating the American Longrifle.** 3rd ed. (Illus.) 110p. pap. George Shumway Publisher. $10.00.

Carmichael, Jim. **The Modern Rifle.** (Illus.) 352p. 1976. Stoeger. pap. $5.95.

Carmichael, Jim. **The Modern Rifle.** (Illus.) 1975. Winchester Press. $12.50.

Chamberlain, Peter & Gander, Terry. **Allied Pistols, Rifles and Grenades.** 1976. pap. Arco. $3.95.

—**Axis Pistols, Rifles, and Grenades,** 1977. pap. Arco. $4.95.

—**Submachine Guns and Automatic Rifles: World War 2 Facts Ser.** 1976. pap. Arco. $3.95.

Colby, C. B. **Firearms by Winchester: A Part of U.S. History.** (Illus.) (gr. 4-7). 1957. Coward, McCann & Geoghegan. $5.29.

—**First Rifle: How to Shoot It Straight and Use It Safely.** (Illus.) (gr. 4-7). 1954. Coward, McCann & Geoghegan. $5.29.

Davis, Henry. **A Forgotten Heritage: The Story of the Early American Rifle.** 1976. Repr. of 1941 ed. Gun Room Press. $9.95.

Edsall, James. **The Golden Age of Single Shot Rifles.** Pioneer Press. $2.75.

—**The Revolver Rifles.** Pioneer Press. $2.50.

Grant, James J. **More Single Shot Rifles.** (Illus.). Gun Room Press. $12.50.

—**Still More Single Shot Rifles.** 1979. Pioneer Press. $17.50.

Hanson. **The Plains Rifle.** Gun Room Press. $11.95.

Hatcher, Julian S. **The Book of the Garand.** new ed. Edwards, Douglas & Wick, Patricia, eds. (Illus.). 1977. Repr. of 1948 ed. Pine Mountain Press. $22.50.

Huddleston, Joe D. **Colonial Riflemen in the American Revolution.** (Illus.) 70p. 1978. George Shumway Publsher. $18.00.

Kindig, Joe. Jr. **Thoughts on the Kentucky Rifle in its Golden Age.** annotated 2nd ed. (Illus.). 561p. 1980 George Shumway Publisher. $59.50.

Lachuk, John. **The Gun Digest Book of the .22 Rimfire.** 1978. pap. DBI Books. $6.95.

Madis, George. **The Winchester Book.** 3rd ed (Illus.). 1979. Art & Reference House. $39.50.

O'Connor, Jack. **Complete Book of Rifles and Shotguns.** rev. ed. (Illus.). 1966. Harper & Row. $12.50.

—**Hunting Rifle.** (Illus.) 1970. Winchester Press. $10.95.

—**Hunting Rifle.** (Illus.) 1975. pap. Stoeger. $7.95.

—**The Rifle Book** 3rd ed. (Illus.). 1978. Knopf. $13.95; pap. $7.95.

Olson, John. **John Olson's Book of the Rifle.** (Illus.). 1974. O'Hara. (OP). $9.95; pap. $5.95.

Otteson, Stuart. **The Bolt Action: A Design Analysis.** 1974. Winchester Press. $12.95.

Page, Warren. **The Accurate Rifle.** Winchester Press. $8.95.

—**The Accurate Rifle.** 1975. pap. Stoeger. $5.95.

Perkins, Jim. **American Boys Rifles.** 1980. pap. Collector Books. $9.95.

Petzal, David. **.22 Caliber Rifle.** (Illus.) 1973. Winchester Press. $6.95.

Pullum, Bill & Hanenkrat, Frank T. **Position Rifle Shooting.** 1973. Winchester Press. (OP). $10.00

Roberts, Ned H. **The Muzzle-Loading Cap Lock Rifle.** (Illus.). 306p. 1978. Repr. George

Shumway Publisher. $24.50.

Rywell, Martin **American Antique Rifles.** Pioneer Press. $2.00.

—**U.S. Muskets, Rifles and Carbines.** Pioneer Press. $2.00

Schedelmann, Hans. **Vienna Kunsthistorisches Die Grossen Buchsenmacher.** (Illus.) 1976. Arma Press. $235.00.

Scott, Robert F., ed. **1982 Shooter's Bible.** No. 73. (Illus.). 1981. pap. Stoeger. $10.95.

Shumway, George. **Pennsylvania Longrifles of Note.** (Illus.). 63p. 1977. George Shumway Publisher. $6.50.

—**Rifles of Colonial America,** 2 vols. (Illus.). 352p. 1980. George Shumway Publisher. casebound ea. $49.50.

—**Rifles of Colonial America,** 2 vols. (Illus.). 352p. (Vol. 1, 352 pp. vol. 2, 288 pp.). George Shumway Publisher. 1980. Vol. 1., Vol. 2. $49.50.

Steindler, R.A. **The Rifle Guide.** (Illus.) 1978. pap. Stoeger. $8.95.

Taylor. **African Rifles and Cartridges.** Gun Room Press. $16.95.

U.S. Rifle Caliber .30 Model 1903. Pioneer Press. $2.00.

U.S. Rifle Model 1866 Springfield. Pioneer Press. 75¢.

U.S. Rifle Model 1870 Remington. Pioneer Press. 75¢.

Wahl, Paul. **Carbine Handbook.** (Illus., Orig.). 1964. Arco. (OP). $6.00; pap. $4.95.

Wallack, L.R. **American Rifle Design and Performance.** 1977. Winchester Press. $14.95.

Waterman, Charles. **The Treasury of Sporting Guns.** (Illus.). 1979. Random House. $24.95.

West, Bill. **Know Your Winchesters: General Use, All Models and Types, 1849-1969.** (Illus.) B. West. $12.00.

—**Winchester-Complete: All Wins and Forerunners, 1849-Date.** (Illus.) 1975. B. West. $33.00.

—**Winchester Encyclopedia.** (Illus.). B. West. $12.00.

—**Winchester Lever-Action Handbook.** (Illus.). B. West. $29.00.

—**The Winchester Single Shot.** (Illus.). B. West. $12.00.

—**Winchester, Cartridges, and History.** (Illus.). B West. $29.00.

Williamson, Harold F. **Winchester: The Gun That Won the West.** (Illus.). 1978. pap. A. S. Barnes. $10.95.

Wood, J. B. **Troubleshooting Your Rifle and Shotgun.** (Illus.). 1978. pap. Follett. $5.95.

The World's Assault Rifles. TBN Enterprises. $19.95.

RIOT CONTROL

Applegate, Rex. **Riot Control: Material and Techniques.** 4th rev. ed. (Illus.). 320p. 1981. Paladin Enterprises. $15.95.

Bassiouni, M. Cherif. **The Law of Dissent and Riots.** 510p. 1971. C.C. Thomas. $31.25.

Deane-Drummond, Anthony. **Riot Control.** 158p. 1975. Crane-Russak Co. $10.95.

Farmer, David J. **Civil Disorder Control.** 1968. pap. Pub Admin. (OP). $3.00.

Momboisse, Raymond M. **Community Relations and Riot Prevention.** (Illus.). 272p. 1974. C.C. Thomas. $13.50.

—**Riots, Revolts and Insurrections.** (Illus.). 544p. 1977. C.C. Thomas. $15.25.

ROBBERY

Astor, Gerald. **Hot Paper.** 1976. Sat Rev Pr. (OP). $8.95.

Behn, Noel. **Big Stick-Up at Brink's!** (Illus.). 1977. Putnam. $10.00.

—**The Brinks Job.** (Illus.). 1978. pap. Warner Books. $2.50.

Conklin, John E. **Robbery and the Criminal Justice System.** 250p. 1972. Lippincott. $5.75; pap. $2.75.

David, Pedro R., ed. **The World of the Burglar: Five Criminal Lives.** 298p. 1974. University of New Mexico Press. $10.00.

Defoe, Daniel. **Street-Robberies Consider'd: The Reason of Their Being So Frequent.** Sill, Geoffrey M., ed. (Illus.). 1973. pap. Carolingian Press. $4.95.

Greene, A.C. **The Santa Claus Bank Robbery.** 1972. Knopf. (OP) $6.95.

Hall, Stuart, et al. **Policing the Crisis: Mugging, the State, and Law and Order.** Roberts, Brian, ed. 1978. Holmes & Meier. $34.75; pap. $14.50.

Macdonald, John M. **Armed Robbery: Offenders and Their Victims.** 456p. 1975. C.C. Thomas. $23.75.

—**Burglary and Theft.** 320p. 1980. C.C. Thomas. $19.75.

National Commission on the Causes & Prevention of Violence. **Violent Crime.** 1970. pap. Braziller. $2.50.

Pinkerton, Allan. **The Expressman and the Detective.** (Illus.). 1976. Repr. of 1875 ed. Arno Press. $16.00.

Webb, Donald G. **Investigation of Safe and Money Chest Burglary.** (Illus.). 124p. 1975. C.C. Thomas. $16.00.

SEARCHES AND SEIZURES

Bassiouni, M. Cherif. **Citizen's Arrest: The Law of Arrest, Search and Seizure for Private Citizens and Private Police.** (Illus.). 144p. 1977. C.C.Thomas. $15.25; pap. $10.25.

Berry, Calvin W. **Arrest, Search and Seizure.** 234p. 1973. Michie. $25.00.

Creamer, J. **The Law of Arrest.** 3rd ed. 653p. 1980. pap. Holt, Rinehart & Winston. $12.95.

Davis, Rex D. **Federal Searches and Seizures.** 1964. C.C. Thomas. (OP). $12.00.

Gardner, Thomas J. & Victor, M. **Principles and Cases of the Law of Arrest, Search, and Seizure.** (Illus.). 552p. 1974. McGraw-Hill. $14.95; instructor's manual $3.00.

Griswold, Erwin N. **Search and Seizure: A Dilemma of the Supreme Court.** 1976. University of Nebraska Press. $7.50.

Harding, Arthur L., ed. **Fundamental Law in Criminal Prosecutions.** 1959. Southern Methodist University Press. $4.00.

Hermann, Michele G. **Search and Seizure Checklists.** 1979. pap. Boardman. $10.00.

Hirschel, Joseph D. **Fourth Amendment Rights.** (Illus.). 1979. Lexington Books. $16.95.

Landynski, Jacob W. **Search and Seizure and the Supreme Court: A Study in Constitutional Interpretation.** 1966. John Hopkins. (OP). $16.00.

Lasson, Nelson B. **History and Development of the Fourth Amendment to the United States Constitution.** 1970. Repr. of 1937 ed. Da Capo. $20.00.

Lundgren, R. V. **Lundgren's Handbook on California Arrest, Search and Seizure Rules.** 1980. Legal Book Corp. $6.95.

Markle, A. **The Law of Arrest and Search and Seizure.** (Illus.). 320p. 1974. C.C. Thomas. $19.00.

Ringel, William E. **Searches and Seizures, Arrests and Confessions.** 550p. 1972. casebound with 1978 suppl. Boardman. $45.00.

Schlesinger, Steven. **Exclusionary Injustice: The Problem of Illegally Obtained Evidence, Vol. 3. (Political Science - Constitutional Law).** 1977. Dekker. $14.75.

Search and Seizure. (Supplemented annually). 1979. looseleaf. Gould. $8.50.

Sobel, Nathan R. **Search and Seizure.** 1964. pap. Gould. $4.00.

Taylor, Telford. **Two Studies in Constitutional Interpretation.** 1969. Ohio State University Press. $7.00.

Tobias, Marc W. & Petersen, R. David. **Pre-Trial Criminal Procedure: A Survey of Constitutional Rights.** (Illus.). 448p. 1972. C.C. Thomas. $21.50.

Varon, Joseph A. **Searches, Seizures and Immunities.** 2 vols. rev. ed. 1974. (Bobbs-Merrill Law) Michie. $60.00.

Weiss, Kenneth L. & Kurland, David J. **Legal First Aid for Today's High Society: Everything You Must Know About Drug Laws and the Rights That Protect You.** 212p. (Orig.). 1979. pap. Legal First Aid. $9.95.

SELF-DEFENSE

Adams, Ronald J., et al. **Street Survival: Tactics for Armed Encounters.** (Illus.). 416p. 1980. Calibre Press. $24.95.

Ayoob, Massad F. **Fundamentals of Modern Police Impact Weapons.** (Illus.). 1978. C.C. Thomas. $15.50.

Baltazzi, Evan S. **Basic American Self-Protection: For Fitness, for Sport, for Self Defense.** (Illus.). pap. Evanel Associates. $4.95.

—**Kickboxing: A Safe Sport — a Deadly Defense.** (Illus.). 100p. 1976. C.E. Tuttle. pap. $6.50.

Barclay, Glen. **Martial Arts and Mental Power.** 1975. pap. St. Martin's Press. $2.95.

Baum, Frederic S. & Baum, J. **Law of Self-Defense.** 1970. Oceana. $4.95.

Biddle, A.J. **Do or Die.** (Illus.). 74p. 1975. Repr. of 1937 ed. Paladin Enterprises. $8.95.

Braun, Matthew. **The Save-Your-Life Defense Handbook.** (Illus.). 1977. Devin Adair Co. $10.00; pap. $5.95.

Butler, Pat. **Self-Defense Complete.** (Illus.). 1962 (Pub. by Faber & Faber) Merrimack Book Service. $4.95.

—**Your Book of Self-Defense.** (Illus.). 1968. (Pub. by Faber & Faber). Merrimack Book Service. $5.95.

Cahn, Rolf. **Self-Defense for Gentle People.** (Illus.). 182p. pap. John Muir. $6.00.

Callum, Myles, **Body-Building and Self-Defense,** 1962. pap. Harper & Row. $2.95.

—**Body-Building and Self-Defense.** (Illus.). 1977. pap. Barnes & Noble. $1.75.

Cheong Cheng Leong & Draeger, Donna F. **Phoenix-Eye Fist: A Shaolin Fighting Art of South China.** (Illus.). 1977. pap. Weatherhill. $7.95.

Choi Hong Hi. **Tae Kwon-Do.** (Illus.). 1965. Wehman Brothers, Inc. $20.00; deluxe ed. large vol. $45.00

Chun, Richard. **Moo Duk Kwan, Tae Kwon Do, Korean Art of Self-Defense.** Johnson Gilbert, et al, eds. (Illus.). 1975. Ohara Publications. $5.95.

Conroy, Mary & Ritvo, Edward R. **Common Sense Self-Defense: A Practical Manual for Students and Teachers.** (Illus.). 1977. pap. Mosby. $8.50.

DeMile, James W. **Power Punch: Bruce Lee's 1 and 3 Power Punch.** (Illus.). 1978. pap. Tao of Wing Chun Do. $3.95.

Demura, Fumio. **Sai Karate Weapon of Self-Defense.** (Ser. 115). (Illus.). 1974. pap. Ohara Publications. $5.95.

Demura, Fumio & Ivan, Dan. **Street Survival: A Practical Guide to Self-Defense.** (Illus.). 1979. pap. Japan Publications. $9.95.

Denning, Melita & Phillips, Osborne. **The Llewellyn Practical Guide to Psychic Self Defense and Well Being.** Llewellyn. $5.95.

Dominy, Eric. **Teach Yourself Self-Defense.** (Illus.). 1963. Emerson. $8.95.

Draeger, D.F. **Indonesian Fighting Arts.** Wehman Brothers, Inc. $12.50.

Draeger, Donn. **Ninjutsu: The Art of Invisibility.** 2nd ed. (Illus.). 1979. pap. Phoenix Books. $4.95.

Fairbairn, W.E. & Sykes. E. A. **Shooting to Live.** 105p. Repr. of 1942 ed. 1974. Paladin Enterprises. $5.95.

Fong, Leo T. **Sil Lum Kung-Fu: The Chinese Art of Self-Defense.** Alston, Pat, ed. (Illus.). 1971. pap. Ohara Publications. $5.95.

Fong Fu-Leo. **Choy Lay Fut Kung Fu.** Wehman Brothers, Inc. $5.50.

Gambordella, Theodore L. **Seven Days to Self-Defense.** (Illus.). 1980. Contemporary Books. $3.95.

Gruzanski, Charles V. **Spike and Chain: Japanese Fighting Arts.** (Illus.). 1968. pap. C.E. Tuttle. $7.50.

Harris, Malcolm. **Effective Unarmed Combat.** (Illus.). 1974. pap. Arc Books. $1.50.

Harvey, M.G. **Comprehensive Self-Defense.** (Illus.). 1967. Emerson Books. $7.95.

Hatsumi, Masaaki & Chambers, Quintin. **Stick Fighting: Techniques of Self-Defence.** (Illus.). 148p. 1971. Kodansha International. $7.95.

Hepler, Don. **Self-Defense Simplified in Pictures.** 1969. pap. C.E. Tuttle. $3.00.

Hibbard, Jack. **Karate Breaking Techniques: With Practical Applications to Self-Defense.** (Illus.). 1980. C.E. Tuttle. $23.50.

Hibbard, Jack & Fried, Bryan A. **Weaponless Defense: A Law Enforcement Guide to Non-Violent Control.** 184p. 1980. pap. C.C. Thomas. $14.75.

Hunter, George. **How to Defend Yourself, Your Family and Your Home.** 1970. pap. Univ. Pub & Dist. (OP). $0.95.

Hyams, Joe. **Zen in the Martial Arts.** 1979. J.P. Tarcher. $10.95; pap. $5.95.

Johnson, R.H. & Blair, J.A. **Logical Self-Defense.** 1980. pap. McGraw-Hill. $9.95.

Joo Bang Lee. **Hwa Rang Do II, No. 134.** 1980. pap. Ohara Publications. $6.95.

Kaneshiro, Hansel S. **Nunchaku for Self-Defense.** (Illus.). 82p. 1971. pap. Kaneshiro. $3.95.

Kauz, Herman. **The Martial Spirit: An Introduction to the Origin, Philosophy and Psychology of the Martial Arts.** (Illus.). 1978. Overlook Press. $10.00.

Khim, P'Ng C. & Draeger, Donn F. **Shaolin: An Introduction to Lohan Fighting Techniques.** (Illus.). 1979. C.E. Tuttle. $19.50.

Kozuki, Russell. **Kozuki's Guide to the Martial Arts.** (Illus.). Date not set. Sterling. $13.29.

Lardner, Rex. **Finding and Exploiting Your Opponent's Weaknesses.** (Illus.). 1978. Doubleday. $4.95.

LeBell, Gene. **Your Personal Handbook of Self-Defense.** 1976. pap. Cornerstone Library. $1.95.

Lederman, Milton. **Ancient Fighting Arts for the Men of Our Times.** (Illus.). 1976. Amity Hallmark. $4.95.

Lee, Jae M. & Wayt, David H. **Hapkido: The Korean Art of Self-Defense.** (Illus.). 1977. pap. Arco. $3.95.

Lee Ying-Arng. **Secret Arts of Chinese Leg Manoeuvres.** Wehman Brothers, Inc. $7.95.

Lipman, Ira. **How to Protect Yourself from Crime.** (Illus.). 1975. Atheneum. (OP.). $9.95.

Logan, Williams & Petras, Herman. **Handbook of the Martial Arts and Self-Defense.** (Funk & W. Bk.) (Illus). 1975. T.Y. Crowell. $10.95.

McGee, John. **Defend Yourself!** 1976. McKay. (OP). $7.95; pap. $3.95.

McGrath, Alice. **Self-Defense for Cowards.** (Illus.). 1973. pap. Thor. (OP). $1.95.

Madison, Arnold. **Don't Be a Victim: Protect Yourself and Your Belongings.** (Illus.). (gr. 3-5). 1978. Messner, Julian. $6.97.

Mager, N. H. & Mager, S.K. **Protect Yourself.** (Illus.). 1978. pap. Benjamin Co. $1.95.

—**Protect Yourself: Complete Guide to Safe-Keeping Your Life and Home.** 1978. pap. Dell. $1.95.

Manners, David. **Teach Your Child Self-Defense.** (Illus.). 128p. 1976. Arco. $8.95.

Martone, John. **Handbook of Self-Defense for Law Enforcement Officers.** (Illus.). 1955. Arco. (OP); pap. $1.50.

Mashiro, N. **Black Medicine II: Weapons at Hand.** (Illus.). 88p. 1980. pap. Paladin Enterprises. $8.00.

Maslak, Paul. **Strategy in Unarmed Combat.** 1977. Wehman Brothers, Inc. $10.00.

Mintz, Marilyn D. **The Martial Arts Film.** A.S. Barnes. $9.95.

Murphy, Hank. **Tang Soo Do.** (Illus., Orig.). 1980. pap. Paladin Enterprises. $8.00.

Musashi, Miyamoto. **A Book of Five Rings: A Guide to Strategy.** Harris, Victor, tr. from Japanese. (Illus.). 144p. 1974. Overlook Press. $9.95.

Nakabayashi, Sadaki, et al. **Judo.** (Illus.). 128p. (gr. 7 up). 1974. Sterling. $6.95.

Neff, Fred. **Everybody's Book of Self-Defense.** (Illus.). 1978. Lerner Publications. $12.95; pap. $7.95.

—**Fred Neff's Compete Self-Defense Manual.** (Illus.). 56p. (gr. 5 up). 1976. Lerner Publications. $4.95.

—**Fred Neff's Foot-Fighting Manual for Self-Defense and Sport Karate.** (Illus.). 56p. (gr. 5 up). 1977. Lerner Publications. $4.95.

—**Fred Neff's Hand-Fighting Manual for Self-Defense and Sport Karate.** (Illus.). 56p. (gr. 5 up). 1977. Lerner Publications. $4.95.

Nishioka, Hayward. **Foot Throws Karate, Judo and Self-Defense.** (Illus.). 1972. pap. Ohara Publications. $4.50.

Ochiai, Hidy. **The Essence of Self-Defense.** 1979. Contemporary Books. $14.95; pap. $7.95.

Otake, Hisuke. **The Diety and the Sword: Katori Shinto Ryu.** (Illus.). 1976. Japan Publications. (OP). $12.95.

Pacala, Lynn. **Self Defense.** 1980. Goodyear. $5.95.

Parsons, Kevin. **Techniques of Vigilance: A Textbook for Police Self-Defense.** (Illus.). 1980. C. E. Tuttle. $35.00.

Pu Gill Gwon. **Skills in Counterattacks, No. 135.** 1980. pap. Ohara Publications. $6.95.

Random, Michel. **Martial Arts.** (Octopus Book). (Illus.). 1978. Mayflower Books. $25.00.

Reisberg, Ken. **Martial Arts.** (Illus.). (gr. 4 up). 1979. Watts, Franklin, Inc. $5.90.

Rhee, Jhoon. **Chung-Gun and Toi-Gye.** Wehman Brothers, Inc. $3.95.

Ribner, Susan & Chin, Richard. **The Martial Arts.** (Illus.). 1978. Harper & Row. $8.95.

Robert, Hank. **Ketsugo.** Wehman, Brothers, Inc. $1.95.

—**Ketsugo.** pap. Key Books. $1.00.

Robinson, Richard. **Kung Fu: The Peaceful Way.** (Orig.). 1973. pap. Pyramid Publications. (OP). $1.25.

Rocca, Antonio. **Self-Defense and Physical Fitness.** (Orig.). Essandress. (OP).

Rowe, Richard & Mallman, Joyce. **Total Self-Protection: The Handbook of Crime Prevention.** (Illus.). 1979. Morrow, William, & Co. $12.95; pap. $6.95.

Sakagami, Ryusho & Sakagami, Setsumei. **Numchaku and Sai: Ancient Okinawan Martial Arts.** (Illus.). 180p. 1974. pap. Japan Publications. $8.95.

Sanchez, John. **Slash and Thrust.** 72p. 1980. pap. Paladin Enterprises. $6.00.

Schultz, D.O. & Slepecky, M. **Police Unarmed Defense Tactics.** 102p. 1973. C.C. Thomas. $5.25.

Seidler, Armond. **Defend Yourself: Scientific Personal Defense.** (Illus.). 1978. pap. Houghton Mifflin Co. $7.75.

Shapiro, Amy. **Martial Arts Language: A Running Press Glossary.** 1978. Running Press. $12.90; pap. $6.95.

Shin Duk Kang. **Techniques in Free Fighting. No. 136.** 1980. pap. Ohara Publications. $6.95.

Smith, Robert W. **Hsing-I: Chinese Mind-Body Boxing.** (Illus.). 140p. 1974. Kodansha International. $8.95.

Soo, Chee. **The Discipline of Self-Defense: Chinese Art of Self-Defense.** (Illus.). 1980. Gordon-Cremonesi Book. $14.95.

Soo, K.P. **Palgue: 1-2-3.** Wehman Brothers, Inc. $4.50.

Tamura, V. **Common Sense Self-Defence.** Wehman Brothers Inc. $4.95.

Tegner, Bruce. **Black Belt Judo, Karate and Jukado: Advanced Techniques.** rev. ed. (Illus., Orig.). 1980. pap. Thor. $3.95.

—**Bruce Tegner's Complete Book of Self-Defense.** (Illus.). 1975. Thor. $6.95; softcover $4.95.

—**Instant Self-Defense.** (Illus.). 1965. pap. Grosset & Dunlap, Inc. $2.95.

—**Kung Fu and Tai Chi: Chinese Karate and Classical Exercises.** rev. ed. (Orig.). 1973. pap. Thor. $2.95.

—**Self-Defense: A Basic Course.** (Illus.). 1979. Thor. $5.95; pap. $3.95.

—**Self-Defense for Boys and Men: A Physical Education Course.** rev. ed. (Illus., Orig.). (gr. 9 up). 1969. Thor. $4.95.

—**Self-Defense Nerve Centers and Pressure Points for Karate, Jujitsu and Atemi-Waza.** rev. enlarged ed. (Illus.). 1978. pap. Thor. $2.95.

Tegner, Bruce & McGrath, Alice. **Self-Defense for Your Child: Practical Defenses and Assault-Prevention.** (Illus.). 127p. (Orig.). 1976. Thor. $4.95; pap. $2.95.

—**Self-Defense and Assault Prevention for Girls and Women.** 1980. pap. Thor. $2.95.

Trias, R. A. **Hand Is My Sword.** Wehman Brothers, Inc. $10.00.

Tsirakis, Jack K. **The Art of Jeet-Kung-Tao.** 1977. Exposition Press. $10.00.

Walston, Gerald. **The Legal Implications of Self-Defense: A Reference Text for the Martial Arts.** 1979. Vantage Press. $6.95.

Wyness, G. B. **Practical Personal Defense.** (Illus.). 103p. 1975. pap. Mayfield Publishing. $4.50.

Yamashita, Tadashi. **Shorin-Ryu Karate Japanese Art of Self-Defense.** Adachi, Geraldine, ed. (Illus.). 1976. pap. Ohara Publications. $4.50.

SHERIFFS

Rudman, Jack. **Chief Deputy Sheriff.** (Career Examination Ser.: C-1173). pap. National Learning Corporation. $10.00.

—**Deputy Sheriff.** (Career Examination Ser.: C-204). pap. National Learning Corporation. $8.00.

—**Senior Deputy Sheriff:** (Career Examination Ser.: C-1665). pap. National Learning Corporation. $10.00.

—**Supervising Deputy Sheriff.** (Career Examination Ser.: C-1666). pap. National Learning Corporation. $10.00.

SHOTGUNS

Barker, A. J. **Shotguns and Shooting.** new ed. Brown, Robert K. & Lund, Peter C., eds. (Illus.). 84p. 1973. Paladin Enterprises. $6.50; pap. $4.00.

Boy Scouts of America. **Rifle and Shotgun Shooting.** (Illus.). 80p. (gr. 6-12). 1967. pap. Boy Scouts of America. $0.55.

Brister, Bob. **Shotgunning: The Art and the Science.** (Illus.). 1976. Winchester Press. $12.95.

Burch, Monte. **Shotgunner's Guide.** 1980. Winchester Press. $12.95.

Crudgington, I. M. & Baker, D. J. **The British Shotgun: 1850-1870.** Vol. I. (Illus.). Date not set. (Dist. by Arco). Barrie & Jenkins. $21.95.

Garwood, G. T. **Gough Thomas's Gun Book.** (Illus.). 1970. Winchester Press. (OP). $8.95.

—**Gough Thomas's Second Gun Book.** (Illus.). 1972. Winchester Press. (OP). $8.95.

Hastings, Macdonald. **Shooting — Why We Miss: Questions and Answers on the Successful Use of the Shotgun.** 1977. pap. McKay, David, Co. $3.95.

Hinman, Bob. **Golden Age of Shotgunning.** (Illus.). 1972. Winchester Press. (OP). $8.95.

Knight, Richard A. **Mastering the Shotgun.** (Illus.). 1975. Dutton, E.P. (OP). $7.95.

Laycock, George. **Shotgunner's Bible.** 1969. pap. Doubleday. $2.95.

Lewis, Jack & Mitchell, Jack. **Shotgun Digest.** 2nd ed. 288p. 1980. pap. DBI Books. $8.95.

McCawley, E. S. **Shotguns and Shooting.** 1965. pap. Van Nos Reinhold. $5.95.

McIntosh, Michael. **The Best Shotguns Ever Made in America.** 1980. McKay, David, Co. $14.95.

—**Best Shotguns Ever Made.** (Illus.). 1981. Scribner's. $12.95.

—**Best Shotguns Ever Made in America: Seven Vintage Doubles to Shoot and to Treasure.** 1981. Scribner's. $16.95.

O'Connor, Jack. **The Shotgun Book.** (Illus.). 1978. Knopf, Alfred, A. $15.00; pap. $8.95.

Olson, John. **John Olson's Book of the Shotgun.** (Illus.). 1975. Jolex. (OP). $9.95. pap. $6.95.

Robinson, Roger H. **The Police Shotgun Manual.** (Illus.). 168p. 1973. C.C. Thomas. $13.50.

Scott, Robert F., ed. **1982 Shooter's Bible.** No. 73. (Illus.). 1981. Stoeger. pap. $10.95.

Stanbury, Percy & Carlisle, G. L. **Shotgun and the Shooter.** 1978. (Dist. by Arco). Barrie & Jenkins. $11.95.

Thomas, Gough. **Shotgun Shooting Facts.** 1979. Winchester Press. $10.00.

—**Shotguns and Cartridges for Game and Clays.** 3rd ed. (Illus.). 254p. 1976. Transatlantic Arts Inc. $15.00.

Wallack, L. R. **American Shotgun Design and Performance.** 1977. Winchester Press. $13.95.

Waterman, Charles. **The Treasury of Sporting Guns.** (Illus.). 1979. Random House. $24.95.

Whillett, Roderick F. **The Good Shot.** (Illus.). 155p. 1980. A. S. Barnes. $12.95.

Wood, J. B. **Gun Digest Book of Firearms Assembly-Disassembly: Shotguns, Pt. V.** 1980. pap. DBI Books. $8.95.

—**Troubleshooting Your Rifle and Shotgun.** (Illus.). 1978. pap. Follett. $5.95.

Zutz, Don. **The Double Shotgun.** (Illus.). 1978. Winchester Press. $14.95.

STATE POLICE

Bramstedt, Ernest K. **Dictatorship and Political Police: The Technique of Control by Fear.** 1976. Repr. of 1945 ed. AMS Press. $17.50.

Coakley, Leo J. **Jersey Troopers: A Fifty-Year History of the New Jersey State Police.** (Illus.). 1971. pap. Rutgers University Press. $2.75.

Mayo, Katherine. **Justice to All: The Story of the Pennsylvania State Police.** 1971. Repr. of 1917 ed. Arno Press. $18.00.

Pennsylvania State Federation of Labor. **American Cossack.** 1971. Repr. of 1915 ed. Arno Press. $9.00.

Preiss, Jack J. & Ehrlich, Howard J. **Examination of Role Therapy: The Case of the State Police.** 1966. University of Nebraska Press. $15.95.

Rudman, Jack. **State Trooper.** (Career Examination Ser.: C-757). pap. National Learning Corporation. $8.00.

Smith, Bruce. **State Police, Organization and Administration.** 1969. Repr. of 1925 ed. Patterson Smith. $12.50.

TERRORISM

Alexander, Yonah & Finger, Seymour M., eds. **Terrorism: Interdisciplinary Perspectives.** Date not set. John Jay Press. $15.00.

Bassiouni, M. Cherif. **International Terrorism and Political Crimes.** 624p. 1975. C.C. Thomas. $36.25; pap. $25.00.

Burton, Anthony M. **Urban Terrorism.** 1976. Free Press. $12.95.

Camus, Albert. **Neither Victims nor Executioners.** MacDonald, Dwight, tr. 1968. World Without War. pap. $2.95.

Cole, Richard B. **Executive Security: A Corporate Guide to Effective Response to Abduction and Terrorism.** 200p. 1980. (Pub by Wiley Interscience). Wiley, John & Sons. $19.95.

Cooper, H.H. **Hostage-Takers.** (Illus.). 100p. 1981. pap. Paladin Enterprises. $12.00.

Crelinsten, Ronald D., et al, eds. **Terrorism and Criminal Justice.** (Illus.) 1978. Lexington Books. $15.95.

Dobson, Christopher & Payne, Ronald. **The Carlos Complex: A Study in Terror.** 1977. Putnam's, G.P., Sons. $8.95.

The Terrorists: Their Weapons, Leaders and Tactics. 1979. Facts on File. $14.95.

Dreyfuss, Robert. **Hostage to Khomeini.** (Illus.). 260p. 1981. pap. New Benjamin Franklin House. $3.95.

Farhi, David. **The Limits to Dissent: Facing the Dilemmas Posed by Terrorism.** Aspen Inst Human. $4.00.

Freeman, Charles. **Terrorism in Today's World.** (Illus.). 96p. 1980. (Pub. by Batsford England). 1980. David & Charles. $14.00.

Friedlander, Robert A. **Terrorism: Documents of International and Local Control 1977-1978.** 2 vols. Oceana. $75.00 set.

Green, Gil. **Terrorism — Is It Revolutionary?** 1970. pap. New Outlook. $0.50.

Hacker, Frederick J. **Crusaders, Criminals, Crazies: Terror and Terrorism in Our Time.** 1977. Norton, W.W. & Co. $9.95.

Havens, Murray C., et al. **Assassination and Terrorism: Their Modern Dimensions.** Orig. Title: The Politics of Assassination, Prentice Hall. 200p. 1975. pap. Sterling Swift. $5.95.

Laqueur, Walter. **Terrorism.** Little, Brown & Co. $15.00; pap. $5.95.

—**The Terrorism Reader.** 1978. Temple University Press. $15.00.

Lineberry, William P., ed. **The Struggle Against Terrorism.** 1977. Wilson, H.W. $5.75.

Liston, Robert A. **Terrorism.** (gr. 7 up). 1977. Elsevier/Nelson Books. Repr. $7.95.

Lodge, Juliet. **Terrorism: A Challenge to the State.** 256p. 1981. St. Martin's Press. $25.00.

Lowe, E. Nobles & Shargel, Harry D. **Legal and Other Aspects of Terrorism.** 1979. pap. Practising Law Institute. $20.00.

Merleau-Ponty, Maurice. **Humanism and Terror.** 1969. pap. Beacon Press. $4.95.

Mickolus, Edward F. **Transnational Terrorism: A Chronology of Events, 1968-1979.** 1056p. 1980. Greenwood Press. $75.00.

Miller, Abraham H. **Terrorism and Hostage Negotiations.** 134p. 1980. Westview Press. $16.00.

Mukerjee, Dilip. **Terrorists.** 1980. Vantage Press. $8.95.

O'Ballance, Edgar. **Language of Violence: The Blood Politics of Terrorism.** (Illus.). 1979. Presidio Press. $12.95.

Ochberg, Frank, ed. **Victims of Terrorism.** 1979. Westview Press. $18.75.

Parry, Albert. **Terrorism: Past, Present, Future.** 768p. 1976. Vanguard Press. $17.50.

Private Security Advisory Council. **Prevention of Terroristic Crimes.** 1978. pap. Paladin Enterprises. $4.00.

Protecting Industrial-Business Facilities and Personnel from Terrorist Activities. 1977. pap. Reymont Associates. $5.00.

Schonborn, Karl L. **Dealing with Violence: The Challenge Faced by Police and Other Peace Keepers.** (Illus.) 376p. 1975. C.C. Thomas. $21.50; pap. $16.50.

Shultz, Richard H., Jr. & Sloan, Stephen, eds. **Responding to the Terrorist Threat: Security and Crisis Management.** Date not set. Pergamon Press. $25.01.

Siljander, R.P. **Terrorist Attacks.** 1980. C.C. Thomas. $33.50.

Trent, Darrell & Kupperman, Robert, **Terrorism: Threat, Reality, Response.** 1979. Hoover Institution Press. $14.95.

Trotsky, Leon. **Against Individual Terrorism.** pap. 1974. Pathfinder Press. $0.50.

Truby, J. David. **How Terrorists Kill: The Complete Terrorist Arsenal.** 1978. pap. Paladin Enterprises. $6.00.

Wilber, Charles G. **Contemporary Violence: A Multidisciplinary Examination.** (Illus.). 176p. 1975. C.C. Thomas. $13.75.

Wilcox, Laird M. **Bibliography on Terrorism Assassination, Kidnapping, Bombing, Guerilla Warfare and Countermeasures Against Them.** 1980. pap. Editorial Research Service. $8.95.

TRAFFIC COURTS

Hood, Roger. **Sentencing the Motoring Offender.** 1972. Heinemann Educational Books. $12.95.

Warren, George. **Traffic Courts.** Repr. of 1942 ed. Greenwood Press. $12.50.

TRAFFIC POLICE

Arco Editorial Board. **Bridge and Tunnel Officer — Special Officer.** 2nd ed. (Orig.). 1969. pap. Arco. $5.00.

Auten, James H. **Traffic Crash Investigation: Report Manual and Workbook.** (Illus.). 152p. 1972. pap. C.C. Thomas $13.75.

Baker, J. Stannard. **Traffic Accident Investigation Manual.** 1975. Traffic Institute. $18.00.

Basham, Donald J. **Traffic Accident Management.** (Illus.). 232p. 1979. C.C. Thomas. $15.25.

—**Traffic Law Enforcement** (Illus.). 176p. 1978. C.C. Thomas. $10.75.

Booth, Weldon L. **Police Management of Traffic Accident Prevention Programs.** (Illus.). 360p. 1980. C.C. Thomas $29.50.

Collins, James C. **Accident Reconstruction.** (Illus.) 308p. 1979. C.C. Thomas. $23.75.

Grant, H. **Vehicle Rescue.** (Illus.). 1975. pap. R.J. Brady. $14.95.

—**Vehicle Rescue Instructor's Guide.** 1975. R.J. Brady. $7.95.

Landstreet, Barent F. **The Drinking Driver.** 128p. 1977. C.C. Thomas. $13.75.

Lauer, A.R. **The Psychology of Driving: Factors of Traffic Enforcement.** (Illus.). 352p. C.C. Thomas. $13.50.

Leonard, V.A. **Police Traffic Control:** 176p. 1971. C.C. Thomas. $8.50.

McGrew, D.R. **Traffic Accident Investigation and Physical Evidence.** (Illus.). 132p. 1976. pap. C.C. Thomas. $16.00.

Rivers, R.W. **Traffic Accident Investigator's Handbook.** (Illus.). 336p. 1980. C.C. Thomas. $39.75.

Rudman, Jack. **Parking Enforcement Agent.** (Career Examination Ser.: C-572). pap. National Learning Corporation. $8.00.

—**Senior Parking Enforcement Agent.** (Career Examination Ser.: C-793). pap. National Learning Corporation. $10.00.

Schultz, Donald O. **Police Traffic Enforcement.** 1975. William C. Brown. (OP). $7.95.

Southwestern Law Enforcement Institute. **Traffic Law Enforcement: A Guide for Patrolmen.** (Illus.). 116p. 1971. C.C. Thomas. $7.50.

Turner, David R. **Traffic Control Agent.** 160p. 1973. pap. Arco. $5.00.

Weston, Paul B. **The Police Traffic Control Function.** 4th ed. (Illus.). 420p. 1978. C.C. Thomas. $15.25.

UNITED STATES—IMMIGRATION BORDER PATROL

Arco Editorial Board. **Patrol Inspector.** 4th ed. (Orig.). 1977. pap. Arco. $8.00.

Colby, C. B. **Border Patrol: How U.S. Agents Protect Our Borders from Illegal Entry.** (Illus.). 48p. (gr. 4-7). 1974. Coward, McCann & Geoghegan. $5.29.

Rudman, Jack. **Border Patrol Inspector.** (Career Examination Ser.: C-90). pap. National Learning Corporation. $8.00.

—**Immigration Patrol Inspector.** (Career Examination Ser.: C-362). pap. National Learning Corporation. $8.00.

WHITE COLLAR CRIMES

Benson, George C. & Engeman, Thomas. **Amoral America.** 294p. 1975. Hoover Institution Press. $8.95.

Bequai, August. **White-Collar Crime.** (Illus.). 1978. Lexington Books. $15.95.

Carrol. **White Collar Crime.** 1981. Butterworth. $18.95.

Edelhertz, Herbert & Rogovin, Charles, eds. **A National Strategy for White-Collar-Crime Enforcement.** 1980. Lexington Books. price not set.

Goff, C. & Reasons, C. **Corporate Crime in Canada: A Critical Analysis of Anti-Combines Legislation.** 1978. pap. Prentice-Hall. $7.95.

Leibholz, S. W. & Wilson, L.D. **User's Guide to Computer Crime: Its Commission, Detection and Prevention.** 1974. Chilton Book Co. $9.95.

—**White Collar Crimes 1978.** 1978. pap. Practising Law Institute. $20.00.

WITNESSES

Cannavale, Frank J. & Falcon, William D. **Witness Cooperation.** 1978. pap. Heath, D.C., Co. $6.95.

Cannavale, Frank J., Jr. & Falcon, William. **Witness Cooperation: With a Handbook of Witness Management.** 1976. Lexington Books. $19.95.

Graham, Fred. **The Alias Program.** (Illus.). 1977. Little, Brown & Co. $8.95.

Livingston, Hazel. **Officer on the Witness Stand.** 1967. pap. Legal Book Corporation. $1.50.

National Lawyers Guild. **Representation of Witnesses Before Federal Grand Juries.** 1976. looseleaf with 1978 rev. pages. Boardman. $50.00.

—**How to Be a Witness.** 1971. Oceana. $5.95.

Tierney, Kevin. **Courtroom Testimony: A Policeman's Guide.** (Funk & W Bl.). 1970. T.Y. Crowell. $7.95.

—**How to Be a Witness.** 1971. Oceana. $5.95.

Wall, Patrick M. **Eye-witness Identification in Criminal Cases.** 248p. 1975. C.C. Thomas. $12.00.

Yarmey, A. Daniel. **The Psychology of Eyewitness Testimony.** (Illus.). 1979. Free Press. $15.95.

Index